Musical Symbolism in the Operas of Debussy and Bartók

Musical Symbolism in the Operas of Debussy and Bartók

Trauma, Gender, and the Unfolding of the Unconscious

Elliott Antokoletz

with the collaboration
of Juana Canabal Antokoletz

OXFORD

UNIVERSITY PRESS

OXFORD

UNIVERSITY PRESS

Oxford University Press, Inc., publishes works that further
Oxford University's objective of excellence
in research, scholarship, and education.

Oxford   New York
Auckland   Cape Town   Dar es Salaam   Hong Kong   Karachi
Kuala Lumpur   Madrid   Melbourne   Mexico City   Nairobi
New Delhi   Shanghai   Taipei   Toronto

With offices in
Argentina   Austria   Brazil   Chile   Czech Republic   France   Greece
Guatemala   Hungary   Italy   Japan   Poland   Portugal   Singapore
South Korea   Switzerland   Thailand   Turkey   Ukraine   Vietnam

Library of Congress Cataloging-in-Publication Data
Antokoletz, Elliott.
Musical symbolism in the operas of Debussy and Bartók : trauma,
gender, and the unfolding of the unconscious / Elliott Antokoletz with the
collaboration of Juana Canabal Antokoletz.
p.   cm.
Includes bibliographical references and index.
ISBN 978-0-19-536582-5
1. Debussy, Claude, 1862–1918. Pelléas et Mélisande.
2. Bartók, Béla, 1881–1945. Kékszakállú herceg vára.
3. Symbolism in music.
I. Antokoletz, Juana Canabal. II. Title.
ML1705.A41 2003
782.1′092′2—dc21
2003006592

Printed in the United States of America
on acid-free paper

To our parents
Esther Leiter Antokoletz and Jack Antokoletz
Consuelo Villanueva Canabal and Pedro Canabal
and to Tia Josefina Villanueva

Preface

I gor Stravinsky asserted that "music is, by its very nature, essentially powerless to express anything at all, whether a feeling, an attitude of mind, a psychological mood, a phenomenon of nature, etc."[1] The notion that music permits only the illusion of expression evokes several basic questions. Does the nonverbal medium of music have at least some capacity to represent or symbolize, if not express, human thought and emotions? If so, what is its intrinsic means of conveying them? And how does music translate imagery and feelings from their manifestations in other media into its own unique representation? Such questions of correspondence among artistic media had preoccupied the first Symbolist poets since the end of the nineteenth century. Claude Debussy himself addresses this issue:

> Perhaps it is better that music should by simple means—a chord? a curve?—try and render successive impulses and moods as they occur, rather than make laborious efforts to follow a symphonic development which is laid down in advance and *always arbitrary*, and to which one will inevitably be tempted to sacrifice the development of feelings.[2]

According to Marcel Schneider, "Debussy, in fact, did not want to describe the spectacle of the sea, not even the feeling that one has in front of the ocean; he wanted to become the sea itself and not to lend it its voice. His music describes nothing; it only suggests a world inside man."[3] The intention of this study is to explore the means by which music can represent nonmusical manifestations through the subjective interpretation of two composers of Symbolist opera, Claude Debussy and Béla Bartók.

Symbolic interpretation has held an increasing fascination for writers and scholars since the inception of the Symbolist literary movement. Based on the proliferation of scholarly writings on the subject in various disciplines, this fascination in part seems to be because of the capacity of symbolic interpretation to transcend the boundaries of any single discipline—philosophical, literary, artistic, or musical—and to reveal the deepest levels of expressive meaning by enriching the associative connections among them. It is by means of a new level of symbolic perception in the early twentieth century that the various disciplines seem to be revealed essentially as creative manifestations of a given common message, however elusive that message may be. This is one reason why musicologists today do not study music in isolation, but as one more manifestation of cultural concerns. Music thus becomes part of the cultural canvas in which contemporary themes are expressed and perhaps given form.

Because of the abstract quality of musical art, which lends itself to a diversity of cognitive and affective associations perhaps more readily than any other medium, it seems that any attempt at a clear definition of symbolism in music has remained more elusive than in the fields of literature and the fine arts. In attempting to come to grips with the basic notions of what constitutes the Symbolist conception in the pioneering operas of Debussy and Bartók, one is drawn into the various dramatic and musical issues surrounding the Symbolist and Impressionist aesthetics in an ever-expanding palette of sources that comprehends the various disciplines (musicological, theoretic-analytical, philosophical, psychoanalytical, and historical). Each of these sources is in its own way relevant to the meaning of the literary texts and their musical settings.

A working knowledge of certain disciplines, especially that of psychoanalysis, is important in exploring the fundamental issues of trauma and unconscious motivation that underlie human interaction in the new dramatic field of late-nineteenth-century literary symbolism. This realization came about in conversations with my wife when we speculated about the role of unconscious motivation in the tragic stories of the works whose music I was analyzing at the time. Both of us have learned to take the matter of the unconscious seriously. Her daily work as psychologist involves attentive listening to her patients' narratives with the aim of helping them understand what they might be telling themselves in their dreams and free associations. Although I analyze music rather than people, the knowledge that I had gained through my personal analysis with Dr. Bertrand Cramer at the New York Psychoanalytic Institute and, later, with Dr. Clarence R. Parker, founder of the Dallas Institute for Psychoanalysis, has been most helpful not only in my personal life but also in understanding the role of the unconscious in dramatic works.

This book has been a journey that my wife and I undertook together. Her contribution has not only enriched my own understanding and approach to the psychological discipline in general but also has added new insights based on a clinical, yet interpretative, dramatic approach so crucial to the study of human dynamics and interaction. What is evident after many years of research into the subject matter and related primary-source and secondary-source materials is the remarkable degree of interdependent, multidisciplinary concepts and principles necessary for acquiring an integrated understanding of the Symbolist aesthetics as well as coming to a basic definition of this aesthetic movement both on the historical and theoretic-analytical levels of the operas.

Perceptual complexities arise from this special capacity of symbolic interpretation to transcend the multidisciplinary boundaries and to link these disciplines at the highest levels of artistic as well as psychological meaning. Without these complexities, one might otherwise find less common *synesthetic* ground for the mutual expression of the various disciplines.[4] At the same time, one might assume that the elusiveness because of these perceptual complexities on the symbolic level must have at least contributed to the earliest audience responses, which had revealed so little unity in support of these operas. Rejection of both the Debussy and Bartók operas seems, despite some favorable reviews in the case of *Pelléas et Mélisande*, to have been motivated by a lack of genuine public comprehension of the new musical language itself, let alone the interpretative message of the composer in setting the Symbolist text. Radical transformation of the traditional tonal system was partly responsible for the critical attitudes toward the two operas at their initial reception. While the new musical language was understood and appreciated by many at the first performance of the Debussy opera at the Opéra-Comique in Paris on 30 April 1902, there were still those who opposed its "stammering phantoms" and lack of melody, a characteristic that Debussy felt the need to defend.[5] In any case, it was a new kind of music that the public now encountered, based on a new means of harmonic construction and progression that unfolded within a highly innovative harmonic, melodic, and rhythmic structural conception. The style of the opera was previously unknown, except perhaps in Debussy's own little-known earlier work.[6] But beyond the difficulty of musical comprehension lay the issue of its deeper interpretative, symbolic function.

Through her study of the varied critical opinions, Jann Pasler points to the divergent cultural and social forces that motivated public attitudes at the first performances of Debussy's *Pelléas et Mélisande*.[7] However, she shows that studies of the opera's reception by early critics—both proponents and opponents—have not disclosed the exact reasons for the various positions taken. By her examination of many early reviews, Pasler provides documentation showing that the controversy surrounding Debussy's opera extended far beyond the circumstances of the initial productions, the debates continuing for the next ten years. Apparently, the original controversy was ignited more by the differences of social and musical values held by the various public factions in the opera's first audiences than by the inherent qualities of the opera itself.[8] In any case, support came from a group of intellectuals comprising artists, students, pupils from the Conservatoire and writers who were able to promote the work successfully. Some strategy was used by the director of the Opéra-Comique, Albert Carré. When subscribers began to vacate their seats, he brought in gallery attendees to fill the empty orchestra and balcony seats. Among those supporters who converted critics from their negative attitudes during the dress rehearsal were Paul Dukas and Gustave Doret.[9]

Because of the conservative tastes of the Hungarian public in the early years of the century, Bartók's opera, *Duke Bluebeard's Castle*, found even less public support than the Debussy opera. It was originally rejected in a competition for a national opera in 1911 because its genuine Hungarian qualities were unrecognizable to an audience accustomed to hearing Italianate and Germanized settings of Hungarian texts. *Bluebeard* finally had its première in Budapest on 24 May 1918. With the collapse of the postwar revolutionary regime in 1919, however, both *Bluebeard* and the second of Bartók's three stage works, *The Wooden Prince* ballet, were banned because of the political exile of their librettist, Béla Balázs, and it was not performed again in Budapest until 1937. However, the reasons for its lack of acceptance appear to extend beyond these cultural and political attitudes surrounding the work, as it was not until 10 June 1974 that it was to have its première at the New York Metropolitan Opera; its next performance at the same institution did not occur again until 16 January 1989.[10] The infrequency of its performance raises questions of musical perception of the new operatic idiom, and the dearth of theoretic-analytical studies pertaining to intrinsic musical issues has left many such questions unanswered.[11] By coming to grips with the radical changes found in the musical language of both the operas of Debussy and Bartók, we can deepen our understanding not only of the nonverbal art of music itself but also the new psycho-dramatic symbolism with which music was conjoined to produce a meaningful musico-dramatic unity.

Acknowledgments

I wish to express my gratitude to Dr. Benjamin Suchoff (Former Successsor-Trustee of the Estate of Béla Bartók and Head of the New York Bartók Archive) for our fruitful discussions of Bartók's opera and for his invaluable editorial suggestions. I am indebted to Professor Jann Pasler (Musicology, the University of California at San Diego) for her reading of the chapters at an early manuscript stage, and for her astute evaluation of the sociocultural context in which Debussy and the French Symbolists were creating their new ideas. To Professors Carl S. Leafstedt (Musicology, Trinity University, Texas) and Judit Frigyesi (Musicology, Bar-Ilan University, Israel): I am grateful for their sharing with me their dramaturgical, historical, and cultural insights into Bartók's opera. Their recent books on Bartók attest to the depth of their research and thought. I am grateful to the University Research Institute at the University of Texas at Austin for support of my research on the book, providing funds for translation of Bartók's letters by my former student Alicja Usarek, and for other practical and editorial matters by my student Michael J. Malone. Kristina Deli was helpful in pointing out published material in translating from the Hungarian material about the relation between Bartók and Balázs. I am grateful to Victoria Lopez-Meseguer and Cesar Ballester for our discussions of Maeterlinck's theater works and for bringing useful material to my attention. Discussions with my son, Eric Antokoletz, about nineteenth-century philosophical developments, which had a direct bearing on the musical context and thought of both Debussy and Bartók, added insight and depth to certain chapters. To my wife, Juana Canabal Antokoletz, I am most indebted not only for her significant contributions to this book but also for her love and support throughout the long period of its completion. I should also like to thank Maribeth Anderson Payne, former editor at Oxford, for her interest in publishing this book, and I am grateful to the new music editor, Kim Robinson, for her help in bringing this book to publication. Finally, I should like to thank the editorial assistant, Eve Bachrach, and the production editor, Robert Milks, for their intelligent and careful work in the production process.

Acknowledgment is gratefully made to several publishers for use of the musical examples. Credit is given as follows:

Pelléas et Mélisande [public domain]. First edition of piano-vocal score published 1902 by E. Fromont, Paris. Copyright transferred to Durand in 1905. Reprint edition by Edwin F. Kalmus (New York) of the 1907 publication of piano-vocal score. European-American Music Distributos Corporation is sole U.S. and Canadian agent for Alfred A. Kalmus. Full score, originally published in 1904 by E. Fromont, Paris, reprinted 1985 by Dover Publications, Inc. Minneola, N.Y.

Duke Bluebeard's Castle [public domain]. Originally published by Universal Edition A.G., Vienna, Austria, 1921 [1922]; full score, 1925, 1963. Copyright renewed 1949 by Boosey & Hawkes, Inc., New York. Universal Edition (London) Limited. Copyright 2001 by Dover Publications, Inc., Minneola, N.Y.

Elektra [public domain]. Piano-vocal score Copyright 1908. 1909 by Adolf Fürstner. U.S. Copyright Renewed. Copyright assigned 1943 to Hawkes & Son (London) Ltd. (A Boosey & Hawkes company) for the world excluding Germany, Italy, Portugal and the former Territories of the U.S.S.R. (excluding Estonia, Latvia and Lithuania).

Wozzeck: Full Score, Copyright 1926 by Universal Edition A.G., Vienna. Full Score, Copyright Renewed. English translation Copyright 1952 by Alfred A. Kalmus, London. English translation Copyright Renewed. Pocket Score, Copyright 1955 by Universal Edition, A.G., Vienna. Copyright Renewed. European-American Music Distributors Corporation is sole U.S. and Canadian agent for Alfred A. Kalmus and Universal Edition Vienna.

Contents

1. Backgrounds and Development: The New Musical Language and Its Correspondence with Psycho-Dramatic Principles of Symbolist Opera   3

2. The New Musical Language   14

3. Trauma, Gender, and the Unfolding of the Unconscious   30

4. *Pelléas et Mélisande*: Polarity of Characterizations: Human Beings as Real-Life Individuals and Instruments of Fate   55

5. *Pelléas et Mélisande*: Fate and the Unconscious: Transformational Function of the Dominant Ninth Chord; Symbolism of Sonority   84

6. *Pelléas et Mélisande*: Musico-Dramatic Turning Point: Intervallic Expansion as Symbol of Dramatic Tension and Change of Mood   117

7. *Pelléas et Mélisande*: Mélisande as Christ Symbol — Life, Death, and Resurrection — and Motivic Reinterpretations of the Whole-Tone Dyad   147

8. *Pelléas et Mélisande*: Circuity of Fate and Resolution of Mélisande's Dissonant Pentatonic–Whole-Tone Conflict   173

9. *Duke Bluebeard's Castle*: Psychological Motivation: Symbolic Interaction of Diatonic, Whole-Tone, and Chromatic Extremes   182

10. *Duke Bluebeard's Castle*: Toward Character Reversal: Reassignment of Pentatonic and Whole-Tone Spheres   207

11. *Duke Bluebeard's Castle*: The Nietzschean Condition and Polarity of Characterizations: Diatonic-Chromatic Extremes   234

12.   *Duke Bluebeard's Castle*: Final Transformation and Retreat into Eternal
      Darkness: Synthesis of Pentatonic/Diatonic and Whole-Tone Spheres   248

13.   Symbolism and Expressionism in Other Early Twentieth-Century
      Operas   262

      Epilogue   291

      Notes   295

      Works Cited   331

      Index   341

Musical Symbolism in the Operas of Debussy and Bartók

WITH JUANA CANABAL ANTOKOLETZ

Backgrounds and Development

The New Musical Language and Its Correspondence with Psycho-Dramatic Principles of Symbolist Opera

By the end of the nineteenth century, many comforting beliefs about what it meant to be human and the accompanying rules and traditions inherent in that notion had been brought into question. Charles Darwin's theory of evolution challenged mankind's special connection with a divine creator, and even the idea of a deity external to man was replaced, among many, by reliance on the scientific method as the only acceptable avenue to truth. The appearance of man and woman on earth was accountable to the relentless forces of evolution, governed by the principle of survival of the fittest rather than by the special touch of a divine creator. Carried to an extreme, such notions replaced the ideals of tolerance and religious freedom of the Enlightenment and justified the conquest and exploitation of "inferior primitive" populations.[1] The transformation from agrarian to industrial economy in various countries forced the exodus of peasants from rural to urban areas in search of work. The need for mass labor fostered exploitation and impersonal relationships between owner and worker, which in turn led to the development of socialist ideas that further challenged the social structure. Questions of gender and power also began to surface more prominently as women no longer wanted to follow Paul's dictum of being subservient to men: they were beginning to contemplate equality.[2] At the same time, ties between church and state came into question as the last vestiges of royalty's claim to a divine mandate had vanished not only from nations, but also from the basic unit of the family. However, although God's presence may no longer have been felt in traditional places of worship, it had not vanished. It had found shelter in the unconscious,[3] that mysterious realm of the human mind that Pierre Janet, Josef Breuer, and Sigmund Freud had begun to explore in a systematic way by the end of the nineteenth century.

New Tendencies in Literature, Psychology, and Music

New emphases on the internal (unconscious), the external (notion of fate), and the transformational (symbolic) link between the two, are fundamental in defining the "modernism" of opera around the turn of the century. The intention in this book is to show how two early-twentieth-century operas—Claude Debussy's *Pelléas et Mélisande* (1893–1902) and Béla Bartók's *Duke Bluebeard's Castle* (1911), based on the Symbolist plays of the Franco-Belgian poet Maurice Maeterlinck and his Hungarian disciple Béla Balázs—represent the first large-scale attempts in the new era to establish more profound correspondences between unconscious communication so fundamental to Symbolist poetry and the more abstract nonverbal principles of the new musical language. The dissolution of traditional harmonic functions and the establishment of a new musical sound world in early-twentieth-century opera was concomitant with, and to an extent dependent on, new tendencies in literature and psychology. As traditional harmonic functions were no longer used to construct musical narratives, new principles of harmonic construction and progression led to the establishment of the new musical language. These musical principles, which are primarily based on *symmetrical transformation* of traditional harmonic constructions,[4] reflect a new awareness by composers of the possibilities for creating an expressive correspondence between poetic and musical art-forms. As the sense of directed tonal motion and resolution inherent in the major-minor scale system began to be dissolved by the incorporation of modal and symmetrical pitch formations, more subtle correlations between music and certain psychological phenomena of Symbolist drama became possible. The replacement of traditional notions of harmonic functions by the more static, irresolute tonality of impressionism appears to be inextricably connected in the operas with the traumatized psychological condition of the characters. In the case of Debussy's *Mélisande* or Bartók's *Bluebeard*, for instance, musical symbolism underscores how the effects of trauma and the disavowed emotions that accompany them afflict the characters throughout both works.[5]

Maeterlinck made a significant effort toward elucidation of what he and his contemporaries viewed as the uncertain and perilous terrain that men and women entered as they sought intimacy with each other. His treatise on women was a philosophical exploration of this subject.[6] His *Pelléas* play demonstrated a keen awareness of the contradictions inherent in the gender roles of his time and the traumatic effects that such interactions brought about in the protagonists. Similar concerns were the focus of an intellectual circle of avant-garde writers, artists, and composers in Budapest that included Balázs and Bartók.[7] Furthermore, there are puzzling autobiographical correspondences between the dramatic developments of both operas and the personal dilemmas of the authors.[8] This is not surprising, as they were passionate men whose romantic relationships were bound to include the contradictions and struggles that arose from cultural gender prescriptions of the time. We can view the creative process and the work of art itself as a means of resolving painful emotional dilemmas and arriving at symbolic representation of a primitive intuition or awareness that remains unformulated prior to the artist's engagement with the artwork.[9]

Psychiatric Reconceptualizations of Trauma in the Late Nineteenth Century

Contemporary research with traumatized patients, aided by a refinement of neurological assessment techniques, supports the view that trauma often causes severe psychological symptoms as well as significant alterations of neurological patterns that may not be reversible. For instance, alterations in stress-hormone secretions in post-traumatic stress disorder may lead to problems with attention; traumatized people have difficulty in evaluating sensory stimuli and mobilizing appropriate levels of physiological arousal.[10] Psychological and neurological factors often interact with one another and tend to have mutually reinforcing negative effects. One essential requirement for a person to be considered a possible candidate for a post-traumatic stress disorder diagnosis is that he be exposed to a catastrophic experience far beyond the realm of ordinary human life. A traumatized person in a constant state of hyper-arousal may cope by "numbing" his responses to important cues in daily life. This may impair the person's functioning and contribute to low self-esteem and anticipation of negative outcomes.

Bessel A. Van der Kolk suggests that in contrast to the current understanding of both organic and psychological factors in the etiology and symptomatology of trauma, in the late nineteenth century two contrasting views of trauma were held. One viewed the psychological symptoms of trauma as produced by organic causes,[11] while the other considered emotional reactions as primary.[12] Prevailing gender stereotypes affected how trauma was conceptualized. Soldiers who had been in combat suffered from "irritable heart." Women with similar symptoms were more likely diagnosed as suffering from hysteria, which tended to be viewed as only affecting women.[13]

It was the work of Jean-Martin Charcot that led to a greater acceptance of the view that a psychological idea could create physical symptoms. Charcot was committed to the Positivist philosophy of Auguste Comte, and he was the first to establish a systematic scientific study of traumatized patients.[14] He later became interested in the study of hysteria. His many writings and weekly scientific meetings, which were attended by his students, international colleagues, scholars, and journalists, had significant influence in literature and everyday thought. Writers such as Emile Zola, who sought to portray his characters without the filter of social stereotypes or conventional good taste, learned from Charcot's clinical demonstrations of patients with extreme symptoms. Zola's portrayal of characters in his literary works paralleled Charcot's stark realism in his clinical lectures.

Charcot's primary interest, however, was in identifying and describing pathological conditions. Propelled by scientific enthusiasm and the anticlerical mood of his time, he brought into the realm of science diverse psychological conditions such as hysteria, spiritual phenomena, the occult, and even demonic possession.[15] Some of these conditions had been previously treated by religious rituals, some extreme, others by a military that would execute traumatized soldiers for cowardice.[16] Charcot was limited in his approach to these conditions. He was more concerned with the precise description of symptoms and the development of a diagnostic taxonomy than in understanding the individual patient. He carefully studied his patients' responses to treatment by the use of graphs and other quantitative measures that recorded muscle contractions, respiration, pulse, and secretions to describe the course of the illness. His treatment included medicine and behavioral interventions, such as cold showers for uncooperative patients. But he did not listen to his patients, nor did he inquire about their histories.[17]

Although Janet was undoubtedly influenced by Charcot, he had conducted psychiatric research for six years prior to his arrival at Salpetrière, an old hospital complex in Paris that Charcot and his followers used for research based on the scientific method to diagnose and classify illness. Janet's method differed from Charcot's in that early in his work he decided always to examine the patient himself, to make precise annotations of what the patient said, and to obtain a comprehensive history of the patient's life and past treatments.[18] His development of "psychological analysis," which was the term he used for his method of treatment, was also an original contribution. He was able to remove chronic symptoms from some of his patients by inducing somnambulistic states in which he helped the patient recall the traumatic incident that had triggered the symptom. He then helped the patient to confront the irrationality of the patient's "fixed idea" (that had been precipitated by the trauma and had maintained the patient's symptoms) and transform it into a realistic one that would bring about a better adaptation and relieve the symptoms. In subsequent sessions, he would conduct a systematic analysis of the patient's symptoms and would implement the above procedures to effect a cure.[19]

Sigmund Freud spent a brief time in Salpetrière, where he was exposed to Charcot's teachings and his notion that physical symptoms could be elicited by an idea. Prior to his visit to Salpetrière, Freud had been intrigued by the case of a young woman treated by his friend and colleague Josef Breuer. Subsequently they published the case study and theoretical formulations "On the Psychical Mechanism of Hysterical Phenomena: Preliminary Communication."[20] This work suggested that traumatic memories were kept outside of normal consciousness and remained the source of hysterical symptoms because they had not been appropriately "abreacted." This term referred to the accompanying affect and motor responses associated with the idea (such as crying or anger). The recall of the pathological idea and the affect discharge that accompanied it made it possible for the memory to be integrated with the person's experiences and other associations that make the traumatic memory lose its power.[21] Freud's future work would lead him to the development of psychoanalysis, or the "talking cure." There was much that the early works of Janet and Freud shared in common, a fact that evoked some bitter controversy,[22] which is beyond the scope of our discussion.

What is important for this discussion is that the authors of the *Pelléas* and *Bluebeard* texts lived at a time that coincided with a more systematic study and treatment of mental disorders and an increased awareness of the power of unconscious processes to influence human behavior: the rational man of the Enlightenment was being transformed into the psychological man of the twentieth century.[23]

Symbolic Meaning of the New Musical Language and the Language of Trauma

The means by which these two pioneering operas transform the harmonic structures of the traditional major-minor scale system into a new musical language and how this language conveys the psycho-dramatic meaning of the original plays by Maeterlinck (*Pelléas*, 1892) and Balázs (*Bluebeard*, 1910) are inextricably connected to the new dramaturgical and psychological principles that were emerging in literature at that time. With the reaction against the realism of nineteenth-century theater, many authors began to develop a new interest in psychological motivation and a level of consciousness immersed in metaphor, ambiguity, and symbol.[24] The Symbolists were the most significant group to oppose Naturalism during the second half of the nineteenth century. In addition to Maeterlinck and Balázs, some of the most prominent of these new dramatists were Henryk Ibsen, August Strindberg, William Butler Yeats, Anton Chekhov, Ernst Toller, James Joyce, and other figures of diverse national backgrounds.[25] In Vienna, these new literary assumptions were primarily manifested in the dramas and novels of Hugo von Hofmannsthal, Jacob Wassermann, and Arthur Schnitzler, who founded the group known as "Young Vienna" in 1900 in opposition to the German Naturalist school of drama. Wearied by the "intolerable erotic screamings" of *Tristan und Isolde*, Hofmannsthal concerned himself with psychological motivation, more lucid character delineation, and the symbolic transcendence of external reality.

In his Symbolist plays, Maeterlinck was to transform the internal concept of unconscious motivation into an external one, in which human emotions and actions are entirely controlled by fate. In Maeterlinck's characters, fate and the unconscious appear essentially to be different manifestations of the same force against which the human being has no recourse. Opera composers had to expand traditional musical means in order to express the underlying psychological states—even pathological conditions—of their characters. The new musical language could, in correspondence with a literary style that hinted at rather than stated the message, convey a level of understanding that the characters may or may not express in words. It is not primarily pictorial representation that is evoked by this synthesis but, rather, a less tangible, more mysterious realm that exists beyond the limits of external, objective reality. With the advent of the Symbolist movement in literature in the late nineteenth century, this notion was never more evident. Marcel Schneider points out that the Symbolist poets "aimed at transcending the appearance of things and suggesting the invisible and the eternal by means of symbols."[26]

Béla Balázs, author of the *Bluebeard* play, exhibited a lifelong interest in psychological processes.[27] His writings suggest a keen awareness of the symbolic meaning of dreams. Even the journey inside Bluebeard's castle resembles a dream, a fact that is stressed in the original introduction to the play. Balázs's fascination with psychological processes and his self-reflection through journaling was in synchrony with the times in which he lived and shared by his contemporaries. Interest in the study of dreams was manifested in the publication of several treatises on the subject that anteceded Freud's publication of his technique of dream interpretation.[28] One of the most read at the time was "Dreams and the Means to Direct Them," written by the Marquis Hervey de Saint-Denis, professor of Chinese language and literature at the Collège de France.[29] The book describes a detailed account of the technique that Hervey used to record and control his dreams, as well as a discussion of the different theories about dreams. The Dutch psychiatrist and writer Frederik Van Eeden began to study his dreams by using Hervey's methods in 1896.[30] He reported his observations in the novel *The Bride of Dreams*[31] one year after Balázs completed his *Bluebeard* play. Although we have not come across direct evidence of Balázs's awareness of Freud's writings, it is conceivable that Balázs knew of Freud's work since Freud had published his work on the interpretation of dreams in Vienna in 1902[32] and briefly discussed Friedrich Hebbel's tragic drama *Judith* in "The Taboo of Virginity" (1918).[33] Balázs had a special interest in Hebbel's work and had completed his doctoral thesis on Hebbel's literary theory.[34] Balázs and Bartók belonged to the young group of Hungarian intellectuals who were trying to find new artistic expression in Hungarian roots. One of these young intellectuals was György Lukács, with whom Balázs maintained an intimate friendship throughout his life. Lukács developed a theory of artistic expression[35] in which he viewed art as a medium toward the expression and integration of all the suffering and paradoxes of the soul."[36] Bartók admired Balázs's poetry and ability to use words to express feelings and he was aware of the powerful reflection in his music of the vicissitudes of his emotional life.[37]

Cross-Sensory Analogies, Metaphors, and Synesthesia

But how would the dramatic meaning be symbolized in music, by Debussy, Bartók, and others? The dramaturgical meaning is deepened and elaborated by the internal logic of the abstract musical design, that is, by various associative levels of leitmotivic, harmonic, formal, and other structural phenomena that play either an immediate or teleological role in the projection of the purely musical message. The musical integrity of each of these operas serves a level of signification that goes beyond any direct correspondences between literary and musical spheres. Stéphane Mallarmé, pioneer of the Symbolist movement, considered music an entirely self-sufficient language that is founded on its own governing principles, a language that can be said to serve its own expressive purposes. Although the terms "poetry" and "music" are often used as metaphorical interchanges between these two worlds of artistic expression, Paul Verlaine, for one, did not want to substitute the "sacred laws of music" for the "sacred laws of poetry," and Debussy himself claimed that "these two arts can never exchange their various powers."[38] Debussy's argument against Richard Wagner's endless melody in favor of his own quasi-recitative style was in part based on the notion that "symphonic development and character development can never unfold at exactly the same pace,"[39] an assertion that further entertains the notion of two independent systems of artistic expression that nevertheless address the same narrative. They do this by expanding, illuminating, revealing, or hiding different aspects of the drama. Together, they ultimately contribute to a more thorough depiction of the complexity of human interactions. Daniel Stern points to Lawrence E. Marks's concept of "the Doctrine of Equivalent Information," according to which "the different senses can inform about the same features of the external world."[40] Stern explains that "Artists, especially poets, have taken the unity of the senses for granted. Most poetry could not work without the tacit assumption that cross-sensory analogies and metaphors are immediately apparent to everyone. Certain poets, such as the French Symbolists during the nineteenth century, elevated the fact of the cross-modal equivalence of information to a guiding principle of the poetic process." Like the Symbolist poets, certain musicians and artists around the turn of the century also explored the relation of the senses according to the notion of "synesthesia," based on a process in which some human sensation is elicited by an external stimulus, for example, as when a particular smell is induced by a particular color.

It is in Maeterlinck's play, and Debussy's operatic setting of it, that we have the perfect embodiment of the symbolist ideal of Mallarmé.[41] The latter was inspired by Wagner's conception that led to the *Gesamtkunstwerk*, or the fusion of the arts (music, poetry, and staging),[42] but unlike the Wagnerian profusion of characters from Norse mythology within the context of an elaborate stage design, his own conception of the ideal theater was to be devoid of sets, scenery, and costumes. Mallarmé's stage existed only "in the imagination of the reader, who constituted a perfect audience of one."[43] Mallarmé's works were intended to evoke vague and fleeting moods purely by means of the rhythm and sound of the poetic verses. This musical quality of his poetry, unhindered by actual musical notation, "formed an abstract ideal toward which poetry might aspire." According to Paul Dukas, one of the staunch supporters of Debussy's opera and the Symbolist aesthetics:

> Verlaine, Mallarmé, and Laforgue used to provide us with new sounds and sonorities. They cast a light on words such as had never been seen before; they used methods that were unknown to the poets that had preceded them; they made their verbal material yield subtle and powerful effects hitherto undreamt of. Above all, they conceived their poetry or prose like musicians, they tended it with the care of musicians, and, like musicians, too, they sought to express their ideas in corresponding sound values. It was the writers, not the musicians, who exercised the strongest influence on Debussy.[44]

In the Maeterlinck play, a sense of vagueness and passivity is induced by repetitive, often disconnected statements, a language that "transformed dialogue into incantation and drama into ritual." In Maeterlinck's drama, everyday objects acquire symbolic associations and the character verbalizations are often vague and incomplete. They seem to beg for additional elaboration of what is left unsaid. What is left unsaid will be said by Debussy's music. Debussy himself informs us that a critic reproached his score because it assigned the melodic phrase always to the orchestra, never to the voice.[45] Although this technique points to the general influence of the Wagnerian conception, Debussy's own comment points to a fundamental stylistic divergence from the latter: "[The music] stands aside as soon as it can, leaving [the characters] the freedom of their gestures, their utterances—their joy or their sorrow. It is this that one of my critics understood so well—M. Fourcaud of *Le Gaulois*—perhaps without realizing it, when he spoke of *Pelléas et Mélisande* in terms of a 'declamation in notes, scarcely accompanied'."

The impact of the Wagnerian *music drama* is evident, nevertheless, in Debussy's opera, which Debussy referred to as a *drame lyrique*.[46] His musical idiom reflects the more profound Wagnerian approach not so much in terms of tangible stylistic reference but in Wagner's tendency toward sonic objectification of the metaphorical image. This tendency, which was to become pervasive as Wagner's operatic conception evolved toward music drama and the *Gesamtkunstwerk*, is exemplified in Debussy's opera as well. For instance, the dominant ninth chord at the opening of act 2 of *Pelléas* is associated with the old well that used to cure the blind. Now, as the well no longer has the capacity to give sight, the dominant ninth chord, which evokes a traditional sonic quality that is clearly defined by its tertian harmonic construction on a definite chordal root, is transformed into the whole-tone collection, which exhibits a more modern quality that is ambiguous because of its tonally irresolute *cyclic-interval* construction.[47] This transformation of a well that gives sight into one that does not is musically objectified in the transformation from clear dominant ninth to irresolute whole-tone sphere.

In Wagner's early operas *Rienzi* and *Der Fliegende Holländer*, primitive leitmotivic constructions had been employed within the more traditional Romantic style of Weber and Marschner. In *Tannhäuser* and *Lohengrin*, recurrent associative themes were to be more pervasively transformed within the more coalescent forms and textures as the fairy-tale stage acquired greater symbolic significance. As Wagner moved toward increasing fusion of the arts, the leitmotifs were to go far beyond their former role as texturally isolated configurations. In his music dramas, the leitmotifs now entered into an intimate alliance with every step of the dramatic narrative. This new, more pervasive role of the leitmotifs corresponded with the more intense absorption of natural phenomena into the supernatural realm of purely symbolic meaning. Marcel Schneider asserts that "the Wagnerian influence, the Mallarméan notion of suggestion, the lessons that can be extracted from Debussy's work and diffuse mysticism founded more on spiritual and esthetic intuitions than on religious dogma contribute towards forming what we can call: 'symbolistic music'."[48] Thus, the symbolism in Debussy's opera forms a perfect union between Wagner and himself, in spite of his own conscious disavowal of the Wagnerian influence in *Pelléas et Mélisande*.[49]

Symbolist Opera as a Modern Phenomenon

Maeterlinck's aesthetic approach, based on symbolic representation of the human condition as driven by forces beyond one's understanding and control, attracted many composers to use *Pelléas* as a subject for musical expression. This attraction to the *Pelléas* play by composers as diverse as Jean Sibelius, Arnold Schoenberg, Gabriel Fauré, Giacomo Puccini, and Cyril Scott, as well as Debussy, attests to the existence of something special in Maeterlinck that was directed toward stimulation of a "new and universal musical consciousness."[50] It is in this development, which came from the Symbolist move toward abstraction through metaphor, ambiguity, and the avoidance of historically realistic subjects, that we find the signal for the first modernistic wave in music. Composers sought to express the more abstract psycho-dramatic conception of the Symbolist poets in highly individualized styles based on a musical language removed from established tonal notions. These musical conditions suggest a correlation with the Symbolist poets' attempt to "distance the language utterance from the extralinguistic situation. It plays down the 'here' and 'there,' the socially concrete situation."[51] At the same time, the move toward artistic individuality at the turn of the century is emphasized by Péter Pór:

> The pathos, direction and gestures of [Nietzsche's] philosophy proclaimed the possibility and necessity of the integral personality; their message was freedom and destiny, and fate (as Nietzsche would put it: the willing of Fate), while on the artistic plane they professed the grand style—everything that seemed to have been terminated, if not exterminated, by modern industrial society and its philosophy: positivism. . . .
>
> This is why Ady [the Hungarian Symbolist poet] responded so strongly to the "sacred, drunken words" of transcendence, self-realization and unbounded pride:

in a decade of careers and works that facelessly merged into one another, he saw it and followed it as the way of creating real life and real literature, in other words: individuality."[52]

To what degree is Maeterlinck's literary art based on direct expression or symbolic abstraction? André Beaunier, for one, suggests that literature had become divided into two main types by the time Debussy's opera was presented to the public in 1902: "There are essentially two types of art of which one consists of direct expression, and the other proceeds by symbols. A symbol is an image that can be used to represent an idea, thanks to secret correspondences that we do not know how to analyse."[53] Smith, by contrast, takes issue with Beaunier's clear-cut division of categories, asserting that although Mallarmé's writing is dictated primarily by its elusive symbolism, Beaunier's distinctions do not apply unequivocally to Maeterlinck's play. In *Pelléas*, "external events are charted with the utmost clarity and simplicity, whatever else is alluded to in the dialogue. Indeed, it is difficult to imagine any opera in which some semblance of a plot would be entirely absent."[54] The simplicity hides the meaning of the plot, and thereby contributes to its symbolic value.

Symbolism ventured into "internal" reality (wishes, feelings, and conflicts) and sought to express it through "external" reality (for instance, a castle that weeps, or a forest where the sun does not enter). This step toward greater differentiation of the internal world by means of symbol was permitted by a new awareness that man's perception of what he thought to be "reality" was actually colored by his wishes and fears. Furthermore, this conscious distinction between the "internal" (subjective) and "external" (objective) realities is significant in the identification of the symbolist literary movement as a "modern" phenomenon. The modern artist's new awareness of the possibilities for probing levels that exist below the surface of the human body was permitted in part by the invention of X rays, a development that led the artist toward abstraction. At the same time, the modern writer's new awareness of the possibilities for probing (unconscious) levels that exist below the surface of the human mind was permitted by the new developments in dynamic psychology and psychoanalysis. These differences between what is physically and psychologically abstract and concrete are essential to modern literary and artistic thought, and may best be expressed in the definition of "Symbolism" as proposed by Henri de Régnier: "A symbol is, in effect, a comparison and an identity of the abstract with the concrete, comparison in which one of the terms remains implied."[55]

A definition of "Symbol" as it might be narrowed to its particular use by the Symbolist poets can be drawn from the application by the leading Czech theorist Jan Mukařovsky to the Czech Symbolist poet Karel Hlaváček, in whose poetry the Symbolist metaphor reverses the relation between the "thing" and the "image."[56] Whereas in conventional poetry the "thing" was the theme and the "image" exemplified it, in "Symbolism the image assumes materiality and the thing is merely its accompaniment,"[57] for instance, "a door that sighs as it is opened." A more general definition of "Symbolism" as it pertains to modern dramatic usage also lends insight into the way the individual composer may express the nonverbalized emotions of the characters in the music. The notions of *natural* and *conventional* signs are essential, especially in combination, for understanding the symbolic links between the external (more objective) and internal (subjective and psychological) contained within both local and more global contexts of the Symbolist operas.[58] *Natural* signs as an inherent type of symbolism (smoke signifying fire) are manifested in music by means of literal word-painting. For instance, textural reference to the sky or light might be expressed by a rising melodic line. *Conventional* signs, which represent an acquired (noninherent) type of symbolism, are manifested in music by the use of musical notation. The latter serves to express specific dramatic meaning by means of systematic musical association. For instance, analogous to the evocation of meaning as acquired by words, which in and of themselves are no more than verbal sounds that have come to signify non-verbal ideas and corresponding musical structures through an evolving process of association, musical notation seems to acquire a similar function by means of consistent association with concepts, events, and other nonverbal phenomena. Both types of signs can be observed and interpreted throughout these Symbolist operas.

A discovery of the way that each composer creates symbolic associations, that is, by interweaving musical structure with dramatic events, permits an understanding at the deepest levels of meaning in these works. In Symbolist works, the symbol becomes more important than the object it represents. For instance, while the descent into the castle vaults by Golaud and Pelléas is based on literal (that is, objective) pictorialization by descending scales played by string instruments and bassoons in their lower registers, what is most striking in this scene and throughout Debussy's opera on the whole is the arbitrary (that is, subjective) association of the whole-tone scale with the scent of death in this descent. Even though there is nothing obvious about the whole-tone scale that might project a literal meaning for death or for the realm of fate, the unconscious, or darkness, nor about the diatonic scale that might project the essence of the natural realm (human leitmotifs, etc.), we nevertheless sense that each one of them resonates with different extremes of dramatic polarity in the text.[59] In *Bluebeard*, for instance, the basic "Blood" motif, characterized by half-steps, is gradually manifested in the intrusion of this dissonant element into the opening pentatonic folk mode (i.e., a scalar structure entirely devoid of half-steps) as Judith becomes aware of blood on the castle walls. However, psychological tension in the unbroken musical fabric is created not only by the manifest details but also by the latent symbolic and metaphorical questions that these details invoke with regard to our own perception of reality. Such questions are explicit in the Prologue: "The curtains of our eye-lids are raised. But where is the stage . . . In me? In you?" It is the intention of this book to show how Debussy and Bartók use both literal qualities of the musical structures and personal conventions to create such symbolic associations.

In addition to a reaction against Positivism, Realism, and Naturalism, the struggle of the Symbolists to preserve a place for human mystery and spirituality could be seen also as a reaction toward the dehumanization brought about by technology. Theodor Adorno refers to "the concept of shock as one aspect of the unifying principle of the epoch. It belongs to the fundamental level of all modern music, even of that which stands at extremes."[60] Shock implies an unexpected and usually violent event that frightens and overwhelms the person, so his ability to cope with life and gain some sense of mastery or control is diminished. Certainly, the characters in *Pelléas* and *Bluebeard* seem to be at the mercy of forces beyond their control. Adorno traces the social origin of shock to the pressures of modern industrialism and its massive power machinery, which overwhelms the individual and forces him to become aware of his nothingness.[61] Such dehumanizing trends could lead to the development of compensatory defenses, in which narcissistic isolation and grandiosity bolster the denial of human vulnerability and interdependence. These polarities could be easily expressed in the cultural trend to accentuate gender differences. Both *Bluebeard* and *Pelléas* reflect the artists' efforts to create form from these cultural challenges. The conflict between the individual and modern industrial society also led to a questioning of established political institutions and an interest in Socialist ideology by some Symbolist writers.[62]

Both the Debussy and Bartók operas, which are reduced to a bare minimum of characters and actions, provide an artistic synthesis of the inherent cultural contradictions of the late nineteenth and early twentieth century. The composers and the writers of these works introduce and elaborate themes of loneliness, unrequited longing for intimacy, grief over the loss of traditional values, and the shock element at a level of reality entirely steeped in metaphor. The following chapters will discuss how the unconscious conflicts unfold and are expressed in the characters' interactions, and the means by which the musical narrative develops, complements, and enriches the literary narrative as well as deepens its symbolic significance.

2

The New Musical Language

Sources and Evolution of the New Musical Language

In the evolution toward the breakdown of the major-minor scale system, the ultra-chromaticism of German late-Romantic music and the pentatonic-diatonic modalities of peasant music represent what appear to be the two main opposing sources for the development of new principles of pitch organization in the early twentieth century. While the ultrachromaticism of Wagner's *Tristan und Isolde* reached its most intensive stage of development in the more dissonant chromatic tonality of Richard Strauss's *Elektra* (1906–1908), a reaction against the ultrachromaticism of the Wagner-Strauss period led non-Germanic composers in two new directions. On the one hand, composers turned toward their own national treasures in literature, the arts, and folklore, because of increasing nationalistic demands in the decades prior to World War I. On the other hand, as cultural life in Hungary and other countries was becoming reoriented toward that of France after a long tradition of Germanic influences, composers of divergent national backgrounds found a new source for their musical language in the works of Debussy.

Bartók's appointment in 1907 as a piano teacher at the Academy of Music in Budapest permitted him to settle in Hungary and continue his investigations of his native folk music and, at the urging of Zoltán Kodály, who was appointed as composition teacher there at the same time, to study the music of Debussy thoroughly.[1] From documentation housed in Bartók's personal library now in the Budapest Bartók Archívum, we know that Bartók purchased in Budapest copies of several works by Debussy, including the *String Quartet* (in October 1907) and, between 1907 and 1911, a number of the piano works such as *Pour le piano*, *L'isle joyeuse*, *Images I* and *II*, and *Préludes I*.[2] Bartók's own *Quatre nénies*, op. 9a (1910) reveal significant connections with the Debussy works, not only in the use of a French title but also in the prominent use of pentatonic formations and other Debussyian characteristics, as in the *Andante* movement. More extensive similarities between the musical languages of these two composers may be seen in the use of modal and whole-tone formations, for instance, in Bartók's *First String Quartet* (1908-1909) and his opera *Duke Bluebeard's Castle* (1911), the opening strikingly similar to that of the Andante from the *Quatre nénies*.

Although there is no mention by Anthony Cross that Bartók purchased a copy of Debussy's opera score, Bartók himself said that the kind of musical recitation used in *Bluebeard's Castle* was first created by Debussy in *Pelléas et Mélisande* and some of his songs.[3] Furthermore, Bartók was surprised to find in Debussy's music the same kinds of pentatonic phrases that characterized his own Hungarian folk music, and attributed this feature in Debussy's music to the influence of the Russian nationalists.[4] The cultural exchanges between France and Russia in the early pre–World War I–era account in part for the absorption of pentatonic and modal phrases from Russian folk music into the French impressionistic idiom. This inclination toward the pentatonic and modal constructions of folk music led to a nonfunctional basis on which a new kind of tonality was to be established.[5] In turn, many composers in the late nineteenth and early twentieth centuries began to derive new kinds of scale constructions, primarily pentatonic-diatonic, whole-tone, and octatonic, from the modalities of their native folk music. However, it was Debussy and especially Bartók who transformed these folk modalities most radically into a new kind of chromatic, twelve-tone language as a vehicle for their Symbolist messages. The emergence of a new system of pitch organization also fostered a new autonomy of metric and rhythmic approaches. With the dissolution of traditional tonal functions, in which the concepts of consonance and dissonance had been inextricably tied to the regular barline, greater freedom in metric and rhythmic organization was permitted. Composers using folk music sources, especially from the borderlands of Western culture (Eastern Europe, Russia, Asia, and Africa), introduced *unequal beat patterns* both from dynamic dance rhythms in strict style (*tempo giusto*) and free vocal style (*parlando rubato*), the latter playing a particularly important role in the quasi-recitative vocal style of both the Debussy and Bartók operas.

Transformation of Traditional Diatonic Pitch Constructions

After almost a century, the Debussy and Bartók operas are, for us, still "modern," still exemplars of what in the twenty-first century we continue to call "contemporary music." Can we imagine anyone at the time of their composition looking back the same span of years and regarding Bellini's *Norma* as a modern work? (One cannot cite Wagner or Verdi in drawing such an analogy, as neither would yet have written his first opera.) The difference is emblematic of a qualitative change in the foundational premises of the musical language, a revolutionary transformation manifested in the music composed in the space of the same decade by Alexander Scriabin, Schoenberg, Anton Webern, Alban Berg, and Stravinsky, as well as Debussy and Bartók. The implications of this revolutionary change in the language of art music are still problematic and controversial today.

Given the elusive quality of the new literary expression at the turn of the century, as characterized by the evanescent imagery so fundamental to Symbolist drama in particular, traditional harmonic functions of the major-minor scale system with its singular harmonic construct—namely, the triad and its supertertian (seventh chord and ninth chord) extensions—could no longer accommodate the new literary assumptions based on a myriad of kaleidoscopic details capable of evoking a sense of mystery, suggestion, allusion, and symbolic transcendence of familiar, tangible phenomena. The new musical language, of necessity, had to comprehend a diversity of new pitch-set or intervallic types that could serve the multicolored dramatic moods in ways that were not possible with the more homogeneous components of traditional tonal harmony. Originating in the Eastern European folk sources, it is inevitable that these two operas should reveal irreconcilable differences from the prevailing supranational German and Italian operas of the nineteenth century in details of phrase, rhythm, and pitch organization as well as in their large-scale formal construction. Rather, the general stylistic and technical assumptions of *Bluebeard's Castle* have direct connections with the impressionistic style and musical language of Debussy's *Pelléas et Mélisande*. Beyond Bartók's reference to the similar kind of musical recitation (*parlando-rubato* rhythm) used in his and Debussy's opera,[6] an affinity between them is prominently suggested by their common absorption of pentatonic-diatonic folk modalities into a kind of twelve-tone language. This principle, which points to a more general synthesis of divergent pitch materials, is revealed by Bartók's own statement:

> It became clear to me that the old [folk] modes, which had been forgotten in our music, had lost nothing of their vigor. Their employment made new rhythmic combinations possible. This new way of using the diatonic scale brought freedom from the rigid use of the major and minor keys, and eventually led to a new conception of the chromatic scale, every tone of which came to be considered of equal value and could be used freely and independently.[7]

The free use of the anhemitonic pentatonic scale (represented by any one of five rotations on the piano's black-key collection) as well as the heptatonic modal permutations of the diatonic scale (as represented by any one of seven modal octave segments on the piano's white-key collection) led to a weakening of the hierarchical pitch relations inherent in the traditional dominant-tonic progressions and the possibility for diversifying the singular tertian harmonic vocabulary. What emerged was a new conception of diatonicism based on equalization of the modal scalar degrees, that is, the elimination of any tendency by one pitch to gravitate to another. This trend within the diatonic spectrum appears to have paralleled a similar one in late Romantic chromatic music, so composers of divergent stylistic backgrounds began evolving a new concept of the relations contained within the chromatic continuum.

The tendency to equalize the tones of the chromatic continuum and weaken tonal motion was foreshadowed in the nineteenth century by the infusion of *pitch symmetry*,[8] most prominently as the basis of harmonic root progression, into traditional triadic contexts. In the music of Franz Schubert, Frédéric Chopin, Hector Berlioz, Franz Liszt, Mikhail Glinka, and others, chordal root progressions often outlined consecutive motions by a single interval, commonly by the minor third, major third, or major second. Symmetrical pitch relations in the nineteenth century also were manifested in certain types of vertical harmonic construction, as well as in the linear root progressions. Because of the dictates of the traditional tertian system, however, symmetry in harmonic construction was limited to the dominant ninth, diminished seventh, and French augmented sixth chords.[9]

These practices led to pervasive use of *pitch symmetry* and the *interval cycles* as the primary means of integrating large-scale compositional structure in many twentieth-century compositions.[10] While symmetrical properties emerged from the chromatic tonality of late-nineteenth-century Romantic music in the works of certain German and Viennese composers, the concept of symmetry was to a large extent commonly derived by French, Russian, and Hungarian composers from the pentatonic and modal materials of Eastern European folk-music sources. Pentatonic and modal scales often generate symmetrical pitch constructions in works of the latter group of composers, these scales themselves being transformed into cyclic-interval (symmetrical) collections. The pentatonic scale (for example, the black keys on a piano) is often employed explicitly in its symmetrical permutation, Eb–Gb–Ab–Bb–Db, with two of its whole steps encompassed by its two minor thirds (the only form of the scale found in Hungarian folk music). A distinction is often made between the scalar and cyclic-interval forms of the same collection. The scalar content (Eb–Gb–Ab–Bb–Db) can be reordered as a segment of the cycle of fifths: Gb–Db–Ab–Eb–Bb. Larger diatonic collections are also often exploited as both scale and cycle within the same composition. For instance, the Dorian form (D–E–F–G–A–B–C–D) of the white keys of the piano is the one symmetrical modal permutation of the diatonic scale, which is also often ordered as a seven-note (symmetrical) segment of the cycle of fifths: F–C–G–D–A–E–B.

Other types of symmetrical pitch collections, some often associated with or derived from *pentatony* or *diatony*, have come to be associated with certain composers. (Debussy and Bartók, for instance, have prominently employed the whole-tone and octatonic scales.) These varied types of symmetrical collections (whole-tone, octatonic, and permuted forms of the pentatonic and diatonic scales) are all often revealed explicitly as part of a larger uniform field of pitch relations based on the interval cycles. Although we may find extremely contrasting aesthetic and stylistic ideals in the music of composers coming from divergent national backgrounds, common approaches to the use of multifaceted types of pitch constructions reveal a new kind of unity in the early twentieth century, the significance lying in the growth toward a new kind of tonal system and new means of progression. A more relevant view of established concepts of pitch construction (such as pandiatonicism, extended tonality, "wrong-note" intrusions into diatonic spheres, etc.) is suggested by principles of the *equal-division system*, to which belongs the concept of *nonfunctional diatonicism*. As a result, traditional chord functions were either minimized or dissolved altogether, as in Debussy's orchestral *Nocturnes* (1893–1899); the disappearance of the leading tone in new scalar constructions, or the omission of either the third or fifth degrees of the seemingly traditional tertian chords, led to a chordal staticism that acquired a *coloristic* rather than *functional* meaning. Instead, some sense of motion was achieved by means of gently insistent rhythms, changes of timbre, and harmonic changes that are often produced by parallel chord motion.

Symmetrical and Cyclic-Interval Properties of the Dominant Ninth Chord and Other Traditional Harmonic Constructions: Russian Nationalist, French Impressionist, and Hungarian Composers

In the music of the Russian Nationalists, French Impressionists, and Hungarian composers (Kodály as well as Bartók), there is a common bond in the inclination toward the pentatonic and modal constructions of folk music, such constructions forming a nonfunctional basis on which a new kind of tonality (or sense of pitch-class priority) is established. The basic principles underlying these historical developments were stated by Bartók:

> The early researches . . . into the youngest of the sciences, namely musical folklore, drew the attention of certain musicians to the genuine peasant music, and with astonishment they found that they had come upon a natural treasure-store of surpassing abundance.
>
> This exploration . . . seems to have been the inevitable result of a reaction against the ultrachromaticism of the Wagner-Strauss period. The genuine folk music of Eastern Europe is almost completely diatonic and in some parts, such as Hungary, even pentatonic. Curiously enough, at the same time an apparently opposite tendency became apparent, a tendency towards the emancipation of the twelve sounds comprised within our octave from any system of tonality. (This has nothing to do with the ultrachromaticism referred to, for there chromatic notes are only chromatic in so far as they are based upon the underlying diatonic scale.) The diatonic element in Eastern European folk music does not in any way conflict with the tendency to equalize the value of semitones. This tendency can be realized in melody as well as harmony; whether the foundation of the folk melodies is diatonic or even pentatonic, there is still plenty of room in the harmonization for equalizing the value of the semitones.[11]

With the tendency to equalize the twelve tones, symmetrical pitch collections began to appear in the latter part of the nineteenth century as textural devices or local structural elements. Although symmetrical formations contributed to the dissolution of traditional tonal functions, they also contributed to the establishment of a new means of progression. Furthermore, the means by which both Debussy and Bartók employed symmetrical pitch formations in their operas and other early works was to pave the way toward a new sense of pitch-class priority. The growth toward this new system of establishing pitch-class priority was already apparent in the Russian nationalists' and, subsequently, French and Hungarian composers' operations on symmetrical pitch constructions.

Works of the Russian nationalist and French impressionist composers contain prominent examples of pitch symmetry. The opening of the Clock Scene at the end of act 2 of Mussorgsky's *Boris Godunov* (1871) is entirely based on symmetrical pitch constructions and progressions. A prominent example is seen (p. 155 of the score) in the alternation of two transpositions (B–D♯–[F♯]–A–C♯ and E♯–A–[C]–D♯–Fx) of the symmetrical dominant ninth chord, with the common axial tritone (D♯–A) held as an ostinato in the bass and reiterated in the voice (ex. 2-1).[12] Such progressions resulted in subdivisions of the octave into interval cycles in contexts otherwise based

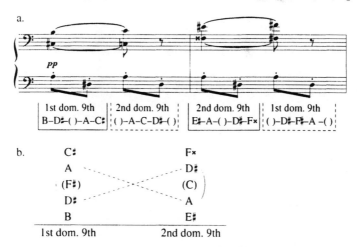

EXAMPLE 2-1. Mussorgsky, *Boris Godunov,* act 2, Clock Scene (p. 155), alternating dominant-ninth chords based on common tritone pivot and axis of symmetry

on traditional triadic harmony. In this example, the tritone cycle is the basic interval of progression between the two dominant ninth chords. While the dominant ninth chord is a traditional tertian construction, it is its symmetrical intervallic properties that are exploited in this passage. The primary connection between these two symmetrical dominant ninth transpositions is their common tritone, D♯–A (or A–D♯), which is held as an ostinato in the bass and reiterated in the voice. This tritone (D♯–A), which serves as a common pivot in the progression, also symmetrically encompasses the implied axes (F♯ and C, respectively) of the two chords (ex. 2-1b). While these axes are only implied, each dominant ninth symmetrically progresses to the axis of the other transposition, that is, C♯–B of the first (B–D♯–[F♯]–A–C♯) moves to axis C–C of the second ([ ]–A–C–D♯–[ ]), while Fx–E♯ of the second (E♯–A–[C]–D♯–Fx) moves to axis F♯–F♯ of the first ([ ]–D♯–F♯–A–[ ]). Thus, the invariant segment (axial tritone D♯–A) functions as a common pivot in the progression between the two transpositions of the "set." This procedure, employed by Nikolay Rimsky-Korsakov as early as 1867, foreshadowed the concept of invariant set-segments in serial compositions and also served as a new means of establishing pitch-class priority (i.e., based on an axis of symmetry). This type of symmetrical progression, based on transpositions of the dominant ninth chord, also applies to other symmetrical constructions such as the diminished seventh and French augmented sixth chords, the latter particularly relevant to the opening of Debussy's opera in terms of the axial concept. Whereas the concept of an *axis of symmetry* actually plays a limited role in Debussy's *Pelléas et Mélisande*—it is more prominent in certain pieces such as "Voiles" from *Preludes I* (1910)[13] and employed more extensively throughout many of Bartók's works—the concept of a pivot (i.e., common element) between two symmetrical (or, for that matter, nonsymmetrical) pitch collections is essential to the harmonic progressions in both the Debussy and Bartók operas.

EXAMPLE 2-2. Debussy, *La mer* (no. 62, m. 4, horns and trumpets), melodic statement of whole-tone scale in conjunction with triadic harmonic basis

In the late-nineteenth and early twentieth centuries, the (symmetrical) whole-tone scale began to appear with increasing prominence. Near the end of Debussy's *La Mer* (1905), a melodic statement of the whole-tone scale appears in conjunction with a triadic harmonic basis (ex. 2-2), the latter not founded on the precepts of traditional dominant and subdominant voice-leading properties.[14] The key of Db is simply asserted at the cadential point of this excerpt by the Db tonic triad. Such fusions of diatonic and whole-tone spheres is prevalent in both the Debussy and Bartók operas.

According to Schoenberg, the conscious use of the whole-tone scale has two forerunners.[15] In the first case, the melodic projection of the augmented triad results in whole-tone segments by splitting any one of the projected major thirds of the triad into two whole tones by way of passing tones. All these symmetrically divided major thirds taken together result in the complete whole-tone scale. In the second case (ex. 2-3), the melodic projection of major thirds from a dominant seventh chord with its fifth degree either augmented or omitted will result in melodic whole-tone segments by the same usage of passing tones. The latter case is similar to the first, since the altered seventh chord can be understood as an augmented triad with added seventh. Such an altered dominant seventh chord gives us four of the six tones of the whole-tone scale, G–[ ]–B–[ ]–D#–F. Schoenberg also points out that if the latter is further expanded into a ninth chord, G–B–D#–F–A, five of the six whole-tones will result. (Contained within the latter is the "French Augmented Sixth" chord, B–D#–F–A, a significant traditional construction that lies exclusively within the whole-tone spectrum.) An additional example is given by Schoenberg to illustrate a "traditional" resolution of a six-note whole-tone chord to a C-major triad (ex. 2-4). This six-tone chord results from the simultaneous raising and lowering of the fifth degree: G–B–[D]–F–A to G–B–[C#–D#]–F–A. The significance of the transformations of these traditional tertian constructions into the symmetrical whole-tone scale has been summarized by Schoenberg: "The whole-tone chords, regarded as vagrant chords, have at least the same possibilities for connection as the augmented triad. Depending on the degrees to which they are referred, they can be used for modulations and modulatory episodes."[16]

The chromatic alterations of such tertian harmonic constructions in extremely chromatic contexts are prominently found in, among others, the works of the German late Romantic composers and in Schoenberg's own works. At the same time, such tertian harmonic constructions (dominant ninth, full or half diminished seventh, and French augmented sixth chords) as well as the pentatonic and modal characteristics that Debussy acquired, largely through the influences of the Russian Nationalists, are the basis of an equally significant tendency toward the breakdown of the traditional

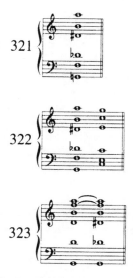

EXAMPLE 2-3. Schoenberg, *Harmonielehre*, exx. 319–320. Melodic projection of major thirds from dominant-seventh chord with fifth degree either augmented or omitted, resulting in melodic whole-tone segments by the usage of passing tones

EXAMPLE 2-4. Schoenberg, *Harmonielehre*, exx. 321–323. Additional example given by Schoenberg to illustrate "traditional" resolution of six-note chord to C-major triad, six-note chord resulting from simultaneous raising and lowering of fifth degree: G–B–(D)–F–A to G–B–(C♯–D♯)–F–A tonal system and the formation of a new one based on equal or symmetrical sub-divisions of the octave. While Modest Mussorgsky and Debussy played important roles in the evolution toward a new system of pitch relations, each represents only a part of that multifaceted development that is entirely encompassed by Bartók's compositional evolution, his *Duke Bluebeard's Castle* being an early culmination. Mussorgsky never transcended, on the large-scale level of a work, the traditional concepts of tertian harmonic construction and tonality, but he did prominently employ folk music elements. Debussy, who was only indirectly influenced by folk music—it remained for him an "exoticism"—went beyond the precepts of tradition in his extensive employment of symmetrical (e.g., whole-tone and pentatonic) constructions. Thus, it was primarily with Bartók in the early part of the twentieth century that the first scientific investigations of folk music were exploited for the purpose of profoundly altering the foundations of the traditional major-minor scale system, and it was his opera, in conjunction with the new developments in literature and dramaturgy, that served as a significant landmark in the evolution away from traditional tonality.

Interaction of Pentatonic, Diatonic, Whole-Tone, and Octatonic Sets by Means of Common Subcollections or Cells

In the Debussy and Bartók operas, diatonic and whole-tone collections function primarily as nonfunctional pitch-sets, which are fundamental in the generation of both the melodic and harmonic materials. One of the ways in which progression can occur between these basic pitch-sets is by means of pivotal subcollections, or cells, that is, segments common to the larger sets.[17] For instance, within the diatonic sphere, the symmetrical dominant ninth chord (e.g., C–E–G–Bb–D) may be reduced to its half-diminished seventh substructure ([ ]–E–G–Bb–D) and partitioned equally into two contrasting types of interlocking three-note cells, D–E–G and Bb–D–E.[18] The first cell (D–E–G) is also a subcollection of a larger pentatonic-diatonic collection (e.g., A–C–D–E–G), the second cell (Bb–D–E) also a subcollection of the larger whole-tone collection (e.g., Bb–C–D–E–F#–G#). Both cells are established as primary intervallic constructions, which are assigned a primary symbolic role in both operas. In its complete form, the dominant ninth chord (C–E–G–Bb–D) also can be partitioned into these two cell types and their literal inversions: D–E–G/G–Bb–C and Bb–D–E/Bb–C–E. These inversionally related cell forms in each pair are exploited in both operas, for instance, for symbolizing the basic dramatic polarity between Pelléas and Mélisande, and the contrasting diatonic/whole-tone cell types are used to symbolize the polarity between the more global human (pentatonic/diatonic) and fatalistic (whole-tone) spheres. While the first cell type (D–E–G) belongs to the larger pentatonic/diatonic set (e.g., A–C–D–E–G), where it is joined with its literal inversion (D–C–A), the second cell (Bb–D–E) appears as a common segment to both diatonic (either in the Lydian form, Bb–C–D–E–F–G–A, or any of its seven modal permutations) and whole-tone (Bb–C–D–E–F#–G#) set types. In the diatonic set, Bb–D–E is limited to an interlocking with its inversion (Bb–C–E), whereas in the whole-tone set Bb–D–E is interlocked with the latter (Bb–C–E), its transposed inversion (D–E–G#), and several other transpositions and transformations.

The three-note cell, B♭–D–E, plays a more extensive pivotal role in *Bluebeard*, where it serves as a common subcollection among three different set types, the two primary ones (diatonic and whole-tone) and the octatonic scale (e.g., B♭–B–C♯–D–E–F–G–G♯). In other words, the cells are subsets of diatonic, whole-tone, and octatonic sets. In the octatonic set, this "whole-tone" cell appears in four transpositions (B♭–D–E, C♯–F–G, E–G♯–B♭, and G–B–C♯) as well as its four inversions (B–C♯–F, D–E–G♯, F–G–B, and G♯–B♭–D). (These relationships are exploited in certain door scenes of *Bluebeard*.) The joining of the latter cell (B♭–D–E) with its overlapping inversion (D–E–G♯) produces the larger, symmetrical French sixth chord (B♭–D–E–G♯), which is one of two equivalent tetrachordal partitions (B♭–D–E–G♯ and C♯–F–G–B) of the octatonic collection (B♭–B–C♯–D–E–F–G–G♯). At the same time, the French sixth chord is a subcollection of the complete whole-tone scale, and it is in this capacity that important musico-dramatic symbolizations are produced in connection with Fate, especially in *Pelléas*. These interactions of the larger modal and symmetrical sets by means of the pivotal functions of common cells are the primary means of melodic and harmonic progression throughout both operas and are essential in the symbolization of the basic dramatic and psychological polarities.

A Twelve-Tone Language Based on the Concept of the Interval Cycle

The concept of the *cell* as a common pivotal element between the larger sets is outlined here in some detail because of its pervasive role in defining the musical surface of the two operas. Although both operas are founded on a kind of twelve-tone language, the concept of a *set* or *series* in either Debussy's or Bartók's music is fundamentally different from that of Schoenberg's twelve-tone system. Whereas the twelve-tone set in Schoenberg's music "functions in the manner of a motive" and must therefore "be invented anew for every piece,"[19] the use of a special "twelve-tone set" in Debussy's and Bartók's music is analogous to the precompositional assumptions of the major and minor scales in traditional tonal music.

What is this special twelve-tone set that functions as scale rather than ostinato twelve-tone motive to form the basis of Debussy's and especially Bartók's nonserial composition? The concept of the *interval cycle* — a series based on a single recurrent interval (e.g., the cycle of fifths or chromatic scale) — appears to lie at the core of both composers' evolution. Debussy, Bartók, Stravinsky, and other early-twentieth-century composers transformed the pentatonic and modal scales of folk music into whole-tone, octatonic, and other types of symmetrical/cyclic-interval collections. In their compositions, the interval cycles and the folk modes together replace the traditional major and minor scales as the background source for deriving new kinds of harmonic and melodic formations.[20] The total complex of interval cycles consists of one cycle of minor seconds, two of whole tones, three of minor thirds, four of major thirds, only one of perfect fourths, and six of tritones.[21] While the minor second and perfect fourth represent the only two interval classes that will each generate all twelve tones within a single cycle, the combination of partitions within each of the other cyclic-interval groups (for instance, the two whole-tone scales or three minor-third cycles) is required to produce all twelve tones.

In certain sections of *Bluebeard's Castle*, the interval cycles can be shown to belong to a more complex unifying principle based on systematic interlocking of the cyclic partitions (fig. 2-1).[22] These partitions provide the framework for the organic development of a special symmetrical cell, G♯–A/A♯–B (ratio 1:1),[23] which emerges in correspondence with the dramatic symbol of "blood." In connection with this emerging symbol in the opening sections that lead to the first door, combinations of semitones move from unobtrusive contexts (as part of larger thematic statements) to being the primary foreground event. More specifically, successive cyclic-interval interlockings suggest a scheme of contracting interval ratios—1:4, 1:3, 1:2, 1:1—over a broad terrain.[24] The organic process on the deep-level structure of the music itself, which is inextricably linked to this abstract scheme outlined in figure 2-1, has been described by Bartók as "extension in range," in which chromatic material is expanded into diatonic themes, or the reverse, which he referred to as "chromatic compression."[25] Through "extension in range" or "chromatic compression," Bartók said that "we will get variety on the one hand, but the unity will remain undestroyed because of the hidden relation between the two forms." The general tendency of the intervallic ratios is toward increasing dissonance (the most dissonant being the 1:1 ratio, based exclusively on two semitones a semitone apart) in association with the main dramatic idea. The main foreground statement of the 1:1 cell (G♯–A/A♯–B) in the "Torture Chamber," the first of the seven doors to be opened by Judith, is part of the progression of contracting ratios that begins with the gradual infusion of semitones into the opening anhemitonic pentatonic "Castle" theme.

In certain scenes of both operas, especially *Bluebeard*, we also find another manifestation of the interval cycles based on the systematic interlocking of cyclic-interval partitions. The process shown in figure 2-1 outlines a succession of various cyclic-interval combinations based on the expansion/contraction of interval ratios, in which the semitone serves as the common link among all the compound sets. The scheme shown in figure 2-2 outlines an intervallically expanded relation between two extended, intercalated segments of the cycle of fifths (F–A–C–E–G–B–D–F♯–A–C♯–E–G♯–B–D♯–F♯–A♯–C♯–E♯), which are interlocked alternately by major thirds and minor thirds in place of the semitonal separation (as in C–C♯–G–G♯–D–D♯–A–A♯–E–E♯–B–B♯–F♯). The sequential pattern of figure 2-2 appears to serve as background source for one of the basic types of harmonic construction in the opera—the seventh chord. This harmonic construction is manifested in the scheme in two adjacent forms—major third/major seventh (e.g., D–F♯–A–C♯) and minor third/minor seventh (e.g., B–D–F♯–A or F♯–A–C♯–E)—each built on alternate steps of the sequence.[26] These variant seventh chords, which have their sources in traditional tertian harmony, are absorbed in the opera into a nonfunctional context, often based on parallel motion of the seventh chords. Such motion occasionally can be shown on the surface level in *Pelléas*, but more explicitly in *Bluebeard*, to be the result of the larger sequence generated by the primary intervals (perfect fifth and minor third/major third) of the two chord types. This phenomenon has been referred to as a "chain of major and minor thirds" by János Kárpáti,[27] who demonstrates that Bartók, without intending to follow a dodecaphonic series, has arrived at a structure closely approximating it in principle—he explores systematic chains of fifths with common third. He also discusses triads with major-minor third structures as "dual" or "alter-

2 times interval-cycle 2 (ratio 1:1, C–C♯/D–E♭, etc.)—chromatic scale:

```
┌──┬──┬──┬──┬──┬──┬─ ─ ─ ─ ─ ┐
C C♯ D E♭ E F F♯ G G♯ A B♭ B (C
└──┴──┴──┴──┴──┴──┘ ─ ─ ─ ─
```

2 times interval-cycle 3 (ratio 1:2, C–C♯/D♯–E, etc.)—octatonic scale:

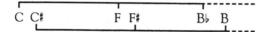

2 times interval-cycle 4 (ratio 1:3, C–C♯/E–F, etc.):

```
┌──┬────────┬──────────┬─ ─ ─ ─ ┐
C C♯        E F        A♭ A    ─ ─ ─(C
└────────┴────────────┴─ ─ ─
```

2 times interval-cycle 5 (ratio 1:4, C–C♯/F–F♯, etc.):

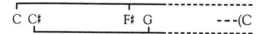

2 times interval-cycle 6 (ratio 1:5, C–C♯/F♯–G, etc.):

```
┌──┬──────────────┬─ ─ ─ ─ ─ ─ ┐
C C♯            F♯ G          ─ ─ ─(C
└──────────────┴─ ─ ─ ─ ─ ─
```

FIGURE 2-1. Ratio 1:1 system, interlocking compound cycles

native" structures, which means they still can be justified separately, and, while appearing together, preserve their original modal content. He discusses the meaning of this structure also in the context of Edwin von der Null's as well as Ernő Lendvai's theoretical concepts (i.e., Lendvai's 1:3 scale model). Kárpáti also explains that if the two equivalent kinds of third can appear within the stable frame of a fifth, then one arrives logically at the dual root and fifth situated around the stable third. In *Contrasts*, the motif of the Lydian fourth becomes equivalent to the dual third-structure of sound. This phenomenon of the "chain of thirds" is fundamental to both linear and harmonic construction in certain Bartók works already prior to *Bluebeard*, for instance, in the early *Violin Concerto* (1907–1908),[28] but appears more systematically in later works, such as the second of the *Three Studies*, op. 18, for piano (1918), and the "Scherzo alla bulgarese" movement of the *Fifth String Quartet* (1934).[29]

A hybrid form of these two seventh chords in the chain of thirds is essential in the transformation of the original major third/major seventh form (D–F♯–A–C♯) of the "Stefi Geyer" motif in the 1907 *Violin Concerto* into the more funereal (minor third/major seventh) form, F–A♭–C–E, of the *First String Quartet* (1908–1909). In

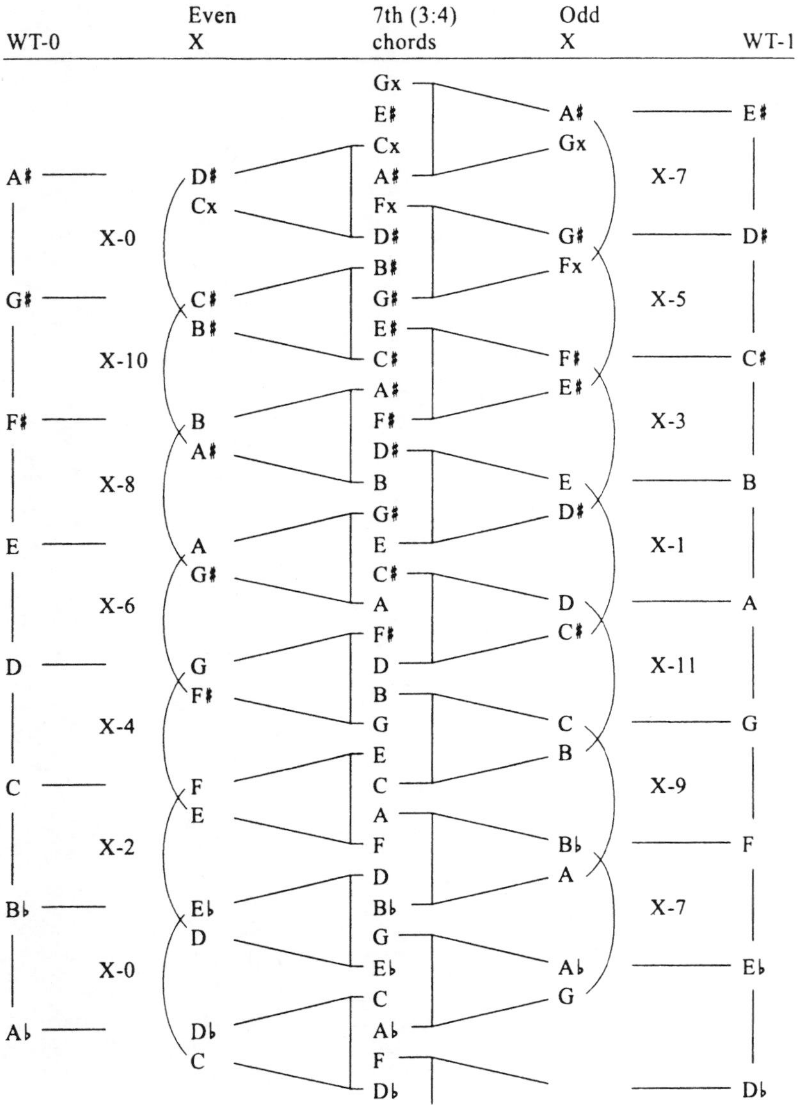

FIGURE 2-2. Ratio 3:4 system, interlocking compound cycles, seventh chords: X- motif in *Bluebeard*, chromatic tetrachords equal transpositions of "Blood" motif; seventh chords equal "Judith" ("Stefi") motif

Bluebeard, a transposition of the latter form, G♭–A–D♭–F (in enharmonic spelling, F♯–A–C♯–E♯), outlines Judith's opening vocal statement. This hybrid variant (minor third/major third/major third) lies outside the scheme of alternating major and minor thirds, so its juxtaposition with the corresponding chordal form in the chain (e.g., F♯–A–C♯–E♯ against either F♯–A♯–C♯–E♯ or F♯–A–C♯–E) produces chromatic conflict between their third or seventh degrees.[30] The hybrid form of the seventh chord has twofold symbolic significance in the opera[31]: one, it serves to increase dissonance in the realization of the semitonal "Blood" motif (based on interval ratio 1:1), and two, its adjacent major thirds (F♯–[A–C♯–E♯]) permit the chord to serve as a link in the transformation from diatonic to whole-tone (fatalistic) spheres. Thus, the "chain of thirds" serves as background source—a kind of harmonic framework—for progression between consonant and dissonant textures, a significant intervallic principle for the realization of the opera's symbolism.

The Symbolist Ideal and Corresponding Musical Processes

These musical processes can be shown to correspond with the dramatic message, in accord with the Symbolist ideal, by means of both local and deep-level harmonic construction. For instance, the intrusion of *fate* into the *human* realm is symbolized in both operas by special pitch-set intrusions of the whole-tone set (fate) into the pentatonic/.diatonic (folklike, human) sphere. The harmonic analyses deal largely with the different ways in which these pitch-set interactions can occur, how they are identified with specific dramatic events, and how they shape certain leitmotivic transformations throughout the work. These processes are similar in both operas to the extent that, in spite of their stylistic differences, there seems to be no doubt of the influence of the Debussy opera on that of Bartók in terms of musical intention, technique, and even basic pitch-set relations.

Debussy's operatic rendition of Maeterlinck's *Pelléas et Mélisande* paved the way for Bartók's musical interpretation of Balázs's *Bluebeard's Castle*, and the symbolism of *Bluebeard* appears to have a direct affinity with that of *Pelléas*.[32] In *Pelléas* the notion of fate is expressly stated by several of the characters, for instance, in act 1, scene 2, when Arkel asserts that "that will be because we never see but the under side of fate, ay, and that too of our own fate," or in act 4, scene 4, when Pelléas finally realizes that he has "played and dreamt with all the snares of destiny" around him. In *Bluebeard*, fate is expressed by the inexorable unlocking of the seven doors, the succession leading to endless darkness. Musically, the whole-tone scale (which underlies the "Fate" motif) is pivotal in transforming diatonic materials ("Human"-motifs), the multiple interactions between these two categories of pitch-sets forming the musico-dramatic basis for the entire opera. These interactions of whole-tone and diatonic spheres also underlie the same dramatic symbolism in Bartók's opera. Bluebeard's opening vocal sections are primarily diatonic, Judith's primarily whole-tone, Judith thus intruding like destiny into Bluebeard's internal world.

Bartók's opera finds common ground with Debussy's in more than just its general Symbolist assumptions. Debussy's and Bartók's musical messages are expressed within clearly articulated architectural frames in both overall form and local phrasal details. These formal frames stem uniquely from the sociocultural contexts within which each composer was deeply rooted. Debussy's formal and textural approach, based on distinct planes and layers that are often articulated by constant repetition of phrase pairs, suggests an affinity with the mosaic patches of color in French Impressionist painting that sacrifice representational line. At the same time, Bartók's rejection of urban civilization and his magnetism to music of the villages similarly led him to a structural approach that contrasted with the more continuous organic constructions of Wagner's music dramas. Bartók's structural and textural articulations, which are similar to Debussy's in certain ways, are especially significant in revealing the composer's roots in the folk music structures themselves. The folk sources provided for Bartók a structural foundation on which many levels of expression could be conjoined. Like *Pelléas, Bluebeard* consists entirely of distinct forms often based on folk-like quaternary structures, which sometimes suggest a rondo type of format (e.g., ABAB or AABA, etc.) within scenes. Furthermore, much of the melodic and harmonic fabric is developed by means of modal variation, an articulative principle that appears to be derived from the process of thematic variation found in the folk music sources. From the modal material of their operas, both composers derive the basic leitmotifs that are central in generating the musico-dramatic fabric and contrasting formal structures.

The modernistic affinity of both operas is also seen in the relation between music and language. Bartók's investigations of the old Hungarian folk tunes permitted him to break with the established nineteenth-century tradition of translating Western languages into Hungarian for opera performance, a tradition that had inevitably led to distortions in Hungarian accentuation. Bartók preserved the Hungarian language accents strictly in his musical setting of the Balázs libretto. Furthermore, the archaic syllabic structure is set almost entirely in the old "parlando-rubato" folk style, producing a kind of contemporary "recitative opera" similar to that pioneered by Debussy.[33] As a manifestation of the French reaction to Wagner's *Tristan* idiom, *Pelléas* was influenced in part by Debussy's interest in the French Baroque, especially Lully's approach to recitative, in which the musical setting was geared to the precise and realistic declamation of the French text. In *Pelléas*, the recitative style is always sensitive to the rhythm and meaning of the text. Typical single-note repetitions and a constrained vocal range together form a vehicle for the expression of the characters' intentions.[34] In *Bluebeard*, the Hungarian text—and this is true of the orchestral phrases as well—is appropriately based on eight syllables per line, which is one of the isometric stanzaic patterns that the composer found in the oldest of the Hungarian folk melodies. These music-text relationships in both operas are based on special premises that could only have been established by the liberation of meter and rhythm that was permitted by the disappearance of traditional tonal functions in the early twentieth century. By means of these new syntactical relations between rhythm and pitch, both composers were able to arrive at new and greatly expanded possibilities for symbolic representation.

As the intended inception of a new and genuinely Hungarian operatic tradition, Bartók consciously fused in *Bluebeard* the fundamental musical elements of Eastern European folk music with Debussy's Impressionist techniques. Both of these historical sources had begun to challenge the hegemony of German late Romantic music in the late nineteenth and early twentieth centuries. Finding common ground in their Symbolist assumptions, both the Debussy and Bartók operas are exemplars of the trend in the first decades of the century toward a new means of musical expression and integration of the entire musical fabric. Because of the free use of the folk modes and the disappearance of the triad as the fundamental harmonic premise, which led to the dissolution of the hierarchical pitch relations inherent in the traditional dominant-tonic progressions, greater emphasis had to be placed on the *intervallic (cell) properties* of both the harmonic and melodic constructions as a means of establishing local and large-scale structural coherence. It may be inferred from these observations of the musical language that the primary integrative means for these new musical contexts, based on the tendency to equalize the elements of the chromatic continuum, are derived from the interaction of discrete pitch-sets. The specific intervallic constructions of such sets (especially pentatonic/diatonic and whole-tone) are exploited by both Debussy and Bartók as a means of reflecting the dramatic relations based on polarity, interaction, and transformation between human and fatalistic realms. It is in this radical transformation of both the musical language and aesthetics, in which states of mind are explored in vague and mysterious contexts that go below those levels of reality characteristic of nineteenth-century Naturalist theater, that we find the modernistic sources of these Symbolist operas.

3

JUANA CANABAL ANTOKOLETZ

Trauma, Gender, and the Unfolding of the Unconscious

The nonverbal quality of music makes it a powerful medium for the expression of what cannot be verbalized.[1] The study of trauma often focuses on those aspects of events that defy their rendering in language, and music might be and often is an appropriate vehicle for the expression of the emotional sequela of tragic events. Both *Pelléas et Mélisande* and *Duke Bluebeard's Castle* are tales of traumatic events as well as of traumatized people. The authors tell their tales in words, but they also acknowledge that words are incomplete vehicles for communicating the feelings and truths that their characters experience. Thus, it is no wonder that composers rushed to create music that would convey what the story line left unexpressed. The works are chosen because of their powerful depiction of gender conflicts and their traumatic resolution, as reflected in the verbal dialogue as well as the musical structure. The stories invite us to a reflection of the effect of power inequalities in relationships as well as within the historical context within which the operas were created.

Personal and Social Factors in the Development of Trauma

Both operas reflect an increasing cultural awareness of human vulnerability to the detrimental psychological impact of traumatic events. Both works also reflect the authors' attempts to grapple with the social and psychological tensions created by challenges to traditional gender roles of the time.[2] The challenge to gender roles was only part of a more pervasive questioning of the social order and the institutions that maintained that order.[3] The stories contain pervasive themes of isolation and loneliness, which are expressed symbolically (e.g., Bluebeard's ambivalent response to Judith's desire to open the doors, or the dense forest of Allemonde in Debussy's opera in which there are places where the sun never shines). The stories also reveal a lack of faith in traditional sources of knowledge or protection (e.g., a well whose waters used to heal the blind but now has lost its healing power).

The characters in Maeterlinck's "static" theater (1889–1894), which includes the *Pelléas* play, exist under the pervasive influence of fate. It is a world that is arbitrary and cruel, and in which the only certainty is death.[4] The protagonists move like sleepwalkers uprooted from a painful dream.[5] In *Bluebeard's Castle*, Judith seems driven to a journey that leads her to a tragic end. The modern preoccupation with an inward look to the inner self is reflected in symbols (underground vaults, dark castle, closed doors). Although the manifest theme in both works appears to be a love story, the underlying themes reveal the contradictions in socially sanctioned roles and power differentials at the time in which the works were written.

The difficulties of finding a satisfactory resolution to the characters' dilemmas, as attested by the tragic endings in both works, lead us to identify another type of trauma, one embedded in the social fabric of the times. A theme common to both operas is the frequency in which the characters are engaged in rigidly structured interactions. The main characters show no room for compromise, nor are they willing or able to understand one another. Within this context, the gender interactions in both works lead to extreme positions, in which only surrender, subversion, domination or coercion are possible (e.g., Golaud's "rescue" of and marriage to Mélisande in spite of her early protests, or Bluebeard's surrender of the keys to Judith, an action that later leads to her demise). The underlying social tensions and the ensuing discontent cut across social and gender categories. Echoes of this more general struggle are evident in *Pelléas et Mélisande*, in which social and gender issues are interwoven in the fabric of the work.[6]

Mutual Recognition and Gender

The creation of both operas coincided with the beginnings of psychoanalysis and psychodynamic psychology. Debussy, Maeterlinck, Balázs, and Bartók were contemporaries of Pierre Janet and Sigmund Freud. The latter two, as clinicians, discovered the psychological effects of traumatic events by listening to their patients and trying to find a way to ameliorate their pain.[7] Although using different perspectives, both Freud and Janet viewed the unconscious as a realm that could be understood and rendered less destructive by awareness and new learning. Maeterlinck and Balázs, relying on the philosophical positions of the time, viewed the unconscious as part of fate, a universal will.[8]

Although framed within the perspective of destiny, or the unconscious will, both works struggle with the notion of a self divided by contradictory impulses and driven by unconscious motivation. The rigidity of gendered social prescriptions at the time in which the stories were written leads to the development of psychological defenses that lock the protagonists in ongoing, mutually traumatizing interactions. *Pelléas* and *Bluebeard* reveal the tragic consequences of the use of narcissistic defenses to cope with fears of vulnerability and intimacy.[9] Narcissistic defenses are defined here as primitive mechanisms that include an exaggerated sense of grandiosity, alternation of idealization and devaluation of others, and a retreat into isolation and avoidance of conflict to counteract feelings of grief and emptiness.[10]

The gender issues that existed around the turn of the twentieth century, and that were explored in both works, continue to be sources of debate and analysis to the present. Klaus Theweleit's analysis of novels, essays, and journals written in the Germany of the 1920s by members of the Freikorps[11] reveals rejection of "the feminine within" as a pervasive theme in these writings. It is "the woman within" that represents the greatest threat for these men. The soft, fluid, boundless perception of the female body, which is "a subversive source of pleasure or pain," is contrasted with the machinelike, clearly defined male body, which is "devoid of all internal viscera." Theweleit views the psychological organization revealed in the writings of the Frei-korps as manifesting narcissistic pathology, not as a regression to the "oceanic feeling" of merging with the mother but, rather, as an inability to find warmth and affection in another person because of early deprivation and rejection.[12]

Writing in 1984, Jessica Benjamin suggested that Western society, by placing issues of race, gender, or social class as avenues for distinguishing subject from object—or the privileged one (who becomes the subject) to dominate the other (who is relegated to the role of the object)—does not provide a healthy ground for the maintenance of mutually satisfying relationships.[13] Benjamin suggests that the notion of an autono-mous person denies the mutual dependency that exists between men and women and more generally within members of the society itself. Within this context, domination becomes intrinsic to the Western society paradigm. Benjamin suggests that acknowl-edgment of mutual dependency and the need for mutual recognition constitutes an alternative to either submission or domination in gender relationships.[14]

Stressing the emotional cost of gender prescriptions, Nancy Chodorow notes that gender inequalities may cause narcissistic injuries because they restrict the manner in which a person, who belongs to one or the other gender, may be permitted to express connection, dependence, independence, differentiation, agency, and initiative.[15] Lay-ton refers to Lisak's observations that both genders suffer "self-mutilation,"[16] because "each one is forced to extirpate from the self characteristics that are experienced as parts of the self, yet coded by the culture as belonging only to the other gender."[17]

Within these formulations, the gender dilemmas in the *Pelléas* and *Bluebeard* dra-mas (expressing the gender dichotomies of their time) could be seen as attempts of their authors to understand and grapple with the traumatic "self-mutilation" that the sociocultural context created for them. In contrast to the Freikorps writings, *Pelléas* and *Bluebeard* held together the painful awareness of the nonviability of the narcis-sistic solution. The characters in both works are hampered by social restrictions that prevent them from engaging in a mutually validating relationship. The need for ab-solute control of the other leads to the destruction of the relationship and to isolation and loneliness.[18]

Language and Meaning

We know from our own experiences that words cannot completely express our feel-ings and perceptions. We make our initial encounter with the world and early care-takers as nonverbal beings but, by the time that we begin to be able to understand and use language to code our experiences and communicate with others, we already have acquired an impressive amount of knowledge via modalities other than language. Those modalities—sound, sight, touch, and kinesthetic sensations—are a very impor-tant part of our memory and our sense of self, and some of them will never be encoded in verbal language. Daniel Stern, who has done considerable work with infants, iden-tifies the emergent self, core self, and a subjective self as states of being that precede and coexist with the verbal sense as ways that relate to us and others (including the noninterpersonal world).[19] It is in those states of being, in which language is not included, that art finds its tremendously compelling power.[20] Maeterlinck writes that "even those who can speak the most profoundly realize—they, perhaps, more than others—that words can never express the real, special relationship that exists between two beings."[21] The Symbolist use of language in both operas, in which meaning is not overtly expressed, offers an opportunity for the music to provide alternative narratives to what is left unsaid by the characters.

Language, Developmental Social Malattunement, and Trauma

We are familiar with traumatic reactions to catastrophic experiences, such as wars or unexpected human violence, which defy what we have learned to expect from our common interactions with the world. Such experiences often disrupt the common neurological paths that we use to process information, and may remain stored in dissociated ways, unencoded in language, and set aside as unwelcome fragments from what we know and experience as our selves.[22] We know from the study of traumatized people of the profound suffering that trauma causes, and to how persistently those fragments of self refuse to go away. They remain invisible prisons that isolate survivors from thoughts, feelings, and events that, while protecting them from terror, impoverish their emotional and intellectual life, or they reappear in the form of frightening dreams, altered emotional states, and symbolic enactments of the traumatic events.

There are also other reasons why some experiences might not be easily translated into language. The feeling of being understood by the other is a source of well-being that is evident from our own experiences and verified by infant observation.[23] Understanding, misunderstanding, attunement, and malattunement occur prior to the advent of language, and are correlated with the caretaker's ability to respond to the infant in the infant's mode of communication (movement, touch, sounds, and changes in stimulus intensity). From a developmental perspective, the acquisition of language, which occurs in an interpersonal context, confines the knowledge that we can share with others and what we can tell ourselves. As we become more able to express our thoughts and feelings in words, we are able to articulate a more complex understanding of our experiences and ourselves. In some instances, we sense a contradiction between what we feel and see, and what others can validate for us. We might be reluctant to express feelings and thoughts that we sense are disruptive to the maintenance of our relationships with those we love, or with the social network that sustains our lives. Thus, language becomes a barrier, an unwritten divide between what we know and what we sense we are supposed to know.[24] We see this use of language in many of Mélisande's utterances, in which her responses are evasive and disconnected. We also see this in Judith's relentless disregard for Bluebeard's pleas and his lack of response to her pleas later in the play. This use of language becomes a more subtle yet powerful form of additional traumatization for the characters. In addition, in as much as ordinary language expresses "so much of the control and manipulation over the individual by the power structure," the use of language may be one of the ways in which the characters resist domination or attempt to maintain it.[25]

Fate and Trauma

Maeterlinck's characters reflect the author's belief in the inexorable unfolding of fate. They have little choice but to be passive observers as the drama of their lives—and their deaths—unfolds. Debussy's musical interpretation further expresses this polarity between the human element (feelings, spontaneity, unpredictability) and fate (mechanical quality, passivity, predictability). A few months before he completed *Pelléas et Mélisande*, Maeterlinck was concerned about his reputation as "a poet of terror."[26] Halls suggests that Mélisande's story was closer to a tale of real human interactions that included affection and love in contrast to his previous works in which terror and fear prevailed. However, Mélisande appears in the play as a terrified young woman who has endured much horror, and her life in Allemonde is not any better. She enters Allemonde as victim of trauma and dies in Allemonde as victim of trauma.

Mélisande and Gender

Although Mélisande's identity remains obscured in the opera, we learn from other sources that she was one of Bluebeard's wives, and it was Bluebeard from whom she was running away when Golaud found her in the forest. In contrast to Judith and Ariane, the two other wives of Bluebeard who appear in the Maeterlinck and Balázs plays, Mélisande appears frail, confused, and driven by forces she does not understand. However, these differences do not diminish the intensity and life-and-death quality of the conflict between the spouses. Her identification as one of Bluebeard's wives, as well as her actual interactions with Golaud, Pelléas, and Arkel, raises the issue of gender as another polarity and important variable to consider in understanding both the opera and the play.

Mélisande's beauty is portrayed as almost irresistible to both Golaud and Pelléas. Both of them had ignored the danger signals that were present in their first encounter with her. Gender polarities are dramatized at the outset, beginning with Golaud and Mélisande. Golaud is the hunter in pursuit of a beast that he has wounded. Instead of the beast, he finds Mélisande who, just like Golaud's beast, was running away from someone who had injured her. Golaud is taken by the beauty of this young girl, but ignores forewarnings of her ultimate rejection of him. Mélisande's first greeting reveals her fear of being harmed by this stranger ("Do not touch me"), and her subsequent allusion to his graying hair suggests that she is aware of their age difference. Golaud's reply "[that it is only] a little, here at the temples" is a defensive reply that reveals his need to minimize its significance. Golaud also tries to talk her out of her fear of him "Why do you look so surprised?" When she exclaims that he is a giant, an observation that emphasizes their difference in size and physical strength, he replies that he is "a man like the rest." We may find greater empathy with Golaud's dilemma if we look at their interaction as a possible dialogue between an inexperienced therapist and a traumatized patient. Golaud is the powerful therapist, who has all the answers and wants to talk this traumatized patient out of her pain by offering support and a corrective emotional experience. But by disregarding Mélisande's feelings, he disenables her—after all, her feelings and the validity of what she has experienced are at the essence of who she is, and all this had motivated her to escape from her oppression by another man. He further undermines her self-confidence and underestimates her strengths by asserting that she has no other options but to go with him. The dialogue also points out ways in which Golaud may have transferred to Mélisande his own disavowed fears and his own need for support and rescue. Hints of his own suffering are suggested by his assertion that he is just a man and, like Mélisande, he, too, is lost.

The influence of Maeterlinck's life-experiences colors his descriptions of the environmental surroundings and passionate interpersonal relationships in Allemonde. Maeterlinck himself referred to the similarities between the castle and forest in *Pelléas et Mélisande* and the castlelike structure of his father's home and vast land holdings. Maeterlinck received such a strict religious Catholic upbringing that one of his schoolmates and close friends said that, in their youth, they were taught to be mindful of the pervasive presence of death rather than life.[27] This remark resonates with the dark atmosphere in Allemonde and the painful consequences of the young lovers' passion.

The contrast between Maeterlinck's religious upbringing and the example of his powerful father, who as a landowner found many mistresses among his subordinates, conveyed contradictory messages. In his actual relationship to women, he seemed to have been influenced by his father. He acknowledged having more than one mistress at a time and may have seen aspects of himself in Pelléas, as we learn that for a period of time he and his father shared the same mistress.[28] He also said that the idea of a jealous Golaud might have come to his mind at a time in which he unwittingly found his first lover in the hands of another man. The need to resolve the contradictions between his religious upbringing and the life he led may have inspired the topics of many of his writings such as those on spirituality, life after death, and the relationship between men and women. Halls suggests that Maeterlinck's gloomy religious upbringing contributed to the bouts of depression he suffered throughout his life.[29]

Maeterlinck suggests that women have communications with the unknown, which are denied to men, "for women are indeed the veiled sisters of all the great things we do not see."[30] But why is it that women can see what men cannot see? Golaud asks Mélisande if she ever closes her eyes (score, p. 16),[31] to which she replies that she closes them at night. Mélisande's constant alertness seems to be a response to fear. She is frightened rather than insightful. Unfortunately, her hypervigilance is justified: the figure of Bluebeard casts a long shadow on Golaud. She is caught between the power differences between herself and Golaud and by the intensity of her desires, which eventually leads to her destruction. Maeterlinck's suggestion of women's position as "nearest of kin to the infinite,"[32] seems to refer to her willingness to abandon herself to her desires and to the power of fate. This places her on a collision course with social restrictions. Mélisande (woman) can see through the inhumanity and falsehood of the restrictions arbitrarily imposed on her,[33] and she is not willing or able to go along with them. Her dialogue with Pelléas in the first "Well" scene (score, p. 63) is a symbolic expression of her predicament. She wants to reach deep into the well but, as she tells Pelléas, her hair is longer than her arms, even longer than herself. Maeterlinck suggests that women "are more largely swayed by destiny than us. They submit to its decrees with far more simplicity; nor is there sincerity in the resistance they offer."[34]

Golaud seems also to be driven by fate when he hints at what he "must" do if he discovers "a forbidden" liaison between the young couple just because "it is customary." The privileged position of the man is shown by his ability to invoke a social dictum that transforms his act of rage and jealousy into an act of duty. Melisande, instead, must be punished because she has failed to behave as a possession. There is no social sanction for a woman's desire.

The abuse of power of the strong versus the weak takes place at different levels in the play. In his first encounter with Mélisande, Golaud commands her to leave the forest with him in spite of her protests. Later we learn that they are married in spite of the great age difference between them. Golaud abuses Yniold, his young son, by forcing him to spy on Mélisande and Pelléas until he has Yniold in tears. He also physically abuses Mélisande in the presence of his elderly grandfather, ignoring the latter's pleas to stop his behavior. He attacks Pelléas and kills him in spite of the fact that his younger brother has no sword nor offers any resistance. Perhaps the greatest abuse of power is the total disregard for the well-being of his two children, Yniold and Mélisande's unborn child, both of whom are left as orphans and with Golaud's legacy of the death of Pelléas and Mélisande.

Abuse is also revealed in the wide social class differences between the ruling family and the peasants.[35] Pelléas and Mélisande find homeless, silent people sleeping in the grotto at night. Arkel and Golaud refer to the people dying of hunger. Their reactions suggest that they view the situation as unpleasant, but they do not reveal any responsibility for their plight or acknowledge any desire or ability to help ameliorate it. In this Symbolist play, one cannot fail to make the connection between the starving lowly peasants and the young lovers' hunger to find love and sensuality in each other. The underlying connection is highlighted by the juxtaposition of Golaud's despotic rejection of Mélisande, his search for his sword and his announcement to Arkel, with much irritation and annoyance, that they just found the body of another peasant. That evening, Golaud kills Pelléas and injures Mélisande (a minor injury that results in her death, nevertheless) when he finds them embracing in the garden.

But Golaud is, of course, a victim himself, as his attempts to control his destiny by force do not lead to fulfillment but to destruction of what he so strongly desires. He is also trapped in a prison stronger than himself, and we wonder what that prison might be. We might find a clue in Maeterlinck's assertion that women "alone can still smile at [the infinite] with the intimate grace of the child, to whom its father inspires no fear."[36]

What is this loss of "grace" caused by fear of the father, fated on boys but not on girls? It is a precursor of Freud's view of women having "a defective superego,"[37] although Freud attributed it to anatomical differences rather than to differential treatment by their fathers. Golaud's loss of grace could have been the internalization of a rigid moral code of values that allows no consideration for feelings or interpersonal realities. In Golaud's case, there also seems to be a sense of entitlement, which allows him to ignore Mélisande's initial rejection and feelings as well as the complexities of the situation.[38] The "loss of grace" could be the injuction to guide our actions by abstract principles without regard to the context in which they are applied, as Maeterlinck could have been taught during his early religious training. Perhaps Maeterlinck's journey toward formulating a more benevolent but spiritual view of life was his attempt to regain "a state of grace." Golaud himself appears trapped in a rigid moral code when he remarks with anger but also regret (score, p. 218): "I don't play the spy. I shall wait on chance; and then . . . Oh, then! Just because it's customary."

It is easy to understand why Mélisande needed to free herself from the ring and the crown, which were considered valuable and precious gifts. Anna Freud, pointed out, in her essay on "losing and being lost," that "in losing" an object the loser may be unconsciously expressing anger against the giver of the gift and may also show a lack of affective connection with the giver. The loser also may identify with the lost object, feeling herself lost. All these interpretations are plausible in Mélisande's case.[39]

But the material value of both gifts as well as their symbolic meaning (royalty or a special status in the case of the crown, and a promise of faithfulness or token of ownership in the case of the ring) lead us to explore once more the gender polarities and inequality of power in Mélisande's world. Both men, the donor of the crown (Bluebeard) and Golaud, give Mélisande very special gifts. For instance, Golaud is deeply upset when he learns of the loss of the ring (score, pp. 99–100): "I would rather have lost all I possess than have lost that ring! You don't know what it is. You don't know where it came from." We know, from the rest of the story, that the loss of the ring also signifies Golaud's awareness of Mélisande's attraction to Pelléas, and the frailty of the marital bond as symbolized by the ring. But Golaud's attraction to Mélisande seems to have been a mirage, an idealization of her since, as he confessed in his letter to Pelléas (score, p. 27), after six months of marriage to her, he knows no more about her than on the day they met. Mélisande was as mysterious as the women to whom Maeterlinck attributed both a kinship with the infinite and a possession of the vision not given to men.

One wonders whether Mélisande's destiny, men's attraction to her, and their need to control her, all leading to their mutual destruction, are reflected in the dynamics of men-women relationships at the time the opera was written and, more specifically, in the personal experiences of Maeterlinck and Debussy. Certainly, Debussy had his share of passionate relationships and disappointments as well as involvement in triangular relationships, such as those portrayed in the opera. Debussy refined his opera at a time in which he felt very alone and had suffered the rejection of three women he had proposed to marry. Two of the women in his life, Gaby, with whom he lived for twelve years, and Lilly, his first wife, attempted suicide when they felt abandoned by Debussy. In the case of Lilly, the unpleasantness of the situation was aggravated by Debussy's affair with a married woman of wealthier means, who finally became his second wife.[40] Passion, ambivalence, and guilt were prevalent during this period, which also coincided with the success of *Pelléas*. Thus, the passionate triangular entanglements, the jealousy, and the guilt prevalent in the opera found a clear echo in the life of the composer. According to Georgette Leblanc, in one of their early encounters, Maeterlinck told her "he had always had several mistresses at once. . . . It was a pastime like any other. But as for happiness, it didn't exist outside of pleasure or a good constitution."[41] Complaining about the multitude of distractions that interfered with his composing, an older Debussy would write to his friend, "first, the family, which clutters and obstructs me. . . . Then there come the Mistresses, or the

Mistress, upon whom one does not even rely, so happy is one to give oneself to her, even to the point of oblivion."[42] Women were thus loved and feared, sought after and rejected.

The opera does not end in absolute chaos or hopelessness because, prior to her death, Mélisande gives birth to a baby girl, but there is uncertainty about what fate will bring to her daughter. Mélisande herself does not appear to feel hopeful. Her first words to her are also her last, since she dies soon afterward (score, pp. 298–299): "She doesn't smile. She's very small. She's going to cry. I'm sorry for her." Arkel himself utters the last words in the opera, which reveal an uncertain future for the little girl: "The child mustn't stay here in this room. It must live in her place now. It's the poor little thing's turn."

If Allemonde were the real world, there would be little hope for Mélisande's little girl. She is orphaned almost at birth at the hands of her rageful, jealous father, who is now overcome by grief and who implies that he also may die soon. There also would be little hope for the infant, if she is to take her mother's unfortunate place, as Arkel pronounces. But we know from other experiences that Arkel's pronouncements, rather than reflecting wisdom, have at times contributed to the tragedy, as when he stopped Pelléas from visiting his friend and thereby facilitated his entanglement with Mélisande.

Thus, we are left alone to answer the question about Mélisande's little girl. There are signs of hope. There are the silent women, whose presence supports Mélisande at her death, whose silent strength and refusal to listen to Golaud's orders to leave disarm him. Perhaps they provide that quiet, holding environment for the baby that the family cannot provide. It is they, who are supposedly powerless, who provide a powerful, calming presence at Mélisande's deathbed.

There is also Golaud's sobs, his last utterances in the opera, a perfect symmetry to Mélisande's sobs, which constitute her first utterances in the opera. If part of the Allemonde tragedy is the irreconcilable gender polarities of strong versus weak, oppressor versus victim, then Golaud's pain is an acknowledgment of the disastrous consequences of narcissistic entitlement.

Arkel seems to say so (score, pp. 304–306): "Careful . . . careful. We must speak quietly, now. We mustn't worry her any more. The human soul is a very silent thing. The human soul likes to take its departure alone. She suffers so timidly. But the pity of it, Golaud, the sadness of everything one sees. Oh! Oh!"

Mélisande and Trauma

The character of Mélisande is an important focal issue in the opera. Her presence in the castle seems to be a promise for a renewal of life. Each one of the male characters is drawn to her in a different way, but it is this attraction (in the case of Pelléas and Golaud) that transforms the promise of hope into a force of destruction. There is a vitality of passion and sensuality in Mélisande that seeks expression in spite of great risk to herself and others around her.

What kind of person is Mélisande that she has such power, yet does not possess the ability to use it on her own behalf nor those she says she loves? Golaud meets her for the first time, alone, sobbing, and lost in the depths of the forest. We learn that she is frightened and that awful things have happened to her, which she cannot talk about. As the story develops, we do not learn much more about her history, except that she had to run away from a painful situation. Her main torturer gave her a golden crown, which she "accidentally" had dropped into the well by the time Golaud had found her.

The "clinical data" thus presented shows basic symptoms of Post-Traumatic Stress Disorder: she has endured events beyond normal human experience; she avoids places or things that remind her of that event; and she has moments in which she suffers intrusive symptoms, and other moments in which she appears "numb," dissociated, and not responding appropriately.[43]

One of the effects of trauma is that it reduces choices. A traumatized person may become more passive and less able to respond to the requirements of the present, because her energy is consumed by coping with feelings and memories of events too overwhelming to be processed, understood, and integrated with the rest of her life. Thus, a traumatized person is more susceptible to external pressures and is more at the mercy of situations and people than others who have not suffered similar experiences. Mélisande's behavior is consistent with these characteristics: she follows Golaud out of the forest and later marries him even though her early encounter with him suggests not only that she does not find him appealing but also that she is frightened of him. She is unable to contain her feelings of attraction for Pelléas and acts on them impulsively without considering safer alternatives.

Dissociation is another possible response to unbearable circumstances. By isolating the traumatic event from the rest of her experiences, the victim is able to protect herself from its potentially disorganizing impact.[44] One of the problems of using dissociation, however, is that what is experienced is not integrated. Therefore the traumatic material is not understood and a person's reactions to it, or to events that trigger memories of the trauma, are difficult to manage. Part of the treatment of trauma lies in the recovery of traumatic memories, which then can be stored as something that happened in the past, so the person is free from reexperiencing the overwhelming effect triggered by the initial trauma in her daily life. In her 1954 interview, Maggie Teyte, one of the earliest to play the dramatic role of Mélisande, suggested that Golaud's violent mistreatment of Mélisande serves as "an archaic shock treatment"; "It is only after Golaud has pulled her violently by the hair that she returns to her senses and is whole-heartedly able to accept affection."[45] Up to that point, Mélisande did not want to be touched, either by Golaud or Pelléas. Teyte suggests that "through brutality she has lost her mind and through brutality it has been restored." Golaud's abusive treatment of Mélisande thus seems to be a prelude to the intensification of her relationship to Pelléas. Unfortunately for Mélisande, Golaud's "therapeutic intervention" was not done in a neutral, safe atmosphere. Instead of helping her to differentiate the past from the present, it repeated the past and thus contributed to further traumatization. This, of course, is one of the potential risks of trauma, the unconscious search for a repetition of similar conditions with the hope of mastering the situation (Freud's notion of repetition compulsion)[46] or diminished ability to discriminate dangerous from nondangerous stimuli that may lead to poor judgment with serious consequences.[47] Halls remarks that Mockel,[48] one of Maeterlinck's early critics, suggested that sadism was Maeterlinck's prominent theme.[49] Golaud's brutal treatment of the young lovers elicits sorrow and compassion that are voiced by King Arkel at Mélisande's deathbed. Mélisande's new partner is as dangerous as the one she left behind.

Mélisande and Her Social Environment

Van der Kolk has suggested that society prefers to blame victims for their misfortunes rather than to believe that they have no control over what happens to them. He suggests that the presence of victims challenges our belief (at least in the Western world) that human beings essentially have mastery over their fate.[50] Because we do not want to believe in this lack of control, it is understandable that some critics might see Mélisande more as instrumental in her own destruction rather than as a victim of Golaud's cruelty. Debussy also suggested that, in spite of her weaknesses, Mélisande had significant strengths. The social structure in *Pelléas et Mélisande*, however, is one of unequal power, and Mélisande, who is female, young, and an outsider, has very little political or physical power in comparison with Golaud. She does, however, manage to express her desires, although her previous trauma and the oppressive surroundings make it difficult for her to do it in a self-assertive manner or to take responsibility for most of her actions. It is interesting that in the two instances in which Mélisande frees herself from the symbols of oppression (the golden crown and Golaud's golden wedding band) she does not do it purposely, or at least does not admit it to herself. The crown "fell in while I was crying" (score, p. 11). As for the ring, "I thought I had it in my hands . . . and yet it fell all the same" (score, p. 70).

Thus, we could say that it is Mélisande's hidden desire for freedom and self-expression that is stronger than her (conscious) self. It is her need for self-expression that prompted her "to lose" her ring and earlier dispose of the golden crown. In this instance, "fate" can be seen as representing Mélisande's true self fighting for self-expression. It is interesting that in Mélisande's case self-expression leads to self-destruction. In Mélisande's situation, there is no room for self-expression. She is the unwilling wife of a powerful man, who ignores her wishes and forces his love on her. The price for self-expression is her death. Halls has suggested that the story brings into focus the clash between natural law and social law, and challenges the imperative to maintain the marriage vow under all circumstances.[51] However, we may not see Mélisande's death as meaningless. Using Donald Winnicott's concept of a true self, we could view Mélisande's death as that part of her self that, finding no way of facilitating the expression of the true self, chooses self-destruction rather than absolute denial of her essence.[52]

Maeterlinck's insight into human psychology predated Winnicott's essay on the true self, a concept that Winnicott developed out of his clinical work with patients. Maeterlinck postulates the presence of an unconscious life (to which he attributes creative and mystical qualities) where our true self resides. He distinguishes the true self from our intelligence as free from the limitations of space and time, both being barriers to our grasping the essence of things.[53]

Prior to the fatal outcome, the increasing tension in the play is brought about by the counterposition between the growing attraction of Pelléas and Mélisande toward each other and Golaud's mounting suspicions. Mélisande evolves, however briefly, from a puppetlike creature to a woman capable of defiance and passion, as evidenced by her behavior during her last encounter with Pelléas (act 4, scene 4, p. 257). She is also capable of deception, not only with Golaud but also with Pelléas; for example, she tells him that she was delayed in meeting him because her husband had bad dreams and because she caught her dress on the nail of a door (act 4, scene 5). The text leaves the reader to suspect that this might be a fabrication, as there is no allusion to Golaud's bad dreams or doornails in narrative prior to their encounter. She omits telling Pelléas of Golaud's threats and of the violent treatment she received earlier that day, which could have been the actual reason for her torn dress. By withholding this information, she fails to alert Pelléas of the increasing danger of their situation.

Mélisande's behavior defies the barriers of time and space that Maeterlinck suggests are impediments for the perception of the true essence of things. She is at the wrong time in the wrong place. When Pelléas declares that the doors are locked and that it is now too late to go back to the castle, Mélisande responds "so much the better." She seems freer to follow the promptings of that inner self without being distracted by the external aspects of the situation. This is perhaps a remnant of a romantic ideal, although the victory, if any, is tragic and subtle rather than triumphant. At the time that he wrote *Pelléas*, Maeterlinck viewed human beings as unable to alter the designs of destiny. In his later writings, he gave a greater role to our ability of use our reason to alter destiny.

The tragic outcome suggests awareness and a protest against the power inequalities of the situation. Mélisande's price for legitimate self-expression is death. As with Judith's story in *Bluebeard*, there is no space for the expression of the woman's desire—although, in Maeterlinck's play, this condition seems to affect peasants, children, and Pelléas as well.

Transcending the obvious interpretations of Pelléas and Mélisande as adulterers, Maeterlinck's symbolic references portray the young lovers as innocent victims (e.g., sheep being carried to slaughter (act 4, scene 3, p. 223); Arkel's reference to Mélisande's eyes, "I see nothing in them but great innocence (act 3, scene 4, pp. 179–180), Yniold's response to Golaud's questions about Pelléas, "No, daddy, he is not mad, he is very good" (act 4, scene 2, pp. 209–210).

Pelléas's death, however, cannot be easily labeled as claim for self-expression. He had wanted to leave the castle prior to Mélisande's arrival, but was prevented in doing so by his grandfather, who admonished him about family obligations. By postponing his departure, Pelléas became entangled in a dangerous situation that ended his life. Contrary to Mélisande, whose marriage to Golaud provided her with limited options for a vital life, Pelléas finally has the opportunity to leave the castle after learning of his father's improvement. His words denote hope for a new life, "Already the whole house seems to be reviving. One can hear people breathing, walking about" (act 4, scene 1, p. 192). He has reservations about his last encounter with Mélisande: "It is late. She isn't coming. It would be better to leave without seeing her" (act 4, scene, p. 233–234). His attraction to her overrules his hesitation and ends his hope for a new life.

Throughout the story, Pelléas functions as a compliant character whose duty to the family seemed to have been to defer the satisfaction of his needs on behalf of other family members.[54] At the end, Pelléas realizes that he, too, is caught in the snares of destiny from which there is no escape. Maeterlinck's narrative of the lovers' last encounter suggests another level of meaning. The dialogue between the lovers portrays a passionate Pelléas, but Mélisande's passion is mixed with dread and dissociation, which leads her to be deceptive rather than forthcoming.

In the passionate declaration of their mutual love, Pelléas, wanting reassurance, asks Mélisande if she is telling him the truth about loving him, or if she is lying just to make him feel better. Mélisande responds that she never lied, except to Golaud (score, p. 247). Pelléas does not seem to realize that if Mélisande could lie to Golaud she also may lie to Pelléas himself. Pelléas "hears only the beauty of her voice: for him, the medium is the message."[55] We suspect that Mélisande had just lied about the reasons for her torn dress and her delay in meeting Pelléas.[56] She had earlier declared that she had loved Pelléas since the moment she met him, but later says that she, like Pelléas, did not love him at the beginning because she was afraid. When Pelléas fears that Mélisande may not be thinking of him because her eyes were somewhere else, she responds that she was seeing him somewhere else (score, p. 254). This ambiguous response may be another evasion, because Mélisande's distractions could be associated with her anticipation of Golaud's presence or memories of previous traumas. She acknowledges that she is both happy and sad (score, p. 255).

In any case, Mélisande is not candid with Pelléas. Her dissociative defenses contribute to her denial of the danger that awaits them. The sudden change in Mélisande's reactions illustrates the extent of her initial denial. She had first expressed defiance, "All the better," when Pelléas remarked that the castle doors are now closed to them, then terror when Golaud confronts them, and she flees crying that she is a coward (score, p. 267). By not telling Pelléas of Golaud's violent behavior and threats, she fails to provide him with information that could have prevented their death, or at least to provide him with more choices. Mélisande's traumatic experiences contribute to the tenuous quality of her attachment to others and make her more vulnerable to her impulses, less capable of considering the needs of another person.[57]

Different Perspectives in the Pursuit of Understanding Bartók's *Bluebeard* Opera

Duke Bluebeard's Castle, the artistic depiction of the legendary story of a wife-murderer in the combined visions of Béla Balázs and Béla Bartók, may be discussed from different perspectives. Like the opera itself, the different perspectives are likely to convey different layers of meaning. These layers attest to the complexity of the work and of human interactions as well as the corresponding feelings that Bartók and Balázs attempted to convey. Rather than claiming a "royal path" to the understanding of Bluebeard's soul, the present interpretation is offered as another layer of meaning that may enrich rather than negate or contradict the accounts of others who have embarked on the same journey, that is, the search to understand the lessons and to appreciate the beauty of *Bluebeard's Castle*.

The Bluebeard Ballad, History, and Cultural Context

Balázs transformed his original idea of a one-act *Don Juan and Bluebeard* play (in which Don Juan was to be Balázs incognito)[58] to the *Bluebeard* play, published in 1910. The creation of the story of *Duke Bluebeard* and his struggles with intimacy and love occurred at a time in which these three men—Balázs, Zoltán Kodály, and Bartók—were facing similar issues in their own lives. Life and art entered the duke's castle and transformed it in ways that reflected personal events as well as artistic and sociopolitical pressures of the time.

Balázs was twenty-six years old at the time of the play's publication, and his personal and professional life was in transition. The *Bluebeard* story resonates with Balázs's personal inquiry into the meaning of life, the nature of intimacy, psychological self-knowledge, and gender relationships. The symbolic meaning of the castle as Bluebeard's soul, and the approach-avoidance conflict in exploring its chambers, represented by Judith's and Bluebeard's struggle, resonate with Balázs's passionate search for understanding his own psychological processes, which are clearly reflected in his journal.[59]

Balázs as well as Bartók and Kodály belong to the younger generation of writers and artists trying to find a place for themselves in their respective vocations and pursuing romantic liaisons. Balázs, like the duke, experienced alienation from the more established writers and artists.[60] Perhaps Balázs found validation for his ideals and ambition and support for his male identity, embattled by the death of his father when he was thirteen years old, in the friendships of Kodály, Lukács, and, later, Bartók. He shared with Kodály and Bartók an interest in folk ballads and music and a desire to create a truly Hungarian voice in the arts. Lukács became his lifelong intellectual comrade, who shared his interests in aesthetics, philosophy, and politics.

Balázs was torn between his intellectual artistic strivings and his sensual passions for which he could find no easy outlet: "I can't get a mistress because I have no time to look for one, and I can't work because my sexual fury doesn't leave me in peace."[61] The duke's story could be seen as Balázs's attempt to portray his own agony at his inability to find sensual comfort and affective intimacy with his male friends or intellectual, artistic kinship with his female friends. The barrier was perhaps more imposed by sociopolitical stereotypes of the time than by Balázs's actual experiences: his female friends were intelligent, sensitive women. However, he had very intense relationships with his male friends, with whom he felt greater affinity. For instance, about his friendship with Kodály, he wrote in his diary, "could not part from Zoltán. This is a mystical destined belonging."[62] The duke's story could represent Balázs's attempts to draw a line in the sand and protect his allegiance to patriarchal hegemony from female intrusion. The story's outcome documents Balázs's awareness of the tragedy of splitting talent, intelligence, and sensuality along a gender divide.

Around the time that the *Bluebeard* play was published, Balázs felt he was drifting apart from Kodály. This was after the latter's marriage to Emma Gruber, their mutual patron and supporter. Although Bartók welcomed the manuscript, Kodály found "no affinity with it."[63] Balázs felt Kodály's apparent rejection very deeply, even though Kodály's distancing could have been the result of his attempts to consolidate his relationship with Emma in the earlier stages of their marriage and a concomitant reevaluation of earlier relationships, including his close friendship with Balázs. Ko-dály's lack of interest in the *Bluebeard* play did not discourage Balázs from dedicating his first volume of collected poems to him in 1911. The first poem in this collection, dedicated to a friend, reiterates the conviction that friendship among men is superior to friendship between men and women, a belief that Balázs and Lukács shared at that time.[64] Balázs's comments further suggest that he viewed Emma as consciously trying to increase the distance between Kodály and himself.

Not surprisingly, the three characters of the play (the Castle, Bluebeard, and Ju-dith) express different aspects of the conflicts that Balázs was struggling with at the time he wrote it. In Judith, Balázs saw himself in the way she pushed forward in ex-ploring the inner soul of the other, in ways that created disruptions in the relation-ship.[65] Judith's choice of the dangerous, risky life to join Bluebeard and abandon the conventional life offered by her family and her betrothed resonates with a basic theme in Balázs's life and work.[66] The author viewed his play as "the ballad of inner life."[67] The use of an inanimate object, the Castle, as one of the play's characters who repre-sents the duke's soul, with its own physiognomy, for instance, voice and actions, fore-shadows the importance that Balázs was to place on the symbolic value of objects in the new language of visual images created in film. The vitality of objects as conveyors of meaning rather than as "dead corpses" was also one of Balázs's father's teachings. Simon Bauer[68] wanted his son to learn a craft, "not to master it," but so that the young Herbert Bauer would see man-made objects as "creations" and not as empty and dead objects surrounding him like "corpses."[69]

Balázs's "ballad of inner life" may well have represented a developmental crisis, a journey in exploring and processing important issues of vocation and his relation-ship to women. From a psychological viewpoint, there was no one more important to the early development of Balázs's identity as a man than the figure of his father, who may well have colored the portrayal of the Castle. Although Balázs's own accounts re-flect admiration for his father's intellectual accomplishments, his integrity, and his di-rect involvement in Balázs's education, discipline, and guidance, there is no question that Balázs viewed his father's life as a sad, tragic one. The depressive, silent suffering of the Castle and its protective walls might not only be seen as an abstract symbol of the man's soul but also as the shadow of Simon Bauer's own tragic story.[70] The tears, violence, and cruelty suggested by the Castle's contents had been experienced in the flesh by Balázs's father and indirectly by Balázs in the manner in which his father's his-tory affected his own.

Balázs, Bluebeard, and Trauma

Although Balázs acknowledges the duke as encompassing aspects of himself and the richness that the women in his life brought to him, the play ends with an affirmation of the inability of men and women to relate to one another, echoing Balázs's pro-nouncements in his 1911 publication. The work itself maintains a constant tension between the opening of the doors and the revelations of horrible secrets, which are rendered harmless by Judith's ultimate discovery that the wives were not dead after all, but alive and kept in splendid riches by the Duke. It is Judith who has committed the crime of intrusion, for which both she and Bluebeard are sentenced to eternal darkness. The play maintains a constant tension between signs of violence and cruelty (blood on the walls, on the jewels, on the instruments of torture) and a denial of violence and cruelty, as seen in the Duke's love for Judith, his willingness to submit to Judith's requests, and the final revelation of his former wives' existence. In some ways, it resembles a childhood story; for example, Little Red Riding Hood's grandmother is not dead, but alive inside the wolf's stomach.[71] Both *Bluebeard* and *Little Red Riding Hood* acknowledge trauma and loss and, at the same time, deny them. In *Bluebeard*, Balázs's insight into the nature of psychological trauma is evident in the suggestion that trauma and loss are not less real when the characters in the play do not die. The trauma comes, instead, from the lack of mutual acknowledgment of the other's existence and individuality.[72] Unlike *Little Red Riding Hood*, the *Bluebeard* ballad does not end happily. Balázs, a man of his time, acknowledges the complexity of intimate relationships.

The general atmosphere of the play is one of pending threat, a feeling that Balázs knew very well. His earliest visual images, documented in his journal, are his accounts of two dreams: a threatening wild horse that nearly collides with him, and a peaceful night scene that slowly changes to fill him with terror. Balázs acknowledges that he was terrified of darkness until he was twenty years old.[73] Balázs's early life included painful losses and unexpected changes, which could have contributed to the young boy's expectations of dread. His father's sudden removal from his teaching post in Szeged, a sophisticated city, second in population to Budapest, and his transfer to the remote rural town of Lőcse when Balázs was five years old was very painful to Balázs's parents and drastically altered his father's professional and literary aspirations. Yet, young Herbert's early memories portrayed this event as a change engineered by fate to foster the young child's development, although it resulted in a profound loss for the family. Balázs's transformation of this tragic event into an opportunity for positive change attests to his healthy resiliency.[74] However, young Herbert's interpretation could also belie his assuming responsibility for an event far beyond his control to counteract feelings of helplessness and loss.

Judith's journey into the castle also may be seen, like Balázs's reaction, as a strategy to counteract feelings of helplessness and lack of control. Her eagerness to bring light into the castle could be interpreted as a counter phobic defense to Balázs's fears of darkness. It also resonates with his active and at times insensitive efforts to control the lives of his friends or scrutinize the content of their souls.

The emphases on masculine symbols of power in the castle and the foreboding bloodstains warns us that it is more than the "inherent incompatibility between men and women" and the resulting loneliness that is hidden within the walls of the castle. Balázs was aware of how much violence and cruelty could be inflected toward one another without spilling one drop of blood. He reports that a teenage boarder shattered his healthier acceptance of sexual love when, as a ten-year-old boy, he was the unexpected witness and uninformed assistant to the rape of a young servant girl.[75] Balázs felt that this experience had a profound and detrimental effect on his view of love relationships between men and women. It was a sweet-sour tacit cooperation between two young males to subjugate the initiative and autonomy of a young woman. Remnants of this tacit allegiance, or perhaps a different expression of it, may be seen in Balázs's and Lukács's early belief in the inherent superiority of men's intellect and the ultimate irreconcilable differences between men and women. In this case, violence is not committed in a physical sense but in a psychological one; that is, an inability to accept the other in the full richness of her or his being. A personal event that brought to light the serious consequences of interpersonal alienation toward women by both Lukács and Balázs occurred in 1911, when Irma Seidler, who had become romantically involved with Balázs after being rejected by Lukács, committed suicide by throwing herself into the Danube.

Bartok's Opera, *Duke Bluebeard's Castle*: Historical and Biographical Notes

When Bartók welcomed Balázs's invitation to set the *Bluebeard* ballad to music, he had been married for a few months to his piano student, Márta Ziegler, thirteen years his junior. Just two years before, Bartók had suffered the severe disappointment of the rupture in his relationship with Stefi Geyer. At that time, he had attached one of Balázs's poems to the manuscript score of the violin concerto that he wrote for Geyer and that he gave to her as a parting gift. Bartók and Balázs shared a sense of loneliness that would stay with both men throughout their lives.[76]

Judit Frigyesi places *Duke Bluebeard's Castle* in the context of the artistic, existential, and historical dilemmas that existed in Hungary when Balázs and Bartók created this work. Within this perspective, Bluebeard's kingdom, if any, seems to reside in the inner regions of his soul. In this way, he represents a reaction against German romanticism and the acknowledgment of the human mind as divided between the conscious self and those unconscious regions that human beings dread to recognize as part of themselves.[77] An awareness of the unconscious had become accepted in scientific circles by the work of Charcot, Janet, Breuer, and Freud. These ideas were already present in the writings of Nietzsche, and there is clear evidence that Bartók and Balázs were avid readers of Nietzsche.[78] Bluebeard is not a hero of romanticism. He does not struggle with and overcome powerful external enemies or conquer vast kingdoms: although the content of the castle's chambers in his kingdom include arsenals and a vast domain, their diffuse quality makes them mysterious, undefined, and without clear external reference. Bluebeard's tragic heroism does not belong to the man of the Enlightenment who views mankind as being able to master the external and internal world and to do so with a measure of benevolence toward others by the appropriate exercise of reason.[79] His heroism corresponds to that ideal of late-nineteenth-century man that involves a willingness to accept all aspects of us from the most noble to the most unpleasant ones. Reiff has suggested that the twentieth century gave rise to psychological man.[80] The latter's journey involves the awareness and containment of the extreme and contradictory impulses that inhabit our conscious and unconscious mind in contrast with the man of the Enlightenment, who idealizes the supremacy of reason.

Frigyesi, in pursuing a thoughtful analysis of the poetic output of the young Hungarian artists, who were part of the circle of Balázs and Bartók, wants us to understand how much the duke is very much a man connected with his time and place, a voice that tells and shares the narrative of his contemporaries, a man that in his solitude and loneliness has much to share with his neighbors. And, it is perhaps this paradox—

loneliness versus attunement—that is one of the many others that the castle contains and that makes it a Symbolist work, attempting to expose and integrate the contradictions of its time.[81] Thus, in this view of the work, the drama does not have two protagonists (Bluebeard and Judith), as the opera suggests, or three characters (Bluebeard, Judith, and the Castle), as suggested by the Balázs play, but only one character, Bluebeard, who, like in Jungian dream symbolism, confronts different parts of himself in a struggle toward self-integration. Within this perspective, Judith's role is to help Bluebeard's soul "to see (and to be seen) and to allow its mystery to slip away."[82]

In a letter to Márta Ziegler, Bartók reveals his willingness to explore and express all feelings, not only those that are comforting and flattering but also those that challenge an idealized vision of ourselves. He writes: "It is only in our times that there is place for the painting of the feeling of vengeance, the grotesque, and the sarcastic. For this reason the music of today could be called realistic because, unlike the idealism of previous eras, it extends with honesty to all real human emotions without excluding any."[83] These thoughts are consistent with the views of Lukács who, a few years earlier, had arrived at a coherent view of the function and aesthetics of the art of that time: "The essence of art is form; it is to defeat oppositions, to conquer opposing forces, to create coherence from every centrifugal force, from all things that have been deeply and eternally alien to one another before and outside this form"[84]

The duke's story conforms to these aesthetic guidelines. The content of its seven chambers, the feelings portrayed in the Balázs script, and Bartók's score opened up a vast horizon of feelings and associations that range from tenderness and love to horror, isolation, and loneliness. The *Bluebeard* score seems to have been a final artistic solution to the painful ending of Bartók's relationship with Stefi Geyer. A letter to her describing the complexity of his feelings attests to the emotional roller coaster that Bartók experienced at that time.[85]

By what means is the artwork able to conquer the "opposing forces" that are introduced at the beginning of the story: the desire to know oneself, even those parts of the self that may horrify us versus the desire to let go, to keep those doors to self-knowledge forever closed? Frigyesi suggests that Judith's intrusiveness is a loving act, the encouragement from "the other" that is always necessary for us to know ourselves.[86]

This interpretation is consistent with the existential dilemmas of the time: the feeling of alienation and powerlessness,[87] and the loss of faith in a benevolent creator and religious institutions. If there was hope, one had to find it in oneself and in one's unconscious. The manifest content of the drama portrays a conflict between a man and a woman and many writers have interpreted the work along those lines. The argument can be made for a more general statement about alienation. Bartók himself candidly acknowledges his difficulties in feeling close to anyone.[88]

It is not possible to disregard the meaning of Bluebeard's story as a reflection of the vicissitudes of men-women relationships at the time the work was written. The issue was not only an important one in the personal lives of Balázs and Bartók but also one confronting the social fabric of the cultural world in which they lived.

Carl Leafstedt's comprehensive review of the transformation of Judith, the self-sacrificing and courageous biblical heroine into the destructive, sexualized, envious man-murderer as depicted in Strauss's *Salome* and Hebbel's *Judith*, attest to the anxiety that the feminist movement engendered with its demands for greater autonomy and self-determination for women.[89] Similarly, Leafstedt's comprehensive documentation of the transformation of Bluebeard, the wife-murderer, into an unhappy, lonely man, whose cruelty could have been a response to unhappiness and repeated disappointments, reflects a greater awareness of the complexity of psychological motivation. As Leafstedt indicates, Bluebeard became a "man to be pitied as well as feared."[90]

Leafstedt enriches his discussion of the *Bluebeard* story by using concepts from Hebbel's theory of literary analysis, which had been the focus of Balázs's doctoral thesis. He suggests that Balázs's poem dramatizes Hebbel's tragic view of human life, which must submit to the equilibrium prescribed by the universal will or face destruction. In Balázs's play, Judith is the Romantic heroine, compelled by the universal will within her to seek love and self-expression. In the dark confines of the castle, women could know a man's soul only at the expense of their love and her destruction. Her compulsive strivings toward liberating Bluebeard's castle from darkness, even after achieving a relatively peaceful stage at the fifth door, destroys the balance, which must be restored through her destruction. Darkness again returns to the castle that is enveloped by endless night.[91]

A Feminist View from a Castle That Is Not

When Judith enters Bluebeard's castle, she leaves behind the patriarchal protection of her father, her brothers, and her betrothed to follow an uncertain destiny with the duke. This early beginning maintains an uneasy tension, which challenges and maintains contemporary gender stereotypes. Judith forsakes the patriarchal protection of her family and relatives for a life with Bluebeard. However, she makes it clear that Bluebeard "will lead" and that "she will follow." It is his castle, not hers, that she will labor to rescue from darkness to light.

The primary distinction regarding the ownership of the castle by Bluebeard announces one of the ways in which the play maintains gender stereotypes of the time and fails to resolve their contradictions. Judith is now on a journey to help Bluebeard face dreaded or unresolved aspects of himself, but there is no allusion to her own castle, her own self, or dreaded aspects of herself that need healing. This dichotomy preserves rigid gender stereotypes that will result in the final destruction of the couple's relationship.[92]

If the castle is a symbol for Bluebeard's soul, "the castle that is not" is a symbol for Judith's predicament. It becomes a symbol for a definition of a woman's desire by its absence. Claire Kahane suggests, from a perspective consistent with that of Luce Irigaray and Jessica Benjamin, that it is the lack of an available symbolic representation for a woman's desire that "fuels female rage."[93] In Bluebeard's discourse, there is no room for Judith to express desires for treasures that she has found herself, for battles that she has fought, for tears that she has shed.

Within this perspective, neither Judith nor Bluebeard has arrived at a stage of mature autonomy, which would involve both the surrender of the narcissistic position and freedom from relationships that require absolute surrender.[94] Kernberg's description of the development of a primitive internal structure, "the grandiose self," as a response to early emotional deprivation and trauma, is helpful in understanding both

Bluebeard and Judith's dilemma. A grandiose view of oneself is a protection against traumatic disappointment and fear of abandonment. It allows the person to deny dependency on others. Others are either idealized or devalued in order to maintain the illusion of personal omnipotence and grandiosity. The narcissistically flawed individual needs the other to validate his or her grandiosity and omnipotence, so must control the other in order to prevent any responses that would challenge his or her sense of entitlement and power. The person thus loses the capacity to depend on others and is able to protect him/herself "from emotional conflicts with others by withdrawing into . . . splendid, grandiose isolation."[95] The relationship between Judith and Bluebeard was defined within the boundaries of domination versus submission.[96] This was unavoidable, as they were both trapped within the boundaries of rigid gender stereotypes. The failure of their relationship is due to their inability to accept each other—and themselves—as interdependent human beings, fallible and with limitations, yet capable of agency and initiative. There was no room in the castle for the space required for two equals to interact and love one another. Judith and Bluebeard could not resolve their differences as respectful adversaries who must consider each other's needs and find alternatives to meeting them without obliterating each other.

This perspective provides an alternative explanation for the tortured relationship between Judith and Bluebeard. Bluebeard wants recognition from Judith. He needs for her to see and accept aspects of himself, some of which he fears. He seems to know and experience the healing power of releasing his open wounds to the healing light of the gaze of another, a process that facilitates his own ability for self-acceptance. But the conditions that he places on Judith, "never question what you see," deny her the recognition of her own subjectivity. Bluebeard's interactions with Judith suggest that he is not able to recognize her as an independent center of initiative and agency, a person that has her own needs for self-knowledge and self-acceptance. Bluebeard is seen as not fully trusting Judith to give him freely the recognition that he seeks. When Judith enters the castle, her future options will be determined by what Bluebeard chooses to give her or not to give her, what he will allow her to see or not to see. When she transgresses the boundaries and Bluebeard passively surrenders the additional keys, the hopelessness of their relationship is sealed. Bluebeard's need for coercive control of Judith's reactions suggests narcissistic vulnerabilities. He cannot accept his human limitations and by allowing Judith to see them, risk potential abandonment and disappointment. He needs Judith to offer unconditional acceptance, but he cannot risk her independent choices.

Within this context, the suffering and violence suggested by the pervasive presence of blood in the castle becomes clear. It signifies the suppression of "the other's" reality and subjectivity. It is interesting that Bluebeard's coercive control of Judith is expressed by the situation (the imprisonment by the castle walls and Bluebeard's control over its forbidding contents) than by Bluebeard's behavior, which has characteristic masochistic qualities (he complains about Judith's requests but submits to them, he pleads with her to be careful but does not stop her, he begs for her love). As has been observed by others, Bluebeard's behavior becomes more assertive after the fifth door is opened, but his rage is never expressed directly. He cannot accept Judith's vitality and independent choices. After her transgression, he assigns her a place in the lifeless chamber of his memories, in spite of her pleas for him to look at her, to acknowledge her existence: "I am still here," she says. Bluebeard ignores her, and with protests of love and appreciation that ring hollow, proceeds to burden her with symbols of his grandiosity and power that she does not want (e.g., "not the crown," she begs).

In Bluebeard's castle, the man is entitled to unquestioned power and grandeur and the woman is entitled to them only through the love and generosity of the man that loves her. Judith can only enjoy these benefits if she renounces her agency. The only manner in which she is allowed to express initiative is by accepting submission.

Within these restricted molds, Judith's choices to express power, ambition, and a sense of entitlement as emerging from her own subjectivity must be disavowed. The need for coercive control is fueled by narcissistic rage. She then overvalues the power and control that her renunciation of her own agency and submission to Bluebeard grants her. It is the narcissistic entitlement of the masochistic position. Although Judith asserts that she is motivated by love to bring light into Bluebeard's darkness, and prompts him to unlock all aspects of himself, she is increasingly insensitive to his feelings. The magical power of masochistic thinking is implied by her logic, she has left everything for Bluebeard; he must now surrender to her. The compulsive quality of her behavior, the lack of satisfaction of what she finds, even after achieving the fifth door, reveals the futility of her journey, because she has not acknowledged her desire for a life of her own.

The final dissolution of the relationship after she discovers Bluebeard's other wives is preceded by painful, almost delusional jealousy that is expressed in a repetitive chant in which Judith compares herself unfavorably to each one of the other three wives. Judith's behavior further portrays the sense of a narcissistically injured person, who has no inner resources to maintain a favorable autonomous view of herself. Thus, she cannot accept Bluebeard as a person with an autonomous life and relationship. The awareness that there are aspects of Bluebeard's life that do not include her—that he has autonomy—is threatening to her. If he has autonomy, he could choose to leave her. This is too threatening to Judith, who does not experience herself as a vital autonomous person, and whose sense of inner cohesion depends on Bluebeard, for example, Judith's responses to the treasure chamber.

Judith is perhaps more herself, more in contact with her own pain, her vulnerability, her need for recognition of Bluebeard, and of her own subjectivity when she desperately begs Bluebeard to acknowledge her, "I am still here." But Bluebeard does not hear her. Instead, he praises her beauty, assigns her a place among his other wives, and continues to ignore her subjectivity. She is now another one of his leftover objects.

Thus, Judith and Bluebeard are both victims and perpetrators. Trapped within the boundaries of rigid gender stereotypes, they are unable to accept each other and themselves with all the richness, vulnerabilities, and limitations that the human condition entails. Imprisonment does not do well for human love. And it is here where we could infer another meaning for the pervasive presence of blood in the castle.

A Reevaluation of the Duke Bluebeard Story within an Autobiographical Perspective

At this point, it is interesting to review Balázs's personal and professional life around the time in which the *Bluebeard* play was created. We know the closeness of Balázs's and Lukács's personal and emotional friendship, and how at the time of the play's creation both men were involved in elucidating man's relationship to woman. The parallel between Bluebeard's treatment of Judith, and Lukács's description of his feelings about the rupture of his relationship to Irma Seidler are striking, "The ice age has begun. I have died but she lives within me; to the extent that anything can live within me. Quietly. Without reproaches. Without pain."[97] This is further stressed in the dedication of his book, *Soul and Form*, to her: "What I want to accomplish can only be carried out by a man who is alone. True solitude, however, can only be bought at the price of, and after, the deepest experience of intimacy."[98] The importance of Irma, the real woman, receded and became disposable as the "ideal Irma." She was replaced in Lukács's heart and mind as an object of philosophical explorations. Although Lukács's replacement of the "real Irma" by "its symbol" may have been helpful to his professional development, it was devastating to Irma. Agnes Heller, in a thoughtful and detailed exposition of the correspondence between Lukács and Irma Seidler, describes the struggle between Lukács the philosopher and Irma the woman. Lukács could only relate to Irma as a symbol, the passion that she elicited in him as a subject for philosophical analysis. Irma just wanted to love and be loved: "She [Irma] put an end to the philosophical parables once and for all with her finale gesture of suicide. It was she, and not the philosopher himself, who cast into doubt and rendered equivocal the philosophy of *Soul and Form* with this final gesture. And through her death she earned the right to share this story [the story of their relationship], not merely as its object, but as its subject as well."[99]

There is strong evidence that Lukács's relationship to Irma had a powerful influence on Balázs. In 1910, the year prior to Irma's death, Balázs wrote a short story, "Friendship [Baratsag]," under the pen name "Happened," which is reported to have been inspired by the writer's seduction of Irma to avenge Lukács.[100] In the voice of the protagonist, Balázs asserts, "I have humiliated my best friend for a woman I did not love, and debased a pure-hearted woman." And later, in a statement reminiscent of Balázs's accounts of the early episode when, at age eleven, he was the unknowing assistant to a rape, the fictionalized Balázs says, "Ervin [who stands for Lukács in the story] just cried and cried. I felt ashamed. The male in me was humiliated, conquered and insulted." In addition, according to Zsuffa, a few months prior to Irma's death, Balázs had her read his play, "The Blood of the Virgin," in which the friendship of two men "triumphs over earthly love—at the price of a woman's life."[101]

Further information about the context of Balázs's *Bluebeard* play may be inferred from the transformation of his original idea to write *Don Juan in Budapest* into the story of *Duke Bluebeard*. There is no question that the character of Don Juan appealed to Balázs, and, like Don Juan, Balázs documented his "conquests."[102] Balázs was aware of the destructive impact of his actions on the women he conquered. Writing to Lukács about the suicide of a girl he had seduced, he said, "You may have already read it in the papers or heard from Edith that a girl died here. This time I am positive. I am not the cause only the occasion of her death. What counts is that death is my companion. I am a public danger."[103]

Thus, the information gathered here suggests that the philosophical, benevolent ending of the *Bluebeard* play reveals Balázs's awareness of the destructive effects of the lack of recognition of the woman's subjectivity and needs, and his feelings of remorse.

Those very human feelings, in addition to the philosophical inquiry of men-women relationships, found expression in the blood and horror contained within the castle's walls.[104]

A View from a Door That Was Not

The beginning scene in Hebbel's *Judith* portrays a magnificent, sexually potent Holofernes, longing for a confrontation with an enemy who will dare to face him. He longs for an adversary, one who may be as magnificent and powerful as he is. Kahane suggests that what Holofernes wants is a narcissistic double. Instead, Hebbel "gives him Judith."[105] One wonders if Holofernes's longing for an adversarial reflection of himself and his disappointing encounter with Judith (whom he uses and then discards with fatal consequences) have some resonance in the *Bluebeard* tale. Bluebeard's Judith, after all, was a woman, and Balázs had made it clear in his poems and literary output, contemporary with his creation of *Bluebeard*, that friendship between men was far more complete and satisfying than the relationship between men and women. Simply put, it is difficult to find happiness in a lover that we devalue and that we see as inferior to ourselves. Such a lover may not offer the challenge that a good adversary can provide. Someone that we can feel is an equal to ourselves, whom we may be able to admire and challenge and engage in fair battle, a battle that may confront us with our limitations and strengths, that may sharpen our skills without causing our mutual destruction.[106] Neither Bluebeard nor Judith was able to serve as a good adversary for the other. Disagreement and differences never became an object for negotiation and debate. Bluebeard and Judith rigidly interchange roles, from being the one who submits to the other to being the one who dominates the other. They could not create a space in which differences of needs or opinions could be negotiated.

Although Lukács, whose aesthetic theory had great influence on Balázs and Bartók, was aware of the need to open the doors and invite discordant emotions to challenge the chains of absolute rationality, neither Balázs nor Bartók could see a way out of the domination versus submission dichotomy. Women were still seen as inferior, closer to the forces of nature. Openness to a woman meant danger of enmeshment to irrational forces. Bluebeard became psychologically aware but isolated.

The rigid either-or alternative, submission versus domination, surrender versus coercion, could be seen as having some adaptive functions if they do not lead to the destruction of both or either one of the partners. Submission could be viewed as an opportunity to be recognized by the other, to give up control to the other, with the hope that one may be free to explore and be oneself. Accepting that she will follow Bluebeard, Judith may have an opportunity to find herself and be recognized by another. The relationship that is available to them, however, is not one of mutual recognition but of mutual idealization. Bluebeard becomes the idealized figure of the powerful father with whom she could identify. She will feel powerful by being with him. But acquiring a sense of power through idealization implies that she cannot tolerate weakness in the idealized other (hence her frightened, paranoid responses to the "blood," Bluebeard's vulnerabilities). True liberation requires a relationship of mutual recognition, in which she, too, is able to experience her own power and freedom to be curious, to use her mind and express assertiveness. As a counterpart, Judith is also an idealized figure for Bluebeard. She is the most beautiful of his wives, and her love will bring light to his castle. However, she cannot exist in the castle as a whole person with her vulnerabilities and needs.

Reflections on Modernity

Maeterlinck's characters, Golaud in particular, find the challenge of modernity too much to bear. Rather than see all aspects of himself and others, to accept ambiguity and endure contradictions, he wants certainty, he wants to know "the truth," as if there was only one truth, one relevant question: "Did Mélisande and Pelléas love each other in a 'forbidden' way?" He cannot look at himself and see his graying hair, his stage in life, and accept the offer of his father to find a wife that would solidify the old order. As a child of modernity, he rejects the past, rejects his grandfather's advice, and finds Mélisande. But he cannot see Mélisande's youth or pain, he can only see his needs and Mélisande as a suitable object for the satisfaction of his needs. His reactions return him to the role of the all-powerful patriarch without the traits of wisdom, benevolence, or concern for others that the paternal role could also entail. Within this point of view, Golaud could be seen as showing the negative side of modernity. It is the dark side of Modernity that, facing the self with all its complexities and nuances of darkness and light, closes its eyes and projects the evil outside of itself.[107] Golaud cannot accept the contradictions and uncertainties of the situation, and so reacts with a sense of entitlement and without regard for the needs of others.

In Allemonde, the pervasive, melancholy air of the castle is accentuated—or perhaps created—by the absence of the father. This absence of one capable of guiding and protecting the family pervades the mood of the castle. Arkel, the king of Allemonde, is old and blind, his well no longer returning sight to the blind. Golaud, who has the power and strength of the father, is so concerned with his own needs and so blinded by his sense of entitlement that his power, rather than providing security to the family, constitutes a greater threat to them than the starving peasants. There is no equivalent force capable of counteracting his power, and so his destructiveness is left unchecked. Mélisande, who in her own way could be seen more in the role of the adversary than the harmless Pelléas, has been weakened by previous victimization and can only maintain some sort of self-respect by losing her life rather than accepting Golaud's oppression.

The challenge of modernity, its invitation to accept the self with all its contradictions, is also too much for the characters in the *Bluebeard* play. The suggestion that isolation or enmeshment are the only avenues for relatedness places Judith and Bluebeard's interaction in a narrow narcissistic paradigm. Bluebeard opens his doors to Judith, perhaps needing her presence to face all the hiding places where less desirable aspects of his soul are exposed. However, he only wants her to behave as a reflection of his glorious, narcissistic self. He wants her to see the diamonds but to ignore the blood. Judith's task, then, is similar to the therapeutic dilemma of a therapist treating a patient with a narcissistic disorder. In urging the patient to confront the aspects of himself that he wants to ignore, without sensitivity to his fears, the therapist may cause additional traumatization to the patient. In a treatment informed by an understanding of the psychology of the self,[108] Bluebeard needed to experience Judith (therapist) as a benevolent figure that could both see Bluebeard's sufferings and shortcomings as well as his strengths, and, through her own empathy and understanding, help Bluebeard develop compassion and empathy for those parts of himself that terrified him. This process also would entail assisting him to remember and explore the life journey that had led him to accumulate his treasures, his weapons, and create the suffering that he may have inflicted on himself or others. Judith, with her own narcissistic vulnerabilities, was not up to the task. She failed to provide the validation that he needed. Instead of providing understanding and empathy for the parts of Bluebeard's soul that he wanted to ignore, but that he knew he needed to face, she reacted to them with horror and disgust. How could she react otherwise? There is no acknowledgment of the existence of her soul, and a castle of her own with hidden chambers that also needed healing. The wounded healer could not heal the wounded because she had no way of acknowledging and grieving her own pain.

In the context of the gender issues contained within *Bluebeard* and *Pelléas et Mélisande*, it is helpful to consider Julia Kristeva's identification of "abjection,"[109] which she describes as the violent repudiation of that which threatens to detract from the defined borders of the ego and the effort to be separate from the heterogeneous. Kristeva suggests that which is excluded—the mother, the feminine. Benjamin's theoretical formulations of human psychology support Kristeva's position. Benjamin refers to the pleasure in mutual recognition and reciprocal interaction between the baby and the mother.[110] She suggests that Western society's overvaluation of work and remunerated productivity and undervaluation of work associated with child rearing and home care creates an artificial dichotomy. It fosters the idealized image of man as an autonomous, independent being, and allows men to deny their dependency on the mother and reject any "commonality" that they may have with her. Women as caretakers must renounce their own subjectivity (that they also have needs, ambitions, and desires). Subjectivity is a male prerogative.[111]

This point of view adds another dimension to the death of Mélisande and Pelléas, who was, after all, a man capable of affection and tenderness, and whose character could conceivably be played by a woman, as discussed earlier. Tenderness, vulnerability, and acknowledgment of dependency were excised from Allemonde by the stroke of Golaud's sword, and so was the hope for "new life" promised by the presence of Melisande. Kristeva's concept of abjection would seem to be most applicable also to Bluebeard's story. It clarifies Judith's horror at the sight of blood and Bluebeard's attempts to gloss over its presence. The feminine is rejected, encased in the dark walls of the castle. Bluebeard remains incomplete and alone.

4

Pelléas et Mélisande

*Polarity of Characterizations: Human
Beings as Real-Life Individuals
and Instruments of Fate*

When one enters the Kingdom of Allemonde, one's sense of time and space dissolves. Allemonde acquires what Freud describes as the quality of the unconscious, in which time and space no longer serve as measuring rods for the relationships among people, objects, and events. For instance, when Mélisande refers to "long ago," we do not know whether she means ten years, a month, or other such measurement of time. This creates a feeling of anxious uncertainty because, as biological beings, we exist in a definite relation to our environment. But as psychological beings, the omnipresence of our unconscious life, which is unrestrained by time and space, allows for infinite wonderment or horror. The connection made between the unconscious and Allemonde resonates with Maeterlinck's notion of Fate. The power of the unconscious to rule our lives may be perceived or expressed externally as Fate.

Ignacio Matte Blanco suggests that unconscious mental processes are governed by symmetrical relationships, in which the whole and a part may belong to the same set (e.g., a dog and its color may be substituted for each other in a dream), while in conscious mental processes the concept of dog and the concept of white would belong to different sets and could not be interchanged for one another. In musical terms, the diatonic scale would be more likely to be associated with the human realm and consciousness because of the nonsymmetrical hierarchy of its components, that is, each diatonic tone has a distinctive function within a larger diatonic mode, while symmetrical pitch formations would be more likely to resonate with the realm of fate and the unconscious because of the equalization of the individual components.[1]

The means by which Debussy transforms the harmonic materials of the traditional major-minor scale system into the new musical language of *Pelléas et Mélisande* and the techniques by which he adapts this language to the expression of the psychodramatic symbolism of the Maeterlinck play mark a significant development in the relation between musical language and text. Within Debussy's pioneering musical conception, the various parameters of phrase construction, rhythm, texture, and instrumental timbre are inextricably connected to the role of pitch relations in reflecting the dramatic symbology. In this regard, instrumental timbre often supports the dramatic and psychological associations according to a sort of "leit-sound" conception (timbre associated with a particular dramatic event, mood, or character), which is analogous to the notion of "leitmotif," although not used in that capacity to the same degree as the pitch-related materials. The mosaic construction of Debussy's orchestral textures, based on pervasive phrasal repetition and the juxtaposition of contrasting instrumental timbres and figurations, is ideally suited to the realization of one of the primary dramatic principles of the opera: polarity between individuals as real-life beings and as instruments of fate. This principle and some of the basic musico-dramatic polarities subsumed under it are outlined in table 4-1.

The intrusion of *fate* into the human realm is musically articulated by a distinctive harmonic coloring for each of the individual textural planes. Although directed motion in the musico-dramatic narrative seems to be produced simply by the plot in and of itself, a sense of progression is induced on the local level by means of special transformations from one type of pitch-set to another: diatonic to symmetrical, or vice versa. Pitch-set transformation is essential for linking the otherwise separate mosaic-like planes and layers and also for drawing them into the intricate web of symbolic associations. Immersed in the mood of fate, the introverted characters never seem to struggle against the relentless force of their destinies, and so the music floats quietly along much of the time in one or another pitch-set coloring. In particular, as part of the denial of free will, in which the characters never reveal the full range of their emotions, a static musical quality is produced primarily by the intervallic symmetry of certain types of pitch-sets (especially whole-tone) and the symmetrical harmonic sub-collections derived from them. The "somewhat stable character" of a symmetrical chord can be attributed to "its self-evident structure."[2]

Although the opera is permeated by nonsymmetrical pitch collections (including the traditional major and minor triads) as well as symmetrical ones, properties of the former in the organic growth of the opera can generally be understood as having latent symmetrical possibilities. That is to say, nonsymmetrical collections often emerge in the course of a passage or scene as segments of larger symmetrical formations, as in the case of a given nonsymmetrical three-note cell (say, Bb–D–E), which might be expanded into the dominant ninth chord (C–E–G–Bb–D), French sixth chord (Bb–D–E–G#), or complete whole-tone scale (Bb–C–D–E–F#–G#). The means by which various nonsymmetrical pitch collections (both traditional and nontraditional) are symmetrized in the opera constitute an important part of this study. In addition to symbolizing the *fatalistic* side of the main dramatic polarity, that is, human beings as instruments of fate as opposed to their status as real-life beings, nonfunctional symmetrical formations also contribute to the general atmospheric quietude that is often elicited by the musical descriptions of wells (or fountains) and scenery,[3] which are themselves presented as symbolic manifestations.

Debussy's aesthetic intentions are revealed in his conversation in October 1889, with his Paris Conservatory professor Ernest Guiraud, as recalled by Maurice Emmanuel.[4] In expressing his opposition to the Wagnerian approach, Debussy prophetically anticipated his discovery of the Maeterlinck play and the new aesthetic approach to mood and characterization: "I dream of texts which will not condemn me

TABLE 4-1 Musico-Dramatic Polarities

Human as real-life being	versus	Human as instrument of fate
Diatonic scales		Whole-tone scales
(pentatony, major/minor, modality)		(symmetry, interval cycles)
(traditional, folklike)		(nontraditional, abstract)
Conscious		Unconscious
Verbal		Nonverbal
Light		Dark
Bondage		Freedom
Life		Death

to perpetrate long, heavy Acts, but will provide me, instead, changing scenes, varied in place and mood, where the characters in the play do not argue, but submit to life and fate."[5] Debussy's static musical language, based on parallel seventh and ninth chords, modal and whole-tone melodies and harmonies, and chromatic fragments within his mosaic-like handling of the structure, provides an ideal medium for the absorption of worldly objects into the fatalistic realm. All these musical features are most evident in the orchestra, the vocal line always unfolding in a quasi-recitative style that is sensitive to the French language. The orchestra, which always carries the melodic phrase, suggests emotion, while the vocal line, which often dwells on a single note, expresses the characters' intentions. This relation of voice and orchestra is one aspect of the principle of polarity. As an essential manifestation of this principle, the voice-orchestra relation may be viewed as an interweaving of "action" and "reflection," in which the music passes "from *information* to *reflection*, from the *fact* to the *symbol*. . . . The vocal line frees itself from diction to gain its autonomy: the texture of the orchestra changes its meaning: from *support* it is transformed into *sharing*."[6]

Except for the opera's distinct subdivisions into acts and scenes, traditional operatic clarity is sacrificed in that there is no notion of distinct recitatives and arias within the local scenes. However, in spite of this structural ambiguity and Debussy's nonfunctional harmonic progressions, discrete musical substructures in the form of local textural planes and layers may be discerned within each of the scenes in correspondence with Maeterlinck's otherwise clear dramatic framework. Furthermore, while Debussy himself generally opposed the "Wagnerian formula"[7] and repudiated the blatant usage of leitmotifs in his own opera, in which he tells us that there is no "guiding thread" and that "the characters are not subjected to the slavery of the leitmotif,"[8] the individual leitmotifs are usually assigned distinctive pitch-set colorings and tend to serve an articulative function in his formal substructures.[9] In other words, the leitmotif conception is integrally linked to the conception of pitch-sets and their polarized interactions, both closely tied to the symbolic meaning of the drama. The leitmotifs often serve as local culminating points for melodic/harmonic interactions and shifts from one area to another in correspondence with the psychological and dramatic direction.[10] Ultimately, however, these leitmotifs remain extremely supple and are never obtrusive. They appear more like "shadows" that accompany the characters.[11] Debussy "wanted music to have a freedom that was perhaps more inherent than in any other art, for it is not limited to a more or less exact representation of nature, but rather to the mysterious affinity between Nature and the Imagination."[12]

In contrast to the more organic flow of the material in Wagner's music dramas, however, Debussy's orchestral leitmotifs occur in separate phrasal and sectional planes. Structuralization is achieved by means of frequently paired repetitions of the textural planes, a feature also reflected in the characters' frequent word repetitions, especially Mélisande's. Such repetitions result in a seemingly less-than-real character, one whose emotional disconnection seems to indicate the effect of traumatic experience. Furthermore, each plane is defined by static harmonies derived either from the diatonic-modal or whole-tone scales, depending on its relative position in the symbolic polarity between the human and fatalistic spheres. Debussy's approach to the musical language of *Pelléas* has been aptly contrasted with that of *Tristan:* "Whereas Wagner's different harmonic fields are momentary, within a constant flow of chromatic harmony, Debussy's range far further, into modal, whole-tone, diatonic 'white-note', even octatonic areas, creating—by the range of possibilities for the presentation of any one motif— a language of extended flexibility with which to respond to Maeterlinck's interplay of themes and symbols."[13]

The fundamental dramatic premise of polarity in the opera is manifested in two dramatic concepts, one in which the individual characters are instruments of *fate*, the other in which they are real human beings capable of love, hate, and jealousy. Notwithstanding the contrasting musical aesthetics of Wagner and Debussy, the Maeterlinck libretto is reminiscent of the *Tristan* plot. Golaud finds Mélisande lost in the forest, falls in love with her and marries her. Later, he becomes jealous of his half-brother Pelléas, who has been meeting with Mélisande. Before killing Pelléas, Golaud drags Mélisande by her hair from left to right and back and forth, the motion invoking the image of the Cross. She forgives him—as Christ forgave us for our sins—just before she dies at childbirth. Events seem preordained as the introverted characters move without resistance toward their fate, a notion that is suggested by Maeterlinck's own philosophical questions: "Do I need to be told whether she whom I take in my arms to-day is jealous or faithful, gay or sad, sincere or treacherous? Do you think that these wretched words can attain the heights whereon our souls repose and where our destiny fulfils itself in silence?"[14]

Act 1, the Prelude: Its Structure and Leitmotifs Associated with the "Forest," "Fate," "Mélisande," and "Mélisande's Naïveté"

Static, contrasting phrasal planes provide the mosaic-like structural foundation on which distinctive musical elements interact to reflect the dramatic principle of polarity. A general outline of the Prelude provides the framework for understanding how these interactions serve in the realization of this fundamental dramatic principle. The Prelude's rounded form is built entirely from successive pairings of phrase segments. While the two segments within each pair of phrases are almost identical thematically, the larger binary periods are distinguished from each other by their differing thematic motifs,[15] these differentiations supported by contrasting instrumental assignments. The opening antecedent phrase (p. 1, mm. 1–4, muted cellos, double basses, and bassoons)[16] introduces the somber "Forest" motif in two almost identical halves. The low instrumental register, which immediately establishes a sense of darkness, later serves to evoke the same mood for the castle and its surroundings, where we are told that the sun never shines. The "Forest" motif is followed by a contrasting consequent phrase (mm. 5–6, oboes, English horn, and clarinets), which Lawrence Gilman refers to as the "Fate" motif.[17] While this motif is also constructed in two almost identical parts, it is only half the length of the "Forest" motif. The musico-dramatic significance of this proportional reduction will be revealed in the adjacency between the ending of the Prelude and opening of the forest scene.

Some scholars have identified Gilman's "Fate" motif more commonly with "Golaud."[18] One reason for this association might be that Golaud's entry into the forest (in a whole-tone context) is in the same relation to the Prelude's closing statement of the "Forest" motif as Gilman's whole-tone "Fate" motif (at mm. 5–6) is to the Prelude's very opening statement of the "Forest" motif. Gilman's assignment of the motif to fate seems more plausible, nevertheless, since the motif at its initial statement (mm. 5–6) and at other prominent occurrences is based on the whole-tone collection, the sonority most pervasively associated with fatalistic moods and events throughout the opera. The symbolic association of this motif with Golaud is less convincing because, in spite of Emmanuel's interpretation in favor of this association, it does not accompany the first nor many other appearances of Golaud. When it does accompany this character, the text usually refers to a significant fatalistic event, for example, Golaud's hunt after the boar (p. 4, m. 4, and p. 17, m. 3 ff.), which will lead him to his first encounter with Mélisande. Conversely, the motif pervades much of the action where Golaud is not present. Furthermore, Debussy's own manuscripts suggest another theme for the original "Golaud" motif (see score p. 14, m. 8, which is identified as such by Gilman) and, later in the compositional process, Debussy invented yet a new motif for Golaud, perhaps during work on act 1.[19] After that, Debussy's compositional development and revision show increasing use of the latter consistently in connection with Golaud.

Regardless of motivic assignment, Golaud emerges as the primary instrument of fate, though he himself, like all the other characters, is incapable of achieving his goals in the face of the inevitable. For one thing, his human will is powerless against the timelessness of the ancient forest.[20] He has made no progress from the moment he has entered the forest, "I shall never get out of this forest," to the moment he attempts to leave it with the mysterious young woman, "I don't know. I'm lost, too."[21] This sense of weakness and futility exceeds Golaud's relation even to the forest. One of his last statements in the final act reveals his ultimate incapacity to comprehend the overwhelming force of his own destiny: "I shall die here in blindness." This inability to struggle against fate is generally reflected in the harmonic relation between modal (diatonic) and symmetrical (whole-tone) spheres. The intrusion of the latter into the former renders the diatonic sphere powerless to achieve any sense of tonal direction. The dissipation of tonal energy is due to the static harmonic quality of symmetrical, cyclic-interval construction.[22]

Golaud as Political Symbol

The figure of Golaud is almost a caricature of the wealthy and powerful man whose power is more apparent than real. Golaud is driven by his impulses, insensitive to the needs of others, and bound by "the masculine principle orientated towards materialism."[23] Represented by a castle set in an indefinite time and place in the legendary world of Allemonde, the mysterious scenario of the opera tells us almost nothing about the subjects that live under the political rule of the royal family. The power of the establishment seems entirely out of proportion with the condition of its subjects. On the one hand, Prince Golaud shows an unempathic, detached attitude toward the starving, homeless beggars in his kingdom. On the other hand, all who live within the castle are obsessed with the mysterious little Mélisande—she is perceived by old King Arkel, for instance, as the main hope for bringing life to the castle—rather than with an unseen people whose existence is barely suggested in the opera. In spite of Golaud's claim of love for Mélisande, his treatment of her is as insensitive as his attitude toward his subjects. We need only cite Golaud's response to Mélisande's threat of suicide when he offers to retrieve her crown from the pond: "Yet it would be very easy to get it out." It is also significant that by marrying Mélisande, Golaud does not fulfill a prearranged marriage to a woman of a prominent family that would have contributed to Allemonde's power.[24] However, in spite of the apparent disregard for Mélisande's social status, he treats her as his property and shows no understanding of her predicament as a young, traumatized person.[25]

The dominant class in France, by submitting to compulsive greed and materialistic, acquisitorial urges, ignored the misery and suffering of the non-privileged classes. This condition invokes Adorno's statement regarding the individual's sense of helplessness before the modern industrial machine.[26] This idea is also applicable to other power struggles of the time, such as the plight of Dreyfus under the military establishment,[27] or the struggle by the feminist movement to change traditional gender roles. Maeterlinck's *Pelléas et Mélisande* and his *Ariane et Barbe-Bleue* both attest to the artistic explorations of the conflicts between men and women. These conditions suggest, in a growing materialistic age, a sense of helplessness before fate and the desire for individual expression. This helplessness seems applicable to individuals regardless of class, the plight of Golaud himself serving as a paradoxical symbolic representation of this futile condition, analogous to that of the French military leaders, who were destined to fail in their case against Dreyfus.

A widening dichotomy between the wealthy and the poor in the increasingly industrialized society of the Third Republic can be linked to this materialistic notion. Following recovery from the defeat of Napoleon III by Bismarck in the Franco-Prussian War of 1871, France entered a new era of prosperity and colonial expansion, and regained her position as a prominent international cultural center. It was under these conditions that the "untaxed rich lived in shameless luxury and systematically brutalized *le peuple* with venal journalism, inspiring promises of progress and expanding empire, and cheap absinthe."[28] The Maeterlinck-Debussy opera seems to symbolize these polarized, unbalanced social conditions under which the individual human being had little or no recourse toward achieving true political self-determination.

Polarity as an Internal Principle of Musico-Dramatic Structure

The general notion of polarity, which underlies these social conditions, is also reflected in some of the internal dramatic issues of the opera. This notion is established by the very opening phrase/period construction in preparation for the remaining planes and layers of the Prelude. After a modified repeat of the entire opening period (p. 1, mm. 8–13), the main "Mélisande" motif (p. 1, mm. 14–15, oboe over layered figurations in the strings), which Debussy himself identified as "Thème initial de Mélisande,"[29] is presented in two identical segments to form an antecedent phrase to her closely related "Naïveté" motif (p. 2, mm. 1–2). Just prior to the return of the "Forest" motif at the end of the Prelude, a more rhythmically complex texture of thematic layers is produced by means of simultaneous combination of the "Naïveté" and "Fate" motifs (p. 2, mm. 3–4), which are distinguished from each other by the contrasting woodwind and brass timbres. This phrase is balanced by a consequent phrase (p. 2, mm. 5–8), which presents both motifs in succession; a skeletal form of the "Naïveté" motif ends the period. In this penultimate passage, the usual consecutive repetitions of the motifs are replaced by their inversions, which are now stated simultaneously with their basic forms to produce a sense of structural (phrasal) fusion. This tendency to maintain the individuality of pure instrumental timbres, especially in such coalescent passages based on the juxtaposition, overlap, or simultaneity of materials, permits sonority to acquire a structural function as well as symbolic association. In a 1908 interview, Debussy said that:

> Musicians no longer know how to decompose sound, to give it in its pure state. In *Pelléas*, the sixth violin is just as important as the first. I try to employ timbre in its pure form; like Mozart, for example. We've learned too well to mix timbres; to throw them into relief with shadows or masses of sound without letting them play with their own meanings.[30]

Already, with Debussy, pure sonority had begun to acquire a structural role almost as prominent as that of the melodic and harmonic dimensions.[31] Analogous to the use of distinct melodic/rhythmic motifs, Debussy's concern for the individuation of pure instrumental sonorities also allows for symbolic association. In those places where these timbres emerge from the general orchestral fabric as primary surface phenomena, their symbolic associations can be identified with some consistency.[32] As outlined by Arthur B. Wenk, direct associations may be shown between the horn and Golaud, trombone/tuba and violent death, trumpet and peaceful death, oboe/English horn and Mélisande, harp and water, timpani and darkness. Extended associations may be shown between horn and darkness/death, oboe and Mélisande's sadness, English horn and Mélisande's pain/suffering, harp and water, renewal, freshness, or change, timpani and impending disaster or death. Wenk also points to more superficial uses of timbre, in which instrumental devices such as string tremolo, flautando, sul ponticello, or harmonics serve to articulate certain structural points. Some of these devices may have pictorial significance. For instance, the use of sharp pizzicato may represent sharp objects such as the bristles of Golaud's beard (in act 3), the point of Golaud's sword (in act 4), or a moment of sudden comprehension as when

Mélisande is distracted by something in the water (in act 2), and so on. We also may cite the descending harp arpeggiation when Mélisande drops her ring into the well (in act 2). Wenk also points to other sonic categories that Debussy uses for pictorialization, including spacing, registration, and dynamics.

On this mosaic structural foundation (based on motivic, harmonic, phrasal, and timbral planes and layers), special relationships are established from the beginning of the opera between the contrasting diatonic and whole-tone sets that reflect the fundamental interactions between the polarized dramatic spheres. From the outset, pentatonic/diatonic collections are identified with those motivic figures that come to represent the natural or human sphere, whole-tone collections becoming identified with the "Fate" motif. In the Prelude, the two whole-tone collections are generated from the whole-step components of the pentatonic scale in connection with the symbolic meaning of the drama, that is, the gradual permeation and transformation of the natural or human realm by "Fate." The opening "Forest" motif, which is based exclusively on a D pentatonic collection, D–E–G–A–C, polarizes two of the pentatonic whole-steps, C–D and G–A, registrally. This motif is immediately absorbed and transformed by "Fate" (ex. 4-1) as the lower pentatonic whole-step, C–D, moves linearly to A♭ (m. 5) to draw this whole-step into the whole-tone sphere (A♭–C–D). This foreshadows the subsequent transformation (ex. 4-2, a and b) of the diatonic "Awakening Desire" motif, A–C–D (in act 2, p. 77, m. 4ff., oboe), into the linearly implied whole-tone form, A♭–C–D (p. 86, m. 2), as Mélisande refers to fate, "It's something stronger than myself."

In the Prelude (m. 5), the pentatonic C–D is also reinterpreted harmonically as the axis of the larger symmetrical French sixth chord, A♭–C–D–F♯ (see ex. 4-1),[33]

(French-
Aug.-6th
with axis C–D)

EXAMPLE 4-1. Prelude, p. 1, mm. 1–6, pentatonic "Forest" and whole-tone "Fate" motifs

a. **En animant peu à peu et sourdement agité**
   With increasing animation and suppressed excitement

D-dominant-ninth collection (D–F♯–A–C–E) in larger A-Dorian mode
(A–[ ]–C–D–E–F♯–[ ]), containing motif, A–C–D

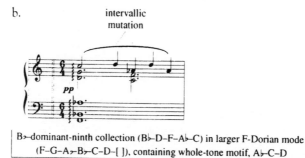

b.
intervallic
mutation

B♭–dominant-ninth collection (B♭–D–F–A♭–C) in larger F-Dorian mode
(F–G–A♭–B♭–C–D–[ ]), containing whole-tone motif, A♭–C–D

EXAMPLE 4-2. Transformation of (a) the diatonic "Awakening Desire" motif, A–C–D (in act 2, p. 77, m. 4ff., oboe), into (b) the linearly implied whole-tone form, A♭–C–D (p. 86, m. 2)

which is established as a substructure of the complete whole-tone collection, A♭–B♭–C–D–E–F♯.[34] It is significant that C–D will appear as the boundary of the symmetrical dominant ninth chord, C–E–G–B♭–D, which is associated with the well at the opening of act 2 (p. 55, m. 10), the well coming to serve as one of the primary instruments of fate. More specifically, the whole-tone tetrachordal substructure, B♭–C–D–E, of the C dominant ninth chord forms the basis of the "Well" motif in the oboes and clarinets (ex. 4-3). At Golaud's entrance into the forest (p. 3, m. 1), the upper pentatonic whole-step, G–A, from the opening "Forest" theme is also drawn into the whole-tone sphere, where it appears analogously as the axis of the other whole-tone collection, E♭–F–G–A–C♭–D♭, in the initial ascending triplet ordering (ex. 4-4). This whole-tone axial link is significant, since Golaud also will serve (like the well) as one of the primary instruments of fate. The axial (symmetrical) position of these pentatonic whole-steps within the respective whole-tone collections contributes to the sense of harmonic stasis.[35]

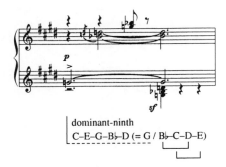

EXAMPLE 4-3. "Well" motif (p. 55, m. 10), whole-tone tetrachordal substructure, Bb–C–D-E, of the C-dominant-ninth chord (C–E–G–Bb–D) in oboes and clarinets.

EXAMPLE 4-4. Golaud's entrance into the forest (p. 3, mm. 1–2), upper pentatonic whole-step, G–A, from opening "Forest" theme drawn into whole-tone-1 sphere as axis of symmetry (in initial ascending triplet ordering)

Mélisande and Fate

Maeterlinck's own statement regarding the affinity of women with destiny provides insight into the interaction between the whole-tone sphere and Mélisande's pentatonic theme near the opening of the Prelude. The following statement by Maeterlinck provides external support for the symbolic interpretation of Mélisande's character as a relentless force, and it contributes to the early establishment of this basic notion, as represented by the contextual interaction of the whole-tone sphere with Mélisande's theme, in preparation for Golaud's first encounter with that mysterious creature of fate:

It would seem that women are more largely swayed by destiny than ourselves. They submit to its decrees with far more simplicity; nor is there sincerity in the resistance they offer. They are still nearer to God, and yield themselves with less reserve to the pure workings of the mystery. And therefore is it, doubtless, that all the incidents in our life in which they take part seem to bring us nearer to what might almost be the very fountainhead of destiny. . . . They lead us close to the gates of our being.[36]

The basic musical premises for this symbolic connection are established from the outset. Following the initial juxtaposition of the pentatonic "Forest" motif and the whole-tone "Fate" motif as the basis of the opening phrasal framework, Mélisande's main motif emerges in connection with a new pentatonic segment (see p. 1, mm. 14–15, oboe), in enharmonic spelling, Ab–Bb–C♯, which suggests the tritone transposition of the opening pentatonic "Forest" motif (D–E–G–A–C). In a context based on increased figural activity, this passage draws the human element more intensively into the fatalistic realm by means of simultaneous transformation of this pentatonic construction (Ab–Bb–C♯) into the whole-tone set (ex. 4-5). The harmony of the accompanying strings forms the French sixth chord, Bb–D–E–Ab, which is a whole-tone transposition above the original one, Ab–C–D–F♯ (m. 5). The specific harmonic position of the chord, as it unfolds in the thirty-second-note figuration (Ab–Bb–D–E), produces a whole-tone expansion of the "Mélisande" motif (Ab–Bb–C♯ to Ab–Bb–D) in the three lower notes. The larger, symmetrical French sixth chord (Ab–Bb–D–E) can be interpreted as a joining of the latter whole-tone segment (Ab–Bb–D) with its inversion (Bb–D–E), both occurring throughout the opera. This intrusion of "Fate" on "Mélisande" produces a single pungent dissonance between the pentatonic C♯ and whole-tone D.

This whole-tone transformation of the pentatonic "Mélisande" theme is confirmed later, in the first Interlude (p. 24, m. 3), in which the motif itself is expanded in each of the two parallel lines to F♯–Ab–C and D–E–Ab, respectively, and drawn exclusively into the complete WT-0 collection as Golaud and Mélisande exit together. Thus, all the themes that have been presented to this point are drawn into the atmosphere of the forest and fatalistic realms through a progressive integration of the contrasting pentatonic and whole-tone sets in a growing continuum of thematic and textural planes. Segments common to both sets are the basic links between these planes.

EXAMPLE 4-5. Whole-tone transformation, Ab–Bb–D–E, of the pentatonic "Mélisande" theme, Ab–Bb–C♯ (p. 1, mm. 14–15)

Act 1, Scene 1: First Meeting of Golaud and Mélisande:
Hybrid Diatonic/Whole-Tone Form of "Fate"
and Golaud's "Love" Motif

The moment Golaud enters the forest, the authority of the gray-bearded prince who controls a kingdom of beggars and starving people, and the strength of the hunter who has just lost his way and the trail of his wounded prey, are brought into question by the ensuing events. The music itself seems to invoke the question and to reflect the conditions that surround the princely figure whose powerful physical appearance belies an emotional dependence on the helpless creature he is about to encounter. Immediately following the Prelude, the musico-dramatic action begins with an ascending statement of the WT-1 cycle, Eb–F–G–A–Cb–Db (p. 3, m. 1), which is symmetrical around one of the original pentatonic dyads, G–A, and defined both harmonically and vocally by an interval-4 chord (Db–F–A). This sudden appearance of the WT-1 cycle, which produces a shift away from the prominence of WT-0 in the Prelude, reflects Golaud's concern as he becomes lost while hunting that he "shall never get out of this forest." Because this WT-1 passage follows the Prelude's recapitulation of the diatonic "Forest" motif directly, it establishes itself as the structural replacement of the original WT-0 collection as the basis for the "Fate" motif (see p. 1, m. 5). In connection with the fatalistic implication of Golaud's question, this replacement function of the complementary whole-tone cycle (WT-1) is supported by the triplet "Fate" rhythm in both voice and orchestra. The proportional relation of the initial statement of the "Fate" motif (at mm. 5–6) to the "Forest" motif (mm. 1–4) at a ratio of 2:1 (as mentioned earlier) is altered now, as the triplet rhythm of "Fate" extends the WT-1 figuration at Golaud's entry into the forest to four and one-half measures (more than twice its original length). This extension complements the last statement of the "Forest" motif to produce a sense of increasing engrossment in the highly static mood of the whole-tone sphere.

From the music, we sense that the snares of destiny are already set from the moment the curtain rises and Golaud enters the forest. Golaud's vacillations between statements of certainty and uncertainty are reflected in orchestral alternations between segments of the two whole-tone scales. A momentary return to a segment of the original WT-0 collection (C–Bb–Ab–Gb) in the orchestra (p. 3, mm. 6–7) is directly associated with Golaud's greater certainty, "Yet I thought I had given it a mortal wound, and here are traces of blood." The adjacency of these alternating whole-tone segments produces diatonic intersections, the first in Bb minor (p. 3, mm. 5–6). These orchestral alternations also induce a shift from the initial whole-tone chord (Db–F–A) of this passage to a series of diatonic triads, and the voice moves to a diatonic fourth, F-Bb (p. 3, mm. 4–5). As Golaud has lost sight of the boar, the whole-tone collections cease to alternate and they become equally fused in a diatonicized form of the "Fate" motif (p. 4, m. 4). In correspondence with Golaud's realization that he is lost and must retrace his steps, this diatonicized form of the motif, which is precisely that of its second occurrence in the Prelude (see p. 1, m. 12ff.) to the point that it even includes the original G–A dyad as the upper diatonic whole-step, retraces its steps to the original WT-0 form of the motif (compare p. 4, m. 8, with p. 1, m. 5). The latter is correspondingly supported by the original whole-tone axis (C–D) in the voice as part of the complete WT-o collection in the harmony. This cadential motivic articulation rounds out what may be considered the first main subsection of this scene. Thus, the return to—and structural prominence of—the original whole-tone (WT-o) form of the "Fate" motif, together with Golaud's premonitory questions, have prepared us for the first fateful event of the opera: Golaud's encounter with Mélisande.

The Prelude also establishes another relationship between diatonic and whole-tone spheres that will play an increasingly significant role in the musico-dramatic interactions of the opera. Within the half-diminished seventh chord (F–Ab–Cb–Eb) of Mélisande's linearly stated "Naïveté" motif (see p. 2, m. 1), her transposed pentatonic motif (Eb–F–Ab) is implicitly interlocked with an intervallically expanded form (Cb–Eb–F), which suggests the larger, symmetrical whole-tone sphere of "Fate." As Golaud becomes enamoured of Mélisande (p. 7, mm. 1-2), "Oh, you are beautiful!" his vocal line outlines a form of her original half-diminished seventh construction (in root position, G♯–B–D–F♯). The specific registral position of the notes of this melodic construction (D–F♯–G♯–B) reveals an overlapping of whole-tone and pentatonic segments (D–F♯–G♯ and F♯–G♯–B). The significance of this hybrid (pentatonic/whole-tone) statement is revealed by the accompanying "Love" motif of Golaud, based on the "Fate" rhythm, the strings evoking the sense of Golaud's stirred feelings for the distraught girl. Because the emotions are essential in controlling human actions, we may assert that they are a primary mover of fate, as emotions are, for the most part, an unconscious force. It is evident that the half-diminished seventh outline of Golaud's vocal line (D–F♯–G♯–B) represents a partial whole-tone transformation of—that is, fatalistic intrusion into—the purely pentatonic form (F♯–G♯–B–C♯) of the "Love" motif in the uppermost violin line of the orchestral accompaniment. Ultimately, in this phrase, both the half-diminished seventh and pentatonic constructions belong to the larger E mixolydian mode (E–F♯–G♯–A–B–C♯–D) exclusively, that is, they are subcollections of the diatonic sphere, which serves as point of departure for whole-tone transformation associated with the awakening of Golaud's passion for the mysterious girl.

The subtle changes of color and shade that elicit the atmospheric nuances in a French Impressionist painting are often induced by the slightest intrusion of a single, contrasting hue. Like the enhancement of a given color by means of juxtaposition with its complementary color, the juxtaposition of specific details in the musical score also invokes mood change. Analogous to principles in painting, the larger musical context within which the smaller details interact is essential in establishing the specific quality of the mood change. In other words, the expressive meaning of a particular note depends entirely on the larger harmonic context within which it is set. At the same time, conversely, the harmonic quality is affected by the local microscopic juxtapositions, in which a single alteration of the local content can produce a radical transformation of the harmonic palette, say, from pentatonic to whole-tone, or vice versa. At the awakening of Golaud's passion (p. 7, mm. 1-2), notes C♯ and D represent the only pitch-class difference between the opposing sets—pentatonic (F♯–G♯–B–[C♯]) and hybrid half-diminished seventh/whole-tone (F♯–G♯–B–[D]) constructions (the latter implying the presence of the WT-o segment, D–F♯–G♯). This recalls the "dissonant" function of these two notes (C♯ and D) in the Prelude (see p. 1, m. 14f.), in which "Mélisande's" oboe motif (A♭–B♭–C♯) had come into conflict with the figuration (A♭–B♭–D–E) in the bassoons, English horn, and strings to produce the same dissonance (C♯ vs. D) by the simultaneous statement of the whole-tone and pentatonic spheres. However, at Golaud's "Love" motif, the dissonance is somewhat subdued by the absorption of both notes into the more homogeneous string texture. This softening of the dissonance seems more appropriate to this more tender mood. The half-diminished seventh construction (G♯–B–D–F♯) of Golaud's vocal line (see p. 7, mm. 1–2) is expanded into the larger dominant ninth chord, E–G♯–B–D–F♯ (cadential chord of the orchestral "Love" motif), by the addition of one note, E. Furthermore, the entire harmonic progression that supports this statement of the "Love" motif is based on alternation of the E–dominant ninth or half-diminished seventh construction ([E]–G♯–B–D–F♯) and pentatonic variant (C♯–[E]–G♯–B) of the uppermost violin line ([F♯]–G♯–B–C♯). Both the half-diminished seventh chord and the dominant ninth, which appeared originally on D (see p. 2, mm. 3–4) as an expanded melodic variant of the half-diminished seventh "Naïvete" motif, serve throughout the opera as prominent hybrid constructions in transformations between the naturalistic (diatonic) and fatalistic (whole-tone) realms. Thus, the dramatic mood changes are induced by minimal changes of local pitch details, elucidated by timbral identifications and associations.

Influences on the Musical Language and Aesthetics of *Pelléas et Mélisande*

Debussy's attendance at the Paris Exposition Universelle in *1889* brought him into contact with the exotic sonorities, rhythms, scales, and modes of Javanese, Chinese, North African, and other musics outside Western European culture. It was also at this time in Paris that Debussy heard Mussorgsky's opera Boris Godunov, in which the dominant ninth chord of the "Clock" scene is exploited for its symmetrical rather than functional properties. In the early *1890s*, as Debussy began to develop his Impressionist/Symbolist aesthetics, in works such as the *String Quartet* (1893), *Prélude à l'aprés midi d'un faune* (1894), the orchestral *Nocturnes* (1893–1899), and *Pelléas et Mélisande* (1893–1902), he tended increasingly to minimize traditional chord functions, often using only part of a chord by omitting the third or fifth degree. He also enriched chords by adding tones that might either extend the triad to supertertian constructions (seventh or ninth chords) or be used as nontertian elements (added sixths, etc.) to heighten the harmonic color and thus the dramatic mood. The most radical departure from traditional harmonic construction and progression was in the use of symmetrical and other harmonic formations often in parallel motion. Such progressions eliminated the need for logical preparation and resolution of dissonance. Symmetrical pitch construction and parallel harmonic motion rendered chords static, so they could be exploited for their individual color rather than any traditional harmonic function.

Accordingly, the dominant ninth chord (E–G♯–B–D–F♯) at the cadence of the "Love" motif (see p. 7, m. 2), like most occurrences of the dominant seventh (or dominant ninth) chord throughout the opera, is employed primarily for its sonic quality and leitmotivic possibilities. However, at those less common occurrences in which the chord of the dominant does serve a harmonic function as part of a perfect cadence, it seems to symbolize personal closeness. At the cadence of Golaud's "Love" motif (p. 7, m. 2), the unresolved E dominant ninth is associated with Mélisande's resistance to personal contact, "Don't touch me, don't touch me, or I'll throw myself in the water." In the preceding passage (p. 5, mm. 8–10), when Golaud tells us that she cannot hear him yet, nor can he see her face, a dominant ninth harmony (G–B–D–F–A) is prolonged. It resolves to the C tonic in the "Forest" motif as he approaches her and touches her shoulder.[37] In act 1, scene 2 (p. 28, mm. 9–10), when Geneviève reads Golaud's letter, which expresses uncertainty regarding Arkel's willingness to receive his new bride, "If, however, he agrees to welcome her as he would welcome his own daughter," the C dominant ninth harmonization (C–E–G–B♭–D) of the "Mélisande" motif resolves to the F major tonic with added sixth (F–A–C–D) on "would welcome." Later in this scene, when Arkel asks Pelléas to come nearer so he may see him where it is lighter (p. 34, mm. 9–14), the C dominant seventh chord resolves to the F major tonic.

Maeterlinck's portrayal of a relentless force against which human beings are powerless is apparent in both the dialogue and the music at the initial encounter of Golaud and Mélisande. Their interaction leads her to ask him (p. 17) why he has come here, the deeper meaning suggested by his response that he does not know himself. He "was hunting in the forest, chasing a wild boar." In other words, Golaud is driven by an unknown force more powerful than himself. The boar itself seems to serve as a kind of symbol of Mélisande in that they are both running away from predators. They are both wounded, Mélisande by psychological trauma, and the wounding of the boar by Golaud portends the final wounding of Mélisande. Conversely, both the boar and Mélisande are potential threats to Golaud. Accordingly, Mélisande's vocal statement linearly interlocks an inverted transposition of her pentatonic pitch-cell (E♭–G♭–A♭) with the whole-tone "Fate" cell (D–G♭–A♭) at the basic pitch level (tonic) of the opera. The orchestra answers, then, with the "Fate" motif (p. 17, m. 3), in exactly the same woodwind scoring as the original occurrence of the motif in the Prelude (p. 1, mm. 5–6). In the present passage, the meaning of Golaud's words, which refer back to losing his way while hunting, is reflected by the increasingly unstable harmonic fluctuations between dominant seventh/half-diminished and whole-tone chords (p. 17, m. 3). Therefore, both whole-tone collections are mixed in these diatonic and whole-tone alternations in support of the ambiguous text.

"Golaud," "Mélisande," and "Fate" Motifs

The latter occurrence of the "Fate" motif (p. 17, m. 3) is a focal point for the subsection that begins with "Golaud's" motif (ex. 4-6, p. 14, m. 8). In correspondence with the trend of the text—from the description of Golaud (*real-life* being) to statements that seem to invoke *fate*—the diatonic harmonies that support "Golaud's" motif (dominant ninths on C♯, E, and F) move toward increasingly pure whole-tone formations. At the cadential chord of this motivic statement (p. 15, m. 1), the harmonic

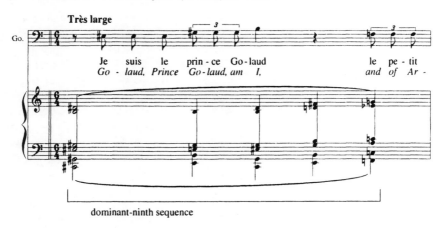

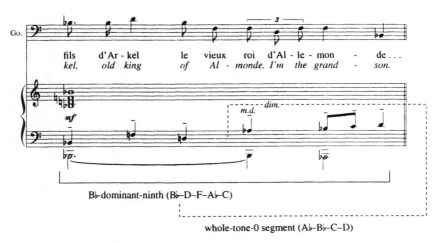

EXAMPLE 4-6. "Golaud's" motif, p. 14, m. 8, dominant-ninths on C♯, E, and F moving toward pure whole-tone formations; cadential chord of motivic statement, p. 15, m. 1, harmonic partitioning of B♭-dominant-ninth chord (B♭–D–F–A♭–C) exposing first linear segment (upper bass line) based on whole-tone components, A♭–B♭–C–D, of B♭-dominant-ninth

partitioning of the B♭ dominant ninth chord (B♭–D–F–A♭–C) exposes the first linear segment (first bassoon) based on the whole-tone components, A♭–B♭–C–D, of the latter.

Transformation from diatonic (human) to whole-tone (fatalistic) spheres begins most prominently when Mélisande, weeping (pp. 12–14), has just dropped her shining crown into the pond. As Golaud offers to retrieve it for her, she threatens suicide: "No, no, I don't want it. I don't want it anymore. I would rather die—die here and now. . . . I don't want it. If you recover it, I shall throw myself in instead." This portends the events that will lead to her death. These ominous events include especially the loss of her ring in the well, her seduction of Pelléas when her hair unfolds from the tower at night, the discovery of their meetings by Golaud, and the setting of the sun in the sea as an indication of the coming of winter when Mélisande is on her deathbed.[38] Her death is the inevitable outcome of her unconscious actions based on her motivation to be free from her marital bond to Golaud. Thus, it seems she is never really free from Golaud in life, and that the more pervasively she is under the control of her unconscious, the less one sees her marriage to Golaud or her love for Pelléas as "a matter of free choice, as is shown subjectively in the fatal compulsion [she] feels so acutely when [she] is in love [with Pelléas]. The compulsion can exist even when [she] is not in love, though in less agreeable form."[39]

Musically, this moment at the pond (p. 12, mm. 5–9) is symbolized by the first recurrence of the same whole-tone scale (G–A–B–C♯–D♯–E♯) that accompanied Golaud's entry into the forest. The somewhat urgent sonority of the muted-horn figure at Golaud's first notice of the shining crown at the bottom of the pond (p. 11, m. 5) is replaced (p. 14, m. 3) by the lighter rendition of this figure in the flutes and clarinets (both passages symbolized by the same glittering key of C major) as Golaud's insistence on retrieving the crown begins to weaken. Subdued by Mélisande's threat, Golaud is rendered helpless, a condition that is indicative throughout much of the opera of the emotional control that the woman can project over the man. This static affect of Golaud's powerless response is supported by the sonic context. The whole-step (G–A), which formed the axis of symmetry of Golaud's whole-tone ("Fate") scale, and that will be associated with virtually every appearance of Golaud throughout the opera, now moves to a primary position in the scale as its two lowest notes (p. 12, m. 5ff.). The association of this dyad with Golaud's original entry into the forest (see ex. 4-4) is further supported by the harmony at Mélisande's declaration that she would rather die (p. 12, m. 8); above the G–A tremolo (downbeat), both orchestra and voice present the same augmented triad (C♯–F–A, or D♭–F–A) of Golaud's original vocal statement and underlying orchestral chord reiterated above the G–A axis of the ascending triplets. It appears, then (p. 13, mm. 7–8), in enharmonic spelling (A–Fx), as both the boundary and axis of symmetry of the WT-1 scale (A–B–C♯–D♯–E♯–Fx/A–B–C♯–D♯–E♯–Fx). Thus, the music suggests that Mélisande's fate, which has freed her from Duke Bluebeard, will soon bind her to Prince Golaud. Debussy's intentions were to deal more with feelings than with actions,[40] prominently with the feeling of fear and the air of mystery.[41] One of the rhythmic patterns identified with fear is a repeated-note triplet figure in the vocal part when, for instance, Mélisande becomes terrified by Golaud's offer to retrieve her crown from the pond. The woman's association of the crown with death is more explicitly realized at the end of Bartók's opera, when Judith grows "numb with death" as she is crowned by Bluebeard.[42] The man's disregard for the woman's emotional response to the crown appears to contribute to her extreme sense of isolation and her treatment as idealized object, which lead to her ultimate destiny.

A kind of word-painting is also evident in this and other sections in the handling of orchestration and registral placement of instrumental sonority in connection with the physical position of objects. For instance, as Golaud refers to Mélisande's crown at the bottom of the well (p. 13, mm. 3–6 and p. 13, m. 11ff.), the orchestration, comprising low strings and bassoons, is maintained exclusively below middle C. The same orchestration and registral placement can also be observed at similar dramatic moments throughout the opera. This occurs in passages of the underground "Vault" scene (act 3, scene 2) and in the scene in which Golaud, lying in bed wounded (act 2, scene 2, p. 77, mm. 2–3), describes how he had become trapped under his horse. At Pelléas's description of the darkness of the grotto (act 2, scene 3, p. 105, mm. 5–7), a fuller orchestration is used (strings and bassoons in oscillating or tremolo figuration, and tuba), but all are maintained below middle C.

Test of the Will and the Dual Symbolic Role of Mélisande as Real-Life Being and Instrument of Fate

In this test of the will between man and woman, Golaud fears any action on his part that might lead to harm of the young woman, and Mélisande is increasingly frightened by the thought that she might once again come under the oppression of another man's crown from which she has just freed herself. At the moment, it is the force of the woman's emotional state that controls the interactions between the two characters. In this emotional power struggle, it is Mélisande who prevails,[43] the test entailing more than just the struggle over the issue of the crown. For Roger Nichols, the "specious outer shell of Golaud—his lineage" belies the man's real emotional condition, which surfaces with Mélisande's probing questions. Golaud has also lost his way, and in this respect appears to be as helpless as Mélisande. In spite of Nichols's insight into Golaud's motivation that stems from his concern for the young woman's safety if she were to be left alone in the forest (it is perhaps Golaud who is afraid of being alone in the greater forest of his own lonely life), the final outcome does not leave Mélisande as victorious as Nichols suggests. Mélisande leaves the forest with Golaud, or, better yet, Golaud leaves it with Mélisande, a symbolic substitution for the wounded beast whose pursuit has caused him to lose his way. Furthermore, Mélisande will eventually enter another man's (Golaud's) castle and lose control of her own life once again.

The musical fabric is in close alliance with every dramatic and emotional nuance. As Mélisande comments on Golaud's gray hair and beard, the orchestra unfolds several transposing statements of Mélisande's "Naïveté" motif (p. 15, m. 2ff.). The characteristic dominant ninth or half-diminished seventh construction of this motif is clearly established by the third statement (p. 15, mm. 4–5). The latter, based exclusively on the D dominant ninth collection (D–F♯–A–C–E), together with the preceding half-diminished seventh construction, G♯–B–D–F♯, assures continuation of the impure, ambiguous diatonic/whole-tone fabric. The presence of subcollections from both whole-tone collections (as well as the more obvious manifestations of diatonic constructions) is therefore implied in these motivic and harmonic adjacencies: the half-diminished seventh implies the presence of a WT-1 segment (D–F♯–G♯), the D dominant ninth a WT-0 segment (C–D–E–F♯). The final motivic statement and its harmonies (p. 16, m. 2) produce a more complex (hybrid) collection.

The overall trend from the WT-1-oriented C♯ dominant ninth construction of "Golaud's" motif to the WT-0-oriented B♭ dominant ninth (p. 15, m. 1) and D dominant ninth outlines of Mélisande's "Naïveté" motif (p. 15, mm. 4 to p. 16, m. 1), which is completed at the more persistent syncopated ostinato rhythm (p. 16, m. 6 ff.) that leads to a full statement of the "Fate" motif (p. 17, m. 3), prepares us for more portentous questions and responses of fatalistic import (p. 17, m. 2 ff.). When Mélisande asks Golaud why he has come here, her vocal line acquires an angular, more twisted contour. This may be interpreted as a modification of Golaud's "Love" motif (compare B–C♯–B–G♯–F♯–F♯ at p. 7, mm. 1-2, with G♭–A♭–G♭–G♭–G♭–D–D–D–E♭ at p. 17, m. 2, in which the last two notes are reversed to produce the more twisted contour). This absorption of an orchestral theme into the vocal recitative, which incorporates rhythmic details of the theme as well, supports the symbolic meaning of Mélisande's question about why he has come here. Golaud's reference, then, to the hunt is followed directly by a shift of his attention directly to Mélisande, especially her youth. Her response, however, is unrelated to his question, an indication of her increased anxiety. For Mélisande, the fear of renewed oppression by this gray-bearded prince (in place of the blue-bearded duke) would certainly induce her traumatic symptoms. Golaud's preceding inquiry (p. 16, mm. 6–7) as to why she looks so surprised is based exclusively on the French sixth chord, B♭–C–E–F♯, which belongs to the basic WT-0 collection. At his next statement, the latter is transposed to C–D–F♯–A♭, both chords producing the complete and pure WT-0 collection for the first time in this subsection. As was shown earlier, "Mélisande's" motif is infused, then, with the basic WT-0 form of the "Fate" motif (D–G♭–A♭). Thus, the renewal of her oppression in what might seem to be the guise of love entails the continuation of a cycle of events and situations of the greatest fatalistic import for Mélisande.

These whole-tone infusions not only provide that special mood appropriate to the fatalistic implications of their questions but also invoke a more profound sense of the larger fatalistic significance that the character of Mélisande seems to have had for Maeterlinck himself. Golaud is immediately taken by this mysterious, helpless young woman, and it is the emotional content—already anticipated by his "Love" motif (p. 7)—which seems to play an important part in the evocation of the fatalistic mood at this moment. Maeterlinck's Symbolist message goes beyond the moral and social implications of the dramatic context. A new symbol is evoked in the present scene in connection with Mélisande, that of Love, which enters almost unobtrusively into the darkness of the ancient castle. But the brief light provided by this symbol is just as suddenly quelled, after having brought with it jealousy, murder, and untold misery. Thus, the equation of love and death, so essential to the *Tristan* story, also informs this Debussy opera on the deepest symbolic level.[44]

This symbolic interpretation, which is one of several levels of symbolic expression in this opening scene, is projected into the overall message of the opera: love draws Golaud fatalistically to Mélisande from the outset, and it will be Golaud who will serve, through jealousy and murder, as the instrument for quelling that love, oppressing the woman, and bringing about her ultimate fate: "In the play, Death is enthroned . . . but Love has come to challenge its hegemony, another force, asserts Maeterlinck, among those invisible powers that weave the pattern of our lives. . . . In

Pelléas there is affection and love, but Love is not to be welcomed, for it can only encompass disaster, leaving Death even more firmly ensconced as the arbiter of Man's destiny."[45] A statement of "Mélisande's" motif (p. 18, mm. 2–3), which is immediately followed by the relentlessly pulsating syncopation and other elements of the "Fate" rhythm, articulates the beginning of another subsection, in which it reflects the preceding ambiguous mixture of the two alternating whole-tone collections and hybrid diatonic (dominant seventh and half-diminished seventh) chords. As Golaud observes Mélisande and questions her about herself, "You look very young. How old are you?" the upper line of the strings, which play her motif (B–C♯–E), and her vocal line (G♯–A–B–D) together outline the (diatonic) B Dorian mode (B–C♯–D–E–[ ]–G♯–A) exclusively. While the initial harmony of her motif forms the E- dominant ninth chord (E–G♯–B–D–F♯), which is derived from this mode, the cadential harmony alters it to form a hybrid diatonic/whole-tone construction (E–G♯–B–D♯–F). At the same time, while the upper harmonic segment (B–D♯–F) forms an inverted WT-1 transformation of her motif, the two remaining notes of the chord (E–G♯) imply the other, complementary WT-0 collection (the intervening chord, F–A–C♯, is exclusively whole-tone). This pitch-set trend regarding transformation toward the whole-tone sphere (in the ensuing passage, which is weighted more toward WT-0 more often associated with Mélisande or Pelléas than Golaud) appears to be connected with Mélisande's increasingly evident role as an instrument of fate, that is, by means of her emotional state, which seems to cast a certain power over Golaud.

The whole-tone harmonic infusion into Mélisande's linear diatonic context also anticipates the symbolism of her death inherent in her comment, "I'm beginning to feel cold." The fatalistic implication of this reference to "cold"—that is, as cold as *fate*—is borne out in act 2, scene 1 (p. 57), in which Pelléas, meeting with Melisande at the well, describes the water as being "as cool as winter." The loss of her wedding ring in the well begins the sequence of events that will inevitably lead to their demise.[46] This fatalistic implication is also borne out when Mélisande, on her deathbed, will refer to the coming of winter (near the end of the opera). The significance of Pelléas's words may also be inferred from Maeterlinck's own explicit reference to "the icy hand of destiny."[47] At the present reference (p. 18, m. 4f.), Mélisande's vocal line infuses her inverted diatonic motif (D♯–F♯–G♯) with the expanded whole-tone form, D–F♯–G♯. Under her cadential (diatonic) D♯, the linear motivic form (D♯–F♯–G♯) is closed off, then, by its vertical projection. The entire scene ends (p. 22) with the "Fate" motif, as Golaud and Mélisande leave together. The first orchestral Interlude (forty-seven measures) intensifies the material of the Prelude through the simultaneous use of the "Forest" and "Fate" motifs.

Act 1, Scene 2 (A Room in the Castle): First Explicit Text Reference to "Fate"

As Arkel and Geneviève discuss Golaud's letter to Pelléas that informs him of his marriage to Mélisande, Arkel's reaction provides the first explicit text references to fate (p. 30), "because we only see the reverse side of fate, only the reverse side even of our own," then, more prominently at the ending of this subsection (p. 32), "Let it be as he wishes: I have never set myself athwart of destiny; he knows his own future better than I do. Perhaps nothing ever occurs that is useless." In correspondence with the dramatic trend of this subsection, the music moves from pervasive occurrences of half-diminished seventh and dominant ninth chords (with occasional intrusions of whole-tone segments) to a pure and complete occurrence of the whole-tone (WT-0) collection. The latter, which coincides with the rhythm of the suggested "Fate" motif (p. 32, m. 9, beat 4, through m. 11, beat 2), contributes to the cadential articulation of this subsection.

The emergence of the whole-tone "Fate" configuration at the cadence is emphasized by its contrast with the preceding passages of this subsection. The pure recitative style is supported, during the first two-thirds of the reading of Golaud's letter (p. 26, m. 1 to p. 28, m. 8), almost entirely by sustained chords in a diatonic context based on functional tonality. The remainder (to p. 29, m. 7) is articulated by two statements of "Mélisande's" motif, supported by a less stable, nonfunctional series of seventh and ninth chords. As the letter is read, whole-tone elements also intrude gradually into the harmonic and melodic dimensions. The first part is subdivided into two large halves, each half also exhibiting a binary construction.[48] The pairs (or groups) of phrases within each part (A and B) are defined by analogous harmonic progressions, first (part A) in C major (I–V65, I–V65), then (part B) in A minor (i–V– VI7, i–V–VI7–iv7), the latter extended by the whole-tone harmony, Ab–Gb–C–E (p. 27, m. 2). Parts A' and B' parallel this harmonic/tonal scheme, but with significant local modifications. The initial C major tonic triad in part A is replaced by a whole-step (C–D) in part A', the next chord (V65: B–D–F–G) modified in A' first by the omission of the original vocal G, then by the addition of A to form a vii7 chord (B–D–F–A) at the cadence of part A'. These changes imply the increasing presence of the whole-tone sphere, the latter now containing the whole-tone cell, B–[ ]–F–A. In correspondence with the increasing symbolic gesture implied in the reading of Golaud's letter, we may consider the distinction between the narrative role and the symbolic significance of objects as well.[49] For instance, the lamp, as referred to by Golaud in his letter to Pelléas (read by Geneviève in act 1, scene 2), is an object that seems to require no symbolic interpretation, as the lighted lamp is simply used as a signal to welcome Golaud and his new bride. At Geneviève's request (in the last line of the scene) that Pelléas be sure to "light the lamp this evening," this object acquires symbolic significance, since her statement evokes the polarity of light versus dark. Thus, the meaning of the object, as observed by Richard Langham Smith, is transformed with the move "to a different plane of expression, where Beaunier's 'direct expression' recedes, and a symbolic framework begins to make itself apparent."

The progression in part B' is extended (p. 28, mm. 7–8) by a modulation down a whole-step from A minor to G minor (V–i), the latter moving, then, to the C dominant ninth chord (C–E–G–Bb–D) as the basis of the first statement of "Mélisande's" motif. The whole-tone (WT-0) significance of this chord (i.e., Bb–C–D–E, the G initially isolated in the voice), which is exactly the same one that underlies the "well" motif in act 2, scene 1 (see ex. 4-3, p. 55, m. 10), will be manifested fully in the course of that scene. The series of tonally unrelated ninth and seventh chords (p. 29, mm. 1–3), the parallel fifths in the bass outlining both whole-tone scales (E–D–[C#]–C–Bb–G# and B–A–[G#]–G–F–[ ]), lead to the second statement of "Mélisande's" motif a half-step higher, on the C# dominant ninth chord, C#–E#–G#–

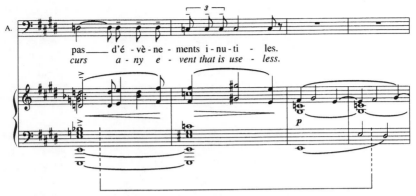

WT-0: B♭–C–D–E–F♯–G♯ (except G, m. 9, beat 1, and D♯, m. 12, beat 3)

EXAMPLE 4-7. Culmination (p. 32, end of m. 9 to beginning of m. 12) on complete WT-0 collection at prominent implication of *fate*

B–D♯. The latter prominently implies the other whole-tone (WT-1) collection, B–C♯–D♯–E♯/G♯. The latter, which supports the statement, "I shall see it from the bridge of our vessel," shifts to basic WT-0 at the prominently placed French sixth, F♯–A♯–C–E, which articulates the beginning and ending of the final statement of the letter, "if not, I shall sail on farther and never come back." These fluctuations between the two whole-tone spheres seem to reflect the alternations between the notions of staying or leaving. The entire subsection culminates (ex. 4-7), then, on the complete WT-0 collection at the implication of *fate* (p. 32, end of m. 9 to beginning of m. 12).

"Pelléas" Motif

Often, dramatic events of the opera seem to reveal a special relevance to the broader philosophical thought of the playwright. The very first appearance of Pelléas may be interpreted as such an event, its symbolic meaning suggested by his tearful emotional state and the circumstances that have induced it. Not only has he learned that his friend is going to die but also that the latter has a foreknowledge of exactly when his death will occur. In retrospect of other prophetic statements in the opera, we may assume that it is Pelléas's own death that is forecast, symbolically, at his first appearance. Pelléas quotes his own father's premonitory statement (in act 4, scene 1, pp. 191–192), as the latter himself was recovering from an illness: "'Is that you, Pelléas? Why, I'd never noticed it before, but you have the serious, friendly expression of people who haven't long to live. You must go on your travels; you must go away.'" These statements are a parallel to those made by Arkel at Pelléas's very first appearance (p. 34, mm. 9ff.): "Is that you, Pelléas? Come a little closer so that I can see you in the light," at which point Pelléas requests leave, that is, to "make a voyage," to visit his dying friend, a visit which Arkel opposes. Such a premonition of death is expressed by Maeterlinck, in his essay on "The Pre-Destined," which provides some insight into these events associated with the character and symbolism of Pelléas:

> For it was thus that my brother died. And though he alone had heard the warning whisper, be it ever so unconsciously—for from his earliest days he had concealed the message of disease within him—yet surely had the knowledge of what was to come been borne in upon us also. What are the signs that set apart the creatures for whom dire events lie in wait? Nothing is visible, and yet all is revealed. They are afraid of us, for that we are ever crying out to them of our knowledge, struggle against it as we may; and when we are with them, they can see that, in our hearts, we are oppressed by their destiny.[50]

Although Maeterlinck believes that "we diminish a thing as soon as we try to express it in words,"[51] such textual parallels as the foregoing are essential in establishing the symbolic significance of an event or character. Nevertheless, it is the nonverbal musical details that can provide insight into thoughts and feelings more directly than any evocation of the opera's most explicit parallel dramatic events and statements, or any of Maeterlinck's other poetic creations are able to. The musical context deepens our perception of the symbolic message. Although the musical trend is once again from the diatonic to whole-tone sphere, the means by which the musical fabric unfolds is often specific to a given dramatic event. Pelléas's entry into the room (ex. 4-8) may be interpreted as a symbolic answer to Geneviève's question (p. 33, m. 9), "What are we going to do?" Pelléas's diatonic (A–major) theme, which is played by the flutes,[52] is harmonized mostly by two half-diminished seventh chords, G#–B–D–F# and F#–A–C–E, which together yield an impure form of the F# Aeolian mode (F#–G#–A–B–[C]–D–E–F#) that reveals five notes of WT-0 (G#–F#–E–D–C) when rotated to begin on A (A–B/C–D–E–F#–G#). The whole-tone components (D, F#, and G#) of the initial half-diminished seventh chord (G#–B–D–F#) are confirmed immediately as such by the orchestral extension of its boundary interval (the ostinato dyad, F#–G#) to the five notes of WT-0 outlined earlier (i.e., the whole-tone partition generally associated with Pelléas and Mélisande, in contrast with the WT-1 collection of Golaud), as Arkel asks, "Who's that coming in?" Arkel's vocal part itself is based exclusively on a WT-0 transposition of the basic "Fate" cell, C–E–F#, Geneviève's answer, "'It's Pelléas," exclusively on the pentatonic form (A–B–D) of Pelléas's leitmotif (B–C#–A–D–A). These prominent occurrences of the whole-tone cell, on C, and Pelléas's pentatonic cell, on A, are local projections of the main keys of Geneviève's letter-reading, in C major and A minor, the former key transformed here into WT-0.

As Arkel and Geneviève puzzle over what they might do about Golaud's rejection of his arranged marriage to Princess Ursula and his request that they accept Mélisande, Pelléas's motif is based on the rhythm of "Fate." Arkel has been talking about never going against fate (p. 32). At this initial appearance of Pelléas, the two accompanying half-diminished seventh chords, G#–B–D–F# and F#–A–C–E, each interlock a perfect fifth (originally associated with the diatonic set) with a tritone, originally associated with the whole-tone set (see the opening of the Prelude).

These intervallic associations were already established in the opening "Forest" and "Fate" motifs, their harmonic interrelations here suggesting the seeds for trans-

EXAMPLE 4-8. Entry of Pelléas (p. 33, mm. 9–12 to p. 34, mm. 1–4), accompanying half-diminished-seventh chords to his diatonic (A-major) theme transformed into WT-o (G♯–F♯–E–D–C) at Arkel's question and Geneviève's answer

formation to "Fate" by way of Pelléas. More specifically, the combined tritones (G♯–D and F♯–C) from these two half-diminished seventh chords together imply the presence of the original French sixth chord (in enharmonic spelling, A♭–C–D–F♯), which initiated the first appearance of the "Fate" motif (see p. 1, m. 5). Just as the pentatonic whole-step ostinato, C–D, of the opening "Forest" motif became the axis of symmetry of this whole-tone French sixth chord in the "Fate" motif, the symmetrically related dyad, F♯–G♯ (in enharmonic spelling, F♯–A♭, in the original French-sixth chord), which functions as a diatonic ostinato under Pelléas's motif, also serves analogously as a common link to the whole-tone sphere (see ex. 4-8, p. 34, mm. 1–4), so Pelléas seems to symbolize a nonverbal answer to the querries of Arkel and Geneviève.

This symbolic role of Pelléas is borne out in act 2 (p. 55 ff.), scenes 1 and 2, in which his pentatonic motif (A–C–D) is transformed into the whole-tone "Fate" cell (A♭–C–D) in correspondence with the dramatic reference (See ex. 4-2b). The act opens with a diatonic transposition of the motif (C♯–E–F♯), as Pelléas and Mélisande meet at the well in the park. The whole-tone form first appears as the "Awakening Desire" motif (ex. 4-9, p. 62, m. 3), as Pelléas warns Mélisande not to toss her ring about, "Take care! Take care! Mélisande." The diatonic form emerges in act 2, scene 2 (See ex. 4.2a, p. 77, m. 4, and p. 81, m. 1), as Mélisande tends to the wounds of Golaud, who has fallen from his horse. In the course of their interaction, Mélisande begins to weep (p. 82, mm. 1–3). At this point, her motivic rhythm is set to the intervallic structure of Pelléas's transposed motif, E♭–G♭–A♭, which is a literal inversion of her own motif (A♭–B♭–C♯). When Golaud asks (p. 85) if it is Pelléas who has done her harm, she responds with an implied reference to fate, "It isn't anybody. You couldn't understand me. It's something stronger than myself." Correspondingly, the original contour of the "Pelléas" motif, which is set in the "Fate" rhythm, appears in its whole-tone transformation (A♭–C–D). Against the latter, the harmony unfolds several diatonic forms of the "Pelléas" motif: F–A♭–B♭, D–F–G, and its inversion C–D–F. This dramatic moment is yet another parallel to Pelléas's initial appearance, at which Arkel asks if it is Pelléas, or the parallel in act 4, based on Pelléas's reference to the same question by his father. In all these cases, Pelléas is not easily seen or he is outside of the light. And in these cases, death is either imminent or is the source of weeping.

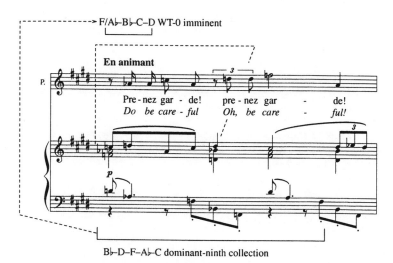

EXAMPLE 4-9. Whole-tone form of "Pelléas" motif first appearing as the "Awakening Desire" motif (p. 62, m. 3)

Transformation from pentatonic to whole-tone forms was foreshadowed at the very opening of the opera, where the ostinato dyad, C–D, together with the upper boundary note (A) of the pentatonic "Forest" motif (C–D–E–G–A), implied the presence of the pentatonic form of the "Pelléas" motif, A–C–D (see ex. 4-1). Dyad C–D then moved linearly to A♭ in the bass to outline the whole-tone form, A♭–C–D, the latter also projected vertically in the first chord (A♭–C–D–F♯) of the exclusive whole-tone "Fate" motif. This whole-tone form (A♭–C–D) of Pelléas's motif is that which accompanies (p. 86, mm. 1–2) Mélisande's evasive response to Golaud's question about Pelléas and, in connection with the latter, her reference to that which is stronger than herself. Maeterlinck himself indirectly provides insight into this event when he tells us that "facts are nothing but the laggards, the spies and camp followers of the great forces we cannot see,"[53] a statement that suggests that Mélisande's apparent lie to Golaud is really a truth on a deeper symbolic level, a truth that further establishes the character of Pelléas as something beyond simply human form.

Act 1, Scene 3 (Before the Castle): "Mélisande" and "Fate" Motifs

Fluidity of musical transformation between polarized pitch-sets corresponds most prominently with an increased focus on the polarity between light and dark in the gardens around the castle (in act 1, scene 3). The dialogue between Geneviève and Mélisande in this scene, while reflecting the mood of the garden, the forest, and the sea, tends at the same time toward a sense of staticism and abstraction because of the persistent reference to light and dark—what Richard Langham Smith characterizes as "idle discussion."[54] This sense of abstraction also may be because of linguistic disconnection. Fragmented and unrelated statements tend to become descriptive and divorced from dramatic direction, thereby lending a focus to their more abstract symbolic role. Maeterlinck's own observation, in his essay on "The Tragical in Daily Life," is most elucidating with regard to the deeper abstract meaning of the dialogue and the Symbolist aesthetic in general:

> for there must perforce be another dialogue besides the one which is superficially necessary. And indeed the only words that count in the play are those that at first seemed useless, for it is therein that the essence lies. . . . You will see, too, that it is the quality and the scope of this unnecessary dialogue that determine the quality and the immeasurable range of the work. . . . One may even affirm that a poem draws nearer to beauty and loftier truth in the measure that it eliminates words that merely explain the action, and substitutes for them others that reveal, not the so-called "soul-state," but I know not what intangible and unceasing striving of the soul towards its own beauty and truth.[55]

The symbolism of light and dark that emerges from the descriptive dialogue of this scene evokes powerful associations to life and death, conscious and unconscious, real-life world and realm of fate. The garden is dark, the forest so thick it blocks the sun, and the sea light, yet gloomy. Mélisande's observation (p. 40, mm. 1–2) of "those forests all round the palace!" foreshadows the later reference to the castle and its dark underground vaults with stagnant water and stench of death (p. 144), thereby suggesting that darkness and death are associated with the castle. Furthermore, the unconscious—that which cannot be seen—is suggested by Geneviève's reference to the mist (p. 46, mm. 3–4), which hangs over the sea and might prevent them from seeing the ship that "comes into the beam of the light." Geneviève's reference to the light, yet gloomy sea (pp. 43–44) seems to be reflected symbolically in the very last scene of the opera (pp. 295–296), in which Mélisande dies as she watches the sun set into the sea; hence, light and darkness associated with her life and ultimate fate, respectively.

This scene appears to be in several dramatic parts. In the first, Geneviève and Mélisande describe the garden darkened by the forest around the castle, but observe some light coming from the sea. In the next, they hear Pelléas approaching, and discuss the sea with him; he comments (pp. 44–45) on a vessel on which "[y]ou could sail off without knowing and never come back again." In the last part, Pelléas, at the request of Geneviève, escorts Mélisande down the dark path. In anticipation of their meeting at the well (act 2, scene 1), this scene is pervaded by the "Mélisande" and "Fate" motifs, which are already prominent in the preceding orchestral Interlude, where they are juxtaposed with "Golaud's Love" motif (p. 38).

The scene opens with "Mélisande's" pentatonic motif in the oboe (D♯–F♯–G♯–B), against which "Pelléas's" motif is imminent as it is interwoven in the murmuring string accompaniment. The primary harmony is the B dominant ninth chord (B–D♯–F♯–A–C♯), embellished by the F♯ half-diminished seventh (F♯–A–C–E). As we have seen from the outset of the opera, both types of construction—pentatonic and dominant-ninth/half-diminished—are readily transformed into whole-tone segments by means of minimal alteration of their components. In the second phrase (p. 39, m. 3), the pentatonic form of "Mélisande's" motif is transformed into a second-inversion G♯ half-diminished seventh outline (D–F♯–G♯–B) by the lowering of the original D♯ to D. Both pentatonic (F♯–G♯–B) and whole-tone (D–F♯–G♯) cells are manifested linearly, while the chords representing Pelléas remain uneqivocally diatonic.

The cadential figuration of the orchestral introduction shifts (at p. 39, m. 6) to a diatonically expanded form of the very opening pentatonic construction of the "Forest" motif (C–D–E–F–G–A), where the dyad C–D was articulated in the lower ostinato figuration, the dyad G–A in the upper. One significant difference is that the original "Fate" rhythm, which followed the "Forest" motif in the Prelude, now supplants the latter to produce a more intense infusion. This is modified into a type of undulating ostinato figuration based on two notes, which continues throughout the following dialogue between Mélisande and Geneviève. This rhythmic figure seems to be associated consistently with darkness and foreboding,[56] as expressed in the dialogue between the two women.

I might digress for the moment to point out that the latter rhythmic figure (associated with darkness and foreboding) is also recognizable in act 2 when Pelléas, in the darkness, cannot distinguish the entrance to the grotto from the night and, in act 3, when Mélisande, in the tower, fears that her doves will be lost in the night. The most striking association of this two-note rhythmic ostinato with fear occurs in the "Vault" scene (p. 144, mm. 6–7, m. 10 ff., and p. 145, m. 5 ff.), in which Golaud will frighten

Pelléas by leading him through the dark chasm, the stench of death rising from its stagnant waters. A syncopated rhythmic figure is used in the same scene when Golaud makes the lantern flicker (p. 146) to frighten Pelléas, these rapid alternations between light and dark perhaps symbolizing the threateningly thin line between life and death. A syncopated figuration is also used earlier (opening scene, p. 20) in connection with Golaud's warning to Mélisande that she will be frightened if she insists on remaining alone in the dark forest. Yet another syncopated figure appears (act 3, scene 1, pp. 137–138) when Mélisande is startled by the sound of Golaud's footsteps as her hair is entangled in the branches during her midnight meeting with Pelléas at the tower. In association with the sense of impending doom, Wenk reveals a certain insight, which gives some support to his contention that the motif of "Fate" and that of "Golaud" are one and the same: "The dramatic situations in which these patterns occur suggest an association of fear and darkness with the character of Golaud. All three types of rhythmic pattern are represented in Golaud's leitmotif: the alternation of two pitches, the repetition of a pitch, and the syncopation produced by tying across the main beat."[57]

The first part of the present scene culminates in a statement of "Mélisande's" motif (p. 41, m. 4), transposed to C♯–D♯–F♯. At Mélisande's claim that she "can hear a noise from down below," we get the first explicit statement of "Pelléas's" motif in this scene, C♯–D♯–A♯, this harmonic inversion (in "root" position, A♯–C♯–D♯) of "Mélisande's" motivic pitch content initiated by the same two notes (C♯–D♯). Three motifs—"Pelléas," "Mélisande," and "Fate"—predominate in the remainder of the scene in correspondence with the dramatic trend. At Pelléas's forbidding comment (p. 44, m. 6 ff.) that one could set sail and never return (this reference to permanent

EXAMPLE 4-10. p. 53, mm. 5–6, Mélisande's pentatonic motif in parallel fourths to produce secondary whole-tone forms, successive whole-tone forms in the bass (B♭–C–E/ E–F♯–A♯) outlining larger segment of WT-0, B♭–C–E–F♯.

departure perhaps invokes the sense of death), the orchestra plays a series of parallel dominant ninth chords that descend by whole tones from F♯ to B♭ (p. 45, mm. 1–3), thus linearly unfolding both complete whole-tone scales simultaneously. The last chord, on B♭, initiates a tremolo figure under the "Fate" motif sung by the boatmen, "Heave Ho! Heave Ho! Ho!"

At the cadential point of this statement of the "Fate" motif, the bass descends by one more whole-step to A♭, which initiates a tremolo on the basic tritone A♭–D. In the Prelude (see ex. 4-1, p. 1, m. 5), this tritone had represented the first extension and transformation of pentatonic-dyad D–C to whole-tone-cell D–C–A♭, this form manifesting itself at prominent points in the opera as an intrusion of "Fate" into the "Pelléas" motif, D–C–A. As the two walk down the path together (p. 53, mm. 5–6), the pentatonic form of "Mélisande's" motif in parallel fourths unfolds simultaneously with the whole-tone form. While the successive pairings of pentatonic forms are transposed by the tritone, so the intersecting notes (e.g., p. 53, m. 5: in parallel fourths, A–C♯–D♯ and E–G♯–A♯) produce secondary whole-tone forms, the successive whole-tone forms in the bass (B♭–C–E/E–F♯–A♯) outline a larger segment of WT-0, B♭–C–E–F♯ (ex. 4-10). These intersections heighten the effect just before the return to the pure pentatonic form of "Mélisande's" motif to round out the scene. Thus, the dramatic fabric weaves itself whole as various interrelated symbols (light and life, darkness and death) unfold within a relentless web of musical motifs and figurations that deepen these dramatic notions with their more global symbolic associations. Eventually, all of these symbols are drawn into the more pervasive shadow of fate in an ominous "Vengeance" motif that emerges with the apprehension of a shipwreck (p. 50, mm. 2–6) — for, indeed, it was a ship that brought Golaud and Mélisande to the castle at Allemonde.

5

Pelléas et Mélisande

Fate and the Unconscious:
Transformational Function
of the Dominant Ninth Chord;
Symbolism of Sonority

End of Act 1: Anticipation of Meeting of Pelléas and Mélisande;
and Act 2, Scene 1: "Pelléas" and "Well" Motifs;
Transformational Function of the Dominant
Ninth Chord

The whole-tone scale began to assert itself with increasing frequency during the first decade of the twentieth century, not only as an integral part of the harmonic palette of Debussy and other modern composers but also as part of a new theoretical consciousness that was manifested prominently in the writings of Arnold Schoenberg.[1] Beyond his mere description of the whole-tone scale, Schoenberg showed how traditional tertian constructions might be transformed into this symmetrical scale "consisting of six tones equidistant from one another." One of the examples given by Schoenberg (see ex. 2-4, earlier) is directly relevant to the whole-tone transformation of the dominant ninth "Well" motif in Debussy's opera, for instance, in act 2, scene 1 (see the first occurrence of the motif in ex. 4-3 earlier, C–E–[G]–B♭–D, and its transformation in ex. 5-1, that is, transposed to G♯–B♯–[D–E]–F♯–A♯). Schoenberg's whole-tone chord is shown without any suggested tonal function, that is, simply as a consequence of the registral isolation and chromatic splitting of the fifth degree of the dominant ninth chord. The transformational function of the latter in Debussy's opera is, in terms of harmonic focus and symbolic expression, highly significant at this meeting of Pelléas and Mélisande at the well.

Act 2 opens (p. 55) with a form of the pentatonic "Pelléas" motif, C♯–E–F♯, which is a variant of its original occurrence (p. 33, mm. 10–11). This variant, a literal inversion of the basic pentatonic "Mélisande" motif (A♭–B♭–C♯), is based on the "Fate" rhythm, played by the flute in the C♯–Aeolian mode. At the cadence of this modal statement (p. 55, m. 3), The C♯ tonic is harmonized deceptively as the ninth of the dominant ninth chord, B–[ ]–F♯–A–C♯. Although derived from this mode (C♯–D♯–E–F♯–G♯–A–[B]–C♯), this chord, which is built on the seventh degree (B), serves as a tonal disruption. It initiates new figurations in paired phrases, the harmonic progression contributing further to the tonally static, disconnected mosaic texture that seems simply to set the evanescent mood. The F♯ minor seventh chord arpeggiations (F♯–A–C♯–E) of the two harps, which extend the held B dominant ninth chord to an eleventh (B–[ ]–F♯–A–C♯–E), serve as the harmonic link between both the opening C♯ Aeolian mode and B dominant ninth/eleventh chord to the following, otherwise unrelated D dominant ninth chord (D–F♯–A–C–E) by altering only one note (C♯ to C). It is striking that the B dominant ninth chord is missing its third degree (D♯), which allows for a somewhat smoother pivotal connection to the alternating D dominant ninth chord.

These two dominant ninth chords imply the presence of the two whole-tone collections, respectively. If we reorder B–[D♯]–F♯–A–C♯ as F♯/A–B–C♯–[D♯], the primary manifestation is WT-1. If we reorder D–F♯–A–C–E as A/C–D–E–F♯, the primary manifestation is WT-0. Following the alternations of these two unrelated dominant ninths (on B and D) in the paired phrases, the F♯ minor seventh chord (F♯–A–C♯–E) returns as the exclusive basis of the retransition (p. 55, mm. 5–6) to a variant of the "Pelléas" motif, C♯–D♯–B–E–B. The latter, which adds the D♯ previously missing from the B dominant ninth, extends the linear F♯ minor seventh chord to F♯–A–C♯–D♯–B, the WT-1 tetrachord (A–B–C♯–D♯) of the complete B dominant ninth chord appearing as an adjacency now. This transformation serves as preparation for the "Well" motif (p. 55, m. 10), a musico-dramatic object associated prominently with *fate*.

According to Schoenberg, who had composed his symphonic poem *Pelleas und Melisande* at about the same time that Debussy completed his opera (1902), he and other composers of the time came to the use of the whole-tone scale independently from Debussy.[2] Furthermore, Schoenberg contrasts Debussy's use of the scale with his own, stating that for Debussy the scale and its harmonic subcollections serve an expressive impressionistic function as "tone color" rather than being used for "the sake of their harmonic and melodic possibilities: the chords for the sake of their connection with other chords, the scale for the sake of its peculiar influence on the melody."[3] While Schoenberg's notion of the scale as "tone color" in Debussy's music is commonly acknowledged, a kind of functionality (albeit nontraditional) also may be assumed from the pervasive transformational relations between whole-tone and other types of harmonic construction. Although traditional notions of linear functionality (that is, dominant-tonic voice-leading) are only suggested on occasion, and seem to assert themselves only on some subliminal level of harmonic progression because of the prevalence of disconnected mosaic textural blocks and layers, a new type of harmonic function may be traced on the local level of Debussy's music. Schoenberg's own statement about the harmonic and structural possibilities of whole-tone chords in modulations and modulatory episodes,[4] which he believes are beyond Debussy's purely coloristic usage, can actually be shown to apply to Debussy's opera, as manifested in a certain logic contained in the relations of adjacent constructions. In Debussy's nontraditional modulations from one type of harmonic construction (e.g., symmetrical) to another (e.g., modal/diatonic), or vice versa, the most pervasive are those voice-leadings, expressed or implied, based on minimal chromatic alterations in combination with common (sustained) tones.

Transformation from diatonic (human) to whole-tone (fatalistic) spheres begins at the first statement of the "Well" motif (p. 55, mm. 10 ff.), in anticipation of the loss of Mélisande's ring. At this focal point, the motif is based on a new dominant ninth transposition, C–E–G–B♭–D, its four whole-tone (WT-0) components separated timbrally from the fifth degree (G/B♭–C–D–E), that is, the two oboes play the main whole-tone motivic figure against the contrasting, articulated G of the muted horns, with less prominent interjections of mixed chordal components by the flutes and harp. It is significant that the whole-tone dyad, C–D, which forms the boundary of the symmetrical dominant ninth chord (C–E–G–B♭–D) as well as the axis of symmetry of the "Well" motif's whole-tone tetrachord (B♭–C–D–E), was already established as the primary transformational element between pentatonic and whole-tone spheres at the opening of the Prelude (see ex. 4-1 earlier), where it moved from its ostinato position in the pentatonic "Forest" motif to its axial position in the initial French sixth chord (A♭–C–D–F♯) of the "Fate" motif.

After some unfolding of modal and pentatonic scales in the orchestra and vocal line, respectively, we get a new statement of the "Well" motif (ex. 5-1, p. 57, mm. 1–2) as Mélisande becomes intrigued with the well: "Oh, how clear the water is!" At this point, the whole-tone segment, B♭–C–D–E (in divided violins and violas), of the motif's timbrally partitioned C dominant ninth chord is transposed to F♯–G♯–A♯–B♯ (p. 57, m. 2) to complete the WT-0 set (B♭–C–D–E/F♯–G♯–A♯–B♯). The latter transposition of the motif, which accompanies Pelléas's observation that "it's as cool as the winter,"[5] that is, like "the icy hand of destiny,"[6] is harmonized not by an "expected" G♯ dominant ninth chord (G♯–B♯–D♯–F♯–A♯, or D♯/F♯–G♯–A♯–B♯) but, rather, by a whole-tone transformation of the latter by the splitting into, and replacement of, its "expected" fifth degree (D♯) by its adjacent half-steps, D and E. The resulting whole-tone collection, D–E–F♯–G♯–A♯–B♯, is supported by the explicit scalar whole-tone segment in the voice (D–E–F♯–G♯–A♯). As Pelléas tells Mélisande about the abandoned well, that "It seems it used to work miracles," D♯ and D are juxtaposed in the voice. The latter note serves as the intersection (p. 57, mm. 5–6, voice) between a transposition of "Pelléas's" pentatonic motif, D–F–G, and the whole-tone "Fate" cell, D–F♯–G♯, which intersects, in turn, with the original transposition of "Mélisande's" pentatonic motif, G♯–A♯–C♯ (in enharmonic spelling, A♭–B♭–C♯). Thus, the alteration of a single note (fifth degree) of the dominant ninth produces an almost "magical" quality as it transforms the diatonic (human) into the whole-tone (fatalistic) realm.

Instrumental Timbre as Signifier

The role of instrumental timbre in the symbolic expression of the drama appears to be primarily contextual, that is, its symbolic significance appears to be established primarily by internal, parallel identifications, although certain scholars have attributed some inherent qualities to instrumental sonority.[7] Perhaps, some combination of its intrinsic and associative (contextual) potential may be assumed. In any case, in addition to pitch-set connections between the well and Mélisande's death, instrumental timbre contributes to the symbolic association of these focal events. The reference to "winter" reveals an even more direct, deep-level symbolic connection between the well and fate at the second statement of the "Well" motif (p. 57, mm. 1–2). The subtle change of instrumental timbre at this return of the motif appears to support the more

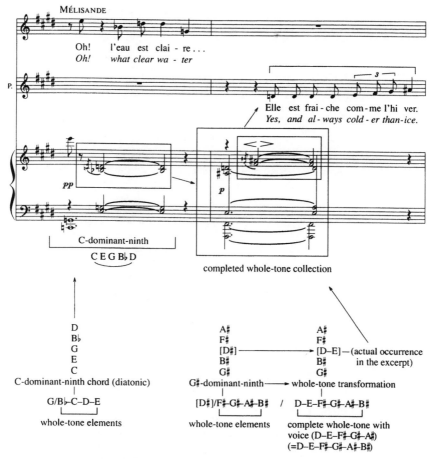

EXAMPLE 5-1. "Well" motif (p. 57, mm. 1–2), whole-tone transformation of dominant-ninth chord

explicit symbolism now provided by the text. At the reference to clear water, winter, and the abandoned ancient well, the basic grace-note figure of the "Well" is articulated first by horns (supported by harp), then flutes. Wenk associates the horn timbre with Golaud, or darkness and death,[8] the latter two appearing to be symbolized by the reference to "winter." Wenk also associates the harp timbre with water, or renewal, freshness, and change, which appears to be symbolized by reference to the past (changed) miraculous powers of the well to heal (renew) the eyes of the sightless. The "fatalistic" significance of these timbral associations is borne out at the end of the opera by the musical context surrounding Mélisande's death.

Mélisande's death is the inevitable outcome of those events that stem from her meeting with Pelléas at the well. When she loses her ring in the well (p. 67), the descending harp glissando is followed by a rhythmic reminiscence of the well's grace-note figure precisely in the horn and flutes. As Mélisande lies on her deathbed at the end of the opera (pp. 295–296), she perceives the setting of the sun in the sea as the coming of winter. This imagery evokes that of the ring falling into the cold water of the well, a symbolic interpretation supported by the last iterations of the "Well" motif (short-long rhythmic figurations) at her reference to the setting sun. Earlier (p. 60), when Mélisande tries to see the bottom of the well, Pelléas tells her, "Nobody has ever seen it. It may be as deep as the sea." This statement provides an additional confirmation of the direct association of the sea with the well. Here, the reminiscence of the "Well" motif's grace-note figure is again articulated by the portentous horn timbre in juxtaposition with the woodwinds, especially flutes (p. 296, m. 1). We may compare the latter instrumentation with that of the "Well" motif's grace-note figures (at p. 57, mm. 1–4). Prevalence of the same instruments (horns and flutes) at the grace-note figure supports the association of the well and ring to the sun setting over the sea in winter, and with Mélisande's death, as the flute and horn (with harp) take over the long-short "Well" rhythm in the last six measures of the opera.[9] The flute plays this rhythmic figure in counterpoint with the "Mélisande" motif, the latter doubled by the trumpet, which, according to Wenk, has a direct association with "peaceful death."[10] Symbolic associations between the individual dramatic moments and the chameleon-like changes of timbre, register, dynamics, and other parameters, which are in constant alliance with the mosaic textural details of the opera, are concomitant with, yet inherently independent from, the myriad details of harmonic (pitch-set) projection. Hence, each of these parameters would warrant an entire associative study in and of itself, and so, can only receive intermittent attention in connection with primary focal issues and events in this discussion.

Power of the Unconscious

Although the influence of unconscious memories and thoughts had been explored by practitioners of "animal magnetism,"[11] their insights were overlooked as animal magnetism fell into disrepute and their findings dismissed.[12] It was Charcot who was to grant the use of hypnosis scientific status in his investigation of mental disorders and specifically hysteric patients at Salpetrière. Charcot also suggested a link between hysterical symptoms and the patient's thoughts. Although Charcot's approach was descriptive and his research focused on physiological measures and visual data—he used drawings and photographs to illustrate his findings or to draw conclusions—he did not listen to his patients' stories or take in-depth clinical histories. Charcot's immoderate adherence to positivism and the extreme reactions of some of his associates, which left no room for mysticism or mystery of the human spirit, found a counterpart in the Symbolist movement, which gave an artistic expression to the power of mystery and unconscious forces. Paradoxically, Charcot influenced many clinicians, including Janet and Freud, who sought ways of exploring the patient's unconscious thought processes in order to ameliorate the psychological symptoms.

These activities in psychology provide some historical support for our attempt at a more modern psychological interpretation in connection with the symbolism, in *Pelléas et Mélisande*, of such focal elements as "The Blindmen's Well," which Pelléas tells us no longer has the power to cure the eyes of the sightless. In answer to Mélisande's question about the loss of this power of the well, Pelléas says (p. 58): "Since the king is almost blind himself, people don't come here any longer." Freud himself believed that man was not in control of his destiny, because internal unconscious forces could influence his actions.[13] Healing of the blind signifies the power to give insight, that is, to bring to consciousness that which is unknown (or unconscious), hence, to acquire a certain control over one's destiny. Because old king Arkel himself is blind, probably a metaphor for the loss of faith in traditional religious beliefs and institutions, neither the well nor the established authority could provide guidance. Thus, the ultimate fate—tragedy and death—of the characters is determined by the power of the unconscious, through which no one can see.

It was only shortly before his death that Pelléas was finally to become conscious of the "snares of destiny" all around him (act 4, scene 4), his hidden unconscious forces thus becoming conscious too late, as he now likens himself to a blind man who should flee from his burning house. Yet, the question arises as to why he could not take destiny in hand by fleeing before the fatal blow, given that he was now aware of his desires and the potential danger associated with them. Freud hypothesized that the unconscious entails more than what has been repressed. There are unconscious elements which have never belonged to the conscious sphere, and so the mechanism of repression could not be applied to them.[14] According to Freud, these unconscious elements are *instincts*, which lie somewhere between the biological and psychological and thus have no capacity for transference to conscious thought.[15] It follows from this Freudian notion that Pelléas's inability to divert the final catastrophe might be attributed to the death instinct.[16] Being conspicuously unarmed, Pelléas continues to embrace Mélisande even though he knows that Golaud would soon fall on him with sword in hand. Given this dilemma, we can surmise that a kind of equivalence exists between unconscious motivation—the instinctual kind in this case—and fate, that force against which the characters never seem to struggle. This force, according to Maeterlinck, differs from "passive misfortunes (such as the death of a person we adore) which simply come towards us, and cannot be influenced by any movement of ours. Bethink you of the fatal day of your life."[17] In Pelléas's case, however, this force, in Maeterlinck's own words, seems to come from "some irresistible impulse, towards an inevitable catastrophe." Thus, in spite of Pelléas's new insight into the role of destiny in all these events, one of the unconscious elements—the death instinct—was to remain hidden, and so could persist as a dynamic force up to the very moment in which fate would reveal its final hand in the demise of the two lovers.[18] Freud observes how "striking are those cases where the person seems to be experiencing something passively, without exerting any influence of his own, and yet always meets with the same fate over and over again . . . we may venture to make the assumption that there really exists in psychic life a repetition-compulsion, which goes beyond the pleasure-principle."[19]

Music as Message Encoder of the Unconscious

Music encodes the message of the unconscious and provides insight into this special scene at the well (act 2, scene 1). As Pelléas describes the mysterious powers of the well—that it used to be able to heal the eyes of the blind—two more statements of the "Well" motif appear (p. 58, mm. 1 and 6) in juxtaposition with several repetitions of the "Fate" motif, the first statements of the latter to appear in this act. What transpires at this moment of the drama is a tightly interwoven set of musical interactions that symbolize the fatalistic meaning of the two lovers at the well. This miraculous object no longer gives man conscious control over his destiny, that is, sight to the blind. Embedded in Pelléas's vocal line (p. 57, mm. 5–6) at these final two statements of the "Well" motif are the inverted tritone-related "Pelléas" and "Mélisande" motifs (D–F–G and G♯–A♯–C♯). The inversional relation of these two strictly diatonic cells is essential in the symmetrical completion of the whole-tone collection. In connection with the first of these final two motivic statements (p. 58, m. 1), the contour of Pelléas's vocal line telling Mélisande that "They still call it the 'Blind men's Well'" is linearly outlined by the pitch content of the E dominant ninth chord (E–G♯–B–D–F♯), the transposed "Well" motif now based exclusively on the whole-tone tetrachord (D–E–F♯–G♯) derived from this dominant ninth construction. The latter tetrachord (D–E–F♯–G♯) is a whole-tone expansion of the "Pelléas" motif (D–F–G) at the same transpositional level. In connection with the final statement of the "Well" motif (p. 58, m. 6), the contour of Mélisande's vocal line, which expresses awe at "How solitary it is—there's not a sound to be heard," is linearly outlined by the slightly modified pitch content of the B♭ dominant ninth chord ([ ]–D–F–A♭–C– [G]). Its pure form is confirmed by the first orchestral chord (B♭–D–F–A♭–C), the transposed "Well" motif now based exclusively on the whole-tone tetrachord (A♭–B♭–C–D) derived from this dominant ninth. The latter tetrachord (A♭–B♭–C–D) is a whole-tone (fatalistic) transformation of the "Mélisande" motif (G♯–A♯–C♯, or A♭–B♭–C♯) at the same transpositional level. The tritone-related whole-tone tetrachords of both statements of the "Well" motif (D–E–F♯–G♯/A♭–B♭–C–D) imply the presence of the complete WT-0 collection, which has been associated with the mood of fate from the outset. The same transformational process was evident at the first occurrence of the "Mélisande" motif in the Prelude (m. 14-15), in which the thematic statement of her cell (A♭–B♭–C♯) was altered to A♭–B♭–D in the accompanying figuration.

Such transformations between the pentatonic/diatonic and whole-tone spheres usually continue in more fragmented and ambiguous ways when they are only adumbrations of the more dynamic dramatic moments of fatalistic consequence. The "Vault" scene of act 3, scene 2, for instance, is among the most explicit symbolic references to Pelléas's ultimate fate (his death), and so is based on the most dynamic, unequivocal generation of the complete (symmetrical) whole-tone cycle from primary "leitmotivic" cells. In the present scene, a subliminal though portentous moment of fatalistic import occurs when Mélisande tosses her wedding ring into the air and drops it into the well (p. 67). Symbolic musical transformations correspondingly remain subtle and incomplete, yet highly effective in preparing for the fulfillment of a complex web of musico-dramatic associations. It is inevitable that the loss of the ring will arouse Golaud's suspicion of Mélisande's affair with Pelléas and lead to tragedy, and so the basic leitmotivic pitch-cell segments associated with the human realm and fate become increasingly enmeshed in the generation of the main larger sets. The falling motion of the ring is depicted by a descending harp arpeggio, which is set within a context permeated by the persistent "Fate" rhythm. The arpeggio unfolds an incomplete F♯ dominant ninth chord, that is, half-diminished seventh chord, [ ]–A♯–C♯–E–G♯, which may be interpreted as an ambiguous interlocking of the original pentatonic "Mélisande" segment, G♯–A♯–C♯ (an enharmonic spelling of A♭–B♭–C♯), with a whole-tone segment, E–G♯–A♯.[20] This symbolic pitch-cell interaction is anticipated (p. 61) by the E♯–half-diminished seventh arpeggiation (E♯–G♯–B–D♯) that accompanies Mélisande's prophetic words to be associated with the ring, "No, no, I want to dip both my hands in." This arpeggiation alternates with a G♯–minor seventh harmony, G♯–B–D♯–F♯, which also unfolds in the vocal line. The rhythmic placement of the vocal pitches in relation to the two alternating harmonies in the orchestra serves as evidence for the pentatonic/whole-tone transformational relation between these two seventh chords. The F♯ and G♯ of the voice are interpreted harmonically as part of the G♯–minor seventh chord, whereas the G♯, B, and D♯ are interpreted harmonically as part of the E♯–half-diminished seventh chord. The first seventh chord construction implies the presence only of the pentatonic "Mélisande" cell (F♯–G♯–B and its inversion, D♯–F♯–G♯), that is, without whole-tone significance, while the second seventh-chord construction implies the presence of both the pentatonic "Mélisande" cell (D♯–E♯–G♯) and its whole-tone ("Fate") transformation (B–D♯–E♯). The difference between the two seventh chords (E♯–G♯–B–D♯ and G♯–B–D♯–F♯) is a single change of pitch, from F♯ to E♯ and back.

As Mélisande tries to see the bottom of the well and to reach down into the water (p. 61), Pelléas wants to take hold of her hand so she will not slip, but she insists on dipping in both her hands. Mélisande's next comment (p. 62), "It seems as if my hands are ill to-day," provides psychological insight into her actions. The inability of her hands (her controlling element) to reach the water suggests that her consciousness—that is, her hands are under voluntary control—is not working well. Only with her sensual hair,[21] which dips inadvertently into the well, can she reach the water (p. 63): "'Yes, it's longer than my arms, it's longer than I am." Also significant at this moment is Mélisande's distraction by something she has suddenly seen in the water. The imagery of a shining object evokes an association to the pond where she had dropped her crown. With regard to timbral association, Debussy's use of pizzicato (with harp in the present passage) appears to be associated with some moment of sudden conscious realization: her attention being drawn to an object in the water, Golaud's subsequent realization that her wedding ring is missing from her finger, or Pelléas's quandary in the love scene about what has all of a sudden awakened him.[22]

We may infer that Mélisande's sensuality (her hair) has a greater reach than her cognition (her hands). In other words, her passion or instincts, which are symbolized by her hair, reach further than herself or her conscious mind. Mélisande's restlessness contrasts with Pelléas's peaceful feeling about the well (see p. 59), "It's always extraordinarily quiet. You can almost hear the water sleeping," thereby reflecting her lack of an internal self-object in contrast with his internal self-reliance. Thus, Mélisande's unconscious, the motivating force that leads her on, is associated with her uncontrollable fate; Pelléas cannot control either Mélisande's hands or hair from dipping into the well.

At Mélisande's reference to her hands (p. 62), the distinction between these pentatonic and whole-tone cells is made more explicit. The whole-tone cell, B–D♯–E♯, is extracted from the previous half-diminished seventh arpeggiation to form an orchestral ostinato against a new transposition of the "Mélisande" pentatonic motif in her vocal line (E♯–Fx–A♯). In contrast to the arpeggiation, these transpositions of the whole-tone and pentatonic cells are divergent in that they are not partitions of the same half-diminished seventh chord. Rather, they are nonliteral inversions of each other (B–D♯–E♯/E♯–Fx–A♯), the pentatonic whole-step (Fx–E♯) of the "Mélisande" motif playing a dual role as it is extended by the whole-tone cell of the orchestra to form part of a larger segment of WT-1 (Fx–E♯–D♯–B).

The significance of these interactions between "Mélisande's" motif and the orchestral statements of the "Fate" cell is manifested in the next passage, at the appearance of both the "Awakening Desire" motif and a transformation of Golaud's "Love" motif (p. 62, mm. 3 and 4, respectively). The latter motivic juxtaposition, which suggests the first emergence of one of the fundamental dramatic conflicts (that is, between Pelléas and Golaud), is articulated by the two whole-tone collections associated with the two brothers, respectively. Pelléas expresses a momentary start, "Oh! Oh! Take care! Take care! Mélisande! Mélisande!" as she leans over to dip her hands into the well. This whole-tone polarity has been foreshadowed in Mélisande's two statements about her hands. In contrast to the orchestral ostinato based on the WT-1 transposition of the "Fate" cell (B–D♯–E♯) underlying her second phrase, Pelléas's "Awakening Desire" motif outlines the original WT-0 transposition of the "Fate" cell, A♭–C–D, that is, a whole-tone transformation of the "Pelléas" motif (A–C–D).

The cell (A♭–C–D) at this point forms part of the larger B♭ dominant ninth chord (B♭–D–F–A♭–C). Cell A♭–C–D is expanded, then, to a larger whole-tone tetrachord, A♭–B♭–C–D, as the basis of the descending triplets of Golaud's transformed "Love" motif. This WT-0 tetrachord retains four of the five notes of the B♭ dominant ninth, that is, without the latter's fifth degree (F), which belongs to the other whole-tone (WT-1) collection. This single "odd" note (F) initiates, then, a sequential transposition of the triplets of Golaud's "Love" motif, in which F–E♭–D♭–C♭ replaces D–C–B♭–A♭. It should be recalled at this point that it is the WT-1 collection that was associated with Golaud from the time of his first entry into the forest, and it will continue to be associated primarily with Golaud in special ways throughout the remainder of the opera. Analogous to the tetrachordal expansion from A♭–C–D of the "Awakening Desire" motif to A♭–B♭–C–D, the WT-1 tetrachord (C♭–D♭–E♭–F) is an expansion of the preceding "Fate" cell ostinato, B–D♯–E♯ (in enharmonic spelling, C♭–E♭–F). The tritone transposition (F–A–B) of the latter replaces A♭–C–D as the basis of the next statement of the "Awakening Desire" motif. In turn, F–A–B is expanded to a WT-1 tetrachord, F–G–A–B, of Golaud's "Love" motif.

The boundary tritone (F–B) of the latter is projected into the linear structure ([F]–D–C–[B]–A♯–F♯) of Pelléas's next vocal statement, "Oh! your hair!" this WT-1 tritone coming into conflict with a larger segment from the other whole-tone (WT-0) collection, D–C–A♯–F♯. The WT-1 note, F, together with the WT-0 dyad, D–C, forms part of Mélisande's pentatonic cell in the initial linear adjacency (F–D–C), the same three-note segment contained at the apex of the "Awakening Desire" theme (p. 62, m. 3). The symbolic connection between Mélisande's hair and the awakening of Pelléas's desire is thereby reflected in this whole-tone fusion within the pentatonic cell extracted from the "Awakening Desire" theme. At this point, however, tritone F-B from WT-1 is replaced in prominence by tritone F♯–C from WT-0. This forms the boundary of the accompanying whole-tone figure, F♯–G♯–A♯–B♯ (p. 63, m. 1), the latter expanding WT-0 of the vocal line to five notes (F♯–G♯–A♯–C–D).

Furthermore, the structure of the original interlocking pentatonic/whole-tone form (F–D–C/D–C–A♭) of the "Awakening Desire" theme is extended downward in the voice by one whole-tone (F–D–C/C–[ ]–A♯–F♯). The significance of this intervallic mutation and whole-tone extension of the thematic structure is twofold. First, it suggests a pictorial (downward) representation of Mélisande's "falling" hair, and, second, it extends the original whole-tone components (D–C–A♭) to the larger WT-0 collection in symbolic anticipation of the *falling* of Mélisande's wedding ring into the well, which signifies her separation from Golaud.

This connection between her "falling" hair and the imminent loss of her ring is supported by her preceding statement, "If there's something shining at the bottom, perhaps you could see it." Mélisande's hair is also symbolic of her intimacy with Pelléas, as seen later, in act 3, when she leans her unbound hair out of the tower window (p. 120) to entwine him sensuously (p. 127f.). Mélisande's eventual destruction is also symbolized by her hair, by which Golaud drags her in the form of a cross.

The conflict between dramatic spheres associated with Pelléas and Golaud, respectively, becomes increasingly explicit (p. 64ff.) as the scene moves relentlessly toward a crucial dramatic moment: loss of the wedding ring in the well. Pelléas's probing question (p. 64, mm. 2–4), "It was beside a spring that he found you, wasn't it?" suggests an equation between the well, where his desire for Mélisande is awakened, and the original pond, where Golaud had found her. When Pelléas asks if Golaud had come close to her at that first encounter, she falsely tells him that Golaud wished to kiss her. Pelléas's question and Mélisande's fabrication represent a seductive testing of each other. Her lie about the kiss, her distraction by something in the well, and her tossing of the ring in the air—this time conscious control is suggested by her statement that her "hands do not shake" (p. 66)—represent a heightening of the polarity between Mélisande's passion for Pelléas and her rejection of Golaud. The latter is revealed in her statement that she did not want Golaud to kiss her and also in her ensuing action in which she is about to toss her wedding ring into the air. At the pond where Golaud had found Mélisande, there was also another conjugal symbol—the crown of Bluebeard—which she had also thrown into the water. In both cases (pp. 7 and 66), reference is made to the danger that Mélisande herself might fall into the water, and, in both cases, it is she who instigates that danger.

Having lost the ring in the well, Mélisande does not assume responsibility for her actions. She does not see the role she plays in the events, since she is controlled by her unconscious (p. 70, mm.7–8): "Yet I thought I had it in my hands. I had already closed my hands, and yet it fell all the same." But Maeterlinck believes that women are more open to the "pure workings of the mystery. And therefore is it, doubtless, that all the incidents in our life in which they take part seem to bring us nearer to what might almost be the very fountainhead of destiny."[23] Pelléas is more rational than Mélisande. He says that another ring can be found for her, but Mélisande's pessimistic notion that there will never be another ring reveals her wish for freedom from her marital bond, that is, as symbolized by the ring of Golaud and, earlier, by the crown of Bluebeard. Her motivation toward freedom seems obvious from her action of having thrown the ring (p. 71) "too high towards the sun."

These polarities are evident at every turn of dramatic events. The rays of the sun evoke one of the basic symbolic polarities of the opera—light (the human element, or consciousness) versus dark (fate or the unconscious). Mélisande's conscious act of tossing the ring into the bright sunlight has fatalistic (unconscious) consequences (her ultimate freedom in death), as her action causes the ring to fall into the darkness of the well (p. 72): "It was striking twelve o'clock just when the ring fell in." The light of the sun—her consciousness and her desire for freedom—is further symbolized by the connection between her reference to the noon-day sun in this scene and her comment later (act 3, scene 1, p. 116, "Hair" scene), in which we learn from her that she was born on a Sunday at noon.[24]

This symbolic connection between her birth at noon and the loss of the ring in the sun's rays perhaps represents rebirth for Mélisande in this context—liberation from Golaud—evokes in us the sense that Mélisande refers to her birth because she wishes to return to a time when she was free. Here, in the tower, Mélisande is reaching again (toward destruction) with her instincts or her sensuality (her hair), more explicitly toward Pelléas now: "My hair is waiting for you all down the tower." Interpretation regarding the equation between Mélisande's birth and her freedom (in death) is further supported by the final event of the opera. Mélisande's daughter, who looks like she could be her sister and who has her own life to live, "'It's the poor little thing's turn," is born just before Mélisande dies as the sun sets. The fate that will befall Mélisande's offspring, however, remains ambiguous at the end of the opera. The birth of her daughter at the time of the sunset and Mélisande's death may be interpreted, in any case, as a manifestation of polarity and, at the same time continuity on a deeper conceptual level: darkness (setting of the sun) and death are balanced and continued by the light of a new life. Furthermore, Golaud's sobs, his last utterances in the opera, constitute both a perfect symmetry and a polarity with Mélisande's sobs, which constitute her first utterances in the opera. If part of the Allemonde tragedy is the irreconcilable gender polarities, of strong versus weak, oppressor versus victim, Golaud's pain and repentance may be the beginning of healing: his ability to abandon his posture of narcissistic entitlement and invulnerability and acceptance of his own neediness and weakness that he had disavowed and projected onto Mélisande. Both the symbolic and psychological significance of these basic polarities from the point of view of the reader's understanding may be clarified by certain symbolic premises of symmetry-asymmetry, as discussed by Ignacio Matte-Blanco,[25] according to whom we find that what an individual (for instance, a writer like Maeterlinck) expresses can be approached from two different perspectives:

> (1) As a *product*, that is, considered independently from its producer, in its structure, its meaning, its relation to other aspects of the reality of the world which are external to the individual who created the product in question; and also from the point of view of objective truth, falsehood or imprecision.
>
> (2) As a *manifestation* or *indication* of what goes on in the individual at the moment of its production or in the period around that moment. It is obvious that in order to study it from this point of view we have to consider at least some aspects which are different from those considered in the first case.
>
> The differences between both cases result from the fact that in each case the same piece of reality is seen or considered in a different configuration or *gestalt*, which makes more visible some aspects, and not others, of the reality in question. Nothing prevents us, however, from seeing the same reality from both angles of observation.

Hence, in the case of the polarity between Mélisande's death (darkness) and the new life (light) of her daughter, for instance, the notion that the latter will continue on the same fatalistic path as her mother (continuity based on an asymmetrical conception) is balanced by the interpretation that her daughter will break the fatalistic pattern of her mother, hence serving, instead of her mother, as the one to usher in the new era, a role that Arkel had originally assigned to Mélisande (this contrasting polarity of roles based on a symmetrical conception). According to all aspects considered, both interpretations might be meaningful, and entail both symmetrical-asymmetrical principles that lead to deeper-level ambiguities in relation to the individual, who functions in the opera simultaneously as real-life being (one who may be capable of asserting a will through conscious awareness) and as instrument of fate (one who remains in the grip of unconscious forces).

Act 2, Scenes 1 and 2: Consequences of the Lost Ring—Varied Repetition and Development of Motifs in Transformation from Pentatonic to Whole-Tone Spheres

In his discourse on women, Maeterlinck speaks about how the woman, chosen for the man by Fate, awaits him at the designated hour on the road that he must cross.[26] Maeterlinck's notion of predestined love provides insight into one of the main symbolic focal points of the opera: the meeting of Pelléas and Mélisande at the well. Mélisande's actions at the well have far-reaching consequences in connection with future events, over which she has no conscious control. Maeterlinck's own philosophical statement seems to apply to Mélisande, that is, as one of those "who attempt to force the hand of Fate. Wildly pressing down their eyelids, so as not to see that which had to be seen—struggling with all their puny strength against the eternal forces—they will contrive perhaps to cross the road and go towards another, sent thither but not for them." In the present scene, one of the primary events—loss of the wedding ring—has come to pass and Mélisande will take the alternative road to conceal the truth from Golaud. Her increasing anxiety over the loss of the ring informs the ending of act 2, scene 1 (p. 70ff.), her words suggesting, prophetically, that the two lovers can never experience conjugal fulfillment: "No, no, we shall never find it, and we shan't find another one, either." She senses the truth because she herself is capable, as we know from her disposal of the crown and now the ring, of actively (albeit innocently) paving the way toward her destruction, her ultimate fate. She ponders an excuse regarding loss of the ring (p. 72), "What shall we tell Golaud if he asks where it is?" to which Pelléas immediately responds, "The truth! The truth!" Insight into Mélisande's fatalistic inclination as siren of destruction may be further gleaned from Maeterlinck's view of Fate and the woman:

> There are times when destiny shuts her eyes, but she knows full well that, when evening falls, we shall return to her, and that the last word must be hers. She may shut her eyes, but the time till she re-open them is time that is lost. . . .
> It would seem that women are more largely swayed by destiny than ourselves. They submit to its decrees with far more simplicity; nor is there sincerity in the resistance they offer. They are still nearer to God, and yield themselves with less reserve to the pure workings of the mystery.[27]

The significance of Pelléas's advice to Mélisande, that she tell the truth to Golaud about the ring, is suggested musically. The well is a symbol of a miraculous power that used to give sight to the blind—a metaphor for insight or truth. We may also associate Pelléas's reference to the "truth" (p. 72) more literally with the well because that is where the ring was actually lost. We get a return of the original C♯ Aeolian sixteenth-note figuration that had directly followed the first statement of the "Well" motif (p. 56, m. 1ff.). At its original ocurrence, the C♯ figuration served as a transitional link between the primarily diatonic (C dominant ninth, G/B♭–C–D–E) content of the "Well" motif and its whole-tone transformation (p. 57, mm. 1–2), where the words suggested the objective coldness of *fate*. The C♯ Aeolian pentatonic substructure (C♯–B–G♯–F♯–E–C♯), which is pervaded both by the pentatonic "Pelléas" cell (C♯–B–G♯, or F♯–E–C♯) and its "Mélisande" inversion (F♯–G♯–B) and is directly associated with Pelléas's C♯ Aeolian theme that opened the scene, accompanies Pelléas's question that literally pertains to the well, "Don't you know where I've brought you?" But where is it that he has brought her, symbolically speaking? The premonitory implications of Pelléas's question is supported by the C♯ tonality, precisely the tonality that will accompany Mélisande at her death in the very final measures of the opera.

The scene ends (p. 72ff.) with a more clearly defined manifestation of the transformational process from pentatonic to whole-tone spheres. Pelléas's suggestion that Mélisande tell the truth to Golaud is articulated cadentially by the final return of the C♯ Aeolian figuration which, as in the opening of this scene, serves a transitional function to the whole-tone world of Fate (established at p. 73, m. 4 ff.). In this case (ex. 5-2), not only is the whole-tone collection associated directly with the "Fate" motif, but the C♯ Aeolian figuration itself is transformed first into the original pentatonic collection (C–D–G–A) of the opening "Forest" motif and, then, exclusively into the complete WT-1 collection (B–D♭–E♭–F–G–A) as it appears in block juxtaposition with the "Fate" motif.

Shortly after the change of key signature (p. 73, m. 2), transposition of the C♯ Aeolian figuration to the "white-key" pentatonic figure, C–D–G–A (see ex. 5-2), recalls the basic pitch relations of the Prelude to the opera. These pitch relations underscore the parallel dramatic function between this passage and the Prelude. In the opening scene immediately following the Prelude, Golaud had become lost in the woods while hunting a wild boar. That event led to Golaud's encounter with Mélisande, who had dropped her shining crown (symbolizing her former bond to Bluebeard) into a pond, and Golaud's eventual marriage to her. In act 2, scene 2, Golaud has fallen from his horse while hunting and is lying on his bed with Mélisande at his bedside. This event leads to his discovery that Mélisande has lost her wedding ring. Mélisande's earlier disposal of the crown symbolizes her escape from bondage to Bluebeard,[28] loss of the ring her freedom from marriage to Golaud. While the woman's feelings seem to symbolize her freedom from an oppressive social structure, the dramatic message of Maeterlinck is that the woman's freedom will inevitably lead to her death.

The musical process supports the dramatic message, which is based on the causal relation between the woman's symbolic freedom from her marital bond and her eventual death. Transposition of the C♯ Aeolian figuration to C pentatonic, C–D–C–A–G–A (see ex. 5-2; p. 73, m. 3), produces four of the five notes of the Prelude's open-

EXAMPLE 5-2. Act 2, scene 1, p. 73, mm. 3–10, C♯-Aeolian figuration transformed into original pentatonic collection of "Forest" motif and complete WT-1 collection, in block juxtaposition with "Fate" motif

ing statement of the "Forest" motif (C–D–E–G–A, originally interpreted as D pentatonic by means of the rhythmic structure). The omission of the single note, E, from the C pentatonic collection at this point—the E is provided by the C major chord on the fourth beat—permits the exclusive figural focus on the two pentatonic dyads, C–D and G–A, which were originally projected as the axes of symmetry of the two whole-tone collections, respectively (see ex. 4-1 and ex. 4-4 earlier). In correspondence with the dramatic parallel, the C pentatonic figuration, which inverts the position of the two dyads from their original registral ordering (C–D/G–A) in the "Forest" motif to G–A/C–D in this closing figuration, moves directly to the "Fate" motif as before. The registral inversion of the two pentatonic dyads permits G–A, which was associated originally with the WT-1 sphere of Golaud as he became lost in the forest, to be identified with the "Fate" motif in the bass layer (see ex. 5-2; p. 73, m. 10). The "Fate" motif, as in the Prelude, is based exclusively on the complete whole-tone collection, with one significant difference: the original WT-0 partition, Ab–Bb–C–D–E–F# (with C–D as its axis), is replaced by the WT-1 partition (of Golaud). The original occurrence of the latter (p. 3, m. 1 ff.) in the orchestral figuration that introduced the first appearance of Golaud had transformed pentatonic-dyad G–A of the "Forest" motif into the axis of symmetry of the ascending WT-1 scale, Eb–F–G–A–Cb–Db. At the present occurrence of the "Fate" motif (p. 73, mm. 4–5), G–A forms the local axis of the upper line (F–G–A–B), which forms part of the complete WT-1 collection, and is exclusive to the sustained bass notes throughout the remainder of the passage, which includes the cadential statement of the "Fate" motif.

The replacement of the original WT-0 partition by WT-1, and the shift in prominence from dyad C–D (of Pelléas) to G-A (of Golaud), suggests, in terms of these pitch relations, an abridgment of the Prelude's structural proportions in anticipation of the reappearance of Golaud. The significance of these dyadic relations in this dramatic parallel is supported by the earlier suggestion of the registral reversal of C–D and G–A in the first Interlude of act 1, between scenes 1 and 2 (p. 22 ff.), after Golaud reveals his predicament to Mélisande, "I don't know. I'm lost, too." In the simultaneous combination of the "Forest" and "Fate" motifs within that Interlude (on p. 23), the combination having earlier served to intensify the thematic/phrasal pairings of the Prelude, transposition of the original "Forest" motif from D–A–G–A to G–D–C–D had placed C–D in the uppermost position one and one-half octaves above the uppermost notes (G–A) of the accompanying "Fate" motif. Furthermore, the block juxtapositions of the sixteenth-note figuration and the "Fate" motif in the present Interlude of act 2 are also analogous to the phrase/period pairings between the "Forest" and "Fate" motifs in the Prelude (see ex. 4-1 earlier). In the latter section, the successive phrase pairings in the opening double period were condensed to the simultaneous combination of the "Mélisande Naïveté" and "Fate" motifs, which immediately preceded the final return of the "Forest" motif. The latter also appeared in simultaneous combination with an intervallic and rhythmic transformation that suggested a diminished form of the two-note "Fate" motif.

The shift to the WT-1 partition of Golaud in the "Fate" motif (near the end of act 2, scene 1, p. 73, mm. 4–5) is foreshadowed directly by the intrusion of dyad D#–G against one of the basic dyads (G–A) of the pentatonic figuration, the combination producing a form of the "Fate" cell, D#–G–A (see ex. 5-2). A transposed inversion (B–Db–F) of the latter appears, then, as the initial harmonization of the "Fate" motif. The same form of the whole-tone cell (B–Db–F) also initiates the following return of the sixteenth-note figuration, the original pentatonic content now transformed entirely into the complete WT-1 collection of Golaud. This transformation is produced by means of one intervallic mutation in the linear progression. The minor third gap in the original linear pentatonic statement (D–C–A–G), which implied the presence of inversionally related forms (D–C–A and G–A–C) of the "Pelléas" and "Mélisande" cells, is expanded to a major third in each of the two tritone-separated parallel lines. This produces the simultaneous linear WT-1 transformations separated by the tritone, C♯–B–G–F and G–F–C♯–B, both together implying the presence of two inversionally related whole-tone cells (C♯–B–G and F–G–B). This interpretation is borne out by the overlapping linear bass figure (p. 73, m. 8), G–C♭–D♭ (an enharmonic spelling of the upper linear pitch content, G-B-C♯). These whole-tone transformations are also implied in the tritone adjacencies (F–B and G–C♯) of the combined lines. Thus, the intrusion of fate into the world of the two characters—Pelléas and Mélisande—is symbolized musically by the whole-tone set, in this case, the WT-1 cyclic partition generally associated with Golaud.

The intrusion of fate is manifested in the C-pentatonic form of the "Pelléas" motif later (p. 86, m. 2) in connection with the more evident textual reference to fate, when Mélisande refers to something that is stronger than herself (see ex. 4-2b). At that point, the pentatonic form of the "Pelléas" motif (C–D–A) is transformed again into the "Fate" cell (C–D–A♭) by the expansion of the minor third to the major third, this time within the WT-0 sphere of Pelléas. The same transformation was already foreshadowed in the bass line at the very opening of the Prelude, where *fate* intruded into the forest. But now, once again, a shift occurs from one brother to the other, as Golaud's presence is imminent. In the Interlude (pp. 74–75) leading to act 2, scene 2, the "Golaud" and "Fate" motifs are ominously sounded by the horns and bassoons, a slightly chromaticized form of the pentatonic "Mélisande" motif (D♭–[D]–E♭–G♭) emerging shortly thereafter (p. 74, mm. 16–17).

Act 2, Scene 2: A Room in the Castle—Golaud, Mélisande, the Ring, and Transformation of the "Pelléas" Motif

The dramatic parallel between act 2, scene 2, and the beginning of the opera—a parallel based on analogous intrusions of fate—is further borne out here. Debussy himself had said to Henri Lerolle that "this has not been without some agitation; [this] scene between Golaud and Mélisande in particular! For it is there that one begins to anticipate the catastrophes."[29] An ominous statement of the "Fate" motif introduces Golaud's attempt to explain the events of his hunting accident to Mélisande. His bewilderment (p. 77) over the sudden bolting of his horse for no apparent reason and his speculation that his horse might have seen something unusual invoke an association with his first, unexpected encounter with the mysterious Mélisande, which also occurred while he was hunting.

Mélisande's apparently unconscious wish to turn away from Golaud, as manifested in the loss of her wedding ring, seems also to have some connection with Golaud's fall from his horse in that yet another symbolic association is established at this point (p. 77, m. 4). The oboe plays a variant of the pentatonic "Pelléas" motif, C–D–A–C–D (see ex. 4-2a), which was heard (p. 62, m. 3) in the orchestra in the whole-tone form of the "Awakening Desire" motif, C–D–A♭–C–D (see ex. 4-9), in connection with the meeting of Pelléas and Mélisande at the well in the midday heat. Pelléas's warning that Mélisande "Take care!" had portended the loss of her ring. While Golaud's comment in the present scene about his horse seeing "something unusual" is ambiguous, both the musical context and his next statement regarding the bolting of his horse at the twelfth stroke of the clock provide the answer: Golaud had fallen from his horse at noon, precisely the moment when Mélisande had dropped her ring into the well, and the latter event occurred shortly after Pelléas's desire was awakened. Maeterlinck provides insight into the sources and fatalistic significance of catastrophe:

> we are in the hands of strange powers, whose intentions we are on the eve of divin- ing. At the time of the great tragic writers of the new era, at the time of Shakespeare, Racine, and their successors, the belief prevailed that all misfortunes came from the various passions of the heart. Catastrophes did not hover between two worlds: they came hence to go thither, and their point of departure was known. Man was always the master. Much less was this the case at the time of the Greeks, for then did fa- tality reign on the heights . . . To-day it is fatality that we challenge, and this is per- haps the distinguishing note of the new theatre. It is no longer the effects of disaster that arrest our attention; it is disaster itself, and we are eager to know its essence and its laws.[30]

It is Mélisande's shift of attention from Golaud to Pelléas and her passion for him that is the source of Golaud's increasing jealousy and the relentless move toward their ultimate fate. The symbolization of this shift from one brother to the other is further suggested by Pelléas's question just prior to the loss of the ring (p. 64): "It was beside a spring that he found you, wasn't it?" that is, it is now Pelléas, rather than Golaud, who "finds" Mélisande beside a well. Pelléas's statement, which compares the two well events, also supports the dramatic parallel between this scene (act 2, scene 2) and the opening scene of the opera more directly. Golaud, like Mélisande, is driven by un- conscious forces that unchain destructive events. The "blindness" of Golaud's uncon- scious and the forceful (fatalistic) nature of the beast within him is symbolized at the opening by his being led astray during the hunt for the boar and now by the bolting of his horse, which "galloped blindly like a mad thing straight into a tree!"

Yet, the beast (Golaud's unconscious) has the ability to sense the mysterious. This is suggested by Golaud's thought (p. 77) that his horse bolted because he was able to sense something strange. The polarity between seeing "something unusual" versus not seeing, "blindly like a mad thing straight into a tree," is powerful because it involves at least two ideas: not seeing what is external to us because it is painful (in this case, Golaud does not want to see the vast differences between him and Méli- sande that ultimately make it impossible for their relationship to be successful); and not wanting to see, that is, not wanting to be conscious of, nor to own painful feelings and impulses which, left unexamined, may lead to destructive actions. Golaud's horse, or that part of himself that is conscious of his desires and his vulnerability, has a hard time accepting the limitations imposed by external reality ("a tree," or the fact that others may have feelings and needs for autonomy and self-expression that may not be compatible with his), and so, always gets out of control. The most extreme conse- quences of this are manifested later when Golaud kills Pelléas after dragging Méli- sande by her hair.

Yet another symbolic interpretation may be made regarding events associated with the well. According to Pelléas, the well no longer has the power to cure the blind. While the loss of the well's "miraculous powers" suggests that all are blind to fate and the unconscious, an apparent contradiction arises. Old King Arkel, who is almost completely blind, is the only one who is aware of, and refers explicitly to, fate (see

p. 32): "I have never set myself athwart of destiny." Debussy himself expressed in a letter to Ernest Chausson that Arkel "comes from beyond the grave and has that objective, prophetic gentleness of those who are soon to die."[31] Furthermore, according to Debussy, Arkel is the only one who understands Mélisande. Maeterlinck himself seems to have believed that for some people insight emerges more from darkness, or the unconscious, as he suggests in his *The Treasure of the Humble:*

> Which of us has not met, more than once, along the paths of life, a forsaken soul that has yet not lost the courage to cherish, in the darkness, a thought diviner and purer than all those that so many others had the power to choose in the light? Here, too, it is simplicity that is God's favourite slave; and it is enough, perhaps, that a few sages should know what has to be done, for the rest of us to act as though we knew too.[32]

"Circle of Light" as Symbol of Fate

Other references to light and dark in *The Treasure of the Humble* can provide still deeper levels of insight into this symbolic polarity in *Pelléas et Mélisande*, in which such references also seem to evoke the sense of futility in seeing our destiny, because we can never escape from it. Maeterlinck symbolizes fate as a "circle of light": "For indeed we can never emerge from the little circle of light that destiny traces about our footsteps; and one might almost believe that the extent and the hue of this impassable ring are known even to the men who are furthest from us."[33] For instance, later in the opera, in act 4, scene 4, as Pelléas sees the snares of destiny all around him (p. 233, mm. 1–2) and likens himself to "a blind man fleeing from his burning house," the actions of the two lovers take them in and out of circles of light. Intending to meet with Mélisande for the last time in order to escape his fate, Pelléas is constantly impelled to stand outside the circle of light (p. 236, mm. 6–7): "don't stay on the edge of the moonlight." But Mélisande wants to remain in the light. Her apparent wish (though certainly an unconscious one) for the two lovers to be snared by fate (caught in the light) points to her symbolic role as siren of destruction (p. 237, mm. 4–5): "I want to be seen."

In terms of the musical symbolization of the dramatic events in this scene (act 2, scene 2), the "Awakening Desire" motif (p. 77, m. 4 ff.), an indication of the shift of focus toward Pelléas, is initiated by the pentatonic dyad (C–D) associated with Pelléas, while the pentatonic dyad (G–A) associated with Golaud is reduced to a sustained A and absorbed into the pentatonic sphere of Pelléas (see ex. 4-2a). In the preceding statement of the "Fate" motif (p. 76, m. 3), in which the dyad C–D initiates a diatonic ascent (C–D–E–F–G–A) that culminates with the dyad G–A, the C–D is introduced by another pentatonic dyad, A♭–B♭. This linear adjacency simultaneously produces a whole-tone interpretation (A♭–B♭–C–D) of dyad C–D in anticipation of the whole-tone transformation of the "Pelléas" motif (C–D–A) to C–D–A♭ (p. 86, m. 2) at Mélisande's allusion to Pelléas and *fate*.

Transformation into the whole-tone sphere is imminent at both of these motivic focal points ("Fate," p. 76, m. 3, and "Awakening Desire" motifs, p. 77, m. 4ff.), which are harmonized by C dominant ninth (C–E–G–B♭–D) and D dominant ninth (D–F♯–A–C–E) chords, respectively. The significance of these two transpositions of the dominant ninth chord lies in their role in reflecting the dramatic pull between the two polarized dramatic spheres. In this section, one sphere is symbolized by Golaud, who may be seen in his attempts to maintain the status quo as a personification of the oppressive social structure, the other by Pelléas, who embodies the emotional force toward change. The C dominant ninth and D dominant ninth chords have symmetrically embedded within them the two notes of Golaud's dyad (G–A) as their respective fifth degrees (C–E–[G]–Bb–D and D–F#–[A]–C–E). These two notes serve as the single elements of diatonic resistance against whole-tone transformation of these dominant ninth constructions and, consequently, of the basic pentatonic- dyad, C–D, the two notes serving as the respective roots of these chords and initiating both motifs.

Whole-tone transformation of the C dominant ninth chord is imminent in the second chord of the "Fate" motif (p. 76, m. 4), where omission of the fifth degree (G) permits the remaining four notes (C–E–[ ]–Bb–D, or Bb–C–D–E) to outline a whole-tone tetrachord, exclusively. Whole-tone transformation of the D dominant ninth chord is imminent in the linear figurations that unfold against the pentatonic "Awakening Desire" motif (p. 77, m. 4 ff.; see ex. 4-2a). While the latter motif (C–D–A–C–D) and tremolo figure (C–E–F#), together, produce the pitch content of the D dominant ninth chord (D–F#–A–C–E), the specific pitch-class partitioning produces a divergence between them into the two opposing (pentatonic and whole-tone) spheres, one forming the "Pelléas" cell (A–C–D) as the basis for "Awakening Desire," the other a transposition of the "Fate" cell (C–E–F#). This relation differs from the earlier passage (p. 62, m. 3), in which the pitch content of the "Fate" cell (Ab–C–D) in the vocal line was identical to that of the whole-tone form of the "Awakening Desire" motif in the orchestra, so no pitch-class conflict occurred between them at that point. In this passage, by contrast, the two cells (A–C–D and C–E–F#), respectively, mutate and transpose the latter (Ab–C–D). Thus, while these motivic relations are derived from the earlier passage, dramatic development is now induced by the conflict between their pitch-set forms. This polarity is reinforced by the vocal line, which also belongs to the D dominant ninth chord ([]–F#–A–C–E). The first three vocal notes (E–F#–A), which invert the pentatonic "Pelléas" cell (A–C–D), outline the "Mélisande" cell, the last three notes (C–E–F#) duplicating the "Fate" cell of the tremolo figure.

As the dialogue between Golaud and Mélisande progresses to the main dramatic points of the scene—Mélisande's fatalistic allusion to Pelléas (p. 86), Golaud's discovery that the wedding ring is missing from Mélisande's hand (p. 95), and Golaud's increasing vehemence (p. 99)—the same motivic/pitch-set constructions continue to intensify in their interactions, mutations, and fluctuations between the two polarized spheres. As Mélisande begins to weep for no apparent reason, the oboe, which we can generally associate with Mélisande's sadness, sounds a mournful variant of her motif, D–Eb–Gb–Ab (p. 82, m. 2). While Golaud's portentous question joins the pentatonic forms of both the "Mélisande" (Eb–F–Ab) and "Pelléas" (F–Ab–Bb) cells, this oboe variant of the "Mélisande" motif fuses the pentatonic form (Eb–Gb–Ab) of the "Pelléas" cell with its "Fate" transformation (D–Gb–Ab) linearly. The D of the latter is supported harmonically by a more explicit form of the "Fate" cell, Ab–Bb–D (p. 82, m. 1), precisely the transposition that was embedded in the harmony against the first linear statement of the pentatonic "Mélisande" motif (Ab–Bb–C#) in the Prelude (p.

1, mm. 14–15). This oboe variant also suggests a motivic fusion in that the contour also resembles the "Awakening Desire" motif (see p. 62, m. 3, vocal line especially; see ex. 4-9).

The tritone boundary of the hybrid motivic form (D–A♭, which is the basic one from the opening of the Prelude) is contracted in the following unambiguous statement of the "Mélisande" motif in the strings (p. 82, mm. 5–6) to form the original pentatonic cell (A♭–B♭–D♭) from her first motivic statement in the Prelude (in enharmonic spelling, A♭–B♭–C♯, p. 1, mm. 14–15). At the present linear occurrence, the respelling of the original C♯ as D♭ indicates some release from the basic conflict between diatonic and whole-tone spheres (i.e., the tendency of C♯ to lead upward to D), Mélisande's words implying that she would like to be free from the present situation, that is, the bonds of fate: "I am sick in this place." This contrasts with the Prelude, in which the pentatonic C♯ and whole-tone D were in simultaneous conflict with each other in the melody and accompaniment as *fate* intruded into the human realm. The harmonic underpinning of the pentatonic "Mélisande" motif at these words contains only a suggestion of Pelléas and fate. The linear bass motion from C♭ to B♭ suggests, in conjunction with the linear motivic statement, the harmonic juxtaposition between a transposition of the "Pelléas" cell (A♭–C♭–D♭) and the "Mélisande" cell (A♭–B♭–D♭). The C♭ in the first simultaneity also produces a vertical intersection between transpositions of the pentatonic "Mélisande" (E♭–F–A♭) and whole-tone "Fate" (C♭–E♭–F) cells, which are partitions of the larger half-diminished seventh chord (F–A♭–C♭–E♭).

While this local fusion of the "Mélisande" (A♭–B♭–D♭) and "Fate" (C♭–E♭–F) cells in the orchestra only suggests the meaning of Mélisande's response to Golaud's questions, certain musical associations become more evident at the varied repeat of their text. A musico-textual parallel emerges within the context of these intensified motif/cell fusions and fluctuations. At her first response to Golaud's question, "Why are you crying all of a sudden?" Mélisande's vocal line at "I feel ill here" outlines a transposition of the pentatonic "Pelléas" cell in the same motivic contour (B♭–D♭–B♭–E♭) as Pelléas's whole-tone vocal line (A♭–C–A♭–D) that unfolded simultaneously with the first orchestral statement of the "Awakening Desire" theme (p. 62, m. 3). At Golaud's further questioning, Mélisande's parallel response, "My lord, I'm not happy here," reiterates a varied segment of her pentatonic ("Pelléas") response, this time in the form of the whole-tone ("Fate") variant, D–F♯–G♯. This cell transformation in Mélisande's vocal line is significant not only in establishing a psychological parallel between Pelléas and fate, but in linking Mélisande's unhappiness to uncontrollable human feelings. That is, the orchestra introduces her statement with the "Awakening Desire" motif. Mélisande's vocal statement of the "Fate" cell at this point (p. 83, m. 4) is at the tritone transposition (D–F♯–G♯) of Pelléas's vocal statement of the "Fate" cell (A♭–C–D) that unfolded with the original occurrence of the "Awakening Desire" motif (p. 62, m. 3). This produces maximal pitch-class intersection (i.e., basic tritone, A♭–D) between these vocal statements of the two characters. The dramatic meaning underlying the structural parallel in this passage (pp. 82-83), which is based on whole-tone transformation of the pentatonic cell at Mélisande's reiterated response, is articulated by an orchestral fusion of the "Fate" rhythm and "Mélisande" motivic contour accompanying Golaud's words, "What has happened then?"

In the next textual subsection (p. 83, m. 5 to p. 86, m. 2), the dramatic direction is toward increasing specificity of Golaud's questions and Mélisande's responses. He asks, "Has some one done you a wrong?" to which she answers, "It isn't that." This dialogue is paralleled, then, by their more explicit questions and responses, "Is it the King? Is it my mother? Is it Pelléas?" "No, no, it isn't Pelléas. It isn't anybody. You couldn't understand me. It's something stronger than myself." Maeterlinck's own question, in his essay on the predestined, about "who can tell us of the power which events possess—whether they issue from us, or whether we owe our being to them?"[34] suggests that Mélisande is perhaps not primarily concealing the truth (although on a more concrete level that appears to be the case), but that she is living "under the shadow of an event that has not yet come to pass." Golaud's and Mélisande's statements are articulated in the orchestra by three strategically placed motifs, the first (p. 84, m. 4) unfolding a variant of the "Fate" motif, the second (p. 85, m. 5ff.) the "Awakening Desire" motif, and the third (p. 86, m. 2), the "Pelléas" motif. The somewhat obscured variant of the "Fate" motif, which coincides with Golaud's question, "But you must be keeping something from me," may be interpreted as concealment of the attachment between Pelléas and Mélisande.

We come to one of the most significant focal points not only of this subsection but also of the larger scene in general. The whole-tone transformation of the "Pelléas" motif into the "Fate" cell (p. 86, m. 2) symbolizes Mélisande's reference to something more powerful than herself (see ex. 4-2b). It is at this point where the human being is identified most explicitly—both textually and musically—as an instrument of *fate* and, furthermore, where human feelings are identified as the basic motivating force that will lead to destruction. The linear contour of Pelléas's transformed motif, C–D–Ab (p. 86, m. 2), which recalls the Prelude's very opening bass-line transformation of pentatonic dyad C–D of the "Forest" motif into the whole-tone cell (Ab–C–D) of the "Fate" motif, outlines a whole-tone segment of the underlying Bb dominant ninth harmonization (Bb–D-F-Ab–C), this motivic segment bounded by the basic tritone, Ab–D. The preceding C dominant ninth chord (C–E–G–Bb–D), which harmonizes the reiterated D of Mélisande's words that link Pelléas to fate, recalls the harmonization of the initial occurrence of the "Well" motif (p. 55, m. 10).[35] Most striking is the specific registral spacing of this chord (C–G–E–Bb–D), which recalls that of the first recurrence of the "Well" motif (p. 57, m. 1) accompanying Mélisande's words, "Oh, how clear the water is." In the latter harmonization of the "Well" motif (see ex. 5-1), C–G was held in the bass, while the tritone Bb–E formed the boundary of the motif. Then, accompanying Pelléas's words that implied *fate*, "It's as cool as winter," the reiterated D of Pelléas's vocal line had served as the altered fifth degree of the transposed dominant ninth chord to form its whole-tone transformation (G♯–B♯–[D]–F♯–A♯), the latter prominently foreshadowing the basic tritone (G♯–D) that will outline the transformed "Pelléas" motif (p. 86, m. 2).

The symbolization of Pelléas by this special motivic (whole-tone) statement is enhanced at this crucial moment in the opera by the pastoral-like timbres of the flute and violin. The flute, in particular, is also used to color Pelléas's motif at his very first appearance (p. 33, m. 10) and again at the more pastoral opening of the "Well" Scene (p. 55), where he brings Mélisande in the midday heat. The use of the flute timbre in association with Pelléas appears to have a more general symbolic significance in connection with this gentle character type in Debussy's music, for instance, in the *Prélude à l'après-midi d'un faune* (1894), inspired by Mallarmé's poem, in which the flute symbolizes the faun's dreaming, and in *Syrinx* (1913) for solo flute that, like the latter work, also seems to invoke the image of Pan, a god of the Greeks and Romans who was part human, part goat.[36] He came from a rural area of Arcadia, where shepherding was an important occupation. In ancient times, the worship of this mythological creature spread to urban areas of Greece and Rome, where he became a symbol of pastoral love and music. He was depicted with nymphs, satyrs, and muses, and shown playing the syrinx (or panpipe), which he supposedly invented. As part of this symbolic imagery, Mélisande herself seems to display certain qualities of a nymph or muse, who often comes across, because of her simple, disconnected, and repetitive verbal utterances, as well as her inextricable connection with wells, ponds, the sea, tears, and other aquatic manifestations, as a somewhat unreal, mysterious mythological creature like the mermaid Mélusine.[37] Thus, Debussy's careful choice of instrumental color enhances and broadens our interpretation of the symbolic meaning of the characters, the environment in which they act, and their psychological motivations and behavior.

The harmonic parallel between Mélisande's fatalistic reference to something *stronger* than herself and the well is further developed by Pelléas's reference to the miraculous *powers* of the well (p. 57). His vocal line at that point began with the reiterated D and cadenced on D as part of his pentatonic cell, F–G–D. The latter was transformed, then, into the whole-tone "Fate" cell (D–F♯–G♯) by the elision of the cadential note (D) with the following raised notes (F♯–G♯) of his cell at the opening of his next vocal statement. This whole-tone cell transformation, like the main transformation of his motif later (p. 86, m. 2), is also outlined prominently by basic-tritone D–G♯ (i.e., A♭–D). Pelléas's disclosure to Mélisande (p. 57) that "it opened the eyes of the blind. They still call it the 'Blind men's Well'" also serves another parallel. Mélisande's statement to Golaud (p. 85, m. 6) that precedes her allusion to fate, "You couldn't understand," may be associated with this reference to the blind. What is most striking in this parallel is the symbolization of the clear water of the well as capable of miraculously healing the blind. It is the water of the well in which Mélisande loses her ring that is instrumental, however indirectly, in Golaud's enlightenment, that is, in opening his eyes. It is the loss of Mélisande's ring that will awaken Golaud's suspicions and unleash those emotional forces (jealousy and anger) that will initiate the course of events leading to vengeance.

The main transformation of the "Pelléas" motif (p. 86, m. 2), although exclusively whole-tone in and of itself (C–D–A♭), represents a fatalistic intrusion into the diatonic sphere at this point, where it belongs ultimately to the larger B♭ dominant ninth harmonization (B♭–D–F–A♭–C). The latter is partitioned linearly into the whole-tone content of the transformed motif (A♭–C–D) and vertically into the pentatonic content of the basic form of the "Pelléas" motif in the three sustained notes (F–A♭–B♭). This hybridized collection (i.e., B♭ dominant ninth chord, B♭–D–F–A♭–C) together with the preceding harmonic construction (C dominant ninth chord, C–E–G–B♭–D), both associated directly at this point with control of Mélisande's own life by that which is stronger than herself, contain a significant musical reference to the very first occurrence of the "Mélisande" motif in the Prelude (p. 1, mm. 14 ff.). In that passage, fatalistic (whole-tone) intrusion into the human (pentatonic) realm was symbolized by the orchestral figurations against her theme. Those figurations were based exclusively on the interlocking of two tritones (basic Ab–D and Bb–E), which together formed the larger whole-tone (French sixth) tetrachord, Ab–Bb–D–E. It is precisely these two tritones that are embedded symmetrically in the Bb dominant ninth (Bb–D–F–Ab–C) and C dominant ninth (C–E–G–Bb–D) chords, respectively, against Mélisande's implied reference to *fate*.

This association between the two passages (p. 86, m. 1 and p. 1, m. 14) is supported by the first chord against Mélisande's statement on the reiterated D. In the Prelude, one had sensed the intrusion of fate (whole-tone collection) into the "Mélisande" realm most prominently by the conflict between her pentatonic note, C♯ (in Ab–Bb–C♯) and the whole-tone element, D (in the French sixth figuration, Ab–Bb–D–E). The initial chord (C♯–G♯–E♮–B–D) accompanying Mélisande's vocal statement is bounded by C♯ and D, the root of the chord (C♯) appearing in conflict with the reiterated D of her vocal line. Resolution of this particular conflict occurs within the whole-tone transformation of the "Pelléas" motif, where the initial, expanded whole-tone dyad, C–D, replaces the C♯–D juxtaposition, the C–D expansion prepared harmonically in the root progression from C♯ to C against Mélisande's reiterated vocal note (D).

When Golaud asks Mélisande (p. 86, m. 4) what she wants him to do, the same variant of the "Fate" rhythm from the preceding passage (p. 84, m. 4) returns. However, it is transposed and infused with certain intervallic mutations as the deep register of the bassoons seems to capture Golaud's increasingly suspicious and dark mood. At the initial occurrence of the "Fate" rhythm (p. 84, m. 4), the whole-tone variant of the "Pelléas" cell seemed to answer Golaud's question regarding concealment. (Again, in connection with the mood of Golaud, this is characteristically presented in the dark register of the low strings, and as part of the complete WT-1 collection.) At this recurrence, Golaud's question is answered by a contraction of the whole-tone form of the "Pelléas" cell, Ab–C–D, to the basic pentatonic form, D–C–A. (The whole-tone form, Ab–C–D, is characteristically presented as part of WT-0, and in the lighter register of the flute and first violins.) Although this explicit occurrence of the "Pelléas" cell (D–C–A) supports the association of the preceding whole-tone transformation (C–D–Ab), that is, in accord with Golaud's offer to help Mélisande against that which is stronger than herself—namely Pelléas and fate, the upward shift of one note (Ab to A) also plays a local transitional function in the musico-dramatic symbolism. As Golaud asks Mélisande, "Do you want to leave me?" the C dominant ninth chord that harmonized Mélisande's reiterated D returns, but now under a linear vocal statement of a transposition of the pentatonic "Pelléas" cell (G–Bb–C).

At the next recurrence of the "Fate" rhythm variant (p. 87, m. 1) at Mélisande's response, "Oh no, it isn't that," the pentatonic note, A, of the "Pelléas" cell (A–C–D) is retained while the C–D is shifted up to C♯–D♯ to produce a new transposition of the whole-tone form of his cell (ex. 5-3). This would seem to suggest that Mélisande actually wants to be free from her uncontrollable (fatalistic) involvement with Pelléas. This interpretation is supported by her reassurance to Golaud, "I should

EXAMPLE 5-3. Act 2, scene 2, p. 87, mm. 1–6, obsessive repetition of "Fate" rhythm, reduced to whole-tone cell (A–C♯–D♯), whole-tone-cell sequence representing shift away from WT-0, to which Pelléas's dyad C–D belongs (see p. 86, mm. 2 and 4), to WT-1, to which Golaud's dyad G–A belongs

like to go away with you. I can't go on living here any longer," her statements accompanied by the obsessive repetition of the "Fate" rhythm, reduced now only to the three notes of the whole-tone cell (A–C♯–D♯). The latter represents a shift away from WT-0 (to which Pelléas's dyad C–D belongs) to WT-1 (to which Golaud's dyad G–A belongs). This is confirmed by the shift first from A–C♯–D♯ of WT-1 to B♭–D–E of WT-0 (p. 87, m. 3), then to the cadential transposition, E♭–G–A (next measure). The held G–A of this final statement therefore replaces the held C–D of the initial statement, so the entire orchestral sequence symbolizes the shift of emphasis from Pelléas (C–D) to Golaud (G–A), a shift motivated by Mélisande's wish to escape the grip of *fate*. We may recall that these two dyads enframed the very opening statement of the "Forest" motif, these dyads then projected as the axes of symmetry of the two whole-tone collections, respectively. Here, dyad G–A is the axis of the combined WT-1 cells: E♭–G–A–D♭.

Transposition A–D♭–E♭ (in enharmonic spelling, A–C♯–D♯), the transposition that indicated a shift away from WT-0 and Pelléas's dyad (C–D) earlier in this passage (p. 87, mm. 1–2), reappears at the cadence as the basis of the abridged "Fate" variant accompanying Mélisande's words, "I feel I might not live much longer." The implications of this musico-textual association are twofold: the first is based on her feeling that she cannot live without Pelléas; the second is based on her premonition that she will be destroyed by Golaud if she remains with Pelléas. The latter is suggested in these cadential measures (see ex. 5-3) by the interlocking of the transposed "Fate" cell associated with Golaud (E♭–G–A) with its tritone transposition, A–D♭–E♭ (i.e., enharmonic spelling of the initial A–C♯–D♯), associated with the loss of Pelléas (A–C–D). Ultimately, in the entire passage to this point (p. 86, m. 4 to p. 87, m. 6), the transposed "Fate" cell (A–C♯–D♯ and E♭–G–A) seems to symbolize the identity between the loss of Pelléas and the death of Mélisande.

Act 2, Scene 2: Events Leading to Golaud's Anger and His Demand That Mélisande Search for the Ring

The flexibility of Debussy's musical language allows for great subtlety of symbolic association with the text. Concomitant with the dramatic and musical techniques of Maeterlinck and Debussy, respectively, based on musico-textual repetitions and alternations within the general mosaic textures of the opera, emphasis is shifted back to Pelléas in correspondence with the gist of Golaud's persistent questioning (p. 88). Elements of the pitch materials associated with Pelléas begin to resurface, though somewhat concealed within the background structures of the successive phrases in correspondence with Mélisande's attempts to conceal Pelléas's true feelings for her. Golaud's question, "Come, is it Pelléas, perhaps?" is introduced by two triads (C–F–A and D–G–B), the second-inversion positions bringing notes C and D of Pelléas's pentatonic (C–D–A) or WT-0 (C–D–A♭) cell into the bass against a four-note WT-1 segment (F–G–A–B) in both orchestra and voice (p. 88, m. 4).

Golaud's further reference to Pelléas, "I don't think he talks to you very much," brings new intrusions of the whole-tone transformation of his cell (A♭–C–D) into the superstructure of both the orchestral and vocal parts: the vocal line is bounded temporally by Pelléas's basic tritone, G♯–D, while the first two accompanying chords together are bounded registrally by his basic dyad, C–D, and the bass line descends to D at the cadence. In contrast to the negative form of Golaud's textual statement, Mélisande provides a relatively affirmative response, "Oh yes, he talks to me sometimes," so the basic pentatonic form of the "Pelléas" cell (D–C–A) emerges as a prominent component of the vocal line. This is the first occurrence of the basic transposition of his cell since the variant statement of the "Fate" motif in the orchestra (p. 86, m. 4). The cell then emerges as a prominent foreground event at Mélisande's revealing statement, "I've seen it in his eyes," and in the accompanying orchestral material, in which one of the cell components (C) serves as linear preparation for the orchestral statement of the cell by means of its alternation with one of the components (B) of the WT-1 form of the "Fate" cell (F–A–B). The latter, which belongs to the musical realm of Golaud, is also the "Pelléas" inversion of the "Mélisande" form (F–G–B) in Golaud's previous vocal line (p. 88, m. 4).

This repetition of the process of the preceding measures, that is, based on the pitch-class intrusions and conflicts between the same primary WT-1 and WT-0 components, is supported by a repeat of the descending linear bass motion to the cadence on D (p. 88, mm. 8–10). This musical parallel supports a hidden textual parallel as well. Golaud's negative statement that Pelléas does not often speak to Mélisande is paralleled by Mélisande's negative reference, "I don't think he likes me," while her statement that he speaks to her at times is paralleled by her statement, "I've seen it in his eyes. But he speaks to me when we meet." In spite of her statements feigning Pelléas's negativity toward her, the orchestra reveals the truth at the appearance of the transposed "Awakening Desire" motif of Pelléas (p. 89, m. 3), which is initiated by one of the basic components (A♭) associated with the basic whole-tone form (A♭–C–D) of the "Pelléas" motive. While the other two notes (C and D) are absent from this transposition of the "Awakening Desire" motif, the accompanying tremolo figuration (p. 89, m. 7) against the transposed third statement of the motif introduces D and C under the reiterated vocal note, D, the A♭ appearing as the intervallically mutated motif's cadential and highest note (E♭–G–A♭).

The fourth orchestral statement of the "Awakening Desire" motif (p. 90, mm. 1–2) begins to acquire the dotted element of the "Fate" rhythm as the dialogue between Golaud and Mélisande progresses toward the climax of the scene. This occurrence of the "Awakening Desire" motif underlines Mélisande's allusion to the true reason behind Pelléas's apparent (that is, feigned) aloofness toward her, "But it isn't that, it isn't that," her statements contradicting Golaud's assumptions. This transposition of the "Awakening Desire" motif is articulated cadentially by Golaud's dyad, G–A, in anticipation of the shift of focus back to Golaud, "Can't you get used to the life we lead here?" The polarity between Golaud and Pelléas intensifies in anticipation of Golaud's discovery that the ring is lost. Golaud's attempt to discover the cause of Mélisande's sadness (pp. 90-94) leads him to the notion that it may be the gloomy castle that upsets Mélisande. His descriptions (pp. 90–91) are reinforced by Mélisande's (p. 92), "Yes, it's true . . . one never sees the sky here." The contrasting images of the gloomy castle and the sky evokes an association to the "Well" scene (pp. 66–67). In anticipation of the moment when Mélisande dropped her ring into the water, Pelléas warned her not to toss her ring about above such deep water, observing, in contrast, how it shines in the sun, that is, before it falls in.

The harmonic underpinning at Golaud's description (p. 90) of the castle as "very vast and cold" supports the interpretation regarding the association between the dark abyss of the castle and the deep water of the well. Golaud's vocal line is based on three notes, D–E–C, which is bounded temporally by Pelléas's dyad, D–C. The cadential note (C), which articulates "profond," is harmonized by a C-major triad, the latter extended upward by thirds (to B♭–D–F) in the next measure to imply the presence of a C dominant eleventh collection, C–E–G–B♭–D–F. The C dominant ninth substructure (C–E–G–B♭–D), supported by the addition of G and B♭ to D–E–C in the voice, is precisely that which formed the harmonic basis of the "Well" motif at its first occurrence (p. 55, m. 10) and recurrence (p. 57, m. 1) in the first scene of this act, in which Mélisande referred to the clear water and Pelléas to the coolness of the ancient well. This reference to "ancient" is also paralleled by Golaud's reference to the oldness of the castle and the people who live in it.

Golaud's reference to "all those ancient sunless forests" is supported by a sliding progression of parallel chords (p. 91, mm. 8–9), which unfold the entire WT-1 collection associated with Golaud and seem to reflect (by means of the harmonic parallelism) the archaic quality expressed in the text. Golaud's dyad, G–A, is the axis of symmetry of the initial chord, F–G–A–B, which is also linearly projected in the upper line of this progression and is prominent in the descending segment of the vocal line. The axial function of the dyad G–A within the WT-1 collection recalls the same function in the ascending orchestral figuration at the opening of the first scene of the opera, where Golaud was lost in the forest. Furthermore, the registral partitioning of the chord isolates the three-note "Fate" cell, F–A–B, which generates the descending sequence of transpositions of the cell in parallel motion. The initial cell transposition (F–A–B) and the larger tetrachord (F–G–A–B) are imminent in the preceding phrases, hidden, for instance, in the inner voices of the orchestra at Golaud's implicit reference to darkness, "very cold and very deep" (p. 90, m. 11). Thus, the parallel text reference to the latter, that is, in the following reference to "woods without any sunshine," is supported by these WT-1 "Fate"-cell manifestations.

Correspondingly, on the other side of this polarity between the spheres of Golaud (dark) and Pelléas (light), the orchestral figure supporting Golaud's words, "But we can brighten it all up if we want to," is initiated now by Pelléas's dyad, D–C. This also forms the registral harmonic boundary or axis of the symmetrical C dominant ninth chord (C–E–G–B♭–D) that initiates the three-chord sequence under the words, "Besides, joy," the bass in the last two chords moving from A to A♭. The larger bass progression (p. 91, mm. 3–6) that culminates on these two notes (D–C–B♭–A–G–C–A–A♭) implies the presence of a background-level transformation of the pentatonic "Pelléas" cell (D–C–A) into the whole-tone "Fate" form (D–C–A♭) of his cell, the A♭ articulated at the vocal cadence under the reiterated statement of "la joie." The entire passage is then articulated (p. 92, mm. 2–3) by the most explicit statement of the "Fate" motif in the scene thus far. The motif is initiated by dyad C–D, the cadential segment of the accompanying bass line unfolding the pentatonic form of the "Pelléas" cell (D–C–A), which then pervades both the orchestral and vocal lines at Golaud's words, "I'll do whatever you want."

The diatonic sixteenth-note figuration from the opening of scene 1 of this act (p. 56) reappears (p. 92, m. 8) as a kind of ritornello figure, the significance of its return seeming to lie primarily in its symbolic associative role. The transposed figure is presented in counterpoint against a descending segment, D–C–B–A, which implies the presence of the pentatonic "Pelléas" cell, D–C–A. The transposition of the figuration on A permits a prominent suggestion of the cell within the harmonic content of the first beat. At its original occurrence (p. 56), the figuration was associated with the meeting of Pelléas and Mélisande at the well, where even the trees could not shield them from the heat of noon. In the present passage, Mélisande expresses her longing to be able to see the sky, "I saw it for the first time this morning," which Golaud assumes is the cause of her weeping. His attempt to console her by holding her hands leads him to discover that the wedding ring is missing. This dramatic sequence, in which Mélisande's reference to the sky is followed by Golaud's reference to her hands and the lost ring (p. 95), seems to parallel the earlier dramatic sequence progressing from Mélisande's reference to her hands (p. 66, m. 6), "My hands don't shake," Pelléas's observation of how the ring shines in the sun, and loss of the ring as Mélisande drops it into the well.

In anticipation of Golaud's realization that the ring is missing (p. 95, mm. 1–3), the lower tremolo figuration of the orchestra and his vocal line imply the presence of the pentatonic "Pelléas" cell, A–C–D. The original intrusion of the whole-tone sphere into the "Mélisande" motif (p. 1, mm. 14–15), based on the conflict between her pentatonic C♯ (in A♭–B♭–C♯) and the whole-tone D of the accompanying figuration (A♭–B♭–D–E), a conflict that resurfaced as Mélisande connected Pelléas with Fate (p. 86), is further manifested here. At Golaud's portentous words, "Oh, what tiny hands they are—I could crush them like flowers," the first two chords over the D pedal (A–C♯–D and A–C–D) now resolve the original C♯/D (pentatonic/whole-tone) conflict in the "Pelléas" cell, as C♯ moves down to C. The background-level structure of the entire vocal phrase implies, furthermore, the presence of the WT-0 expansion (G♯–C–D) of the "Pelléas" cell in conflict with the pentatonic form (A–C–D). Earlier (p. 72), Pélleas had advised Mélisande to tell Golaud the truth about the ring, but now she does not (pp. 95–98) because of her guilt feelings, that is, her unconscious desires that underlie her symbolic role as siren of destruction.[38] However, Golaud's inquiry as to the whereabouts of their marriage token (p. 96, mm. 5–6) suggests its answer in the "Pelléas" cell, which pervades Golaud's vocal line and places emphasis on the "Pelléas" dyad, C–D.

Fragments of the ritornello sixteenth-note figuration (now augmented to eighth-notes) begin to pervade the ending of this subsection of the scene (p. 97, mm. 4 ff.) leading to Golaud's "Vengeance" motif (p. 99, m. 5). The text in this passage is based on Mélisande's attempt to conceal the actual place where the ring was lost, "You know that cave by the sea? Well, that's where it is . . . it must be there," but the ritornello (water) figure is associated with that stifling day under the trees by the well. In anticipation of Golaud's anger, his dyad (G–A) reemerges, first in the upper part of the ritornello figuration (E–F–G–A) and the punctuating chords (p. 97, mm. 4–5), and finally as the principal structural notes of the "Vengeance" motif itself (G-E♭–G–B♭–A), the ominous quality induced by the trombones and tuba. The dyad G–A is then sustained in the tremolo figure and held G.

This statement of the "Vengeance" motif (p. 99, m. 5) is a convergent point for several polarized elements that have been appearing in juxtaposition and conflict throughout the scene (ex. 5-4). Golaud's dyad (G–A) is part of a larger linear manifestation of a WT-1 transposition of the "Fate" cell, Eb–G–A, which appears in counterpoint with the "Pelléas" cell at its basic transpositional level (D–C–A) in the bass line of this measure. Furthermore, the minor form of the A dominant ninth chord (A–C♯–E–G–Bb) under the tail figure (G–Bb–A) of the motif contains C♯, which replaces the preceding C. This juxtaposition (C vs. C♯) has, as we shall see, a similar significance to the same juxtaposition that leads to the transformed "Pelléas" cell, p. 86, mm. 1–2; see ex. 4-2b earlier). Three of the five notes (G–A–C♯) of the A dominant ninth chord imply the presence of a WT-1 form of the "Mélisande-Fate" cell. In the chromatic extension of the "Vengeance" motif (p. 99, m. 6), B replaces Bb to suggest the major form of the A dominant ninth (A–[ ]–E–G–B), which gives us another three-note segment of WT-1 (G–A–B) that belongs to the sphere of Golaud.

At the end of this chromatic extension, C is again replaced by C♯, which is sustained in the tremolo figure to reinforce the reiterated C♯ of the voice. At this point, the vocal C♯ is part of a longer, more explicit linear manifestation of the whole-tone form of the "Mélisande" cell (G–A–C♯), which is also projected vertically into the last chord of the tremolo. This WT-1 segment is a fusion of Golaud's dyad (G–A) and this whole-tone form (G–A–C♯) of the "Mélisande-Fate" cell, or, put another way, the latter is an extension of the sound world of Golaud. This seems to symbolize Golaud's words, "I would rather have lost all I possess than have lost that ring." The vocal C♯ then moves to D, the juxtaposition of these two notes at this crucial point echoing the original pentatonic/whole-tone conflict between Mélisande (Ab–Bb–C♯) and Fate (Ab–Bb–D) (see p. 1, mm. 14–15; see ex. 4-5 earlier).

The implications of Golaud's reference to "loss" is indicated, then, by the abrupt shift from C♯ back to C, the latter belonging to the basic WT-0 form of the "Pelléas-Fate" cell, Ab–C–D, in the chord under "bague" (ring). Thus, we see a parallel between this passage and Mélisande's earlier statement that linked Pelléas to fate (p. 86, mm. 1–2). This conflict between C♯ and D and its resolution in the C-D of the WT-0 form of the "Pelléas-Fate" cell (G♯–C–D) was already prepared in the preceding passage (p. 99, mm. 1–4), as Golaud insisted that Mélisande find the ring.

This transformation back to the WT-0 sphere of Pelléas in correspondence with Golaud's reference to the "loss" of his possessions is articulated by the second, modified statement of his "Vengeance" motif (p. 100, m. 2). The latter, which reflects his increasing anger and his insistence that Mélisande retrieve the ring before the rising tide of the sea gets it first, now expands his WT-1 sphere more prominently within the increasingly chromatic context leading to the end of the scene. This statement of the motif expands the WT-1 components of the combined melodic and harmonic content of the first motivic statement (WT-1/WT-0: C♯–Eb–G–A/Bb–C–D–E) to a more foreground five-note segment (Cb–Db–Eb–F–G) in the tail figure and accompanying chord of the second motivic statement, under a residual element (Ab) from the WT-0 form of the "Pelléas" cell in the voice. In the remainder of the scene, the chromatic figurations result in increased mixture of cellular material from both whole-tone spheres as Golaud's insistence becomes focused more explicitly on Pelléas and on the retrieval of his own possession: the ring.

The sliding chromatic descent in octaves in the bass under this statement of the "Vengeance" motif is articulated cadentially (p. 100, m. 3) by the Bb dominant ninth

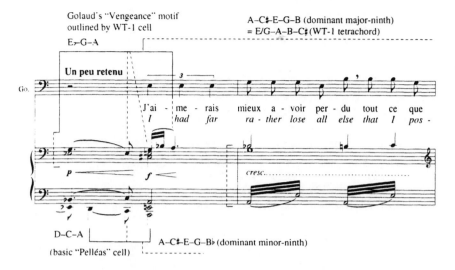

EXAMPLE 5-4. Act 2, scene 2, p. 99, m. 5, "Vengeance" motif as convergent point for several polarized elements

chord, B♭–D–F–A♭–C, into which the basic WT-0 form of the "Pelléas" cell (A♭–C–D) is projected vertically. Both text and harmonic progression suggest a musico-dramatic parallel once again with the original well scene. Golaud's demand that Mélisande retrieve the ring from the sea, no matter how dark it is, recalls the dialogue between Pelléas and Mélisande (pp. 58–59), in which the two lovers talked of the magical powers of "The Blind Men's Well." The basic link between these two passages is the common reference to water. The earlier passage (p. 58, mm. 2–6) also unfolded a descending chromatic progression in the rhythm of the "Fate" motif, which cadenced at the "Well" motif on the B♭ dominant ninth chord. Mélisande's awareness of "How solitary it is—there's not a sound to be heard" seems to have some parallel in her more fearful protestation (p. 100, m. 6), "I daren't, I dare not go there alone."

The significance of this parallel is supported by two symbolic associations, the first between the power of the well to cure blind men and the awakening of Golaud's awareness of Mélisande's affair with Pelléas. The second is based on Golaud's explicit reference to Pelléas. In both passages, the basic WT-0 form of the "Pelléas-Fate" cell is projected vertically as part of the cadential B♭ dominant ninth harmonization of both the "Well" and "Vengeance" motifs (p. 58, m. 6, and p. 100, m. 3). The latter is followed by Golaud's demand, based on jealous motivation, that she go with anyone she likes and that she ask Pelléas to go with her.

With the anticipatory reference to Pelléas (p. 101, mm. 1–2), the basic pentatonic form of the "Pelléas" cell, A–C–[C♯]–A–D, emerges in the vocal line. At the same time, the one "odd" note (C♯), which leads upward to D in this statement, recalls the original C♯–D conflict that was produced by the intrusion of *fate* into the realm of "Mélisande" (see p. 1, mm. 14–15). This C♯–D juxtaposition reflects Mélisande's dilemma at this point, which is intensified by the option given her by Golaud of asking Pelléas to go with her. Golaud's demand that she go immediately to retrieve the ring, which symbolizes their marriage and Golaud's possession of Mélisande, appears to be reflected in the vocal line, which interlocks the "Fate" cell, E♭–G–A, with the pentatonic "Mélisande" cell, G–A–C, both cell transpositions intersecting at Golaud's dyad, G–A. The orchestral Interlude (pp. 103-104) leading to act 2, scene 3, is a motivic and cellular summary of the events that have transpired thus far in this act.

Act 2, Scene 3: Before a Dark Grotto:
Feigned Search for the Ring

The delicate ostinato that opens scene 3 (p. 105) is pervaded by the whole-tone ("Fate") form (A♭–C–D) of the "Pelléas" cell. As the two lovers enter the grotto to carry out their feigned search for the ring, Pelléas speaks with great agitation, "'Yes, this is the place, here we are." One other note (F) expands the Pelléas "Fate" cell (A♭–C–D) to a larger half-diminished seventh collection, D–F–A♭–C, or implied B♭ dominant ninth chord, [B♭]–D–F–A♭–C. This musico-dramatic context suggests a symbolic association with the "Well" scene, that is, the original loss of the ring in the well is alluded to by the pretended search for the ring in the grotto. The dominant ninth chord, which is one of the primary hybrid (diatonic/whole-tone) pitch sets of the opera, again serves as an intermediary stage between the diatonic (human) and whole-tone (fatalistic) spheres. As the atmosphere of the grotto is described in this passage (p. 105, mm. 5–8), "It's so dark that you can't distinguish the entry of the cave from the darkness all round," a new textural block based on the triplet figure of the "Fate" motif suggests that the characters are drawn ever tighter into the snares of destiny. The incomplete B♭ dominant ninth chord ([ ]–D–F–A♭–C) is replaced (in the vocal line and primary chord of the ostinato at the textural change, p. 105, mm. 5–7) by an incomplete form of the original C dominant ninth construction (C–E–G–B♭–[ ]) of the "Well" motif, as Pelléas alludes to the grotto's *darkness*—the "Well" scene had contained Mélisande's opposite allusion to the well's *clear water* (see p. 57, m. 1), which was set exclusively to the same C dominant ninth construction.

The Principle of "Expressive Doubling" as Means of Signifying
Dualistic Human Modes of World Perception

This distinction between the earlier brightness of the noon-day sun and the darkness of night may be considered a kind of *expressive doubling*,[39] that is, variant meanings manifested in two musico-dramatically related situations, in which meaning is determined purely by internal (contextual) association rather than a priori assumption. Regarding Lawrence Kramer's notion of *expressive doubling*, his exploration reveals not only connections between works that form a "coherent group" but also differentiates meanings unique to those individual works that otherwise exhibit similar structures between works within the larger group. In his goal toward providing a wider cultural framework for approaching the issue of musical meaning and expression, Kramer further asserts that "the practice of expressive doubling is closely bound up with the utopian esthetics and subject/object polarity of early Romantic culture."[40] He points to the dualistic human modes of world perception that underlie, for instance, William Blake's sequence of illustrated poems *Songs of Innocence and Experience* (1794), E. T. A. Hoffmann's novella *The Golden Pot* (1813), based on "the conjunction and opposition of two ideal worlds," and J. M. W. Turner's use of "expressive doubling" in his paired paintings *Shade and Darkness — The Evening of the Deluge* and *Light and Color (Goethe's Theory) — The Morning After the Deluge — Mosses* [sic] *Writing the Book of Genesis* (1843). Kramer then cites the Scherzo movement of Beethoven's Fifth Symphony, in which the "meaning" of the da capo structure, based on a profound stylistic reinterpretation of the scherzo return after the trio section, differs from the aesthetic message of the same structure in the Scherzo of the String Quartet, op. 74 ("Harp"). Although both scherzo movements reveal several common structural and stylistic features, including key, rhythmic motive, and "whispery" return, they convey contrasting messages on a higher level of interpretation: in the symphony the scherzo persists in its dynamic energy and sense of struggle, while in the quartet it dissipates it.

Kramer's definition of "expressive doubling" as "a process that submits a well-defined Gestalt to reinterpretation and evaluation" is also exemplified in Debussy's opera by the present comparisons of dramatic events or objects and their underlying musical cross-references. The remaining text of the grotto scene bears out the reflexive (that is, contextually determined) connection between this and the earlier "Well" scene: Pelléas refers to the starless night, suggesting that the two lovers wait till the moon (counterpart of the noon-day sun) has broken through the great cloud bank. He then warns of the dangerous places within, and the narrow path between two pools where the bottom has never been found — this recalls the well. He invites Mélisande into the grotto (p. 108) because "You must be able to describe the place where you lost the ring if he asks you about it."

The incomplete C dominant ninth construction (C–E–G–B♭–[ ]) is explicitly linked up with the incomplete B♭ dominant ninth (i.e., D half-diminished seventh construction, [ ]–D–F–A♭–C) in the larger chain of thirds (C–E–G–B♭–D–F–A♭–C). This occurs (p. 105, downbeat of m. 7) at the intersection between the seventh degree (B♭) of the C–E–G–B♭ vocal line and the incomplete B♭ dominant ninth chord (B♭–D–F–[ ]–[ ]), the return of A♭ (downbeat of the next measure) and C extending and completing this supertertian chain of dominant ninths (C–E–G–B♭–D/B♭–D–F–A♭–C).

The significance of these two dominant ninth constructions as links to the fatalistic realm in this passage is seen primarily in their whole-tone potential. That is, hypothetical omission of the diatonic fifth degrees (G and F, respectively) from C–E–[ ]–B♭–D and B♭–D–[ ]–A♭–C reveals five notes of the WT-0 collection exclusively: A♭–B♭–C–D–E. The latter is the tritone transposition of the five notes of Pelléas's WT-0 vocal line (D–E–F♯–G♯–A♯) in the "Well" scene (p. 57), where he presents the metaphor, "It's as cool as winter." Furthermore, the specific way in which these two dominant ninth chords are left incomplete in this passage (C–E–G–B♭–[ ] and [ ]–D–F–A♭–C) suggests a more profound significance in the relation of the two lovers to their fate. While the whole-tone components of the latter ([ ]–D–F–A♭–C) yield the whole-tone ("Fate") form of the "Pelléas" cell (A♭–C–D), which is manifested unequivocally throughout much of the passage (p. 105, m. 1 ff.), the whole-tone components of the former (C–E–G–B♭–[ ]) yield the inversion (B♭–C–E), which is the whole-tone ("Fate") form of the "Mélisande" cell. It is the form of the "Pelléas" cell that prevails in this scene, however, in correspondence with his dramatic initiative.

As Pelléas and Mélisande stand in the darkness of the grotto (p. 110), we get a variant of the "Fate" motif that closed the preceding scene. The "Fate" motif is then transformed into a radiating stream of instrumental timbres (flutes, oboe, English horn, harp glissandi, string tremolo, and pianissimo cymbals), as Pelléas refers to the light that illuminates three white-haired paupers. As they talk of the paupers in the cave, the flute and oboe—these are the two instrumental timbres most prominently associated with the pastoral mood of Pelléas and the sadness of Mélisande, respectively—trace a lamenting line almost to the end of the scene, where the quiet postlude echoes the "Fate" motif in the winds.

6

Pelléas et Mélisande

Musico-Dramatic Turning Point: Intervallic Expansion as Symbol of Dramatic Tension and Change of Mood

Subtle mood fluctuations have been manifested, throughout the first two acts, in static (nonfunctional) pitch-set interactions between the contrasting, mosaic planes and layers, in which whole-tone (fatalistic) intrusions into the pentatonic/ diatonic (human) sphere have been serving a highly localized coloristic function to create the opera's impressionistic shades. At the same time, these local coloristic (modal/ whole-tone) shimmerings form a larger integrated harmonic pallette, a chameleonic fabric that seems to function as a kind of mysterious textural "ether" for linking the multiplicity of basic themes and their transformations.

At the center of the opera, act 3 brings us to what may be considered one of the most significant turning points in the symbolic action. At this juncture, the polarized pentatonic/diatonic and whole-tone spheres, while still serving a local coloristic role, acquire a more global structural significance in conjunction with dramatic developments and long-range symbolic associations. Especially by way of act 3, in which the atmosphere of darkness—tower scene at night and underground vault—permits a greater "capacity for telepathy and prophecy and, by extension, [a greater association] with the pre-conscious or subconscious,"[1] it seems that the nonfunctional modal and whole-tone sets can acquire, in the psychological sense, "linear" (cross-referenced) associations on the larger structural level of the opera.[2]

In his essay on "cross correspondence,"[3] Maeterlinck goes beyond the mere poetic expression of psychic forces as developed in his *Pelléas* play by probing more deeply into the question of telepathy as scientific fact, not only in terms of its role in communicating with the dead during a transitional period in which memory may linger in an incorporeal state, but in terms of a mystery that may have its place as much in this world (i.e., between living souls) as in the other.[4] Because of our association of darkness with the *unconscious* in the opera (for instance, as is symbolized by the underground vaults of the castle) and the power of the unconscious to compel the characters toward their ultimate fate (that is, death), we may link the opera's symbolism with certain notions of telepathy as set forth by the advocates of Psychic Force.[5] Maeterlinck's quote from Crookes's article reveals the importance of unconscious suggestion and telepathic communication as a basis for Maeterlinck's own symbolic thought. The "Vault" scene is a premonitory symbol of Pelléas's death. As Golaud leads Pelléas into the dark underground vaults, for instance, he first asks Pelléas if he has never yet found his way down into these vaults, and then asks him if he can smell the stench of death that rises from the stagnant water. Pelléas has thus been forewarned of his death at the hand of Golaud, this subliminal suggestion seeming to draw Pelléas relentlessly toward a working out of that destiny in his subsequent actions. We can only assume that Golaud's forewarning remains hidden within Pelléas's unconscious mind, since it is only on the final night (pp. 232–233) that Pelléas will reveal to Mélisande how he has been "playing like a child around a thing whose existence [he] did not suspect." The element of unconscious suggestion may also be observed in Pelléas's reference to himself as a "child," which appears to be taken over— that is, used vicariously by Pelléas—from Golaud's own metaphorical application of the word to both Pelléas and Mélisande when he found them together at the tower at night (see p. 139). Maeterlinck asserts, in his discussion of "cross correspondence,"[6] that such phenomena can be attributed to the "special character and the as yet imperfectly recognized difficulties of telepathic communication," and that unconscious suggestions may perhaps "make their way into certain forgotten corners which the intelligence no longer visits and thence bring back more or less surprising discoveries; but the intellectual quality of the aggregate will always be inferior to that which a conscious mind would yield." These notions of telepathic communication and unconscious suggestion appear to underlie the moods of both love and death in the events of the following two scenes.

Act 3, Scene 1: One of the Towers of the Castle: Mélisande's Hair as an Object of Manifold Symbolic Significance, the Seduction of Pelléas in the Magic of the Night, and the Threatening Arrival of Golaud

Fundamental clues to symbolic association among what may be considered primary dramatic issues—loss of innocence, punishment and destruction of the two lovers by Golaud, and Mélisande's forgiveness of Golaud before she dies at childbirth—emerge most prominently in act 3. The basic pitch-set interactions contribute increasingly to the larger architectural shapes of the scenes in correspondence with these dramatic developments, which are essential to an increased sense of plot direction. One of the basic tendencies of pitch-set development in this act (for instance, from act 3, scene 1 through the opening of scene 2) is toward long-range intervallic expansion. Both chromatic and pentatonic figurations progress to predominantly whole-tone constructions as the sensuous mood changes to a more ominous one by the opening of scene 2. At that point, the whole-tone sphere is associated more directly with Golaud's jealousy and violence.[7] Consequently, these pitch-sets acquire a larger structural function within these two scenes, that is, beyond their earlier predominantly local coloristic functions, as they become associated directly with primary dramatic focal points. This is demonstrated in the following musico-dramatic description.

Mélisande's hair is the primary focus for symbolic association in acts 3 and 4, first as an object of seduction that reveals the woman in all her sensuality, later as an instrument of her punishment when Golaud drags her by her hair in a motion that simulates the Cross (act 4, scene 2, pp. 215-216): "Ah ha! Your long hair is useful for something at last. To the right and then to the left! To the left and then to the right! Absalom! Absalom! Forward! Back!" The dual significance of Mélisande's hair, which is used to symbolize her as both sensuous woman and "Christ" figure, seems, thus, to play an essential role in the more global polarity between Mélisande as real-life being and as instrument of fate.

Act 3 begins with the delicate sonorities of the harp, flute, and strings (in pizzicato and sustained harmonics), which together set the mood for this most sensuous moment of the opera. This instrumentation, which is strikingly similar to that which introduced the "Well" scene (opening of act 2), supports an event that is both parallel to and polarized with the earlier one. In act 2 (p. 55), the two lovers had met at the well in the brightness of the noon-day sun, whereas, in act 3 (p. 115), they meet in the darkness of the starry mid-night sky. In both cases, the sensuous, seductive mood will lead to a culminating moment associated either indirectly or directly with Golaud: in act 2 Mélisande loses the wedding ring given to her by Golaud, in act 3 Golaud himself interrupts them as Mélisande's unbound hair is caught in the branches. The opening scene of act 3 is particularly striking, perhaps even unusual in the opera, for its sense of dramatic buildup in the transformation of moods. The sensuality of Mélisande, her seduction of Pelléas, increasing suspicion of Golaud, and threat of mortal danger together point the direction of the plot toward the dramatic peak of the opera. This progression of changing moods, which culminates in the dark, forbidding, and sinister atmosphere of the castle vaults (act 3, scene 2), is essential in shaping the musico-dramatic form of scene 1.

The scene begins with Mélisande alone at the tower window, combing her long unbound hair which she describes as "waiting for you all down the tower." The appearance of Pelléas is musically anticipated in Mélisande's unaccompanied recitative, which is pervaded by surface reiterations of the "Pelléas" pentatonic cell, B–D–E. Pelléas would like to see Mélisande move from the shadows, to lean out of the window under the shining stars of the lovely night so he may see her unbound hair and touch her hand. While leaning out as far as she can, her hair suddenly falls and envelops him: "Oh! Oh! my hair is falling right down the tower!" Then begins the sensuous episode with Mélisande's hair (p. 128), accompanied by murmuring figurations in the violas, cellos, harp, and horn, as the clarinet sings the "Mélisande" thematic variant above kaleidoscopic harmonic changes, which induce an intense but restrained passion. Pelléas's rhapsodic description of Mélisande's hair suggests what may be interpreted as the first distinctive metaphor for sexual union as he is engulfed by her tresses down to his knees: "I'm holding it in my hands, I'm holding it in my mouth, I'm holding it in my arms, I'm putting it around my neck. . . . Look, look, it comes down from such a height, and yet it covers me as far as my heart, it even covers me as far as my knees!"

As Pelléas refers to Mélisande as his prisoner for the night, text and music move from moderation to growing animation and passion. Startled by doves flying down from the tower in the darkness (p. 135), Mélisande seems to have found the means for diverting attention away from Pelléas's seductive teasing. At this point, the string tremolo linearly joins a pentatonic variant of her motif (at its original pitch level, G♯–A♯–C♯–A♯–G♯) with the whole-tone form of the "Pelléas" motif (G♯–F♯–D–F♯–

G♯). The registral boundary (C♯–D) of both forms together (C♯–A♯–G♯/G♯–F♯–D) recalls the original dissonance in the Prelude (p. 1, mm. 14–15) between the pentatonic "Mélisande" cell (A♭–B♭–C♯) in the oboe and the whole-tone "Fate" form (A♭–B♭–D–E) in the strings. The string figuration, which recalls the same timbral quality of the whole-tone transformation in the original passage (p. 1, mm. 14–15), now absorbs both forms of the motif into a single color as they are linearly projected in the present passage. This subtle reduction from oboe and strings to strings alone in correspondence with motivic fusion produces a sense of transformation toward the more mysterious quality associated with the original whole-tone sonority.

A change of mood ensues as Golaud enters by the winding stairway (accompanied by the ostinato "Fate" rhythm), the two lovers becoming frightened that he may

EXAMPLE 6-1. Act 3, scene 1, three new motifs: (a) magical quality of "Night" (p. 115, m. 6 [show mm. 4–6]), (b) Pelléas's "Ardor" (p. 120, m. 3), and (c) Mélisande's "Descending Hair" (p. 127, mm. 1–3)

have overheard them. As Golaud questions them about their activities, this culminating moment of the scene (p. 138, mm. 9–10) is accompanied by a sombre statement of his "Vengeance" motif (compare with the original "Golaud" motif, p. 14, m. 8, and "Vengeance" motif, p. 99, m. 5). The instrumentation (horns, bassoons, and low strings), which is essentially the same for all three musical events, contributes to the symbolic association among these events and provides yet another example of the use of timbre in a kind of "leit-sound" capacity. Golaud's final words provide an ironic polarity to, even denial of, their seductive activity: "Stop playing in the dark like that. You're just a pair of children. What children you are! What children!" and he exits with Pelléas.

Scene 1 is structurally articulated by three new motifs (ex. 6-1)—the magical quality of "Night" (p. 115, m. 6), Pelléas's "Ardor" (p. 120, m. 3), and Mélisande's "Descending Hair" (p. 127, mm. 1–3)—which are followed by thematic variants of "Mélisande" (p. 128, mm. 1–2) and Golaud's "Vengeance" (p. 138, m. 9). Within this structural deployment of motifs, the symbolic use of figuration and instrumentation is especially poignant, the prelude unfolding a quiet arabesque that sets the mood in anticipation of Mélisande's flowing hair. The opening arabesque, based on pitch-class B in alternation with the "Night" motif in the suggested key of E minor/major (p. 115. m. 6ff.), is part of a larger ambiguous tonal polarity between B and E, which resolves to E at the end of her recitative (p. 117). The prolongation of tonal ambiguity to the cadential point contributes, within the context of the figural arabesque, to the general mood of Mélisande's seductive action.

Intervallic Expansion as Basis for Dramatic Tension and Change of Mood

Within the opening arabesque, subtle fluctuations between the two basic dualistic modal spheres—pentatonic/diatonic and whole-tone—produce new, more chromatic elements. These local chromatic intrusions establish the initial conditions in preparation for a larger structural projection of expanding intervals, basically from semitone to whole-tone in connection with developing dramatic tension based on the change of mood from the sensuous to the ominous. A similar procedure occurs in Bartók's *Bluebeard*, from the pentatonic "Castle" theme and Judith's initial whole-tone statement to the chromatic "Blood" motif. This points, if only by coincidence, to a striking resemblance between the Debussy and Bartók operas. Bartók referred to the principle most fundamental to the organic processes of his music, especially after 1926, as diatonic "extension in range" of chromatic themes and the reverse, chromatic "compression" of diatonic themes, though there is evidence of it in his 1911 opera and other early works.[8] In the opening lyrical diatonic string theme of the present scene in Debussy's opera (p. 115, mm. 3–5), A–F♯–A–D unfolds against pitch-class B of the harp (see ex. 6-1a). This already suggests an adumbration of the contour (but not the mood) of Golaud's "Vengeance" motif, which will be stated by the horns, bassoons, and low strings at Golaud's appearance (p. 138, m. 9). The final note (D) of the lyrical theme moves to D♯ in the held chord, B–D♯–F♯ (at m. 6) to produce the first chromatic alteration. Under this chord, the "Night" motif itself, played by the flute and oboe, alternates the pentatonic "Pelléas" (or "Mélisande") cell (G♯–F♯–D♯)

with its chromatic variant (G–F♯–D♯) to produce another chromatic conflict (G♯–G). The phrase ends with the chromatic variant (G–F♯–D♯), so the descending phase in the fluctuations between G♯ and G is given priority. This chromatic descent is further emphasized by the next note, F♯, thereby implying the presence of a three-note chromatic descent (G♯–G–F♯). The "Night" motif then serves as a kind of ritournelle that punctuates the ensuing vocal recitatives.

This tendency toward chromatic descent and intervallic expansion has long-range significance in this scene both in the transformation from one motif to the next and in the larger interval-expansion process. In Mélisande's unaccompanied recitative (p. 116), in which she refers to her hair waiting for Pelléas down the tower, the pentatonic cell (E–D–B) becomes preeminent. The association of this cell with Pelléas at this point is supported by the basic contour (D–E–B) of his original motif, the contour identification established at his first appearance (p. 33, mm. 10 ff.; see also his theme at the opening of act 2, p. 55). This cell is part of a larger pentatonic segment, G–A–B–D–E, which cadences on C♯. The C♯ disruption of this pentatonic collection is significant in that the cadential motion from D to C♯ appears to represent a more background-level continuation of the initial chromatic fluctuations between D♯ and D (p. 115, mm. 5–6 and 13–14).[9] The general tendency of these two chromatic adjacencies (D♯–D and D–C♯) implies the presence of a larger chromatic descent, D♯–D–C♯. In the transposed "Night" motif that punctuates Mélisande's recitative (p. 117, m. 1), the initial dyad (C–B) suggests a further extension of the chromatic descent to D♯–D–C♯–C–B.

The significance of this background-level chromatic descent, which in and of itself contributes to the sensual mood of Mélisande's hair combing in the night atmosphere, may in part be attributed to the appearance of Pelléas's "Ardor" motif (p. 120, m. 3; see ex. 6-1b). The contraction of the long-range chromatic descent into the foreground level in this new motif (D–C♯–C–E–B) produces a musical intensification that seems to symbolize Pelléas's increasing passion. The motif itself seems to be nothing more than a chromatic elaboration of Pelléas's pentatonic cell or motif (D–E–B) as it appeared in Mélisande's recitative (p. 116). The C♯ disruption of the pentatonic collection in the latter, that is, as part of the cadential dyad (D–C♯) of the first two phrases, may be interpreted as the beginning of the chromatic elaboration in the "Ardor" motif. The initial dyad (C–B) of the transposed "Night" motif that punctuated the end of the recitative (p. 117, m. 1) may be interpreted, in turn, as an adumbration of the ending of the "Ardor" motif (D–C♯–C–E–B). The latter interpretation is supported by the larger group of pitch adjacencies at the opening of the transposed "Night" motif, in which a sustained E appears in counterpoint with C–B to foreshadow the three cadential notes of the "Ardor" motif (see ex. 6-1b). Both motifs are then presented in close proximity (p. 122, mm. 4–5) as Mélisande leans further out of the window (ex. 6-2). The transpositional level (B–A♯–A–C♯–G♯) of the "Ardor" motif at this point (p. 122, mm. 5–6) further extends the chromatic descent of the motif's original content (D–C♯–C–E–B). Both transpositions together (D–C♯–C–E–B/B–A♯–A–C♯–G♯) outline a long-range temporal boundary of tritone D–G♯, which is manifested more locally in the vocal line above the orchestral statement of the motif that accompanies Pelléas's passionate utterance to Mélisande: "Give me your hand, put your little hand to my lips." The sixteenth-note scalar figuration at the

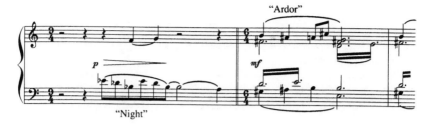

EXAMPLE 6-2. Act 3, scene 1, p. 122, mm. 4–5, "Night" and "Ardor" motifs in close proximity as Mélisande leans further out of window; transpositional level (B–A♮–A–C♯–G♯) of "Ardor" motif further extends long-range chromatic descent (D–C♯–C–E–B/ B–A♮–A–C♯–G♯), with tritone boundary (D–G♯) manifested locally in vocal line

vocal cadence (p. 123) is initiated by a whole-tone tetrachord (D–E–F♯–G♯), which is bounded by this tritone. These foreground-level condensations further support the increasing dramatic passion. Foreground condensation is also evident on the phrasal level, the preceding paired statements of the descending chromatic "Ardor" motif spanning two measures, the ascending paired statements of the whole-tone/Lydian scale being reduced to one measure.

The first significant intervallic expansion from chromatic to whole-tone is represented by this whole-tone tetrachord (D–E–F♯–G♯) in the ascending sixteenth-note figuration (p. 123, m. 1), the larger scale unfolding a gapped form of the D Lydian (diatonic) mode, D–E–F♯–G♯–[ ]–B–C♯. The next paired statements of the "Ardor" motif re-expand the phrase structure to two measures. The descending scalar counterpoint against the motif, which forms a counterbalance to the preceding scalar ascent (its trills simulating the sixteenth-note figuration), plays a significant role in the expansion from chromatic to whole-tone/diatonic intervals in anticipation of the whole-tone "Descending Hair" motif. The latter is played by the sensuous strings in *fortissimo* (p. 127, mm. 1 ff.). The first four trilled notes, D–C♯–C–B (at p. 123, m. 2), which confirm the connection between the simultaneously stated "Ardor" motif (D–C♯–C–E–B) and the previously unfolded background-level chromatic descent (i.e., from the cadential D–C♯ in the opening of Mélisande's recitative, p. 116, to the initial C–B of the transposed "Night" motif, p. 117, m. 1), imply the presence of two interlocking whole-tone dyads, D–C and B–C♯. This interpretation is supported by the preceding gapped Lydian scale, that is, the latter ends with B–C♯, which is a WT-1 disruption of the WT-0 tetrachord, D–E–F♯–G♯. The final note (B) of the descending trilled chromatic tetrachord (D–C♯–C–B) initiates a WT-1 segment (B–A–G) within the longer line, this trichord expanded in the repeated statement of the descending trills (mm. 3–4) to tetrachord B–A–G–F.

The significance of these musical developments lies in their anticipation of, and connections with, the pitch-set structure of the "Descending Hair" motif, these musical connections supporting the organic dramatic buildup of increasing passion. While belonging to the larger D Dorian (diatonic) scale (D–E/F–G–A–B/C) in this passage, both this WT-1 tetrachord (B–A–G–F) and the tritone transposition (Ab–Bb–C–D) of WT-0-tetrachord D–E–F♯–G♯ are precisely those that will outline the upper and lower layers of the "Descending Hair" motif (p. 127, mm. 1–2). The tritone transposition (F–Eb–Db–Cb) of tetrachord B–A–G–F is also found to be aligned in one of the inner layers with one other whole-tone tetrachord (G–F–Eb–Db), both together outlining the complete WT-1 collection in the lower inner lines (see ex. 6-1c). The latter WT-1 tetrachord (G–F–Eb–Db), which is apparently the only new one in this sliding progression of descending parallel dominant seventh chords, was actually implied already in the passages of increasing passion. Its presence was first implied in Mélisande's recitative by the single tritone (G–C♯) of the E Dorian mode (E–F♯–G–A–B–C♯–D–E), where it outlined a form of the intruding whole-tone ("Fate") cell, G–B–C♯ (p. 116, mm. 3–4 and 5–6). As Pelléas complains (p. 124, mm. 3–4) that he "can only see the branches of the willow that overhangs the wall," tritone G–C♯ is prominently embedded in the vocal line (G–Bb–C♯–D), which contains one semitone and a pair of minor thirds. The minor third, which is enclosed temporally by whole-step orchestral ostinati (see the preceding D–E–F♯ triplets and the following G–A sixteenths), is an expansion of the latter interval in this sensuous (harmonically full) "divisi" string passage that interrupts the developing "Night" and "Ardor" motifs.

The harmonic accompaniment under this vocal statement of Pelléas (p. 124, mm. 3–4), which contains two incomplete interval-3 cycles (G–Bb–C♯–[ ] and Eb–F♯–A–[ ]) in the upper and lower accompanying instrumental layers, respectively, foreshadows the larger, exclusive octatonic segment (G–A–Bb–C–Db–Eb) that follows directly (p. 124, m. 4). This octatonic collection juxtaposes vertical statements of the primary interval-3 cycle (G–Bb–Db) with the tritone transposition (A–C–Eb) of the other interval-3 cycle (Eb–F♯–A) of this passage, the ostinato layers linearly unfolding whole-tone dyads, G–A, Db–Eb, and Bb–C. In the upper harmonic unfolding of the parallel dominant seventh chords that comprise the "Descending Hair" motif, we get pairs of parallel diminished triads a whole-step apart, each pair (D–F–B and C–Eb–A, Bb–Db–G and Ab–Cb–F, etc.) forming a six-note segment of an octatonic collection. This was foreshadowed by the identical procedure just discussed in the ostinato figuration that followed Pelléas's vocal statement (p. 124, m. 4). While the octatonic segments in the "Descending Hair" motif summarize the intervals of the expansion process stemming from the beginning of the scene, that is, semitone, whole-tone, and minor third, the whole-tone dyads of the earlier ostinato figuration are extended downward now to larger whole-tone tetrachords in the "Descending Hair" motif. Thus, the whole-tone cycle is given priority in this context, and serves as a primary focal point in the developing dramatic structure.

Passion and Sensuality: Diatonic and Chromatic Saturation

The parallel harmonic motion underlying the initial occurrence of the "Descending Hair" motif (p. 127, mm. 1–2) represents a type of nonfunctional progression that often accompanies strong feelings of passion or sensuality. Such progressions may sometimes be comprised of what Wenk refers to as *diatonic saturation*,[10] the principle observed in the first variant of the motif (p. 128, mm. 5–6; ex. 6-3). This diatonic (ambiguous E♭ major) transformation of the original whole-tone form corresponds with the increased human passion expressed in the text, in which Pelléas refers to Mélisande's flowing locks around his neck. According to Wenk, the progression "embellish[es] a single [vii7] chord [D–F–A♭–C], saturating it, as it were, with the remaining pitches of the scale to which it belongs." This procedure contributes to the pivotal function of the generating tertian harmony (dominant seventh chord in the initial motivic statement, half-diminished seventh in the motivic variant) in the transformation from one symbolic realm (fatalistic whole-tone) to the other (human diatonic). Thus, the chromatically saturated whole-tone form of the initial motivic statement (p. 127, mm. 1–2) is replaced by the diatonically saturated form at the heightened expression of human feelings. Wenk's identification of similar passages based on the principle of diatonic saturation in *Pelléas* and other Debussy works, in which he imputes a common symbolic significance, supports the premise that the diatonic set is primarily associated with the human or natural realm:

> diatonic saturation occur[s] when moonlight floods the grotto at the end of Act II, when the fragrance of freshly-watered flowers fills the air in Act III, when Pelléas and Mélisande declare their love in Act IV, and later when they exclaim, "All the stars are falling!," and in Act V when Mélisande is blinded by the evening sun. Debussy seems to have retained the symbolic associations of this procedure in certain of his later works. *La cathédral engloutie* [The sunken cathedral], from the first book of piano preludes (1910), depicting a cathedral engulfed by the sea, employs diatonic saturation almost throughout the composition.[11]

Mélisande's sensuality, as symbolized by her hair, represents—like her emotions—one of the most significant forces in the characters' move toward their destiny. Pelléas mistakes her hair for a beam of light (p. 118), but her hair also blocks his view of the starry sky (p. 130), "I can no longer see the sky through your hair."[12] While we may associate light with consciousness (even insight), Mélisande's hair ultimately blocks

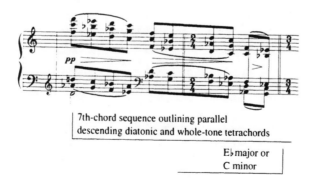

EXAMPLE 6-3. Act 3, scene 1, p. 128, mm. 5–6, first variant of "Descending Hair" motif, diatonic (ambiguous E♭-major) transformation of original whole-tone form; pivotal function of tertian harmony (dominant-seventh chord in initial motivic statement, half-diminished-seventh in motivic variant) in transformation from one symbolic realm (fatalistic whole-tone) to the other (human diatonic)

the light, that is, her sensuality (hair) seems to symbolize an unconscious inclination toward destruction. This interpretation is supported by Maeterlinck's own words: "And if the sky is hidden from you, 'does not the great starry sky,' asks the poet, 'spread over our soul, in spite of all, under guise of death.'"[13] At the end of the opera, it is Mélisande who, on her deathbed, cannot recognize Golaud (p. 279, mm. 2–4) because of the glare of the evening sun in her eyes.

Golaud begs Mélisande to tell him the truth about her love for Pelléas because soon she is going to die, and he after her (p. 290). He blames himself for their fate, telling her that now he can see all, but he loved her so (pp. 284–285). The final dialogue between Golaud and Mélisande provides a link between Mélisande's love for Pelléas as the primary motivating force of Golaud's jealousy and the symbolic polarities identified with the human realm and fate: light and dark, seeing and not seeing, conscious and unconscious, insight and blindness (Golaud is afraid he will go to his grave as one that is blind), truth and lies (he begs Mélisande not to lie at the moment of her death), life and death (ultimate fate). Thus, we may interpret the message of the symbols and final outcome in terms of the force of human emotions, which are both real and inevitable. According to Debussy himself, "The drama of *Pelléas*— which despite its atmosphere of dreams contains much more humanity than those so-called documents of real life—seemed to suit my purpose admirably."[14] Debussy also acknowledged the autonomy of the characters' emotional expression in his opera:

> Above all I respected the characters themselves—their ways. I wanted them to have their own expression, independent of me. . . . On hearing opera, the spectator is accustomed to experiencing two distinct sorts of emotion: on the one hand the *musical emotion*, and on the other the emotion of the characters—usually he experiences them in succession. I tried to ensure that the two were perfectly merged and simultaneous. Melody, if I dare say so, is antilyrical. It cannot express the varying states of the soul, and of life. . . . I have never allowed my music to precipitate or retard the changing feelings or passions of my characters for technical convenience. It stands aside as soon as it can, leaving them the freedom of their gestures, their utterances— their joy or their sorrow. It is this that one of my critics understood so well—M. Fourcaud of *Le Gaulois*—perhaps without realizing it, when he spoke of *Pelléas et Mélisande* in terms of a "declamation in notes, scarcely accompanied."[15]

Golaud, Fate, and the WT-1 Collection

Debussy's musical setting may not "precipitate or retard" the changing feelings or passions, but it seems to symbolize them on the deepest level of his musical language. A prominent linear foreground occurrence of the "Fate" cell, Db–F–G (vocal line) occurs at Pelléas's first explicit reference to Mélisande's hair (p. 127, mm. 6–7), which he describes as "coming down" on to him. This gapped manifestation of the whole-tone tetrachord (Db–Eb–F–G), which is outlined in the lower inner layer of the "Descending Hair" motif, first emerged as part of a longer line in Mélisande's opening recitative (p. 116), where its tritone transposition (G–B–C♯) was contained in the cadential segment (G–B–[D]–C♯). The symbolic significance of the whole-tone "Fate" cell (Db–F–G), which occurs as an isolated foreground event at Pelléas's reference to Mélisande's hair (p. 127, mm. 6–7), is more fully revealed when Golaud enters by the winding stairway. Mélisande's startled words (p. 137, mm. 4–5), "I think it's Golaud!" are expressed by the same linear statement of the cell (Db–F–G). This musical connection (that is, the identical form of the "Fate" cell) between Pelléas's reference to Mélisande's sensuously unfurling hair and Golaud's appearance provides a portentous sign for the direction of the drama.

It is significant that the latter transposition of the "Fate" cell (Db–F–G) is part of the WT-1 collection, which has been associated with Golaud since his very first appearance in act 1. His opening vocal statement (p. 3), which was a prelude to his first meeting with Mélisande, outlined the augmented (WT-1) triad, A–F–Db (see ex. 4-4 earlier). At Golaud's appearance on the stairway (p. 137), where he is about to encounter Mélisande and Pelléas in a compromising situation (her hair is twisted around the branches in the dark), the WT-1 "Fate" cell (Db–F–G) is preceded in Mélisande's vocal line (p. 137, mm. 1–2) by a permutation (Db–A–F, in enharmonic spelling, C♯–A–F) of the same augmented triad that initiated Golaud's first appearance in the opera. Furthermore, the ominous mood of the "Fate" cell (Db–F–G) is enhanced by the ostinato rhythm of the "Fate" motif, which is also associated frequently with Golaud.

The portentous quality of the augmented triad, which belongs to the whole-tone sphere, is already imminent in the "Night" motif at the beginning of this scene (p. 115, m. 6; see ex. 6-1a). The chromatic fluctuation between G♯ and G in the juxtaposition of the pentatonic "Pelléas" cell (G♯–F♯–D♯) and its variant (G–F♯–D♯), while foreshadowing the chromaticism of Pelléas's "Ardor" motif, expands the held B major chord alternately into a minor seventh chord (G♯–B–D♯–F♯) often identified with both the "Pelléas" and "Mélisande" (pentatonic) cells (i.e., D♯–F♯–G♯ and its inversion, F♯–G♯–B) and a quasi-whole-tone construction (G–B–D♯–F♯) containing the augmented (whole-tone) triad associated with Golaud and the fatalistic realm. At the cadence of Mélisande's recitative (p. 117, m. 1), the transposed "night" motif unfolds C–B–G♯ against a held E to outline a more transparent linear transposition (C–E–G♯–B) of the quasi-whole-tone construction containing another augmented triad (C–E–G♯) as Pelléas enters by the path to encounter Mélisande.

Other musical elements also appear to play a significant symbolic role in the dramatic development between the "Descending Hair" motif and the arrival of Golaud. Golaud's "Fate" cell (Db–F–G) is harmonized as part of the larger dominant ninth chord, Eb–G–Bb–Db–F. At Pelléas's reference to Mélisande's hair (p. 127), the cell is harmonized by an incomplete form ([ ]–G–Bb–Db–F) of the same dominant ninth chord in anticipation of the complete form of the chord to be associated with Golaud's appearance. As Pelléas continues to describe Mélisande's hair, "Your hair, Mélisande, all your hair has fallen down from the tower," the C dominant ninth transposition (C–E–G–Bb–D) begins to intrude against segments of the Eb dominant ninth to produce an ambiguous hybrid, more chromatic harmonic context. Pelléas's vocal line (at p. 127, mm. 8–9) first unfolds C–G, then D♯–A♯ (in enharmonic spelling, Eb–Bb), the first implying the basic fifth of the C dominant ninth, the second the basic fifth of the Eb dominant ninth. The orchestral layers support these harmonic implications. In the preceding measure (p. 127, m. 7), the final eighth note and tremolo figure together outline C–E–G–Bb. In the next measure (p. 127, m. 8), the final vocal note and tremolo figures together outline Eb–G–Bb–Db. While the Eb dominant ninth chord is obscured in the first half of the next measure (p. 127, m. 9) by enharmonic spellings, D♯–[ ]–A♯–C♯ (= E♭–[ ]–B♭–D♭), and several chromatic tones, the C dominant ninth (C–E–G–B♭–D) emerges complete and exclusive at the end of the measure.

The emergence of the C dominant ninth chord in juxtaposition with the incomplete E♭ dominant ninth provides a significant musical clue for dramatic symbolic association. The C dominant ninth was originally associated with the "Well" motif (p. 55, m. 10, and p. 57, m. 1). In that scene, Mélisande is looking into the "clear water," where she will drop her ring eventually, her vocal line outlining a transposition of the "Fate" cell (B♭–D–E). At its return in the "Hair" scene (p. 127, end of m. 9f.; see ex. 6-1c), the C dominant ninth chord is based on the same registral isolation of its whole-tone tetrachord (B♭–C–D–E) as had characterized the "Well" motif. Thus, a symbolic musical connection is established between Mélisande's shining ring falling into the well and her hair descending from the tower at night, both events eventually discovered by Golaud. The symbolic connection between these two events is supported by the contrasting light-dark imagery in Mélisande's opening recitative (pp. 116–117), "I was born on a Sunday, on a Sunday at noon," and "I'm doing my hair for the night." Furthermore, Pelléas associates her hair with light, "Is that what I can see on the wall? I thought you had a light."

Dramatic Parallels and Polarities

What follows is an increasing number of dramatic parallels between light and dark metaphors associated with the two events referred to above: the falling of Mélisande's ring into the well in the sunlight of mid-day and the unfolding of her hair from the tower in the darkness of night. These metaphors are evident in Pelléas's statements, "There are countless stars," "but the moon is still over the sea," and "Don't stay in the shadow, Mélisande." The imagery of the moon over the water provides a particularly prominent metaphor of the sun over the well, and the reference to the "shadow" invokes an association to the linden tree near the well through which the sun never can shine (p. 59). These metaphors, which connect key events in the Maeterlinck text, seem endless. The connections between Mélisande's ring and hair, light and dark, and the water of the sea and well, all hark back to the first fatalistic event, in which Golaud discovered Mélisande lost in the dark forest where she had just thrown her crown into the pond, an image later recalled when Mélisande's hair dips into the well at mid-day. Conversely to Kramer's principle of "expressive doubling,"[16] in which he *differentiates* meanings unique to those individual works that otherwise exhibit similar structures, the fundamental polarity between freedom and bondage provides a *common* conceptual framework for a larger series of metaphorically related events: Mélisande's freedom from the crown, a signifier of her former marital bond to Bluebeard; freedom from the wedding ring, a signifier of her marital bond to Golaud; freedom from her bound hair, a signifier of her released emotions as her unbound hair engulfs Pelléas in the darkness of night (her hair is later used by Golaud as an instrument of punishment as he drags her by her hair in the form of the Cross), and Pelléas's explicit statements (p. 132) which reveal that he is able to keep her as his prisoner for the night because her hair is snagged by a willow branch.

Harmonic and timbral interactions are essential in establishing metaphorical cross-relations and parallels among these dramatic polarities, all contributing to the buildup toward the main dramatic goals of the last two acts and the ultimate fulfillment of the lovers' destiny. The chromatic fluctuation between G♯ and G in the arabesque of the "Night" motif (p. 115, m. 6; see ex. 6-1a), which had produced harmonic alternations between the diatonic minor seventh chord (G♯–B–D♯–F♯) and its more expanded quasi-whole-tone form (G–B–D♯–F♯) that contains the augmented triad, acquires a greater structural and dramatic prominence in the sensual hair episode in anticipation of Golaud's entry (p. 137). These polarized harmonic events (diatonic and whole-tone) provide musical metaphors for the dramatic polarities, which otherwise reveal parallel (metaphorical) concepts.

The repetition of these balanced harmonic spheres in all of the parallel dramatic events provides the common musical framework for a more abstract level of musico-dramatic association. This episode begins (p. 128) with alternations between a G Phrygian variant of the "Mélisande" motif in the clarinet and a diatonic variant of the "Descending Hair" motif under Pelléas's rhapsodic phrases. The explicit indication of restrained passion, partially effected by the murmuring accompaniment (in strings, harp, and horn) under the exclusively diatonic forms of both orchestral motifs, serves as a point of departure for the increasing animation and passion of the two lovers, and for modal transformation toward increasing whole-tone configurations during the course of the remaining portion of the scene.

Subtle chromatic inflections in both vocal line and accompaniment, first between G and G♭ (p. 128), then G♯ and G (p. 129), produce pitch configurations that refer back to the chromatic "Night" motif as well as the local whole-tone cell constructions (e.g., "Fate" cell, G♭–B♭–C, p. 128, mm. 2–3, vocal line) that portend the culminating dramatic events of the scene. As in the opening statement of the "Night" motif in this scene (p. 115, m. 6), the orchestral juxtaposition of G♯ and G plays a significant role in the transformation from diatonic to whole-tone spheres (especially the WT-1 sphere of Golaud), and contributes to the increasing dramatic tension. Under the second segment of Mélisande's motivic variant (p. 129, mm. 3–5), the lower three notes of the linearly stated G♯ minor seventh outline, G♯–B–D♯–F♯ (doubled by Pelléas's vocal line), are transformed by means of the G into the augmented triad (G–B–D♯) of WT-1, as in the "Night" motif. In the upper three orchestral lines, it is the complete WT-1 cycle (G–A–B–C♯–D♯–E♯) that emerges now as the more prominent foreground collection, partially intermixed with the remaining notes (D–E–F♯–G♯, i.e., WT-0 tetrachord) in these lines. The latter collection implies the presence of a WT-0 transposition of the "Fate" cell, G♯–F♯–D, which is the tritone transposition of D–C–A♭. This transposition (D–C–A♭) is precisely the one that accompanied Mélisande's allusion to something stronger than herself—Pelléas (p. 86, m. 2) and fate. Thus, while transposition G♯–F♯–D of Pelléas's "Fate" cell represents an expansion of the diatonic "Pelléas" cell (G♯–F♯–D♯) contained in the "Night" motif in the direction of WT-0, the G of the more chromaticized segment (G–F♯–D♯) of the "Night" motif is the primary pivotal element in the transformation of the diatonic "Pelléas" cell into the WT-1 sphere associated with Golaud.

Following the next diatonic statement of the "Descending Hair" motif (p. 129, mm. 5–7), which overlaps and extends Mélisande's thematic variant, Golaud's "Fate" cell and the WT-1 cycle are manifested with increasing prominence. These manifestations occur in increasingly distinct juxtapositions with the WT-0 sphere of Pelléas and Mélisande, the polarity of the whole-tone spheres stemming in this scene from the chromatic fluctuations between G♯ and G of the "Night" motif. As Pelléas's passionate involvement with Mélisande's hair intensifies (p. 129, m. 7ff.), a transposition of the "Pelléas" pentatonic cell, D–F–G, which initiates his vocal line, is simultaneously transformed by the C♯ of violin I into the basic WT-1 transposition (C♯–F–G) of Goulaud's "Fate" cell. The entire harmonic content of the orchestra and voice at this point (p. 129, m. 8) is based on a five-note segment (F–G–A–B–C♯) of the WT-1 collection, plus one "odd" note, D. The latter note represents the single difference between the pentatonic cell (D–F–G) and its whole-tone form (C♯–F–G), so D and C♯ again serve as conflicting elements as part of a higher level conflict between harmonic spheres. The conflict between precisely these two notes is striking considering that the upper melodic line of the orchestra unfolds a "Mélisande" motivic variant similar in rhythm and contour to her original motif in the prelude (p. 1, mm. 14–15). At that point (see ex. 4-5), the same conflict occurred between C♯ of her pentatonic motif (A♭–B♭–C♯) and D of the WT-0 accompaniment (A♭–B♭–D–E), in which D of the arpeggiation served to transform the pitch content of her motif into a WT-0 transposition of the "Fate" cell (A♭–B♭–D). In the sensual "Hair" scene (p. 129, m. 7), the reverse relation occurs—D in the voice, C♯ in the accompaniment—as we move toward the WT-1 sphere in anticipation of Goulaud. This conflict is intensified (p. 129, mm. 9–10) as D moves prominently into the bass to form a pedal under the "Mélisande" motif, which is bounded by tritone C♯–G of the "Goulaud-Fate" cell.

As Pelléas describes the entwining of Mélisande's hair around his heart, two new notes (A♭ and C) from WT-0 enter into his predominantly WT-1 vocal phrase ([D]–F–G–A–[A♭]–C♯–[C–A♭]–A). These two new notes (A♭–C) and the initial D, which are the exclusive representations of WT-0 in this vocal phrase, together imply the presence of the basic transposition (A♭–C–D) of Pelléas's "Fate" cell. At the same time, the emergence of D as a pedal against the linear statement of the dyad A♭–C and the reinforcement of the latter dyad by its own harmonic projection (at p. 129, m. 9, beat 3, and m. 10, beat 3) contribute, together, to the developing tension between the two whole-tone spheres. It is striking that Pelléas's A♭–C dyad is linearly adjacent to G and A, the latter two notes implying the presence of the basic WT-1 dyad (G–A), which was originally associated with Goulaud's very first appearance in the forest (p. 3, mm. 1 and 3, that is, where G–A formed the axis of symmetry of the ascending complete WT-1 scale). The dyad G–A also belongs to the tritone transposition (G–A–C♯) of the "Goulaud-Fate" cell (C♯–F–G), both transpositions imminent in the present passage.

The conflict between the two whole-tone spheres is also intensified in this passage by the absorption of the single WT-0 component (E) of Mélisande's thematic variant (C♯–E–G-E) into a larger five-note segment (A♭–B♭–C–D–E–[F–G]) of WT-0 at the two points where dyad A♭–C is projected vertically (last chord of p. 129, both mm. 9 and 10). The harmonic alternations between WT-1, F–G–A–B–C♯–[D–E] (p. 129, mm. 8-9, etc.), and WT-0, A♭–B♭–C–D–E-[F–G] (end of p. 129, both mm. 9 and 10), result in linear chromatic dyads in several of the layers: A–A♭, C♯–C (vocal line), C♯–C, A–A♭, and B–B♭ (clarinet and basses). The local fusion of chromatic and whole-tone materials at this more passionate dramatic moment is a telescoping of the overall tendency of the scene thus far: the progression, stemming from the G♯–G fluctuations of the "Night" motif, has developed into the longer chromatic descent of the "Ardor" motif and the layers of descending whole-tone (subsequently diatonic) tetrachords of the "Descending Hair" motif. In general, the overall progression from one motif to the next has been based essentially on expansion from chromatic details to whole-tone and diatonic collections. Thus, the divergence (polarity) between whole-tone and chromatic materials serves as a musical metaphor for the tension of the lovers' increasing passion and their impending destiny, which are inextricably connected both musically and dramatically.

Increasing Passion and Impending Fate: Chromatic (Octatonic) Compression of the Whole-Tone Set by Common Tritone Projections

While the more dense chromatic context of the combined whole-tone partitions seems to be a general reflection of the darkness of the night and the fullness of Mélisande's tresses that block the moonlight and stars, as expressed in Pelléas's statement (p. 130, mm. 7–9) that he can no longer see the sky through her hair, the chromatic obfuscation and momentary dissolution of the two whole-tone cycles near the beginning of this vocal statement (by the disruptive F♯ minor triad on the last beat of m. 7) suggests a more direct connection—musically and symbolically—to the chromatic cell (G–F♯–D♯) that initiated the original statement of the "Night" motif; E♭–F♯ is linearly contiguous in the cello and violin in the present passage, the G embedded in the following C major chord. At this point (p. 130, mm. 8–9), a new pair of shortened (two-chord) phrase segments, which reduce the original whole-tone tetrachordal layers of the "Descending Hair" motif to tritone layers, radically transforms the two whole-tone cycles into a more chromatic (that is, octatonic) context. While each linearly outlined tritone in the "Descending Hair" motif (see p. 127, mm. 1–2) originally enframed a whole-tone tetrachordal layer, each tritone (C–F♯, E–A♯, and G–C♯) in the condensed triadic progression (C–E–G to F♯–A♯–C♯) of the present passage (p. 130, mm. 8–9) is reinterpreted exclusively as a member of a larger six-note octatonic segment, C–C♯–[ ]–E–F♯–G–[ ]–A♯. This gapped octatonic segment, together with the preceding two triads (E♭–G♭–B♭ and F♯–A–C♯), generates the complete octatonic collection (C–C♯–E♭–E–F♯–G–A–B♭) exclusively. One of the layers, E♭–F♯–G (p. 130, mm. 7–8, as described earlier), in this progression of octatonic triads implies the presence of the initial segment (in enharmonic spelling, D♯–F♯–G) of the "Night" motif. The intervallic structure of the transposed inversion (e.g., C–C♯–E or F♯–G–A♯) is also implied in the gapped six-note octatonic content (C–C♯–[ ]–E–F♯–G–[ ]–A♯), which is formed by the C major and F♯ major triads.

The more complex fusion of the cellular (intervallic) characteristics of the "Night," "Well," and "Descending Hair" motifs and their larger symmetrical pitch-set manifestations (octatonic and whole-tone) in this passage contribute not only to the accumulating musico-dramatic tension, but also to the tighter musical and symbolic connections among these motifs in terms of their common fatalistic significance. Although the octatonic and whole-tone collections represent a more general polarity on one level (whole-tone versus chromatic, essentially), together they represent a singular sphere on one side of a higher-level polarity—both collections represent a deeper move into the realm of symmetrical pitch construction, such constructions having fatalistic significance in contrast to the pentatonic and larger nonsymmetrical modal pitch constructions associated with the natural human realm. In the first of the two triads—Eb–Gb–Bb and F♯–A–C♯ (p. 130, m. 7)—that precede the two-chord octatonic phrase segments, the triadic root (Eb) ends the descending five-note WT-1 layer (B–A–G–F–Eb) of the "Descending Hair" motif. At the same time, the remaining third (Gb–Bb) of this triad ends the descending series of parallel major thirds that unfold the two WT-0 tetrachords (E–D–C–Bb and C–Bb–Ab–Gb) simultaneously. While these WT-0 tetrachords, which are initiated by the original major thirds (E–C/D–Bb) of the "Well" motif, together yield the complete WT-0 collection that was only implied by the "Well" motif originally, the next triad (F♯–A–C♯) transforms the Eb minor triad from its dual WT-1/WT-0 function into an octatonic function. These two minor-third-related triads (Eb–Gb–Bb and F♯–A–C♯) and the following tritone-related triads (C–E–G and F♯–A♯–C♯) together produce the complete octatonic collection (C–C♯–Eb–E–F♯–G–A–A♯) in contrapuntal synchronization with Pelléas's vocal statement. The intervallic structure of the vocal line combines the cyclic intervals (F♯–A–C and Bb–C) of the larger octatonic and whole-tone collections, respectively. The increasingly explicit octatonic and whole-tone—symmetrical—significance of the three motifs deepens both their musical and symbolic role in producing a sense of inevitable motion toward the fulfillment of the main events.

Pelléas's statement (pp. 130–131) that his "hands can't hold it all—it spreads out onto the branches of the willow" expresses his *loss of control* of Mélisande's unbound hair, and his reference to *falling* once again invokes a symbolic association to the *loss of control* of the ring as it had *fallen* into the well. In connection with both events—falling of Mélisande's ring and her unbound hair—we get pitch-set transformations in more complex combinations. The WT-1 collection re-emerges with greater clarity and prominence now in Pelléas's vocal line (G–A–B–C♯–D♯), the latter generated from the original axial dyad, G–A (see p. 3) associated with the imminent appearance of Golaud. The accompanying orchestral material juxtaposes two dominant ninth chords, D–F♯–A–C–E and B–D♯–F♯–A–C♯, precisely the two that alternated (p. 55, mm. 3–4) in preparation for the primary dominant ninth chord (C–E–G–Bb–D) of the "Well" motif. The original manifestations of these three dominant ninth chords at that meeting of the two lovers—the dominant ninth construction has been shown to be maximally whole-tone—are now projected into the deep-level structure of the "Descending Hair" scene, where they serve as the basis for increasingly distinct, conflicting musico-dramatic juxtapositions of the two whole-tone partitions, WT-1 associated with Golaud, WT-0 with Pelléas and Mélisande.

The original interaction between the cellular variants (octatonic G–F♯–D♯ and pentatonic G♯–F♯–D♯) of the "Night" motif and the whole-tone versus minor seventh ambiguity of the accompanying held chord (p. 115) is projected into a context of more complex figurations (p. 131). While this projection of the basic cellular elements of the "Night" motif provides long-range structural unity and continuity in the developmental process, it also reestablishes the basic generative material of the scene as a point of departure for a new stage of development toward symbolic fulfillment. The larger pitch-set implications (whole-tone, octatonic, and diatonic) of the cellular components of the "Night" motif are manifested now in their more complete and explicit forms, the growth and interaction of these sets seeming to symbolize the inevitable move toward the dramatic climax of the scene.

The original pentatonic cell (G♯–F♯–D♯), which is manifested in the upper two layers of the triplet figure (p. 131, m. 4 ff.), replaces the G–F♯ of the upper instrumental line in the preceding three measures, these two notes implying the presence of the initial (octatonic) cell (G–F♯–D♯) of the "Night" motif. At the same time, the pentatonic cell (G♯–F♯–D♯) forms part of a minor dominant ninth chord, G♯–B♯–D♯–F♯–A (m. 4), which also has octatonic rather than whole-tone significance because of the use of the minor ninth (A) in place of the more common major ninth (A♯) in the opera. The minor dominant ninth—and therefore its pentatonic segment (G♯–F♯–D♯)—belongs exclusively to the larger six-note octatonic segment (G♯–A–[ ]–B♯–[ ]–D♯–E♯–F♯) of this measure. The progression from the WT-1 vocal line to octatonic collection reiterates the pitch-set tendency of the preceding progression (p. 130), but in a figurally reinterpreted context. The basic cells of the "night" motif thereby acquire multiple pitch-set functions within the context of increasing passion, seduction, and the imminence of Golaud.

The symbolic connection between two focal events—Pelléas's reference to Mélisande in the "Descending Hair" Scene (p. 132, mm. 1–5) as his prisoner for the night and Mélisande's reference (p. 86, mm. 1–2) to something stronger than herself, that is, her feelings for Pelléas, which make her a prisoner of fate—is even more striking if we consider the larger harmonic context, which is identical at both dramatic points. At Mélisande's symbolic allusion to Pelléas, the "Fate" cell, A♭–C–D (p. 86, m. 2), appears as an explicit linear surface structure in the form of the "Pelléas" motif, the vertical projection of the larger B♭–dominant ninth chord to which it belongs intruded upon by one "odd" note, G (see ex. 4-2b). This note (G) and the fifth degree (F) of the B♭ dominant ninth chord are the only elements of the harmonic content not belonging to the WT-0 collection of the Pelléas "Fate" cell. They foreshadow the WT-1 sphere at the appearance of Golaud. In the "Descending Hair" scene (p. 132, mm. 3–4), cell A♭–C–D is again manifested as part of the larger B♭ dominant ninth chord, but obscured now by its vertical projection into a completely different figuration. Within this harmonic context, the WT-1 dyad (G–F) and WT-0 dyads (A♭–B♭ and C–D) are all projected similarly in the linear voice leading. However, in correspondence with the tendency of the drama toward the whole-tone sphere of Golaud, the G–F dyad achieves greater prominence by its duplication in the vocal line.

In correspondence with Pelléas's passionate references to Mélisande as his prisoner, which is symbolized by the *strands* of her hair, the fatalistic instrument that binds her in this case to Pelléas and the branch of the willow, G♯ (= A♭) and G of the original "Night" motif initiate larger whole-tone *strands* associated specifically with the original form of her "Descending Hair" motif (p. 127, mm. 1–2). At Pelléas's declaration (p. 132, m. 5), "You are my prisoner to-night, all night long," the orchestral WT-0 dyads (C–D and A♭–B♭) are joined linearly in the voice to form the WT-0 tetrachord, A♭–B♭–C–D, and the WT-1 dyad (G–F) of the preceding vocal statement is extended to the WT-1 trichord, E♭–F–G, in the orchestra. At Mélisande's cries (p. 132, mm. 8–9), "Pelléas! Pelléas!" a new transposition of Pelléas's "Fate" cell (G♭–B♭–C) expands the WT-0 tetrachord to five notes (G♭–A♭–B♭–C–D) of the WT-0 collection. At Pelléas's words (p. 133, mm. 1–2), "I'm tying it, tying it to the willow branches," a segment (G♭–A♭–B♭) of the latter unfolds above a WT-1 tetrachord (C♭–D♭–E♭–F), which implies an extension of the WT-1 trichord, E♭–F–G (p. 132, mm. 5–7) to five notes (C♭–D♭–E♭–F–G) of the WT-1 collection. The primary segments of the two whole-tone collections in this passage are tetrachords A♭–B♭–C–D (p. 132, m. 5) and C♭–D♭–E♭–F (p. 133, mm. 1–2), which are associated directly with the words "prisoner" and "bound," respectively. It is significant that these two whole-tone tetrachords are precisely two of the four tetrachordal *strands* (A♭–B♭–C–D, C♭–D♭–E♭–F, F–G–A–B, and D♭–E♭–F–G) that had unfolded in parallel motion to produce the original "Hair" motif (p. 127, mm. 1–2). While the third tetrachord (F–G–A–B) is related to one of the two basic whole-tone tetrachords (C♭–D♭–E♭–F) of this passage by its common tritone boundary (C♭–F, or B–F), the remaining tetrachord (D♭–E♭–F–G) of the "Hair" motif will emerge as primary at Golaud's appearance (p. 137, mm. 3–5). At that point, this tetrachord is manifested prominently in the form of the "Fate" cell (D♭–F–G) at Mélisande's fearful realization, "I think it's Golaud!" and as the basic whole-tone construction of the underlying E♭ dominant ninth harmonization (E♭–G–B♭–D♭–F). Cell D♭–F–G was already foreshadowed at Pelléas's first reference to Mélisande's unbound hair (p. 127, mm. 6–7), "'your hair is coming down on to me!"

The peak of Pelléas's passionate entanglement with Mélisande's hair (p. 134), "Can you hear my kisses along your hair?" which corresponds with the most intense affirmation of Mélisande's attachment, "My hands are free and you can't leave me," is interrupted by a seemingly insignificant event. Mélisande is startled by some doves, which fly out of the tower and encircle them in the darkness. As they fly overhead, the tremolo figure in the strings unfolds a variant of the "Mélisande" motif at the original pitch level, A♭–B♭–C♯ (in enharmonic spelling, G♯–A♯–C♯). The placement of this dramatic event between Pelléas's reference to Mélisande's eternal attachment to him and the subsequent shift of her attention to the sound of Golaud's footsteps elicits a symbolic interpretation, induced partly by the transitional structural role of this passage, that is, in preparation for the dramatic culmination of this scene. As one of several possible interpretations, the doves perhaps represent that part of Mélisande that would like to fly away, a freedom that she can only experience vicariously through these doves. At the same time, her words belie a sense of loss, "They're my doves, Pelléas. Let's go now, leave me; they would never come back," perhaps even loneliness. But Mélisande's identification with the doves is even more significant if we consider that, just as she cannot be free, doves, unlike some other types of birds, always return to their roost.

These conflicting needs of Mélisande are the basis of the condition that has imprisoned her, her fate stemming from these internal (subconscious) forces against which she cannot and will not struggle. Her dual emotional bonds to the two men are manifestations of her internal dilemma. On the one hand, her emotional attraction to Pelléas—and his to her—threatens her marital bond to Golaud, from whom she seems frightened to take leave. On the other hand, as suggested earlier by Mélisande's plaints to Golaud (p. 87), "I should like to go away with you. I can't go on living here any longer," her attachment to Golaud exceeds the mere formality of matrimony. After all, she was able to escape from her bondage to Bluebeard, as we know from the opening of this and the *Ariane et Barbe-Bleue* play.

Emergence of Pelléas, Then Golaud, in the Darkness; Mélisande's Dilemma Symbolized by Heightened Dramatic Polarity and Complex Pitch-Set Interactions

In correspondence with the emergence of the two men—first Pelléas, then Golaud—in the darkness of the night, Mélisande's dilemma is symbolized musically in this and the culminating passages of the scene by a heightened distinction, polarity, and at the same time interlocking of the pitch-set materials identified with the individual characters. The pentatonic/whole-tone cell transpositions associated with Pelléas and Mélisande, on the one hand, and Golaud, on the other, are generated at their basic pitch levels from the basic G and G♯ details of the "Night" motif with increased clarity. As the doves fly out of the tower (p. 135), Mélisande's motif in the tremolo figure is initiated prominently by pitch-class G♯. Her pentatonic cell at its original pitch level, G♯–A♯–C♯, is joined linearly at the G♯ with its mutated (whole-tone) inversion, G♯–F♯–D, the latter WT-0 form the tritone transposition of Pelléas's basic "Fate" cell (D–C–A♭). This linear pentatonic/whole-tone combination (D–F♯–G♯/G♯–A♯–C♯) recalls the initial occurrence of Mélisande's motif in the prelude of the opera (p. 1, mm. 14–15), where the boundary notes (C♯ and D) appeared in harmonic conflict, that is, based on intrusion of *fate* (whole-tone) into the human (pentatonic/diatonic) realm, as Golaud's entry into the forest and his encounter with Mélisande were imminent. With the imminence of Golaud in this scene, it is the upper note (C♯) of Mélisande's motif, rather than its lower-note (G♯) link to the tritone transposition of Pelléas's WT-0 "Fate" cell (G♯–F♯–D), that serves as the pivot to the inversion (C♯–A–G, p. 136, mm. 2–3, voice) of Golaud's WT-1 "Fate" cell (D♭–F–G, p. 137, mm. 4–7). This Mélisande-Golaud connection is confirmed by the transposition of her motif to C♯–D♯–F♯ in the violins (p. 136, mm. 2–3), where it is joined linearly now with Golaud's cell inversion (C♯–A–G) and tritone transposition (G–B–C♯) of the main form (D♭–F–G) that is assigned to the following explicit reference to him in the voice, horn, and oboe (p. 137, mm. 3–6). This pentatonic/whole-tone combination in the violins and voice (p. 136, mm. 2–3) gives us F♯–D♯–C♯/C♯–A–G.

The intervallic expansion of Mélisande's pentatonic cell, C♯–A♯–G♯ (p. 135, opening string tremolo) to the inverted form, C♯–A–G, of Golaud's basic WT-1 "Fate" cell (D♭–F–G) in Mélisande's vocal line (p. 137) produces a shift from the WT-0 note (G♯) to the WT-1 note (G), that is, the basic semitone (G♯–G) of the "Night" motif. (The string tremolo recalls the same timbre that introduced the first whole-tone intrusion against Mélisande's motif in the Prelude, a significant symbolic gesture in this context in which Golaud is about to appear.) This shift from one whole-tone sphere to the other in connection with Mélisande's expressed fear that her doves will all be *lost* in the dark invokes an association to Golaud's first words in the opera (p. 3), where he was *lost* in the forest. At that point, we had the same shift from the predominance of the WT-0 collection (see opening of the prelude) to the

WT-1 collection. At the same time, the shift in Mélisande's vocal line (p. 136, m. 2, through p. 137, m. 2) to Golaud's WT-1 cell (first C♯–A–G, then D♭–F–G, both joined locally in voice and orchestra, p. 137, m. 1f.) within the context of the complete WT-1 collection, G–A–B–C♯–D♯–F (see p. 136, mm. 7–8, string tremolo), points to a deeper symbolic meaning. The loss of the doves implies their freedom, to which we may associate Mélisande's own wish to fly away as she apprehends Golaud's appearance on the stairway, "Let me lift up my head. I can hear footsteps. Let me go! It's Golaud!" The augmented triad of Mélisande's vocal line (F–A–C♯, pp. 136–137) is a permutation of the identical segment that had accompanied Golaud's first words in the opera. Furthermore, the axis of symmetry (G–A) of the opening whole-tone scalar ascent, E♭–F–G–A–C♭–D♭ (p. 3, m. 1), which was established in the orchestra in connection with the loss of Golaud in the forest, is manifested now (p. 136, m. 7) as an isolated segment of the WT-1 cell (C♯–A–G) in direct connection with Mélisande's words, "They will get lost in the darkness." In the first situation, it was a fleeing boar that led Golaud astray and to his encounter with Mélisande. Now, it is fleeing doves that distract Mélisande and direct her attention to the approach of Golaud.

The WT-1 collection is momentarily interrupted in the vocal line (p. 137, m. 2) by the WT-0 dyad, A♭–B♭, which is established by the following D♭ as part of Mélisande's basic pentatonic cell, A♭–B♭–D♭ (see p. 137, mm. 2–3). The pentatonic D♭ serves as a transitional link as it initiates the basic WT-1 cell of Golaud (D♭–F–G). This fleeting reference to the WT-0 sphere of Pelléas and Mélisande (i.e., by means of the linear interpolation of Mélisande's A♭–B♭ dyad between F–G and D♭ of the WT-1 cell) serves as the basic link in the shift of Mélisande's attention from Pelléas to Golaud. As Mélisande refers to Golaud, dyad A♭–B♭ is projected into the orchestra as the only WT-0 element among several WT-1 instrumental layers. At this focal point in the scene (p. 137, mm. 3 ff.), Golaud's WT-1 cell (D♭–F–G) unfolds both in the voice and the upper two orchestral layers, the undulating dotted half-notes recalling the "Forest" motif, the triplet/eighth-note figure the "Fate" motif rhythm. These motivic references, as at the opening of the opera, anticipate Golaud's appearance.

The lower layers of this variant of the "Forest" motif, in contrary motion to the upper layer, draw the cell into a larger context of whole-tone layers. As the sensuous play with Mélisande's hair comes to an end by the twisting of her hair in the branches and the sound of Golaud's footsteps, the orchestral figurations (p. 137, mm. 3 ff.) suggest one final, dissipating reference to the whole-tone strands of the "Hair" motif. In the woodwinds, dyads G–F and E♭–D♭ together unfold the WT-1 tetrachord, D♭–E♭–F–G, while the dyad B♭–A♭ implies an abridgment of the WT-0 tetrachord, A♭–B♭–C–D. Both tetrachords had unfolded in the lower two string layers of the "Hair" motif (see ex. 6-1c). (These instrumental families, winds and strings, when presented as choirs rather than solos, are most often associated with Golaud and Mélisande, respectively, the strings providing a more sensual quality, the winds a somewhat more ominous one.) At the same time, the harmonic content maintains the diatonic association with the parallel dominant seventh chords of the "Hair" motif, but the progression is reduced to two tertian constructions, on E♭ and D♭. The E♭ chord outlines a complete dominant ninth construction (E♭–G–B♭–D♭–F), but the D♭ chord is limited to a triad (D♭–F–A♭) plus a dissonant G. If we interpret the single note A♭ as the "odd" element, then the remainder of the D♭ chord (WT-1 cell D♭–F–G) is simply a component of the larger E♭ dominant ninth chord. Thus, the WT-1 tetrachordal construction, D♭–E♭–F–G (and its cellular subcollection, D♭–F–G), of the E♭ dominant ninth chord emerges as the predominating structure of the passage. The note A♭, which represents the basic transpositional level of the Pelléas and Mélisande cells throughout the opera, is the only "odd" (that is, WT-0) element of the passage.

The enharmonic reinterpretation of Mélisande's original pentatonic cell (A♭–B♭–C♯) as A♭–B♭–D♭ in her vocal line (p. 137, mm. 3) also contributes to the shift of emphasis from the WT-0 to WT-1 sphere of Golaud, as Mélisande refers to his approach. The reinterpretation of C♯ as D♭, which was already manifested (p. 137, m. 1) in the cross relation between the vocal C♯ and chordal D♭, weakens the original conflict in the Prelude (p. 1, mm. 14–15) between the pentatonic C♯ of Mélisande's motif and the WT-0-related D of the arpeggiations as D♭ now forms part of the "Golaud" WT-1 cell. In contrast to the original upward tendency of C♯ to D in the Prelude, the orchestral D♭ now moves down to C, which is maintained in the remainder of the passage as the basis of the "Fate" rhythm. This reinterpreted tendency of the original C♯ (as the enharmonic D♭ moves down to C) contributes to the weakening of the D (or A♭) area of Pelléas. The momentary return (p. 138, mm. 1–4) of his whole-tone "Fate" cell (A♭–C–D) in the combined vocal line and C pedal (exclusively as part of the larger WT-0 collection) appropriately coincides with his anxiety about her hair being caught in the branches. As he warns her to remain still, the C pedal of the "Fate" rhythm moves down by one half-step to B to begin Golaud's "Vengeance" motif (p. 138, m. 9). The latter is derived from the earlier "Golaud" motif (p. 14, m. 8).

At its first appearance in act 2, scene 2 (p. 99, m. 5, and p. 100, m. 2), the "Vengeance" motif had been presented in two statements in the trombones and tuba, the second statement more vehement than the first. According to Wenk, the trombones and tuba are directly associated, in the opera, with "violent death."[17] As Golaud discovers the two lovers in the dark, questions their actions, and warns Mélisande not to lean out of the window or she will fall, the "Vengeance" motif is again presented in two statements (p. 138, m. 9, and p. 139, m. 4), first in the bassoons, horns, and low strings, then in the upper strings. This instrumentation, which represents a softening of the "more violent" earlier timbral forces, seems to correspond with the more ambiguous level of Golaud's anger. At the earlier statements of the motif, Mélisande's loss of the ring was intolerable for him. In these more recent statements of the motif, denial now colors Golaud's feelings as he treats the two lovers like children. This time, the contrast between the two motivic statements is more subtle, the second transforming the exclusively diatonic, half-diminished seventh content (B–D–F–A) of the first into the whole-tone cell contour (D–F♯–[A]–G♯) of the second within a highly chromaticized harmonization. This transformation from diatonic to whole-tone/chromatic, the tendency in keeping with the general direction of the pitch-set transformations of this scene, reflects the symbolic significance of Golaud's words, "you'll fall ... Don't you know it's late? It's close on midnight." The parallel association of Mélisande's "fall" from the window with Golaud's reference to the "loss" of the ring at the initial occurrence of the "Vengeance" motif (p. 99, m. 5) is supported by the musical association. At that initial statement of the "Vengeance" motif, the whole-tone "Fate"-cell (E♭–G–[B♭]–A) had also defined the linear contour. The chromatic harmonization with its linear half-step manifestations in both cases may be identified with the character of the "Night" motif. It is striking that in both passages, Golaud's threatening words are followed by events in the darkness, the first in which Golaud insists that Mélisande search for the ring in the grotto that night, the present passage in which he refers to the mid-night hour. The latter reference also foreshadows the opening of act 2, scene 2, directly, where Golaud will guide Pelléas through the underground vaults of the castle.

As Golaud, laughing nervously, departs with Pelléas, the tritone transposition (D–F♯–G♯) of Pelléas's WT-0 "Fate" cell in the second statement of the "Vengeance" motif (p. 139, m. 4) is transposed to its basic pitch level (A♭–C–D) in the first chord (A♭–C–D–F) of the Interlude (p. 140), where it initiates the "Fate" motif. The melodic note, F, is the one "odd" element in this primarily WT-0 chord. At the same time, the upper thematic layer (F–G) of the motif belongs to the WT-1 sphere of Golaud, the second note (G) harmonized by the larger WT-1 segment, B–E♭–F–G. The one "odd" note in this primarily WT-1 chord is the A♭ pedal. Thus, the Interlude begins with an equal representation of the two men in connection with the dramatic setting. The "Mélisande" motif returns, after two transposed statements (on A and E♭), to its basic pitch level (on G♯) at the Modéré (p. 141).

Act 3, Scene 2: The Vaults of the Castle; Scene 3:
A Terrace at the Entrance of the Vaults: Dark and Light;
Scene 4: Before the Castle: Golaud's Expression of Jealousy;
Primary Manifestation of the Whole-Tone Cycles and Their Cells

The sound of Golaud's nervous laughter diminishes as he exits with Pelléas into the darkness of the night, the scene ending (p. 141) with an echo of his "Vengeance" motif in the muted trumpet over a sustained chord in horns and woodwinds. This passage is an ominous prelude to the entry of Golaud and Pelléas into the dark vaults of the castle.[18] The mood of the vaults and Golaud's words portend tragedy and death as Golaud's jealousy becomes increasingly evident. The darkness of the underground vaults invokes a symbolic association to Mélisande's crown, ring, and descending hair, since these are linked with the watery depths of the wells and the darkness of night, which we have equated with unconscious motivation, that is, fate.

There are no new motifs in act 3, scenes 2 and 3, but musical commentary on the implications of the action and dialogue provides a more pointed expression of the mood transformation that had occurred in the preceding scene. The musical tendency of that scene, in which the chromatic details of the "Night" and "Ardor" motifs served as point of departure for diatonic and whole-tone expansion in the "Descending Hair" motif and "Fate" cell (linked with the apprehension of Golaud's arrival), reaches its most intensive stage of pitch-set differentiation at the opening of the vault scene. This new focal point is expressed in the most lucid juxtaposition of diatonic and whole-tone spheres thus far in this act. The opening of scene 2 contains a sublimated reference to the "Forest" and "Fate" motifs that opened the opera, an association supported by the somber mood. The initial pair of phrases (p. 142, mm. 1–2) not only recalls the undulating contour of the "Forest" motif, but is identified with the latter by the linearly stated pentatonic dyads (C–D and G–A) that pervade the string

EXAMPLE 6-4. Act 3, scene 2, "Vault" scene, p. 142, mm. 1–14, sublimated reference to "Forest" and "Fate" motifs by linearly stated pentatonic dyads (C–D and G–A) in bass and upper two lines (mm. 1–2); single chromatic change to A♭ on last beat recalls original intrusion (p. 1, m. 5) of WT-0 "Fate" motif

lines (ex. 6-4). The single chromatic change to A♭ on the last beat of both measures is precisely the same alteration that led to the original intrusion (p. 1, m. 5) of the WT-0 "Fate" motif. In the vault scene, the unobtrusive A♭ has two functions: as in the forest scene, it prepares for the shift to the exclusive WT-0 figuration (C–D–G♭–A♭–B♭) of "Fate"; and, as in the preceding tower scene, its linear voice-leading function (A to A♭) recalls the linear half-step element of the "Night" motif.

The local half-step fluctuation (A–A♭) within the otherwise pentatonic/diatonic material of the initial pair of phrases ("vault" motif) and the re-emergence of the gapped whole-tone "Fate"-cell (C–D–G♭, D–G♭–A♭, G♭–A♭–C, etc.) within the larger WT-0 sphere of Pelléas set the musical pattern for an increasing sense of conflict as Golaud begins to lead Pelléas through the dark vaults. The second statement (p. 142, mm. 5–6) of the "Forest" variant (or "Vault" motif) is based on a harmonic reinterpretation of the pentatonic line. The first two chords together produce the complete WT-0 collection, the third chord a WT-1 segment. This pattern is continued (p. 142, m. 7) by an abridgment of these alternating whole-tone chords, now providing equal representation of the two whole-tone collections. The first chord implies the presence of two inversionally related forms of the WT-0 "Fate" cell of Pelléas (A♭–B♭–D/D–F♯–A♭), the second chord two inversionally related forms of the WT-1 "Fate" cell of Golaud (B–E♭–F/F–G–B). The latter collection closes the passage as a more explicit manifestation of the "Fate" cell.

These alternations between the two whole-tone collections seem to symbolize the tension between Golaud and Pelléas. At the same time, they produce a linear chromaticism that recalls the half-step element of the "Night" motif, associated now with the forbidding darkness of the vaults. As Golaud leads Pelléas downward, the complete WT-0 collection, associated with Pelléas, emerges in its most prominent and exclusive manifestation in the opera thus far (p. 142, m. 10 ff.). The motivic and rhythmic disposition of the WT-0 collection produces several striking symbolic associations. The collection is presented in two distinct phrasal pairings, the first based on descending-ascending scales in syncopated counterpoint and articulated by the "Fate" rhythm, the second based on pairings of grace-note/half-note chords built on two transpositions (D–E–A♭ and F♯–B♭–C) of the whole-tone "Fate" cell. The actual harmonic inversion of the first transposition (E–A♭–D) permits whole-step voice-leading (E–F♯, A♭–B♭, D–C) to the second chord (F♯–B♭–C). In combination with the short-long rhythm, the two-chord progression suggests the "Well" motif.

The symbolic association between the descent of the two brothers into the vaults and the unfolding of Mélisande's hair as she had reached into the well (see p. 62), "Take care! Take care! Mélisande! Mélisande! Oh, your hair!" which was followed by the loss of her ring in the well shortly thereafter, is heightened by a parallel between the latter statements of Pelléas to Mélisande and Golaud's warning to Pelléas (p. 143), "Take care. . . . You've never been down into these dungeons?" Golaud's question seems to invoke a reference to the "Blind Men's Well," the associated passages (pp. 57–58 and p. 143) also referring, respectively, to "an old abandoned well" and Pelléas having descended into the vaults "long ago." The ultimate link between the depths of the well and the darkness of the vaults seems to be their common symbolic representation of the unconscious, or fate, that is, that which cannot be seen.

The darkness of the unconscious, that is, the unknown, as suggested by Golaud's question, is symbolized musically by a more prominent intrusion of the half-step element (A–A♭) of the "Night" motif into Golaud's vocal line and accompanying instrumental layers (p. 143, mm. 4–5). As shown earlier, the half-step portends (or reflects) the juxtaposition of the two whole-tone collections. While Pelléas's WT-0 collection dominates the remainder of the scene, Golaud's WT-1 collection interrupts the latter at a significant point (p. 144, mm. 8–10) as a symbol of portending death, played by bassoons, horns, and low strings. According to Wenk,[19] the horns evoke a direct association to Golaud, an indirect association to darkness and death, thereby supporting the symbolic association of the WT-1 collection to Golaud throughout the opera. The threat to Pelléas appears more explicit now in Golaud's ominous statements, "Well, here's the stagnant pool I was speaking about. Do you smell the scent of death that rises from it? Let's go to the edge of this overhanging rock and lean over a little. It will strike you in the face." Precisely at "visage," the WT-0 dyad, C–D, which is part of Pelléas's "Fate" cell (Ab–C–D) in the longer vocal line (p. 144, mm. 6–7), is interrupted by the complete WT-1 collection of Golaud, the latter replacing the original WT-0 collection in the inversionally related syncopated scales. According to Wenk,[20] the timpani (ostinato on C–D) provides a direct association to darkness and an extended association to impending disaster and death. The scalar contour provides a pictorial representation of the "up" and "down" references in the text.

As a musical response to the dialogue about the chasm (pp. 145–146), a series of half-step reiterations associated with the "Night" motif closes the scene. The text at this point refers to the flickering light of the lantern on the dark walls, the stark contrast only serving to heighten the gloominess of the vaults while anticipating the emergence of the two brothers from the stifling air. The WT-0 motif from the opening of the scene returns in the interlude (p. 147, m. 3), where it serves a re-transitional role between the half-steps of darkness and the pentatonic/diatonic sphere associated with the sunlight and air of the terrace at the entrance of the vaults (act 3, scene 3). The WT-0 motif in the double basses is transformed (p. 147, m. 7 ff.) into an ascending figuration in the harps in pictorial representation of the dramatic action. According to Wenk, spacing and registration play an important symbolic role, in which "changes in placement mark important movements on stage, such as the ascent of Golaud and Pelléas from the castle vaults to the terrace by the sea."[21] In anticipation of light and air, the motif appears in a figuration of extreme lucidity in the original arch-shaped contour of the motif. The sense of light and air is supported by the extension of one major-third gap into a complete major-third cycle within the larger WT-0 figuration (Ab–Bb–C–E–Ab–C). These whole-tone arpeggiations are first transformed at the crescendo (p. 148) into a pentatonic/diatonic (E–F♯–G♯–A–C♯–E–F♯–A–C♯–E), then D-dominant ninth construction (D–F♯–A–C–E) at the opening of scene 3, the change of mood expressed by Pelléas's relief, "Ah! I can breathe at last!" The transfer of arpeggiations between flute and harp in the move from scenes 2 to 3 indicate an important movement on stage, the harp symbolizing the water of the sea and the sense of renewal, freshness, and change. Thus, this momentary move from the sense of death to one of life is reflected in the instrumentation and the tendency from whole-tone to diatonic, the reverse of the tendency established at the opening of the opera, in the "Descending Hair" scene, and at the opening of the vault scene.

Textual alternations between these contrasting moods continue throughout scene 3, the WT-1 sphere of Golaud symbolizing the more sinister sense of death, the progression from the WT-0 sphere of Pelléas to the pentatonic/diatonic one the brighter sense of life. At Pelléas's thought that he was going to be ill in the enormous caverns (p. 149, m. 6), the juxtaposition of an E dominant seventh (E–G♯–B–D) and C dominant ninth (C–E–G–Bb–D) chord produces linear half-step voice-leadings (G♯–G, B–Bb, and B–C) that recall the darkness of the "Night" motif. Following the two chords, which contain maximal reference to Pelléas's WT-0 collection (E–G#–[ ]–D and C–E–[ ]–Bb–D), Golaud's WT-1 "Fate" cell interrupts in the form of the gapped French augmented sixth harmony (F–A–B–D#) at Pelléas's reference to "tomber" ("fall"). A cellular segment (D#–F–A) of the latter unfolds explicitly in the vocal line at Pelléas's implication of death, "Down there the air is moist and heavy like leaden dew, and there are thick shadows like poisonous dough." In contrasting exclamation of relief, "And now, all the air from the sea," the WT-0 to diatonic/pentatonic material returns in the "joyeux et clair" arpeggiations.

Polarity and Golaud's Increasing Jealousy

A sense of increasing polarity characterizes the remainder of act 3 and some of the following scenes as well, as Golaud's jealousy increases. Scene 3 of act 3 moves from Pelléas's fluctuating references to light and shade—first in his exuberant descriptions of the flowers in the sunlight of noon, then the flowers in the shadow of the tower, the children bathing in the sea, then the need for his mother and Mélisande to be taken to a shady quarter—to Golaud's first unequivocal expression of jealousy. He now tells Pelléas that he had overheard everything the night before and warns him that it must not be repeated, since the slightest of shocks might bring misfortune for the pregnant Mélisande. The direction of the scene, in which this prophetic statement of death is in stark contrast to Pelléas's description of the flowers in sunlight, most directly establishes the pattern for the overall development in the final acts of the opera.

In act 3, scene 4, Golaud turns to Yniold, his young son from his former marriage, as an incestual tool which he uses to confirm his suspicions by forcing him to spy on Pelléas and Mélisande. The notion of incest is partly manifested in Golaud's identification with Yniold, as he likens himself to a new born baby that is lost in the forest (p. 169, mm. 6–7), and his vicarious experience of seeing the lovers through Yniold's eyes. Conversely, Yniold says that he is told by them that he will grow up as big as his father. When Golaud asks Yniold how they kiss, Yniold demonstrates by kissing him on the mouth. Most striking are certain parallels between the present scene with Yniold and Golaud's first meeting with Mélisande in the forest. In both scenes, Golaud refers to being lost in the forest and tells Yniold how he, too, has forsaken him. Mélisande and Yniold similarly refer to Golaud's gray beard, Mélisande and Yniold both cry, both are afraid of being hurt, and Golaud reassures them he will not hurt them. In the earlier scene, Golaud refers to the stray boar he was hunting and in this scene he is distracted by a wolf that he sees pass by.

In correspondence with Golaud's increasing jealousy, a complex set of ambiguous motivic-cellular interactions and syntheses develop. As in the preceding scenes of this act, there is an increased sense of dramatic direction in contrast to the relatively more descriptive, static events of the first two acts. The Interlude that leads into scene 4 closes with a new pentatonic/diatonic oboe motif (C#–G#–F#–G#–C#) associated with Yniold (p. 158, m 4), the pentatonicism characterizing all of the motifs of the opera in their original associations with the characters as human beings. This initial C# minor linear statement of the motif stands out in marked contrast with the preceding WT-0 figuration. This C# transposition serves as a significant enharmonic

EXAMPLE 6-5. Act 3, scene 4, p. 158, mm. 4–19, "Yniold" motif and introduction to appearance of Golaud and Yniold; ambiguous interlocking of symbolically related elements: initial figure (C–Db–F–G, with held C) of scene 4 joins Golaud's WT-1 "Fate" cell (Db–F–G) with C of Yniold's C-major triad to suggest C-Phrygian mode; held C and F–G of Golaud's cell suggests cell (C–G–F) derived from transposition of "Yniold" motif

link to the WT-1 "Fate" cell (D♭–F–G) of his father, which is embedded in the larger figure that opens scene 4 (p. 158, m. 13). The second statement of the motif, on B♭ (m. 9), closes the Interlude precisely with the cadential note, D♭ (m. 12).

The brief orchestral introduction that leads to the appearance of Golaud and Yniold, the latter of whom is now identified explicitly by the C major triad in Golaud's vocal line as the child is asked to sit on his father's knee, presents an ambiguous interlocking of several symbolically-related elements (ex. 6-5). The initial figure of the scene (C–D♭–F–G, with sustained C) joins Golaud's WT-1 "Fate" cell (D♭–F–G) with the C of Yniold's triad to suggest the C Phrygian mode. In this modal context, the sustained C, together with F–G of Golaud's cell, implies the presence of a cell (C–G–F) derived from an implied C transposition of Yniold's motif, C♯–G♯–F♯ (see p. 158, m. 1). The held C, which represents a diatonic extension of Golaud's WT-1 "Fate" cell (C/D♭–F–G/C) also serves as a pivot to the WT-0 sphere of Pelléas, the following new notes (B♭ and G♭) absorbing the C into the "Pelléas-Fate" cell, C–B♭– G♭. The latter is then expanded into a larger, exclusively WT-0 segment (G♭–A♭–B♭– C, plus E of the voice. Thus, the implied "Yniold" cell (C–G–F) serves as a musical link between Golaud's D♭–F–G and Pelléas's G♭–B♭–C in anticipation of the ensuing dramatic events.

This hybridized introductory passage serves structurally, then, as a kind of ritornello (p. 159, mm. 6–7), which punctuates Golaud's statement that reveals his jealousy of Mélisande, "You've forsaken me, too; you're always with your little mummy." This ritornello statement presents equal representation of Golaud's WT-1 "Fate" cell (D♭–F–G) and Pelléas's WT-0 "Fate" cell (C–B♭–G♭), in which Yniold's cell (C– G–F) again serves as a link: the one intrusion (C) into the WT-1 cell foreshadows Pelléas's intrusion into the sphere of Golaud; the one intrusion (D♭) into the WT-0 cell symbolizes the reverse. Subsequent variant forms of the ritornello figure, which are presented simultaneously with vocal statements, shift the balance between these two whole-tone spheres in distinct juxtapositions between the whole-tone "Fate" cell and some "odd" (that is, non-whole-tone) element in correspondence with the dramatic trend. In these juxtapositions of WT-1 and WT-0 (P. 160, m. 8), which follow statements of Yniold's pentatonic cell (p. 160, mm. 5–6), Golaud refers to someone with a lantern (apparently Pelléas). Correspondingly, there is a shift to D♭–E♮–G♭–A♭, which transposes the initial ritornello figure up one half-step (from C–D♭–F–G to D♭–E♮–G♭–A♭) to produce a reversal of whole-tone representation—the transposition is based on a complete form of Pelléas's WT-0 cell plus Golaud's D♭. There is a direct correlation between Golaud's observation that "there's someone going through the garden with a lantern," specifically, "with a lantern," and Pelléas's WT-0 cell within the larger vocal line; as in the preceding scene, light is associated with the WT-0 sphere of Pelléas.

Two statements by Golaud to Yniold (p. 163, mm. 1–2), "I'm not talking about the light" and "I'm talking about the door," provide a more explicit contrast between light and dark (door signifies privacy or darkness). The paired accompanying phrases seem to reflect this polarity. Above the undulating triplet figure of the "Fate" motif, two whole-tone-related dyads appear in alternation. The first dyad (C–D), together with the whole-tone dyad (F–G) of the triplet, forms a pentatonic tetrachord (F–G–

C–D), which implies the presence of the "Yniold" cell (C–G–F) and its inversion (G–C–D). The second dyad (B–Eb), together with the same F–G dyad of the "Fate" rhythm, produces a WT-1 segment (F–G–B–Eb), which implies the presence of a transposition of the WT-1 "Golaud-Fate" cell (B–Eb–F) and its inversion (F–G–B). As in the previous scenes, the latter cell is again associated with darkness. The WT-1 dyad (F–G) of the triplets moves to a half-step dyad (B–C), the combination unfolding the WT-1 "Fate" cell (F–G–B) plus one "odd" note (C). This recalls the basic pitch-set (intervallic) relations of the initial ritornello figure, C/Db–F–G (p. 158, opening of the scene), based on the primary transposition of the "Golaud" WT-1 cell plus the "odd" note (C) of the implied "Yniold" cell (C–F–G). In both cases, Yniold's pentatonic cell, which serves as a link between the respective whole-tone spheres of Pelléas and Golaud, is the same. At Golaud's order to Yniold not to put his hand in his mouth (p. 163), Yniold's action suggesting inhibition and fear as to what he had seen, the first chord (B–C–Eb–F) modifies the linear triplet segment (F–G–B–C). The new "Golaud" WT-1 cell segment (B–Eb–F, i.e., inverted tritone transposition of F–G–B) is also combined with the same "odd" element (C).

As Yniold's agitation increases (p. 164), his pentatonic motif reappears in parallel fourths and thirds at his words, "Daddy, you've hurt me!" Within this parallel harmonization, we find a hidden manifestation of the basic transposition on C (C–G–F–G, interwoven in second flute and oboes), which emerges as the exclusive form at Golaud's bribing words (p. 165, mm. 4–5), "I'll give you a present tomorrow," that is, if Yniold will inform on Pelléas and Mélisande. The first two notes (C–G) of the motif are harmonized by the C dominant ninth chord (C–E–G–Bb–D), which gives priority to the WT-0 area (Bb–C–D–E), the next two notes (F–G) harmonized by the F dominant ninth (F–A–C–Eb–G), which gives priority to the WT-1 area (Eb–F–G–A). Thus, Yniold's diatonic theme serves as a link between the respective, imminent whole-tone spheres of Pelléas and Golaud.

The direction of the scene, in which Yniold comes to spy on Pelléas and Mélisande, is further indicated by the subtle intrusion of a chromatic tetrachord associated

EXAMPLE 6-6. Act 3, scene 4, p. 174, m. 6ff., chromatic tetrachord, D–C#–C–B (originally as counterpoint to pentatonic "Pelléas" motif), in agitated ostinato figure, as Yniold answers Golaud's question about lovers' kiss

with Pelléas's first appearance in the opera (see ex. 4-8 earlier). The first explicit manifestation of a chromatic tetrachord (F–Gb–G–Ab) in this scene unfolds under the ritornello figure accompanying Golaud's question (p. 162, mm. 5–6), "Who doesn't want it opened?" The chromatic tetrachordal construction can be traced back to the linear chromatic descent (D–C♯–C–B) of Pelléas's "Ardor" motif (p. 120, m. 3) and, originally, to this transposition of the descending tetrachord in the lower flute line in counterpoint with the "Pelléas" motif (p. 33, mm. 10–11). This transposition (D–C♯–C–B) emerges subsequently (ex. 6-6) as the basis of an agitated ostinato figure (p. 174, mm. 6 ff., again played by the flute), as Yniold answers Golaud's question about the lovers' kiss. The tetrachordal ostinato unfolds in counterpoint against a highly varied version of the "Pelléas" motif in the lower lines, so this passage is a transformation of that (p. 33) which introduced Pelléas's first appearance. Pelléas's motif pervades the remainder of the scene and is joined by Mélisande's motif (p. 180, mm. 2–4) as Golaud lifts Yniold to spy on them. As in the "Hair" and "Vault" scenes, references to "light" and "dark" continue (p. 177 ff.) and the triplet figure of the "Fate" rhythm becomes pervasive as the dramatic tension builds to the end of the scene.

7

Pelléas et Mélisande

Mélisande as Christ Symbol—
Life, Death, and Resurrection—
and Motivic Reinterpretations
of the Whole-Tone Dyad

Act 4, Scene 1: A Room in the Castle:
Pelléas's Fate Foreseen by His Father

Pelléas and Mélisande seem to be cast most obviously as instruments of fate in Act 4, which represents the dramatic climax of the opera. The capacity of certain characters to intuit the main fatalistic events is also demonstrated most lucidly at this dramatic highpoint, as revealed in the perceptive utterances by both Pelléas's ailing father and the blind King Arkel. The main symbolic polarities of light-dark, life-death, youth-age, and blindness-foresight are invoked by present dramatic events and reflected in Debussy's corresponding musical setting as Pelléas informs Mélisande of his father's recovery from illness (i.e., return to life) after his close encounter with death (p. 191). It seems almost as though his father's own brush with death has endowed him with the capacity to foresee his son's death. Pelléas reveals concern over his father's premonitory statement by conveying it to Mélisande: "you have the serious, friendly expression of people who haven't long to live." Pelléas is warned, furthermore, that he "must go away," but Pelléas cannot heed his father's warning because Pelléas himself cannot see his own destiny until it is too late, until only moments before the fatal blow is dealt him by Golaud.[1]

It is striking that Pelléas had earlier requested leave to visit his dying friend Marcellus (in act 1, scene 2, p. 35),[2] but Arkel had insisted (unlike Pelléas's father, who warned his son that he must "make a voyage") that Pelléas should remain with his dying father, instead. Because of his lack of insight into his own destiny, Pelléas becomes an instrument of that destiny. Although he finally reveals (pp. 232-233) some insight, specifically that he has been "playing like a child around a thing whose existence [he] did not suspect," playing and dreaming "with all the snares of destiny around him," he ultimately remains incapable of struggle against his fate. Maeterlinck's own questions and observations provide insight into the condition, indeed the dilemma, of his characters, especially the thoughts, actions, and predetermined circumstances of Pelléas:

Who can tell us of the power which events possess—whether they issue from us, or whether we owe our being to them? Do we attract them, or are we attracted by them? Do we mould them, or do they mould us? Are they always unerring in their course? . . . Whence is it that they come to us; and why are they shaped in our image, as though they were our brothers? Are their workings in the past or in the future; and are the more powerful of them those that are no longer, or those that are not yet? Is it to-day or to-morrow that moulds us? Do we not all spend the greater part of our lives under the shadow of an event that has not yet come to pass? . . .

It is death that is the guide of our life, and our life has no goal but death. Our death is the mould into which our life flows: it is death that has shaped our features.[3]

The insightful words of Pelléas's father lead us to draw parallels between events entailing premonitory perceptions by those men who are close to Pelléas. For instance, we may compare Pelléas's visit to his father's bedside, where his father has forecast Pelléas's death, with the scene of the dark underground vaults of the castle, where Golaud had frightened Pelléas with his reference to "the scent of death." The latter event supports the equation between darkness (the unconscious, or unseen) and fate. A parallel may also be drawn between his father's premonition and Pelléas's very first appearance in the opera (p. 34). Pelléas recounts how his father, recovering from his illness (p. 191), "He knew me. He took my hand, and in that strange manner he's had ever since he's been ill, he said: 'Is that you, Pelléas?'"

Immediately following the musical statement of the "Pelléas" motif at his very first appearance (in act 1, scene 2, p. 34), it was Arkel who had originally posed the question: "Is that you, Pelléas? Come a little closer so that I can see you in the light." The descending chromatic tetrachord, D–C♯–C–B, which was hidden in the counterpoint under the original diatonic statement of the "Pelléas" motif (p. 33, mm. 10–11; see ex. 4-8 earlier), reemerges as a primary foreground event in the first oboe (p. 191, mm. 9–11) at Pelléas's quotation of his father's question "Is it thou? Pelléas?" It is striking that at Pelléas's original appearance, it was his friend Marcellus who was going to die. The significance of this chromatic tetrachord in connection with his father's premonition of Pelléas's death—D–C♯–C–B belongs to the symbolic realm of Pelléas—is all the more striking in view of the tetrachord's manifestation in the agitated ostinato of the preceding scene (p. 174), where Yniold's description of the kiss of the two lovers had heightened Golaud's jealousy, an emotion which will motivate Golaud's final violent action against his brother. Whereas the basic "Pelléas" motif itself had appeared in the scene of Golaud's jealousy (p. 174, m. 6 ff.) in a highly modified form in the counterpoint of the oboe and clarinets against the tetrachordal ostinato (D–C♯–C–B) of the flute, the motif is now manifested (pp. 191–192) in a transposed statement (G–A–E–A–E) consisting of a slight intervallic mutation of the original occurrence, B–C♯–A–D–A (see p. 33, mm. 10–12). It is also striking that the chromatic tetrachord of Pelléas (D–C♯–C–B), which directly precedes the transposed form of his motif (G–A–E–A–E) in this passage (p. 191, m. 10) will become the linear thread of the "Ardor" motif (see p. 120, mm. 3–4) as it symbolizes his increasing passion for Mélisande.

The present phrasal and transpositional modification of the "Pelléas" motif in the flute intensifies the meaning of the text and its symbolic associations.[4] It is separated from, that is, it follows rather than appears in counterpoint with, the chromatic tetrachord (p. 191, mm. 9 ff.). This phrasal separation gives greater importance to both diatonic motif and chromatic tetrachord. The direct correlation of the tetrachord with his father's statement about Pelléas's appearance of one who will not live very long (p. 191, m. 10, to p. 192, m. 2), also suggests its more prominent musical status. Furthermore, the specific transpositional level of the "Pelléas" motif at this point provides yet another level of dramatic association. The motif, which is initiated by none other than Golaud's WT-1 dyad (G–A), is linked directly with the statement predicting Pelléas's death, which will be inflicted precisely by his jealous half-brother. The G–A dyad, which appeared as the axis of symmetry of the ascending whole-tone triplet figure (E♭–F–G–A–C♭–D♭) that first introduced Golaud as he had been hunting a wounded boar (p. 3), now appears in Pelléas's vocal line (p. 191, mm. 5–8) as the axis of symmetry of the linear WT-1 tetrachord, F–G–A–B, just prior to his father's premonition of Pelléas's death.

The entire scene is enframed by a sixteenth-note ritornello-like figuration that recalls the first meeting of Pelléas and Mélisande at the well (p. 56). At the earlier ritornello figuration, which implies the presence of the "Pelléas" motif at a transposition level (G♯–B–C♯) that contains one of the primary elements (G♯) associated with Pelléas, the text refers to the stifling heat of the sun at noon. At the opening of the present scene (p. 189), the ritornello figuration, which implies the presence of the "Pelléas" motif at the new transpositional level (E–G–A) that contains Golaud's WT-1 dyad (G–A) and unfolds in linear counterpoint against an explicit statement of this transposition, G–A–E–A–E (p. 189, mm. 7–10), is also associated with the meeting of Pelléas and Mélisande. This time, as Pelléas's words suggest darkness (p. 190), "I must talk to you this evening," the ritornello and motif shift momentarily (p. 190, m. 1 ff.) to the original pitch level (on G♯) in the "Well" scene, the latter transposition supporting the symbolic association of the two scenes. The association with the "Well" scene becomes explicit (p. 193), as they plan to meet in the evening at the blind men's well. A local reference to a variant of Yniold's motif in the ritornello (p. 189, mm. 11–12) provides a transitional link between these opposing transpositional levels, the lowest layer (second bassoon, A–G–F) representing the WT-1 sphere of Golaud, the upper three layers (clarinets, E–D–C, C–B♭–A♭, and F♯–E–D) together producing a complete WT-0 extension of the Pelléas realm.

The symbolic connection between old Arkel and the ancient well, one blind but also able to foresee fateful events (for instance, in act 4, scene 2, p. 202, he "foresees" that Mélisande will be the one to open the door to a new era), the other formerly able to give sight to the blind—hence, conscious (that which is seen) versus unconscious (that which is unseen), or fate—is one of the central themes of symbolic polarity in the entire opera. We may identify other significant polarities in this scene as metaphors of the latter. The polarity between life and death pervades the scene. The warning to Pelléas of his death contrasts with the revival of his father and all the castle (p. 192). The symbolic identity between death and night is also suggested as Pelléas tells Mélisande that their meeting at the well this night will be their last. It is striking that his statement is punctuated by Mélisande's vocal line based on the same WT-1 augmented triad (A–C♯–F–A) that unfolded in Golaud's very first statement (see p. 3). Mélisande's opposite response, in which she tells Pelléas that she shall always see him, establishes the dark-light polarity as well.

The development of these symbolic associations and the fulfillment of primary dramatic events reaches the highpoint in act 4, scene 2. The scene is characterized by stark contrast between Arkel's gentle, life-invoking comments to Mélisande and the violent entry of the enraged Golaud. The contrast in this scene (pp. 201–202) between Arkel's comments to Mélisande, "I have always noticed that all young, fair creatures create around them young, fair and happy events. And now it is you who are going to open the door to the new era that I foresee," and the prediction in the preceding scene of Pelléas's death supports the life-death polarity that emerges with increasing significance and urgency in this act. We also find a symbolic link between this life-death polarity and the youth-age polarity expressed by Arkel in his description of Mélisande's youth and beauty versus his own age. Arkel's words establish this link between the two pairs of polarizations directly (pp. 203–204), "old men need to put their lips, now and then, to a woman's brow or a child's cheek, in order to go believing in the freshness of life and to drive away for a moment the threat of death."

Act 4, Scene 2: Mélisande as Symbol of Resurrection as Foreseen by Arkel; Golaud's Vengeance and Mélisande's Hair as Symbol of the Crucifixion

The sixteenth-note ritornello figuration that ends act 4, scene 1, shifts harmonically at the opening of scene 2 (p. 197, m. 6, beat 1) to a five-note segment (E–F♯–G♯–A♯–B♯) of WT-0, the whole-tone collection associated primarily with Pelléas and Mélisande (ex. 7-1). The intrusion of one "odd" note (C♯) on the next beat transforms the WT-0 collection into an F♯ dominant ninth chord (F♯–A♯–C♯–E–G♯), in which one note, B♯ (= C), is replaced by C♯. This progression from whole-tone to dominant ninth (diatonic), which is the reverse of the progression entailed in the first whole-tone transformation of the "Well" motif (see p. 57, mm. 1–2), serves to establish, momentarily, the more joyful human mood expressed in the ensuing text (pp. 198–202), in which Arkel tells us that the father of Pelléas has been saved from death and that the young and fair Mélisande will be the source for new life in the castle.

In contrast to the association of pitch-class C♯ (or D♭) with the ominous WT-1 "Fate" cell of Golaud discussed earlier, this intrusion of C♯ into the WT-0 collection as the fifth degree of the F♯ dominant ninth chord supports Richard Langham Smith's contention that the tonality of F♯ major, which symbolizes "light" and the striving for Mélisande as an "ideal," is often prepared by its dominant, C♯ major.[5] He asserts that "in the broadest way, frustrated or unconsummated preparations for F♯ major occur in the first three acts, frequently to mirror some aspect of the light-imagery, or to suggest the rising desire for union with Mélisande. These preparations are consummated only in the final love-scene between Pelléas and Mélisande (Act IV, scene 4), where the dominant finally resolves into a new motif, clearly in the aspired-to key of F♯ major." However, as will be discussed later, the association of C♯/F♯ to light (or life) in this passage is ambiguous. This association is perhaps even contradictory in terms of the light-dark symbolism, since Arkel's words also express a forbidding mood (p. 200), "bewildered look of someone constantly awaiting a calamity, in the sunshine, in a beautiful garden." This contradiction is more apparent than real, however, since light (life,

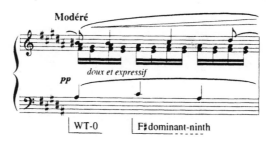

EXAMPLE 7-1. Act 4, scene 1, to opening of scene 2 (p. 197, m. 6, beat 1), sixteenth-note ritornello figuration, harmonic shift to five-note segment (E–F♯–G♯–A♯–B♯) of WT-0, replacement of B♯ by one "odd" note (C♯) transforming WT-0 collection into F♯ dominant-ninth chord (F♯–A♯–C♯–E–G♯)

love) is inextricably connected with darkness (death) in the opera, that is, reference to one of these conditions almost always foreshadows, or invokes its opposite. For instance, Smith cites Pelléas's reference (p. 236, mm. 6–7) to "the edge of the moonlight,"[6] after which Pelléas expresses his fear of being seen (p. 237, mm. 1–3) and that this is perhaps the last time they shall ever meet (p. 242, mm. 3–4).

The darker association of C♯ is imminent within this seemingly brighter (more optimistic) context, nevertheless. In the reversed progression—whole-tone to dominant ninth—in the first measure of this scene (p. 197), the C♯ intrusion that induces the change to the F♯ dominant ninth (F♯–A♯–[C♯]–E–G♯) also initiates a transposition of the "Mélisande" pentatonic motif (C♯–D♯–F♯). The latter (notably dyad C♯–D♯) also belongs to the darker realm of Golaud's WT-1 collection. Recall the transposition of his "Fate" cell on C♯ (in enharmonic spelling, D♭–F–G) at his appearance in the "Descending Hair" or "Tower" scene at midnight. The connection between the C♯–D♯ dyad of this initial statement of the "Mélisande" motif (in the brighter register of the violins) and Golaud is subsequently confirmed in this scene (p. 205, mm. 7–8) in the darker register of the violas and cellos, where the "Fate" motif, based precisely on this dyad (C♯–D♯), accompanies his agitated appearance. The "Mélisande" motif is transposed, then, in the next statement to the original pitch level, A♭–B♭–C♯ (in enharmonic spelling, G♯–A♯–C♯), which now belongs primarily to the WT-0 sphere, that is, except for the C♯. The final transposition of the "Mélisande" motif transforms the pentatonic structure into the WT-0 "Fate" cell, E–F♯–A♯ (violins doubled by the horns). This cadences (p. 197, mm. 16–17) with the initial WT-1 dyad (D♯–C♯) of her pentatonic motif that began the passage, expanded (within a quasi-diatonic collection, D♯–C♯–B–A–G/F♯–E) into a five-note segment of WT-1 (D♯–C♯–B–A–G) against the "odd" WT-0 half notes (F♯ and E) in these two cadential measures. The WT-0 interpretation of the latter two notes (F♯ and E) may be supported by a comparison of the cadential measures with the preceding two measures, in which the hierarchical relation between the two whole-tone collections is reversed in the quasi-diatonic collection, B♯–A♯–G♯–F♯–E/D♯–C♯. In the latter, F♯ and E belong to a five-note segment of WT-0, while the cadential D♯ and C♯ represent the "odd" WT-1 half-notes (see ex. 7-1 earlier). Furthermore, while C♯–D♯ initiates the first (pentatonic) statement of the "Mélisande" motif (p. 197, mm. 6–8), E–F♯ initiates the third (whole-tone) statement (p. 197, mm. 14–16). Thus, in connection with the successive appearances of Arkel and Golaud, the lighter and darker moods as symbolized by the special details of the musical fabric seem to be weaving their net relentlessly around Mélisande.

Mélisande's motif unfolds over a more fragmented form of the "Fate" ostinato as Arkel tells Mélisande how he has been observing her life at the castle (p. 199) and her look of one awaiting a calamity. Life and death, which are mixed increasingly in Arkel's statements (p. 200, mm. 1–2), are musically identified with an ascending-descending wedge-shaped progression in crescendo, which seems to depict this duality literally. This pattern gives way to a mysterious sixteenth-note figuration, as Arkel claims she is "too young and too beautiful to live day and night under the shadow of death." This cross-like figure becomes more continuous and incorporates the "Mélisande" motif within it (e.g., p. 201, m. 7 ff., last beat, F♯–A–F♯–E; m. 11ff., B–D–B–B♭, etc.) as Arkel's words about the reliance on events themselves begin to link Mélisande with fate.

Mélisande and Fate

What is the connection between Mélisande and fate? What can Arkel mean by his assertions (pp. 200–201) that now everything is going to change, that it is Mélisande (p. 202) who will open the door to the new era that he foresees, and (p. 204) his need to believe in the freshness of life to drive away the threat of death? The association between Mélisande and fate and the cryptic meaning of Arkel's statements emerge with increasing clarity in the following sequence of events. Arkel's dualistic statements throughout the first part of this scene, in which he invokes life, youth, and beauty in opposition to death, are interrupted by Golaud's agitated appearance (p. 205), accompanied by the "Fate" rhythm based on the WT-1 dyad, C♯–D♯. This dyad recalls (in enharmonic spelling) the D♭ inverted transposition of Golaud's "Fate" cell (D♭–F–G) at his ominous appearance (p. 137) in the "Hair" Scene, which was also marked by the "Fate" rhythm at that point. The C♯–D♯ transposition of the "Fate" motif (p. 205, mm. 7–8) may be identified with the "Mélisande" motif (C♯–D♯–F♯) at its first occurrence in this scene (p. 197, mm. 6–8, first Violin I); the cadence on D♯–C♯ (p. 197, m. 17) also introduced Arkel's first vocal statement initiated by this dyad. As Golaud, with blood on his brow (p. 205, m. 12), threatens that "Pelléas is going this evening," his "Fate-motif" dyad, C♯–D♯, is expanded to a chromatic tetrachord, C♯–D–D♯–E (p. 205, mm. 7–9). This construction had formed the counterpoint to Pelléas's motif at his very first appearance in the opera (p. 33, mm. 10–12, second flute).

Instrumental timbre contributes to the musical symbolism. Transpositions of the chromatic tetrachord had subsequently formed the flute counterpoint against Pelléas's diatonic motif (p. 174, m. 6 ff.; see ex. 6-6 earlier), which was identified at that point with danger to the two lovers and Golaud's jealousy. At Arkel's present reference to blood on Golaud's brow (p. 205, m. 12), the tetrachord is transposed to E♯–

F♯–G–A♭ (now in the low strings) as the basis of the "Fate" rhythm, thereby further extending Golaud's C♯–D♯ dyad chromatically. This progression at Golaud's entrance, which primarily comprises chromatic tetrachords (in the low strings, a timbre appropriate to Golaud's character), may be outlined as follows: C♯–D♯/C♯–D–D♯–E/E♯–F♯–G–A♭/A–B♭. Thus, the specific instrumental timbres at these separate occurrences of the tetrachord (flute, then low strings) seem to support the respective symbolic associations of this intervallic construction.

The first literal clue to Melisande's primary symbolic role is suggested by Golaud's claim (p. 206) that the blood on his brow was produced by a "thorn hedge." In view of certain forthcoming events, this may perhaps be interpreted as a metaphor for the crown of thorns that Christ wore under the burden of the Cross. This speculation is based on the imminence of Mélisande's own symbolic "crucifixion." As Golaud's rage intensifies, he asks first for his sword, which Mélisande, trembling, finds on the prayer stool. She is reassured by Golaud, however, that she is not going to be killed. As Golaud becomes accusatorial, repeated statements of Mélisande's "Naïveté" motif (p. 208) are joined by rhythmic elements of the "Fate" motif in support of the increasingly direct dramatic force. But Arkel can see in Mélisande's eyes a great innocence only, to which Golaud responds sarcastically with yet other metaphors associated with the crucifixion (pp. 210–211): "They are greater than innocence!. They are purer than the eyes of a lamb. They could give God lessons in innocence! . . . One would think the angels of heaven were for ever celebrating a christening there."

As Golaud's sarcasm turns to vehemence, new forms of several basic motifs unfold in combinations and juxtapositions in anticipation of the violent climax of the scene. A strange variant of the "Mélisande" motif (p. 212, mm. 4–5) is now accompanied by the ascending form of the chromatic tetrachord, A♭–A–B♭–C♭, then B♭–B–C–C♯, the descending form originally used in counterpoint against the "Pelléas" motif both at his first appearance (p. 33) and at Golaud's jealousy (p. 174). This "Mélisande" variant and the "Pelleas" tetrachord together seem to reflect the meaning behind Golaud's jealousy and sarcastic question, "I have no hidden thoughts. . . . If I had, why shouldn't I express them?" This motivic combination leads to the triplet figure suggesting "Fate," its contour (D–F♯–G–F♯) outlining Mélisande's motif (p. 213, mm. 2–8), which is gradually expanded into the more angular figure (p. 214) of two alternating tritones (F♯–C/B♭–E) as Golaud seizes Mélisande by her hair. As he forces her down on her knees, a variant of her whole-tone "Hair" motif unfolds in his vocal line (p. 215, mm. 8–9), "Your long hair is useful for something at last." Then, his words and actions seem to symbolize the Cross as he drags Mélisande by her hair, "To the right, then to the left! To the left, and then to the right! Absalom! Absalom! Forward! Back!"[7] The triplet figuration begins to break up into a crosslike pattern (p. 216) in the viola and cello. This exclusively WT-0 figuration is reinforced by the augmented triplet figure in the clarinets and bassoons. The latter figure, in parallel major thirds (first occurrence, G♯–B♯/F♯–A♯), recalls the "Well" motif (see p. 57, m. 2, flutes) at its original suggestion of ultimate fate, that is, "as cool as winter." The symbolic association of the well with Mélisande's ultimate fate is further developed, now, by the violent imagery of her "Crucifixion." It is striking that the "Well" motif (whole-tone tetrachord) in the latter passage occurs, as in the "Well" scene, as part of the larger, complete WT-0 collection. Thus, the motivic and harmonic identification between these two passages contributes to the common symbolic meaning of these otherwise highly contrasting dramatic moments.

In correspondence with the dramatic symbolism, the pairs of major thirds above the jagged crosslike triplets (p. 216) suggest a fusion of the "Well" motif and a dyadic fragmentation of the whole-tone tetrachordal "Hair" motif, both motifs prominently associated with fate. This fusion seems to grow out of the descending segment of the strange "Mélisande" variant (see p. 212, m. 5). The scene closes (p. 218, m. 12) with a whole-tone variant of Golaud's "Vengeance" motif, played by the trombones and tubas as a timbral reflection of the violent mood,[8] above a partial statement (Ab–A–Bb–[ ]) of Pelléas's chromatic tetrachord, and then Arkel's words (p. 219), "If I were God, I should have pity on the hearts of men." But it is Mélisande who, as a Christ figure on her deathbed (p. 282), answers Golaud's plea, "Yes, I forgive you."

The symbol of Christ—life, death, and resurrection—was suggested earlier by Arkel's prophecy (p. 202) that Mélisande will be the one to open the door for a new era. Arkel seems to bear out this metaphor of resurrection more prominently at the end of the opera (pp. 309–310), where he declares that Mélisande's child must live on in her place. This metaphor is articulated by the closing instrumental passage in C# major (p. 310, m. 2 ff.; ex. 7-2), in which a series of suspensions in the descending parallel triads over reiterations of the tonic note (C#) lead to a dirgelike theme in the two flutes and muted trumpet (p. 310, m. 7). This theme is none other than Mélisande's motif in quasi stretto at two transpositional levels: the original one of the opera (in enharmonic spelling, G#–A#–C#) and its perfect-fourth transposition (C#–D#–F#). The trumpet, according to Wenk, symbolizes "peaceful death,"[9] which is entirely appropriate to the mood of this ending.

These tonal materials are crucial in fulfilling one of the main symbolic messages of the drama. The significance of these two motivic transpositions, in which the original form contains the C# tonic as its upper boundary note, the other the C# tonic as its lower boundary note, lies in the meaning of the original dissonant intrusion of the whole-tone "Fate" sphere into the pentatonic "Human" sphere of Mélisande at the opening of the opera (p. 1, mm. 14–15). At that point, the pentatonic form of her motif (Ab–Bb–C#) was expanded intervallically in the accompanying figuration (Ab–Bb–D–E) to the whole-tone "Fate" form by the alteration of one note, C# to D. This dissonance between the pentatonic C# and the whole-tone D represents the first simultaneous transformation from one pitch-set to the other. This musical event is a microscopic reflection (or telescoping) of the opening D pentatonic and closing C# major tonalities of the opera. The shift from D to C# is reflected locally in the final cadence of the suspensions on D (p. 310, m. 6), the latter then moving down one half-step to the C# transposition of the "Mélisande" motif in the trumpet. At the same time, the basic tritone (G#) of D, which hovers above this resolution in the tremolo figure, prepares for the basic G# transposition of Mélisande's motif in the flute. The original intrusion of "Fate" is thereby fulfilled in the final resolution of D to Mélisande's diatonic note, C#, in which her resurrection is symbolized in the new life of her daughter. But the destiny of that new life, hence Mélisande's own fate, comes into question now as Golaud's "Fate" cell, Db–F–G (in enharmonic spelling, C#–E#–Fx), is embedded in the cadential C#–major (or Lydian) figuration. This ominous echo of his

EXAMPLE 7-2. Act 5, p. 310, mm. 2–12, metaphor of resurrection as Mélisande gives birth before she dies, articulated by closing instrumental passage in C♯ major; suspensions in descending parallel triads over reiterations of tonic note (C♯) lead to dirge-like theme in the two flutes and muted trumpet (p. 310, m. 7)

"Fate" motif seems to suggest that the continuation of life and its events remain bound within the cycle of fate. In more practical terms, the woman, as represented by Mélisande and her daughter, cannot be free from the power structure as represented by Golaud.

Act 4, Scene 3: A Well in the Park: Symbol of the Sacrificial Lamb; Scene 4: Love Duet and the Death of Pelléas

Act 4, scene 3, which often was omitted from performance at the Opéra-Comique, functions simply as an episode both dramatically and musically. However, while the scene presents no new themes or recognizable recurrences, it is essential in elucidating the basic symbolic message. As Yniold attempts to move a heavy stone to retrieve his golden ball (p. 223), a variant of the "Fate" rhythm in the strings yields to an obsessive ostinato pattern, which emerges in correspondence with the distant sound of bleating sheep. This figuration continues as the plight of the sheep becomes increasingly evident. First Yniold hears "the sheep crying." He observes, then, that "The sun's gone in" and that "They're frightened of the dark." The shepherd's pelting of the sheep with stones to keep them on their path invokes the image of Christ—the sacrificial lamb—who was stoned as he was forced to Calvary under the burden of the Cross. In answer to Yniold's questions, the unseen shepherd suggests the slaughter of the sheep as he tells Yniold that they are not on their way to the stable. The *unseen* shepherd, who guides the sheep, may be equated with *invisible* fate, which guides all life and events. A deeper symbolic meaning in this event may also be gleaned from Maeterlinck's own words in "The Deeper Life," which can provide a clue to the ultimate symbolic message of Mélisande's death. Her fate is portended by the slaughter of the innocent sheep and Arkel has seen only a great innocence in her eyes (p. 210), but which Golaud sarcastically compares to the eyes of a lamb just before he crucifies her symbolically. According to Maeterlinck:

> Then it is no longer necessary that a great king should die for us to remember that "the world does not end at the house-doors," and not an evening passes but the smallest thing suffices to ennoble the soul.
>
> Yet it is not by telling yourself that God is great and that you move in His radiance, that you will be able to live in the beauty and fertile depths where the heroes dwelt. You may perhaps remind yourself, day and night, that the hands of all the invisible powers are waving over your head like a tent with countless folds, and yet shall the least gesture of these hands be imperceptible to you. . . . Beauty and grandeur are everywhere; for it needs but an unexpected incident to reveal them to us.[10]

The harmonic progression underlying the implied "Fate" rhythm provides another level of insight into this dramatic symbolization, and prepares us for the dramatic events of act 4, scene 4. The initial harmonic construction of the triplets (p. 225, mm. 11–12), above a sustained fifth (F–C), outlines the A-pentatonic collection (A–C–D–E–G). The latter is a permutation of the pentatonic collection of the "Forest" motif (C–D–E–G–A), which opened the opera. At that point, the pentatonic whole-step ostinato (D–C) of the bass was transformed by the linear motion to A♭ (p. 1, m. 5) to outline the first statement of Pelléas's WT-0 "Fate" cell (A♭–C–D). In the present scene (p. 225), the oscillating A pentatonic triplets contain an unobtrusive manifestation of Pelléas's pentatonic form (A–C–D), which analogously moves (p. 226, mm. 1 ff.) to the whole-tone form (A♭–C–D) within a larger five-note segment (A♭–B♭–C–D–E) of WT-0. It is significant that just as this is the last night of life for the sheep, act 4, scene 4 begins (p. 232) with Pelléas's realization that it is the last night for Mélisande and him. The same form of his WT-0 "Fate" cell, A♭–C–D (in enharmonic spelling, G♯–C–D), is also prominent here. Manifested as a held orchestral dyad C–D and vocal G♯, the cell coincides with "last night," which is followed directly by Pelléas's realization that he has been "playing like a child round a thing I did not suspect was there. I have been playing in a dream, round the snares of fate." This also suggests two other metaphorical associations with act 4, scene 3, one in which the child Yniold was playing around an immovable stone (inexorable fate), the second in which the unseen shepherd (symbol of invisible fate) was guiding his flock. It is at the end of act 4, scene 4 that Golaud will strike down Pelléas (p. 266), precisely at the site of that fatalistic symbol, the well.

The harmonic progression in the triplet figuration of scene 3 (p. 226, mm. 1 ff.) recalls that of the "Well" scene (see p. 55), thereby linking the latter with the opening of scene 4 and the inevitable move toward Pelléas's destruction at the edge of the well. The original transformation of the C dominant ninth chord of the "Well" motif into the WT-0 collection is expanded in act 4, scene 3 into a more complex set of diatonic/whole-tone interactions. As Yniold refers to the weeping of the sheep and to the end of the sunshine, the orchestra unfolds five notes of WT-0 (A♭–B♭–C–D–E) under a sustained G. This collection implies the presence of the C dominant ninth chord (C–E–G–B♭–D) as it was partitioned in the "Well" motif (i.e., with isolated fifth, G), plus A♭. The tension between the diatonic fifth (G) and the extra whole-tone element (A♭), the conflict representing the single difference between these two pitch-set spheres (diatonic and whole-tone), entails essential notes associated with the "Fate" motif transpositions of Golaud (G, or its tritone D♭) and Pelléas (A♭, or its tritone D), respectively.

Act 4, Scene 4: Structure and Proportion in the Service of Musico-Dramatic Development and Emotional Climax

The structural design of act 4, scene 4 is maximally geared toward local dramatic development and also to the establishment of the entire act as the primary culminating point for musico-dramatic development on the more global level of the opera. The Symbolist poets were particularly interested in the symbolism of numbers and numerical proportions both for the possibility of creating secret (even mystical) encodings and for the more concrete potential of controlling, shaping, and balancing the local as well as large-scale structure and design.[11] Roy Howat points out that the first work in which Debussy used the Golden Section (GS) proportions and symmetrical organization was *Pelléas et Mélisande*, the shape already suggested in the Maeterlinck play.[12] It is striking that Debussy used these proportions to heighten and establish the love duet (act 4, scene 4) as the climax of the opera. Scene 4

> accumulates its tension in a clear sequence of events. . . . Its main dramatic pivot, after Pelléas's and Mélisande's declaration of love, is the point of literally no return, as Pelléas and Mélisande, in the garden, hear the castle doors lock for the night (top line

of page 255 in the Durand vocal score, at the double-bar). This divides the scene's total of 1316 crotchet beats in exact G.S. of 813:503 (taking the scene's musical beginning as the 6/4 on p. 232 of the Durand vocal score)—as accurate as anything yet traced in this book. Pelléas's and Mélisande's declaration of love (p. 244 in the Durand vocal score) is placed over the exact halfway point of these first 813 beats.[13]

Act 4, scene 4 may be analyzed into three large parts, as articulated simultaneously by the musico-textual meaning as well as the GS and symmetrical formulas, the succession of contrasting events producing the final buildup of tension toward the end of the scene where Golaud falls on Pelléas with his sword during Pelléas's embrace with Mélisande. The first section (p. 232, m. 6–p. 244, m. 2), in which Pelléas is awakened for the first time to the existence of fate, is an expression of hopelessness as Pelléas realizes that his relationship with Mélisande is destined to come to an end this night. The second section (p. 244, m. 3–p. 255, m. 2), based on mutual confessions of love, is an expression of the most ecstatic, tender, and nostalgic feelings. The third section (p. 255, m. 3–end), in which the two lovers realize that they have just been locked out of the castle, comprehends extreme contrasts of mood between rapturous embrace and the fear of Golaud's vengeance. In this final section, tension increases dramatically in anticipation of Golaud's violent appearance and the inevitable move toward tragic doom, all of this invoking a striking parallel to the events leading to the "love-death" of Tristan and Isolde. The increase of passion to the moment of greatest intensity and the final declaration of love seem to be dependent on Pelléas's realization that he has arrived on the brink of his ultimate fate. Maeterlinck indirectly provides us with some insight into Pelléas's psychological condition:

> we must accustom ourselves to live like an angel who has just sprung to life, like a woman who loves, or a man on the point of death. If you knew that you were going to die to-night, or merely that you would have to go away and never return, would you, looking upon men and things for the last time, see them in the same light that you have hitherto seen them? Would you not love as you never yet have loved? Is it the virtue or evil of the appearances around you that would be magnified? . . . Would not everything, down to actual evil and suffering, be transformed into love, overflowing with gentlest tears?[14]

Various musical factors, in terms of both local content and the larger structure and design of this scene and the opera as a whole, deepen our understanding of these psychological (even philosophical) questions and issues invoked by Maeterlinck. At the opening of act 4, scene 4, Pelléas is introduced by the descending chromatic counterpoint, which has been associated with his motif, and by the held boundary interval (C–D) of the C dominant ninth chord (C–E–G–B♭–D). This basic WT-0 dyad (C–D) emerges, as it did in the very opening "Forest" motif, as a primary foreground event. Its direct contrapuntal combination with whole-tone dyad G♯–F♯ in the lower bass octaves and initial notes of Pelléas's vocal line produces a more immediate transformation of the C–D dyad into the whole-tone sphere than had occurred either at the first juxtaposition of the "Forest" and "Fate" motifs (p. 1, mm. 4–5), in the "Well" scene (p. 57), at Mélisande's cryptic suggestion that links Pelléas to fate (p. 86, m. 2), or in the triplets accompanying the bleating of the sheep that are being led to the slaughter by the unseen shepherd (p. 225, mm. 11–12 to p. 226). This passage at the opening of scene 4 of this act bears the most direct resemblance to the inversionally related whole-tone lines that were framed temporally by the dyad C–D (p. 142, mm. 10 ff.) in connection with the descent of Pelléas and Golaud into the dark vaults of the castle, where the stench of death arising from the stagnant water was premonitory of Pelléas's death. In musical terms, the WT-0 configuration at the opening of scene 4 (p. 232, mm. 9–11) implies the presence of a long-range symmetrical transformation of the C dominant ninth chord associated primarily with the "Well" motif—Pelléas will die at the well in this scene. If we split the fifth degree (G) of the C dominant ninth chord (C–E–G–B♭–D), which is in itself a symmetrical formation, into its upper and lower half-steps (G♯ and F♯) while retaining the C–D boundary, the present symmetrical WT-0 tetrachord (C–F♯–G♯–D) is produced. This is a symmetrical permutation of the very first chord of the original "Fate" motif (p. 1, m. 5), A♭–C–D–F♯ (in enharmonic spelling, G♯–C–D–F♯), in which the dyad C–D of the "Forest" motif was absorbed into the "Fate" motif as the axis of symmetry. Thus, the WT-0 configuration at the opening of act 4, scene 4, which unfolds toward Pelléas's death by the end of this scene, ties together many of the primary symbolic events at this crucial point in the drama by means of musical association and symbolization.

Pelléas's further realizations (p. 233) support these long-range symbolic connections. His reference to the snares of destiny all around him and the likening of himself to a blind man, "I shall run away shouting with joy and grief, like a blind man fleeing from his burning house," which symbolize the powers of the well, are represented musically by the encirclement of his basic motif (p. 233, mm. 4–5) by a complex of varied figures of referential significance (ex. 7-3). The twisting chromatic descents in the "Fate" triplets, which seem to reflect Pelléas's textual imagery of the surrounding snares of destiny, anticipate the chromatic counterpoint originally associated with the "Pelléas" motif (see p. 33, mm. 10–11, Flute II and Flute III). In answer to his question, "Who was it that woke me suddenly?" the two statements of his motif are each introduced by a rapid flourish of the complete WT-0 scale (B♭–C–D–E–F♯–G♯–A♯), which has been associated primarily with Pelléas's fate. But what is it exactly that has awakened him all at once? It is his love for Mélisande, the emotion that serves as the primary mover of fate, the emotion that Pelléas will soon confess to her. The second statement of his motif is then extended by the descending eighths and triplets to form a variant of Pelléas's C♯ Aeolian theme that had introduced the "Well" scene (see p. 55). The present thematic statement in scene 4 of this act transforms the original Aeolian descent into a hybrid mode in which the WT-0 scale (G♯–[A]–F♯–E–D–C–[B]) associated most often with both Pelléas and Mélisande is preeminent.

One may observe a still more significant parallel between this and the original "Well" scene. It was at their first meeting at the well that Pelléas's "Awakening Desire" motif (C–D–A♭–C–D) first emerged in the orchestra (p. 62, m. 3; see ex. 4-9). In act 4, scene 4, in which their final meeting is also at the well, the "Awakening Desire" motif reemerges in the horns and strings (p. 242, mm. 1–2), directly following two statements of the "Well" motif in the horns and harp. The close identification of the "Awakening Desire" motif, C–D–A♭–C–D (p. 242), with the whole-tone form of Pelléas's motif, C–D–A♭–D–A♭ (p. 86, m. 2), clarifies the meaning of Mélisande's assertion about something stronger than herself. At the "Awakening Desire" motif in the present scene, Pelléas asks Mélisande if she knows why he wanted to meet her

EXAMPLE 7-3. Act 4, scene 4, p. 233, mm. 1–4, powers of well as symbolized by figural encirclement of "Pelléas" motif; twisting chromatic descents in "Fate" triplets that reflect "snares of destiny" and anticipate chromatic counterpoint associated with "Pelléas" motif

here tonight. We soon find that it was to declare his love for her, and it is the emotion of love that was implied by Mélisande's reference to something stronger than herself, hence the connection between their love and their fate. Furthermore, Wenk's association of the horn (darkness, death) and harp (change) timbres seems to capture the mood of the text: this is the last time they shall ever meet and Pelléas must go away forever.

Several other motifs emerge in the passages that intervene between Pelléas's motif (p. 233, mm. 4–5) and the reemergence of the "Well" and "Awakening Desire" motifs (pp. 241–242). Pelléas's vocal fragments imply the presence of the pentatonic "Mélisande" cell, E–F♯–A (p. 233, mm. 7–8), as he urgently expresses to her his need to take flight at this late moment. He tells her that he has never gazed on her gaze (p. 235, mm. 1–2), as though it were a hundred years since he has seen her, and

Mélisande's cell (G♯–B♭–C♯) reemerges at its original pitch level, above which the motif itself unfolds at the tritone transposition, D–E–G–E–D. This combination of transpositions (G♯–B♭–C♯/D–E–G) contains the original dissonance between C♯ and D (see p. 1, mm. 14–15), where the whole-tone ("Fate") sphere had intruded into Mélisande's pentatonic set. At this point, however, the note D does not have whole-tone significance but, rather, simply echoes the original intrusion. This conflict is intensified by the cadential articulation of the motivic D by the C♯ dominant ninth chord with minor ninth (C♯–E♯–G♯–B–D). The conflict is to be resolved only later, after Mélisande's death, by the final, pure C♯–major harmony which, as mentioned earlier, replaces the opening D pentatonic tonality of the opera.

"Shadows" Motif

Pelléas asks Mélisande not to stay on the edge of the moonlight (p. 236, m. 6 ff.), and this is reflected by the emergence of the "Shadows" motif, E♭–D♭–E♭–G–E♭–D♭–E♭. The chordal roots that underlie the progression of tertian and supertertian sonorities (on D♭, B♯♯, D♭, E♭, D♭, B♯♯, D♭) imply the presence of a transposition (in enharmonic spelling, A–C♯–D♯) of Golaud's whole-tone "Fate" cell. The prominence of the dense horn timbres above the low cello tremolo portends the appearance of Golaud and the association to darkness, and death.[15] The whole-tone transformation of the "Mélisande" pentatonic motif in the uppermost horn line of the "Shadows" motif appears only in association with the idea of sheltering darkness and concealment. The whole-tone form of the "Mélisande" cell (D♭–E♭–G), which is bounded by the basic tritone of Golaud's WT-1 "Fate" cell (D♭–F–G), is somewhat concealed by the diatonic tertian harmonizations. What follows are polarized references to shade and light. Pelléas's reference to concealment from the moonlight by taking refuge within "the shadow of the lime-tree" recalls the analogous event in the original "Well" scene (p. 56), where the trees served as protection from the stifling heat of the sunlight. The significance of this parallel between these two scenes seems to lie primarily in the symbolism of their passion, that is, stifling heat and protection from being seen. At Pelléas's reference to the late hour (p. 238, m. 3), the dotted rhythm of the "Fate" motif emerges in correspondence with increasing passion.

In the second section of this scene (p. 244 ff.), the peaceful, ecstatic mood of mutual confessions of love contains barely a hint of the disruptive force that will emerge in the third section. The unaccompanied declarations of love (p. 244, mm. 3–4) together outline the C dominant ninth chord (C–E–G–B♭–D), which refers primarily to the WT-0 fatalistic sphere (C–E–[ ]–B♭–D) of the two lovers. The one note (fifth degree, G), which signals the WT-1 sphere of Golaud, is extended to a three-note WT-1 segment (A–G–F). This seems to symbolize the danger suggested by Pelléas's statement that he could hardly hear what Mélisande said, in other words, to indicate Mélisande's fear of being overheard. The symbolic implications of these pitch-set relations are developed at the following orchestral entry, where the figural contour of the four solo cellos (with sustained harmonies in the violins and violas) suggests a variant of the "Well" motif. Both text and harmonization reveal a striking parallel to the original meeting of the two lovers at the well (see p. 57, mm. 1–2). The parallel between Pelléas's words, "The ice has been broken with red-hot irons! You said that

EXAMPLE 7-4. Act 4, scene 4, p. 244, mm. 6–8 to p. 245, mm. 3–5, alternating C-dominant-ninth and its whole-tone transposition, with chordal roots (D and C of Pelléas) and fifth degrees (A and G of Golaud) in lowest two lines, A–G representing intrusion of WT-1 into WT-0 sphere; transposition of dominant-ninths by major third to F♯ and E, combining content of transpositions (on C, D, E, and F♯) that permits completion of WT-0 collection

in a voice that came from the ends of the earth!" and his words at their earlier meeting, "It's as cool as winter. This is an old abandoned well," is supported by the similar scalar pitch construction of his vocal phrases. The present passage outlines an impure variant, D–E–F♯–[ ]–B♭–[ ]–G♯ (i.e., within the complete vocal pitch content: D–E–[F]–F♯–[G]–G♯–B♭–[C]), of the earlier ascending five-note segment (D–E–F♯–G♯–A♯) of WT-0. The text in both cases implies coldness and a sense of distance in time and space, their passion thawing out that coldness.

While the passage in the earlier "Well" Scene (p. 57) alternated the primary C dominant ninth chord with an altered form of the G♯ dominant ninth chord, that is, transformed into WT-0 (G♯–B♯–[D–E]–F♯–A♯) by the splitting of its implied fifth degree (D♯ into D–E), the present passage (p. 244, m. 6 to p. 245, m. 3) alternates the C dominant ninth chord with its whole-step transposition (D–F♯–A–C–E). This harmonic progression (ex. 7-4), which alternates the chordal roots (D and C) and fifth degrees (A and G) in the lowest two lines—the latter dyad (A–G) represents an intrusion of the WT-1 collection into the otherwise exclusively WT-0 sphere—also recalls the very opening "Forest" motif, the scene in which Golaud was the first to enter. As Pelléas repeats his words (p. 245), "I hardly heard you. . . . You love me?" the two dominant ninths are transposed up by major third to F♯ and E, respectively. These transpositions mirror that in the "Well" scene (p. 57), in which the C dominant ninth chord was transposed down by major third to the altered (that is, whole-tone) form of the G♯ dominant ninth. As in that passage, the combined content of these transpositions, on C, D, E, and F♯ (see ex. 7-4) permits completion of the WT-0 collection. The new WT-1 dyad, C♯–B (second cello line from bottom), together with the first WT-1 dyad, A–G (same cello line), implies the presence of the larger WT-1 tetrachord, G–A–B–C♯. This tetrachord is bounded by the basic notes (G and its tritone, C♯) associated with Golaud's WT-1 "Fate" cell. As Mélisande responds to Pelléas's questions about her love, "Always. . . . Ever since I first saw you," it is the WT-1 dyad B–C♯ of the transposed chordal block (p. 245, mm. 1–3) rather than A–G–F of Pelléas's vocal line (p. 244, m. 5) or A–G of the first chordal block (p. 244, mm. 6–7) that intrudes into the otherwise exclusive WT-0 vocal line.

"Ecstasy" Motif

The mutual confessions of the two lovers invoke the "Ecstasy" motif (p. 245, m. 7, horn and divided violins), a diatonic construction which soon acquires a somewhat more whole-tone character (p. 250, m. 6, strings, horns, and woodwinds) in correspondence with the increasing passion expressed in the text, that is, in correspondence with the prime mover of their fate (ex. 7-5). The establishment of the new key signature (p. 245) seems to support Smith's interpretation that F♯ major is the "aspired-to" key that reflects some particular aspect of the "light-imagery."[16] He argues that the dominant preparations of this key are fulfilled only in this final love scene, in which the C♯ dominant ninth harmony resolves to F♯ major as the basis of the new motif. Pelléas's words seem to capture this imagery: "Your voice sounds as if it has passed over the seas in springtime! I have never heard it till now." Smith convincingly demonstrates that while the F♯ major tonality is prepared as early as act 1 by a stepwise tonal progression to F♯ major at certain focal points associated with "light,"

Debussy's placement of the unresolved C♯ dominant seventh chord in connection with Mélisande is primary in inducing a sense of longing for this key and "light":

> Since Mélisande is the agent through whom man may achieve "the light," it is logical that the agency of the dominant chord should at first be associated with her. Can it be fortuitous that the first occurrence of the chord of C♯, with a dominant seventh, is at the moment of Golaud's first attraction to Mélisande? ... Golaud has a glimpse of the light as he looks into Mélisande's eyes. ... The frustration of Golaud's unsuccessful attempt at physical contact with Mélisande is portrayed in F♯ minor [see pp. 20–21]. These two instances are the closest to the "light" that Golaud ever gets.[17]

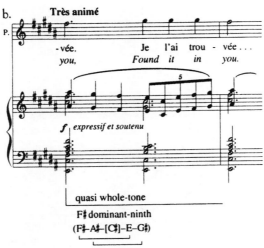

EXAMPLE 7-5. Act 4, scene 4, (a) p. 245, m. 7, horn and divided violins, diatonic form of "Ecstasy" motif; (b) p. 250, mm. 5–6, strings, horns, and woodwinds, more whole-tone character of "Ecstasy" motif, in correspondence with increasing passion of text

The change of key signature from six sharps to five in the second statement of the "Ecstasy" motif (p. 250, m. 5) lowers E♯ to E, which permits the melodic line to outline the F♯ dominant ninth chord (F♯–A♯–C♯–E–G♯). The ordering of the chordal pitch content gives priority to the WT-0 tetrachord (A♯–G♯–F♯–E/C♯), analogously to that of the C dominant ninth chord (E–D–C–B♭/G) of the "Well" motif (see p. 55, m. 10). This explicit surface (thematic) ordering of the dominant ninth construction in the "Ecstasy" motif suggests a musical connection between this motif and the original harmonic disposition of the dominant ninth chord at the "Well" motif, the symbolic connection between the two motifs being obvious in this scene: the height of their ecstasy is expressed, here, at the well during this final meeting. The intervening passages between the two occurrences of the "Ecstasy" motif support the tendency from diatonic to whole-tone as Pelléas's passion leads to increasingly explicit descriptions of Mélisande's beauty. In correspondence with Pelléas's increasing passion, his chromatic "Ardor" motif (p. 248, m. 2), that is, based on the descending chromatic thread (B–A♯–A–G♯), intrudes against a triplet figure that juxtaposes components (C♯–D♯ and C–E–F♯) of the two whole-tone collections, the linear combination producing a more chromatic octatonic segment (C–C♯–D♯–E–F♯).

Fusion of Light and Dark: Octatonic Fusion of Pentatonic and Whole-Tone

In terms of tonal symbolism, in which the note C is increasingly associated with "darkness," in opposition to the "light" key of F♯ major, the octatonic scale (C–C♯–D♯–E–F♯–G–A–A♯) represents a fusion (i.e., intensification) of the "light-dark" polarity, because it contains the basic harmonies (C–E–G and F♯–A♯–C♯) of both tritone-related keys equally.[18] The tritone symbolization of darkness is thus intensified by extending the three interlocking tritones of the whole-tone ("Fate") scale to the four contained in the more chromatically compressed octatonic scale. As part of the dramatic symbolism of this culminating scene, both the whole-tone "Fate" (F♯–G♯–B♯, in enharmonic spelling, F♯–G♯–C) and pentatonic (F♯–G♯–B) forms of the "Mélisande" cell are sustained alternately in the clarinets and oboe (p. 248, mm. 3–4) as part of the larger octatonic collection (D♯–E♯–F♯–G♯–A–B–B♯), the note A supplied by the last chord (m. 4) in the inverted form of the pentatonic cell (F♯–A–B). The pentatonic cell is also embedded in the larger pentatonic vocal line. Mélisande's expression of love (p. 244), which is heightened now by Pelléas's metaphorical description of her voice, "It is like pure water on my lips," is supported by this octatonic fusion and transformation of the pentatonic and whole-tone spheres. That is to say, the fusion of light and dark in this culminating scene of the opera may be identified symbolically with the intensification of the human-fate (pentatonic-whole-tone) polarity. With regard to the fusion of light and dark, Smith observes the following:[19]

> Although it was Act IV scene 4 . . . that Debussy composed first, it is in the final part of this act that the harmonic fields and keys are at their least stable. Before the hand of destiny is explicitly evident from the text, it is clear from the instability of Debussy's music that Pelléas and Mélisande's declaration of love is not the final *dénouement* of the opera. A later discussion of light and dark causes the rich chords previ-

ously associated with the shade of the *tilleuls* to deliquesce into half-diminished chords. . . . Mélisande, the "forewarned," remarks "Si, si, je suis heureuse, mais je suis triste . . . " (Yes, yes, I am happy, but I am sad . . .); and at once the noise of the closing of the castle gates is heard. Paradoxes and opposites abound in text and music from here onwards. . . . The darkness is now of a dual significance. Not only is it a haven for the declared love of the hopeless pair, but [soon] Golaud makes his presence felt. . . . What was the initial love-scene theme in F♯ major is now heard in the "dark" key of C major. (VS, p. 258)

The pervasive mood of darkness in act 5 is also reflected by the increased prominence of Phrygian and octatonic materials.[20] As Pelléas's apprehension is expressed from the outset of the love scene (act 4, scene 4), Mélisande's ambiguous pentatonic motif (D–E–G–E–D) is absorbed into the larger octatonic sphere, G♯–B♭–B–C♯–D–E–F–G (for instance, see p. 235, mm. 1–3, in which one note, A, in the vocal line is the only element that does not belong to this particular octatonic collection). At the opening of act 5 (p. 268), the "Mélisande" motif itself is transformed unambiguously into an octatonic segment, E–F–A♭–F–E–F–C♯–D (i.e., C♯–D–E–F–[ ]–A♭). The tension of the octatonic tritones is intensified, then, in the second motivic statement (p. 268, mm. 3–4) by the intrusion of two chromatic elements (C and A) in Violin II.

In the love scene (p. 248, m. 2), the last whole-tone triplet figure, C–D–E, which further chromaticizes the octatonic segment (C–C♯–[D]–D♯–E–F♯), is itself extended linearly to a five-note segment (C–D–E–F♯–G♯–[ ]–B♯) of WT-0. At the same time, the first sixteenth-note figure (E♯–D♯) extends the preceding WT-1 dyad (C♯–D♯) of the triplets to three notes (C♯–D♯–E♯) of WT-1. These whole-tone interactions not only form the basis of the figuration surrounding the "Ardor" motif but also intensify the motif's chromaticism (C–B–A♯–A–G♯) by extending it to the larger chromatic collection of eleven pitch classes (G♯–[ ]–F♯–E♯–E–D♯–D–C♯–C/C–B–A♯–A–G♯). Thus, the progression from the mood of light to that of darkness and fate by means of increasing passion underlies these pitch-set associations.

Strikingly, the one missing element from the larger chromatic collection is the note G, which has been prominently associated with Golaud. This pitch-class enters into the passage as part of the held chord, G–A–C♯ (p. 248, m. 5). This subtle intrusion of Golaud's WT-1 "Fate" cell, which is bounded by his basic tritone (G–C♯), once again portends his appearance, this time the fatal one for Pelléas and Mélisande. The cell alternates with its diatonic ("Mélisande") form, G–A–C, which is also embedded in Pelléas's "white-key" pentatonic vocal line as he describes her voice as purest water that falls on his hands. The symbolic significance of these interactions between whole-tone and pentatonic sets is all the more evident if we consider that the pentatonic vocal content (E–G–A–C–D) is identical to that of the "Forest" motif at the very opening of the opera, which had set the mood for Golaud's first appearance. This symbolic association is supported by the ensuing sixteenth-note figurations (p. 249, mm. 5–6 especially), in which Golaud's WT-1 dyad (G–A) emerges prominently as part of the same pentatonic context that is now closer in contour to the opening four measures of the opera. While both pentatonic/diatonic passages are cadenced similarly by WT-0 cells (A♭–C–D–F♯, p. 1, m. 5, and C–E–F♯ in the bass line, p. 249, m. 6), the present passage replaces the linear "Forest" motif with the "Mélisande" form (D–E–G). Its upper note (G) and cadential note (A), which is the "odd" element within the final WT-0 chord (C–E–F♯–[A]), draws Mélisande closer to the sphere of Golaud (G–A dyad and WT-1), as Pelléas's praise of Mélisande's beauty reaches its culmination. This symbolism is further established by the following transformation of Mélisande's pentatonic motif into the WT-1 form, F–G–B (p. 250, m. 1 ff.), where it is accompanied by, as well as linearly interlocked with, the inversion (G–B–C♯) of Golaud's basic WT-1 "Fate" cell (G–A–C♯). The entire phrase is based exclusively on five notes of WT-1 (F–G–A–B–C♯).

The initial intrusion of the WT-1 "Fate" cell, G–A–C♯ (p. 248, m. 5), follows the two slurred chords, WT-0 (F♯–G♯–B♯) and pentatonic (F♯–A–B), which together form another octatonic segment (B♯–B–A–G♯–F♯). This time it is Golaud's WT-1 "Fate" cell (G–A–C♯) that fills in and seals off the latter chromatically (C♯–B♯–B–[ ]–A–G♯–G–F♯). Chromatic intensification also occurs in Pelléas's vocal line, in this case by means of "black-key/white-key" pentatonic complementation. The general tendency from chromatic to whole-tone material during this impassioned section is completed by the final transformation from pentatonic to whole-tone material in the sixteenth-note figurations. The WT-1 transformation of the original "Mélisande" pentatonic motif (p. 250, m. 1 ff., winds), which is supported by the WT-1 figuration (strings), is a focal point in this interval-expansion process. At the return to pentatonic/diatonic material just before the second occurrence of the "Ecstasy" motif, Golaud's WT-1 dyad (G–A) emerges prominently in the upper line of both the figuration and the dotted rhythm of the "Fate" motif. The priority of WT-0 is momentarily reestablished in the first four notes (A♯–G♯–F♯–E) of the "Ecstasy" motif (p. 250, m. 5) (see ex. 7-5b earlier) Thus, three primary motifs—"Ardor," "Mélisande," and "Fate"—emerge at the culmination of the interval-expansion process in correspondence with the buildup of passion in this love duet.

Golaud's Vengeance and the Fulfillment of Fate

The change of mood and sense of doom (p. 251, m. 3 ff.), which is invoked by the text (Pelléas cannot hear Mélisande breathe anymore and asks her why she looks at him so sadly), anticipates the final section of act 4, scene 4 and the dramatic fulfillment of their destiny. Pelléas's adulation of Mélisande's loveliness, which is accompanied by the more whole-tone form of the "Ecstasy" motif, is closed off by a diminuendo and final more expressive whole-tone statement of the "Mélisande" motif (C–D–F♯), which is now part of its larger WT-0 sphere. The entire harmonic content at this point forms the original "French augmented sixth" chord, C–D–F♯–G♯ (see p. 1, m. 5), which implies the presence of Pelléas's basic WT-0 "Fate" cell, A♭–C–D (see the opening bass line of the opera) and its tritone transposition (D–F♯–G♯). The basic tritone boundary (D–G♯), which emerges as an unaccompanied foreground event at Pelléas's question, "Where are you?" foreshadows the occurrence of this basic tritone as the intervallic frame of the "Vengeance" motif at Pelléas's death by Golaud's sword (p. 267, m. 8 ff.). As Pelléas falls at the edge of the well (p. 266, m. 11 ff.), the "Fate" motif is declaimed by four horns (Wenk: "Golaud, darkness, and death") in unison over a string tremolo, which is prominently based on G♯ as part of the larger harmonic content. As Mélisande takes flight through the woods, the latter, G♯–B–C, expands to Golaud's "Vengeance" motif, A♭–C–E–D (p. 267, mm. 8–9), which implies the presence of Pelléas's original "Fate" cell, A♭–C–D. The cadential note (*sforzando* D) of the motif is held against the tremolo octaves (G♭–G♭ and A♭–A♭), all three notes together forming the tritone transposition (in enharmonic spelling, D–F♯–G♯) of Pelléas's WT-0 "Fate" cell.

Mélisande's final vocal statement (p. 267, mm. 2–9), a chromatic descent (F♯–F–E–D♯–D–C♯–C–B–B♭–A–A♭) that ends on A♭, recalls the descending chromatic tetrachord (D–C♯–C–B) that has been associated consistently with the "Pelléas" motif. The descending tetrachordal construction had emerged prominently in connection with Golaud's jealousy and his imminent threat to the two lovers (e.g., p. 174). The latter association of the chromatic tetrachord reveals its broader symbolic meaning, in which Golaud's jealousy and ultimately his vengeance are inextricably connected to Pelléas's passion. The following two statements of the "Vengeance" motif each end with exclusive foreground harmonic occurrences of Pelléas's original WT-0 "Fate" cell, A♭–C–D (tremolo A♭ and motivic cadential notes D–C at p. 267, mm. 13 and 15).

The latter cell had initiated the earlier change of mood (p. 251, m. 3) as part of the larger French sixth collection, C–D–F♯–G♯, which, in turn, could be traced back to the very first statement of the WT-0 "Fate" motif (see ex. 4-1b earlier). As Pelléas tells Mélisande (p. 251, m. 4 ff.) that he cannot hear her breathe anymore, his "Fate" cell (D–F♯–G♯) is found embedded in the larger vocal contour of her phrase, "that's because I am looking at you," and in the single chord (B–D–F♯–G♯) of this excerpt. In the ensuing dialogue (p. 252 ff.), the polarity between darkness (the shadows) and light explicitly symbolizes the dual emotions of happiness and sadness in this section, as reflected by the return of the "Shadows" motif (p. 252, mm. 1–2).

As an increasing sense of doom is expressed by Pelléas's awareness (p. 253, m. 1) that there is so little time left to the two lovers, Golaud's basic WT-1 dyad (A–G) intrudes once again into the WT-0 sphere—the first three vocal segments, F♯–E–D–C–[G], E–F♯, and F♯–[A]–C (to the first beat of p. 253, m. 3) are otherwise based exclusively on WT-0. The orchestra prominently unfolds imitative statements that join the WT-1 dyad (A–G) with a WT-0 tetrachord (F♯–E–D–C). The WT-1 sphere is then extended and interlocked with WT-0 (p. 253, mm. 3–4) in both voice and orchestra as the lovers seek safety in the darkness. These whole-tone interactions culminate (p. 255, mm. 1–2) in a more chromatically compressed (octatonic) form of the "Mélisande" motif (G–A♭–C♭). This is a significant adumbration of Mélisande's "Dolorous" theme (E–F–A♭), which begins act 5 (p. 268), and Mélisande's deathbed scene. This sadder, more expressive transformation of her motif serves as point of departure for the climactic buildup of violence in the final section of the present scene (p. 255, m. 3 ff.). As Mélisande confides in Pelléas that she is happy but sad too, this form of her motif (G–A♭–C♭) is fused with the WT-1 form (F–G–C♭) of her "Fate" cell, the inversion (F–A–B) prominently initiating the final section (p. 255, m. 3). Both whole-tone forms of the cell (F–G–B and F–A–B) were simultaneously implied in her vocal line (p. 253, mm. 3–4) at the first extension (F–G–A–B) of WT-1: "I'm closer to you in the darkness."

Startled by the sound of the closing doors (p. 255, mm. 3–5), Pelléas's terse vocal statements alternate with two orchestral statements of a surging figure based on the progression from the WT-1 "Fate" cell, F–A–B, to its inverted major-third transposition, A–B–D♯, the two forms together forming the larger WT-1 "French-sixth" symmetry, F–A–B–D♯. A harsh, ominous rumbling follows in the low strings to begin a variant of the "Fate" rhythm, which leads (crescendo) to Golaud's motif (p. 256, mm. 4–5), at Pelléas's realization that the big chains have fallen (ex. 7-6). Golaud's motif is comprised primarily of the WT-0 "Fate"-cell of Pelléas (F♯–D–F♯–[A]–G♯) with neighbor note (A) in the upper instrumental line, which unfolds above the pentatonic form of the "Pelléas" motif (E–C♯–E–[G]–F♯) with neighbor note (G) in the bass line. It is striking that the two neighbor notes (G and A) again reflect the threatening intrusion of Golaud. The ensuing "Fate" rhythm (p. 256, m. 6 ff.) is initiated by the E dominant ninth chord (E–G♯–B–D–F♯), the WT-0 structure (D–E–F♯–G♯) within it implying the presence of the inversionally related "Pelléas" (D–F♯–G♯) and "Mélisande" (D–E–G♯) "Fate" cells bounded by the primary WT-0 tritone (D–G♯). At the second crescendo (p. 256, mm. 8–9), the reiterated chord (A–C–D♯–G, above the E pedal) of the "Fate" rhythm moves to Golaud's basic WT-1 dyad (A–G) as the registral boundary of the initial chord (G–D–F–A) of the ascending harmonic sequence (p. 256, m. 10 ff.). In correspondence with Pelléas's exclamation that it is too late, this boundary dyad (G–A) also initiates linear WT-1 tetrachordal outlines on the quarter beats in the uppermost (A–B–C♯–D♯) and lowermost (G–A–B–C♯) instrumental parts. The weak neighboring eighths correspondingly outline two WT-0 tetrachords (uppermost line, C–D–E–F♯, and lowermost line, B♭–C–D–E), respectively.

At the end of this harmonic sequence, which is based primarily on the WT-1 sphere of Golaud, Mélisande's cry that it is "All the better!" is accompanied by a pentatonic transformation of Golaud's motif (F–D–F–A–G) in the horns and cellos, the cadential neighbor motion again based on Golaud's primary WT-1 dyad (G–A). The association between these motivic statements and Mélisande's exclamations points to one of the key symbolic issues of the opera. The woman's apparent wish to be free from her matrimonial bond is expressed by her exclamations of relief in response to the closing of the gate, her conflicting needs being resolved by submission to fate. Emotional freedom by means of this power beyond human control is expressed more explicitly by Pelléas, "Things no longer depend on our wish! All is lost, all is saved!" The fulfillment of their love inevitably at the cost of their lives suggests the "love-death" symbolism of Wagner's *Tristan und Isolde*. It is significant that this passionate love duet of Pelléas and Mélisande serves a similar dramatic function in Debussy's opera as the love duet in the Wagner music drama. In both works, love is fulfilled only in death.

The succession of several highly individualized motifs in the remainder of the scene contributes to the increasing contrast of moods, the interaction drawing the music toward its tragic conclusion. As the lovers embrace and Pelléas describes the throbbing of his heart (p. 258, m. 12), an exotic interaction of shifting tonalities introduces the "Rapture" motif, which may be interpreted as a variant of the "Ecstasy" motif. Golaud's WT-1 dyad (A–G) initiates the larger diatonic motif, the significance indicated by Mélisande's apprehension of someone lurking behind them. Under her vocal statement, the basses, trombones (Wenk: "violent death"), and timpani (Wenk: "impending disaster, death, darkness") present a quiet statement of the "Vengeance" motif (p. 259, m. 1), which is outlined by the basic WT-0 cell of Pelléas (C-A♭–C–

EXAMPLE 7-6. Act 4, scene 4, p. 256, mm. 4–12, Golaud's motif, based on WT-0 "Fate"-cell of Pelléas (F♯–D–F♯–[A]–G♯) and neighbor-note A in upper violin I, above pentatonic form of "Pelléas" motif (E–C♯–E–[G]–F♯) and neighbor-note G in contrabass, neighbor-notes G and A reflecting threat of Golaud; at p. 256, m. 8, new chord (A–C–D♯–G) in "Fate" rhythm and initial chord of ascending harmonic sequence (p. 256, m. 10ff.) bounded by Golaud's WT-1 dyad (A–G)

[E♭]–D) and harmonized by its lower whole-step transposition (G♭–B♭–C) in anticipation of Pelléas's fate at the hands of Golaud. As Mélisande insists that she has
heard a noise, the motif is repeated. While Pelléas believes he hears only Mélisande's
heartbeat in the darkness, the orchestra confirms Mélisande's fears by unfolding the
original WT-1 augmented triad (C♯–A–F) of Golaud's vocal line at his very first entry
into the forest while hunting (see p. 3). At Mélisande's third, most emphatic assertion
(p. 259, mm. 7–10) that she "heard the dead leaves rustle," Golaud's "Vengeance"
motif is drawn entirely into his WT-1 sphere. The upper line unfolds a transposition
of his "Fate" cell (B–D♯–F), with added whole-tone appoggiatura (D♯–B–D♯–[G]–
F) above the basic transposition of the cell (G–B–[D♯]–C♯). Another transposition
(F–A–B) in the bass complements these parallel motivic forms to produce the complete WT-1 collection.

The sense of mood contrast, which is heightened by new statements of the "Rapture" motif (p. 260, violins, pianissimo), propels the music toward the peak of dramatic
intensity. The text itself suggests a mixture of extreme moods. Mélisande's preoccupation with the length of their shadows and Pelléas's more romantic reflections on how
they intertwine all the way to where the flower garden ends and how they are kissing
far off, are colored by the darkness of the shadows. The sinister implications of these
observations are immediately confirmed as Mélisande sights Golaud hiding behind a
tree at the end of their shadows. The descending motivic figure (p. 261, mm. 1–2),
which is initiated by Golaud's basic WT-1 dyad (A–G), fuses a variant of Golaud's
earlier "Love" motif (see p. 7, mm. 1–2) with the "Rapture" motif, these new statements are, like the previous ones, also initiated by Golaud's WT-1 dyad (A–G). This
hybridized figure is interrupted by a pianissimo statement of the "Vengeance" motif,
which is again outlined by the basic Pelléas "Fate" cell (A♭–C–[E♭]–D), this time just
before Mélisande sees Golaud.

At Pelléas's startled interjections, the dotted rhythm of "Fate" appears above a
chromatic bass figure in alternation with the "Vengeance" motif. As Pelléas is frozen
by the sight of Golaud with sword in hand and by his fear that Golaud had seen them
kiss (p. 262), the chromatic figuration recalls the chromatic tetrachord associated
with Golaud's jealousy, which was provoked when Yniold had told him of the kiss
between Pelléas and Mélisande. This figuration is transformed, now, into an exclusively WT-1 form (p. 262, mm. 5–8). Continual alternations of these chromatic and
whole-tone forms are joined (p. 263) by more insistent manifestations of the dotted
rhythm as Pelléas urges Mélisande to take flight while he holds Golaud at bay. Henceforth, as Pelléas's doom approaches, most of the figurations of this scene interact
with greater rapidity. But Mélisande insists on remaining with him, and their final des-
perate embrace serves as a prelude to Pelléas's death. The "Rapture" motif (p. 265,
mm. 5–6) leads, in crescendo to fortissimo, to the last statements of the "Ecstasy"
motif (p. 266, mm. 5–10), as they give wholly to each other once more. Pelléas's "Fate
cell (A♭–C–D), which articulates the motif by harmonizing the basic A♭ (p. 266, mm.
5, 7, and 10), prepares for the prominent G♯ in the tremolo figure as Pelléas is struck
down. This cell also prepares for the final statements of the "Vengeance" motif, which
is based on the complete form of the cell (A♭–C–D) as Golaud pursues Mélisande
through the woods.

Several earlier events may be identified, by means of a common tonal emphasis, as symbolic adumbrations of Golaud's deadly attack on Pelléas. The note G♯ (or A♭) has been associated with the basic pitch level of Pelléas's whole-tone "Fate" cell, A♭–C–D (p. 86, see ex. 4-2b earlier), which served originally as the pivotal element from the "Forest" to "Fate" motif (p. 1, mm. 1–5), and that of Mélisande's basic motif, A♭–B♭–C♯ (p. 1, mm. 14–15). It was soon established (in act 1, scene 3, pp. 44–45, mm. 4–5) by the G♯ minor chords and A♭–D tremolo (one of the many string techniques used by Debussy "to set off individual moments in the drama without establishing consistent symbolic references"[21]) at the first allusion to the gloomy darkness of the sea over which the storm was brewing. The A♭ of this tritone tremolo was the goal of the descending whole-tone bass progression, F♯–E–D–C–B♭–A♭, the scale generally identified as a primary symbol of "Fate." It is no coincidence that the "symbolic tempest" of that scene is manifested in the same tonality (string tremolo on G♯–B) at the point where Golaud strikes down Pelléas (pp. 266–267).[22] The tremolo now precedes the "Vengeance" motif, which is outlined by Pelléas's "Fate" cell (A♭–C–[ ]–D).

8

Pelléas et Mélisande

Circuity of Fate and Resolution of Mélisande's Dissonant Pentatonic – Whole-Tone Conflict

Act 5: A Room in the Castle: Mélisande's Forgiveness of Golaud and Her Death

For the increasing sense of darkness and death, which has been developing throughout the opera, it is significant that Debussy varies and intensifies the basic motivic materials of the preceding acts rather than bringing in new ideas at this culminating point, act 5. This musical technique supports the long-range unfolding of Maeterlinck's symbolic structure.[1] Maeterlinck's general contention is "that Time is a mystery which we have arbitrarily divided into a Past and a Future, in order to try to understand something of it,"[2] but that while on some level of human consciousness man knows the Future, he "cannot make use of its knowledge."[3] However, even though this knowledge resides in the unconscious, Maeterlinck does seem to believe that man ultimately has some control over his destiny. This notion has significant implications regarding the psychology and motivation of his characters—for instance, Mélisande, whose emotions (and perhaps her subliminal knowledge of the Future) lead her and Pelléas toward destruction. The following assertion by Maeterlinck thus supports my stated premise that there is a definite equation between Fate and unconscious motivation:

> One would say that man had always the feeling that a mere infirmity of his mind separates him from the Future. He knows it to be there, living, actual, perfect, behind a kind of wall around which he has never ceased to turn since the first days of his coming on this earth. Or rather, he feels it within himself and known to a part of himself: only, that importunate and disquieting knowledge is unable to travel, through the too narrow channels of his senses, to his consciousness, which is the only place where knowledge acquires a name, a useful strength and, so to speak, the freedom of the human city. It is only by glimmers, by casual and passing infiltrations that future years of which he is full, of which the imperious realities surround him on every hand, penetrate to his brain. . . . At all times, man has tried to . . . pierce the partitions that separate his reason, which scarcely knows anything, from his instinct, which knows all, but cannot make use of its knowledge.[4]

In addition to the exclusive recall of musical material from previous acts, act 5 nevertheless evokes some new questions, which are left unanswered and open for speculation. This act, in one continuous scene, serves several musico-dramatic functions. First, it rounds out the overall arch shape of the opera as the quiet mood returns after the climactic buildup of passion, rage, and vengeance. Second, it ties together and further explores some of the basic symbolic issues of the first four acts.[5] This act itself may be analyzed into a kind of ternary dramatic arch form, the dialogue of the central section (p. 281, m. 7–p. 293, m. 3) echoing the love of Pelléas and Mélisande and revealing the jealousy and frustration that still lurks in Golaud's prodding questions to Mélisande. The beginning of this section contains a recapitulation of the opening "Forest" motif (p. 279, mm. 7–8), but now on C♯ rather than D, as Mélisande, surprised to see how Golaud has aged, harks back to the first time they had met. The orchestration, too, is modified, the bassoon maintaining some of the original brooding quality of the low strings and bassoon, the doubling by the oboe adding a certain plaintive quality as a degree of nostalgia is expressed in Mélisande's reminiscence.[6] This recapitulation contributes to a rounding out of the opera's overall structure. In connection with this background-level structural reference, the long-range replacement of D by C♯ recalls the first significant "dissonance" of the opera (p. 1, mm. 14–15), where the whole-tone "Fate" cell, A♭–B♭–D (as part of the larger French-sixth chord, A♭–B♭–D–E), intruded against the pentatonic "Mélisande" motif, A♭–B♭–C♯, to produce a clash between C♯ and D.[7]

In the first part of the ternary arch-form of this act, we find Mélisande on her deathbed, surrounded by the grieving figures of Arkel, Golaud, and the physician. The act opens (p. 268) with the succession and juxtaposition of several expressive motifs (ex. 8-1): the "Dolorous" form of the "Mélisande" motif in the violas with harp accompaniment (E–F–A♭–F–E–F–C♯–D), which recalls the earlier plaintive variant sounded by the oboe expressing Mélisande's weeping as Golaud questioned her (see p. 82, mm. 1–2); the "Pity" motif in the two flutes (p. 268, mm. 5–8), which seems to be derived from Golaud's earlier "Love" motif (see p. 7, mm. 1–2); and a gentle variant of the "Fate" motif, which is initially hinted at by the subtly darkened timbre of the muted horns (p. 268, m. 14 ff.) in counterpoint with an intervallically expanded form of the "Dolorous Mélisande" motif in the cellos (A–B♭–D–B♭–A–B♭–F♯–G), as Mélisande lies wounded on the bed in one corner of the room. The physician's words at this point imply that something more powerful than Golaud—perhaps Pelléas's death and Mélisande's attachment to him—is responsible for her own demise: "She's not going to die from such a little wound. . . . So it isn't you that killed her, my lord." Realistically, however, one must ask how it could not have been Golaud who has caused Mélisande's fatal injury. The physician's suggestion of some more mysterious force invokes a larger issue related to gender. The blame would seem, somehow, to be shifted from the man's responsibility to the woman's, some unseen violent action by the man being downplayed within the context of the Maeterlinck play.

The true cause of Mélisande's death may perhaps be attributed to unconscious psychological forces related to trauma rather than the supposedly "insignificant" physical wound inflicted by Golaud. This interpretation regarding the cause of Mélisande's demise is supported by the construction of the orchestral motifs. Arkel's prophetic insight (p. 269, m. 8) that the omen is not a good one is introduced (p. 269,

EXAMPLE 8-1. Act 5, p. 268, mm. 1–16, succession and juxtaposition of expressive motifs: "Dolorous" form of "Mélisande" motif in violas with harp accompaniment; "Pity" motif in two flutes (mm. 5–8); and gentle variant of "Fate" motif in muted horns (m. 14ff.)

m. 6) by the return of the opening form of the "Dolorous Mélisande" motif (in enharmonic spelling, E–F–G♯–F–E–F–C♯–D) in counterpoint with the gentle "Fate" variant. In the three statements of the "Dolorous" motif that have unfolded thus far (E–F–A♭, A–B♭–D, and E–F–G♯), the upper boundary note is either A♭ (= G♯) or D. This tritone provides a subtle hint that the essence of Pelléas (and his WT-0 cell, A♭–C–D), whose presence is still felt after the tragic ending of the preceding act, underlies Mélisande's mood and is obviously the direct human source affecting it. The third occurrence of the "Dolorous" motif (p. 269, m. 6) is reinforced in the bass by another variant (G♯–B–D), in which both notes of the tritone (G♯–D) now form the boundary interval. Arkel's prophetic words of doom are then articulated by a crescendo figure (p. 270) built from the B♭ dominant-ninth chord (B♭–D–F–A♭–C), which absorbs the D–A♭ tritone into a larger segment (A♭–B♭–C–D) of the WT-0 sphere.

Arkel's reference to the eternal coldness of Mélisande's soul (p. 270, mm. 3–4), which evokes an association to the coldness of the well (see p. 57), is punctuated (p. 270, m. 5) by the first prominent statement of the "Fate" motif in this act. The chromatic bass line (G–G♯–A–G♯) in the cello counterpoint under this statement is based on a symmetrical encirclement of Pelléas's G♯ by Golaud's G–A dyad, which may perhaps elicit some symbolic association to Golaud's statement of remorse that he has "killed for no reason." This shift of focus to Golaud suggests the beginning of a transition to the middle section of the act.

In the presence of Arkel and the physician, Golaud's jealousy begins to resurface (p. 271), "They kissed like little children." While his rationalization momentarily serves as defense against his most painful feelings, his statement also portends his actual mood and intentions, which surface in the central section of the act. We may glean several meanings from his statement: denial, then jealousy, and finally his need for absolution from guilt for having killed Pelléas and mortally wounding Mélisande. Golaud's probing questions, intended to elicit Mélisande's reassurance, are explicit from the opening of the central section (p. 281): "Mélisande, are you sorry for me as I am for you? Mélisande, do you forgive me, Mélisande?" The emotional intensity of his questioning is heightened by the upward whole-tone/diatonic progression (A–B–C♯–D♯/E), which seems to contradict the whispery quality of its actual setting in unaccompanied recitative style. The whole-tone intervallic construction produces a sense of expansion as it follows the more chromatic intervals of Mélisande's "Dolorous" motif, E♯–F♯–A–F♯–E♯ (p. 281, mm. 5–6, bassoon, violin, and cello), her motif already appearing in contrapuntal conflict with the whole-tone harmony.

Mélisande's reassurance comes with her words of forgiveness, underlined by her more peaceful pentatonic "Gentleness" motif, D♯–C♯–A♯–F♯–G♯. But this is not the reassurance that Golaud is seeking from her. His quiet statements of admission of wrongdoing are gradually transformed into a surgent expression of anxiety and jealous demanding (see p. 286), that Mélisande "must speak the truth to someone who is going to die." His own statement seems deceptive because, in this operatic version of the play, it is only Mélisande who dies. From the dialogue between the servants in the last act of the original spoken play, we learn that Golaud committed suicide after killing Pelléas and wounding Mélisande. Given that act 5 of the opera version is based only on the second scene of the play's last act, we have only Golaud's suggestion about, rather than the realization of, his death. Whether his statements in the opera libretto are deceitful or really true, the elimination of the suicide act permits a greater focus on Mélisande's death, which becomes one of the primary symbolic manifestations of ultimate fate in the opera. In any case, we may discern a deeper meaning in his assertion that without knowing the truth, he would never be able to "rest in peace." Any implication that Golaud dies in the opera is left ambiguous. The main issue is that Golaud's relentless effort to extract the truth from Mélisande reveals his need to find some justification for having committed murder, in other words to achieve some sense of absolution of guilt.

His initial words that express his urgent need to know (p. 286, mm. 2–8) are supported by a progression of alternating complete and incomplete dominant ninth chords: F♯–A♯–C♯–E–G♯, [ ]–G♯–B–D–F♯, D–F♯–A–C–E, [ ]–E–G–B♭–D, and so on. This basic harmonic construction, which pervades the opera, has been associated with the fatalistic realm ever since its transformation into the whole-tone collection in connection with the well and the meeting of Pelléas and Mélisande. It is in the present passage (p. 286) that Golaud faces his last chance to learn the truth from Mélisande about their love. These *fortissimo* dominant ninth chords, unlike those in the "Well" scene (p. 57, mm. 1–4; see ex. 5-1 earlier), now remain untransformed, leaving the whole-tone realm unrealized, although imminent in both the construction of the dominant ninth chord and in the voice-leading of the first four chords built on F♯, [E], D, and [C]). Correspondingly, Golaud's question will remain unanswered on this issue of Mélisande's emotional attachment to Pelléas, which has led to the death of the two lovers. It is almost as though an affirmative answer from Mélisande would, in Golaud's mind, have justified his vengeful action. In any case, Mélisande's death is an indictment against the social power structure, as symbolized by Golaud. It signifies the irreconcilable conflict between the woman as real-life feeling being and her ultimate fate, which is fulfilled because of her inability to repress her emotions, such repression permitting her to adhere to the conditions set down for her by the omnipotent controlling prince. The sense of power inequality in the opera becomes, in the final analysis, a dramatic premise by dint of—if nothing else—simply implementing the "Impressionist-Symbolist" technique of vague assertion. That is to say, there is never a hint that Mélisande actively consents to a proposal of marriage by Golaud. Such an event or statement is noticeably missing. It seems, then, that marriage is a *fait accompli* simply by some sense that Golaud seems to have wished it so. The only assertive action in this connection is made by Golaud, however vaguely, when he approaches Mélisande at their initial encounter, and subsequently in his letter sent home to Pelléas.

The third (and final) section of this act (p. 293 ff.) begins with Golaud's request that Arkel and the physician reenter the room after his unsuccessful attempt to extract the truth from Mélisande about her love for Pelléas, "It's useless . . . she's already too far gone. . . . I shall never know! I shall die here in blindness." His realization that he is fated to die as a "blind" man, which brings to mind the old well that can no longer heal the blind, is accompanied (p. 293, mm. 9–10) by a sequential pair of chords that alternate two segments (A♭–D–F♯–B♭ and E♭–A–D♭–F) from the two complementary whole-tone collections, the intervallic set associated with "Fate" (ex. 8-2). The descending linear configuration of each pair suggests a transformation of the "Well" motif, the original short-long rhythm replaced now by a more placid, even rhythm as Mélisande moves toward death.

Mélisande's decline is symbolized by her question (pp. 294–295), "Is it true that winter is starting?" and Arkel's query about why she has asked that question. Their statements are accompanied by an emotionally touching phrase in the solo violin, cello, and two clarinets. A still more profound symbolism emerges in both text and orchestra in connection with the coldness of winter and the setting of the sun over the

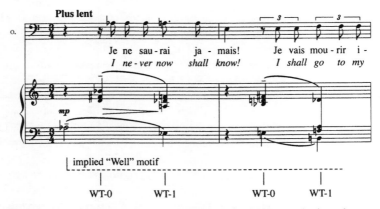

EXAMPLE 8-2. Act 5, p. 293, mm. 9–10, sequential pair of chords that alternate two segments (Ab–D–F♯–Bb and Eb–A–Db–F) from complementary whole-tone collections, descending linear configuration of each pair suggesting transformation of "Well" motif

water. Arkel asks Mélisande if she is cold and would like to have the windows shut, to which Mélisande responds that they should not be shut "until the sun has sunk into the sea." At this point (p. 295, m. 6 ff.), the orchestra, in delicate sonority, unfolds the inversion of the "Well" motif in paired repetitions based on the original short-long rhythm of the linear motivic whole-steps (see ex. 5-1 earlier). This motivic association suggests a symbolic parallel between the fall of Mélisande's ring from the glare of the sunlight into the watery depths of the well—the special moment that initiated the inevitable sequence of events that lead to her demise—and the setting of the sun in the watery depths of the sea as Mélisande lay on her deathbed. The association of the setting sun (Mélisande's death) with the fall of her ring into the well is further supported by a textual comparison with the "Well" scene, especially with the first explicit reference to the cold water of the well (p. 57, mm. 1–2), "It's as cool as winter." The key word here is "winter," which reveals the literal connection with Mélisande's present reference (p. 295, mm. 1–2 ff., and more directly on p. 296, mm. 2–3) to the cold winter and the setting sun.

The ascending fourths figuration in the even eighth-notes that accompany this transformation of the "Well" motif (p. 295, m. 6 ff.) supports the interpretation of the previous, evenly descending-fourths figuration (p. 293, mm. 9–10, bass; see ex. 8-2 earlier) as part of the more disguised transformation of the "Well" motif. At the same time, the present, more explicit transformation of the motif associated with the setting sun serves a more prominent role in the long-range symbolic associations that pertain to Mélisande's fate. Like the original harmonization of the "Well" motif (C dominant ninth, p. 55, mm. 10–11), this inverted occurrence of the motif is also based on the dominant-ninth construction, but transposed to C♯–E♯–G♯–B–D♯. The registral distribution of the C♯ dominant ninth components (p. 295) implies the presence (as in the original C dominant ninth harmonization of the "Well" motif; see p. 55) of the whole-tone transformation of the diatonic sphere; that is, the gapped whole-tone cell (B–[ ]–D♯–E♯) defines the transformed motif exclusively, while the one diatonic element (fifth degree, G♯) of the C♯ dominant ninth (G♯/B–C♯–D♯–E♯) is somewhat isolated in the eighth-note figuration of the bass. At the same time, the sustained C♯ root of the chord anticipates the mysterious C♯ major tonality associated with Mélisande's death at the end of the opera (p. 310) and suggests a tonal link with the original occurrence of the "Mélisande" motif, A♭–B♭–C♯ (see p. 1, mm. 14–15).

By means of an enharmonic spelling (G♯–A♯–[ ]–C♯) of the latter (A♭–B♭–C♯), the C♯ tonal connection between the basic "Mélisande" motif and her death is made more evident. The first simultaneous conflict between diatonic (human) and whole-tone (fate) spheres occurred (p. 1, mm. 14–15) with the replacement of a single note (C♯) of the "Mélisande" motif (A♭–B♭–[C♯]) by D in the accompanying whole-tone figuration (A♭–B♭–[D]–E). In view of certain harmonic events at Mélisande's death, this initial dissonance—a microcosmic musical event produced by the intrusion of Fate—plays a significant role in foreshadowing her death. The clash of D against the C♯ of her motif was already prepared by the D pentatonic tonality of the opening statements of the "Forest" motif. The D became increasingly prominent toward the end of the Prelude in Mélisande's "Naïveté" motif (p. 2, mm. 3–5), where it served as the root of the D dominant ninth chord (D–F♯–A–C–E). It moved to the D Dorian mode in the retransition (p. 2, mm. 6–7) and D Aeolian in the recapitulation of the "Forest" motif. As Mélisande dies and only her new-born daughter remains (p. 310, mm. 3–12; see ex. 7-2 earlier), the procedure is reversed—only a hint of the D–C♯ conflict is heard as the C♯ Phrygian scale unfolds in the descending chain of "Well-motif" suspensions (A–G♯–F♯–E–D–C♯); the cadential point (p. 310, mm. 6–7) is based on the final resolution of D (second modal degree) to the C♯ tonic. The latter defines the pitch level (C♯–D♯–F♯) of the final statement of the "Mélisande" motif, played as a gentle dirge in the muted trumpet. In counterpoint above it, a permutation of the motif at its original pitch level, A♭–B♭–C♯ (now in enharmonic spelling, G♯–A♯–C♯), is heard in the flutes with murmurs of the "Well" motif. Furthermore, in the last six measures, the C♯ Lydian/Ionian bimodal construction, C♯–D♯–E♯–F♯–Fx–G♯–A♯–B♯, which suggests the inversion of the preceding C♯–Phrygian mode, permits local surface echoes of Golaud's "Fate" cell at its basic pitch level, C♯–E♯–Fx. This is an enharmonic spelling of that construction (D♭–F–G) that had appeared so ominously at key dramatic moments in the opera. All of these conflicting elements are resolved in the final, pure C♯ major triad as Mélisande is no more.

This tonal resolution suggests a still deeper-level symbolism. Arkel's last words, which bring the text to a close, suggest that Mélisande's daughter is a kind of mirror image of her mother (p. 309), that "she lies there as if she were her baby's elder sister," and is bound within the same fatalistic structure, "It must live in her place now. It's the poor little thing's turn." This idea is carried further by David Grayson, who hypothesizes that "if her daughter is the Mélisande of the future, then Geneviève is in some respects the Mélisande of the past. . . . Geneviève, too, was brought to the castle as a bride . . . and loved two men who were brothers (or at least half-brothers)."[8] The long-range musical relations seem to symbolize the continuation of Mélisande in her daughter. The final tonality of C♯ was an essential detail in the pitch structure of Mélisande's original motif (A♭–B♭–C♯). The ultimate tonality of C♯, which is associated with the continuation of Mélisande in her daughter, that is, trapped in the same fate, has evolved logically from the C♯ of her original motif (A♭–B♭–C♯). The odd "misspelling" of the expected D♭ as C♯ permits an association between the first statement of Mélisande's motif and the final tonality, which is related to Mélisande's death and her continuation through the life of her daughter, the common C♯ spelling serving as yet another confirmation of this symbolic interpretation. However, the replacement of the oboe (Wenk's interpretation as "Mélisande's sadness") as basis of Mélisande's initial motivic statement, A♭–B♭–C♯ (p. 1, mm. 14–15), by the trumpet (Wenk's interpretation as "Mélisande's peaceful death") as basis of her final motivic statement, C♯–D♯–F♯ (p. 310, mm. 7–8), supports the fatalistic meaning primarily in terms of the connection between her sadness and her death, not the new life of her daughter.

In his symbolic interpretations of the individual tonalities, which he presents within his larger tonal (major/minor-key) outline, Wenk associates C♯/D♭ with "caring" and "solicitousness" for Mélisande.[9] Wenk interprets certain "caring" moments in the final act under the broad rubric of its closing tonality (D♭/C♯ major). For instance, when Arkel asks the dying Mélisande if she is feeling better (p. 297), she responds that she is "not worried any more," and when he asks her if she would like to see her child, she is puzzled. While Wenk's interpretation of these caring moments in connection with the final D♭/C♯ seems to be casting the tonal net a bit too wide, as these local textual statements have nothing to do with D♭/C♯, it does bring to our attention the more general mood that foreshadows this closing tonality of the opera. Instead, a more direct connection of C♯ to Mélisande's (and her child's) sad fate may be observed in Arkel's final words (p. 310), "'It's the poor little thing's turn," in which "caring" turns more explicitly to pity.

Like Wenk, Smith associates the sharp ("light") keys (especially C♯ and its tonic, F♯) with hope and caring in this final scene.[10] Smith cites Arkel's assurance to Mélisande that he can take care of her child (p. 298, mm. 3–4). This is supported by one of the rare cadential resolutions of the C♯ major chord to its F♯ major tonic. Within the following passages, which contain interspersions of whole-tone (p. 300, mm. 1–3, textual suggestion of fate), octatonic (p. 300, mm. 4–7, textual suggestion of ambiguity), descending chromatic figurations (p. 301, mm. 5–8, textual association with weeping), and Lydian/Phrygian constructions on C♯ (p. 310), hints of C♯ major occur in preparation for its final establishment. As Smith points out, this key of "light" is the sharpest one, as represented by its key signature of seven sharps.

Although there is some evidence in the score that supports these tonal associations, the question must be raised regarding the broader symbolic meaning of C♯ major as the final key of the opera. In contrast to its associations with light, hope, and caring, we have seen how the note C♯ also emerged as part of the threatening "Fate" cell of Golaud as well as having appeared (p. 1, mm. 14–15) as the first significant dissonance (against D of the whole-tone harmony in the orchestra) as part of Mélisande's basic motif, A♭–B♭–C♯. Perhaps the message that can be discerned from these polarized interpretations (life and hope vs. death and fate) is one of ambiguity or duality: Mélisande will live on in her daughter, but as a "poor creature" whose "turn" it is to continue in the cycle of fate,[11] the "cyclical" principle of fate being essential to the play. Arkel's words about Mélisande's daughter living in her place points to a pattern of actions and events that are, as Grayson puts it, "destined to repeat generation after generation in a cycle of 'eternal return.'"[12] Grayson points out further that "this cyclical ending, this expression of 'eternal return,' produces a feeling less of hope and comfort than of resignation and fatality." This association of resignation with the idea of "eternal recurrence" also may be observed in twentieth-century continental drama.[13] Edward Lockspeiser's perspective also emphasizes the pessimistic side of the duality between life and hope versus death and fate, but does not explicitly focus on the cyclical concept:

> The drama of *Pelléas* preaches the fatalistic philosophy that man's incapacity to escape from the hidden unconscious forces which determine the course of his life is the tragedy of his existence. In Maeterlinck's pessimistic view there is only one certain reality—death. Death hovers over all his plays, liberating his creatures from their world of dreams. . . . The vogue of this playwright at the beginning of the century was based precisely on a denial of free-will and leads, ultimately, to the despairing predicament of humanity illustrated by such writers of our time as James Joyce, Virginia Woolf or Franz Kafka. The musical counterparts of these later explorations of the unconscious mind are Alban Berg's operas *Wozzeck* and *Lulu;* and it is therefore entirely comprehensible that *Pelléas* has been considered, on the one hand, as a logical extension of *Tristan* and, on the other, as a musical and psychological forerunner of *Wozzeck.*[14]

It must be said, ultimately, that one cannot establish absolute and unequivocal correspondences between music and text. Attempts have often been made to associate certain musical qualities, figures, or elements with particular moods, emotions, or events.[15] However, such nonspecific associations "are best understood by observing the correspondences between music and poetry in a wide range of examples."[16] In Debussy's personal expressive idiom, for instance, there are certain recurrences of specific musical materials—pentatonic, modal, whole-tone, octatonic, and chromatic—within a given work that provide insight into the meaning of the text. In other words, such associations have contextual rather than a priori (precompositional) meaning. Wenk aptly elaborates on this enigmatic issue of meaning in music: "In no way can we say that the pentatonic scale means a pastoral scene or that the whole-tone scale means an escape into another world. Rather we observe a certain pattern in the situations in which Debussy employs these musical idioms, and the awareness of this pattern causes us to look for its significance at each new encounter. . . . The progressive elaboration of a personal musical idiom, on the other hand, leads the composer to associate certain musical idioms with certain classes of ideas regardless of their specific poetic context."[17] The question of musical meaning and its symbolic associations in Debussy's opera is, in any case, explored in this study only in terms of contextual association, not a priori assumptions.

9

Duke Bluebeard's Castle

Psychological Motivation: Symbolic Interaction of Diatonic, Whole-Tone, and Chromatic Extremes

Psycho-Dramatic and Musical Bases

Bartók's opera *Duke Bluebeard's Castle* is closely allied with Debussy's *Pelléas et Mélisande* in its psychological as well as aesthetic and philosophical assumptions. At the same time, basic differences may also be discerned, for instance, in the area of gender relations. The Maeterlinck-Debussy work evokes oedipal questions pertaining to psychological interrelations in the triad of main characters, whereas the Balázs-Bartók opera seems inclined more toward narcissistic questions in the man-woman dyad. These similarities and differences, as manifested on both dramatic and musical levels of the operas, are explored in the ensuing discussions. Whereas the internal concept of unconscious motivation seems to be represented primarily as an external one in the Maeterlinck play, in which human action is entirely controlled by fate, the *Bluebeard* opera libretto of Balázs projects perhaps an even more intense sense of unconscious interplay between the characters.

The equivalence between unconscious motivation and the control by fate, that is, in the sense that the human being has no control over the hidden forces of the soul, entails yet another aspect relevant to psychological assumptions in *Bluebeard*. Adorno's concept of shock in his assessment of musical modernism is particularly relevant to the notion of trauma in the latter.[1] Bartók's opera, limited to a bare minimum of characters, introduces the shock element and a level of reality entirely immersed in the unconscious as well as metaphorical, or symbolic representation. As a symbol of Bluebeard's internal self, blood vividly appears in each of his chambers as the seven doors are forced open by Judith, who relentlessly pries into her husband's private life. Judith herself seems to represent the instrument of relentless time and, at the same time, unrequited love, which draws Bluebeard toward endless darkness, "And always, too, it shall be night. Night . . . night. . . . "[2] The opera begins and ends in darkness after a few brief moments of illumination. The man's life, according to Frigyesi, is hidden (that is, unconscious) as much from himself as it is from the woman: "Underlying the entire design of the play is the realization that the self does not know its secrets and that these can be revealed only if the soul is opened—by the Other."[3]

The symbolism of the drama suggests yet another level of psychological manifestation, which goes beyond the context of the opera itself. We may attribute an autobiographical significance to the subject of the *Bluebeard* opera as an aspect of its symbolism, based on internal as well as circumstantial evidence. An autobiographical significance might be assumed separately and in different ways for both the playwright and composer. As noted earlier, Balázs himself had experienced psychological trauma when, at the age of ten years old, he became an accomplice as a witness of violence against a girl. When a young male boarder at his home attacked their young maid, Balázs aided the boarder to help him pin her down because, as he later confessed, "defeat would have been the defeat of maledom."[4] When the boarder lifted the maid's skirt, Balázs experienced a "so far unknown, frenzied sexual desire" that terrified him. A few years earlier he had witnessed the tender embrace of a pair of lovers in the woods. The original impression of loving tenderness was to become transformed in his mind by the later violent experience, and the original perception of love "now sank back into the darkness of the basest, most brutal instincts. . . . Thus originated in my mind a fateful splitting of healthy, harmonious love. It was an inner discord between animalistic, brutal sexuality and dreamy, spiritual, unphysical love, which for a long time did not appear together, as if one necessarily excluded the other. This for many years became the tragic complication of my life and caused a great deal of psychic confusion, suffering, and misfortune." Balázs kept a diary for many years, from the time he was thirteen, of his external and internal world, and so became his own "lifelong psychoanalyst."[5]

The connection between Balázs's earlier trauma and his *Bluebeard* play seems obvious, the subject of love being colored by violence and blood as light streams forth from each of the doors unlocked by Judith. For Balázs, the light imagery in the play suggests a striking association with the maid's "white thighs gleaming in the twilight dimness of the room." The *Bluebeard* story is, however, a denial of brutality, as Bluebeard's actions are devoid of the more overt violent actions of the sword-wielding figure in the 1697 Charles Perrault tale or the earlier historical figures of the wife murderer on whom the tale is based. In the Balázs play, the only signs of violence are circumstantial—a torture chamber, armory, and stains of blood—and the former wives in the seventh chamber are actually depicted as living and adorned by jewels. Hence, although the play may be interpreted as an expression of Balázs's trauma and guilt, the lack of overt physical violence toward Judith and the former wives diminishes the confessional significance for Balázs and therefore the cathartic psychological function of his artistic creation. The more vague Symbolist expression of the play is all the more striking considering that his "compulsive urge to confess—even his most intimate thoughts and deeds—is a most important factor in his life and artistic oeuvre."[6] The ten-year-old boy's need to protect the power of "maledom" also remains a psychological issue for the adult playwright: Bluebeard's power is revealed when the fifth door opens onto his vast domain and Judith's character conversely diminishes toward extinction. Although the original 1697 Perrault tale requires the woman's two brothers to save her from being beheaded by Blue Beard, in Balázs's *Bluebeard* play there is no one to save Judith from her ultimate fate.

From an entirely different perspective, namely, the autobiographical significance of the play for the composer, accounts given by those who had personal contact with Bartók have pointed to his aloofness and his need to protect his privacy, an attitude reflected in the character of Bluebeard. For instance, according to the composer's elder son, "Bartók was rather reserved when in the company of strangers."[7] At the same time, the issue of male power over the woman in the Balázs play may have also attracted Bartók to set the work as an opera. At a 1910 reading of the Balázs libretto, which was originally intended for Kodály, it was Bartók who was drawn to this subject. It is striking that of all of Bartók's works, he was to choose *Bluebeard* for dedication to his wife, Márta Ziegler, whom Bartók abandoned later for a younger woman, Ditta Pásztory. In the opera, all of Bluebeard's wives are lost as they are inevitably confined to his dungeon. Consideration of the women in Bartók's life—especially the violinist Stefi Geyer, for whom Bartók expressed his first love, and Márta and Ditta—and their significance in connection with the woman in the opera is essential in understanding the opera's Symbolist conception. These gender issues and their consideration within the context of Bartók's espousal of Nietzsche's philosophy during these years—to rise above all and to be emotionally and spiritually independent—are explored in more depth in the following chapters.

All of these aspects—unconscious motivation, concept of fate, shock element, and psychological projection of the playwright or the composer—contribute to the definition of the opera's symbolism. In fundamental ways, the subject of the opera and especially Bartók's approach to its musical setting can provide insight into the composer's personality and creative impulses, and even serve as a mirror of his basic psychological constitution. The converse is also true, in which the study of Bartók's personality and psychological motivations can provide a viable source for uncovering some of the opera's symbolic mysteries.[8] In view of the circumstances of his personal life, especially from the time of his unrequited love for Stefi Geyer (1907–1908),[9] Bartók's attraction to the Balázs play seems to acquire considerable documentary significance. It contributes to our understanding not only of the composer's personal psychological needs, but also provides insight into the traumatic forces of his life (rejection in love) and career (rejection as a composer and his withdrawal from public life in 1912), which were leading him away from Central Europe and the ultra-emotional chromatic idiom of Wagner and Strauss (as exemplified in his *First Violin Concerto, Two Portraits for Orchestra*, and *First String Quartet*) to a musical aesthetics based on the infusion of new sources dominated by the essence of Eastern European folk music. The opera represents an intermediary stage in his lifelong evolution toward coalescence of various aesthetic sources, the German romantic, impressionistic, and folkloristic, which he acquired prior to World War I.

The reasons for Bartók's increasing aversion to urban society and his search for spiritual consolation among the peoples of the villages are rooted in a constellation of factors—personal, political, and social—but his musical expression may perhaps provide the most tangible focus for understanding the composer's changing spiritual needs and his artistic evolution.[10] At the same time, an awareness of Bartók's character and psychological motivations lends support to the interpretation of the artistic creation itself. According to the Hungarian psychiatrist Bertalan Pethő,[11] Kodály described Bartók as "a typical example of the schizothym mental constitution,"[12] that is, introverted, withdrawn. Of the character traits that Kodály described, those that seem to identify the composer most with the protagonist of his *Bluebeard* opera include "cool, rigid, fanatical, hesitating, aristocratic, unsociable, idealistic, eccentric, stubborn, reserved, distrustful, misanthropic." However, this description is qualified by Pethő:[13]

> The limits of Kretschmer's typology and that of the similar introversion-extroversion typology originate above all in their superficiality. Practically, they only describe two types in details: schizothym and cyclothym (introverted and extroverted respectively).... Bartók's writings and his contemporaries' memories permit a typological refinement. Bartók's accuracy and assiduity are well-known,[14] he consciously held preciseness second to none[15] and hated imperfection.[16] ... "He was extremely puritan all through his life," wrote Mrs. Gyárfás, who knew him well in the 1910s.[17]

Pethő outlines an additional listing of mental characteristics known in "personalistic psychology" as the "melancholic" type, which "refers to the well-known relation between melancholy and philosophical immersion (e.g., visualized by Dürer) on the one hand and to the tendency to earnestness, pessimism and neurotic or psychotic depression on the other hand," but he argues against the notion that Bartók suffered from depression. He does, however, point to Bartók's pessimism throughout his life. For instance, during the time of his emigration to the United States, Bartók wrote that "I have lost all faith in people, countries, in everything."[18] As for Bartók's dislike of "imperfection," we may cite Bluebeard as a symbolic representation of his need, at all costs, to prevent the woman from prying into each of the seven doors and exposing the bloody crimes that stain Bluebeard's past. From our observations of Bartók's relationship to Stefi Geyer, or Bluebeard's to Judith, we may also identify the man's narcissistic qualities: self-involvement, based on his need to control or use others to validate the self and, at the same time, to be dependent on others for such validation. Bartók says to Stefi, "Here is a case of human frailty! I anticipated that you might react like this, yet when you actually did so, I was upset. Why couldn't I read your letter with cold indifference? ... Why should I be so affected by your reaction?"[19] And Bluebeard begs Judith, "Judith, love me, ask me nothing." Paradoxically, Bartók, like Bluebeard, who "collected women,"[20] turns out to be a prisoner himself. According to Giovacchini, some patients use "narcissistic defenses" against "their basic vulnerability and feelings of inadequacy.... Kohut (1971) has referred to them as *narcissistic personality disorders*," which seems entirely relevant at least to the character of Bluebeard, whose vast domain is revealed in the context of his efforts to conceal the bloody defects within the chambers of his soul (castle). Giovacchini points out that:

> This character type has been familiar to both professionals and nonprofessionals for centuries. Some of these persons have become leaders and through their charisma have gained immense power. They have been recognized by their sometimes ruthless ambition for fame, prestige, and power and the sometimes obvious fact that they are overcompensating for some real or imagined defect."[21]

These psycho-dynamic qualities within the narcissistic purview are characterized by the polarity of psychological extremes—grandiosity as defense-mechanism against vulnerability—a significant factor that may have contributed to the eternal man-woman problem of irreconcilability because of sexual inequality within the male-dominated power structure. Bluebeard's vast domain is a symbol of that domination. This polarity of psychological extremes, which seems to be an essential factor in understanding the *narcissistic personality disorder*, can be added to the basic list of polarities, that is, between the characters as real-life beings and as instruments of *fate* (see table 4-1 earlier), this list underlying the symbolic message not only of the Balázs-Bartók conception but the Maeterlinck-Debussy as well.

Structural Framework as Basis for Development of Psycho-Dramatic Polarity, Power Inequality, and Symbolic Musical Expression

Bartók's new, personal Symbolist musical context is set within a clearly architectural framework in both overall form and local phrasal details. In contrast with the more continuous organic structures of Wagner's music dramas, this formal approach reveals Bartók's roots in the folk music structures themselves, that is, a musical manifestation of his rejection of the traditional forms and his attraction to the new world of the peasant. The entire opera consists of several distinct forms within scenes, often based on folklike quaternary structures that sometimes suggest a rondo type of format. Furthermore, much of the melodic and harmonic fabric is developed by means of modal elaboration, a principle that appears to be derived from the process of thematic variation found in the folk-music sources. From the modal material of the opera, Bartók derives the basic leitmotifs, which are central in generating the musico-dramatic fabric.[22] The basic "Blood" motif, characterized by half-steps, is gradually manifested in the intrusion of this dissonant element into the opening pentatonic folk mode—a scalar structure entirely devoid of semitones—as Judith becomes aware of blood on the castle walls. However, psychological tension in the unbroken musical fabric is created not only by the manifest details but also by the latent symbolic and metaphorical questions that these details invoke with regard to our own perception of reality. Such questions are explicit in the Prologue: "The curtains of our eye-lids are raised. But where is the stage. In me? In you?"

Psychological development, which is fundamental to the symbolic meaning of *Bluebeard*, is realized by means of two inextricably connected and overlapping formal concepts, one sectional, the other unfolding the dynamic spiritual evolution and transformation of the two characters. Sándor Veress has shown how the large-scale form of the opera is a closed symmetrical construction, an arch-form in three parts:[23] (1) an introduction initially established by the folklike, brooding, F♯–pentatonic "Darkness" (or "Castle") and "Foreboding" motifs; (2) seven scenes demarcated by Doors I–VII, which peak at the uncovering of Bluebeard's vast domain behind Door V in the contrastingly bright key of C major (the most distant key from the opening F♯); and (3) a recapitulation of the "Foreboding" and F♯– pentatonic "Darkness" theme.[24] Julian Grant shows a symmetrical scheme of keys in his outline of Doors II and IV in D♯/E♭, V in C, VI in A, and VII moving from C to F♯.[25] This scheme of a descending cycle of thirds—F♯–D♯–C–A–C–F♯—which seems to reflect the pessimistic outcome, is supported by the progression of changing hues of light through the color spectrum. The first door reveals Bluebeard's torture chamber in a beam of red light, the second door the armory in reddish-yellow, the third door the treasury in gold, the fourth the garden scene in blue-green. The door that opens onto Bluebeard's vast domain is illuminated by an all-encompassing flood of white light. This peak of radiance dims with the gloom of the sixth and seventh doors, one opening onto the lake of tears, the other Bluebeard's imprisoned former wives. The white radiance of the fifth door (in C major) is then polarized by the ultimate darkness that engulfs the lonely figure of Bluebeard, in the original "darkness" key of F♯ pentatonic.[26] The use of color in conjunction with specific tonalities or musical details (themes, motifs, or sections) appears to serve some symbolic role in the musical contexts of works composed during the same period as Bartók's *Bluebeard*. Grant points out that:

> there was a tendency among composers of the period to use external elements as an alternative organizing agent to tonality, and an equation of music with colour is a fleeting, though fascinating, preoccupation. It plays a part in Balázs's and Bartók's scheme for Bluebeard: the first four doors are accompanied by stage instructions specifying the projection of colours. Previous composers, notably Rimsky-Korsakov and Scriabin, had associated keys and harmonies with specific colours; Schönberg in his correspondence with Kandinsky and in *Die glückliche Hand* (1908–13) — a contemporary work of *Bluebeard* and Scriabin's *Prometheus* (with its part for an invented colour-organ) — took the relationship further. Bartók was not so rigorous, though the music for the doors is far more static harmonically than the surrounding music for Judith and Bluebeard. This makes a sole point of contact with another Maeterlinck opera, *Ariane et Barbe-bleue* (1907) by Paul Dukas, a feminist version of the legend that Balázs knew, though Bartók makes no reference to it. In the Dukas, the opening of the doors reveals jewels of different colours, depicted in washes of gorgeously orchestrated static harmony — serving a similar function to the Bartók in bringing stability to an unstable harmonic language.[27]

The sectional arch-form, which is determined primarily by the various musical (modal-tonal) and visual (light and color) factors, actually finds a limited amount of musical reinforcement in spite of the cyclical return of the opening castle material at the end. As Paul Banks points out, "the music is much more concerned with vividly characterising each episode — the martial glare of the armoury, the glittering beauty of the treasure room, the oppressive sadness of the lake of tears — and allowing the material of each episode to evolve organically."[28] Any sense of an overall arch-shape is heightened more by the dramatic psychological process. The distinct vocal styles and personalities of the two characters are established at the outset. Judith's first vocal entry, a prominent (whole-tone related) wide-ranging figure in a characteristically strong Magyar rhythm, contrasts with Bluebeard's reserved (pentatonic-diatonic) repeated-note line in even durational values. By the time Door V (opening on Bluebeard's vast domain) is reached, this contrast is reversed: the man has progressed from reserve to increasingly intense and passionate utterance, while the woman has moved in the opposite direction toward her own extinction. Only when the inevitable occurs and Judith is lost does Bluebeard become emotionally resigned. According to Veress:

> Judith is symbolic of the passionate woman who, because of her love, is thoroughly in the power of the man, and with her warm, protective tenderness desires to free him. Bluebeard, on the other hand, is the rational man whose feelings develop slowly

and who lives his own life and to maintain this would even sacrifice love. Judith is the restless, passionate, demanding one, Bluebeard the reticent character who in his wisdom understands life, and [somewhat paradoxically] in Judith finds the complete fulfillment of his desires.[29]

Veress's interpretation accords with the inevitable loss of Judith and the significance of Bluebeard's last words that now it will always be dark. However, a broader historical study of Judith as a more general female type in literature and art may provide a more profound understanding of the woman's symbolic significance in the Bartók-Balázs operatic setting. The subject of *Bluebeard* suggests the eternally problematical relation of the two sexes. The relation between the two as depicted in the opera is one that the contemporary feminist movement would deplore, but all the more do we have to understand this relation. There are only two characters, a man and a woman. The man is the central character, and it is perhaps partly for this reason that critical studies of the opera have been devoted almost entirely to the Bluebeard character, with little or no systematic attention given to that of Judith.[30]

Gender and Power in the Modernist Conception

The underlying theme of unequal power, a basic aspect of the modernist conception, is implicit in the Bartók as well as the Debussy opera.[31] It is elaborated by several dichotomies that reveal different aspects of the struggle: man versus woman, young versus old, master versus servant, jailer versus prisoner. By focusing on one specific aspect of the power differential in both operas, the relationship between men and women reveals an awareness of the oppressive order and the dread and terror of change. In both works, the female protagonists have been described by critics as embarking on a journey that brings about destruction for them and their lovers. This interpretation, which is consistent with the growing perception at that time of women as dangerous, was associated with anxiety about the role changes advocated by the beginning of the feminist movement. Consideration of the social circumstances surrounding this attitude toward women in the late nineteenth century provides some background for these literary and artistic depictions, and may lend insight into the psychological attitude toward the woman in both operas. Radical changes in the social relations between men and women were taking place in the late nineteenth century. The momentum gained by the international women's movement led to new social roles for women and man's sense that he would no longer be able to maintain his control over women.[32] An extreme example of misogynistic reaction is found in the writings of Otto Weininger: "no man who really thinks deeply about woman retains a high opinion of them; men either despise women or they have never thought seriously about them."[33]

We learn from Maeterlinck's *Ariane et Barbe-bleue*, which was set as an opera by Dukas in 1907, that Mélisande was one of Bluebeard's captive wives. The first time she appears in the opera she is weeping after having thrown the crown that Bluebeard had given her as the price for her bondage into a pond. In a parallel action, she later drops the wedding ring that Golaud gave her into a well. These associations of Mélisande with water throughout the opera (weeping, pond, well, the sea) invoke yet another symbolic association between the woman in Maeterlinck's play and that seductive water sprite in French legend, the mermaid Mélusine, whose connection with the Maeterlinck character seems to go beyond mere alliteration. Mélusine has fallen in love with a human mortal but leaves him when he learns her secret. Like the mermaid, Mélisande is a mysterious creature who also has a secret, and she also is alienated from the social structure in which she has found herself enmeshed, bound in marriage first to Bluebeard, then to Golaud. Mélisande and Mélusine both find themselves in unequal relationships with men, and each woman can maintain only a fleeting link with human society. Whereas Mélisande's emotions symbolize (that is, are the means of achieving) her freedom from an oppressive social structure,[34] the dramatic message of Maeterlinck is that the woman's quest for freedom will lead inevitably to her demise. At the same time, because of the consequences for those men connected with Mélisande, one is led to believe, paradoxically, that for Maeterlinck the woman symbolizes the siren of destruction, a view of women quite common at that time.[35] By way of dramatic analogy, Bartók's Judith, the passionate woman, intrudes into Bluebeard's soul, her uncontrollable feelings determining the destiny of both characters. In the opera, the Bluebeard character represents the reticent, reserved man who cannot reach out to his beloved in the way she desires, and so she pries into the hidden recesses of his soul until man and woman both submit to ultimate fate.

Balázs's philosophical view of the woman apparently stems from Friedrich Hebbel's transformation of Judith, the selfless biblical character, into something more Salome-like. Such historical representations of Judith provide insight into the character and role of Bartók's Judith, but certain depictions in literature and art reveal more direct correspondences to the essence of the woman in the *Bluebeard* opera.[36] Around the turn of the twentieth century, the name of Judith became associated with the seductive woman whose sexual attractiveness leads to man's demise as well as her own, and connections also were made with the figure of Salome. The mistaken identification of Judith for Salome can be documented from the time of the early reception of two paintings by the Viennese artist Gustav Klimt, entitled *Judith and Holofernes* (1901 and 1909), the error stemming from the journal reproduction of the 1901 painting without its label.[37] Judith, like Salome, is depicted as the sexually attractive young woman who holds the head of the man she has decapitated. The biblical story of Judith and Holofernes, in which the Assyrian general is decapitated by the woman, is prototypic of the modern Judith image. However, the modern focus on sexuality and psychological motivation in connection with Judith appears to stem from Hebbel's tragic drama *Judith* (1840), in which the original biblical figure of a widow who kills Holofernes to save her people is replaced by the young virgin bent on personal revenge. Hebbel's *Judith* was performed by Max Reinhardt's Berlin theater company in Budapest just before the publication of Balázs's *Bluebeard* in 1910. Like Judith and Salome, the image of the *femme fatale* also has been manifested in character representations such as Frank Wedekind's Lulu and the anonymous woman in Marie Pappenheim's libretto for Schoenberg's *Erwartung*, as well as Maeterlinck's Mélisande, all of these female types having drawn opera composers to use them in their musical settings.[38]

In analyzing the Bluebeard character, one may cite Bartók's own adoption of the more modern ideas of Nietzsche (of his Zarathustra, especially) during this time in Bartók's life. He invokes Nietzsche by asserting that one must strive to rise above all and to be completely independent and indifferent.[39] He was to recall this idea a few years later when, brought to tears by the young woman with whom he was in love, he expressed shame toward his emotional weakness for what he considered to be his own "human frailty."[40] The sense of loneliness, pessimism, and despair, as manifested in these operas, seems to stem in part from the lack of acceptance by men that women were potentially their equals in both the emotional and intellectual spheres. Balázs himself "invariably approached women with the idea that he was on a higher plane intellectually and emotionally, and it was his task to lead women in their quest for meaning in life. . . . Bartók thought similarly in this matter. But the need to assert male superiority clashed with his natural inclinations to open up toward women more easily than toward men."[41] According to Angelica Bäumer, "The demands of nature time and again drive man into woman's arms, but he no longer finds a haven there, no peace or safety, only coldness, distance and insoluble incomprehension."[42] The image of Bartók's Judith may be placed appropriately within the context of these social developments.

Prologue through Door I (Torture Chamber)

The symbolism of Bartók's *Bluebeard* is derived directly from the French symbolism of Debussy's *Pelléas*. Both the Debussy and Bartók operas belong in essence to the same dramatic sphere of Maeterlinck, and it is in this context that part of the mystery surrounding the woman in Debussy's opera is resolved. We learn from Maeterlinck's *Ariane et Barbe-bleue*, the drama on which Dukas's 1907 opera is based, that Mélisande was one of the escaped wives from Bluebeard's dungeon. The woman as siren of destruction is most evident in the Debussy opera. Musically, the whole-tone collection (basis of the "Fate" motif) is the catalyst for transforming diatonic materials ("Human" motifs), the interaction between the two forming the musico-dramatic basis for the entire opera. This interaction of whole-tone and diatonic spheres also underlies the same dramatic symbolism in Bartók's opera. Bluebeard's opening vocal sections are primarily pentatonic/diatonic, Judith's primarily whole-tone, Judith thus fatalistically intruding into Bluebeard's private life.

As in the Debussy opera, the musical fabric of *Bluebeard* is generated primarily by special "pitch-set" interactions as the basis for symbolic and dramatic expression.[43] The opening F♯ pentatonic set, F♯–A–B–C♯–E, a folk-derived diatonic substructure without semitones,[44] serves as the point of departure for the infusion of semitones as a representation of the emerging symbol of "Blood," and for transformation into the whole-tone sphere in connection with Judith's intrusion into Bluebeard's personal world.[45] His castle may be interpreted as a metaphor for man's soul, hence the identification of the opening F♯ pentatonic theme—we will call this the "Darkness" theme—essentially with Bluebeard himself. These two dramatic aspects—symbol of "Blood" and intrusion of "Fate"—are closely interconnected as Judith's relentless prying opens the wounds of Bluebeard's soul.

In connection with the symbol of "Blood," combinations of semitones move from unobtrusive contexts (that is, as part of larger thematic statements) to being the primary foreground event. The general tendency in the relation of pairs of semitones is

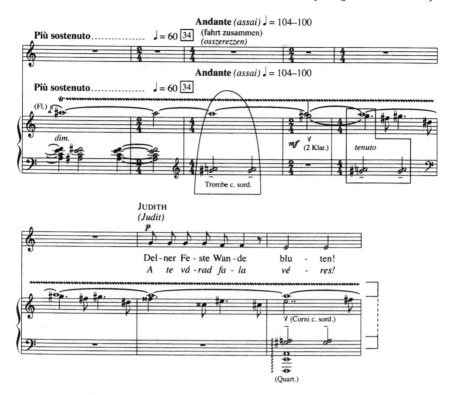

EXAMPLE 9-1. Torture Chamber, Section b1, no. 34f., main "Blood" motif occurrence

toward increasing dissonance, the most dissonant relation being the separation of two semitones by a semitone, in association with the main dramatic idea. The excerpt shown in example 9-1—a prominent foreground statement of a four-note semitonal cell, G♯–A/A♯–B (i.e., interval-ratio 1:1)[46]—occurs in the scene of the torture chamber, the first of the seven doors to be opened by Judith. The text at this point reveals that Judith has just noticed blood in Bluebeard's domain (no. 34, mm. 5–6): "Your castle walls are bloody!" This pair of semitones (G♯–A/A♯–B), the most dissonant relationship between two semitones, is divorced from any traditional modal construction.

Rhythmic Structure and the Hungarian Language

Prior to this point, combinations of semitones generally appear as part of larger modal or polymodal thematic material. An awareness of the underlying rhythmic structure of this material, in which the semitonal "blood" motif is gradually abstracted from larger folklike diatonic/modal constructions, reveals the common ground between

Bartók's and Debussy's operas in more than their musico-dramatic Symbolist assumptions. Both operas suggest a similar approach to the relationship between music and language. Bartók's investigations of the old Hungarian folk tunes permitted him to break with the established nineteenth-century tradition of translating Western languages into Hungarian for opera performance, a tradition that had led inevitably to distortions in Hungarian accentuation.[47] Bartók strictly preserved the Hungarian language accents in his musical setting of the Balázs libretto. The archaic syllabic structure is set by Bartók almost entirely in the old "parlando-rubato" folk style, producing a kind of contemporary "recitative opera" that was pioneered by Debussy.[48] In *Bluebeard*, the Hungarian text — and this is true of the orchestral phrases as well — is appropriately based on eight syllables per line, which is one of the isometric stanzaic patterns that the composer found in the oldest of the Hungarian folk melodies.[49] These music-text relationships are based on special premises that could only have been established by the liberation of meter and rhythm that was permitted by the disappearance of traditional tonal functions in the early twentieth century.

By means of these new syntactical relations between rhythm and pitch Bartók, like Debussy, was able to arrive at new and greatly expanded possibilities for symbolic representation. The opening F# pentatonic "Darkness" theme in *Bluebeard* unfolds in two pairs of four-note phrases, or two larger eight-note pairings of the archaic Hungarian isometric syllabic structure (ex. 9-2a). As Bartók illustrates in connection with the old-style Hungarian folk tunes, each line of the eight-syllable format may be reduced to the rhythmic schemata of 4 + 4.[50] The "Foreboding" motif suddenly appears in overlap with the E–F#–pentatonic cadence (mm. 18–21), its two phrases also articulated in 2 × 8 "syllables." In addition to its increasing rhythmic agitation by means of the following more fragmented and irregular statements — that is, the 4 × 4 measures of the opening pentatonic theme are followed by measure groupings of 2 × 2 plus 2 × 1 (extended by 3) and 2 × 1 (extended by 4) that lead to Recitative Part 1 (no. 2, m. 7) — the "Foreboding" motif introduces the first intrusion of both chromatic and whole-tone spheres into the opening pentatonic theme as Bluebeard and Judith enter the castle.

Four of the F# pentatonic notes (F#–A–B–[ ]–E) are retained in the "Foreboding" motif (ex. 9-2b), which expands the pentatonic segment to an exotic nondiatonic mode, F#–G–A–B–C–[ ]–D#–E. This expanded collection suggests a permutation of E harmonic minor, E–F#–G–A–B–C–D#–E, which explicitly unfolds above the held F# tonic. This combination of an E-based mode and sustained F# supports the cadential pentatonic dyad (E–F#) of the "Darkness" (or "Castle") theme. Three semitones (F#–G, B–C, and D#–E) are thereby introduced into the original pentatonic formation. In the second statement of the motif (mm. 18–19), the collection is further chromaticized by the addition of C#, the one F# pentatonic note missing from the first statement, producing F#–G–A–B–C–C#–D#–E. The latter suggests a permutation of the "bimodal" combination of E harmonic minor and E melodic minor (E–F#–G–A–B–C–C#–D#–E), which unfolds above the held F#. Dissonance and tension are thereby introduced by the sudden incorporation of semitones into the opening pentatonic framework, the organic process both controlled and heightened by the metric-syllabic structure of the archaic Hungarian linguistic syntax.

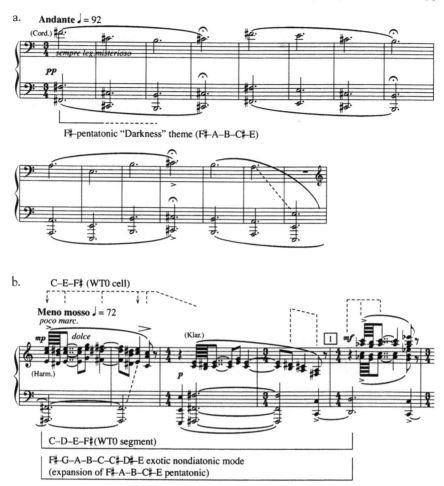

EXAMPLE 9-2. Prologue, (a) mm. 1–16, opening F#-pentatonic "Darkness" (or "Castle") theme, in two pairs of four-note phrases or two larger eight-note pairings of archaic Hungarian isometric syllabic structure; (b) m. 16 through no. 1, "Menacing" or "Foreboding" motif, whole-tone expansion of cadential F#-pentatonic dyad, E–F#

Characterization and the Intrusion of Fate

From the outset of the opera, Bluebeard's message is implied in the question he puts to his new wife (no. 3, m. 6), "Don't you hear the warning bells?" The ominous meaning of Bluebeard's question goes unheeded by Judith, who is portrayed at her initial appearance as the faithful woman, bound to her loved one. Our first impression of Judith seems to be that of the redemptive heroine in Wagner's *Der Fliegende Holländer,* in which absolution of the Dutchman's sins is possible only through the eternal devotion of the woman.[51] However, in Bartók's opera, each new sign of blood and Judith's imminent suspicions of murder induce a gradual change in her attitude. Her faithfulness eventually diminishes to a jealous uncertainty as her relentless actions lead to the encounter with her husband's former wives.

The symbolism contained in the opening musical material portends Judith's character transformation and demise. The semitones of "Blood" begin to permeate the opening pentatonic framework as the whole-tone sphere is introduced into the melodic and harmonic structure of the "Foreboding" motif. The F♯-pentatonic scale (F♯–A–B–C♯–E) implies the presence of a segment from each of the two whole-tone collections, the boundary (F♯–E) belonging to one of these collections, the central three notes (A–B–C♯) to the other. In the linear bass accompaniment of the "Foreboding" motif (see ex. 9-2b earlier), the cadential pentatonic dyad, E–F♯, is expanded to a four-note whole-tone tetrachord, C–D–E–F♯, a segment (C–[ ]–E–F♯) serving as the basic chord of the first phrase (mm. 16–17) as well as the embellished frame of the upper melodic line of the motif. The melodic cadence of the second phrase introduces a gapped segment (A–[ ]–C♯–D♯) from the other whole-tone scale, a transposition of the initial gapped cell (C–[ ]–E–F♯) producing a chromatic conflict with the primary whole-tone collection in the bass.[52] The priority of the latter is reestablished by the initial chord (A♭–C–D) of the next statement (no. 1).

These whole-tone segments (C–[ ]–E–F♯, or C–D–E–F♯, and A–[ ]–C♯–D♯), which are embedded in or accompany the "Foreboding" motif, also imply the presence of the A Dorian/A Lydian modes (A–B–[C–D–E–F♯]–G–A/[A]–B–[C♯–D♯]–E–F♯–[ ]–A). This polymodal combination supports the argument regarding the semitone ("Blood" motif) intrusions into the opening anhemitonic F♯ pentatonic "Darkness" motif by means of polymodal chromaticism. In addition to the whole-tone/diatonic intrusion here, we also may point to the octatonic implication. If we consider one note (B) as an "odd" element within the implied E harmonic minor content of the thematic structure (E–F♯–G–A–[B]–C–C♯–D♯–E, or its pentatonically derived permutation, F♯–G–A–B–C–C♯–D♯–E), then we also have seven notes (F♯–G–A–[ ]–C–C♯–D♯–E) of an octatonic collection. Thus, the basic pitch sets that will be explored throughout the discussion of the opera are already evident in this passage.

In contrast to Judith, Bluebeard expresses uncertainty on entering the castle, questioning his wife's resolve to follow him (no. 5): "Are you stopping, Judith? Would you go back?" The musico-textual syllabic scheme of Bluebeard's first vocal statement serves the expression of his mood. The underlying octosyllabic linguistic structure forms the basis for special phrasal reinterpretations and vocal-orchestral elisions, which permit some sense of musical fragmentation, fusion, and conflict. His first recitative begins with a textual scheme of 4 + 12 syllables, one of the few irregular groupings of the 8 + 8 isometric structure. This reinterpretation permits a special phrasal elision to occur between the final statement of the "Foreboding" motif (no. 2, mm. 1–5) and the overlapping initial entry of the vocal part. Specifically, the first two orchestral motivic fragments of 4 + 4 articulations are melodically extended by four more notes, so the four syllables of the overlapping vocal entry complete the latter as a 4 + 4 rhythmic construction. This technique produces continuity between the orchestral introduction and the first words of the opera, while maintaining an allusion

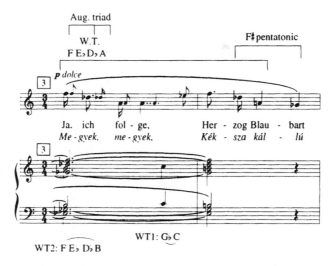

EXAMPLE 9-3. Judith's opening theme, no. 3, further infusion of whole-tone sphere into F♯-pentatonic collection

to the isometric (8 +8) folk structure. At the same time, this cadential four-note orchestral extension outlines a segment (F♯–A–[ ]–C♯–E) of the original pentatonic collection to establish the pentatonic significance of Bluebeard's F♯ octave at his words (no. 2, mm. 4–5), "We have arrived."

In his ensuing phrase, F♯ pentatonic is transposed to D pentatonic, a special transpositional relationship between these two pentatonic collections (F♯–A–B–C♯–E and D–F–G–A–C) implying the presence of certain fundamental pitch-set criteria for further intrusion of the whole-tone sphere and Judith's first statement. Specifically, the boundary whole-tone (F♯–E) of the original F♯–pentatonic collection is replaced by the new whole-tone boundary (D–C) of Bluebeard's D pentatonic statement, both boundaries having unfolded jointly in the bass accompaniment to the "Foreboding" motif (mm. 16–21) as a whole-tone tetrachordal extension and transformation (C–D–E–F♯) of the F♯ pentatonic sphere. Thus, this primary whole-tone tetrachordal cell, which is also basic to the chordal structure of the motif, serves as a link between the two pentatonic transpositions to establish one of the basic musical premises for the intrusion of fate into Bluebeard's world.

While Bluebeard's quiet D pentatonic line is elaborated diatonically by B and E (no. 2, mm. 10–14) to form the larger D Dorian mode (D–E–F–G–A–B–C), Judith responds to his questioning with a contrasting rhythmic and wide-ranging line at her words (no. 3), "I'm coming, Bluebeard, I'm coming," based on further infusion of the whole-tone sphere into the F♯ pentatonic collection. Her vocal statement (ex. 9-3) outlines a descending segment (F–E♭–D♭–A) belonging to the secondary whole-tone scale, the cadential G♭ revealing the presence of the F♯–pentatonic triad (in enharmonic spelling, G♭–A–D♭), so the basic F♯–pentatonic collection is partially transformed into a hybrid whole-tone/pentatonic formation, G♭–A–D♭–E♭–F (i.e., F♯–

A–C♯–E♭–F) at Judith's first utterance. Thus, while the respective boundary whole-steps (F♯–E and C–D) from the F♯– and D pentatonic collections were jointly manifested as a segment (C–D/E–F♯) from the primary whole-tone collection, Judith's whole-tone segment (especially the augmented-triad A–D♭–F) from the secondary whole-tone collection is an enharmonic manifestation of the internal whole-tone segments (A–[ ]–C♯ and F–[ ]–A) of the F♯– and D pentatonic scales, respectively.

Autobiographical Significance and "Fate"

From this vocal statement of Judith, we may be able to glean an autobiographical clue to the opera, one that links the *Bluebeard* opera with Bartók's more explicit autobiographical references in certain earlier works composed in 1908 and 1909. Both the early *Concerto for Violin and Orchestra*, op. posth., and *Two Portraits* for orchestra are based on the same leitmotif, D–F♯–A–C♯, which is also recognizable in the last two pieces of the *Fourteen Bagatelles for Piano*, op. 6, and the *First String Quartet*. The quartet opens with F–A♭–C–E, the minor variant of the chord. This leitmotif has programmatic significance, symbolizing Stefi Geyer, to whom he dedicated the *Concerto*. Bartók explicitly outlined and bracketed Stefi's leitmotif in musical notation for her (ex. 9-4).[53] Bartók's handwritten note in the score indicates that he began to compose the *Concerto* on 1 July 1907 while a guest of Stefi and her family in Jászberény; hence the depiction of Stefi as "the young girl" in the first movement, the "violin virtuoso" in the second.[54] In addition to the romantic feature, these works are also structurally related: Bartók had incorporated the first movement of the then unpublished *Concerto* into the *Two Portraits*,[55] with some alteration, and combined it with an orchestral version of *Bagatelle No. XIV*. In *Bluebeard*, the principal tones of Judith's hybrid F♯ pentatonic/whole-tone construction (Gb–A–Db–Eb–F) outline the minor variant of Stefi's leitmotif, Gb–A–Db–F (in enharmonic spelling, F♯–A–C♯–E♯).

Bartók was drawn to the Balázs libretto of *Bluebeard* only about two years after Stefi's rejection of him in 1908. The drama is based on a dismal attitude toward the woman in the opera, so it is not surprising that Stefi's leitmotif was to be used here as a focal point for the intrusion of the whole-tone collection into the pentatonic/diatonic sphere. It is striking that Bartók's mood associated with the minor-modal variant of the leitmotif is one of "sad misgivings" and a lack of "any consolation in life save in music," a mood that portends the end of their relationship.[56] At this point in the letter, Bartók reiterates his opening statement, telling Stefi that her letter brought him almost to tears. Perhaps we may associate Bartók's reference to tears directly with the sixth door scene of the opera, entitled *Lake of Tears*, which serves as a prelude to the inevitable dissolution of Bluebeard's relationship with Judith.

Considering the nature of Bartók's former close relationship with Stefi, the basic message in his operatic setting provides us with yet another dimension. In his religious and philosophical discussions with Stefi, Bartók revealed his atheistic convictions,[57] his emphatic expression of these views having a twofold significance. First, Bartók may have known at some level that such an imposition of his atheistic beliefs on a woman whom he knew to be "godfearing" and highly sensitive to such issues could only lead to rejection by the woman he loved. The association of Bartók's tears to the *Lake of Tears* seems all the more pertinent in view of Bartók's own admission that he

EXAMPLE 9-4. Stefi's leitmotif in musical notation, as outlined for her by Bartók in 1907 (*Béla Bartók Letters*, ed. János Demény, p. 87).

had expected Stefi to "react like this" to his philosophical arguments. Bartók's statement can perhaps shed light on his fascination with the Bluebeard-Judith relationship and suggest connections between the latter and Bartók's own personal relationships with the other women in his life. As mentioned earlier, it was Bartók who in 1924 was to divorce his first wife, Márta, the woman to whom he had actually dedicated the opera in 1911, in order to marry the younger Ditta Pásztory. Second, Bartók's extreme alienation from the Catholic Church, which represents a radical reversal of his earlier devotion to the faith, and ultimately his denial of the existence of God appear to be profoundly connected to his sense of isolation from his fellow human beings.[58] This feeling evidently stems at least in part from the widening chasm between what Bartók considered to be the intellectual stagnation of his urban culture and his own artistic aspirations and, furthermore, from his pessimism fueled by the increasing indifference toward his music by the Budapest public. These unhappy circumstances undoubtedly contributed to Bartók's espousal of Nietzsche's philosophy.[59] His expressed acceptance of his lonely destiny is striking for more than simply the loneliness itself, since the *inevitability* of this isolation to which he had referred in connection with his personal existence is reflected directly in the message of his opera. Bartók's attitude was already expressed as early as 1905:

> I may be looked after by Dietl or Mandl in Vienna, and I may have friends in Budapest (Thomán, Mrs. Gruber), yet there are times when I suddenly become aware of the fact that I am absolutely alone! And I prophesy, I have a foreknowledge, that this spiritual loneliness is to be my destiny. I look about me in search of the ideal companion, and yet I am fully aware that it is a vain quest. Even if I should ever succeed in finding someone, I am sure that I would be disappointed.[60]

Bartók's belief in the inevitability of his spiritual isolation suggests more than acquiescence, as he fervently espoused the basic tenets of atheism, separation from the Catholic Church, and his aggressive stance toward Stefi on the subject. Bartók's message to Stefi, which implies an actual *need* for isolation, seems to be reflected in Bluebeard's struggle with Judith to protect his privacy and isolation from the outside world. Thus, while the relationship between Judith and Bluebeard appears on the surface to be the converse of that between Stefi and Bartók—that is, Stefi's rejection of

Bartók is reversed in the opera between the man and the woman—Bartók's letter provides us with a more profound insight into his relationship with Stefi. From this relationship we become aware of significant parallels between Stefi and Judith. Bartók's certainty "that he would be disappointed," even if he "should succeed in finding someone," is most evident in the opera, where Judith's prying into Bluebeard's personal life leads him to dissatisfaction with the woman; his abandonment of her, then, as he forces her to join his previous wives behind the seventh door, leads to his own eternal loneliness in "endless night," a metaphor for his death. The latter assumption is supported by Bartók's own comment in his last letter to Stefi Geyer in early 1908: "I have begun a quartet; the first theme is the theme of the second movement [that is, of the violin concerto]: this is my funeral dirge."[61] It is also significant that the very opening F♯ pentatonic ("Darkness") theme, which returns at the end of the *Bluebeard* opera in association with "endless darkness," is similar to the theme in the second of Bartók's *Four Dirges for Piano*, op. 8b (1908).[62]

Ultimately, it is Bartók's need to *control* the woman that seems to lie at the heart of the parallel between Stefi and Judith. In the same letter to his mother, he reveals his conflicted attitude regarding the equality between men and women, the negative side of this conflict pointing to his need for control:

> after giving the subject a great deal of thought, I have come to believe that men and women are so different in mind and body that it may not be such a bad idea after all to demand from women a greater degree of chastity. These matters are too intimate to write about in detail.
>
> But though these considerations might lead one to favour more restraints for women, one has to take into account what happens all too often as a result. (I'm thinking, of course, of the dire consequences of "lapsing" from socially accepted standards, of having to suffer the condemnation of society.) And so finally I come back to where I started: Equal standards for men and women.[63]

The question of control between man and woman is crucial not only in the opera but appears to be significant in Bartók's own life as well. Although the overt action in the opera is motivated by Judith's need to control Bluebeard by her relentless pressure to open the doors of his castle (that is, to open the wounds of his past) and to learn everything about him, there is the powerful and relentless counterpressure of Bluebeard to control Judith's passion and desires for intimacy and to condemn her to an emotional isolation that suppresses the essence of who she is. In his personal life, Bartók reveals to us in his letter to Stefi his need to shape the woman according to his own views, to win the woman over in their ideological and spiritual struggle. He discusses their religious disagreements based on the conflict between his atheism and her "godfearing" stand. Although he asks her permission to develop the two axioms that he has presented earlier[64]—the first stating that *it is man who created God after his own likeness*, the second that *the soul is transitory and the body (that is, matter) is everlasting*—his painstaking discourse presents his views as though they were a foregone conclusion. It is he who must educate Stefi, so she may eventually come to see things his way: "You are still green? Never mind! The important thing is that you should want to mature. . . . Will you allow me to supply you with reading matter from time to time? (Something not too weighty as a start, just to bring you onto the right track)."[65] In spite of Bartók's assertion that "it's only a short time since I was still zealously bent on winning everyone over to atheism. . . . And now I am saying—let everyone do as he likes, it's no business of mine. But there's trouble in store for any pious person wanting to pick a quarrel with me and compel me by law to do this or that,"[66] his attempt to control Stefi's emotional reaction to what he writes becomes evident: "Though you wanted me to write on this subject, I must beg you to harbour no resentment against me for the way in which I've written; I would like you to feel towards me as you have always done in the past."

Stefi rejected Bartók in the early part of 1908, and this led him to characterize her in certain works composed at this time according to two personalities. The *Two Portraits* for orchestra, op. 5, published in 1911, was derived by combining the first movement of the unpublished *Violin Concerto* with an orchestrated version of the last of the *Fourteen Bagatelles* for piano, op. 6. To the first *Portrait* Bartók gave the title "Une idéale," to the second, "Une grotesque." Originally, in the *Bagatelles*, the latter piece belonged to a titled pair: "Elle est morte (Lento funebre)" and "Valse: ma mie qui danse (Presto)." Although there appears to be no direct musical correlation between these characterizations of Stefi in the *Two Portraits* and Judith in the opera, a comparison of certain changes in orchestration of the first (ideal) and second (grotesque) *Portraits* suggests a more general association to the opera. Bartók heightens the sense of the grotesque in the second of the *Portraits* by replacing the more tranquil sounds of certain instruments with sharper ones.[67] The "shrill, hysterical tone" produced by the addition of piccolo, E♭ clarinet, B♭ bass clarinet, several percussion, and the more prominent use of harps, trumpets and trombones in the second of the *Portraits* draws our attention directly to the grotesque sound associated with the "blood" motif in the opera. The scene of the "Torture Chamber" is introduced (at no. 30) by a piercing half-step (B–A♯) violin trill and agitated piccolo/flute interjection as Judith opens the door, producing a blood-red gap in the wall. The main appearance of the "blood" motif (at no. 34; see ex. 9-1 earlier) is then effectuated by the sharp, yet disembodied quality of the muted trumpets on the half-step G♯–A against the original B–A♯ trill figure in the flute, which is overlapped by the "dripping" dotted figure in the clarinets.

Emerging Symbol of Blood

The fusion of whole-tone and pentatonic spheres in Judith's line (see ex. 9-3 earlier), which forms Stefi's leitmotif, also has wider ramifications in connection with the gradually emerging symbol of "Blood." Judith's highest note (F), which belongs to the whole-tone segment (F–D♭–A), and her lowest note (G♭), which belongs to the pentatonic segment (G♭–A–D♭), together imply the presence of a half-step, that is, the complementary interval of the major-seventh boundary (F–G♭), which is one of several prominent half-steps to have emerged in these passages thus far. The first of these prominent half-steps, D–D♭, occurred as a linear disruption of the whole-tone bass line, C–D–E–F♯ (at no. 1, mm. 2–3), the second and third, F♯–F and D♯–D, as the bass of the brief orchestral interlude (no. 2, mm. 6–7) connecting Bluebeard's first two phrases. The connection between the semitones that foreshadow the chromatic

"Blood" motif and the whole-tone (fate) symbol also occurs on a more complex level in the material surrounding Judith's opening statement. The held orchestral chord expands Judith's vocal whole-tone content to five notes (A–B–Db–Eb–F) by the addition of a new note, B, while the cadential pentatonic vocal note (Gb) from the primary whole-tone scale is expanded to a larger whole-tone segment (Gb–C) by the addition of the orchestral neighbor note, C. This chromatic mixture of basic components from both whole-tone collections (C–Gb, in enharmonic spelling, C–F#, from tetrachord C–D–E–F#, that is, boundary elements of the basic F# and D pentatonic formations, and A–B–Db–Eb–F from Judith's statement) is further elaborated in the next interlude (ex. 9-5), which connects Judith's line and Bluebeard's next statement at the beginning of Recitative—part 2 (no. 3, m. 6). The two parallel ascending lines (C–D–E–F# and Ab–Bb–C) in the first four articulations of this interlude together outline the complete primary whole-tone collection, while the held notes (G–A) and boundary notes (Eb–A) of the descending line imply the presence of a gapped whole-tone cell (Eb–[ ]–G–A) from the secondary whole-tone collection. The entire chromatic content that results from these combined whole-tone segments, together with the next prominent half-step (B–C) in the bass, reveals a systematic structural projection and chromatic elaboration of the basic whole-tone tetrachord, C–D–E–F#, that is, the entire content, D–Eb–E–[ ]–F#–G–Ab–A–Bb–B–C–[ ]–D–Eb–E, contains two gaps, one between E and F#, the other between C and D. Thus, the musical premises underlying the dramatic connection between Judith as an unrelenting force (whole-tone sphere) and the anticipation of the "Blood" of Bluebeard's soul (chromatic sphere) are firmly established at the entry of the two characters into the castle.

At the same time, the interval of the semitone seems to symbolize more than simply "Blood." It tends to represent, as Banks suggests, "fear, guilt, pain and sadness— and it gradually dominates the texture as Judith taunts the duke into giving her the key to the last door. It continues to resonate in the bitonal textures towards the end— a somber reminder of the failure of the two characters to establish a true bond. Finally all that is left is the primeval pentatonicism of the opening."[68] In this musical context, which is based on pentatonic/diatonic interactions with the whole-tone sphere and the chromatic filling-in process that results from these interactions, the principle dramatic concepts of "fate," "blood," and the emotional conflicts that can be traced to them, are inextricably connected with each other on the deepest levels of the psychological and musico-dramatic context.

Following this initial dialogue (Recitative—part 1), which establishes the basic polarity between Bluebeard's distinctive pentatonic-diatonic phrases and Judith's whole-tone intrusion into the pentatonic sphere in a folklike quaternary stanzaic scheme of three lines for Bluebeard and one for Judith, the text (Recitative—part 2) introduces a more explicit statement of tension into this marriage as Bluebeard warns Judith (no. 3, mm. 6–11): "Don't you hear the warning bells? Your mother is dressed in mourning, Your father straps on his sharp sword, Your brother saddles his horse. Judith, do you still follow me?" With her reaffirmation that she is coming with him, their respective diatonic and whole-tone spheres undergo the first chromatic transformations. To this point, the three prominently placed orchestral half-steps (the first two at no. 2, mm. 6–7, the third at no. 3, mm. 5–6) have unfolded in a background-level relation separated by whole-steps: F#–F/D#–D/C–B (i.e., interval-ratio 1:2). These three half-

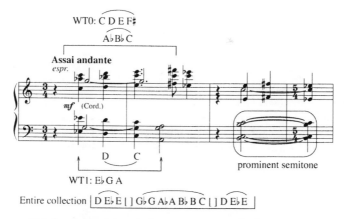

EXAMPLE 9-5. Brief orchestral interlude, no. 3, mm. 3–6, chromatic mixture of both whole-tone collections

steps then move into the foreground in Bluebeard's vocal line of Recitative—part 2 (no. 3, m. 6 ff.) in the form of an octatonic intrusion that transforms his diatonic line into a hybrid diatonic-octatonic formation (fig. 9-1).[69] We may outline the entire pitch content of this vocal phrase (through the high Gb–F) most conveniently in descending scalar ordering: C–B–A–G♯–Gb–F–Eb–D–C–B–A–G. This scale interlocks a complete octatonic scale (C–B–A–G♯–Gb–F–Eb–D) with a G major segment (G–A–B–C–D), or one of the permutations (G–A–B–C–D–Eb–F) of a larger nondiatonic folk mode that Bartók found in Eastern European folk music.[70]

Henceforth, in anticipation of blood, the primary transpositional level of two semitones at interval-ratio 1:1 (G♯–A/A♯–B) emerges with increasing prominence from the modal thematic material into a foreground event. At the return of the "Foreboding" motif (no. 4, mm. 5–6), both of these semitones appear for the first time as

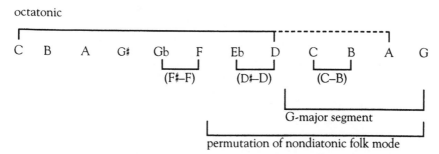

FIGURE 9-1. Bluebeard's vocal line of Recitative part 2, no. 3, m. 6ff., hybrid diatonic-octatonic formation based on foreground occurrence of earlier isolated half-steps at interval-ratio 1:2 (F♯–F/D♯–D/C–B)

basic details within the larger thematic statement to introduce Bluebeard's question (no. 5) about her stopping and wanting to go back. At this point (no. 5, mm. 2–5, flutes and oboes), one of these semitones (G#–A) appears as the upper boundary of the successive eighth-note figures. At Judith's comment (no. 10, mm. 8–9) on how dark his castle is, the pitch content of the accompanying pentatonic collection (D#–F#–G#–A#–C#) is disrupted by a single dissonant note (A) in the voice, implying the presence of a partial statement of the basic 1:1 cell, G#–A/A#–[ ]. With this reference to darkness, the clarinet begins a long sustained melody (no. 10, m. 6 ff.). This two-note *lamenting* figure (in alternating long and dotted-note values) seems to anticipate Judith's wonderment (no. 11, mm. 3–4) about the kind of water that falls onto her hand, as though Bluebeard's castle is weeping. It is striking that the clarinet timbre will again be used later to simulate the dripping of blood (at no. 34, m. 2 ff.), the new weeping—or lamenting—figure appearing in counterpoint against the main statement of the "Blood" motif (G#–A–A#–B), which is presented in anticipation of Judith's first explicit reference to blood. Unfolding in counterpoint against the present turn figure of the string ostinato (no. 10, mm. 6 ff.), this clarinet "theme" contains momentary breaks.[71] After each (e.g., no. 12), the line is contrapuntally reinforced by the addition of bass clarinet, followed by English horn, then flutes. As Bluebeard warns (no. 19, mm. 6–7) that nothing will make his castle glitter, the darker timbre of the English horn ends the long lament (in the postlude, no. 19, m. 10 ff.), which was originally initiated by the clarinet, by expanding the sustained two-note figure to a broader, turning thematic contour, C–D–A–D–C–D–G#–E/D–C–B–A–D. The latter, which emulates the ostinato turn figure of the string counterpoint, intensifies the somber mood. At Judith's first metaphorical allusion to blood (no. 11), that is, as oozing water, one of the semitones (G#–A) of the 1:1 cell (G#–A/A#–[ ]) had already appeared as a primary foreground event in the flutes, oboes, and horns.

Door I (Torture Chamber)

The components of this semitonal cell appear with increasing prominence in correspondence with the growing awareness of blood.[72] As the opening of the first door (Torture Chamber; no. 30 ff.) produces a blood-red gap in the wall, the trilled semitone A#–B appears as a dissonant element against the partially diatonic figurations. This semitone (at no. 33) is briefly diatonicized as part of the scale figures, A#–B–C#–D#–E, and its inversion, B–A#–G#–F#–E# (ex. 9-6), the basic A#–B forming an interval ratio of 1:4 with each of the other two diatonic semitones (A#–B/D#–E and E#–F#/A#–B). Then, at the main dramatic focal point of the symbol of "Blood," (no. 34; see ex. 9-1 earlier), semitone A#–B is dissociated from the latter diatonic context and joined with the other basic semitone, G#–A, to form the dissonant 1:1 cell, G#–A/A#–B. The derivation of an abstract chromatic intervallic cell from traditional modal formations contributes to the expression, direction, and integration of the drama.

The local process by which the intervallically contracted chromatic "Blood" motif or cell (G#–A–A#–B) emerges from the diatonic interval structure of the preceding figuration (as shown in ex. 9-6, scales) is a reflection of the same macroscopic process that has been developing toward this focal point since the beginning of the opera.

EXAMPLE 9-6. Torture Chamber, No. 33ff., trilled semitone A♯–B of "Blood" motif in diatonic interval-ratio 1:4 with two other boundary semitones (A♯–B/D♯–E and E♯–F♯/A♯–B) in ascending and descending scalar figure

Whereas the "Foreboding" motif (m. 16 ff.) had begun partially to fill in the anhemitonic gaps of the opening pentatonic "Castle" theme, the shrill figuration (nos. 33–34) leading directly to the "Blood" motif represents a complete and systematic manifestation of this filling-in principle. A special symmetrical intervallic relation unfolds between vocal lines and accompanying diatonic figuration, this relation providing the

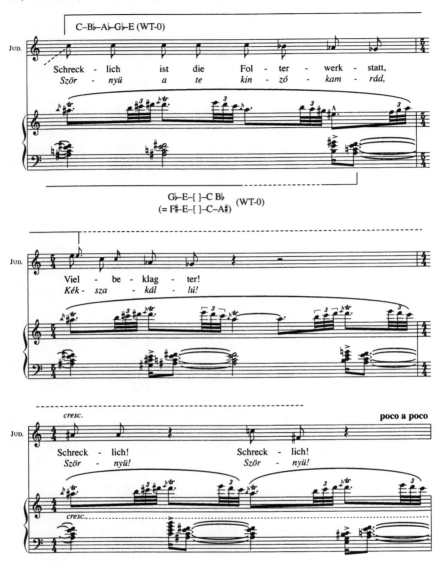

EXAMPLE 9-6 *(continued)*

means for fusing diatonic, whole-tone, and chromatic spheres at this significant point of intervallic compression. While Judith's vocal line exclusively produces a whole-tone transformation of both D pentatonic (implied by Bluebeard's perfect fourths, D–G–C) and F♯ pentatonic (represented by Judith's cadential figure ending on G♭, that is, to imply a whole-tone mutation, E–C–A♭/G♭, of Judith's original hybrid whole-tone/pentatonic motif, F–D♭–A/G♭), the orchestral figurations produce systematic semitonal intrusions into Judith's whole-tone line. The two alternating diatonic orchestral figures, A♯–B–C♯–D♯–E, and its inversion, B–A♯–G♯–F♯–E♮, both contain axial whole-tone trichords, B–C♯–D♯ and A♯–G♯–F♯, respectively. The first trichord produces a chromatic conflict with Judith's WT-0 vocal line (C–B♭–A♭–Gb–E) and, furthermore, complements Bluebeard's cadential WT-0 dyad, C–D, to imply the presence of a chromatically filled symmetry, B–[C]–C♯–[D]–D♯.

The diatonic boundary notes, A♯ and E, of the first diatonic orchestral figure also imply an extension of Bluebeard's cadential dyad (C–D) to a WT-0 tetrachord, A♯–C–D–E, this dyad and Judith's vocal line together forming the complete WT-0 scale (D–C–B♭–A♭–Gb–E). The axial trichord of the second, inverted diatonic orchestral figure, A♯–G♯–F♯, duplicates Judith's axial whole-tone trichord (in enharmonic spelling, B♭–A♭–Gb). At the same time, the boundary notes, B–E♮, of the second diatonic segment (B–A♯–G♯–F♯–E♮) map chromatically into Judith's whole-tone line, C–[B]–B♭–A♭–Gb–[E♮]–E, precisely between the two whole-steps (C–B♭ and Gb–E) that are also vertically projected to form the reiterated "French-sixth" chord (in enharmonic spelling, A♯–C–E–F♯). The "Blood" motif (B–A♯–A–G♯) descends within this minor sixth boundary (C–E) and is extended further downward to Fx (B–A♯–A–G♯–Fx). Judith's line also unfolds within this boundary. Such half-step intrusions into the whole-tone sphere are anticipated in Judith's initial vocal statements (no. 32 ff.), in which her whole-tone-related boundary, E–C (no. 33), is adjoined by half-steps to produce an octatonic, or interval-ratio 1:2 segment, E–Eb/Db–C.

The latter chromatic complementation of the combined descending whole-tone line of Judith and the inverted diatonic orchestral figure (C–[B]–B♭–A♭–Gb–[E♮]–E) is further chromaticized, then, by the "Blood" motif (G♯–A–A♯–B), significantly in descending order: the trill-figure B–A♯ appears first, to which is added A–G♯ (no. 34), then Fx, and so on, in the "dripping" dotted figure of the clarinet. Judith's vocal line (through the "Tranquillo") moves entirely within the ambitus of this descent.

The large-scale development of the contrasting personalities of the two characters is partly reflected in the formal proportions of their paired statements. Judith's dynamic, though brief, interjectory responses (at no. 3 and no. 4, mm. 3–4) within the opening pair of recitatives shifts in part 2 (no. 6) of the second pair of recitatives to an extended and uninterrupted assertion of her will to follow her husband. In the three ensuing monologues (nos. 9–19, m. 4), Judith's vocal part prevails, and her positive attitude is expressed by her desire to let light into the castle. The sectional form of the first door scene (Torture Chamber), a folklike quaternary musical structure outlining a larger binary form—introduction, a1, b1 / a2, b2, introduction—serves to demarcate the polarized attitudes of the two characters, one positive, the other negative.[73] In the first half, the dialogue of both characters refers to elements of torture, fear, and blood, the main occurrence of the "Blood" motif articulated by the music of section b1 (no. 34). In section a2 (no. 36), Judith's assertion, "No! I am not afraid.— Look, it lightens already," is now contrasted by Bluebeard's observation (no. 37) that it is a "Red brook—bloody brook." This polarity is further developed in b2 as Judith speaks of light, love, and the desire to probe, while Bluebeard refers to hiding, trembling, and danger. The larger binary musical form of this scene is, therefore, in general correspondence with the textual references to blood and fear in a1 and b1 versus light and courage in a2 and b2.

In connection with their respective attitudes, the two characters further develop their corresponding pitch-set spheres (diatonic and whole-tone) that have been established from the very beginning. As the orchestra gradually realizes the chromatic "Blood" motif (see ex. 9-1 earlier), Bluebeard's interjections establish his pentatonic-diatonic association in two perfect fourths, C–G and E–B, which are harmonically projected as an inverted C major seventh chord (E–G–B–C) as well. As Bluebeard introduces his torture chamber to Judith, the perfect fourth segment, D–G–C (no. 33, m. 2), suggests the frame of his original D pentatonic recitative (D–F–G–A–C), the held C major seventh chord providing the two notes (E and B) that originally expanded this pentatonic collection to the larger D Dorian mode (see no. 2, m. 7 ff., vocal line). The pentatonic whole-step boundary, D–C, which originally served as a link with the whole-tone sphere, is brought into registral and temporal proximity at this statement, analogous to its original cadential function (see no. 2, m. 9). This pentatonic whole-step is then absorbed into the whole-tone sphere, as Judith unfolds her first whole-tone statement of the passage (C–B♭–A♭–G♭–E). Her first four pitches, C–B♭–A♭–G♭, form the inversion of the original whole-tone tetrachord, C–D–E–F♯, which accompanied the "Foreboding" motif (mm. 16–19).

At this point, the whole-tone tetrachord is linearly extended by a transposition, E–C–A♭, of her original augmented triad, F–D♭–A (see no. 3), this extension having two important consequences: it completes a linear statement of the WT-0 scale beginning with Bluebeard's preceding D–C, and it produces a shift from Judith's original secondary WT-1 collection to the primary one containing the whole-steps (C–D and E–F♯) that bounded the F♯ pentatonic (F♯–A–B–C♯–E) and D pentatonic (D–F–G–A–C) collections associated with the castle and Bluebeard.

This transposition (E–C–A♭) of Judith's original augmented triad also permits a more complete transformation of the F♯–pentatonic collection into the whole-tone sphere. Her original line, F–D♭–A–G♭ (in enharmonic spelling, F–C♯–A–F♯), represented a whole-tone extension of, or deviation from, the F♯ pentatonic structure, whereas in the present passage, the transposition (E C–A♭) draws the cadential G♭ (i.e., F♯) into a WT-0 segment (G♭ A♭ C E) exclusively. It is striking that at her interjections (no. 33, m. 5), "Horrible, horrible," which directly precede the main statement of the "Blood" motif, we get the tritone transposition (F♯–[ ]–A♯–C) of the gapped primary whole-tone cell (C–[ ]–E–F♯) that served as the harmonic frame for the first statement of the "Foreboding" motif. The main harmonic construction at this point is the "French sixth" (whole-tone) chord, A♯–C–E–F♯, which represents a fusion of both cell transpositions (C–E–F♯ and F♯–A♯–C).

10

Duke Bluebeard's Castle

Toward Character Reversal:
Reassignment of Pentatonic
and Whole-Tone Spheres

Doors II (Armory), III (Treasure Chamber), and IV (Garden)

The psychological characterizations of both Bluebeard and Judith begin to show signs of reversal as Judith unlocks the second and third doors (Armory and Treasure Chamber) to unveil the man's power and riches. Bluebeard begins to yield to Judith's relentless demanding (no. 53, m. 7 ff.) as he now tells her not to be afraid, that "it matters no more," a comment that points to the inevitability of her actions. Bluebeard becomes more assertive when giving Judith the keys for the central three doors (III–V), an attitude that contrasts with the more reticent one he exhibits when she opens the first two and last two doors. The first hint of psychological reversal is suggested by Bluebeard's more confident offer to give Judith the keys and by Judith's new indecisiveness as she beholds his treasury, their attitudes appearing to be symbolized by the contrast between darkness and light. For instance, Judith denies being afraid and explains away her hesitancy with the excuse that the lock is hidden in the shadow, or darkness, the golden light that emanates from Bluebeard's treasure chamber providing a brilliant contrast. In the overall arch design of the opera, "the three central doors reveal more positive aspects of the human soul: in these cases it is Bluebeard who urges Judith to open them. The light which they reveal is stronger, and in the case of the fourth and fifth doors, it comes from outside the castle."[1] It is only at the fifth door, however, when Bluebeard's vast domain is revealed, that the contrasting—extroverted versus introverted—psychological characterizations of the two characters are completely reversed: Judith's vocal statement at the opening of the opera progresses from a passionate, wide-ranging vocal style in short-long Magyar rhythm to quiet awe when the fifth door is opened, while Bluebeard's vocal style progresses, conversely, from reserved, narrow-ranged repeated-note figurations to increasingly intense and passionate utterance. However, a contradiction emerges from these developments. As Bluebeard's power is revealed, he himself seems to become humbled by—less able to resist—fate.

Some insight into Bluebeard's psychological transformation, that is, reversal of his characterization, is provided by Frigyesi.[2] According to her interpretation, Bluebeard lacks self-knowledge. This is symbolized by what she believes to be Bluebeard's unawareness of what lay hidden behind each of his castle doors, a condition responsible for his indecisiveness toward Judith's entry into the first several chambers. Frigyesi assumes, therefore, that Bluebeard's ambivalence toward his own secrets is preventing him from realizing that he should actually feel confident in wanting Judith to see what lies behind the doors. It follows logically, then, from Frigyesi's conjecture, that if Bluebeard were aware of the precise contents behind the doors, he would not hesitate to reveal what one might assume to be the glory of his soul, as symbolized especially by his vast domain proudly outspread behind the fifth door.

A contradiction arises, however, from Frigyesi's otherwise plausible interpretation. The torture chamber, armory, and the other doors, all hiding blood behind them, contain secrets that one would hardly want to reveal consciously. Bluebeard would certainly have had to be aware, furthermore, that he himself is responsible for the imprisonment of his former wives behind the seventh door. It follows from this that he also would have to have specific knowledge of the terrible events hidden behind the first six doors, as the extinction of his wives must logically be traced back to them. Behind the sixth door, for instance, Judith finds a lake of motionless water, which Bluebeard tells her was formed by tears. Judith can only surmise from this and all of the preceding events that Bluebeard has had previous wives who have met their doom with him. Judith herself assumes, from her encounter with each of the first six doors, that Bluebeard has murdered his former wives, and it is their blood that she has found behind each door.[3]

Judith's "Fate" Motif and the Leitmotif of Stefi Geyer

A rhythmic variant of Judith's original "Fate" motif and its harmonization in the section that leads to the second door (i.e., Armory, at no. 40, near the end of the Torture Chamber) seem to identify Judith even more prominently with Stefi Geyer, the virtuoso violinist for whom Bartók's love remained unfulfilled. At its first appearance (see ex. 9-3 earlier), I noted that Judith's melodic figure is based on the intrusion of the whole-tone (fate) sphere into the opening F♯ pentatonic construction ("Darkness" or "Castle" motif) to outline one of the basic seventh chord manifestations of Stefi's motif, G♭–A–D♭–F (minor third/major seventh modal form, in enharmonic spelling, F♯–A–C♯–E♯). The harmonic accompaniment to this rhythmic variant of Judith's "Fate" motif (no. 40; ex. 10-1), or variant of her "Danger" motif, is now based on unequivocal transpositions (on C♯) of both major third and minor third modal forms of Stefi's motif, C♯–E♯–G♯–B♯ and C♯–E–G♯–B♯ (compare ex. 10-1 with ex. 9-4).

This major-minor simultaneity produces minor second/major seventh dissonances between E♯ and E, and also between the boundary notes, C♯ and B♯. The initial occurrence of this seventh-chord motif on C♯ (at no. 38, m. 5 ff.) had included only the minor third modal form, C♯–E–G♯–B♯, so the main occurrence (as seen in ex. 10-1), which combines major and minor modal forms just prior to the return of the section that introduced the first door (that is, transition to the Armory scene), is permitted a heightened sense of dissonance, now between the major third, E♯, in

EXAMPLE 10-1. Ending of Torture Chamber scene, no. 40, mm. 1–4, Judith's "Danger" motif, rhythmic variant of Judith's original "fate" motif and its harmonization based on C♯ transpositions of major-third and minor-third modal forms of Stefi's motif, C♯–E♯–G♯–B♯ and C♯–E–G♯–B♯

the orchestra, and minor third, E, in both orchestra and voice. This musical implication of blood (semitone E–E♯) corresponds with Judith's demand that all the doors must open for her. This statement (at no. 40) follows Bluebeard's cryptic reference (at no. 39) to what is behind them. Because the awareness of blood is not yet manifested here, we do not get the basic transpositional level (G♯–A/A♯–B) of the "Blood" motif semitones. Strikingly, Bluebeard's vocal line at this point is based on a nondiatonic collection (unusual for Bluebeard thus far in the opera). This outlines the minor-modal version of Stefi's seventh chord, F♯–A–C♯–[D♯]–E♯, at the exact transpositional level of Judith's very opening vocal statement (but in enharmonic spelling). The melodic contour reveals, therefore, the prominent infusion of the whole-tone sphere ([F–D♭–A]–G♭).

One of Bartók's most characteristic techniques is thereby revealed in the progression from the Romantic tertian seventh chord construction of the "Stefi" leitmotif to the chromatically compressed intervals (semitones) of the "Blood" motif. The presence of the latter is implied, for instance, in the major-seventh boundary or juxtaposed major third/minor third modal variants of the "Stefi" seventh chord leitmotif (see fig. 2-2 earlier). The larger (major third) intervals of the "Stefi" chord also imply the presence of the whole-tone sphere, so the anticipation of blood in the conflicting major (ideal) and minor (funereal) forms of her seventh chord is symbolized in Bartók's characteristic technique based on chromatic compression of diatonic (and/or whole-tone) material.[4] Regarding this principle, Bartók said that "when I first used the device of extending chromatic melodies into a diatonic form, or vice versa, I thought I invented something absolutely new, which never yet existed. And now I see that an absolutely identical principle exists in Dalmatia since Heaven knows how long a time."[5]

We may speculate about the symbolic meaning that Stefi's leitmotif, especially the minor-modal form of the C♯ transposition, C♯–E–G♯–B♯ (No, 38, m. 5 ff., and no. 40), and its dramatic placement at this point in the opera had for Bartók so soon after Stefi Geyer's rejection of him. This is precisely the version of the leitmotif that Bartók outlined for her in his letter dated mid-September 1907 (see ex. 9-4 earlier).[6] The tone of his letter hints that his relationship with her was already under some strain: "I have a sad misgiving that I shall never find any consolation in life save in music. And yet— (This is your "Leitmotiv"). . . . One letter from you, a line, even a word—and I am in a transport of joy, the next brings me almost to tears, it hurts so. What is to be the end of it all?" Bartók construed his expression of these personal emotions as a human weakness.[7] This attitude reflects the strong Nietzschean tone expressed in the same letter (p. 86): "Do you mean to say that you wouldn't have the courage to read Nietzsche's *Zarathustra*, even though you would be intrigued by Strauss's?!" His apprehension that the love between Stefi and himself would be dissolved was soon to be realized, and he expressed his feelings about this by his eventual transformation of the lively, "witty and amusing" second-movement theme of the early *Violin Concerto*, which he was composing (in 1907–1908) for Stefi at the time he wrote this letter, into the slow fugue theme that opens the *First String Quartet* (1907–1909). Because of Stefi's rejection of him around the time he finished the *Concerto*, Bartók referred to this thematic transformation in the quartet, with its more depressed mood, as his "Funeral Dirge,"[8] hence, the duality of emotion that spans the gamut from love to the emptiness of death. The trend from the ideal (in the first movement of the *Violin Concerto*) to the funereal (in the first movement of the *First String Quartet* and *Bluebeard's Castle*) via the shape of the concerto's virtuoso second-movement theme appears to symbolize the final outcome of Bartók's relationship with Stefi. The theme of unrequited love in Wagner's *Tristan und Isolde* is symbolized in the *Violin Concerto* by the spirit of *Tristan*.[9] This connection between the Bartók idiom and that of Wagner is supported by certain musical elements in the score of the *Concerto*:

> The anguished entry of the countersubject (mm. 7–8) dramatizes the fate of Wagnerian "realism" and its great influence. Stefi's "love-motif" and the "grief-motif" of Tristan are fastened here forever, and their motivic complementation is thus made clear. The last note, A, of the subject is the pivot to the countersubject, which sets up the first polarization in the piece. The countersubject (mm. 7–8) begins with F–E; together, this subject/countersubject intersection (at A/F–E) forms the first three notes of Wagner's opera. This angular contour of the subject/countersubject convergence (A/F–E–G–C♯) foreshadows the jagged virtuoso theme of the second movement [ex. 5]. Thus . . . the note A as part of the A–F–E motif eliding subject and countersubject, represents the first implication of the fusion between the ideal and virtuoso. It is the spirit of *Tristan* that emerges as a catalyst.[10]

János Kárpáti points to the dual (love-death) meaning of this transformation of the theme from its lively form in the concerto to its more depressed disposition in the quartet, asserting that the "yearning and resigned musical tone . . . was inspired by [Bartók's] reading of Nietzsche and Schopenhauer. . . . Under such influences it was natural that the composer should express his passionate affection with the same musical character as his torment, resignation and longing for death."[11] In accord with Bartók's emotional transformation associated with Stefi, this "love-death" duality (and identity) evolved in the musical forms and symbolic meaning of the motif during the period of compositional creativity extending from the *Violin Concerto* to the *Bluebeard* opera. The *String Quartet* theme is based on transposition F–A♭–C–E, the minor third modal form of the major seventh chord that also characterizes the C♯ version of Stefi's leitmotif (C♯–E–G♯–B♯) in the present section of the opera (see ex. 10-1 earlier). It is striking that, as presented in Bartók's letter to Stefi (see ex. 9-4), this C♯ transposition of the leitmotif is also harmonically set in a short-long "Magyar" rhythm, which also appears as a funeral-like ostinato figure under variants of Stefi's leitmotif in *Bagatelle No. 13*, op. 6 (1908), entitled "Elle est mort" (She is dead). In the *Bluebeard* opera setting, the depressed mood of the C♯ minor form of Stefi's (now Judith's) leitmotif, which is integrated into Judith's "Danger" motif (no. 40) as part of the bimodal (major-minor third) clash, C♯–E♯–G♯–B♯ versus C♯–E–G♯–B♯, is intensified to the point of fear and trembling, as expressed by the remaining text and premonition of blood.

The funereal short-long "Magyar" rhythm found in Bartók's letter and *Bagatelle No. 13* also appears in the opera in greater agitation (no. 41, m. 6 ff.). This occurs at Bluebeard's fearful utterance, "Beware, beware of my castle. Beware, beware for us, Judith," as a projection of his tortured, angry self. We may conclude that Bartók's idealistic love for Stefi, which was manifested from the opening measures of the *Violin Concerto*, no longer glows in the *Bluebeard* opera. This interpretation differs in a basic way from that of Frigyesi,[12] who links the minor third modal form of the "Stefi" chord (C♯–E–G♯–B♯), as it occurs at the first climax of the first scene (see Molto vivace in her ex. 32), with an emphatic statement about Judith's love. Frigyesi's assertion that "Judith's aggressivity in insisting on her role of changing things in the castle appears to Bartók as an act of passionate love" is a viable interpretation within the opera at large. However, her assumption that "love is obvious from both the thematic and the harmonic designs" in the present ten-measure context differs from the explicit meaning that Bartók himself had given to the "Stefi" chord in its minor third/major seventh form, C♯–E–G♯–B♯. In his letter to Stefi, in which he outlines this form of the seventh chord,[13] he is not referring so much to love (as Frigyesi suggests), but rather to "a state of spiritual intoxication" based on extreme feelings of joy and sadness, which Bartók considers necessary for composing.

The letter thus suggests a different, perhaps even opposite meaning to that based primarily on love, one that was later confirmed in Bartók's statement about this particular harmonic form, C♯–E–G♯–B♯ (as transposed to F–A♭–C–E at the opening of the *First String Quartet*), as his "funeral dirge." In his letter, the motif acquires a more somber quality as Stefi's rejection seems imminent. Immediately preceding the motif, Bartók writes that he has "a sad misgiving that I shall never find any consolation in life save in music," and immediately following the motif he tells Stefi that he has been "in a very strange mood, going from one extreme to the other. One letter from you, a line, even a word—and I am in a transport of joy, the next brings me almost to tears, it hurts so. What is to be the end of it all? and when?" Frigyesi refers to the seventh chord on C♯ as the "dominant" of the opening dark key of F♯, which she asserts is the "polar opposite on the same axis" as C,[14] the latter key of light characterizing Judith's vocal line. However, it should not be assumed that these two tonalities (F♯ and C) are connected in this context by means of the C♯ seventh chord, since the latter (C♯–E–G♯–B♯) is not the dominant seventh chord of F♯, either in terms of its construction or its function. Nor is there enough contextual evidence to assume that if C♯ is the dominant of F♯, then it must also function, by substitution of tonalities on the "same axis" of Lendvai's system, as the dominant of C, that is, of the polar-axis tritone of F♯. There is no functional relation between the C♯ chord and C-major vocal outline, only a contextual juxtaposition. The significance of these tonal/harmonic juxtapositions between the bright C major tonality and the C♯– minor third/major seventh chord lies rather in their extremely dissonant half-step relationship. Thus, it would seem that these dissonant relations point more to emotional conflict and pain rather than passionate love.

The operatic setting appears to be the final stage in the symbolic metamorphosis of Stefi's leitmotif and Bartók's psychological obsession with her, the seventh chord construction and its modal variants (always symbolizing Stefi) migrating from one composition to another during these years of the composer's emotional upheaval. In the *Violin Concerto*, variants of the leitmotif are identified with two contrasting musical images of the beloved, the "idealized Stefi Geyer, celestial and inward," and the lively violin virtuoso depicted as a "cheerful, witty, amusing" young girl. As their relationship came to an end, Bartók still managed to restrain his impulse to characterize her as the "indifferent, cool and silent Stefi Geyer" in a projected third movement, because he felt the music would have been "hateful."[15] However, he soon combined the "ideal," loving image of Stefi from the first movement of the *Concerto* with the grotesque mood of the first of the *Two Romanian Dances*, op. 8a (1909). He then renamed the first movement of the *Concerto* as "One Ideal" and combined it with an orchestrated version of the *Fourteenth Bagatelle*, op. 6, renamed as "One Grotesque" to form the *Two Portraits*, op. 5 (1907–1908). But it is in *Bluebeard* that Stefi's leitmotif undergoes its final metamorphosis beyond the grotesque stage into the violent, blood-ridden (even hateful) scenario of the opera, which progresses toward the inevitable. Judith's "character has a hard, unyielding core over which Bluebeard exerts little control. She makes a decision at the beginning of the opera and pursues it to the end, a course of action which, paradoxically, brings about her own ruin. But something even more vital has been destroyed as well: the fragile love that she and Bluebeard have nurtured during its brief existence."[16] From Leafstedt's account, one cannot help but draw a parallel (albeit a nonliteral one) between the psychology of the characters in the opera and the adamante stance and hopeless love echoed in Bartók's last letters to Stefi.[17]

Kroó's assessment of Judith as a symbol of "passion with all its destructive power" and the "demon whose passion ruins the happiness of both"[18] can, in spite of Kroó's bias, lend some plausibility to the notion that the woman in the opera serves as the instrument for the composer's emotional and psychological catharsis of the pain he suffered from Stefi's rejection. The forces behind Bartók's obsession with Stefi and his unabated need to work out his emotional struggle with her and the woman in Balázs's libretto, both linked by a common musical metaphor (leitmotif assigned to Stefi in his letter of mid-September, 1907, and to Judith in his opera of 1911), may best be understood in terms of the composer's relationship to his parents. Bartók's emotional dependence on his mother throughout his life, for instance, may explain his magnetism toward girls much younger than himself.[19] By controlling younger women, he may have felt instinctively that he could regain the control that his mother exerted over him. Pethő, in citing Bartók, brings to our attention the following[20]:

> When he first suffered his existential crisis, as a young man, he mentioned his love for his mother in the first place as a reason for not committing a suicide.[21] . . . Nearly forty years later, after the death of his mother, this feeling hopelessly kept him in its power: "I could enjoy all pleasures, if I had not the constant feeling that everything comes too late."[22] . . . On the other hand his relationship to the opposite sex [was] characterized by a teaching and elucidating attitude and by the ambition for leading which revealed both his very strong control of consciousness and his spiritual mentality and commitment. His ambition for dominance over women was underlined by submission appearing in his relationships to some men. . . . Such a polarization of dominance and submission would certainly not have come about, if he had not lost his father in his youth and if he had not had to begin to lead a conscious, controlled and responsible life so early.

Thus, Bartók, although older than the women in his life, remains hopelessly infantalized by his dependence on his mother. This may shed light on the Bluebeard character as a metaphor for the composer. Bartók's attachments can help us to understand one of the basic contradictions of Bluebeard's relation to Judith: the wealthy and powerful man of the opera gradually weakens in his resistance against the prying of the woman. Perhaps we also can equate the paradoxical entrapment of Bluebeard (Bartók) with "endless darkness," which represents his ultimate weakness yet, at the same time, his ultimate strength (i.e., his defense against emotional imprisonment and victory over the woman). The changing strong-weak positions between the two characters are not synchronized in the drama, a condition that permits development of the competition for control—Bartók was controlling of, yet dependent on, the woman (Stefi) who eventually rejected him, the same condition characterizing Bluebeard's relationship with Judith except for the reverse in terms of the rejection.[23] Thus, based on the outcome of the opera, the relationship between Bluebeard and Judith may be interpreted, in part, as a metaphor for the psychological/emotional shift from the composer's love for Stefi to his anger and depression.

This shift from love to anger/depression and the increasing sense of danger is encapsulated in Bluebeard's question (no. 39) that he poses to Judith about what the doors are hiding. The answer is implied in the orchestral accompaniment under Judith's abridged statement (no. 40, mm. 3–5), "every door," based on the more emphatic major seventh chordal statements of Stefi's motif (C♯–E♯–G♯–B♯); these are compounded harmonically by the dotted clarinet figure, which invokes the image of dripping blood at the main appearance of the "Blood" motif (no. 34, m. 3 ff.; see ex. 9-1 earlier).[24] This added layer (see ex. 10-1 earlier), in the more agitated diminished rhythm, is generated from the clashing minor third (E) above the major third form of Stefi's seventh chord and resolved at the half-step trill (A♯–B) of the original "Blood" motif. The basic four-note form of the "Blood" motif is also present in this progression: the C♯–B♯ boundary of the seventh chord and the cadential A♯–B trill together imply the presence of the interval 1:1 ratio of two semitones to give us A♯–B/B♯–C♯, a transposition of the original form (G♯–A/A♯–B) as it first emerged in the Torture Chamber; at that occurrence, the dyad A♯–B was also presented as a trill. This musical technique of intervallic reinterpretation permits Bartók to create an inextricable connection between Stefi's original (diatonic) love motif and its transformation into a depressed, frightful, and more abstract (chromatic) form. The A♯–B trill, one of the two main semitones of the "Blood" motif, is carried over into the next (Armory) scene, where it is transformed into a segment of a new diatonic figure based on the complete F♯ Mixolydian mode, F♯–G♯–A♯–B–C♯–D♯–E (no. 42, m. 5 ff.).

Transformation between Judith's (Stefi's) Motif of the Seventh Chord and the Chromatic Motif of "Blood"

The means of transformation from chromatic to diatonic extremes, or the reverse, which characterizes harmonic progression and pitch-set interactions in Bartók's works in general,[25] is manifested as early as his *Eight Hungarian Folk Songs* (1907-1917). In the first song (ex. 10-2), for instance, the exclusive E pentatonic pitch content (E–G–A–B–D) of the folk tune serves as the point of departure for expanded modal pitch collections in the piano accompaniment,[26] the combination producing a larger polymodal chromatic symmetry. The E pentatonic content is projected into the bass line, where it is extended to a complete statement of the E Phrygian mode (E–F–G–A–B–C–D) as the basis for the overall harmonic root progression. While the addition of the Phrygian second and sixth degrees (F and C) to the basic E pentatonic content in the bass line disrupts the pentatonic symmetry (E–[F]–G–A–B–[C]–D), the E Phrygian mode also appears within the local harmonizations, where it belongs to a larger bimodal symmetry. The opening E pentatonic arpeggiation, which forms the exclusive harmonic basis (at mm. 3 and 8) of the first and last notes of the tune (seventh degree, D, and tonic, E), is expanded to the larger E Dorian mode by the addition of the modal sixth (C♯) and second (F♯) degrees: E–[F♯]–G–A–B–[C♯]–D). This modal expansion, which produces the first local disruption of the E pentatonic symmetry, is balanced directly by the lowering of these two modal degrees to F and C (mm. 5–6) to produce the E Phrygian mode E–[F]–G–A–B–[C]–D). Together, these two E modes complement each other to produce the larger bimodal chromatic symmetry, E–F–F♯–G–A–B–C–C♯–D.

While the chromatic segments (E–F–F♯–G and B–C–C♯–D) retain their bimodal meaning in this song, in other works of Bartók—for instance, in the slow movement of the 1926 *Sonata* for piano—such chromatic tetrachordal components are extracted from a similar bimodal combination (mm. 10–12, right hand [R.H.]), A–B♭–B–C–D–E♭–E–F–[ ] (A Aeolian, A–B–C–D–E–F–[ ], embellished by A Locrian elements, B♭ and E♭), and developed in the middle section as abstract four-note cells, for example, D–E♭–E–F (in enharmonic spelling, D–D♯–E–E♯, at mm. 37-41, left hand [L.H.]) and A–B♭–B–C (in enharmonic spelling, A–A♯–B–C, at

EXAMPLE 10-2. First of Bartók's arrangement of *Eight Hungarian Folk Songs* (1907–1917), mm. 3–8, E-pentatonic pitch content (E–G–A–B–D) of folk tune as point of departure for expanded modal pitch collections in piano accompaniment, combination producing larger polymodal chromatic symmetry

m. 37, R.H.). These as well as other transpositions of the cell in this passage (mm. 30–41) together produce the entire chromatic continuum.

In the first several sections of the opera's Armory scene—sections a1 (no. 42, m.7 ff.), a2 (no. 46 ff.) and part of b1 (nos. 48–50)—Bluebeard's vocal line continues to reflect the reserve that has characterized his demeanor thus far, as he begs Judith to be cautious (see ending of a2, no. 47, mm. 4–5), "Beware, beware for us, Judith!" his phrases remaining short, infrequent, often fragmented, and exclusively diatonic. In contrast to the wider, more extroverted major seventh boundary of Judith's (Stefi's) motif, which was asserted prominently near the end of the preceding scene (see ex. 10-1 earlier), Bluebeard's more introverted vocal line implies the slightly contracted minor seventh chordal components of the Hungarian pentatonic scale at prominent structural points. His interjection on C♯–F♯ at the opening of a1 is part of the tonic minor seventh chord, D♯–F♯–A♯–C♯ (oboes/clarinets), his last statement in a2 (no. 47, m.10–no. 48) outlining a complete G minor-seventh chord (G–B♭–D–F) within the larger G pentatonic collection of his vocal line, G–B♭–C–D–F.

In contrast to Bluebeard's character development, a change in Judith's extroverted manner is imminent as she begins to acknowledge the man's power. While her vocal line is still more continuous and prominent than Bluebeard's in the opening sections of this scene, the pitch constructions underlying her phrases are somewhat more diatonic than in the preceding section. Her initial statement (no. 42, mm. 10–12), "A hundred cruel, horrible weapons," reiterates the D♯ tonic key of the second door scene, the orchestral D♯–minor seventh chord (D♯–F♯–A#–C♯) to which Bluebeard's preceding C♯–F♯ interjection belongs (no. 42, m. 8). The descending minor seventh chordal outline (C♯–A♯–F♯–D♯) of her vocal part represents an intervallic contraction of the major-seventh boundary of her original ("Stefi") motif (see ex. 9-3 earlier). At the same time, her second vocal phrase (no. 43) introduces a chromatic conflict between A♯ and A, which prepares us for her first references to blood in this scene (no. 45, m. 4): "Blood dries on your weapons!"[27] This statement is introduced by Bluebeard's question, "Are you afraid?" and by the first interjection in this scene of the other basic half-step, G♯–A (in muted horns/trumpets), of the main "Blood" motif (G♯–A/A♯–B), the first (A♯–B) having initiated this scene as a trill.

The axis of symmetry (A–A♯) of the basic transposition (G♯–A–A♯–B) of the "Blood" motif (see ex. 9-1 earlier) is established in the initial figuration of this scene as the implied axis of the basic diatonic fifth (F♯–C♯) of the opera. The entire figure (upper oboe/clarinet line, C♯–B–C♯–D♯–C♯, lower oboe/clarinet line, F♯–G♯–F♯–E–F♯) outlines the diatonic hexachord (E–F♯–G♯/B–C♯–D♯ around the implied axis of A–A♯), which links the pentatonic/diatonic sphere of Bluebeard with the more abstract chromatic sphere of blood (G♯–A/A♯–B). The figural hexachord is a symmetrical manifestation of the pentatonic/diatonic form expressly built around the tonic fifth, F♯–C♯, of the original "Castle" theme (F♯–A–B–C♯–E), so blood is imminent in, even central to, the infra-structure of Bluebeard's being.

The upper basic half-step (A♯–B) of the main "Blood" motif (G♯–A/A♯–B) seems to be lurking just below the surface of section a1. It is implied in Bluebeard's second statement (no. 43, mm. 3–4), which introduces Judith to his armory. This adds a new note (B) to his initial fifth (F♯–C♯) to give us a new fifth (B–F♯) within his larger, incomplete pentatonic vocal segment, F♯–B–C♯. At this point, the horns add this perfect fifth (B–F♯) to the D♯–minor seventh figure of the orchestra (D♯–F♯–A♯–C♯), the overlap (B–D♯–F♯–A♯–C♯) also implying the presence of the major form of Judith's (Stefi's) seventh chord motif (B–D♯–F♯–A♯). The major seventh boundary of the latter outlines precisely the other half-step/major seventh interval class (A♯–B) of the main "Blood" motif, which had introduced this scene in the form of the trill figure. The B major seventh chord is immediately transformed back into the original minor seventh form, but remaining at the transposed pitch level (B–D–F♯–A). One of the main differences between the major (B–D♯–F♯–A♯) and minor (B–D–F♯–A) modal forms of these transpositions (on B) is in their respective seventh degrees (A♯ and A), the chromatic conflict first introduced in Judith's second vocal phrase (no. 43). Section a1 closes (no. 45, mm. 12–16) with a more prominent manifestation of this conflict (ex. 10-3). Judith's more chromatic (i.e., octatonic A♯–

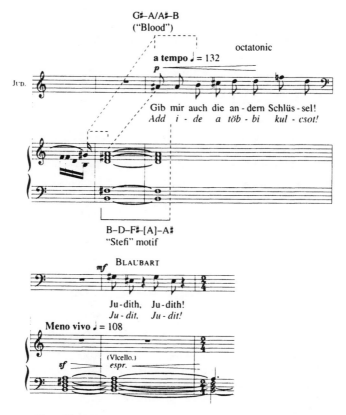

EXAMPLE 10-3. Door II (Armory), section a1, no. 45, mm. 12–16, Judith's more chromatic (octatonic A♯–B–C♯–D–[ ]–F) line initiated by half-step A♯–B, A♯ expanding boundary (B–A) of held B-minor-seventh chord (B–D–F♯–A); vocal half-step (A♯–B) component of basic "Blood" motif (G♯–A/A♯–B) transforms B-minor-seventh chord into minor-third modal form of "Stefi" motif, B–D–F♯–A♯

B–C♯–D–[ ]–F) vocal line is initiated by half-step A♯–B, the A♯ expanding the boundary (B–A) of the held B minor seventh chord (B–D–F♯–A). This vocal half-step (A♯–B), which is a component of the basic "Blood" motif (G♯–A/A♯–B) at its original occurrence, transforms the B minor seventh chord into the minor third modal form of the "Stefi" motif, B–D–F♯–A♯. Thus, the conflict between the major seventh, which has been associated with Judith's intrusion (i.e., as part of the whole-tone transformation of Bluebeard's pentatonic sphere in the Stefi motif, F–D♭–A–G♭, in enharmonic spelling and chordal outline, F♯–A–C♯–E♯, near the beginning of the opera), and the minor seventh, associated with the pentatonic basis of the "Darkness" or "Castle" theme (F♯–A–B–C♯–E), underlies the dramatic development and symbolic message of this scene. The interval-class 1/11 (half-step/major seventh) cell that symbolizes "Blood" is imminent in these relations between the seventh chord variants.

Following the return (at the opening of section a2, no. 46) to the tonic D♯–minor seventh chord in the orchestra and Judith's vocal line, Bluebeard's character now begins to reveal both dramatic and musical change (no. 47, mm. 4–5). Bluebeard's somewhat wider-ranged vocal descent, C♯–A♯–F♯–E, seems to foreshadow his more extroverted expression of later scenes. The original F♯–minor seventh construction (F♯–A–C♯–E) of the pentatonic "Darkness" (that is, "Castle") motif is modified in Bluebeard's vocal line by the raised third degree, A♯, giving us C♯–A♯–F♯–E (in root position, F♯–A♯–C♯–E). This statement reveals the rhythm and contour of Judith's (Stefi's) original seventh chord motif, and is also a modified intervallic inversion of the latter (E–G–B–D♯), which is simultaneously sustained in the orchestra. The progression and combination of these variant seventh chords at this point (no. 47f.) together produce a heightened chromaticism as well: the held chord F–A–C–E♭ moves to a chordal variant, E–G–B–D♯, a half-step below, the latter under Bluebeard's melodic variant, F♯–A♯–C♯–E. Together, these three forms outline a series of half-step related seventh chords (on E, F, and F♯), their combined pitch content implying the presence of a ten-note polymodal context: E–F–F♯–G–[ ]–A–A♯–B–C–C♯–[ ]–D♯, the significance being evident in connection with blood and Judith's relentless quest despite Bluebeard's warning (no. 45, m. 8): "Are you afraid?" Kárpáti's observation of a similar, though more systematic, set of relationships in Bartók's *Contrasts* (1938) has general relevance to the chromatic principle lying behind the unfolding of seventh chords in the opera:

> Although we have stressed that the constructional principle expounded above . . . cannot be considered a dodecaphonic series, its tendency is to fill out the dodecaphonic scale as fully as possible. The three closed "cells" of the chain of fifths with common thirds [see Kárpáti's ex. 12: A–C–C♯–E, B♭–C♯–D–F, B–D–E♭–F♯] provide a dodecaphonic series which is supplemented by a connecting "cell" [C♯–E–F–G♯ and G–B♭–B–D] each to produce a dodecaphonic series. That means that Bartók . . . has once again arrived in his logical arrangement of the musical material at a structure closely approximating to it in principle.[28]

As Judith renews her fervor to have all the doors open (no. 47), her preceding vocal statement, which unfolds a more chromatic (octatonic) line (A–B–C–D–E♭–F) similar to the previous one (A♯–B–C♯–D–[ ]–F) on the same text, "Give me the other keys," is transformed at the next statement of the same text (no. 47, m. 7) into a hybrid whole-tone/diatonic construction, G–A–B–C♯–D♯/F♯. Thus, as a symbol of the intrusion of fate (Judith) into Bluebeard's private world, notes C♯ and D♯ of the vocal D♯– minor seventh segment, D♯–F♯–[ ]–C♯ (see no. 46, mm. 2–4), which is also isolated in the upper staff of the accompaniment, is transformed by its intersection with the initial whole-tone segment (G–A–B–C♯–D♯) of the voice (at no. 47, m. 7). A more complete whole-tone transformation occurs at Judith's next, more passionate vocal statement (ex. 10-4), which opens Section b1 (no. 48, mm. –3-4). Juxtaposed against her reiterated D♯– minor seventh chordal boundary (D♯–C♯), the accompaniment unfolds ascending scales, the first outlining the major seventh chord motif, F–A–C– E, the second the D♯– minor seventh chord with raised seventh (C♯ to Cx). The latter gives us the minor third modal form of the "Stefi" motif, D♯–F♯–A♯–Cx, in which the upper three notes are absorbed into the complete whole-tone scale, D♯–E♯/F♯– G♯–A♯–B♯–Cx–E. These interactions and transformations serve as prelude to the heightened anxiety that characterizes the remainder of the Armory scene. Bluebeard presents his first aria in section b1 (no. 50, m. 3 ff.), as he speaks of trembling, invasion, opening of wounds, and sorrow. Now, his vocal line moves from pentatonic phrases in section b1 through several polymodal chromatic shifts in section b2 (no. 50, m. 8 ff.) in quasi-imitative juxtapositions with the horn (no. 50, mm. 3–7), the modality mutated into an exotic chromatic figure reminiscent of the "Danger" motif. The horn timbre itself, like that in Debussy's opera, seems to invoke the sense of darkness as it is reinforced by the lower woodwinds (bassoon, bass clarinet, and English horn).

EXAMPLE 10-4. Door II (Armory), section b1, no. 48, mm. 1–4, more complete whole-tone transformation at Judith's more passionate statement, based on D♯-minor–seventh chordal boundary (vocal D♯–C♯) above ascending scales: major-seventh-chord motif, F–A–C–E, in first scale, and D♯-minor–seventh chord with raised seventh (D♯–F♯– A♯–Cx), in second scale, upper three notes absorbed into complete whole-tone scale, D♯–E♯/F♯–G♯–A♯–B♯–Cx–E

The inherent interval-class identity between the boundary (major seventh) interval of the diatonic "Stefi" (Judith) leitmotif (F#–A–C#–E#, or its modal variants) and the cyclic (semitone) interval of the chromatic "Blood" motif (G#–A–A#–B, or its transpositions and segments), a connection so essential in the organic musico-dramatic processes, may be shown in the Armory Scene to stem ultimately from operations on the basic F# pentatonic structure (F#–A–B–C#–E, or its minor seventh chordal substructure, F#–A–C#–E) of Bluebeard's original "Castle" theme. The Armory Scene (no. 42) is introduced by a trill based on one of the original semitones (A#–B) of the "Blood" motif, against descending semitone (E#–E–D#–D–C#–C) and whole-tone (C#–B–A–G) lines in the upper counterpoint. In overlap with the trill, the main ostinato figuration (sustained fifth and triplets) of section a' establishes a significant reference to the original "Castle" theme, the sustained fifth (F#–C#) serving as the primary structural interval of the "Castle" theme's pentatonic outline (F#–A–B–C#–E). While the A#–B trill expands the chromatic content of the combined semitonal (E#–E–D#–D–C#–C) and whole-tone (C#–B–A–G) contrapuntal lines to E#–E–D#–D–C#–C–B–A#–A–[ ]–G (no. 42, mm. 1–3, voice and descending upper line), the following held F#–C# seals off the interval-class 2/10 boundary chromatically (E#–[F#]–G) to produce maximal chromatic saturation. The G# of the triplet figure completes the entire chromatic content of the upper contrapuntal lines. The pentatonic fifth (F#–C#) serves as the basic thread in the ensuing progression of seventh chord harmonic variants within the larger stanzaic structure of the scene.

The embellishing motion of the triplet figure draws the sustained fifth, F#–C# (i.e., the primary structural interval of the original F# pentatonic "Castle" theme), into a harmonic context based on two types of constructions so essential to the symbolic polarity of the opera: (1) the Straussian "romantic" major seventh chord (associated with Judith/Stefi), which frames the triplet figure (E–G#–B–D#); and (2), the folklike pentatonic/diatonic material (associated with the "Castle" theme and Bluebeard), which forms the basis of the ostinato figure (E–F#–G#–B–C#–D#, and/or its pentatonic subcollections, E–F#–G#–B–C# or F#–G#–B–C#–D#). The symmetrical placement of the sustained fifth, F#–C#, within the major-seventh chord (E–[F#]–G#–B–[C#]–D#) in this passage suggests the possibility of a link between the pentatonic "Castle" theme and the major-seventh "Stefi" motif). That is to say, the ostinato figuration that opens the Armory scene synthesizes the latter two types of construction, the catalyst being the primary structural interval (F#–C#) of the basic "Castle" theme.

Judith's original statement of the "Stefi" leitmotif, Gb–A–Db–F (in enharmonic spelling, F#–A–C#–E#), was shown earlier to imply a partial whole-tone transformation of Bluebeard's pentatonic "Castle" theme (F#–A–B–C#–E) by the alteration of the seventh degree, E to F (or E#). In the present (Armory) scene, other chromatic alterations of the F# pentatonic structure, which suggest a symbolic significance in connection with the basic harmonic (pentatonic vs. major seventh) polarity between Bluebeard and Judith, also contribute to the musico-dramatic direction toward "Blood." The A#–B trill figure, which leads into the scene, suggests, together with the sustained F#–C#, the major modal transformation (F#–A#–C#–[ ]) of the basic F# pentatonic structure (F#–A–C#–E). The A# of the trill is absorbed, then, into another perfect-fifth figure (D#–A#) in counterpoint with the sustained F#–C#. Both fifths together form a transposition (D♯–F♯–A♯–C♯) of the "Castle" theme's penta-tonic minor seventh chord against the E major seventh outline (E–G♯–B–D♯) of the triplet figure. Bluebeard's ominous question, "What do you see?" built on C♯–F♯, is answered by Judith's words in two tetrasyllabic statements (i.e., octosyllabic structure of the old Hungarian folk-song style) on the D♯ minor seventh chord outline. At her octosyllabic consequent phrase, "Many terrible tools of war," her vocal line introduces the first chromatic conflict, between A♯ and A, above the sustained fifth, F♯–C♯. This produces both major and minor third modal forms of the basic seventh chord (F♯–A/A♯–C♯–[ ]), which emerges more explicitly in the new sixteenth-note figuration, in counterpoint also with the "dripping" dotted-rhythm figure. The F♯ major-minor bimodal juxtaposition, which contains the interval (semitone) associated with blood, plays a crucial role in the unfolding of the original "Blood" motif (G♯–A/A♯–B) in this scene, in that it serves as a long-range link between the initial dyad (A♯–B trill) and dyad G♯–A, which emerges at the first reference to blood in this scene, explicitly in the horns and trumpets (at no. 45, m. 2). Judith's consequent phrase (at no. 43, m. 2) adds G♯, the descending sequence outlining three notes ([ ]–A♯–A–G♯) of the "Blood" motif.

Descending Third Transpositions of Variant Seventh Chords That Produce Chromatic Collisions

Semitones emerge from the major-minor modal variants as well as major-minor seventh variants of the leitmotif, these variants producing chromatic collisions.[29] At the same time, a more pervasive, systematic extraction of semitones develops from a process based on transpositions of the seventh-chord (see fig. 2-2 earlier). From the construction, interaction, and development of the thirds and sevenths of Judith's (Stefi's) diatonic leitmotif comes the chromatic sphere of blood. This results in what Kárpáti refers to, in his discussion of the "Scherzo alla bulgarese" of the *Fifth String Quartet* (1934), as a "chain of major and minor thirds."[30] He asserts that the third chain "is no new phenomenon in Bartók, since the leitmotif of his early works also contains a similar melody forming principle."

The present scene of the opera begins with ambiguous alternations and juxtapositions between the implied F♯ major seventh or minor seventh chord (F♯–A♯–C♯–[ ]) and the D♯ minor seventh chord (D♯–F♯–A♯–C♯) in the eighth-note counterpoint (no. 42, m. 7 ff.). Within the basic initial figuration (i.e., anchored on the sustained F♯–C♯ of the original "Castle" theme), the complete pitch content of the former (F♯–A♯–C♯–[E]), that is, with minor seventh, is suggested by the E of the triplets, while the lower third transposition ([D♯]–F♯–A♯–C♯) is simultaneously implied by the D♯ of the triplets. This foreshadows a procedure in this scene based on supertertian extensions outward from a central intervallic construction (F♯–C♯), the latter itself having seventh chord significance in this passage as well as at the very opening of the opera.

The first chromatic collision (A♯–A), which occurs (at no. 43) between the major/minor thirds of the implied F♯ seventh chord (F♯–A♯/A–C♯–[ ]) and its lower third transposition, D♯– minor seventh chord (D♯–F♯–A♯–C♯), is compounded by a hint of the next lower third transposition (B–D♯–F♯–A♯). The latter is implied by the addition of B in the dotted figure. At Bluebeard's words, "This is my armoury, Judith," the explicit B major seventh harmony elides with the D♯– minor seventh chord under the sustained F♯–C♯, so three transpositional levels of the seventh-chord construction (on F♯, D♯, and B) have unfolded in the chain of thirds thus far (from top to bottom: E–C♯–A♯/A–F♯–D♯–B). The last transposition, on B, is significant in that its major seventh boundary (B–A♯) reinstates the notes of the initial semitonal trill, a significant semitone collision in preparation for more prominent manifestations of the basic symbol of blood. The B major seventh collection (B–D♯–F♯–A♯) is immediately transformed (no. 43, mm. 3–5) into a B minor seventh collection (B–D–F♯–A), which introduces (in addition to A♯–A) yet another semitone collision, D–D♯. At Judith's words, "How very powerful you are, How very cruel you are!" the third degree (D) of the preceding B minor seventh chord is transformed into the root of a new lower third transposition (D–F–A–C) of the basic fifth, F♯–C♯. Momentarily, the sustained F♯–C♯ is changed to A–E (no. 43, mm. 6–7), the juxtaposition implying the presence of the complete minor seventh (pentatonic) construction (F♯–A–C♯– E) of the original "Castle" theme. With a return to the transposition on B, albeit in the minor seventh form, B–D–F♯–A (no. 44), the lower third transposition (G♯–B– D♯–F♯) of the latter emerges against the F♯–C♯ thread. The emergence of the G♯ transposition is significant in that it allows the remaining note (G♯) of the basic "Blood" motif (G♯–A/A♯–B) to enter into the leitmotivic chain of thirds. Thus, from the construction and sequential unfolding of the thirds and sevenths of Judith's (Stefi's) diatonic leitmotif emerges the chromatic sphere of blood.

Kárpáti asserts, in connection with Bartók's *First Sonata* for violin and piano (1921), that "the consequent circumscription of the degrees of the triads that appear in the piano part relates to the chain of thirds that launch the first movement in that a tonal divergence is created between the harmonic and melodic strata."[31] In connection with the opera, we may add that such divergences acquire an even greater significance because of the added dimension of the dramaturgy. In addition to the unfolding of the third-related transpositions of the seventh chord leitmotif, Judith's vocal line (at no. 44), which refers to Bluebeard's fierce power, outlines two minor second–related transpositions, one on G♯, the other on A. The G♯– minor seventh (G♯–B–D♯–F♯) in voice and Trumpet II immediately follows the minor seventh chord transposition on A (A–C–E–G) in voice and oboes. This progression is significant in that the roots of these two chords foreshadow one of the two main "Blood" semitones (G♯–A), the other (A♯–B trill) having initiated the scene. The local adjacency of the three third-related minor seventh chords (D–F–A–C, B–D–F♯–A, and G♯– B–D♯–F♯) in the surrounding contrapuntal figures, in conjunction with Judith's acknowledgment of Bluebeard's power, produces the complete octatonic collection, G♯–A–B–C–D–D♯–F–F♯, a significant intermediary (quasi-chromatic) stage in the transformation from pentatonic/diatonic to chromatic.

The chain of thirds that unfolds toward the chromatic "Blood" symbol is confirmed by the distinct foreground occurrence of dyad G♯–A (no. 45, m. 2) following Bluebeard's question asking her if she is afraid. As Bluebeard reiterates this question, all of the chromatic components (G♯–A–A♯–B) of the "Blood" motif come together as a more foreground event (at no. 45, mm. 11–13, in Violin I (G♯–A) and voice (A♯–B). The latter dyad initiates an exclusive linear (that is, more chromatic) octatonic segment (A♯–B–C♯–D–[ ]–F), as Judith demands the other keys (see ex. 10-3 earlier). Kárpáti's observations on Bartók's *First Sonata* for violin and piano suggest an analogy to procedures already developed in the 1911 opera in connection with juxtapositions, superpositions, and modal alterations of the seventh chord leitmotif:

> Folk music also gave Bartók examples of how to employ certain tonal tensions and colliding intervals. In the present case the violin melody, inspired by a Romanian tune, is accompanied by an ostinato drumbeat of fifths, towered in such a manner that upon each fifth there is superposed a diminished fifth. The total value of the two intervals amounts to 13 (7 + 6) semitones. From that one arrives at the same sound tension that occurred in the material of the first movement. Of course, this tower of fifths can be written out more "sparingly," from which it will appear that the principle of chromatic adjacents is again valid, but that would only be speculation, because music of this character is associated almost inseparably with what one can call "false" or "mistuned" fifths that form a chain. There are similar forms of accompaniment in numerous other Bartók works . . . in which cases of diminishing and augmenting collisions occur as well.[32]

At the point in the Armory scene where the complete tetrachordal content (G♯–A–A♯–B) of the "Blood" motif "collides" within the larger harmonic and vocal pitch collection (no. 45, mm. 11–13), the chain of seventh chords associated with Judith also begins to appear more systematic and extended. These combined harmonic concepts (chromatically compressed "Blood" motif and the diatonic-supertertian extensions associated with Judith) seem to reflect, or symbolize, the polarity (perhaps even identity) of blood and sunlight in the overall dramatic imagery of this scene, that is, these two polarized images are inextricably connected in that the sunlight streams into the castle only if the doors (Bluebeard's wounds) are opened. The harmonic content extends the minor seventh chord B–D–F♯–A–[A♯], which is central to these measures (see ex. 10-3 earlier), by thirds in opposite directions (G♯/B–D–F♯–A–[A♯]/C♯). Most of this collection has already emerged in the preceding passage (from no. 45) when Bluebeard questions Judith about her fear as she notices blood on his armor. The B minor seventh chord (at the *Meno vivo*, no. 45, m. 14) is followed, then, by the D♯ minor seventh chord (D♯–F♯–A♯–C♯) and its linear-thematic outline in the English horn (no. 46), the F♯– minor seventh chord (F♯–A–C♯–E) and its linear-thematic outline in the clarinet, and the D seventh chord variant (D–F♯–A–C), which is juxtaposed with the linear-thematic outline of the A minor seventh chord in the flute and oboe (no. 46, mm. 5–7). Thus far, the entire sequence, in chain-of-thirds ordering, has unfolded the seventh chord transpositions G♯–B–D–F♯, B–D–F♯–A/A♯, D–F♯–A–C, D♯–F♯–A♯–C♯, F♯–A–C♯–E, and A–C–E–G. The first transposition (on G♯) and the last (on A) imply the presence of a hidden (background-level) unfolding of the lower dyad (G♯–A) of the basic "Blood" motif, the other dyad (A♯–B) occurring more locally within Judith's vocal line (at no. 45, m. 13). This sequential chain of seventh chords unfolds as part of section a2 (no. 46ff.) in connection with Judith's reference to the "Beautiful stream of light.—See it! See it!" a contrast with the allusions to blood in section a1 of this door scene.

Henceforth, as Judith renews her demands for Bluebeard to release the remaining keys, the modalities of the seventh chords are altered more radically in concomitance with the move toward greater chromaticism. The larger pentatonic/diatonic scalar col-

EXAMPLE 10-5. Door II (Armory), section a2, no. 46, mm. 4–19, violins, three linearly-stated diatonic seventh-chords reinterpreted as octatonic seventh chords, succession of two octatonic collections (C♯–D♯–E–F♯–G–A–A♯–C and C–D-E♭–F–G♭–A♭–A–B) implying presence of total chromatic continuum

lections within which the seventh chords have been embedded are transformed into symmetrical types of sets (octatonic, whole-tone, and hybrid forms) to reflect Judith's intensified move toward her ultimate fate, so the intervallic construction of the original diatonic forms of the seventh chord is correspondingly altered. At the first prominent crescendo of the Armory scene (no. 46, m. 7 ff.), the violins diverge from the sustained seventh chord (D–F♯–A–C) of the phrase by unfolding a sequence of three contrasting, linearly stated seventh chords: A–C–E–G, F♯–A–B♯–E, and D♯–F♯–Gx-C♯ (ex. 10-5). The total content of these three forms, each still diatonic in construction, comprises a seven-note segment of the octatonic-1 collection, C♯–D♯–E–F♯–G–A–[ ]–C. The second sustained chord (F♯–A♯–C♯) provides the missing A♯ of the octatonic collection (C♯–D♯–E–F♯–G–A–A♯–C). This draws the very first diatonic seventh chords of the scene (F♯–A♯–C♯–[ ] and D♯–F♯–A♯–C♯) into the octatonic sphere. At this point (no. 46, m. 9), both the F♯ chord (F♯–A♯–C♯) and melodic first beat (Gx) together form the dual (major-minor) mode, F♯–Gx–A♯–C♯ (in enharmonic spelling, F♯–A–A♯–C♯), within the basic fifth (F♯–C♯) of the original "Castle" theme that pervades this scene. The remaining notes of this measure (except for the Gx) outlines the minor seventh chord, D♯–F♯–A♯–C♯.

At the *rallent. al tempo*, the D♯– minor seventh chord is enharmonically respelled in the new theme of the violins as an E♭– minor seventh chord, E♭–G♭–B♭–D♭, exclusively. The latter, which has been shown to have octatonic-1 significance (C♯–D♯–E–F♯–G–A–A♯–C, in enharmonic spelling, D♭–E♭–F♭–G♭–G–A–B♭–C) in the preceding linear sequence, is divergent in pitch content from the new sustained chord, F–A–C. Except for one note (F) of the latter, both chords (E♭–G♭–B♭–D♭ and [ ]–A–C) together form a six-note segment of the octatonic-1 collection. However, the "odd-note" F permits the entire seventh chord, F–A–C–E♭, to serve as a pivot to octatonic-0, which unfolds in the voice as a six-note segment, A–B–C–D–E♭–F—the implied F–A–C–E♭ seventh-chord frame of the segment is projected explicitly against it in the harmony. The preceding G♭–E♭ cadential dyad and the follow-

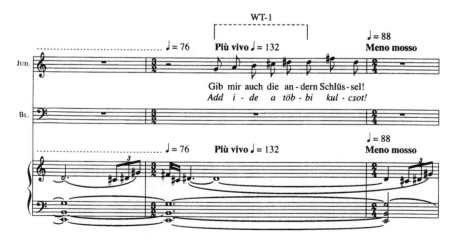

EXAMPLE 10-5 *(continued)*

ing addition of A♭ in the E♭–pentatonic theme together complete the octatonic-o segment (A–B–C–D–E♭–F–G♭–A♭). Thus, the diatonic seventh-chords are reinterpreted as octatonic seventh chords in this section, the succession of the two octatonic collections (C♯–D♯–E–F♯–G–A–A♯–C and C–D–E♭–F–G♭–A♭–A–B) implying the presence of the total chromatic continuum.

The E♭ tonic of the E♭ pentatonic strings (E♭–G♭–A♭–B♭–D♭) is enharmonically reinterpreted (no. 47, m. 4ff.) and transformed into the major-seventh degree of the minor third modal form of the "Stefi" motif, E–G–B–D♯, as Bluebeard warns, "Beware, beware, also for us both, Judith!" Against this chord (see ex. 10-5 earlier), Bluebeard's vocal line outlines the seventh chord (F♯–A♯–C♯–E) containing the basic fifth, F♯–C♯, the combination of sustained chord and vocal line producing a maximal clash of semitones, D♯–E, F♯–G, and A♯–B. As the held chordal seventh (D♯) is simultaneously reinterpreted as a tonic in the cadential pentatonic figure, D♯–F♯–G♯– [ ]–C♯, we get a more extended semitonal clash between chord and melody (D♯–E, F♯–G–G♯). At this point (*più vivo*), as Judith repeats her demand for Bluebeard to release the keys, both constructions (E–G–B–D♯ and pentatonic-segment D♯–F♯–G♯–[ ]–C♯) are reinterpreted in Judith's vocal line (G–A–B–C♯–D♯/F♯) as hybrid modal segments (whole-tone and pentatonic/diatonic), in which the three upper notes (G–B–D♯) of the E–G–B–D♯ seventh chord are expressly filled in by whole-tones (G–A–B–C♯–D♯). This whole-tone transformation of the seventh chord (E–G–B–D♯) is analogous to Judith's first transformation (G♭–A–D♭–F, in enharmonic spelling, F♯–A–C♯–E♯) of the "Castle" theme's basic pentatonic seventh chord (F♯–A–C♯–E) at the opening of the opera.

Within this hybrid-modal line (G–A–B–C♯–D♯/F♯), the predominance of the whole-tone collection has broad implications in connection with the symbolism of "Stefi's" (Judith's) minor third/major seventh modal form of the leitmotif. The E–G–B–D♯ construction is a transposition of the form (F–A♭–C–E) that symbolizes Bartók's "funeral dirge,"[33] so the mood of this form of the seventh chord seems to portend Judith's ultimate fate, especially in light of the demands that will eventually seal her doom and the more immediate musico-dramatic developments from this point on in the scene. Seventh chord E–G–B–D♯ becomes G–B–D♯–F♯ in Judith's hybrid vocal line, the latter form representing a more radical (quasi-whole-tone) transformation of the basic diatonic seventh chord construction. At Bluebeard's question (no. 48), "Don't you know what the door hides?" his pentatonic line, G–B♭–C–D–F, which implies the presence of the minor seventh chord, G–B♭–D–F, is transformed by the orchestral motif, C–D–F♯ (i.e., as part of the larger pitch collection, G–B♭–C–D–F♯), into a more whole-tone–related construction. In other words, the pentatonic minor seventh chord (G–B♭–D–F) is transformed into the more "funereal" form, G–B♭–D–F♯, the whole-tone significance implied in the upper three notes (B♭–D–F♯).

Whole-tone transformation of the pentatonic/diatonic sphere becomes increasingly pervasive in anticipation of the variant of Judith's "Danger" motif (no. 49, mm. 5–6). At the cadence of Bluebeard's ominous question (no. 48), which begins section b', part 1, the pentatonic key note G in the voice is reinterpreted harmonically by the augmented triad, C♯–F–A (the original whole-tone-related form of Judith's first interjection, F–D♭–A, at the opening of the opera), as part of a larger whole-tone segment, C♯–F–G–A. This, in turn, is expanded by the lower tetrachord (F–G–A–B) of the F Lydian scale to a five-note segment of the WT-1 cycle to C♯–[ ]–F–G–A–B. The complete WT-0 cycle emerges, then, in the hybrid septuplet scale, D♯–E♯/F♯–G♯–A♯–B♯–Cx-E, against Judith's vocal dyad, D♯–C♯, which provides the one note (D♯) that was missing from the WT-1 collection. The juxtapositions of both whole-tone collections implies the presence, once again, of the total chromatic continuum.

The significance of the hybrid structure of these diatonic/whole-tone scales is seen in their enframing seventh chord superstructures (see ex. 10-4 earlier). The first scale, F–G–A–B–C–D–E (no. 48), outlines the "Stefi" F major seventh chord (F–A–C–E). The second scale, D♯–E♯–F♯–G♯–A♯–B♯–Cx-E, whose tonic is a whole-tone below the first scale, outlines the "Stefi" D♯ seventh "funereal" form, D♯–F♯–A♯–Cx (in enharmonic spelling, E♭–G♭–B♭–D); the latter is intercalated with its whole-tone transposition, E♯–G♯–B♯–E (in enharmonic spelling, F–A♭–C–E), within the scale. It is at this point (no. 48ff.), in which Judith's "Danger" motif takes shape, that the leitmotif (seventh chord) frames become pivotal in generating both whole-tone cycles in connection with the ominous mood of Judith's actions, which cause the castle to "tremble." The initial two tonal areas of the Armory scene, F♯ and D♯, which are local reflections of the first two tonalities in the opera's overall minor-third scheme (F♯, D♯, [D], D♯, C, A, C, F♯), are projected into the embellishing scales of the "Danger" motif. Beginning with the second, hybrid (diatonic/ whole-tone) scale, the earlier seventh chord functions of pitch-classes F♯ and D♯ are gradually transformed and absorbed into their respective whole-tone cycles in connection with dramatic symbolization.

At Judith's first appearance in the opera (at no. 3), the opening "Castle" theme's F♯– minor seventh pentatonic structure (F♯–A–C♯–E) was altered by the intrusion of the major-seventh degree, F (G♭–A–D♭–F, in enharmonic spelling, F♯–A–C♯–E♯) in Judith's vocal line, so the tonic note F♯ came into conflict with an emergent WT-1 segment, A–C♯–F (i.e., in F♯/A–C♯–F). The latter returns, now, as an essential element of the "Danger" motif (no. 48, harmony; see ex. 10-4 earlier). In this case, this WT-1 triad (A–C♯–F), which plays an important articulative harmonic role in the "Danger" motif, is separated from its seventh chord root (F♯) and is absorbed into a larger segment of WT-1 in the first scale, that is, C♯–F–A is followed by F–G–A–B. Conversely, the second (hybrid) scale (D♯–E♯/F♯–G♯–A♯–B♯–Cx-E), which completes the WT-1 collection by the addition of D♯ in the initial WT-1 dyad (D♯–E♯), now absorbs the F♯ (i.e., G♭) root of Judith's original seventh chord, G♭–A–D♭–F (see ex. 9-3 earlier) into the complete WT-0 scale. The latter scale implies the presence of a WT-0 transposition (F♯–A♯–Cx) of the original WT-1 augmented triad (F–A–C♯) in the symmetrical framework of the WT-0 septuplet segment (F♯–G♯–A♯–B♯–Cx). The significance of this transposition is twofold: (1) it suggests a whole-tone transformation of the basic pentatonic D♯– minor seventh chord (D♯–F♯–A♯–C♯) of this scene into a hybrid pentatonic/ whole-tone construction (D♯–F♯–A♯–Cx) analogous to the original transformation of the "Castle" theme's pentatonic seventh chord (F♯–A–C♯–E) into Judith's pentatonic/whole-tone line (G♭–A–D♭–F, in enharmonic spelling, F♯–A–C♯–E♯); and (2) it provides the final WT-0 transformation of both the pentatonic pitch-class F♯ of the "Castle" theme and Judith's hybrid construction into the complete WT-0 sphere of destiny.

The transition to the third door (Treasure Chamber) entails a further shift of Bluebeard's character toward Judith's more open manner. As Bluebeard gives Judith the third key, his pentatonic phrase, G♯–B–C♯–D♯ (no. 52, mm. 3–4), is transformed into a whole-tone figure in the English horn, A–G–D♯–C♯, which is based on a rhythmic variant of Judith's "Fate" motif. The transition opens, *Più lento,* with a pair of vocal statements between Bluebeard and Judith, based on an analogous whole-tone transformation: Bluebeard sings a variant of Judith's motif, which outlines the minor-modal form of the "Stefi" seventh chord, F–A♭–C–E. The whole-tone component of the latter (augmented triad A♭–C–E) is extended in Judith's vocal line to a five-note segment of the whole-tone scale, A♭–B♭–C–D–E (with one "odd" note, G), and used as the basis for the following brief interlude (no. 53). Three of the four grace-note dyads that embellish the latter (C–E–A♭) outline the complete complementary whole-tone cycle, A–B/D♭–E♭/F–G. As Bluebeard becomes more resigned to the inevitability of Judith's demands and yields to a somewhat more supportive role (no. 53, mm. 7–8) by telling her not to be afraid and that it does not matter anymore, his final variant (A–G♯–F♯–G♯–E–C♯) of Judith's motif fuses his original F♯–minor seventh (pentatonic) content, F♯–A–C♯–E, with the major-modal form of the "Stefi" motif, A–C♯–E–G♯.

Whole-tone infusions into the diatonic sphere prevail in the Treasure Chamber, these pitch-set interactions appearing to symbolize (by means of contextual association) Bluebeard's allusion to the will of fate. Impressed by the vastness of his wealth, Judith's vocal statements diminish in force as the scene unfolds. Her opening simple pentatonic phrases, which together outline A–C–D–E, are transformed by the sustained orchestral chord (D–F♯–A) and triplet figure (G♯–F♯–E–C) into a hybrid diatonic/whole-tone collection (C–D–E–F♯–G♯/A): the third degree (F♯) of the held D major triad extends the upper three notes (C–D–E) of her pentatonic line to a four-note segment of the whole-tone scale (C–D–E–F♯); the triplet figure further extends this to five notes, C–D–E–F♯–G♯; and the whole-tone cycle is completed by the addition of A♯ in the fourth triplet figure (no. 55, m. 10). Judith's longer third statement (nos. 55–56) introduces a chromatic conflict between the third degrees (C and C♯) of her A minor/major bimodal line. The significance of this conflict is twofold. First, the C♯ extends the held D major triad to the major form of the "Stefi" seventh chord, D–F♯–A–C♯, and second, the half-step seems to foreshadow the appearance of blood later in the scene. Thus, the interaction of pentatonic/diatonic, whole-tone, and chromatic spheres is, once again, manifested as one of the fundamental aspects of Bartók's musical language in correspondence with dramatic meaning.

Elements of the basic "Blood" motif (G♯–A/A♯–B), which begin to emerge at the opening of the Treasure Chamber, were imminent in the whole-tone intrusions into Bluebeard's pentatonic/diatonic sphere that brought the Armory scene to a close and prepared for the unlocking of the door to the Treasure Chamber. Judith's vocal line (no. 49, mm. 4–9), which had fused the pitch content of the two basic seventh chords (D♯–F♯–A♯–C♯ and F♯–A♯–C♯–E) of this scene above the last two orchestral statements of her "Danger" motif, was followed by two, more subdued pentatonic phrases sung by Bluebeard, the initial notes (G♯ and A) of these respective phrases implying the presence of one of the two basic semitones of the "Blood" motif. As Bluebeard's vocal line at the end of the transition to the Treasure Chamber was transformed (at no. 53, mm. 7–8) into the contour of Judith's more arpeggiated style, these two notes (A and G♯) of the "Blood" motif had come into closer proximity, as the content of the pentatonic F♯–seventh chord collection (F♯–A–C♯–E) was fused, now, with the major seventh form at the upper third (A–C♯–E–G♯) to give us F♯–A–C♯–E–G♯.

In connection with the implication of blood, this closing passage of the transition between the Armory and Treasure Chamber is even more striking in view of its long-range relation to the opening of the Armory scene. Although the closing vocal and orchestral figurations have nothing to do with that of the opening of the Armory scene, the pitch content is identical, with one exception. Each note of the opening sustained tonic fifth, F♯–C♯ (see no. 42, m. 5 ff.), is linearly embellished by the whole-tone trichords, E–F♯–G♯ and B–C♯–D♯, respectively. This combination of whole-tone trichords produces a diatonic hexachordal symmetry around an implied axis, A–A♯, in which only the A♯ is manifested in the trill figure. In the closing passage of the transition (ex. 10-6), the flutes embellish only the sustained fifth degree, C♯ (i.e., B–C♯–D♯) of the original perfect fifth (F♯–C♯), the voice presenting a contextual re-interpretation of the sustained embellished tonic, F♯ (i.e., E–F♯–G♯), as part of an eighth-note segment.[34] While the cadential C♯ of the voice simply duplicates the sus-tained C♯, the initial note, A, replaces the original A♯ of the semitonal trill (A♯–B). Thus, the two passages complement each other to complete the semitonal axis of symmetry, A–A♯, which is also the axis of the basic "Blood" motif, G♯–A/A♯–B. Its semitonal components begin to emerge, then, at cadential junctures of the counter-point at the opening of the Treasure Chamber.

In the opening portion of the Treasure Chamber, the presence of the two basic half steps of the "Blood" motif (G♯–A/A♯–B) is implied by the appearance of the first dyad, G♯–A (at no. 54, m. 8, and again at no. 55, m. 9), in the adjacency between Ju-dith's cadential note, A, and the initiating G♯ of the violin triplets, and by the second

EXAMPLE 10-6. Door II (Armory), closing passage of transition, no. 53, mm. 7–8, flutes embellish sustained fifth degree, C♯ (i.e., B–C♯–D♯) of original perfect fifth (F♯–C♯), while voice presents contextual reinterpretation of sustained embellished tonic, F♯ (i.e., E–F♯–G♯), with one exception, A (related to axis, A–A♯, of "Blood" motif, G♯–A–A♯–B)

dyad (A♯–B) in the uppermost notes of the last two triplet figures (no. 55, mm. 10–11). The complementary half-step (G♯–A) of the implied "Blood" motif appears, then (at nos. 56–58, horns), as the boundary of the "Stefi" seventh chord motif, A–C–E–G♯, which develops into a horn stretto as an ostinato leading to the complete form (A–B♭/B–C) of the transposed "Blood" motif at the end of this scene (no. 58–no. 59, m. 4).[35] In this ostinato, which outlines the "Stefi" seventh chord (A–C–E–G♯), pitch-class D is added as a cadential tone to complete the exact pitch collection (no. 54, mm. 4–8), A–C–D–E–G♯, of Judith's opening two pentatonic phrases plus the G♯ of the adjacent triplet figure. The "fatalistic" association of this transformation of Judith's pentatonic segment into the "Stefi" motif is further supported by the descending contour of the motif, G♯–E–C–A/D, the first three notes (G♯–E–C) giving prominence to the whole-tone sphere and linking the symbolism of this passage to that of Judith's first vocal statement near the opening of the opera (no. 3).

Whole-tone transformation of the diatonic sphere is further established at the appearance of half-step A–B♭ (at no. 58f.), which transforms the held D major triad into an augmented (whole-tone) triad, D–F♯–B♭. The precise relation of the tetrachordal "Blood" motif, A–B♭–B–C, to the hybrid pentatonic/whole-tone structure of the "Stefi" motif, A–C–D–E–G♯, in which the chromatic tetrachord fills in the one non-whole-tone element (lower pentatonic third, A–C) of the hybrid construction, reveals, on the local foreground level, the extremes of musico-dramatic polarity. The chromatic sphere associated with "Blood" (A–B♭–B–C, to which we can add the raised seventh degree, G♯) is directly juxtaposed with the whole-tone sphere associated with Judith's intrusion into the pentatonic realm of the castle, C–D–E–F♯–G♯–B♭. The latter is formed by the joining of the hybrid—pentatonic/whole-tone—segment, C–D–E–G♯, with the F♯ and B♭ of the held chord. Thus, the basic motif of Judith (or Stefi) is once again revealed as the symbolic link with "Fate" and "Blood," a conception of the woman that accords with the historical transformation from the biblical heroine to the modern image associated with *femme fatale*.

Interaction of Diatonic and Whole-Tone Spheres: Dissonance and the Move toward Ultimate Fate

Judith shows signs of increasing alarm as she approaches the fourth door (Garden scene). Bluebeard now refers to light (no. 59, mm. 6–9), "Open the fourth door. Let there be sunlight—open it, open it," a mood which is contrasted by Judith's words (no. 65, mm. 7–8), "Hidden beneath hard rocks!" The musical symbolism of the preceding scene is still more prominently manifested in this scene, which is an immediate adumbration of the brilliance and vastness of Bluebeard's domain that lies behind the fifth door. The Garden scene is introduced (no. 59, mm. 6–9) by three diatonically related phrases in Bluebeard's vocal line (ex. 10-7), the ascending upper notes outlining the basic whole-tone tetrachord, B♭–C–D–E, as part of the larger B♭ Lydian vocal collection (B♭–C–D–E–F–[ ]–A). The ascending harp glissando (A–B♭–C–D–E♭–F–G–A–B♭–C–D–E♭) suggests, by means of its cadential articulation on E♭, a permuted transposition (E♭–F–G–A–B♭–C–D–E♭) of the B♭ Lydian mode that shifts the priority from the WT-0 tetrachord of the voice (B♭–C–D–E) to a WT-1 tetrachord (E♭–F–G–A). This whole-tone infusion into Bluebeard's dia-

EXAMPLE 10-7. Closing passage of transition, no. 59, to opening of Door IV (Garden), No. 60, m. 5, vocal phrases outline WT-0 tetrachord (B♭–C–D–E) as part of B♭-Lydian collection (B♭–C–D–E–F–[ ]–A); harp glissando shifts priority from vocal WT-0 tetrachord (B♭–C–D–E) to WT-1 tetrachord (E♭–F–G–A); tremolo of two major-seventh chords (A♭–C–E♭–G and B♭–D–F–A) suggests bimodal collection based on two intercalated whole-tone tetrachords (A♭–B♭–C–D/E♭–F–G–A).

tonic sphere is accompanied by a quasi-diatonic string tremolo, partitioned into two alternating major-seventh chords (A♭–C–E♭–G and B♭–D–F–A), which represent the major modal form of the "Stefi" motif. These two chordal transpositions together outline a bimodal collection that also implies the presence of two whole-tone tetrachords, A♭–B♭–C–D/E♭–F–G–A.

The half-step intersection (axis D–Eb) of the latter chordal combination suggests a microscopic reflection of the shift from the preceding D major chord, which was sustained throughout the Treasure Chamber (nos. 54 through 59, m. 5), to the asserted Eb tonality of the Garden scene. At the same time, the implied dual axis of symmetry, Ab–A (i.e., symmetrically related to half-step D–Eb: D/Ab–A/Eb), is manifested in the other symmetrical permutation of the scale, Eb–F–G–A/Ab–Bb–C–D, which is part of the complete "Blood" motif at the center of this scale (G–Ab–A–Bb). The dyad Ab–A is precisely the half-step (in enharmonic spelling, G#–A) that is articulated as part of the incomplete "Blood" motif (Fx–G#–A–[ ]) in section d1 (latter part of this scene, at no. 71). This motivic occurrence accompanies Judith's more timid diatonic statement (no. 71, mm. 2–3): "The stems of your white roses are bloody." At section d2 (no. 72, m. 8), the latter statement of the "Blood" motif is transposed to A–Bb as part of the larger segment, G#–A–Bb–[ ], against a new diatonic statement in Judith's vocal line. The combination of these two partial "Blood" motif statements implies a background occurrence of the complete four-note form, Fx–G#–A–Bb. The latter (in enharmonic spelling, G–Ab–A–Bb) is identical in pitch content to the chromatic tetrachordal axis of the scale based on the two "Stefi" major seventh chords (Eb–F–[G–Ab–A–Bb]–C–D) in the opening string tremolo. Furthermore, the half-step A–Bb (no. 58-no. 59, m. 5), which was associated with blood in the transition leading into the Garden scene, forms the upper half-step of the latter tetrachordal ("Blood"-motif) axis of these two "Stefi" seventh chords. This half-step (A–Bb), which then initiated Bluebeard's vocal line in the Garden scene, is manifested as the other diatonic half-step (i.e., like D–Eb in the harp glissando, A/Bb–C–D/Eb–F–G–A/Bb–C–D/Eb (see ex. 10-7 earlier). Thus, the Garden scene reveals a still more intensive musical interaction and integration of the basic sets (diatonic, whole-tone, and chromatic) in association with the relentless unfolding of dramatic symbolism toward the highpoint of the opera.

The transition to the fifth door (no. 73, m. 4 ff.) represents a significant musicodramatic focal point in the transformation of the diatonic to whole-tone sphere, as Bluebeard appears more acquiescent to his destiny: "See how my castle already lightens. Open the fifth door." His rising vocal line outlines exclusively a tetrachordal segment of the WT-0 collection, D–E–F#–G#, his second, wider-ranging statement outlining a segment (augmented triad G–B–D#) belonging to the complementary WT-1 collection. The latter is accompanied by the dotted-rhythmic figure associated with dripping blood, which also unfolds a segment of the WT-1 collection, D#–F–G. Both voice and orchestra together yield the four-note whole-tone segment, D#–F–G–[ ]– B, which is expanded to a five-note segment (B–C#–D#–F–G–[ ]) by the upper linear whole-tone segment (B–C#–D#) of the chordal ostinato and completed by the ascending five-note segment (Eb–F–G–A–B) that leads into the fifth-door scene to give us Eb–F–G–A–B–C#–[D#]. Against the WT-1 collectional unfolding of the voice and upper orchestral lines, the lower three notes of each chord outline a trichordal WT-0 segment, the succession of segments producing the entire WT-0 collection, D–E–F#–G#–A#–B#. Thus the contrasting whole-tone segments in Bluebeard's two vocal phrases are extended by the orchestra to the complete whole-tone collections, respectively.

The combination of both complete whole-tone collections in this passage produces all twelve tones, thereby permitting a half-step dissonance to occur in virtually every simultaneity (e.g., G/F♯, G/G♯, D♯/E, and F/F♯, at no. 74, mm. 1–6, as well as D/E♭, F/F♯, etc., in the following measures). At the cadence before the fifth door, the primary or initial notes (D and E♭) of the repeated chord (D–F♯–G♯–B) and ascending whole-tone segment (E♭–F–G–A–B), respectively, telescope the earlier half-step shift from the held D major chord that closed the Treasure Chamber scene to the E♭ tonality asserted at the opening of the Garden scene. In the context of the half-step blood signifier (A♭–G in the sharp Magyar short-long rhythm on A♭–G–D, at no. 72–no. 73, m. 3), which is complemented by the trumpet addition of the dyad A–B♭ to imply the presence of the complete chromatic tetrachord that symbolizes blood (G–A♭/A–B♭), the dissonant element becomes a prominent contributor to the tension that increases in anticipation of the emotional outburst and brilliant sonorities of the fifth door. Our understanding of the dramatic role of the chromatic dissonance in this section is deepened by Leafstedt's interpretation of the symbolic function of the clarinet melody, which was associated with the semitonal "Blood" motif in the first door scene, in this transitional segment to the fifth door:

> In the final moments before the music converges onto a pounding, syncopated rhythm that will lead into the moment when Judith throws open the next door, what sounds like an allusion to the clarinet melody of the first door scene [see Nos. 34–35] fleetingly sounds forth at fig. 74—a symbol, perhaps, that for Judith each forward step in the opera is also a step backward toward a fate suggested by the first door.[36]

Duke Bluebeard's Castle

The Nietzschean Condition and
Polarity of Characterizations:
Diatonic-Chromatic Extremes

Door V (Bluebeard's Domain)

In a letter to his mother, dated 10 September 1905, Bartók expresses ambivalence regarding the gender relation of power.[1] His train of thought leads him from vacillation on the issue of equal standards for men and women to certainty that he is destined to a life of spiritual loneliness, based on the belief that his search for the ideal companion can only end in disappointment. But Bartók has learned to accept this irreconcilable state of affairs and offers a note of advice as consolation to others: one must "attempt to achieve a state of spiritual indifference in which it is possible to view the affairs of the world with complete indifference and with the utmost tranquility."[2] He further argues that:

> it is difficult, extremely difficult—in fact, the most difficult thing there is—to attain this state, but success in this is the greatest victory man can ever hope to win: over other people, over himself and over all things. Sometimes I feel that for a brief space of time I have risen to these heights. Then comes a mighty crash; then again more struggle, always striving to rise higher; and this recurs again and again. The time may come when I shall be able to stay on the heights.

In a letter to Stefi Geyer, dated 6 September 1907, Bartók's expression of this need acquires more grandiose proportions.[3] He sees the weaker man's comfort as derived from his ability "to pray to a Powerful Being," with the hope that the "Mighty One will spare him a few crumbs or scraps." In contrast, Bartók sees for himself only that path which will lead him toward "a state of spiritual indifference" as the means for attaining inner emotional strength. Describing himself, in a letter to Irmy Jurkovics, dated 15 August 1905,[4] as a follower of Friedrich Nietzsche, Bartók offers his own formulation of the latter's philosophical thought (italics are Bartók's): "*Each must strive to rise above all; nothing must touch him; he must be completely independent, completely indifferent. Only thus can he reconcile himself to death and to the meaninglessness of life.*" Bartók continues: "It needs a gigantic struggle to rise above all things! How far I am yet from doing so! What is more, the further you advance, the more intensely, it seems, you feel!" The source for this notion is found not only in Bartók's reading of *Zarathustra*, but also in other passages from Nietzsche:[5]

> if [one] were able to grasp and feel mankind's overall consciousness in himself, he would collapse with a curse against existence—for mankind, as a whole, has *no* goals. . . . But does our philosophy then turn into tragedy? Does not truth become an enemy of life? . . . although the aftereffect [of knowledge] described above is possible in some natures, I could just as well imagine a different one, which would give rise to a life much more simple . . . than the present one . . . [such a man who] continues to live on only to better his knowledge must be able to renounce without envy and chagrin much . . . that other men value. He must be *content* with that free, fearless hovering over men, customs, laws . . . which is for him the most desirable of states. He is glad to communicate his joy in this state. . . . But if one nevertheless wants more from him, with a benevolent shake of the head he will indicate his brother, the free man of action.

The perspective of this quote clarifies the optimistic nature of Bartók's own position. His pronouncement of "indifference" in his 1905 letter to Irmy does not imply a lack of feeling, nor does his assumption about the "meaninglessness of life" entail a pessimistic view. On the contrary, he links attainment of the heights—spiritual independence—with the intensification of feelings, and he also believes that an enthusiasm for life is necessary for the capacity to carry out one's work.[6] These issues are relevant not only to Bartók's own life but also they inform the gender relationship in his opera. Bluebeard's need to maintain the privacy of his vast domain (behind the fifth door) and his reticence toward Judith's intrusion into his inner world do not preclude Bluebeard's strong feelings for her. He wants to love and be loved by the woman, but he does not want her to question him or pry into his personal life. With the flood of light streaming into the castle through the fifth door, which represents the peak of the formal and dramatic structure, the characters' emotions as expressed in the earlier scenes are reversed. The man proudly gazes out toward the horizon of his endless domain in all of its brilliance, expansiveness, and grandeur. Concomitant with this sense of achievement, he feels "liberated, redeemed, luminous, grateful in his happiness" and "wants to embrace the woman in his arms." However, she can only see the blood now, as the daylight dims.[7]

The Nietzschean notion of the will toward superiority—striving toward the goal of the *Übermensch* (superman), like his Zarathustra, informs the mood of the fifth door scene. Nietzsche had attacked the Christian ethic because it idealizes the humility and weakness of the common man while repressing the aspirations of the nobility. It is in this scene of the opera—Bluebeard's endless domain—and in Bartók's highly perceptive, personal musical setting of it that we may recognize the strongest metaphor for this Nietzschean precept.[8] But for Nietzsche, the struggle is intensified at the same time by an inherent polarity, which he reveals to us by way of Zarathustra's reply to a youth leaning against a tree, wearily observing the valley below: "But it is with man as it is with the tree. The more he aspires to the height and light, the more strongly do his roots strive earthward, downward, into the dark, the deep—into evil."[9] The fifth door of the opera, which now reveals the expansive world of Bluebeard, appears to be a symbolic manifestation of Bartók's own personal struggle toward the heights he had spoken of in his letters. At the same time, the pull toward evil is imminent as blood mars Bluebeard's domain, the woman's (Judith's) relentless inquiry exposing the bloody scene as she has attempted to let light shine into the castle—into the man's soul.[10] In the first four door scenes of the opera, the struggle for control between the man and the woman leads to a gradual change in their relationship. As Bluebeard's Domain is revealed at the opening of the fifth door, extreme contrast is manifested in a complete reversal not only of the emotional states of the two characters but also their personalities, as Judith is awed by the vastness of Bluebeard's domain.

Polarity of Darkness and Light: Large-Scale and Local Use of Geometrically Expanding Proportional Structure

If we consider the seven door scenes with the large introductory section (and its brief return at the end), the opera yields eight different sections altogether. The placement of the fifth door scene at five-eighths of the way through the opera seems to play a significant role in terms of the musico-dramatic content and its relation to the large-scale structure and design. These structural proportions,[11] which are based on a geometrically expanding scheme, lend themselves to a heightened sense of contrast between the initial darkness encountered on Judith's and Bluebeard's entry into the castle (in F♯ pentatonic/minor) and the light of Bluebeard's endless domain encountered at the opening of the fifth door (in C major). While the musico-dramatic polarity and reversal of characterizations between the man and the woman at this highpoint is also intensified by the overall expanding proportions, the polarity of the two characters is also reflected on various structural levels within the fifth door scene itself. (The structural outline of the scene is given in table 11-1.)[12] The symmetrical quaternary structure of the Hungarian folklike text serves as point of departure for a more complex structural development, the principle of structural extension also seeming to stem from the idea of thematic variants characteristic of authentic Hungarian folk-music sources.

The overall construction of this door scene, which is an asymmetrical or extended binary form (table 11-1), is initiated by section A1, a quaternary structure in which each subsection (a1, a2, a3, a4) is further broken down into four octosyllabic phrases. In subsection a1 (nos. 75–76), Bluebeard's personality is immediately established as predominating, his "fortissimo, quasi parlando" line occupying three of the four phrases, while Judith's part is reduced to a single "piano, senza espressione" line without accompaniment. Furthermore, Bluebeard's text now alludes to light (no. 76, mm. 12–13, and no. 77, m. 8), "And blue mountains far in the distance. . . . Here live the sun, moon and stars," while Judith refers to the redness of blood. Bluebeard's part is still characteristically pentatonic—the Hungarian folkmusic form (A–C–D–E–G) is permuted in this case to C–D–E–G–A—but now Judith's part is also absorbed into the pentatonic sphere (E♭–G♭–A♭–[ ]–D♭), a tritone away from that of Bluebeard's. Strikingly, the complementary relationship of their pentatonic collections implies the presence of a chromatic continuum (C–D♭–D–E♭–E–[ ]–G♭–G–A♭–A–[ ]–[ ]) containing gaps that mark the two basic tonalities (C and G♭, i.e., F♯) of the opera. The Hungarian form of each of these two pentatonic collections (A–C–D–E–G and E♭–G♭–A♭–[ ]–D♭) also implies the presence (in the initial minor thirds,

TABLE 11-1. Door V (Bluebeard's Domain), no. 74, m. 19ff, overall extended binary form of the scene, projection of quaternary folksong structure into several formal levels with increasing irregularity

I.	(no. 75)	(no. 76)	(no. 77)	(no. 78, m. 5)
Section A¹:	a¹	a²	a³	a⁴
Phrases:	3 + 1	3 + 1	4 + 1	1
	Bl Ju	Bl Ju	Bl Ju	Ju
Text:	allusions to light ("Moon and stars")			"Blood"
tonalities:	C maj.	F maj.-G maj.	Ab maj.-E maj.	F min.

II.	(no. 79)	(no. 80)	(no. 82, m. 5)	
Section A²:	a¹	a²	a³	(extended by B)
Phrases:	3	1 + 1 + 3 + 1	2 + 1 + 2	1
	Bl	Bl Ju Bl Ju	Bl Ju Bl	
Text:	"sunlight"	Judith demands to open doors		
tonalities:	C vs. Eb triads to increasing tonal ambiguity			
	(whole-tone intrusion)		held F#-Ab-C w.t.cell in a³	

	(no. 85)	(no. 86)	(no. 87)	
Section B:	b¹	b²	b³ (extension to transition)	
Phrases:	2 + 2	still octosyllabic but ambiguous		
	Ju Bl	Ju Bl overlap	Ju Bl Ju overlap	
Text:	Ju strongest demands to open doors			
tonalities:	"Blood" motif, chromatic in voice and orchestra in b¹			
			whole-tone voices in b³	

A–C and E♭–G♭, respectively) of the remaining cyclic-interval-3 tonal subdivisions of the basic tritone, F#–E♭–C–A–F#. These subdivisions reflect the basic key scheme of the opera. Tritone F#–C locally reflects the background-level polarity between the F# pentatonic tonality of the Prologue and the C major tonality of this scene, a relation that was first reflected in the whole-tone cell, C–D–E–F#, in the harmonic structure of the "Foreboding" motif (see mm. 16–19), and at Bluebeard's and Judith's final utterances just prior to the first explicit appearance of the "Blood" motif (no. 34).

An Aphorism of Nietzsche on Independence: Bluebeard's Strength and Loneliness

For Bartók, spiritual and emotional independence is a goal that can be achieved only by the most difficult of struggles. He speaks of the rise to the heights that is often followed by the mighty crash, and then there is the repetition of this process, at the end hoping someday to be able to remain at the heights. For Bluebeard, however, the optimistic ending does not seem possible without the woman as part of his life. Bluebeard's condition and his destiny can be sensed, perhaps, in an aphorism of Nietzsche on independence:

Independence is for the very few; it is a privilege of the strong. And whoever attempts it even with the best right but without inner constraint proves that he is probably not only strong, but also daring to the point of recklessness. He enters into a labyrinth, he multiplies a thousandfold the dangers which life brings with it in any case, not the least of which is that no one can see how and where he loses his way, becomes lonely, and is torn piecemeal by some minotaur of conscience. Supposing one like that comes to grief, this happens so far from the comprehension of men that they neither feel it nor sympathize. And he cannot go back any longer. Nor can he go back to the pity of men.[13]

This quote from Nietzsche resonates entirely with the basic psychological and philosophical issues surrounding the characters, especially Bluebeard. Bartók's espousal of Nietzsche in the years prior to his creation of the opera in 1911 came from an inner spiritual need, but his philosophical knowledge was not acquired in isolation. Similar philosophical notions surfaced around the same time in the writings of intellectuals such as György Lukács, Béla Balázs, and Endre Ady.[14] According to Frigyesi, the works of Nietzsche and Ady "were among the most widely read and discussed literature of the modern-minded intelligentsia." Because Bartók's friends provided him with copies of these writings, one can assume that Nietzsche's philosophical thought was a significant part of their intellectual discussions. It was through Emma Gruber and Zoltán Kodály that Bartók first came to know many of these musical and literary personages, among them Balázs, who in turn brought Bartók into contact with the learned members of the Sunday circle that centered around Lukács. Thus, such evidence that Balázs must have had a working knowledge of Nietzsche's ideas supports the contention that Nietzschean philosophical precepts inform the dramatic conception of Balázs's mystery play. Nietzsche's writings may thus be considered a viable source for philosophical interpretation of the opera. This assumption is all the more plausible given Bartók's own insightful musical "interpretation" of the Balázs libretto. That is to say, Bartók's highly original musical setting further contributes to our perception of the Nietzschean elements, which are confirmed by Bartók's own stated Nietzschean convictions that lie behind the composer's musical thought.

Bartók's musical processes are indispensable to the full realization of Balázs's dramatic conception based on the Nietzschean symbolic message. The question arises as to how the composer was able to transform his philosophical view of life to the more abstract structural principles of his opera. Frigyesi suggests that "Nietzsche's text alone might have given him the idea for the structural design of his mature pieces. In the Nietzschean worldview, distinct aspects of reality were not linear events in a temporal sequence but existed as contrasts and variants laid out without hierarchy in a metaphysical entity."[15] Frigyesi asserts, then, that "Bartók experienced life in this manner and began to transmit this idea to art around 1907." The following analysis shows how the composer realizes the dramatic conception by means of musical symbolism in the fifth door scene. Judith's music has moved from her earlier whole-tone context to a pentatonic one, but the reversal of pitch-set associations between the two characters is also implicit in the opening chordal accompaniment of this climactic scene, where the whole-tone sphere (originally associated with Judith, at no. 3) conversely begins to intrude into the voice-leading of the triadic progressions that accompany Bluebeard's opening three C-based pentatonic phrases (ex. 11-1). The key

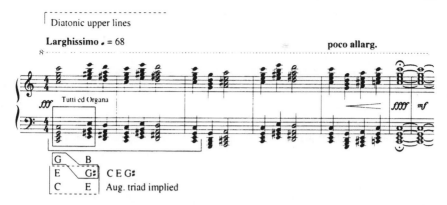

EXAMPLE 11-1. Door V (Bluebeard's Domain), no. 74, mm. 19–24, intrusion of whole-tone sphere into lower voice-leading of modally mixed parallel major triads

of C major is established by the linear content and shape of the outer voices as well as by the prominent metric placement of the tonic triad, while the overall triadic progression itself has little to do with traditional tonal functions. Instead, the parallel harmonic motion produces a series of major triads resulting in modal mixture and the intrusion of tones foreign to the basic key of C major. The content of the two upper lines of these triads is exclusively "white-key" diatonic, the two lower lines of the first seven chords exclusively unfolding five of the six notes of the primary whole-tone scale, C–D–E–F♯–G♯. The latter shifts in the two lower lines of the next two chords (G–B–D and A–C♯–E) to a four-note segment (G–A–B–C♯) of the secondary whole-tone scale.

The relationship between the first two triads (C–E–G and E–G♯–B) of this harmonic progression is most significant in connection with both Bluebeard's transformation from diatonic to whole-tone spheres and the intrusion of the semitonal "Blood" symbol. These two chords together (C–E–G–G♯–B) imply the presence of the C augmented triad (C–E–G♯), a whole-tone-related construction originally associated with Judith (see no. 3). By the end of the scene (no. 89, mm. 21–22), Bluebeard takes over Judith's opening whole-tone/pentatonic theme, the transposition by a major third (to A–F–D♭–B♭) as he urges Judith not to open it. This transposition permits Judith's original augmented triad (F–D♭–A) to remain unchanged. The difference between the explicit tonic triad (C–E–G) and the implied augmented triad (C–E–G♯) in the opening chords of this scene is the half-step between their fifth degrees, G and G♯, an interval that becomes increasingly prominent with the intrusion of blood into Bluebeard's domain.

This conflict between the diatonic (C–E–G) and whole-tone (implied C–E–G♯) spheres is also projected into the background-level tonal scheme of Section A1 of Bluebeard's Domain. While subsection a1 establishes the priority of C major, the first three phrases of subsection a2 (no. 76, mm. 1–14) move from F major to G major at the cadence (see table 11-1 earlier). Following the fourth phrase, which again reveals Judith's quiet vocal tone in the contrasting "black-key" pentatonic area, G major moves up a half-step to Ab major at the opening of subsection a3 (no. 77). The significance of these two keys, G and Ab, that is, as tonal projections of G and G# of the opening C major and E major triads, is confirmed by the shift from Ab major to the latter (E major) for the remainder of a3 (to no. 78). The local structure of 3 + 1 phrases of subsections a1 and a2 and 4 + 1 phrases of a3—these proportions directly underlie the contrast between Bluebeard's power and Judith's timidity—is paralleled in the larger construction of section A1, as subsection a4 (no. 78, m. 3 ff.) shifts to a dissonant, half-step bounded chord (F–Ab–C–F#) in support of Judith's first explicit reference to blood in this scene. Furthermore, basic tritone C–F# emerges as a local event in this chord, while Judith's vocal line is a pentatonic transformation of her original whole-tone/pentatonic theme (see no. 3).

Section A2 (no. 79) is a focal point for the most explicit manifestations of the basic pitch-set interactions of the opera. At this point (ex. 11-2), subsection a1 recapitulates the main key of C major, the chord progression alternating two triads (C major and Eb major) as a telescoping of Bluebeard's initial C-based pentatonic tonality and Judith's Eb–pentatonic tonality from the first and fourth phrases of this scene. This tonal juxtaposition may perhaps be viewed as an adumbration of Door VII, Former Wives, where Judith's prying seals her doom—the Wives' scene is in C minor, the tonic chord fusing components of both the C and Eb tonalities. Bluebeard's vocal line (no. 79) also fuses elements from C and Eb, the "black keys" (Eb and Bb) intruding for the first time into his "white-key" C-based pentatonic frame in anticipation of the inevitable loss of Judith. Against Bluebeard's vocal line, the original gapped whole-tone cell, C–E–F# (symbol of "Fate"),[16] which had appeared as the basic harmonic structure of the "Foreboding" motif (m. 16 ff.; see ex. 9-2b) (that is, the first whole-tone intrusion into the opening F# pentatonic sphere), now appears in its most prominent manifestation. At this point, this primary whole-tone cell (C–E–F#) forms an ostinato pattern based on alternations with its transposition, Eb–G–A, from the secondary whole-tone collection. Both transpositions had already appeared in the brief interlude following Judith's first statement (see no. 3, mm. 3–6), where they were obscurely embedded in the simultaneously ascending and descending instrumental lines. Ultimately, these two cell transpositions represent a whole-tone transformation of Bluebeard's "white-key" pentatonic collection (C–E–G–A, or in Hungarian pentatonic form, A–C–[ ]–E–G) that opened this scene, the addition of the two "black-keys" (F# and Eb) in this ostinato transforming these pentatonic "white keys" into the whole-tone sphere (C–E–F# and Eb–G–A). Both cells together form a six-note octatonic segment (C–[ ]–Eb–E–F#–G–A–[ ]), the Bb from Bluebeard's vocal line expanding the latter to seven notes (C–[ ]–Eb–E–F#–G–A–Bb), thereby resulting in a more dissonant fusion of whole-steps and half-steps in the interval ratio of 1:2 as well.

The large-scale form of the scene further reflects the proportions of the quaternary phrase structure of the subsections as well as the larger quaternary subsectional structure within section A1 (see table 11-1 earlier). Section A2 also unfolds several subsections analogous to A1. However, in place of an "expected" subsection a4, which would have rounded out the quaternary form of section A2, we get a greatly expanded subsection. Because of its extremely contrasting and developmental character, this subsection may be more appropriately interpreted as section B (no. 85). As a macroscopic structural reflection of Judith's reference to blood in the fourth phrase of the

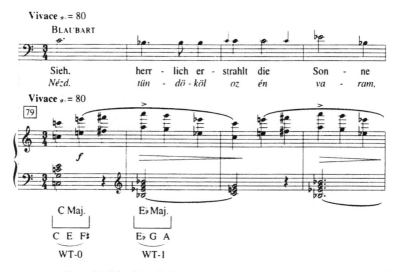

EXAMPLE 11-2. Door V (Bluebeard's Domain), section A2, no. 79, explicit manifestation of original gapped whole-tone cell (symbol of "Fate") in two transpositions from both whole-tone collections, and intrusion of "black keys" into Bluebeard's "white-key" C-based pentatonic frame

first (a1) subsection of section A1, section B is initiated by the most intensive unfolding of the chromatic "Blood" motif (see ex. 11-3 later), which contrasts with the whole-tone and diatonic interactions of the three subsections of section A2.

In anticipation of the "Blood" motif, the tritone transposition (F♯–A♭–[ ]–C) of the basic whole-tone (fate) cell had intruded as a held chord against Bluebeard's diatonic line in subsection a3 of section A2 (no. 82, m. 11 ff.). Against this WT-o chord (ex. 11-3), Judith's original quasi-WT-1 theme (see ex. 9-3 earlier: F–D♭–A/G♭) is recalled in a contour inversion initiated by the same augmented triad from the WT-1 collection, in enharmonic spelling, A–C♯–F/B♭ (no. 83, mm. 5–8), as she demanded that the other doors be opened. Both whole-tone segments (F♯–A♭–C, winds, and A–C♯–F, voice) together produce three semitones, F–F♯, A♭–A, and C–C♯. Furthermore, the sustained WT-o wind chord (F♯–A♭–C) and the violin II ostinato (B–E♭–F/D), the first three notes (B–E♭–F) containing a transposed inversion of the sustained chord (F♯–A♭–C), together form a seven-note octatonic segment, F♯–A♭–[ ]–B–C–D–E♭–F. The first note (A) from Judith's augmented (WT-1) triad (A–C♯–F) completes the octatonic collection (F♯–A♭–A–B–C–D–E♭–F). The latter extends the number of semitones within the still larger nine-note chromatic collection (F♯–[ ]–A♭–A–[ ]–B–C–C♯–D–E♭–[ ]–F), which comprehends the content of all of these final passages of Section A2 (no. 83, m. 5 to no. 85). Each of the three missing notes (G, B♭, and E) is added at a prominent structural point within these passages (see ex. 11-3): the note B♭, which appears only once, serves as a disrupter of Judith's initial WT-1 vocal segment (no. 83, m. 8); G functions as the first WT-1 expander in violin II (at no. 84); and E articulates the cadence of the entire A2 section

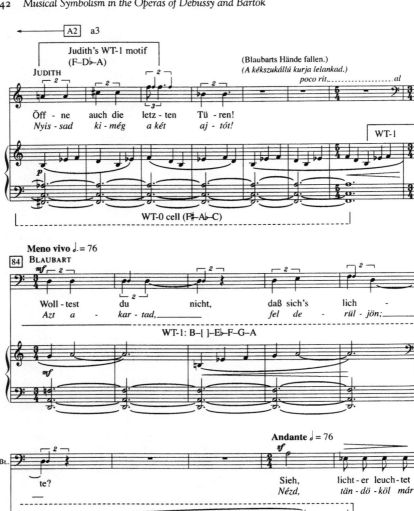

EXAMPLE 11-3. Door V (Bluebeard's Domain), section A2, subsection a3, no. 83, mm. 5–8, contour inversion (A–C#–F/B♭) of Judith's original WT-1 motif (F–D♭–A/G♭), both initiated by same augmented triad from WT-1 collection, against sustained WT-0 chord (F#–A♭–C), both whole-tone segments (F#–A♭–C, winds, and A–C#–F, voice) together producing three semitones, F–F#, A♭–A, and C–C#; nos. 84–85, further extension of WT-1 collection in violin II to B–[C#]–E♭–F–G–A.

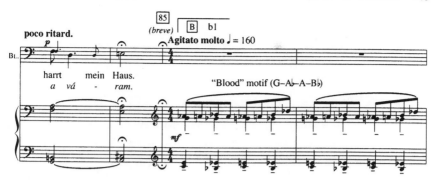

EXAMPLE 11-3 *(continued)*

as the final note of Bluebeard's vocal line (no. 84, m. 12). This note (E) is anticipated five measures earlier as the single disrupter of WT-1 in violin II. It appeared three measures before that in Bluebeard's vocal line, where it was similarly juxtaposed with the WT-1 element (A) of violin II.

Thus, chromatic conflict is increased in two ways in the final passages of section A2 in anticipation of the more dense linear chromatic "Blood" motif that opens section B: (1) by the combination of Judith's ascending whole-tone vocal segment and sustained whole-tone wind chord; and (2) by the combination of the two whole-tone segments of the orchestra to produce the complete octatonic-0 collection. At the same time, Judith's vocal ascent and the violin-II ostinato extend the cyclic-interval content of Judith's original WT-1 motif (see no. 3) to an impure five-note WT-1 segment (A–B–C♯–[D]–E♭–F) in precisely the original registral ordering of the collection (see ex. 9-3 earlier). The boundary interval of the present passage is the chromatic dyad, F–F♯ (enharmonic spelling of F–G♭), which supports the connection with Judith's original thematic statement (F–D♭–A–G♭). The WT-1 content is then extended (in violin II, no. 83, m. 11, to no. 85) to the complete WT-1 cycle, B–[ ]–E♭–F–G–A, the C♯ supplied by Judith's vocal motif, A–C♯–F (at no. 83, m. 6).

Toward the end of section B (nos. 87–89), both vocal parts unfold mutually exclusive segments from the respective whole-tone scales, the juxtapositions producing more general chromatic relations. Against Judith's descending seventh-chord outline (A–F♯–D♯–B), Bluebeard sings a descending WT-0 tetrachord, D–C–B♭–A♭, as he asks her, "Why do you want to? Why do you want to?, Judith, Judith!" while Judith follows with a modified WT-1 version (A–G–E♭–B) of her original whole-tone/pentatonic theme (see ex. 9-3 earlier), at her words (no. 87, mm. 5–6), "Open them, open them!" This modified form is an incomplete inversion of the Violin II figure (B–E♭–F–G–A) from the final measures of Section A2 (see ex. 11-3 earlier). The symbolic significance of these pitch-set interactions is revealed by the accelerated *fff* intrusions of Judith's "Danger" motif (no. 88 ff.) in alternation with the whole-tone/diatonic orchestral figurations as Judith insists upon opening the next door.

Our awareness of Balázs's own personal view of women, as expressed in one of his diary entries, sharpens one's sense of the dramatic dissonance that results from Judith's actions, that is, Judith's increasingly assertive behavior in the opera brings her into conflict with Balázs's real-life belief as to how women should act. Balázs saw himself as intellectually and emotionally superior to women and assumed the role as a guide toward their understanding of life's meaning: "They come to me, into the life-observing tower to look around a little bit ... and to seek advice and encouragement. . . . They regard me as their general. It is not as though I knew the path but because my faith is stronger and I see things more clearly."[17] Balázs's superior attitude toward women often led to their antagonism. Although Bartók's own view of women differed in basic ways from that of Balázs, there was enough common ground between their perspectives regarding gender issues that drew Bartók to Balázs's *Bluebeard* text.

Isometric Text-Verse of Ancient Hungarian Folk Music as Structural Framework for the Final Phase of Character Development and Transformation

Of the isometric stanzaic patterns that Bartók found in the most ancient of the Hungarian folk melodies, many of the underlying text-verses have either twelve, eight, or six syllables per line, the rhythmic style generally *parlando-rubato*.[18] In many other of the ancient Hungarian melodies of isometric stanzaic structure, the underlying text-verses have seven, nine, ten, or eleven syllables, the rhythmic style mostly *tempo giusto*. Bartók's opera is entirely based on the ancient pattern of eight syllables per line. The folklike octosyllabic structure of the opening two vocal phrases, based on the pairing of Bluebeard's WT-0 tetrachord (D–C–B♭–A♭) and Judith's characteristically more wide-ranging WT-1 segment (A–G–E♭–B), establishes the structural framework within which these pitch-set relations can be developed in connection with symbolic expression. Bluebeard's descending WT-0 tetrachord (D–C–B♭–A♭), which unfolds in a 4 + 4-note octosyllabic statement, is simultaneously expanded in the orchestra into a complete WT-0 collection by the lower four-note segment (E–F♯–G♯–A♯) of the longer diatonic line (E–F♯–G♯–A♯/B–C♯). In the enharmonic repeat of the figure, the orchestral whole-tone tetrachord is also linearly expanded into the complete WT-0 scale (F♭–G♭–A♭–B♭–C–D/E♭) in connection with the dramatic (symbolic) trend of the passage, that is, imminent danger and relentless move toward fate as Judith demands that the door be opened. The second, more fragmented pair of vocal segments on "Judit! Judit!" which shortens the first pair of WT-0 tetrachords to the tritone boundary (D–A♭, D–A♭), now forms a 2 + 2-note tetrasyllabic construction. The latter is extended to the "expected" eight syllables by Judith's four-note phrase to round out the phrasal pairing according to the old Hungarian octosyllabic principle of the opera. At the same time, Judith's initial four-note statement (no. 87) has already supplied the four-note segment that is implicitly missing from Bluebeard's octosyllabic (4 + 4/2 + 2 = 12) pairing, so a sense of structural ambiguity, fusion, and intensification is produced.

While Judith's second four-note phrase (no. 87, mm. 5–6) is part of an octosyllabic pattern if considered in connection with Bluebeard's initial twelve-syllable construction (i.e., Bluebeard's 12 + Judith's 4 = 8 + 8), it also seems to have a larger hierarchical significance. On the one hand, her second four-note segment, together with her first (at no. 87), is part of a complete octosyllabic construction (4 + 4). On the other hand, her second four-note segment, because of its separation from her first, also begins a new octosyllabic construction, which is continued as such by the following statements of the two-note "Danger" motif (no. 88, mm. 1 and 3, etc.). As a parallel to Bluebeard's incomplete (4 + 4 + 2 + 2 + [ ]) pairing of octosyllabic constructions, Judith's two separate four-note phrases are also extended by successive two-note fragments ("Danger" motif, at no. 88). The latter have the same structural function as Bluebeard's "Judit! Judit!," so Judith's two vocal phrases and the first two orchestral statements of the "Danger" motif suggest a similar 4 + 4 + 2 + 2 pattern. In turn, the "Danger" motif begins a succession of syllabic groupings of 2 + 8 notes with the following eighth-note figure, this juxtaposition implying a reversal of Bluebeard's initial vocal construction of 8 + 2 + 2, which produces a sense of rounding out the scene as it approaches the cadential (transitional) passage (no. 89 ff.).

An Aphorism of Nietzsche on Women and Its Reflection in the Dual Illusion of Balázs's Judith

The more the man and woman struggle to attain happiness through spiritual union, the more Balázs's message of irreconcilability announces itself and seems to resonate with Nietzsche's perception regarding the basic source of the dilemma between man and woman: "The sexes deceive themselves about each other—because at bottom they honor and love only themselves (or their own ideal, to put it more pleasantly). Thus man likes woman peaceful—but woman is essentially unpeaceful, like a cat, however well she may have trained herself to seem peaceable."[19] Balázs's text seems to reflect this idea if we compare Judith's dependent, loving words at the opening of the opera, "I'm coming, Bluebeard, I'm coming," with her most intrusive, dangerously insistent statements at the structural highpoint (fifth door) of the opera, "Be it my life or my death, Bluebeard," her intention boldly expressed just after Bluebeard has warned her to beware that his castle will not get any lighter. Indeed, the inevitable course of Judith's actions will lead to her demise and to "endless darkness" for Bluebeard.

The succession of irregular octosyllabic overlappings, elisions, and additions contribute to the tense mood of the (transitional) passage (no. 89 ff.). In the unfolding of these ambiguous phrasal constructions, it is primarily Judith's "Danger" motif that induces a sense of disruption as subsection b3 winds down (diminuendo) to the cadence. Within the octosyllabic framework, the "Danger" motif seems to serve as a replacement for (that is, identity with) Bluebeard's two declamatory statements on "Judit! Judit!" This identification of the "Danger" motif with Judith's name is supported by the harmonic context as well. The harmonic underpinning of each of the first two statements of the "Danger" motif is based on two augmented (whole-tone) triads. The first augmented triad in each pair of chords forms part of the larger minor-modal (funereal) form of the "Stefi" seventh chord (first pairing, F–A♭–C–E/G–B–D♮; second pairing, B–D–F♯–A♯/C–E–G♯), which recalls the basic intervallic structure (G♭–A–D♭–F, in enharmonic spelling, F♯–A–C♯–E♯) of Judith's very first assertion that she is coming, as she had entered the castle with Bluebeard (at no. 3). The initial augmented triads (A♭–C–E and D–F♯–A♯) of the first two statements of the "Danger" motif, respectively, which are built on the same tritone elements (A♭ and D) of Bluebeard's two "Judit!" declamations, together extend the WT-0 tetrachord (D–C–B♭–A♭) of Bluebeard's phrase to the complete WT-0 collection. At the same time, the successive eighth-note scalar figurations, which alternate with the "Danger" motif, unfold ascending whole-tone tetrachords that complete the WT-1 collection of Judith's second phrase: after the initial tetrachordal ascent, D–E–F♯– G♯ (no. 88, m. 2), which forms the tritone complement of Bluebeard's WT-0 tetrachord, A♭–B♭–C–D, the following four tetrachordal ascents (A–B–C♯–D♯, F–G– A–B, B–C♯–D♯–E♯, and G–A–B–C♯) outline the complete WT-1 collection. Thus, the basic whole-tone quality of the "Danger" motif, the expanded harmonic projection of it as augmented triads that belong in turn to the larger funereal form of the "Stefi" seventh chord, and the implied presence of the entire chromatic collection by the combination or juxtaposition of both whole-tone collections throughout the passage, provide the relevant musical characteristics that symbolize Judith's fatalistic intrusion and the continual expectation of the appearance of blood in Bluebeard's soul (castle).

The symbolic significance of the octosyllabic interactions that form subsection b3 (nos. 87–89) is elucidated by the more regular octosyllabic constructions of the orchestral figurations, which first accompany the vocal phrases and then alternate with the "Danger" motif. The descending tetrachords and the two-note "Judit!" declamations of Bluebeard's opening phrase are all drawn into the octosyllabic interpretation by the contrapuntal figuration of the orchestra. Then, each of the two-note segments of Judith's descending four-note phrase is also interpreted by the orchestral counterpoint as part of an octosyllabic construction. The only disruption of the octosyllabic pattern is introduced by the two-note statements of the "Danger" motif, which otherwise appear in alternation with the regular octosyllabic orchestral figuration. The latter is soon reduced to four-note segments, while the "Danger" motif is reduced to one note at the beginning of the transition. These single-note representations of the "Danger" motif unfold, then, as part of an octosyllabic pattern in "tre battute."

Echoes of the octosyllabic interactions comprise the remainder of the transition, in which the sequence of one- or two-note segments add up to two separate octosyllabic patterns surrounding the final two octosyllabic vocal statements of Bluebeard. The second orchestral grouping unfolds seven articulations plus one more after Bluebeard's second vocal statement, the latter now revealing the reversal of characterizations as Bluebeard sings Judith's original descending motif (F–D♭–A–G♭) at the major third transposition (A–F–D♭–B♭). This transposition permits Judith's original augmented triad (F–D♭–A) to be retained. Although the original seventh-chord boundary (F–G♭) of Judith's original statement (no. 3) is replaced here by a new boundary (A–B♭), the two preceding glissandi, which are reminiscent of Judith's "Danger" motif, permit her original motivic boundary (F–G♭) to be heard in this significant passage of character transformation. Another aphorism of Nietzsche on independence points to yet another aspect of the dilemma in the characters' relationship, in this case, especially on the part of Judith:

> Not to remain stuck to a person—not even the most loved—every person is a prison, also a nook. . . . Not to remain stuck to some pity—not even for higher men into whose rare torture and helplessness some accident allowed us to look. Not to re-

main stuck to a science—even if it should lure us with the most precious finds that seem to have been saved up precisely for us. Not to remain stuck to one's own detachment, to that voluptuous remoteness and strangeness of the bird who flees ever higher to see ever more below him—the danger of the flier. Not to remain stuck to our own virtues and become as a whole the victim of some detail in us . . . which is the danger of dangers for superior and rich souls who spend themselves lavishly, almost indifferently, and exaggerate the virtue of generosity into a vice.[20]

Duke Bluebeard's Castle

*Final Transformation and Retreat
into Eternal Darkness: Synthesis
of Pentatonic/Diatonic and
Whole-Tone Spheres*

Doors VI (Lake of Tears) and VII (Former Wives)

Complete psychological reversal and extreme divergence between the two characters
are realized by the fifth door scene, the peak of the opera. Through her love and devotion, Judith has faced every danger to achieve total knowledge of the man, to shed
light on the painful secrets of his past, and to find complete spiritual union with him.
But now, the image of the man acquires a new and frightening dimension. His world
darkens further before her as her renewed probing reveals the grief hidden in the still
waters of the lake of tears. György Kroó suggests a transformation of Judith's attitude
that, while corresponding with Veress's assertions regarding the psychological reversal between the two characters, provides a somewhat different perspective as to the
nature of this change:

> The woman through her faith, trust and devotion has gradually overcome the dark-
> ness and sadness of soul, but is now beginning to have doubts. She starts to find the
> man's secrets a burden, just at the moment when Bluebeard has given her everything
> that can be shared. From now on her musical portrait expresses more and more her
> suspicions, curiosity, and the passion of Eve's nature. . . . The theme of Judith's jeal-
> ousy, which silences the melody of the duke's love, grows out of the motif illustrating
> the blood stain. . . . The wife-slaying duke of the saga disappears; the only moving
> force of the tragic denouement will be the woman's blind passion. While woman's
> mediocrity is being exposed, man's idealism is increasingly glorified. Man's love and
> heroic character are sublime and pure, and therefore his realization that he can never
> gain fulfilment in love and is doomed to eternal misery is all the more tragic. . . .
> [Judith] has lost irredeemably any chance of happiness with Bluebeard. She will be-
> come just a dream image of love.[1]

Kroó's interpretation, like Veress's, pertains to the reversal of characterization on
the internal level of the opera itself. A different kind of character reversal may also be
observed in the historical development of the two characters from their ancient literary and artistic depictions to their transformations in modern sources. The murder of

Holofernes by Judith, the self-sacrificing woman in the book of the Old Testament, is in fulfillment of God's interest in saving his people. In the nineteenth century, Hebbel's dramatic transformation of Judith into the tragic figure of the young virgin motivated by anger and personal revenge served as a bridge between romantic and more modern conceptions of the woman. Her seductive power as a symbol of danger to men acquired a more fundamental, evil significance in the early twentieth century,[2] this negative conception of the woman foreshadowed in such realistic writings as Gustave Flaubert's *Madame Bovary* or, more directly, in connection with the Salome of his *Hérodias*. Although Béla Balázs himself was well-versed in the dramas of Hebbel,[3] the woman in Balázs's libretto is presented as a somewhat more abstract, personally nondescript figure, a characterization tempered by the influence of Maeterlinck's symbolist dramaturgy. Balázs's Judith does retain the nineteenth-century literary image of the dangerous woman, but she is devoid of any sense of revenge, explicit evil attributes, or the overt sexual enticement she exudes in Klimt's paintings and other contemporary works.

Conversely to Judith, the figure of Bluebeard has been portrayed as the embodiment of evil—the cruel wife killer—from the early literary sources, which stem from Charles Perrault's "Barbe bleue" tale, in *Histoires ou Contes du Temps passé, avec des Moralités* (published in 1697).[4] Nineteenth-century historical studies have traced the figure of the wife-killer even further back to folklore, for instance, to the Hungarian tale of Márton Ajgó, who is decapitated by the woman, Anna Molnár, whom the man had lured to the tree from which he hanged his former lovers. Other stories, as Kroó informs us, are based on "contrasted notions of Darkness and Light. . . . [t]he figure of Bluebeard stand[ing] for the dark and sinful Night, which slays its betrothed."[5] Of the various literary and musical manifestations of Bluebeard in the nineteenth and early twentieth century,[6] including Offenbach's comic opera (1866), Maeterlinck's *Ariane et Barbe-bleue* (1902), H. Eulenberg's three-act drama *Ritter Blaubart* (1905), Dukas's opera after Maeterlinck's *Ariane et Barbe-bleue* (1907), Anatole France's short story *Les sept femmes de la Barbe-bleue* (1909), Balázs's mystery play *A kékszakállú herceg vára* (1910–1911), and E. Reznicek's three-act opera after Eulenberg's *Ritter Blaubart* (1920), the Symbolist influence has tended to diffuse, even transform the evil quality of the character in certain cases, especially in Bartók's musical setting. Throughout the opera, Bluebeard's words and gestures indicate love, devotion, and remorse. Despite the shield of his impenetrable reserve and the grim reality of the plot itself, he expresses his wish to share his love, wealth, and vast domain with his beloved forever.

The final musical transformation of the characters in Bartók's opera occurs in the transition between the fifth and sixth doors (no. 90, mm. 11–12), where Bluebeard takes over Judith's (Stefi's) original whole-tone/pentatonic theme a major third higher, $A-F-D\flat-B\flat$. Then, the diatonic, whole-tone, and chromatic pitch-set interactions implied in the opening chord progression of the fifth door scene are manifested more explicitly in the repeated arpeggiations at the opening of Door VI (Lake of Tears) (no. 91). This throbbing A pentatonic figuration adds the note G♯ at its apex, $A-C-[\ ]-E-G-G\sharp$ (ex. 12-1) to reveal a more exclusive foreground connection between this note (G♯) and Bluebeard's C major triad at the opening of the preceding scene. In these arpeggiations, G♯ forms a half-step relation not only with the adjacent fifth degree (G) of the C major triad, but also with the lowest note (A), implying the presence of the dissonant interval-ratio 1:1 cell, G–G♯–A–[ ]; an isolated semitone, E–D♯, punctuates this first set of arpeggiations. The outline of the configuration is the "Stefi" motif, A–C–E–G♯, which serves once again as the source for the musical symbolism.

Judith's vocal statements (no. 92, m. 4 ff.) in the opening sections of the *Lake of Tears*, like the initial arpeggiations, acquire an ostinato-like quality as she reiterates the A minor seventh construction (A–C–E–G) derived from the more complex arpeggiations (A–C–E–G–G♯). These static vocal repetitions of A–C–E–G, which now contract the original major seventh boundary of Judith's basic pentatonic/whole-tone motif (A–C–E–G♯) to a minor seventh, reflect the more depressed, lifeless quality expressed by Judith's words (no. 92, m. 4–no. 93): "I see a silent white lake, A motionless white lake." The larger pentatonic significance of her vocal content, as opposed to its whole-tone connection in the arpeggiations of the "Stefi" motif ([ ]–C–E–G♯), is confirmed by the underlying string harmony in section b' (no. 92, m. 4 ff.), voice and accompaniment together outlining A–C–D–E–G, then E–G–A–B–D (ex. 12-2). The pentatonic quality of her vocal line serves, at the same time, as the point of departure for transformation into whole-tone and more chromatic coloring. The accompanying pentatonic bass line, G–B♭–C–D–[ ] (no. 93, m. 2 ff.) is partially transformed, then, into a hybrid pentatonic/whole-tone collection (G–B♭–C–D–E) by the sustained E, which is drawn into a chromatic/octatonic figure (E–F–F♯–F–E/E–D–C♯–B–B♭) at the cadence just before the reiteration of Judith's A pentatonic phrase, C–G–A–E (i.e., A–C–[ ]–E–G) at no. 94. The latter begins a repeat of the same trend of compression, which cadences on the complete form of the "Blood" motif tetrachord (E–F–F♯–F–E–E♭) before the return at section a2 (at no. 95) to the hybrid A pentatonic/whole-tone arpeggiation. Thus, these local progressions toward intervallic compression represents, again, a microscopic reflection of the basic overall tendency toward fate and blood in each scene.

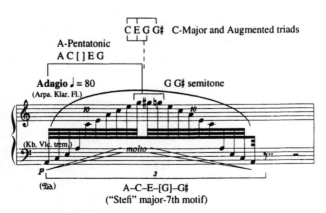

EXAMPLE 12-1. Door VI (Lake of Tears), no. 91, fusion of pentatonic/diatonic, whole-tone (augmented triad), and chromatic in arpeggiations

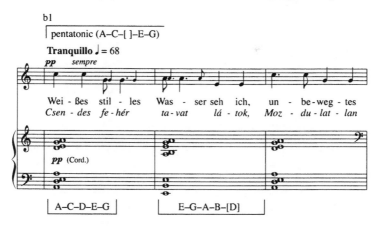

EXAMPLE 12-2. Door VI (Lake of Tears), no. 92, m. 4ff., pentatonic significance of Judith's vocal content, confirmed by underlying string harmony, both voice and accompaniment together outlining A–C–D–E–G, then E–G–A–B–D

Transition from Doors V to VI: Bluebeard's Acquisition of Judith's "Fate" (Pentatonic/Whole-Tone) Motif; The Sexual Instinct and the Death Wish

Bluebeard's acquisition of Judith's "Fate" (pentatonic/whole-tone) motif in the transition from doors V to VI provides a musical clue to the inevitable dramatic outcome: it symbolizes the reversal of characterization and anticipates the loss of Judith. The struggle between the man and the woman culminates in their affirmations of love in the sixth door scene. Admitting to his tears of sorrow, Bluebeard opens his arms and declares his love for Judith, but asserts in no uncertain terms that the last door will never be opened. In contrast, Judith submits to his embrace and, in an increasingly doubtful tone, questions his love for her (no. 103, m. 5 ff.), "Do you truly love me, Bluebeard?" His words reveal a double bind, "Kiss me, kiss me, ask me nothing." The outcome of their struggle is imminent. Section d4 (no. 112, m. 2 ff.) develops the "Blood" motif extensively as Judith acknowledges the meaning of the blood she has seen in each of the chambers (no. 113, mm. 4–5), "I know, Bluebeard, I know what the seventh door conceals. . . . All your former wives are there! Slaughtered, frozen in blood. Oh, the rumors are true, the horrible rumors!"

Considering Judith's foresight into the source of blood, her demand to have the seventh door opened would seem to suggest an inner (unconscious) compulsion—a death wish—to fulfill her ultimate destiny. This assumption is based on her foreknowledge of what lies behind the last door and yet her inability to deter her obsessive desire to open it. As Balázs himself tells us, "[The castle] is lonely, dark, and secretive: the castle of closed doors. It is precisely this tragic obscurity, this suffering withdrawal into seclusion, that attracted the woman with strange power, even though she had heard frightful rumors about murdered women."[7] And so, a more profound psychological dimension is added to the fatalistic message of the opera.[8] In the penultimate scene of the Maeterlinck-Debussy opera, the connection between fate and the unconscious is prominently manifested in Mélisande's shocking utterance, "All the better!" as the fallen castle chains seal the lovers' doom. In the penultimate scene of the Balázs-Bartók opera, similarly, the connection between fate and unconscious motivation is manifested in Judith's demand that the last door be opened, in spite of her knowledge that the source of blood lay within. Bartók's attraction to a subject imbued by the death wish may be interpreted as a projection of his own psycho-social background, especially during the period 1908–1911. As Dorothy Lamb Crawford explains:

> In Hungary, the Nietzsche-influenced poet Endre Ady provoked young Budapest radicals to expose and transcend the moral vacuum of their times [Arpad Kadarkay, *Georg Lukács: Life, Thought, and Politics* (Cambridge, Mass.: Blackwell, 1991), p. 58]. The example of Ady's adult life, much of it lived in relative sexual freedom in Paris, was emulated—frequently with suicidal results—by members of Bartók's intellectual circle in Budapest. With great intensity they debated the "woman question," and notions of sexual polarity derived from the Viennese writer Otto Weininger, who himself had committed suicide after the publication of his widely read book, *Sex and Character*. . . .
>
> Bartók's expressionism occurs in works born of seemingly bottomless despair and manifests itself in two phases: first in the emotionally obsessive 1908–11 period, which culminated in his opera, *Duke Bluebeard's Castle*, and second in the 1915–19 period, which culminated in the bizarre eroticism of the first version of *The Miraculous Mandarin*.[9]

Bartók's works of the first period are pervaded by transformations of the "Stefi" motif, a persistent musical manifestation of "a diary-like preoccupation with changing views and moods in regard to the pain of love. Suicide," according to Crawford, "was apparently on Bartók's mind."[10] His letter of September 1907 to Stefi Geyer is explicit:

> I do not see why you should condemn suicide as such a cowardly act! It's quite the contrary. . . . As long as my mother is alive, and as long as I have some interest in the world, I will not commit suicide. But beyond that? Once I have no responsibility towards *any* living person, once I live all by myself (never "*wavering*" even then) —why should suicide be a cowardly act? It's true, of course, that it would not be a deed of great daring, but it could not be dismissed as an act of cowardly indifference . . .[11]

Regarding the general notion of suicide, Alexander Grinstein explains that "[t]here are a number of themes commonly present in the dreams of patients contemplating suicide. There is often some reference to desperation, to 'no exit or 'no way out,' that they have come to a 'dead end' in a trip."[12] In the opera, this sense of finitude is evident as Judith forces Bluebeard to unlock the seventh door. Indeed, a sense of closure was present from the outset as Judith had unlocked the very first door. As Bluebeard relinquishes the last key, he seems now to accept his death as he identifies each of the four wives symbolically with a different phase of man's life cycle. Judith is recognized as the last—ephemeral—wife who came at midnight, thereby pointing, again, to her association with relentless time and ultimate fate. More specifically, Bartók's personal belief that men and women are essentially different in mind and body and that his own spiritual loneliness was to be his destiny—"I look about me in search of the ideal companion, and yet I am fully aware that it is a vain quest"[13]—provides a still deeper insight. The notion that irreconcilable differences exist between the sexes supports the premise that fate and unconscious motivation are equivalent in the sense that they are different conceptualizations of the same force. In the opera, the woman's "passionate" (unconscious) urge to probe into the deepest levels of the man's soul to achieve union with him will bring the two characters into direct conflict. Because the man would sacrifice love to maintain his own private world, he abandons Judith as she is inevitably drawn into the chamber of his former wives.

Thus, the irreconcilable relation between the sexes is essential to the theme of ultimate fate (death) in the opera. The man himself cannot escape his eternal loneliness (in "endless darkness"), this metaphor for Bluebeard's death reflected in Bartók's letter to Stefi Geyer, after her rejection of him, about his "funeral dirge." In the Lengyel-Bartók ballet pantomime, *The Miraculous Mandarin* (1919), composed one year after the first performance of the opera, sexual union between the man and the woman leads inevitably to the man's death. The Mandarin is lured by a girl into the den of three tramps who proceed to rob him. Their attacks cannot subdue this virtually invincible wealthy Chinese, who dies only after the girl satisfies his desire. In the opera, the demise of both the man and the woman is brought about by the woman's unconscious motivation (death wish, according to evidence in the libretto itself) to fulfill her ultimate fate. In the ballet, the demise of the man is conversely brought about by his "passionate" urge. It is the man rather than the woman who is lured into the room in the latter case, and it is the man who will meet his ultimate fate through his desire for union with the woman. In the section of his book on "Death Symbols," Grinstein writes that "[b]ecause of the common association between death and sexuality in people's minds, either theme may be symbolized by the other. . . . If associations lead to the topic of death when the material is sexual, the therapist should consider the possibility that the patient is expressing his anxiety that the gratification of his sexual wishes will result in his own demise or that of his sexual partner."[14]

The composer's own psychological (or quasi-autobiographical) projection seems to be symbolized in several descending string arpeggiations (no. 120, m. 2ff.) just prior to the opening of the seventh door (ex. 12-3). The first arpeggiation outlines the "Stefi" major-seventh motif ([Gb]–F–Db–Bb–Gb), which is identical in pitch content to Judith's opening statement (no. 3), except for the replacement of the original minor third (A) by the major third (Bb); the presence of the latter (A) is implied by the B♮ neighbor in the cadential segment only. The major third replacement suggests the dissolution of the whole-tone component of Judith's motif in anticipation of the final stage of the drama. In the last two descending statements, Gb–Eb–Cb–Ab–Fb (no. 120, mm. 4 and 7), the major seventh construction of the motif (Fb–Ab–Cb–Eb) is elided with a transposition (Ab–Cb–Eb–Gb) of the pentatonic minor seventh chord. This is an adumbration of the return at the end of the opera to Bluebeard's original, unaltered pentatonic construction, a slightly compressed transformation of both the major seventh and whole-tone-related forms of the "Stefi" harmonic construction. Momentarily, however, at the opening of Door VII (Former Wives), as Judith expects to find the murdered wives, the quasi-whole-tone implication of the "Stefi" seventh chord is reasserted by the expansion of the basic C minor tonic triad (at no. 121) to the funereal form of the seventh chord, C–Eb–G–B (at no. 121, m. 8), by the addition of the major seventh degree, B.

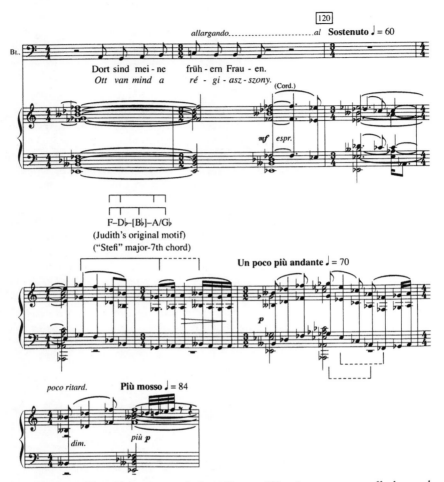

EXAMPLE 12-3. Transition to seventh door (Former Wives), no. 120, m. 2ff., descending string arpeggiations outlining "Stefi" major-seventh motif, [G♭]–F–D♭–B♭–G♭ (identical in pitch content to Judith's opening statement at No. 3), except for replacement of original minor third (A) by major third (B♭); presence of A implied by B♭♭ neighbor in cadential segment

The full significance of the latter chord, C–E♭–G–B, which is the tritone transposition of Judith's very opening vocal construction, G♭–A–D♭–F (see ex. 9-3 earlier), and a representation, furthermore, of the quasi-whole-tone transformation (A–D♭–F) of the initial "Castle" theme's minor-seventh harmonic substructure (i.e., F♯–A–C♯–E is transformed into F♯–A–C♯–E♯, in enharmonic spelling, G♭–A–D♭–F), may be surmised as follows. Judith's opening statement, G♭–A–D♭–F (no. 3), contains three notes (A–D♭–F) of the primary WT-1 collection, the tritone transposition (C–E♭–G–B) at the opening of Door VII containing the remaining three notes (E♭–G–B) of the same whole-tone collection. This long-range complementary pitch-set relation between Judith's initial entry into the castle and her last entry into the seventh chamber to join the former wives provides a sense of completion of the main fatalistic musical symbol of the opera. It is striking that while the two respective augmented triads (A–Db–F and Eb–G–B) imply the presence of a long-range intercalation (A–[B]–Db–[Eb]–F–[G]) of the complete WT-1 cycle, the remaining WT-0 notes (Gb and C) from these two transpositions (Gb/A–Db–F and C/Eb–G–B) of the "Stefi" funereal form reflect the two basic polarized tonalities of the opera.

Although one may argue that these complementary pitch-set relations occur primarily over the long span of the opera, transposition C–Eb–G–B (no. 121, m. 7 ff.) of Door VII was already partially manifested at Judith's opening vocal statement (see ex. 9-3 earlier) by the vocal grace-note, Eb, sustained orchestral B, and neighbor-note C, the remaining harmonic content providing only pitch-class duplications of the vocal line. Thus, the final, complementary transposition (C–Eb–G–B), which contains the remaining elements (Eb–G–B) of the WT-1 collection, is already maximally represented (by C, Eb, and B) in the harmonic content that accompanies Judith's first appearance. Conversely, transposition Gb–A–Db–F of Judith's opening statement is manifested (ex. 12-4) in the harmonic content of Door VII (at no. 121, mm. 4–no. 122, m. 3), which infuses the seventh chord on C (C–Eb–G–B) with the combined

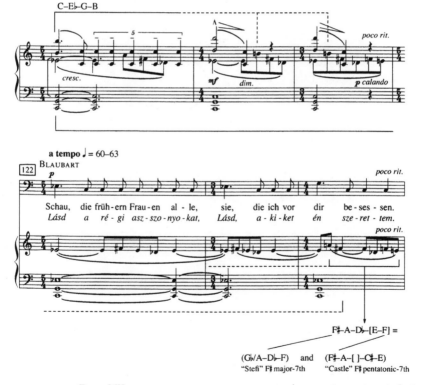

EXAMPLE 12-4. Door VII, no. 121, m. 7 to no. 122, m. 3, harmonic content infusing seventh chord on C (C–Eb–G–B) with combined "Stefi" and "Castle" forms of seventh chord (F#–A–Db–E–F) on Gb in the english horn

"Stefi" and "Castle" forms of the seventh chord (F♯–A–D♭–E/F) on G♭ in the English horn.[15] These pitch-set relations tell us, symbolically, that, on Judith's entry into the castle, her ultimate fate is imminent, and that, on her entry into the last chamber, it is fulfilled, her death wish serving as a prime mover of her fate. Judith's motivation may be further elucidated by means of certain basic psychoanalytical concepts, which were increasingly understood by many early twentieth-century dramatists (such as those in Bartók's literary circle). According to Peter Giovacchini's summary of Freud's hypothesis,[16]

> [Instincts] try to restore earlier states, and in the case of the living organism, instincts attempt to restore the inanimate state. . . . Rather than being concerned with the preservation of life, [the] real aim [of self-preservative instincts] is to permit the organism to seek death in its own fashion. Freud identified this as the *death instinct.* The sexual instincts, however, are in opposition to such forces. They are part of the germ plasm that strives toward unification and life.

Whereas Bluebeard's words just prior to the seventh door evoke the notion of the sexual instinct—he wishes to be unified with Judith (no. 109)—"Judith, love me, ask me nothing," she offers a conflicting, ambiguous message that signifies both the sexual and death instincts: her quest for love (no. 101, mm. 7–8), "Bluebeard . . . love me," shifts to defiance of her internal sense of danger as she stands on the threshold of the seventh door. Judith's entry into the last chamber symbolizes her destructive tendency, but the sexual instinct is simultaneously indicated, hence the common association between death and sexuality.[17]

However, according to Freud, "some symbols have more connection with the uterus than with the [external] female genitals: thus, cupboards, stoves and, more especially, rooms. Here room-symbolism touches on house-symbolism. . . ."[18] We are acquainted already with rooms as symbol. The representation can be carried further, for windows, and doors in and out of rooms, take over the meaning of orifices in the body. In this connection interest in whether the room is open or locked is easily intelligible."[19] Freud also asserts that "a dream of going through a suite of rooms is a brothel or harem dream. But, as Sachs (1914) has shown by some neat examples, it can also be used (by antithesis) to represent marriage."[20] Beyond that, such dreams in which a person travels through a number of rooms may be interpreted as multiple sexual affairs, in this case invoking symbolic significance in connection with Bluebeard's wives.[21] All of these interpretations bear directly on our understanding of the sexual instinct in all of its symbolic meanings in the Balázs libretto. Such interpretations acquire even greater significance in view of the new interests in psychological motivation during an era of increasing awareness of the unconscious and the irrational, especially as reflected in Freud's publications of the time.

Traditional Role of Women and Transition to Equality

Another possible interpretation of Judith's mixed messages can be made along sociological lines. The traditionally submissive role of women in marriage was undergoing a transition in the late nineteenth century to one of greater equality. In this context, Bluebeard symbolizes the traditional man in that he places conditions on his wife that he expects her to obey. Conversely, Judith symbolizes, instead of a traditional woman, a transitional woman who demands equality and full disclosure from her husband. Here, we understand the traditional love relationship as expressed by Nietzsche:

> I will never admit the claim that man and woman have *equal* rights in love; these do not exist. For man and woman have different conceptions of love ... what woman means by love is clear enough: total devotion (not mere surrender) with soul and body, without any consideration or reserve.... Man, when he loves a woman, wants precisely this love from her and is thus himself as far as can be from the presupposition of feminine love. ... A woman's passion in its unconditional renunciation of rights of her own presupposes precisely that on the other side there is no equal pathos, no equal will to renunciation.[22]

For Nietzsche, "it is man who creates for himself the image of woman, and woman forms herself according to this image."[23] Nietzsche's precept resonates, with slight modification, with Balázs's own assessment regarding the meaning of the Hungarian ballad about *Duke Bluebeard's Castle*. Balázs tells us that Judith "doesn't shudder in horror until [Bluebeard] begins to beautify her, to adorn her with jewels. 'Ah, Bluebeard, you are not dreaming, I am your poor, living wife.' But the man covers her with glittering ornaments, and Judith gradually grows numb with death. The man's dream kills her, the very dream she herself conjured up in him. And the dreaming man remains alone once more, his castle again locked and dark."[24]

As she comes to full realization of the main cause of her forebodings, which had begun with the bloody evidence of Bluebeard's murdered wives behind each of the first six doors, Judith falters before Door VII. But then, astonished, she encounters the final unexpected secret (no. 122, mm. 4–5): "They live, they live!— They are alive here!" The allegorical depiction of these women—living, beautiful, and splendidly adorned in the only scene of the opera without textual reference to blood— introduces yet another symbolic dimension to the opera, one that would evoke strong reaction from the modern feminist movement. This thwarting of expectations, that is, as a sort of *deus ex machina*, which contradicts the evidence for the source of blood, practically suggests absolution of the man, even to the point of reversing the evil historical image of the wife murderer in the ancient Perrault novel. We are almost duped into perceiving Bluebeard now as a benevolent figure, a lover of beauty who desires to share his love, riches, and entire being. This image is further enhanced by the more immediate dramatic message of humility, in which Bluebeard, like Judith who stands humbly in line with the other wives (no. 126, mm. 10–11), "Alas, I am wretched and shabby," sinks to his knees with open arms before his three former wives.

Nevertheless, in spite of this twist, in which Bluebeard's former wives are expected to be found murdered but are found living instead, in beautiful adornments no less, the deep-level meaning cannot in the final analysis escape the ultimate conclusion of death. Other symbols support this assumption and provide a degree of realistic continuity in the events of the opera, which are driven by unconscious forces and permit logical consistency in their meaning. As Grinstein explains:

> Beautiful dreams are often dreams of death (Grotjahn, 1980). ... One patient, for example, dreamed of being in a large, peaceful, grassy area where many daisies and other flowers were blooming. Her associations led to the slang expression "pushing

daisies," which means death. When images of sunsets accompany these scenic dreams [we may invoke the final scene of Debussy's opera, where Mélisande's death occurs while she watches the sun set into the sea]—such phrases as "going off into the sunset" or the "sunset years" of one's life (referring to thoughts about aging and death) are frequently given as associations.[25]

This door scene of the former wives directly precedes the ending of the opera, the chronological progression of these scenes permitting sharp contrast between the glittering adornments—jewels, crown of diamonds, and starlit mantle—and the final darkness. Grinstein further suggests that "Dreams in which the color black appears, where there is reference to emptiness [and] darkness . . . may also symbolize death."[26]

Even Bluebeard's music acquires a more melodious quality, exclusively based on his original D pentatonic construction as the scene moves toward its conclusion (no. 135 ff.), "You are beautiful, you are beautiful, a hundred times beautiful." The opening of the scene continues the musical trend of the preceding measures. The opening harmony as well as Bluebeard's initial vocal statement in the introduction of this scene are reduced essentially to a C minor triad. This softening of the earlier C major harmony of Bluebeard's vast domain was already suggested by the infusion of Judith's intimidated Eb tonality in that scene (see no. 75, m. 10). A segment of the latter, for which another level of musical meaning was suggested in connection with the fusion of the basic seventh chords (see ex. 12-4 earlier), is reiterated here in the English horn, F#–Eb–Db–Eb (in enharmonic spelling, Gb–Eb–Db–Eb).

The simple tonic triad (C–Eb–G) of Door VII suggests a reduction of both Bluebeard's pentatonic construction and Judith's (Stefi's) "Fate" chord (see ex. 12-4 earlier), a simultaneous reflection of the dramatic decrescendo of their characterizations. The momentary orchestral expansion of the triad into the funereal (minor-modal) form of the "Stefi" seventh chord, C–Eb–G–B (no. 121, m. 7), partially supports this interpretation of the minor triad as a musical symbolization of Judith (Stefi). At Judith's fragmented, quiet vocal entry on the notes E–Eb (no. 122, mm. 4–5), the significance of the C minor triad as the common element in the fusion concept is further confirmed. While the Eb belongs to the held C minor triad (C–Eb–[ ]), the E simultaneously invokes Bluebeard's C major form from Door V. At the same time, the sextuplet figure adds two new notes, B implying the presence of both the major and minor forms of the "Stefi" motif, C–Eb–[ ]–B and C–E–[ ]–B, A# (in enharmonic spelling, Bb) Bluebeard's basic minor seventh (pentatonic) form, C–Eb–[ ]–Bb.

The "Wives" music, which first appears in part 1 of this scene (at no. 124, mm. 8–10), outlines the major-modal form of the "Stefi" motif (G–B–D–F#) in association with Bluebeard's description of his former wives as lovely visions who live in unforgotten beauty.[27] This major-modal thematic form serves, in the remainder of the scene, to punctuate Bluebeard's successive references to the three wives, the rhythmic structure of the theme gradually revealing (by no. 126, mm. 4–10) its connection with (or reminiscence of) Judith's "Danger" motif. While some chromatic shifts are introduced in the orchestra, both vocal parts remain relatively reserved and diatonic. The last prominent statement of the C minor modal form of the "Stefi" motif, C–D#–Fx–B (i.e., C–Eb–G–B), linearly occurs (at no. 124, mm. 1–3) in juxtaposition with its impure tritone transposition, F#–A–C#–[D#]–E# (ex. 12-5). The latter recalls Judith's opening vocal line (Gb–A–Db–F) and foreshadows the return (no. 138) of Bluebeard's

Andante ♩ = 100

C–D♯–F×–[A]–B (= C–E♭–G–[A]–B)

124

schön - heit - strah -
száz - szor szé -

più *f molto espr.*

F♯–A–C♯–[D♯]–E♯

EXAMPLE 12-5. Door VII, no. 124, mm. 1–3, last prominent statement of C-minor-modal form of "Stefi" motif, C–D♯–Fx–B (i.e., C–E♭–G–B) in juxtaposition with its impure tritone transposition, F♯–A–C♯–[D♯]–E♯

F♯ pentatonic "Castle" ("Darkness") theme before the final darkness. The WT-1 (fatalistic) implications of the augmented triads contained within this tritone-related pairing (C/E♭–G–B and F♯/A–C♯–E♯) are expressly outlined in Bluebeard's vocal line, D♯–C♯–B–A–G (no. 126, mm. 2–6), which unfolds above the expanded statements of the "Wives" theme as he acknowledges the power they have brought him and how his domain and being belong to them.

The interpretation of Judith as an instrument of fate, ultimate darkness and, therefore, of Bluebeard's death, is supported not only by her WT-1 symbolization as unfolded in her opening vocal statement (F–D♭–A/G♭), but by the F♯ (G♭) tonality of the larger "Stefi" motif. This tonality emerges more explicitly in connection with Bluebeard's allusion to darkness (no. 131, mm. 2–4), "I found the fourth at night, Starry, black night." Judith's declamatory statement on dyad F♯–F (no. 131, m. 7 ff.), "Quiet, quiet. I am still here!" further establishes this fatalistic symbolism, as this two-note boundary (F♯–F) of her original motif (F–D♭–A–G♭, or F–D♭–A–F♯) is articulated by her final life assertion in the face of her death and, consequently, the symbolic death of Bluebeard.

Nietzsche, Bartók, Bluebeard, and Judith

It seems inevitable that the young Bartók would be drawn as much to the dilemma embodied in the main character of the Balázs libretto as he was to that in the writings of Nietzsche. The vast power of Bluebeard's Domain, a metaphor for at least certain aspects of Nietzsche's conception of man's "Will to Power," inevitably embodies the man's loneliness and finally his annihilation. Bluebeard cannot bear to look at the blood of his old wounds, opened by the relentlessly prying woman.[28] In correspondence with the text, the opera ends with a return (at nos. 138–139) to the "Foreboding" motif and a segment of Bluebeard's original D pentatonic Recitative (no. 2, mm. 7–9), now in enharmonic spelling, E♯–A–G–D. The adjacency of the first three notes (E♯–A–G) echoes the whole-tone collection of Judith's initial theme. This is supported by Judith's (Stefi's) original augmented triad (F–D♭–A, in enharmonic spelling, F–A–C♯), which is heard as a faint reminiscence in the initial chord of the underlying "Foreboding" motif. Bluebeard's last words, "Night . . . night . . . ," bring a brief return to tritone F♯–C of the original whole-tone scale, that is, that which first intruded into the F♯ pentatonic sphere (m. 16 ff.). This tritone—and with it the whole-tone collection—dissolves as the note C is replaced by the final pentatonic C♯ at the incomplete cadence of the basic F♯ pentatonic "Darkness" theme. The Woman who came at nightfall has vanished and Bluebeard's destiny is realized.

The final manifestation of the F♯ pentatonic "Darkness" theme (in the form of the minor seventh construction, F♯–A–C♯–E) at the end of the opera suggests a significant symbolic reference to Stefi Geyer (ex. 12-6). This is manifested as the funereal minor-modal variant, F♯–A–C♯–E♯, of Stefi's leitmotif (no. 140, mm. 6–11).[29] The latter hybrid (pentatonic/whole-tone) construction (F♯–A–C♯–E♯, with added B♯, in enharmonic spelling, C) belongs to the final conflict between WT-0 (represented by F♯–C) and WT-1 (represented by E♯–C♯–A, which was first manifested in Judith's opening vocal statement as F–D♭–A/G♭). At the final cadence, the latter (E♯–C♯–A) appears as part of the WT-1-infused "Darkness" ("Castle") theme of Bluebeard's soul, in which the pentatonic minor-seventh form (F♯–A–C♯–E) is

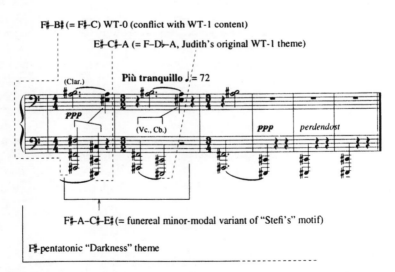

EXAMPLE 12-6. End of opera, no. 140, mm. 6–11, final manifestation of F♯–pentatonic "Darkness" theme, manifested as funereal minor-modal variant, F♯–A–C♯–E♯, of Stefi's leitmotif; hybrid (pentatonic/whole-tone) construction (F♯–A–C♯–E♯, with added B♯, in enharmonic spelling, C) belongs to conflict between WT-0 (represented by F♯–C) and WT-1 (represented by E♯–C♯–A, from Judith's opening vocal statement

transformed into the present version of Bartók's "funereal" form (F♯–A–C♯–E♯). The juxtaposition of the pentatonic fifth degree (C♯) with its whole-tone-related variant (C) had produced one of the first half-step intrusions at the appearance of the "Foreboding" theme at the opening of the opera (mm. 17–18).

In one respect, Bartók's Judith in the *Bluebeard* opera is analogous to Nietzsche's dwarf in *Zarathustra*. Judith has already seen the horrors of Bluebeard's chambers but insists on opening the remaining doors. Once his vast domain is revealed, Bluebeard is doomed to fall from the heights, lonely without the woman to love, weeping and resigned to eternal darkness. Beyond this analogy, we may further ask how one so powerful could be so dependent upon the woman for his survival. The composer, too, could not face what he saw as his own weakness in his relationship with Stefi Geyer: "By the time I had finished reading your letter, I was almost in tears—and that, as you can imagine, does not usually happen to me every day. Here is a case of human frailty. . . . Why couldn't I read your letter with cold indifference?"[30]

The notion of "mediocrity"—of Zarathustra's dwarf—may be understood as the acknowledgment of that part of the self that is vulnerable and can have feelings, attributes that in the past have been assigned primarily to the domain of the woman. Such labeling is a way of undervaluing or disavowing the emotional, vulnerable part of the self. Bartók's own philosophical assertion regarding his "struggle to rise above all things" suggests this attitude: "How far I am yet from doing so . . . the further you advance, the more intensely, it seems, you feel!"[31] The character of Judith, as manifested in Bartók's opera, appears to symbolize the vulnerable side, that is to say, the feeling side of the man's spiritual being.

The ultimate contradiction of the Bluebeard condition lies in the significance of this role of the woman. Although Bluebeard exhibits what seems to be extraordinary power, he can never have the completeness for which he strives. That completeness requires reciprocation by revealing and sharing his entire self with his loved one. Yet, he asks Judith to love him but ask him nothing. For Bluebeard, as for Bartók himself, that self contains the weakness that he must deny to attain ultimate power. The man's dilemma is embodied in Judith's own position, "I demand the truth before me." Paradoxically, it is in that position that the man's potential strength exists, if only he could acknowledge it. Hence, true power lies not at the lonely peak that towers above the rest of humankind, hovering in a questionable autonomy but, rather, in the completeness found in the human relationship that Bluebeard—or Bartók himself—feels he must resist to remain secure in his power. Thus the power for which the man strives is more apparent than real, a premise that we may assert is the ultimate meaning of Bartók's opera.

13

Symbolism and Expressionism in Other Early Twentieth-Century Operas

The Vienna of Sigmund Freud

In Vienna around the turn of the twentieth century, certain new aesthetic assumptions developed by the Symbolist poets in France also were manifested in the dramas and novels of Hugo von Hofmannsthal, Jacob Wassermann, Arthur Schnitzler, and others who reacted against the realism of nineteenth-century theater. These writers, whose literary thought reflected the theories of Freud, were to reveal new psychological insights into the pathological, clinical conditions of their characters.[1] As the seat of the Austro-Hungarian Empire and a scientific and cultural center, Vienna also attracted musical figures such as Johannes Brahms, Anton Bruckner, Gustav Mahler, Richard Strauss, and Arnold Schoenberg. This musical line, which brought the nineteenth century to a culmination, paved the way for the most radical transformations of chromatic tonality into the free-atonal idiom of Schoenberg in conjunction with his more intense Expressionist aesthetics.

Strauss's *Elektra:* Toward Expressionism and the Transformation of Late-Nineteenth-Century Chromatic Tonality

Between 1906 and 1908, Hugo von Hofmannsthal and Richard Strauss began their collaboration with the operatic setting of *Elektra*. In many of his librettos, Hofmannsthal approached the subject of love and hate from a profound human perspective based on a heightened concern for unconscious motivation. It was during this time in Vienna that Freud was developing his theory of psychoanalysis.[2] These psychoanalytic studies were instrumental in establishing the premise of unconscious domination over the conscious mind. The connection between Hofmannsthal's psychological approach to *Elektra* and Freud's theories is a direct one.[3] When the Austrian theater director Max Reinhardt expressed to Hofmannsthal his disinterest in what he considered to be the dullness of the ancient Greek dramatic style, Hofmannsthal was impelled to turn to a study of Rohde's *Psyche* as well as Freud's *Studien über Hysterie* before producing his version of the *Elektra* play in 1903. These psychoanalytic influences obviously led Hofmannsthal to his more intense and powerful version of the original Sophocles model.

In conjunction with these developments in literature and psychology, composers sought new technical means to express the more profound psychological states underlying emotions. The ultrachromaticism of Wagner, Bruckner, and Mahler reached its most intensive stage in the dissonant chromatic tonality of *Elektra*, a landmark in Strauss's operatic development that epitomizes late Romantic music on the threshold of the new chromatic idiom. While the expressionistic quality as well as certain "nontonal" aspects of *Elektra* predate the *free-atonality* of Schoenberg's *Erwartung* (1909) and Berg's *Wozzeck* (1914–1922), Strauss never crossed that threshold. After *Elektra*, in his operas *Der Rosenkavalier* and *Ariadne auf Naxos* (1911–1912), he reverted to classical techniques and forms. *Elektra* foreshadowed certain characteristics of the new idiom, especially in its overall tonal organization based on a specific scheme of chromatic relations. The trend toward equalization of the twelve semitones of the chromatic scale and the dissolution of traditional tonal functions in the compositions of the Vienna Schoenberg circle were already suggested in *Elektra*, where traditional triadic roots are symmetrically distributed around the central tonality of D.[4] In Classical harmonic progressions, the derivation of triads from common or closely related diatonic scales permits maximal intersection of triadic content, whereas in Strauss's opera the symmetrical organization of triadic roots produces maximal chromatic relations between the triadic constructions themselves. Also, the new means by which extreme dissonance is produced within this symmetrical scheme go far beyond Wagner and other German late Romantic composers. Strauss's approach to harmonic progression, dissonance, and the overall symmetrical tonal scheme in *Elektra* represents a radical departure from nineteenth-century chromaticism, the new musical principles providing expanded possibilities for expressing the psychological symbolization of drama.

In his letters to Hofmannsthal, Strauss revealed his intentions of intensifying and concentrating the musico-dramatic structure.[5] He mentioned his keenness on the idea of setting *Elektra* and how he had already cut the play down a good deal for his own private use.[6] Hofmannsthal's responses reveal his agreement with Strauss regarding certain abridgments. One of Strauss's more significant requests to condense the dramatic materials is pivotal:

> write me a drama that's full of action and contrasts, with few mass scenes, but two or three good rich parts. As for our recent conversation about *Elektra*, I believe we can't leave out Aegisthus altogether. He is definitely part of the plot and must be killed with the rest. . . . [However,] it's not a good plan to have all the women come running on-stage after the murder of Klytemnestra, then disappear again, and then, following the murder of Aegisthus, return once more with Chrysothemis. This breaks the line too much. . . . Couldn't we let Aegisthus come home immediately after Orestes has entered the house? And perform the murders in quick succession one after the other?[7]

These correspondences between composer and librettist also provide evidence of Strauss's concern for textual material that could provide the means for maximal musical intensification: "Eight, sixteen, twenty lines, as many as you can, and all in the same ecstatic mood, rising all the time towards a climax."[8]

Strauss was continually intensifying the Hofmannsthal drama as he adapted the play for a libretto. Although he made certain changes in the play for musical purposes, no new words were added. There is, in effect, no libretto, only a less repetitious setting of the play. Strauss's interest in musico-dramatic concentration resulted in a single operatic scene at the royal home, where Elektra broods on revenge after her father, Agamemnon, was murdered by her mother, Klytemnestra, who took a lover, banished her son, Orestes, and degraded her daughter. Strauss also sought to reduce the number of characters, opposing the large operatic ensembles used for crowd scenes in nineteenth-century grand opera. Musically, he reduced the melodic line to a single type, which lies somewhere between *recitative* and *arioso* styles. The entire contrapuntal fabric follows the Wagnerian principle of continuous inner action, in which there is no break in the linear motion of the orchestral writing.[9] Because the tragedy occurs at the end, no intermission is provided. This creates a single, remarkably intense cumulative scene that is set within a large binary (A–B) form (see fig. 13-1 later). Section B, the pivotal point in the drama, begins when Elektra's brooding turns to action, sparked by the terrified screams of Chrysothemis informing her that Orestes is dead. This section (indicated by new rehearsal numbers, 1a, 2a, etc.),[10] in contrast with section A, is characterized by extreme transformation of leitmotifs, rhythmic agitation, and a continual stream of dissonance. The large form is further subdivided into approximately seven smaller sections based on character presentation. After the opening scene with the serving maids, there is little dialogue, as much had been cut from the Hofmannsthal play to accommodate the long sections.

The Hofmannsthal story itself follows the more concentrated version of the ancient Sophocles play, which includes fewer characters and a more localized setting than the Aeschylus and Euripedes versions.[11] Hofmannsthal was to reshape the Sophocles play into a nineteenth-century "Freudian" drama, in which his protagonist appears to have a more dynamic and complex character than that of the Sophocles version. In the Hofmannsthal play, Elektra is motivated by her inability to sublimate her hate for her mother, which stems from her grief over her murdered father. A twist of plot by Hofmannsthal has significant implications regarding certain premises of Freudian psychoanalytic theory. On receiving the false news from her terrified sister of Orestes' death, Elektra's need to avenge her father's murder is frustrated. She turns her anger inward and becomes momentarily depressed and aimless. This is expressed effectively by the orchestra (at nos. 22a to 26a), following the lamenting dialogue between the two sisters. The relentless renewal of her anger and the determination to carry out the revenge herself may be interpreted within the frame of her inability to sublimate her hate for her mother, a result of an unresolved attachment to her father. This can be contrasted with the healthier attitude of her sister, who pleads with Elektra to give up her hate so they may live a more normal life, and that Chrysothemis may fulfill her desire to marry and have children.

The local harmonic progressions and large-scale tonal scheme of the opera appear to reflect the dramatic symbolization. This scheme appears to be determined by Elektra's internal perception of the polarization of her parents according to the "Oedipal" principle. The overall symmetrical organization of tonalities (fig. 13-1), which provides an effective means for establishing tonal polarity as well as symbolic representation of the basic dramatic polarity, serves as the main organizing principle for the constantly shifting keys that often result in multitonal (successive) as well as polytonal (simultaneous) key relations. Each key is established locally as a point of departure or convergence for the tonally ambiguous contrapuntal lines. The opening tonality of D minor serves as axis for the overall series of tonalities associated with the seven main character presentations of the opera. In the Introduction, the opening statement of the central "Agamemnon" motif establishes the priority of D minor. At the point (no. 1, mm. 2–5) at which "Elektra darts back, like an animal to its lair, one arm held before her face," her motif alternates two first-inversion minor triads, on B (D–F♯/B) and F (A♭–C♭/F), a tritone apart. This triadic root relation precludes any common tones between the two triads, so maximal harmonic (chromatic) conflict is produced. This local harmonic progression based on B and F offers the first suggestion of a symmetrical root relation to the axial tonality of D minor (B–D–F). In Elektra's first monologue, B♭ is associated with Agamemnon (no. 36, m. 6), while F♯ (in section 3, especially at no. 130, m. 3 ff.) is associated with Klytemnestra. The tonalities (B♭ and F♯) of the two parents are symmetrically polarized on either side of the B–F motif of the child (Elektra) and, ultimately, the D axis. At the first words of Orestes (no. 123a), "here must I tarry," these two tonalities (B♭ and F♯, in enharmonic spelling, G♭) are locally juxtaposed with D as the roots of three solemn chords. The recognition scene (section 6, no. 148a, m. 9ff.) is exclusively in A♭ major, the latter being the tritone of the original D tonality and therefore representing the dual axis of the symmetrical tonal scheme. The opera ends in C major, the tonality of Elektra's triumph. We may consider the sudden and prominent appearance (last four measures) of the major third degree (E) of the C major tonic triad as part of an implied frame (C–E) for the D axis.

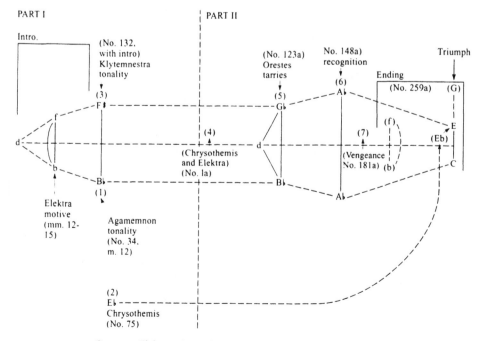

FIGURE 13-1. Strauss, *Elektra*, Overall symmetrical scheme of tonalities

On the local level of the opera, symmetrical root progressions are also basic for producing an entirely chromatic set of tonal and harmonic relations. Here, we find that a single chord may represent an entire key, each expanded into a tonal area most prominently by its augmented sixth chord, which appears as both a melodic and harmonic (leitmotivic) representation of Elektra's "Hate." In the Introduction (ex. 13-1), one of Elektra's two minor triads (on B and F) is expanded into a local tonal area by the first occurrence of the "Hate" motif: the F minor triad (no. 1, m. 5) is abruptly fol-

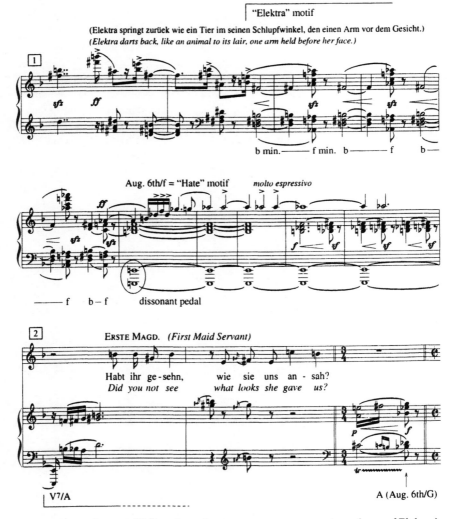

EXAMPLE 13-1. Strauss, *Elektra*, Introduction, nos. 1–5, expansion of one of Elektra's two minor triads (on B and F) into local tonal area by first occurrence of "Hate" motif, augmented-sixth chord (B–Db–F–Ab) of F

EXAMPLE 13-1 *(continued)*

EXAMPLE 13-1 *(continued)*

lowed by its augmented sixth chord, Db–F–Ab–B, over a dissonant E pedal. This pedal then appears (at no. 2) as the root of the V7 of the A dominant, which resolves to A at the 3/4 measure. This resolution to the fifth of the basic key produces an asymmetrical imbalance in the chordal scheme around the D tonal-axis (A–F–D–B–[ ]). Symmetrization then occurs as follows: the resolution to A is immediately disrupted by what appears to be an Eb–dominant seventh construction, which seems to have no functional significance in this multitonal context. Following a return to D major/minor (from no. 3, m. 3 to no. 4, m. 3), which is embellished by local major/minor A dominant seventh statements of the "Agamemnon" motif, the only other tonality to unfold thus far is G major, established by a vii2–1 progression (no. 4, mm. 4–5). The earlier Eb dominant seventh construction thereby seems, in retrospect, to serve as an isolated augmented sixth chord anticipation (in enharmonic spelling, Eb–G–Bb–C♯) of the G tonality. The latter, a fifth below the basic D tonic, provides a long-range symmetrical balance with the A-dominant (m. 7 ff. and no. 2, m. 3 ff.), a fifth above the D tonic. All these tonalities form symmetrical root relations to D (A–F–D–B–G). At the return to Elektra's B–F motif (no. 4, m. 6), a cycle is completed: the original elaboration of the F minor triad by its augmented sixth chord (Db–F–Ab–B) is balanced by a reinterpretation of the new G tonic as the root of the augmented sixth chord (no. 4, m. 5: G–B–D–F, in enharmonic spelling, G–B–D–E♯, with added dissonances) of Elektra's other minor triad (on B).

In Elektra's monologue (no. 34, m. 12, ex. 13-2), which is introduced by the basic tonality of D in the preceding orchestral interlude, Elektra's declamatory statements expressing her loneliness as she stands over her father's grave unfold over a prolonged occurrence of her "Hate" motif—the augmented sixth chord of F (Db–F–Ab–B, with dissonant E pedal). After a brief disruption of this chord at the first cadence (no. 36, mm. 3–4), a resolution to F is suggested at the 6/4 measure. However, F is interpreted as the root of an F dominant seventh chord instead, resolving to Agamemnon's key of Bb minor. The subsequent symmetrical polarization of Bb by Klytemnestra's F♯ tonality (introduction to section 3, especially beginning at no. 130) around the basic D axis is already suggested at this cadential disruption of Elektra's Db–augmented sixth chord in her monologue (see ex. 13-2 later). At Elektra's words, "My father gone to dwell affrighted in the tomb's chill darkness," we get a harmonic shift, on "Klüfte," to the augmented sixth chord of F♯, this chord—D–F♯–A–C (or D–F♯–A–B♯)—resolved simultaneously (that is, polytonally) at this point in the F♯ "Agamemnon" motif (in enharmonic spelling, Gb major/minor). With more explicit references to the Queen (no. 39 ff.), we get increasing intrusions of the "Hate" motif belonging to the tonal sphere of F♯ in connection with Elektra's other minor triad, on B. Thus, a direct polarization of the parents keys (Bb and F♯) is based on their symmetrical organization around the tritone-related chords of the child (Bb/F–B/F♯).

In the intense chromatic idiom of this opera, the symmetrical relationship of the triadic roots is fundamental for producing maximal distinction between triadic content and for contributing to the sense of dissonance. However, dissonances most often occur as a result of the contrapuntal motion of the lines, sometimes simply to produce shock, as with, for instance, the piling up of minor seconds at the point of vengeance. Strauss ventured into new areas of contrapuntal writing in this way and achieved a texture of almost continuous dissonance by the use of suspensions, appoggiaturas, and altered notes. These techniques are particularly pronounced at the midpoint of the

EXAMPLE 13-2. Strauss, *Elektra,* section 1: Elektra's Monologue, no. 34, m. 12ff., augmented-sixth chord (B–D♭–F–A♭) of F prolonged and resolved to F as dominant of B♭ (Agamemnon), after disruption of augmented-sixth of F♯ (Klytemnestra) to prepare for symmetrized polarity moving from B♭ to F♯ in reference to Queen

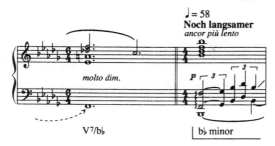

EXAMPLE 13-2 *(continued)*

opera (no. 1a, ex. 13-3), where Chrysothemis cries out that "Orestes is dead." A special technique suggests the proper resolution of nonchordal tones, but the other voices move out from under the resolution, so there is in effect no resolution. The resultant chords produce pseudo-polytonality in an otherwise traditional triadic idiom. The opening of this section is entirely in Chrysothemis's key of Eb, the one tonality not complemented explicitly (by C♯) in the symmetrical scheme around the D axis tonality.[12] This Eb section is introduced by the dominant seventh chord (Gb–Bb–[ ]–Fb) of Cb. Resolution to the latter tone (Cb) occurs over the remote Eb minor tonic triad, which is prolonged by a series of chromatic passing chords. The Neapolitan sixth is stated simultaneously against the held tonic Eb (no. 1a, last beat of m. 4 ff.). Dissonance is produced further as the seventh degree (Cb) of the vii43 of Eb (no. 2a, m. 4, beat 2) becomes a suspension over the tonic triad (no. 3a). Here, it resolves to the fifth degree (Bb) of the tonic triad, a tone that is itself dissonant above the new Eb–A–Db–G harmony. On "tot," the dominant seventh of Eb (upbeat to no. 4a) is unexpectedly reinterpreted as the augmented sixth chord of D minor, the basic key of the opera. The orchestra then plays the writhing motif of the "children of Agamemnon" over the held D minor triad, which represents the central tonality of the opera.[13]

A striking development in the process of symmetrically completing the chromatically related tonal areas begins prior to the appearance of Orestes, when Elektra digs for the murder axe (especially from no. 116a). Against the shrill stream of dissonances that unfold in the chromatically descending violins, we get an irregularly descending series of keys, moving from F♯ minor downward. Elektra's first declamatory statement that questions the intentions of the disguised Orestes (no. 121a) further contributes to the already agitated tonalities in the linear unfolding. At Orestes's first words (no. 123a, and again at no. 124a, mm. 7–9, ex. 13-4a), "here must I tarry," we begin to get the first symmetrization of tonalities around the D center in this section. His three chords (on Bb, D, and Gb) serve as the focus for the fulfillment of this symmetrical process.

In connection with Elektra's psychological motivation, in which her hate serves as the dramatic catalyst for the move toward vengeance and triumph, the augmented sixth chord ("Hate" motif) serves as the basic pivot to the final C major sphere, which represents "Triumph." This trend begins (at no. 110a) when Elektra's brooding turns to action as she realizes she must dig up the murder axe and carry out the act of revenge herself. The augmented sixth "Hate motif" (Db–F–Ab–B) of the F chord in

EXAMPLE 13-3. Strauss, *Elektra*, section 4: Chrysothemis and Elektra, no. 1a, mm. 1–14, turning point of binary form, dissonant quasi-polytonal embellishment of E♭ minor of Chrysothemis as she refers to death of Orestes; moves to D and "Children" motif

EXAMPLE 13-4. Strauss, *Elektra*, section 5: Appearance of Orestes; (a) no. 124a, "Orestes" motif based on symmetrical triadic root motion around D axis (Gb–D–Bb), tonalities referring to parents; (b) no. 127a, further symmetrization by balance of A and G around D

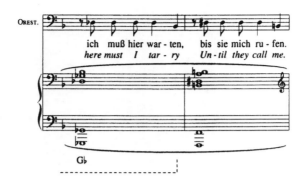

EXAMPLE 13-4 (continued)

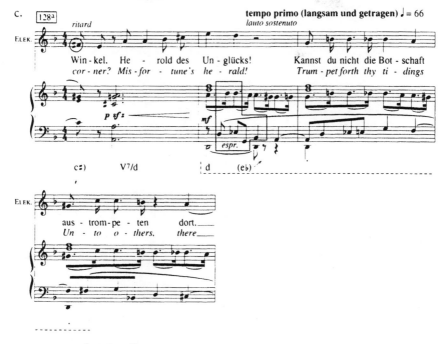

EXAMPLE 13-4 (continued)

Elektra's B–F motif has invariably been accompanied by a dissonant E pedal, which is now for the first time expanded into the key of E minor. As we move toward triumph at the end of the opera, the note E is absorbed into the tonal spectrum of C major. The C tonality already begins to emerge prior to the murder of Klytemnestra and her lover Aegisthus (at the climax of section 7, no. l86a, m. 11, ex. 13-5), and it is in this passage (two measures before no. 186a) that the "Hate motif" (augmented sixth chord) begins to serve as the tonal pivot. As Elektra paces back and forth in anxious anticipation, having forgotten to give Orestes the axe that had been used to murder her father, the B minor triad from her F–B motif is elaborated by its augmented-sixth chord, G–B–D–E♯ (in enharmonic spelling, G–B–D–F). The latter is interpreted simultaneously as the dominant seventh chord of C, the key suddenly appearing over a B tremolo. The scales alternate, then, between C minor and B minor.

At Elektra's final dance of triumph (no. 259a, ex. 13-6), a pivot from the B minor triad of her B–F motif to the triumphal C is produced by the musical catalyst (the augmented sixth chord) that has been equated throughout with the psycho-dramatic catalyst—the "Hate" motif. Here, Elektra's F and B tonalities are each established by their respective augmented-sixth chords (D♭–F–A♭–B and G–B–D–E♯, at no. 260a, mm. 1–2), the one belonging to the B tonality (again in enharmonic spelling, G–B–D–F) serving simultaneously as the dominant of C minor and C major (no. 259a), these modes on C alternately occurring with the last statements of her B chord. But Elektra's triumphal dance ends in her own death, which might be interpreted psy-

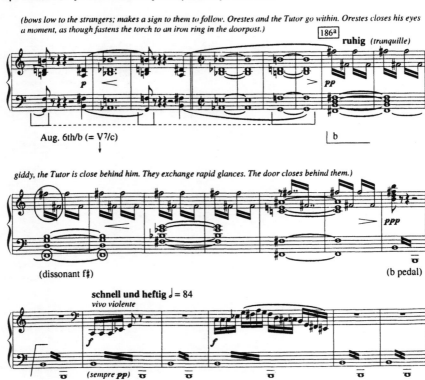

EXAMPLE 13-5. Strauss, *Elektra*, section 7: Anticipation of Vengeance, no. 186a, m. 11ff., augmented-sixth/dominant-seventh "Hate" motif as tonal pivot between Elektra's B chord and Triumph complex of C

EXAMPLE 13-6. Strauss, *Elektra*, Elektra's final Victory Dance, no. 259a, final pivot from the B chord of her B–F motif to the triumphal C effected by augmented-sixth chord catalyst

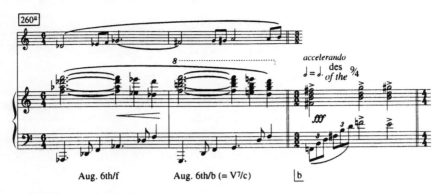

EXAMPLE 13-6 (*continued*)

choanalytically as the result of her inability to resolve her love-hate feelings for her mother. That is, in conspiring toward her mother's death, Elektra must finally punish herself. She cannot triumph without bringing on her own destruction.

With the musical language of *Elektra*, Strauss had gone as far as he ever would from traditional tonality. Progression in this work is determined almost entirely by a single chord function, in which the augmented sixth ("Hate") motif serves as both a modulator and key expander. This anticipates the twentieth-century pitch-set concept of equal linear and harmonic exploitation of a collection. We find the same historical anticipation of the pitch-set premise in Schoenberg's use of the minor seventh chord in his early, still tonal *Gurre-Lieder*. However, it was primarily with the disappearance of the triad itself, when Schoenberg subsequently turned to free-atonality in 1909, that any suggestion of traditional harmonic functions of pervasively occurring "cellular-type" chords were to be entirely dissolved. Nevertheless, Strauss's exploitation of symmetrical root relations in *Elektra*, a work still anchored in vertical triadic construction, prompted the direction toward dissolution of traditional tonal functions and the establishment of a new musical sound world based on equalization of the twelve semitones. This development by Strauss and Schoenberg in particular appears to have inextricably transformed German late Romanticism, creating a new realm of expressionistic intensity. Ethan Mordden places *Elektra* in proper perspective: "a monumental nexus of revenge tragedy, psychological study, and classical reinvestment—the regeneration of old themes via modern interrogation . . . the heroine's monologue, a case for Freud not merely in word-pictures, but in sounds as well, insatiable natterings, outbursts, screaming; Elektra's confrontations with her sister and her mother, the latter scene presaging the expressionism of atonal opera."[14]

Schoenberg's *Erwartung*: Free-Atonality, Expressionism, and Symbolic Meaning

Principles of structural concentration and reduction, nonrepetition and athematicism, as well as cellular variation and transformation, the basis of Schoenberg's new expressionistic and symbolic idiom, developed in the remainder of his atonal compositions prior to World War I. His works composed during this time include his *Five Orchestral*

Pieces, op.16 (1909); the operas *Erwartung*, op. 17 (1909), and *Die Glückliche Hand*, op. 18 (1910–1913); the *Sechs kleine Klavierstücke*, op. 19 (1911); *Herzgewächse* for soprano, celesta, harmonium, and harp, op. 20 (1911); *Pierrot Lunaire*, op. 21 (1912); and the *Four Orchestral Songs*, op. 22 (1913–1916). *Erwartung*, a monodrama in four continuous scenes on a text by Marie Pappenheim, represents Schoenberg's first major breakthrough in transforming the chromatic idiom of Wagner's *Tristan* into an expressionistic and atonal musical language.[15] In the Vienna of Freud, writers and artists turned with greater awareness to the unconscious and the irrational. Schoenberg's monodrama includes one character in an extreme of convulsive expression.[16] The Woman enters the forest to keep a rendezvous with her lover, but the lover has been murdered, and in the dark she stumbles over his corpse. All of nature seems to reflect her anxiety and absorb her innermost feelings. The work is highly symbolic, metaphoric, and ambiguous in that we do not know whether what we see on the stage is supposed to be a representation of a series of events or of a dream. And if a dream, whose dream?

Erwartung is unified by means of related sonorities. Most of the chords have six notes, which generally combine two three-note chords each encompassed by a major seventh.[17] For instance, the symmetrical construction G♭–C–F/B–E–B♭ alternates tritones and perfect-fourths, which pervade the texture in various transpositions, permutations, transformations, and combinations. However, the work is entirely athematic (i.e., without motivic development, repetition, or transformation) to produce an amorphous stream of consciousness. This is because of the dissociation of the sonorities from any recognizably consistent rhythms, thematic contours, or registers, and the result is an ever-changing contrapuntal fabric that supports the relentless unfolding of psychological drama. The opera lasts half an hour, but its singular mood in a context of perpetually *developing variation* (Schoenberg's term) induces a sense of extreme psychological condensation of the entire action into a single moment or, stated in reverse, a single moment based on an anxiety or state of mind expanded to half an hour. There is no real sense of past, present, or future, because psychological time relies, of necessity, on our perception of the temporal ordering of distinguishable events. Schoenberg has concealed the sectional premise of traditional operatic construction, stating that *Erwartung* represents "in *slow motion* everything that occurs during a single second of maximal spiritual excitement."[18]

Alban Berg's *Wozzeck*: Symbol of the Oppressed and Peak of Expressionism

In various ways, each of Alban Berg's earlier atonal works prepared the way for *Wozzeck*, the first of his two operas. In May 1914, Berg saw several performances of Georg Büchner's dramatic fragment *Woyzeck* at the Vienna Chamber Theatre. Shortly thereafter, he decided to set the work as an opera and began to arrange the text, while continuing his work on the *Three Orchestral Pieces*. Later in the year, he completed a fair copy of the score of the Praeludium from scene 1 and the Military March from scene 3, which he sent to Schoenberg. During the next year or so, Schoenberg's teaching came to a halt as his pupils were selected for military duty. Berg spent more than three years in the Austrian army, so the entire short score of *Wozzeck* was not completed until 1919, the final orchestration in 1922.

Büchner's drama, although written in the first half of the nineteenth century, anticipated the morbid reality of Berg's own era. *Wozzeck* can be considered real twentieth-century drama, imbued further by Berg's musical setting of a highly expressionistic quality, in which the emotional and psychological state of the protagonist seems to be projected into every external object, action, and musical fiber. The work has not only become one of the cornerstones of expressionism but also is an historical document of the war years, and a highly personal, autobiographical expression of the composer. Wozzeck, who is a symbol of the oppressed man, refers to himself as "wir arme Leut." He is a poor soldier who is exploited by his superiors and "tormented by *all the world*."[19] Driven by unconscious forces, he eventually murders his unfaithful mistress and drowns himself. In his preoccupation with *Wozzeck* during a short leave in 1918 from his own military duties, Berg wrote a letter to his wife (dated 7 August), in which he revealed his sense of identity with Büchner's character:

> There is a bit of me in his character . . . since I have been spending these war years just as dependent on people I hate, have been in chains, sick, captive, resigned, in fact, humiliated. Without this military service I should be as healthy as before. . . . Still, perhaps but for this the musical expression (for *Wozzeck*) would not have occurred to me.[20]

One of Berg's main concerns in composing *Wozzeck* was the means by which both local and large-scale structural unity could be achieved in the atonal idiom. He could neither rely on the Büchner text for such coherence because of its fragmentary nature nor on the organizational principles of tonal form and development. In part, Berg's solution lay in the use of a series of diverse but coherent traditional forms, which were to "correspond to the diversity in the character of the individual scenes."[21] For the libretto, Berg first reduced Büchner's twenty-five scenes (based on the Franzos-Landau edition of twenty-six scenes of the text) to fifteen, then organized them in three acts of five scenes each. Each scene has a "rounded off" and individual character, yet contributes to the overall unity. While the musical forms are classical and clearly defined, Berg's main accomplishment lay in his ability to draw audience attention away from the "various fugues, inventions, suites, sonata movements, variations, and passacaglias," to the "vast social implications of the work which by far transcend the personal destiny of Wozzeck."[22] Furthermore, in place of traditional tonal relations for support of the structure and psycho-dramatic currents, Berg provided a complex set of musical interrelationships and transformations based on recurrent motifs as well as referential pitch collections, all unfolding in a varied orchestration.

Berg suggested an outline of the scenes based on the main dramatic and musical events.[23] The large three-act form is determined by the dramatic structure and based on a corresponding temporal symmetry in the musical architecture: the three acts form an arch, in which the longer and more complex middle section (act 2) forms a bridge between the symmetrically balanced outer sections (acts 1 and 3). According to Willi Reich's outline of Berg's chart, act 1 ("Wozzeck in his relation to the world around him") is a dramatic *exposition* of the main characters and their relationship to the protagonist. These different character sketches are represented by a series of older musical forms of distinctly different styles. The dramatic "development" of the plot, however, which begins at the end of act 1 (where Marie is embraced by the Drum Major), actually unfolds in act 2, where the succession of scenes represents Wozzeck's gradual realization of Marie's infidelity. Here, a closed symphonic shape of five movements (scenes) is the developmental as well as unifying musical structure. The "catastrophe" and final outcome of the plot are the basis of act 3. The scenes of act 3 are now individual situational sketches (each in the form of an invention on a single musical idea) that balance the character sketches of act 1. Regarding these abstract and clearly organized musical forms, George Perle points out that:

> The musical coherence that the opera has, independently of the staged events, reflects an objective order whose irrelevance to the subjective fate of Wozzeck poignantly emphasizes his total isolation in an indifferent universe . . . this is not to say that the assignment of a specific "absolute" musical form to a given scene is made without reference to specific dramaturgical considerations.[24]

The "Passacaglia" (act 1, scene 4), as one instance, provides a rigid musical structure, which can be seen as reflecting the strict diet that the Doctor has forced on Wozzeck, in his use of him as a "guinea pig" for his medical experiments. The opera is pervaded by musical details of structural or local textual significance, such details having either leitmotivic or nonleitmotivic functions.[25]

The opera generally belongs to the atonal idiom, but there seems to be no single system to which all the pitch relations and harmonic constructions are accountable. Whereas traditional tonal works are based on a priori functional associations of the major-minor scale system, with the triad as the single harmonic referent, in *Wozzeck* we find a diversity of constructions that are given both musical and literary significance primarily by the immediate musical context within which they occur. Differing views regarding this question of the existence of a large-scale, unified system of pitch relations in *Wozzeck* are expressed in several major studies, most significantly by Douglas Jarman, George Perle, and Janet Schmalfeldt.[26] With reference to traditional functional relationships, Perle states that "no comparable generalizations regarding the musical language of *Wozzeck* are offered here, but a first attempt is made to describe certain means of integration and differentiation that are characteristic features of that language."[27] In dealing with those elements of pitch organization that are basic to the context in which themes and motifs unfold, Perle includes detailed discussions of tone centers, vertical sets, chord series, scale segments, and other such recurrent phenomena. Jarman's view is similar to Perle's, in which he refers to an "immense variety of procedures employed [in 'free' atonal music] and the difficulty in classifying these procedures according to neat, self-contained categories. The techniques employed . . . cannot be referred to any generally accepted or understood criteria . . . as can those of tonal music, nor can they be referred to a set of theoretical propositions of the kind upon which twelve-note music is based."[28] Jarman, however, does show how certain motifs in *Wozzeck* are related to isolated larger pitch collections that play a role in large-scale structural unity. In contrast, Schmalfeldt attempts to establish those pitch structures that "serve as fundamental components of the harmonic language"[29] and to demonstrate that motifs are related to, and perhaps may even generate, large-scale pitch structures. She states that "essential yet hitherto unexplored aspects of Berg's harmonic procedure in *Wozzeck* can be uncovered by means of the pitch-class set-analytical method."[30]

Certain pitch constructions, in any case, do seem to have a referential function in the overall working out of the material. In the "Murder scene" (act 3, scene 2), which is one of the primary dramatic focal points in the opera, Wozzeck's obsession is reflected by an insistent "Invention on a Tone B." At the same time, reminiscences of the earlier musical ideas associated with Marie seem to flash through her mind as she is about to die. Underlying these reminiscences, tone B occurs in various temporal, registral, and timbral positions. It is introduced at the end of the preceding scene (no. 71 ff.), where it occurs as a "dissonant" pedal against the bitonal combination of major triads on D and E♭. At Marie's first words in the "Murder Scene," the sustained notes (no. 73, m. 1) harmonically extend the B pedal to a whole-tone tetrachord, B– C♯–E♭–F, encompassed by tritone B–F. The upper boundary tone of this collection (F, in the horn) is also marked by Marie's entry pitch. The first two phrasal segments of Wozzeck's entry, based on F–G–A–]–C♯ (no. 75), together with the B pedal, provide the remaining notes of this whole-tone collection. Again, the vocal entry pitch is F, the tritone of B. This whole-tone cycle is completed by the C♯–D♯ of Violin I, while the ending of Wozzeck's line secondarily unfolds a segment (F♯–]–B♭–C–D) of the other whole-tone collection. The basic tritone, B–F, which emerges more prominently in the double bass (at m. 84), is further manifested as a primary structural element in subsequent passages approaching the murder.

Cyclic-interval fillings of the main tritone, B–F, establish an essential principle of musical progression and dramatic association in the earlier sections of the opera. In the Praeludium of the opening Suite, the cadential tone (D♭) of the Captain's leitmotif (mm. 4–6) overlaps his statement, "Easy, Wozzeck, easy" as Wozzeck shaves his superior officer (ex. 13-7). In correspondence with the Captain's apparent need for control, the reiterated D♭ moves from a "dissonant" (or odd-note) position against whole-tone segment C–D–E (no. 5) to a "consonant" position within a gapped segment B–[ ]–E♭–F of the other whole-tone collection. This completes the basic whole-tone tetrachord B–D♭–E♭–F. While the two whole-tone segments are distinct in the linear partitioning, the entire pitch content of the voice and English horn forms a semitonal filling of tritone B–F (B–C–D♭–D–E♭–E–F); this basic tritone appears as a cadential focal point. The Captain's theme itself opens with two juxtaposed whole-tone segments, F♯–G♯ and C♯–B–F (m. 4), the latter (B–C♯–[ ]–F) foreshadowing the basic whole-tone tetrachord B–D♭–E♭–F immediately.

At the reprise of the Praeludium (A, m. 24 ff.), these musico-dramatic relations are more explicit. While the Captain's thematic material from the very opening of the Praeludium returns slightly varied in the winds at this point, D♭ is reiterated as the basis of both Wozzeck's first explicit "Jawohl" statement and, as before, as the cadential tone of the Captain's theme (mm. 28–30). Whereas D♭ was absorbed into the whole-tone tetrachord B–D♭–E♭–F in the original statement of the Captain's theme (mm. 5–6), it is now part of an expanded whole-tone segment (D♭–E♭–F–[ ]–A–B), which is sustained in the winds in the final measures of the Praeludium (mm. 27–29). This collection is anticipated (at m. 26) in the combined "Jawohl" statement and pizzicato chord (D♭–E♭–F–[ ]–A–B, with one odd note, C). Thus, priority is given to one of the whole-tone cycles (i.e., that which contains the main tetrachord, B– D♭–E♭–F), as it pervades, and then ends the reprise exclusively.

The Pavane begins with the Captain's words (no. 30 ff.), "It makes me afraid for the world to think of eternity," further revealing an obsessive fear of his inability to control the objective world. In this connection, the section is based on a more com-

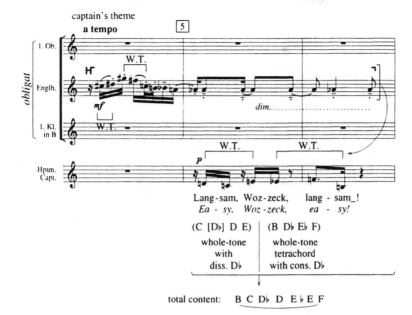

EXAMPLE 13-7. Berg, *Wozzeck*, act 1, scene 1, mm. 4–6, Captain's need for control symbolized by reiterated Db that moves from "dissonant" (or odd-note) position against whole-tone segment C–D–E (No. 5) to "consonant" position within gapped segment B–[ ]–Eb–F of other whole-tone collection to complete basic whole-tone tetrachord, B–Db–Eb–F

plex interaction of the interval cycles (ex. 13-8). The first six triplets of the Captain's transformed leitmotif repeat the whole-tone pitch content of the cadence, the odd note (C) this time being expanded to a tritone (Gb–C) from the other whole-tone cycle. While the prevailing interval-class of this thematic segment (Db–Eb–[ ]–G–A–B) and the accompanying triplet figure (Db–Eb) in the harp and horn is whole tone (no. 30), the sustained chord of the winds reinterprets the whole-tone dyad Db–Eb as part of a four-note segment of the cycle of fourths, or fifths (Db–Ab–Eb–Bb); the entire accompaniment in this measure is based on the larger cyclic segment, Gb–Db–Ab–Eb–Bb. Whereas the earlier combination of whole-tone segments, C–D–E and B–Db–Eb–F, at the cadence of the Captain's theme, mm. 5–6 (see ex. 13-7 earlier), implied the content of a semitonal cyclic segment, B–C–Db–D–Eb–E–F, the combination of whole-tone elements in this passage outlines a segment of the cycle of fourths/fifths. Then (at mm. 33–34), a long descent of fourths, F–C–G–D–A–E–B–F♯–C♯, appears to symbolize "eternity." On another level, increased complexity can also be noted in the absorption of Wozzeck's "Jawohl" rhythm into the Captain's vocal line, at the words "as I think of eternity. 'Eternal, that's 'eternal.'"

Strictness, and an obsessive need for control, is manifested even more obviously in the megalomaniacal character of the Doctor, who uses Wozzeck for his medical experiments. Scene 4 is appropriately based on a strict ostinato pattern in the form of a

EXAMPLE 13-8. Berg, *Wozzeck*, act 1, scene 1, "Pavane," nos. 30–35, prevailing whole-tone interval-class of thematic segment (Db–Eb–[ ]–G–A-B) and accompanying triplet figure (Db–Eb) in harp and horn (no. 30), sustained chord of winds reinterpreting whole-tone dyad Db–Eb as part of four-note segment of cycle of fourths (Db–Ab–Eb–Bb); accompaniment based on larger cyclic segment, Gb–Db–Ab–Eb–Bb, combination of whole-tone elements outlining segment of cycle of fourths (mm. 33–34), endless descent of fourths, F–C–G–D–A–E–B–F#–C#, symbolizing "eternity"

EXAMPLE 13-8 *(continued)*

twelve-tone Passacaglia theme, which underlies a set of twenty-one variations. These are organized into three main sections: variations 1-12, the Doctor's increasing insistence on an ascetic diet for his medical subject and Wozzeck's objections; variations 13–18, the Doctor's psychological exploitation of Wozzeck as a "guinea pig" for his dietary experiments; and variations 19-21, the height of the Doctor's conceit and his cry for immortality, after which there is a return to the dialogue of the opening. At the climax of the scene (no. 612), beginning at variation 19, the Doctor's conceit is musically represented by extreme control of the material. As the Doctor reviews Wozzeck's strict diet, "Eat your beans then, and mutton to follow," his vocal line systematically unfolds two descending whole-tone tetrachords, D♯–C♯–B–A and G–F–E♭–D♭, which together complete the primary whole-tone cycle. Both tetrachords are interlocked by an intersecting segment of the cycle of fourths, A–D–G.[31] At the same time, the Doctor's obsession is supported by a strict three-part canon in the strings, the contrapuntal texture increasing in density as his obsession intensifies, "Don't slacken, and the Captain you'll shave, and cultivate your idée fixe further." The vocal line (at mm. 615–616) also provides a complete descending statement of the other whole-tone cycle. At the climax of the Doctor's conceit (beginning of Variation 20), "Oh! my hypothesis!" the vocal line presents a more emphatic statement of an expanded, descending five-note segment of the primary whole-tone cycle (ex. 13-9). The strings support this statement by a more dense six-part canon, now entirely based

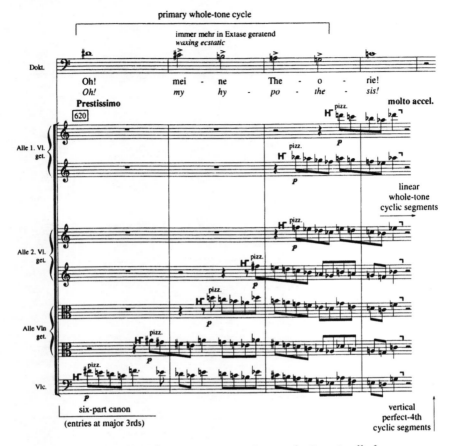

EXAMPLE 13-9. Berg, *Wozzeck*, act 1, scene 4, "Passacaglia," m. 620ff., five-note segment of whole-tone cycle supported by six-part canon based on array of interlocking cyclic collections

on an array of linearly and vertically intersecting cyclic collections. While each string line unfolds both whole-tone cycles in tetrachordal segments as well as complete scales, all the strings are contrapuntally aligned in such a way as to permit a harmonic sequence of perfect-fourth cyclic segments. Furthermore, the sequence of canonic entry pitches outlines the major-third cycle, F#–A#–D–F#–[F]–Bb–D. Overlapping this canon, the winds unfold a series of chords (at mm. 623–637), the outer voices of the winds (piccolo 1 and bass tuba) expanding in inversional motion in connection with the Doctor's most grandiose exclamations, "Oh my fame! I shall be immortal! Immortal! Immortal!" These chords, most built on fourths, lead to the chorale-like final variation (marked *fortissimo*) and the Doctor's last cry for immortality.

These final variations, with their systematic and strict presentation of the interval cycles, are a focus for earlier cyclic-interval development in connection with the trend of the drama. The structure of the twelve-tone Passacaglia theme itself serves as an essential unifying link in this development. The row can be partitioned into alternating segments of the two whole-tone collections: Eb–B–G-C♯/C-F♯–E–Bb/A–F/ Ab–D. However, the concluding three-note segment (F–Ab–D), which forms an incomplete cycle of minor thirds, often functions as a refrain element, a connecting link between variations, and as a disruption of unfolding whole-tone successions. The scene opens (m. 488 ff.) with a cello recitative statement of the Passacaglia theme, which is obscured by the lengthy pitch reiterations in rubato style. This accompanies the Doctor's irregular speechlike vocal line, in which he scolds Wozzeck. The refrain element (F–Ab–D) is first brought out at the Doctor's declamatory "Eh, Eh, Eh!" which refers to his having caught Wozzeck coughing. A recognizable structure within the otherwise irregular phrases is the "Jawohl" rhythm at Wozzeck's "What sir? What, Doctor?" and at the Doctor's words, "you howled like a dog." Then, the Doctor's conceit begins to be revealed in his statement, "You do not get paid every day for such antics, Wozzeck!" which, in contrast to the preceding statements, is based on the first systematic occurrence of descending whole-tone tetrachords (G–F–Eb–Db and B–A–G–F). These are interlocked by a perfect-fourth cyclic segment (Db–Gb–B). In the remainder of the Doctor's moralizing statements (to m. 495), vocal pitch adjacencies form whole-tone extensions of the corresponding cyclic segments in the Passacaglia theme, for example, B–A–G–F of the voice cyclically extends G–C♯, then G♯–F♯–D extends C–F♯–E–Bb to form the entire whole-tone collection, Bb–C–D–E-F♯–G♯, at the words, "This is bad! The world is bad, so bad!" Wozzeck's reference to his own lack of control, "When forced to that [coughing] by nature!" is then punctuated by the disruptive cadential tones of the row in the cello (F–Ab–D). The latter association is established further by the recurrence of this refrain figure in the viola (mm. 496 and 497), where the Doctor refers to "your nature!" and "ridiculus superstition."

The Doctor then proceeds to the first of his explicitly grandiose statements (in the second half of variation 1, m. 498 ff.), "Have I not proved quite clearly that the muscles are subject to the human will?" This obvious reference to the need for strictness and control is manifested in the accompanying *stretto* of whole-tone tetrachords (ex. 13-10). The tritone G–C♯ of the Doctor's vocal line is cyclically extended by one of these tetrachords, Db–Cb–Bbb–G (bassoon), which is bounded by the same tritone. The next stretto of whole-tone tetrachords (mm. 500–502) is then disrupted by the cadential figure, F–Ab–D, as the Doctor scolds Wozzeck for coughing. As the Doctor shifts to a more "scientific" attitude toward the dietary experiments (Variations 2–3), the more "learned" character of the text is reflected in the voice. Here begins what Perle refers to as "Berg's secret art," in which linear symmetries pervade the entire vocal line.[32]

In connection with the Doctor's growing conceit and his obsession with his strict medical experiments, which reach a peak in the final variations, cyclic and symmetrical collections emerge from unobtrusive positions in irregularly organized contexts to being more systematic, local, foreground events. The most prominent of these is the whole-tone cycle, especially its derivative tetrachordal segments. As discussed earlier, the basic transpositional level of the whole-tone tetrachord (B–Db–Eb–F) is significantly manifested in the "Murder" scene in connection with Wozzeck's obsession, or *idee fixe*.

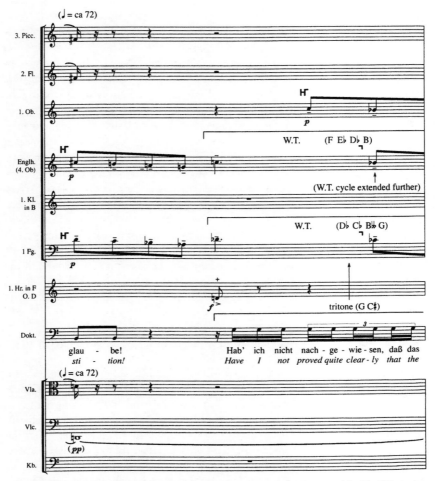

EXAMPLE 13-10. Berg, *Wozzeck*, act 1, scene 4, "Passacaglia," second half of Variation 1, m. 498ff., need for strictness and control manifested in *stretto* of whole-tone tetrachords, tritone G–C♯ of Doctor's vocal line cyclically extended by tetrachord D♭–C♭–B♭♭–G (bassoon), bounded by same tritone, next stretto of whole-tone tetrachords (mm. 500–502) disrupted by cadential figure, F–A♭–D, as Doctor scolds Wozzeck for coughing

The foregoing discussion of Berg's opera is intended, on the one hand, to outline only some of the dramatic functions of the formal organization and several representative thematic constructions. On the other hand, the detailed discussion of one aspect of pitch organization and progression (albeit an essential one) in connection with the psychological development of certain characters is intended to provide some basic insights into Berg's musical thinking. It should be made clear that this work is based on a multiplicity of melodic and harmonic pitch constructions, rhythms, and styles,

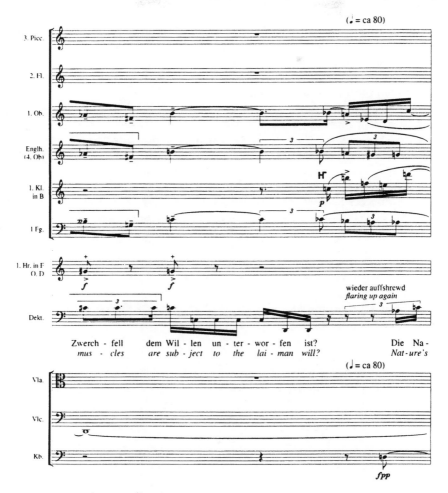

EXAMPLE 13-10 *(continued)*

which defy any single approach to Berg's idiom. While unity is provided by pervasive use of leitmotif, strictly organized forms, and prominent interactions of certain cyclic-interval formations (especially whole-tone formations), the work also includes such contrasting features as mixed-interval and triadic constructions, atonal and tonal passages (though without the hierarchy of functions found in the major-minor scale system), juxtaposition of *Sprechtstimme* and lyric vocal lines (e.g., as in Marie's Bible-reading scene), *parlando* and *arioso* vocal styles, instrumental writing in both chamber and large orchestral textures, irregular, atonally organized phrasal constructions in contrast to folklike symmetrical phraseology, and traditional classical forms that are often mathematically strict in proportions, and in contrast to freely organized passages and sections.

Wozzeck represents a confluence of divergent historical tendencies, in part reflected in these juxtapositions of differing styles and techniques. Composed during a period in which established principles of musical organization were being profoundly altered by Berg and his colleagues, the composer of *Wozzeck* also leaned toward a reconciliation of the principles of pitch organization and rhythm of the new musical language with certain structural and thematic principles basic to the older Austro-German tradition. It is significant, however, that Berg himself never intended either to reform or revolutionize opera through *Wozzeck* but, instead, "simply wanted to compose good music."[33] The technical and stylistic means of composition were obviously secondary to the expression of the poetic text, and, because of Berg's personal circumstances during these bitter war years, the text was deeply colored by his intense personal involvement with the subject matter. Many details of Berg's life during his military service paralleled those of Wozzeck. We have only to cite Berg's exploitation by superiors and assignment to guard duty in Vienna after his complete physical breakdown in November 1915. This incident serves to remind us of the suffering of the opera's tormented soldier, under quite similar conditions; Berg had described indeed his own duties as "imprisonment" or "slavery."

The tendency of Viennese expressionism to move toward one of its most intensive stages of development in this opera was inextricably tied to the political, social, cultural, as well as personal circumstances of Berg during World War I. However, this connection is not so much manifested in the literal historical and autobiographical correlations that one can find in the work but, rather, in the emotional and psychological correspondences between composer and subject. It is the latter that prominently contributes to the unity of purpose and mood, permitting the composer to exploit the possibilities existing in the multiplicity of strict classical forms, as well as in both older and newer techniques, for their special character and logic in the creation of a new idiom.

14

Epilogue

The new musical language that emerged in the early twentieth century seems to have been motivated, at least in part, by the need to reflect—even express—the new literary, psychological, and philosophical principles that surfaced in the new art-form of these symbolist operas. In my book on Bartók's music, I explored the notion of a generalized systematic approach to tonality and progression in his musical language, and I also broached the subject in that of Debussy and other contemporary composers:

> Part of the problem that has existed in determining the basic means of pitch organi-
> zation in Bartók's music is that there has been no theory, comparable to that of the
> traditional tonal system, to draw together all pitch formations in his music under one
> unified set of principles. Yet one senses in Bartók's total output an all-encompassing
> system of pitch relations.[1]

Regardless of the degree to which my own theoretical attempts have succeeded in demonstrating what had seemed—and still does seem—obvious in the actual listening experience (i.e., Bartók's ability to create a sense of unity within diversity), certain basic principles emerged from that study to establish a sonic and structural basis for approaching at least one of the most essential parameters in the realization of the symbolist message in the operas of these pioneering composers. Yet, while one must acknowledge the primary role of the harmonic/melodic dimension in the larger sonic conception of these operas, which are based on the interaction of traditional and more modern types of pitch and intervallic construction, other parameters—including instrumental timbre, thematic/leitmotivic variation and transformation, phrase/period structure and its relation to the larger formal structure and design, as well as general rhythmic style—are explored mainly in connection with, and in complementation to the all-pervasive world of pitch/interval relations. Instrumental timbre and other dimensions are invoked primarily—but not only—where they best elucidate the essential role of pitch organization.

If the balance of parameters in this study seems somewhat skewed, it is because the harmonic spectrum cannot be denied as one of the overriding factors in establishing a sense of dramatic motion, interaction, cross-referential associations, and rapidly changing moods. These moods pervade the kaleidoscopic details of the musico-dramatic fabric of the operas. In short, because the most radical musical changes in the early twentieth century occurred in the area of musical language, based on a revolutionary transformation of traditional tonal and harmonic vocabulary and interrelations, it is this area that composers have most sought to exploit as the primary means for expanding the possibility of expressing the underlying psychological states so fundamental to the symbolist idiom. The transformation of the more linear, defined quality of the traditional major/minor scales into the more diffuse, static effects created by the use of modality, polymodality, and symmetrical pitch-set interactions resonated with the modernistic conception of the human being, who is perennially divided and threatened by the split between the conscious and the unconscious mind. The symbolic connotation of symmetrical pitch relations has similarities with Matte Blanco's concept of "the unconscious as infinite sets."[2] Matte Blanco's work is an attempt to provide a more precise description of what Freud alluded to when he stated that "the dreamwork is not simply more careless, more irrational, more forgetful, and more incomplete than waking thought, it is completely different from it qualitatively and for that reason not immediately comparable with it."[3] In the unconscious, two objects may be represented by or equated to each other because they have accidental rather than essential similarities, or because they are juxtaposed. In the conscious mind, which is ruled by Aristotelian logic, objects are equated only in essential ways when they belong to the same class. In the foregoing study of the two Symbolist operas, meaning is generally inferred by rules that follow the system of the unconscious.

Creative Process and Social Context

The text narratives are affected by the ideological trends of the time, not only in what they say but also in what they omit. Both operas have meanings that must be decoded. In giving a voice to what is left unsaid, I hope to have revealed additional insights into what both operas reveal about human interactions and the historical moment in which these works emerged. The creative process that can be glimpsed through Maeterlinck's and Balázs's writings does not follow a linear, rational, cognitive path. The authors' unconscious processes were actively engaged not only in the germination of the ideas but also in the process of completing the work.[4] One may cite Georgette Leblanc's accounts of how Maeterlinck's characters "wrote" their lives in a manner that at times surprised and saddened the author,[5] and how Balázs used the content of his dreams to create some of his works. Adorno addresses a similar issue in the subject of musical analysis.[6] He suggested that musical analysis is able to uncover the deepest interrelationships "within the compositional process, which has been unconsciously produced."

In spite of the temporal and geographical differences between the beginning of the last century and today, there are many similarities. Gender issues continue to exercise pressures and manifest themselves in different areas in ways in which sights of blood are just as apparent as on the walls of Bluebeard's castle. The tension between isolation/intimacy and the advance of technology continues to exercise great pressures on our psychological well-being, so the problems presented to the inhabitants of Allemonde and Bluebeard's castle are not foreign to us.

In addition to understanding what the authors wanted to convey in creating their works, I explored how, in spite of the patriarchal ideology that informs both operas, the historical truth comes through, that is, the human agony that is created by a society in which only privileged members of the dominant class have a claim to articulation and pursuit of desire.

Analysis of these works from the point of view of dynamic psychology does not detract from the creative accomplishments of the authors in any way. In studying salient aspects of their lives that spurred them to creative action, we may learn how they managed to make sense, "to frame the contradictions of their time" in their artistic productions, an aim which, according to their contemporary, György Lukács, is one of the purposes of art. I hope that the efforts here in using concepts learned from depth psychology to explore these works may have provided another layer of understanding of the psychological underpinnings and clarified issues that would have remained obscure if I had relied more exclusively on information from the authors themselves about the nature of their work.[7] Through artistic means, the writers and composers were able to create formal coherence out of the emotional chaos that emerged from the cultural upheaval of the time. Psychotherapists, in turn, may benefit from their immersion in the psychological dilemmas and choices presented by the characters of both operas. They may gain a more profound insight into the contemporary Bluebeards, Judiths, Mélisandes, Pelléases, Yniolds, and Arkels that often visit their offices.

The painful interactions between the male and female protagonists in both operas dramatize not only the contemporary cultural struggle with gender issues but also the contradictions brought about by the modern preoccupation with integrating all aspects of the self. Modernity challenged the safety of socially assigned roles. Such concerns intensified fear of intimacy and the displacement to the feminine of a sense of vulnerability and diffuse boundaries. Thus, loving a woman could be seen as a threat to the self—the dangerous dissolution of the self boundaries. György Lukács, Béla Balázs's friend, source of inspiration,[8] and support, expressed these themes poignantly in a love letter to a woman friend. Lukács's letter seems to invoke the lonely world of Balázs's Bluebeard, whose locked doors symbolize a kind of mask that hides his soul, a mask that is threatened to be shattered by Judith's actions:

> And so Socrates pressed to his face, like a mask, the impenetrable purity of his words, which never betrayed his own longings and desires, nor made audible the stifled cries of his eternal loneliness. That is why Socrates welcomed death. He knew his soul would gain in death and—who knows? —silence his longings. . . .
>
> My own mask lies at my feet shattered in pieces. My longings and desires reach forth like tear-stained emaciated arms. Spread wide, they are waiting. And yet, were anything to approach, my arms would withdraw for fear of opening up all wounds, aware that if love turned to flesh it would become one with it. The lover and beloved must part. The one who departs carries away part of the beloved's flesh only to increase his loneliness and deepen his wounds.
>
> I don't want to lose you completely, but on my ocean everyone sinks who reaches out for my hand. The hour has struck and I must leave. Where am I going? Who knows? . . . I am going alone.[9]

Notes

Preface

1. Igor Stravinsky, *Autobiography* (New York: Simon and Schuster, 1936; New York: Norton, 1962), p. 52.

2. Letter (dated 18 April 1909) from Debussy to Edwin Evans, published for the first time in Roger Nichols and Richard Langham Smith, *Claude Debussy: "Pelléas et Mélisande"* (Cambridge: Cambridge University Press, 1989), pp. 184–186, appendix.

3. Marcel Schneider, "Symbolist Movement," trans. Edouard Roditi, in *The Symbolist Movement in the Literature of European Languages: A Comparative History of Literatures in European Languages*, ed. Anna Balakian (Budapest: Akadémiai Kiadó, 1982; rev. ed. 1984), p. 473.

4. In psychology, *synesthesia* is "a process in which one type of stimulus produces a secondary, subjective sensation, as when a specific color evokes a specific smell sensation." See *Webster's New World Dictionary of the American Language*, college ed.

5. Lawrence Gilman, in *Debussy's "Pelléas et Mélisande": A Guide to the Opera* (New York: G. Schirmer, 1907), p. 50, discusses this initial reception and controversy. Gilman also lists (p. 47) the next several performances of *Pelléas*: the first took place outside of Paris at the Théâtre de la Monnaie, Brussels (9 January 1907), the second at Frankfort (19 April 1907), and the third was to be given at the Manhattan Opera House in New York shortly thereafter. The original Paris cast included M. Jean Périer as Pelléas, Miss Mary Garden as Mélisande, M. Vieuille as Arkel, M. Dufranne as Golaud, Mlle. Gerville-Réache as Geneviève, M. Blondin as Le petit Yniold, and M. Viguié as Un Médicin, with M. André Messager as conductor, all under M. Albert Carré as director of the Opéra-Comique.

6. See Gilman, *Debussy's "Pelléas et Mélisande,"* pp. 3–4.

7. See Jann Pasler, "Pelléas and Power: Forces Behind the Reception of Debussy's Opera," *Nineteenth Century Music* 10/3 (Spring 1987); repr. in *Music at the Turn of the Century* (Berkeley: University of California Press, 1990), p. 130.

8. See ibid. See also Romain Rolland, *Musiciens d'Aujourd'hui*, 17th ed. (Paris: Librairie Hatchette, 1949), pp. 197–206, and Gilman, *Debussy's "Pelléas et Mélisande,"* p. 47.

9. See Léon Vallas, *Claude Debussy: His Life and Works*, trans. Maire and Grace O'Brien (New York: Dover, 1973; orig. New York: Oxford University Press, 1933), pp. 125–126.

10. See Elliott Antokoletz and George Perle, "*Erwartung* and *Bluebeard*," Program Note in *Stagebill*, for the performance by the New York Metropolitan Opera (16 January 1989).

11. Of the few studies devoted to Bartók's opera, theoretic-analytical discussion of the musical language itself has remained peripheral to dramaturgical considerations. Studies that are based primarily on the theoretic-analytical approach include to some extent Sándor Veress, "Bluebeard's Castle," *Tempo* (London) 13 (1949): 32–38; reprinted in *Béla Bartók: A Memorial Review* (New York: Boosey & Hawkes, 1950), pp. 36–53, which addresses motivic- and harmonic-symbolism, tonalities characterizing the door-scenes, musical expression, harmonic construction, melodic style, and musical form; and Antokoletz, "Bartók's *Bluebeard*: The Sources of Its 'Modernism,'" *College Music Symposium* 30/1 (Spring 1990): 75–95, which explores more intensively the fusion of impressionist musical techniques with the modal structures of Hungarian folk music, transformation of the latter into more abstract, symmetrical (e.g., whole-tone) pitch relations, and the interaction of discrete pitch collections as the basis for symbolic representation. Analysis focuses primarily on the new musical language itself, its relation to the larger structure and design of the scenes, and how Bartók exploited the musical principles to reflect the new dramatic symbolism. Studies focusing on history, dramaturgy, or compositional process include György Kroó, "Duke Bluebeard's Castle," *Studia Musicologica* 1 (1961): 251–340, "Monothematik und Dramaturgie in Bartóks Bühnenwerken," *Studia Musicologica* 5/1–4 (1963): 449–467, "Adatok 'A kekszakállú herceg vára' keletkezéstörténetéhez" [Some data on the genesis of *Duke Bluebeard's Castle*]. *Magyar zenetörténeti tanulmányok: Szabolcsi Bence 70. születésnapjára* (1969): 333 ff. (English translation in *Studia Musicologica* 23 [1981]: 79–123), "Opera: *Duke Bluebeard's Castle*," in *The Bartók Companion*, ed. Malcolm Gillies (London: Faber and Faber, 1993; Portland, Ore.: Amadeus Press, 1994), pp. 349–359, based on symbolic and dramaturgical interpretations as well as an account of the tonalities of the scenes, harmonic construction derived from various folk- and art-music sources, motivic recurrence and development as a significant source of the opera's "symphonic" organic unity, and discussion of the orchestral and vocal styles; and Carl S. Leafstedt, "*Bluebeard* as Theater: The Influence of Maeterlinck and Hebbel on Balázs's *Bluebeard* Drama," in *Bartók and His World*, ed. Peter Laki (Princeton, N.J.: Princeton University Press, 1995), pp. 119–148, and *Inside Bluebeard's Castle: Music and Drama in Béla Bartók's Opera* (New York: Oxford University Press, 1999). All of these draw together a wide array of historical data that provide insight into the dramaturgical thought. Other such studies of the opera are found in *The Stage Works of Béla Bartók*, ed. Nicholas John (New York: Riverrun; London: Calder, 1991), including Paul Banks, "Images of the Self: Duke Bluebeard's Castle"; Simon Broughton, "Bartók and World Music"; Keith Bosley and Peter Sherwood, translators, "Annie Miller [The Ballad of Anna Molnár]"; Julian Grant, "A Foot in Bluebeard's Door"; Mike Ashman, "Around the Bluebeard Myth"; Thematic Guide [to A *kékszakállú herceg vára (Duke Bluebeard's Castle)*]; "'A kékszakállú herceg vára' libretto by Béla Balázs"; and "'Duke Bluebeard's Castle' translation by John Lloyd Davies."

1. *Backgrounds and Development*

1. Henri F. Ellenberger, *The Discovery of the Unconscious: The History and Evolution of Dynamic Psychiatry* (New York: Basic Books, 1970), p. 256.

2. See women's suffrage movement in Constance Rover, *Love, Morals and the Feminists* (London: Routledge, 1970); see also John Langdon Davies, *A Short History of Women* (New York: Viking, 1927), pp. 360 and 379.

3. Maurice Maeterlinck, *The Double Garden*, trans. Alexander Teixeira de Mattos (New York: Dodd Mead, 1904), pp. 68–69.

4. Principles of *symmetrical transformation* are discussed in chap. 2.

5. This outcome is consistent with contemporary psychiatric studies of traumatized populations, as demonstrated by Bessel A. Van der Kolk, "The Body Keeps the Score: Approaches to the Psychobiology of Post-traumatic Stress Disorder," in *Traumatic Stress: The Effects of Over-*

whelming Experience on Mind, Body, and Society, ed. Bessel A. Van der Kolk, Alexander C. Mac-Farlane, and Lars Weisaeth (New York: Guilford Press, 1996), pp. 214–241.

6. Maeterlinck, "On Women," in *The Treasure of the Humble,* trans. Alfred Sutro (New York: Dodd, Mead; London: George Allen, Ruskin House, 1902), pp. 77–94. Originally published in French as *Le Trésor des Humbles* (1897).

7. Judit Frigyesi, in *Béla Bartók and Turn-of-the-Century Budapest* (Berkeley: University of California Press, 1998), p. 196 ff., discusses the attitudes of these Hungarian artists in this era, especially of men toward women, asserting that most men could not accept women as their equals emotionally or intellectually. However, man's stereotypic depictions of women in literature as despotic, demonic, destructive, or naive and childlike "did not necessarily guide his everyday relation to women."

8. See chap. 3, on trauma.

9. According to Marilyn Charles, "The Language of the Body: Allusions to Self-Experience in Women's Poetry," *Psychoanalytic Psychology* 18/2 (Spring 2001): 346, "Art provides a means for translating primary awareness into pattern form that can be used as a way of finding oneself."

10. Van der Kolk, *Traumatic Stress,* pp. 227–232.

11. See Herman Oppenheim, *Die traumatische Neurosen* (Berlin: Hirschwald, 1889), and Eric J. Erichsen, *On Railway and Other Injuries of the Nervous System* (London: Walton and Moberley, 1866) and *On Concussion of the Spine, Nervous Shock, And Other Obscure Injuries to the Nervous System in Their Clinical and Medico-Legal Aspects* (New York: William Wood, 1886), both referred to by van der Kolk, in *Traumatic Stress,* p. 48.

12. See H. Page, "Injuries of the Spine and Spinal Cord," in *Post-Traumatic Neuroses: From Railroad Spine to Whiplash,* ed. M. R. Trimble (London: J. Churchill, 1885), p. 29.

13. See van der Kolk, in *Traumatic Stress,* p. 48.

14. Comte's third (Positivist) stage is particularly relevant to Charcot's thought, in contrast to the second (metaphysical) stage. See n. 24.

15. Christopher G. Goetz, Michel Bonduelle, and Toby Gelfand, *Charcot: Constructing Neurology* (New York: Oxford University Press, 1995), p. 183.

16. Judith Herman, Workshop on Post Traumatic Stress Disorder, New England Institute (Summer 1990).

17. Goetz, *Charcot,* p. 184.

18. Ellenberger, "Pierre Janet and Psychological Analysis," in *The Discovery of the Unconscious,* p. 339.

19. Ellenberger, "Pierre Janet," p. 364.

20. In Sigmund Freud and Josef Breuer, *Studies on Hysteria,* trans. and ed. James Strachey (New York: Avon, 1966), pp. 37–52.

21. Ibid, p. 43.

22. Ibid, pp. xii–xiii, n. 2.

23. Philip Reiff, *The Feeling Intellect: Selected Writings,* ed. Jonathan B. Imber (Chicago: Chicago University Press, 1990), p. 4.

24. Some insight into this development may be gleaned from a study of Auguste Comte's philosophical thought. In his discourse on social evolution, as presented in his *Cours de philosophie positive* (Paris: La Société Positiviste, 1892–1896; 1830–1842); Eng. trans., *The Course of Positive Philosophy* (New York: W. Gowans, 1868; 1853), Comte's theory of intellectual development is presented in what is described as the "Law of the Three Stages": (1) theological, in which cause is ascribed to supernatural forces; (2) metaphysical, in which cause is understood in terms of metaphysical abstraction, or symbol (an object standing for something abstract); and (3) positive, in which phenomena are understood by means of empirical data and the scientific method (based on observation, hypotheses, and experimentation), that is, physical nature and historical background based on that which can be measured. The reaction of sym-

bolist poets against the basic tenets of realism may be seen as a reversion from the third (positivist) stage to the second (metaphysical) stage of Comte's Law. The Symbolist poets under the influence of Baudelaire rebelled against the writings of those influenced by the Positivism of Comte, whose objective and calculated approach to reality was replaced in literature by symbolic representation. Moods and impressions were now simply suggested by the sounds and rhythms of the poetic language. The new aesthetics of Mallarmé, Verlaine, and Rimbaud were further developed in the poetry of LaForgue, Moreas, Regnier, and the dramas of Maeterlinck, as well as in the writings of later symbolists, including Claudel, Valéry, Jammes, and Fort. This symbolist trend in France, which was further developed in the discursive style of Proust, also led to similar developments in all the arts.

25. Ibsen's late plays together with the Wagnerian conception of music drama were the first influences on the Symbolists in the theater.

26. Marcel Schneider, "Symbolist Movement," trans. Edouard Roditi, in *The Symbolist Movement in the Literature of European Languages: A Comparative History of Literatures in European Languages*, ed. Anna Balakian (Budapest: Akadémiai Kiadó, 1982; rev. ed. 1984), p. 473.

27. See Balázs, *Theory of the film*, p. 151, cited by Joseph Zsuffa, in *Béla Balázs, The Man and the Artist* (Berkeley: University of California Press, 1987), chap. 1, n. 5.

28. Sigmund Freud, *The Interpretation of Dreams*, new trans. Joyce Crick (New York: Oxford Univesity press, 1999).

29. Marie-Jean-Leon Hervey de Saint-Denis, *Les Rêves et les moyens de les diriger* (Paris: Amyot, 1867), as cited by Ellenberger in *The Discovery of the Unconscious*, pp. 306–308.

30. Ellenberger, "On the Threshold of a New Dynamic Psychiatry," *The Discovery of the Unconscious*, p. 306.

31. Frederik Van Eeden, *De Nachtbruid* (1909), Eng. trans. Mellie von Auw, *The Bride of Dreams* (New York: Mitchell Kennerley, 1913), as cited by Ellenberger in *The Discovery of the Unconscious*, p. 306.

32. Ibid., p. 783. Ellenberger provides documentation showing that Freud's *Interpretation of Dreams* was, upon publication, widely reviewed and well known on an international scale in medical, psychiatric, psychological, and generally educated circles.

33. Sigmund Freud, "The Taboo of Virginity," in *Sexuality and the Psychology of Love*, trans. Joan Riviere (New York: Collier Books, 1963; *Sammlung*, Vierte Folge, 1918), pp. 84–85.

34. Herbert Bauer, *Hebbel Frigyes pántragizmusa, mint a romantikus világnézlet eredménye* (Friedrich Hebbel's Pan-Tragicness, as the Result of the Romantic Worldview) (Budapest: Franklin Társulat, 1909).

35. György Lukács, "The Metaphysics of Tragedy," in *Soul and Form*, trans. Anna Bostock (London: Merlin, 1978), p. 156.

36. Lukács, "Esztétikay Kultura" (Aesthetic culture), in *Ifjkuri művek* (1902–1918) [Youthful Works], ed. Arpad Timar (Budapest: Magvető, 1977), pp. 434–435, cited by Frigyesi, *Béla Bartók*, p.164.

37. Leafstedt, *Inside Bluebeard's Castle: Music and Drama in Bartók's Opera* (New York: Oxford University Press, 1999), pp. 19–20.

38. Schneider, "Symbolist Movement," p. 471.

39. "Pelléas and Gil Blas: Claudine and Monsieur Croche," *Debussy on Music: The Critical Writings of the Great French Composer*, collected and introduced by François Lesure, trans. and ed. Richard Langham Smith (Ithaca, N.Y.: Cornell University Press, 1977), p. 67.

40. Daniel N. Stern, *The Interpersonal World of the Infant: A View from Psychoanalysis and Developmental Psychology* (New York: Basic Books, 1985), p. 155.

41. As Debussy reacted against the aesthetics of his colleagues at the Conservatoire, he sought other artistic ties by entering into the orbit of the Symbolist poets and Impressionist painters who met at Stéphane Mallarmé's and frequented the cafés. Those who constituted De-

bussy's new circle of friends were Paul Verlaine, Henri de Regnier, Maurice Vaucaire, Pierre Louÿs, André Gide, James Whistler, Claude Monet, Pierre Auguste Renoir, Alfred Sisley, Camille Pissarro, Édouard Manet, Edgar Dégas, and Jacques-Emile Blanche.

42. See "Richard Wagner, Revery of a French Poet," *Revue Wagnérienne* (Geneve: Slatkine Reprints, 1968), as cited by Arthur B. Wenk, *Claude Debussy and Twentieth-Century Music* (Boston: Twayne, 1983), pp. 35–36.

43. Wenk, *Claude Debussy*, p. 36.

44. As quoted in Léon Vallas, *Claude Debussy: His Life and Works*, trans. Maire and Grace O'Brien (New York: Dover Publications, 1973; original publication, New York: Oxford University Press, 1933), p. 52.

45. See the interview by Robert de Flers, "*Pelléas et Mélisande*: A Reply to the Critics," *Le Figaro* (16 May 1902), in *Debussy on Music*, p. 80.

46. This general term has been applied to French operas that do not readily fit into the categories of *opéra comique* or *grand opéra*.

47. An *interval cycle* is a series based on a single recurrent interval (e.g., as in the whole-tone cycle, cycle of fifths, etc.), the sequence being completed by the return of the initial pitch at the octave. The entire set of uni-intervallic cycles is outlined in Elliott Antokoletz, *The Music of Béla Bartók: A Study of Tonality and Progression in Twentieth-Century Music* (Berkeley: University of California Press, 1984), p. 68.

48. Schneider, "Symbolist Movement," p. 474. Insight into Debussy's position with regard to Wagner and the new aesthetic developments in France is also provided by Erik Satie's claim, in one of his lectures, that "he explained to Debussy the need a Frenchman has to free himself from the Wagnerian venture, which didn't respond to our natural aspirations. . . . Why could we not use the means that Claude Monet, Cezanne, Toulouse-Lautrec and others had made known? Why could we not transpose these means into music?" While there is no evidence that Debussy was affected consciously by the Impressionist painters, Satie's statement does draw our attention to Debussy's "Wagnerian venture" as well as his reaction against the German late-Romantic tradition in general.

49. Debussy, "*Pelléas et Mélisande*: A Reply to the Critics," pp. 80–81. By belittling Wagner's use of the leitmotif as the "calling card" type, Debussy was in reality oversimplifying Wagner's complexities. It is, paradoxically, in this more complex conception of Wagner's music dramas that Debussy's own approach to the leitmotif technique in *Pelléas* finds its most direct reference.

50. Edward Lockspeiser, *Debussy* (New York: McGraw-Hill, 1936; rev. J. M. Dent, 1963), p. 209.

51. Anna Balakian, *Literary Origins of Surrealism: A New Mysticism in French Poetry* (New York: New York University Press, 1947; rev. ed. 1966), p. 97, as cited in René Wellek, "What is Symbolism?" in *The Symbolist Movement in the Literature of European Languages*, pp. 26–27.

52. Péter Pór, "The Symbolist Turn in Endre Ady's Poetry," in *The Symbolist Movement in the Literature of European Languages*, p. 366.

53. André Beaunier, *Le poésie nouvelle* (Paris, 1920), p. 14.

54. Richard Langham Smith, "Tonalities of Darkness and Light," in Roger Nichols and Richard Langham Smith, *Claude Debussy: Pelléas et Mélisande* (Cambridge: Cambridge University Press, 1989), p. 108.

55. Henri de Régnier, "Poètes d'aujourd'hui et poèsie de demain," in *Mercure de France*, 35 (1900): 342. "Un symbole est, en effet, une comparaison et une identité de l'abstrait au concret, comparaison dont l'un des termes reste sous-entendu."

56. Jan Mukařovsky, *Kapitoly z ceské poetiky* (Prague, 1948), vol. 2, p. 220.

57. René Wellek, "What is Symbolism?" in *The Symbolist Movement in the Literature of European Languages*, p. 26.

58. These two types of signs have been described as follows: "Those [signs] are natural which, without any desire or intention of signifying, make us aware of something beyond themselves, like smoke which signifies fire," whereas "conventional signs are those which living creatures show to one another for the purpose of conveying, in so far as they are able, the motion of their spirits or something which they have sensed or understood." St. Augustine, in *On Christian Doctrine*, trans. D.W. Robertson, Jr. (Indianapolis and New York: Bobbs-Merrill, 1958), p. 34.

59. Matte Blanco's concept of the unconscious as infinite sets offers a plausible explanation for this association. See my discussion in chap. 4 of how Matte Blanco's concept is helpful in understanding Debussy's depiction of the polarities of fate versus human, unconscious versus conscious. See Ignacio Matte Blanco, *The Unconscious as Infinite Sets: An Essay in Bi-Logic* (London: Duckworth, 1975), p. 106.

60. Theodor W. Adorno, *Philosophy of Modern Music*, trans. Anne G. Mitchell and Wesley V. Blomster (New York: Seabury, 1973), pp. 155–156.

61. Ibid., p. 156.

62. Paulin Limayrac, "La Poèsie symboliste et socialiste," *Revue des Deux Mondes*, N.S. 5 (1844): 669–682. See also Judit Frigyesi, *Béla Bartók and Turn-of-the-Century Budapest*, p. 98, who cites Balázs's devotion to the Communist Party, these activities, like those of the other Hungarian modernists, leading him away from his immediate environment and profession, as did Bartók's and Kodály's turn toward folk-music investigation.

2. The New Musical Language

1. Béla Bartók, "Temoignage (sur Ravel)," *Revue Musicale* 19/2 (December 1938): 436. See also Bartók's 1921 "Autobiography," in *Béla Bartók Essays*, ed. Benjamin Suchoff (New York: St. Martin's Press, 1976), p. 410, which originally appeared in several versions in: *Musikblätter des Anbruch* (Vienna) 3/5 (March 1921): 87–90; *Magyar írás hármaskönyve* (Budapest) 1/2 (May, 1921): 33–36; *Az est hármaskönyve* (Budapest: Az Est Lapkiadó RT kiadása, 1923): cols. 77–84; *Sovremennaya muzyka* (Moscow) 2/7 (1925): 1–6; and *Színházi élet* (Budapest) 17/51 (December 1927): 49–51.

2. Anthony Cross, "Debussy and Bartók," *Musical Times* 108 (1967): 126.

3. Bartók, "Harvard Lectures," in *Béla Bartók Essays*, ed. Benjamin Suchoff (New York: St. Martin's Press, 1976), p. 386. The original publication of the MSS of four lectures given during February 1943 was in *Journal of the American Musicological Society* 19/2 (Summer 1966): 232–243.

4. See Bartók's 1921 "Autobiography," in n. 1 earlier.

5. Elliott Antokoletz, *The Music of Béla Bartók: A Study of Tonality and Progression in Twentieth-Century Music* (Berkeley: University of California Press, 1984), pp. 8 and 13.

6. Bartók, "Harvard Lectures," p. 386.

7. *Béla Bartók Essays*, p. 410, or the original publication of "Selbstbiographie," in *Musikblätter des Anbruch* (Vienna) 3/5 (March 1921): 89.

8. A collection of pitches is *symmetrical* if the intervallic structure of one-half of it can be mapped into the other half through mirroring, that is, literal inversion. The properties of symmetrical inversion are discussed in depth in Antokoletz, *The Music of Béla Bartók*, chap. 4.

9. For some of these manifestations of symmetrical pitch construction and progression in chromatic tonal music of the nineteenth century, see George Perle, "Symmetrical Formations in the String Quartets of Béla Bartók," *Music Review* 16 (November 1955): 301; Philip Friedheim, "Radical Harmonic Procedures in Berlioz," *Music Review* 21/4 (November 1960): 286; Felix Salzer and Carl Schachter, *Counterpoint in Composition: The Study of Voice Leading* (New

York: McGraw-Hill, 1969): 215–221; Gregory Proctor, "Technical Bases of Nineteenth-Century Chromatic Tonality: A Study in Chromaticism" (Ph.D. diss., Princeton University, 1977); Elliott Antokoletz, *The Music of Bela Bartok*, pp. 323–325; and Richard Taruskin, "Chernomoor to Kaschei: Harmonic Sorcery; or, Stravinsky's 'Angle'," *Journal of the American Musicological Society* 38/1 (Spring 1985): 79ff.

10. For a definition of *interval cycle*, see chap. 1, n. 47.

11. *Béla Bartók Essays*, pp. 323–324. The original publication is "The Relation of Folk Song to the Development of the Art Music of Our Time," *The Sackbut* 2/1 (June 1921): 5–11. This essay was also published in *Muzyka* (Warsaw) 2/6 (June 1925): 230–233, and 4/6 (June 1927): 256–259.

12. See Perle, "Symmetrical Formations," p. 302, and Antokoletz, *The Music of Béla Bartók*, pp. 4–5.

13. As shown in Antokoletz, *The Music of Béla Bartók*, pp. 6–8.

14. Arnold Whittall, "Tonality and the Whole-Tone Scale in the Music of Debussy," *Music Review* 36/4 (November 1975): 261.

15. Arnold Schoenberg, *Theory of Harmony*, trans. Roy E. Carter (Berkeley: University of California Press, 1978), p. 391.

16. Ibid., p. 397.

17. A *cell* is defined by George Perle, in *Serial Composition and Atonality* (6th ed. rev., Berkeley: University of California Press, 1991), p. 9, as a group of pitches that "may operate as a kind of microcosmic set of fixed intervallic content, statable either as a chord or as a melodic figure or as a combination of both." Its components, however, are not fixed with regard to order in Debussy's or Bartók's works or the early free-atonal works of Schoenberg.

18. For demonstration purposes only, the specific choice of pitch content for these examples of intervallic construction in the present discussion is largely arbitrary, since most if not all of the transpositions of these cells and the larger sets are employed throughout both operas.

19. Arnold Schoenberg, 1941 essay "Composition with Twelve Tones (I)," *Style and Idea, Selected Writings of Arnold Schoenberg*, ed. Leonard Stein, trans. Leo Black (London: Faber and Faber, 1975), p. 219.

20. See Elliott Antokoletz, "Organic Development and the Interval Cycles in Bartók's Three Studies, Op. 18," *Studia Musicologica* 36/3–4 (1995): 249–261, for a study of a set of principles that were to be manifested most systematically in Bartók's works after World War I. In his prewar works, such as *Bluebeard's Castle*, the interval cycles appear to be relatively ambiguous and nonsystematic because of the highly diversified network of harmonic and melodic constructions within which they unfold. Nevertheless, in the opera, the system of the interval cycles had already begun to play a significant role in the generation, progression, transformation, and integration of the basic pitch-sets in correspondence with the symbolic message of the drama.

21. Intervals larger than the tritone are the harmonic inversions of the corresponding smaller intervals (perfect fifth/perfect fourth, minor sixth/major third, etc.), that is, they form the intervallic complements of the smaller ones in the same interval class. The total system of the interval cycles is outlined in Antokoletz, *The Music of Béla Bartók*, ex. 70.

22. See Elliott Antokoletz, "Organic Development and the Interval Cycles in Bartók's Three Studies, Op. 18," p. 251, and "Organic Expansion and Classical Structure in Bartók's Sonata for Two Pianos and Percussion," in *Bartók Perspectives*, ed. Elliott Antokoletz, Victoria Fischer, and Benjamin Suchoff (New York: Oxford University Press, 2000), p. 93.

23. The term "ratio 1:1" (or "interval-ratio 1:1") is used here to designate the relationship of two semitones to one another in terms of their intervallic separation, that is, two semitones separated by a semitone; "ratio 1:2" designates two semitones separated by a whole-tone, or two whole-tones separated by a semitone; and so on.

24. These intervallic indications have no relation to Ernő Lendvai's terminology for his interval "Models," since he infers Golden Section significance, while I interpret these intervallic relations exclusively in terms of the interval cycles.

25. Bartók, "Harvard Lectures," pp. 379–381.

26. The major seventh chord, with either minor third or major third, has special leitmotivic significance in Bartók's opera, as will be discussed in later chapters.

27. See János Kárpáti, "Alternatív struktúrák Bartók Kontrasztok című művében" [Alternative structures in Bartók's *Contrasts*], *Zeneelmélet, stíluselemzés* (Budapest: Zeneműkiadó, 1977), pp. 103–108; also published in English in *Studia Musicologica* 23 (1981): 201–207. See also Kárpáti, "Tonal Divergences of Melody and Harmony," *Studia Musicologica* 24 (1982): 373–374, for further discussion based on the "chain of thirds" phenomenon.

28. In a more recent study, Alicja Usarek, in "The Genesis and Fate of Béla Bartók's 1907 *Violin Concerto*" (D.M.A. diss., the University of Texas at Austin, 2000), pp. 85–94, suggests that the "chain of thirds" is employed as a nonfunctional vehicle for leitmotivic progression.

29. See Kárpáti, *Bartók's String Quartets*, trans. Fred Macnicol (Budapest: Corvina Press, 1975), p. 233; revised and enlarged as *Bartók's Chamber Music*, trans. Fred Macnicol and Mária Steiner, trans. rev. Paul Merrick (Stuyvesant, N.Y.: Pendragon Press, 1994), p. 376.

30. Kárpáti, in "Tonal Divergences," p. 374, presents the notion of "dual degrees" as a source for such conflicts.

31. See Antokoletz, "Bartók's *Bluebeard:* The Sources of Its Modernism," *College Music Symposium* 30/1 (Spring 1990): 79–80 and 83.

32. See Zoltán Kodály, "Béla Bartók," *La Revue Musicale* 2, no. 5 (March 1921): 213.

33. See n. 3 earlier.

34. Debussy, "*Pelléas et Mélisande:* A Reply to the Critics (Interview by Robert de Flers)," *Le Figaro* (16 May 1902); originally in *Monsieur Croche et autres écrits* (Paris: Editions Gallimard, 1971; see the translation, *Debussy on Music: The Critical Writings of the Great Composer*, ed. François Lesure, trans. and ed. Richard Langham Smith (New York: Alfred A. Knopf, 1977; Ithaca, N.Y.: Cornell University Press, 1977), p. 80.

3. Trauma, Gender, and the Unfolding of the Unconscious

1. Balázs, who would later become a pioneer in the new art of cinematography, viewed film as another avenue for the expression of what cannot be put into words: "The gestures of visual man are not intended to convey concepts which can be expressed in words, but such inner experiences, such non-rational emotions which would still remain unexpressed when everything that can be told has been told"; see Béla Balázs. *Theory of the Film: Character and Growth of a New Art*, trans. Edith Bone (London: Dennis Dobson, 1952), p. 40.

2. Maeterlinck wrote several works exploring gender issues, as in his treatise "On Women," in *The Treasure of the Humble*, trans. Alfred Sutro (New York: Dodd, Mead; London: George Allen, Ruskin House, 1902,), and his play, *Ariane et Barbe-bleue*. Balázs had just published a book of poems, *The Wanderer Sings* (1911), cited in Joseph Zsuffa, *Béla Balázs, The Man and the Artist* (Berkeley: University of California Press, 1987), p. 37, in which he asserted that men's friendship with men was superior to their friendship with women.

3. See Jann Pasler, "Pelléas and Power: Forces Behind the Reception of Debussy's Opera," *Nineteenth Century Music* 10/3 (Spring 1987); repr. in *Music at the Turn of the Century* (Berkeley: University of California Press, 1990), p. 148. Those underlying tensions could be seen in the controversies emerging after the premiere of *Pelléas*, in which those who favored the opera tended to be associated with the Dreyfus movement and vice versa. Similarly, *Duke Bluebeard's Castle* was banned from the stage until 1918 partly because of Balázs's connection with the Communist movement.

4. Rainer Maria Rilke, "Maurice Maeterlinck," in *Oeuvres en prose, recits et essais*, ed. Claude David (Paris: Gallimard, 1993), p. 717.

5. Maeterlinck, "Preface au theâtre de 1901," in *Oeuvres*, ed. P. Gorceix t.I (Bruxelles: Complexe, 1899), p. 495.

6. Social discontent was reflected in the grumblings of the anarchist movement, the organization of workers, and the women's demands for universal suffrage. Steven Huebner, in *French Opera at the Fin de Siècle: Wagnerism, Nationalism, and Style* (New York: Oxford University Press, 1999), p. 454, discusses Charpentier's use of an anarchist theme in his opera, *Louise*.

7. Both Janet and Freud had extensive training in philosophy and the classics as this was part of the graduate education of the time. Their theories about what they observed in their patients was informed by their knowledge in these areas. See Henri F. Ellenberger, *The Discovery of the Unconscious: The History and Evolution of Dynamic Psychiatry* (New York: Basic Books, 1970), pp. 209 and 337.

8. See Susan Youens, "An Unseen Player: Destiny in *Pelléas et Mélisande*," in Arthur Groos and Roger Parker, *Reading Opera* (Princeton, N.J.: Princeton University Press, 1988), pp. 60–66 and 88. See also Carl Leafstedt, *Inside Bluebeard's Castle* (New York: Oxford University Press, 1999), p. 48.

9. It is interesting that Jeremy Tambling, in *Opera and the Culture of Fascism* (Oxford: Clarendon Press, 1996), p. 3, see also pp. 1–24, sees the nineteenth century as a primeval landscape for "fascism," which he says is "to revert out of fear of the critical self-consciousness into pure, spontaneous action." For Tambling, fascism (spelled with a lowercase "f") is not confined to the specific historical period traditionally from 1923 to 1945 in which Fascism (with an uppercase "F") threatened to conquer the world. "Fascism" (uppercase "F") was the epitomy of narcissistic pathology developed into its most pathological extremes.

10. The stories teach us, in synchrony with current developments in psychoanalysis, that the therapeutic task remains incomplete if it only assists the patient in becoming aware of his primitive and archaic sexual lust or unprocessed traumatic memories. It is also necessary to help the patient understand and modify the primitive psychological defenses developed as a response to trauma.

11. Loosely organized private armies of former German imperial soldiers, anticommunists, and other groups that existed in Germany after World War I; see Anson Rabinbach and Jessica Benjamin, foreword to Klaus Theweleit, *Male Fantasies*, vol. 2 (Minneapolis: University of Minnesota Press, 1989), pp. xiv–xv.

12. See ibid., pp. xix and xx.

13. Jessica Benjamin, *The Bonds of Love: Psychoanalysis, Feminism, and the Problem of Domination* (New York: Pantheon Books, 1988), pp.187–189. See also Lynne Layton, "Trauma, Gender Identity, and Sexuality: Discourses in Fragmentation," in Peter L. Rudnytsky and Andrew M. Gordon, eds., *Psychoanalyses/Feminisms* (Albany: State University of New York Press, 2000), p. 219.

14. Benjamin, *The Bonds of Love*, p. 224.

15. Nancy J. Chodorow, *Feminism and Psychoanalytic Theory* (New Haven, Conn.: Yale University Press, 1989), pp. 23–44.

16. See Layton, "Trauma," p. 216, and David Lisak, "Sexual Aggression, Masculinity, and Fathers," *Signs* 16/2 (Winter 1991): 238–262, and "Gender Development and Sexual Abuse in lives of Men," unpublished paper presented at the conference on Trauma and its Sociocultural Context, the University of Massachusetts (1992).

17. Layton, "Trauma," p. 216.

18. Judit Frigyesi, in "In Search of Meaning in Context: Bartók's *Duke Bluebeard's Castle*," *Current Musicology* 70 (Fall 2000): 27, argues that *Bluebeard* ends in "beautiful loneliness." I will offer an alternative view in my analysis of *Bluebeard*.

19. Daniel D. Stern, *The Interpersonal World of the Infant: A view from Psychoanalysis and Developmental Psychology* (New York: Basic Books, 1985), p. 11.

20. See ibid., p. 54. Stern's description of these states of being that coexist with the verbal self and have nonverbal means of encoding and expressing experiences seems to validate the notion that music (probably more akin to the emergent self, which experiences rhythm and vitality) has its own syntax that is parallel to, but not identical to, language syntax. It is significant that Debussy's composition of *Pelléas* was a statement against Wagner's desire to integrate music and words in a common language.

21. See Maeterlinck, "Silence," in *The Treasure of the Humble*, trans. Alfred Sutro, with introduction by A.B. Walkley (New York: Dodd, Mead; London: George Allen, Ruskin House, 1902), p. 15.

22. Bessel A. van der Kolk, "Trauma and Memory," eds. Bessel A. van der Kolk, Alexander C. McFarlane, Lars Weisaeth (New York: Guilford Press, 1996), pp 293–296.

23. Daniel Stern, Beatrice Beebe, Joseph Jaffe, and Stephen Bennett, "The Infant's stimulus World During Social Interaction: A Study of Caregiver Behaviors with Particular Reference to Repetition and Timing," in H. R. Schaffer, ed., *Studies in Mother-Infant Interaction* (London: Academic Press, 1977), pp. 177–193.

24. Daniel N. Stern, *The Interpersonal World of the Infant* (New York: Basic Books, 1985), pp. 174–182.

25. From the point of view of society at large, language also may be used to enforce societal norms. Censorship of free speech is one of the first steps that occur in totalitarian regimes. In more subtle ways, society rules are encoded in the "politically correct" unwritten norms for what and how opinions may be expressed. This is true in formal situations as well as in the area of intimate relationships. For example, Herbert Marcuse, as quoted in the introduction to Theodor W. Adorno, *Essays on Music*, ed. Richard Leppert, trans. Susan H. Gillespie (Berkeley: University of California Press, 2002), p. 67, suggests that Adorno's difficult prose may be his resistance to social oppression: "Ordinary language, ordinary prose . . . expresses so much of the control and manipulation over the individual by the power structure, that in order to counteract this process you have to indicate already in the language your use of the necessary rupture with conformity."

26. Letter to *L'Art moderne* (29 November 1981), p. 380, cited by W. D. Halls, in *Maurice Maeterlinck* (Oxford: Clarendon Press, 1960), p. 31.

27. Georges Rodenbach, *Le Rouet des brumes* (Paris: Sâeguier, 1900), p. 210.

28. Maeterlinck, *Bulles Bleues (souvenirs heureux)* (Monaco: Éditions du Rocher, 1948), p. 128.

29. Halls, *Maeterlinck*, p. 9. Halls also discusses (p. 6) how, as a child, he went through successive tutors because his mother dismissed many of them as result of his father's amorous advances to them. This was bound to create tension for the young Maeterlinck.

30. Maeterlinck, "On Women," in *The Treasure of the Humble*, p. 92. See also Adorno, *Essays on Music*, pp. 64–65: "The splinter in your eye is the best magnifying glass. . . . Seeing now is not a matter of optical mechanics but insight, the driving force behind which in this instance is pain."

31. See chap. 4, n. 16.

32. See Maeterlinck, "On Women," pp. 83–84.

33. See discussion later of the possible meaning of women "not falling from grace." Benjamin, in *The Bonds of Love*, p. 246, n. 4, indicates that Wilhelm Reich in his writings on fascism viewed society as repressing instinct, and so, defended instinct against culture. See Reich, *The Mass Psychology of Fascism* (1933) (New York: Simon and Schuster, 1970) and "What Is Class Consciousness?" in *Sex-Pol: Essays, 1929–1934.*

34. Maeterlinck, "On Women," pp. 83–84.

35. References to social inequalities were made in other contemporary works of the time, such as Charpentier's opera, *Louise*, in which the main characters are workers and the seamstress shop the stage for some of the scenes.

36. Maeterlinck, "On Women," p. 92.

37. Sigmund Freud, "Some Psychical Consequences of the Anatomical Distinctions Between the Sexes" [1925], *Standard Edition*, vol. 19 (London: Hogarth Press, 1961), p. 257.

38. Carol Gilligan, *In a Different Voice: Psychological Theory and Women's Development* (Cambridge, Mass.: Harvard University Press, 1982), p. 174. The work of Gilligan in the United States about differences in male and female moral development suggests that men tend to evaluate situations abstractly, while women tend to view them within the perspective of interpersonal consequences.

39. See Anna Freud, *About Losing and Being Lost*, in *The Writings of Anna Freud, Vol. 14, 1945–1956* (New York: International Universities Press, 1968), pp. 308–310.

40. Edward Lockspeiser, Debussy (New York: McGraw-Hill Book Company, 1936; rev. J. M. Dent, 1963), pp. 76, 87–89.

41. Leblanc, *Souvenirs*, p. 27.

42. Debussy to André Caplet, 22 December 1911, as quoted in Marcel Dietschy, *A Portrait of Claude Debussy* (Oxford: Clarendon Press, 1990), p. xi.

43. American Psychiatric Association, *Diagnostic and Statistical Manual of Mental Disorders*, 4th ed. (Washington, D.C.: American Psychiatric Association, 1994), pp. 428–429.

44. Nancy McWilliams, *Psychoanalytic Diagnosis: Understanding the Personality Structure in the Clinical Process* (New York: Guilford Press, 1994), p. 324.

45. Richard Langham Smith, "The Play and its Playwright," in Roger Nichols and Richard Langham Smith, *Claude Debussy: "Pelléas et Mélisande"* (Cambridge: Cambridge University Press, 1989), p. 19.

46. Sigmund Freud, "Beyond the Pleasure Principle [1920a]," *Standard Edition of the Complete Psychological Works of Sigmund Freud*, vol. 18 (London: Hogarth Press, 1955), pp. 7–64.

47. Bessel A. van der Kolk, Onno van der Hart, and Charles R. Marmar, "Dissociation and Information Processing in Post-Traumatic Stress Disorder," in *Traumatic Stress: The Effects of Overwhelming Experience on Mind, Body, and Society*, ed. Bessel A. van der Kolk, Alexander C. McFarlane, and Lars Weisaeth (New York: Guilford Press, 1996), pp. 303–327.

48. See Halls, *Maeterlinck*, pp. 38–39, and Albert Mockel, in "Chronique littéraire," *La Wallonie* (Liège, 1981), p. 94.

49. Georgette Leblanc describes an incident in which Maeterlinck killed her cat with one shot from his revolver: "A Messalina, like all females of her race, prowled through the garden proclaiming her desires. Exasperated, he opened the window: 'I am going to kill her.' I thought he was joking. The animal stopped short, looked at us fixedly. She received the bullet directly between the eyes." See Georgette Leblanc, *Souvenirs: My Life with Maeterlinck*, trans. Janet Flanner (New York: Dutton, 1932), p. 26.

50. McFarlane and van der Kolk, "Trauma and Its Challenge to Society," in *Traumatic Stress*, p. 28.

51. Halls, *Maeterlinck*, p. 38.

52. Donald W. Winnicott, "Ego distortion in terms of true and false self," *The Maturational Processes and the Facilitating Environment* (New York: International University Press, 1965), pp. 140–152.

53. See Maeterlinck, "Notre Moi Veritable," *Le Temple enseveli* (1902), in *Oeuvres*, ed. P. Gorceix t.I (Brussels: Complexe, 1899), p. 209.

54. Pelléas's role does not place him as part of the patriarchal ruling class. It is noteworthy

that Debussy briefly considered a woman for Pelléas's role (See Lockspeiser, *Debussy*, p. 85) and that Sarah Bernhardt acted the role of Pelléas in Maeterlinck's play in London, in 1904 (see Smith, *Pelléas et Mélisande*, p. 5).

55. Nichols, "Synopsis," in Nichols and Smith, *Pelléas et Mélisande*, p. 75.

56. Pelléas as well as the reader, already has evidence that Mélisande was capable of making up stories to avoid telling the truth, as when she fabricated in detail the story about how she lost her ring.

57. The difficulties of Melisande's character to experience real human closeness and openness to intimacy may have been accurately expressed by Mary Garden's interpretation of the role. A review of her portrayal of Melisande published in *Le Figaro* read: "Miss Garden makes the best of the role of Melisande. Her voice is very attractive, and if her personality appears a little cold, it is because the part demands it." See Michael Turnbull, "Mary Garden" (Portland, Ore.: Amadeus Press, 1997), p. 34; *Le Figaro*, 1 May 1902.

58. Joseph Zsuffa, *Béla Balázs: The Man and the Artist* (Berkeley: University of California Press, 1987), p. 32.

59. Ibid., p. 27. Balázs wanted his diary to reflect his developing self and to dissect his view of life. Zsuffa, Balázs's biographer, indicates that "the anguished cry, 'I must find myself'," echoes through his diary. At age twenty-six, Balázs had completed a doctorate in German philology with aesthetics and philosophy as minors (completed in German in 1908), was working actively in developing a career as a writer, and many of his poems and essays had been published in a new liberal literary review, *Nyugat* (West), highly respected in literary circles.

60. See Zsuffa, *Béla Balázs*, p.31.

61. Ibid., p. 32.

62. Ibid., p. 42.

63. *Magyar Zenetörténeti Tanulmónyok 4. Kodály Zoltán Emlékére*, ed. Ferenc Bónis (Budapest: Zeneműkiadó, 1977), p. 33, as cited by Zsuffa, *Béla Balázs*, p. 36.

64. Included in the first volume of Balázs's collected poems, *The Wanderer Sings*, published in 1911. See Zsuffa, *Béla Balázs*, p. 37.

65. See Diary, MS 5023/16,13–14, as cited by Judit Frigyesi, in *Béla Bartók and Turn-of-the-Century Budapest* (Berkeley: University of California Press, 1998), p. 197.

66. Balázs's involvement in activities that challenged the social system created problems throughout his life (e.g., he lost one of his best friends during early adolescence because he supported an opposing political candidate rather than his friends; he created community turmoil when he warned workers of a reprisal by employers in his home town of Szeged). His activities also caused his later exile from his native Hungary. When he had to leave Vienna to escape Nazi persecution, he chose to go to war-threatened Russia, where he would continue to pursue his socialist ideals rather than the more stable shelter in the United States. The choice of a conventional versus a challenging life was also illustrated in his works; for example, Dr. Margit Szélpál, the heroine of one of his plays written in Berlin around 1906, is torn between following her vocation in science or pursuing a conventional, monotonous life. See Zsuffa, *Béla Balázs*, p. 33.

67. See *"Duke Bluebeard's Castle*, Notes on the Text by Béla Balázs, Circa 1915," Eng. trans. Carl Leafstedt from the Hungarian translation (for inclusion in Balázs, *Balázs Béla: Válogatott cikkek*, 34–37) of the original German, in Carl Leafstedt, *Inside Bluebeard's Castle: Music and Drama in Béla Bartók's Opera* (New York: Oxford University Press, 1999), p. 202.

68. Balázs's actual family name was Bauer.

69. Zsuffa, *Béla Balázs*, p. 12.

70. Ibid., p. 3. The legendary story of his father's unknown roots—allegedly, his great-grandfather had been found as a baby, swaddled in "fine linen with a silver taler under his shirt,"

by a Jewish vendor in a wooden area amid the Carpethian mountains—influenced Balázs's view of himself as a wanderer, unsure of his origins. This insecurity was accentuated by his father's obedient but unenthusiastic and secret compliance with Jewish ritual, his resigned acceptance of his life-long exile to Lőcse, where he and a small circle of friends suffered in silence a lifelong sentence to a monotonous and conventional existence, and lastly his father's premature death from a fatal illness at a time when his literary achievements had provided him with the cherished opportunity to end his exile and return to Szeged.

71. Like *Bluebeard*, the literary source of *Little Red Riding Hood* is found in the Charles Perrault tales of 1697.

72. See Benjamin, *The Bonds of Love*, p. 15.

73. Zsuffa, *Béla Balázs*, p. 5.

74. Balázs's perception of the family's relocation as a reason for celebration, in contrast to his father's experience of it as a profound loss, could have been Balázs's attempts to counteract feelings of loss and disappointment.

75. Zsuffa, *Béla Balázs*, p. 13.

76. Leafstedt, *Inside Bluebeard's Castle*, p. 18.

77. Frigyesi, *Béla Bartók*, p. 236, has suggested that Bluebeard portrays a new form of "Hungarianness" that is not equated with heroism.

78. *Béla Bartók Letters*, ed. János Demény (New York: St. Martin's Press, 1971), Eng. trans. Peter Balabán and István Farkas. Trans. rev. Elizabeth West and Colin Mason (London: Faber & Faber; Budapest: Corvina Press, 1971), pp. 50–51.

79. The view of the Enlightenment did not always lead to benevolent results, since it failed to consider individual differences in abilities and the capacity to cope with life. See Henri F. Ellenberger, *The Discovery of the Unconscious*, pp. 196–198.

80. See Philip Reiff, *The Feeling Intellect: Selected Writings*, ed. Jonathan B. Imber (Chicago: Chicago University Press, 1990), p. 4, who speaks of the economic and religious man, not the man of reason.

81. Frigyesi, *Béla Bartók*, p. 226, argues that "[Balázs's] poem stresses the polarity of love as being both separation and union, both the instance of becoming one with the other, and that of returning to the self."

82. Frigyesi, *Béla Bartók*, p. 228.

83. See Bartók's letter to Márta and Hermina Ziegler (Darázs, 4 February 1909), in *Bartók Béla családi levelei* [Béla Bartók's family letters], ed. Béla Bartók, Jr. (Budapest: Zeneműkiadó, 1981), pp. 187–88, as trans. in Frigyesi, *Béla Bartók*, p. 120.

84. "Esztétikai kultúra" [Aesthetic culture], in *Ifjúkori művek (1902–1918)* [Youthful works], by György Lukács, ed. Árpád Timár (Budapest: Magvető, 1977), 424, 434. See Frigyesi, *Béla Bartók*, p. 164.

85. *Béla Bartók Letters*, ed. János Demény (New York: St. Martin's Press, 1971), Eng. trans. Peter Balabán and István Farkas. Trans. rev. Elizabeth West and Colin Mason (London: Faber & Faber; Budapest: Corvina Press, 1971), p. 87.

86. Frigyesi, *Béla Bartók*, p. 229.

87. Theodor W. Adorno, *Philosophy of Modern Music*, trans. Anne G. Mitchell and Wesley V. Blomster (New York: Seabury Press, 1973), pp. 155–156.

88. See Bartók's letter to Stefi Geyer (20 August 1907), in *Béla Bartók: Briefe an Stefi Geyer, 1907–1908*, ed. Paul Sacher, German trans. Lajos Nyikos (Basle: Privatdruck Ltd., 1979).

89. See Leafstedt, *Inside Bluebeard's Castle*, p. 185.

90. Ibid., p. 162.

91. Ibid., p. 46.

92. Susan McClary, in *Feminine Endings: Music, Gender, and Sexuality* (Minneapolis: University of Minnesota Press, 1991), p. 3, suggests that the conflict between Judith and Bluebeard is fueled by Bluebeard's self-serving patriarchal demands and Judith's inability to submit to them.

93. Claire Kahane, "The Woman with a Knife and a Chicken without a Head: Fantasms of Rage and Emptiness," in *Psychoanalyses/Feminisms*, ed. Peter L. Rudnytsky and Andrew M. Gordon (Albany: State University of New York Press, 2000), p. 184. For Irigaray, see *The Speculum of the Other Woman*, trans. Gillian C. Gill (Ithaca, N.Y.: Cornell University Press, 1985), p. 42.

94. J. Whitebook, "Reflections on the Autonomous Individual and Decentered Subject," *American Imago* 49 (1992): 97–116.

95. See Otto Kernberg, *Borderline Conditions and Pathological Narcissism* (New York: Jason Aronson, 1975), p. 282.

96. Benjamin, in *The Bonds of Love*, p. 221, suggests that the notion of an autonomous person denies the mutual dependency between men and women. Acknowledgment of mutual dependency and recognition suggests an alternative to either submission or domination in gender relationships.

97. Lukács, "Diaries, 27–28 April 1910," in Mary Gluck, *Georg Lukács and His Generation, 1900–1918* (Cambridge, Mass: Harvard University Press, 1985), p. 126.

98. Letter from Lukács to Irma Seidler (22 March 1910), in Gluck, *Georg Lukács*, p. 127. Kadarkay notes that Lukács sent Irma an inscribed copy of *Soul and Form* and a copy of a book celebrating erotic love through Balázs who visited Lukács in Florence in April 1911, one month prior to Irma's suicide. Kadarkay suggests that Lukács's gifts were "a prelude to tragedy" because they may have inadvertently led to Balázs's involvement with Irma and to her suicide (p. 118).

99. See Agnes Heller, *Lukács Revalued* (Oxford: Basil Blackwell, 1983), p. 30.

100. See Balázs, "Baratsag," in *Csend* (Budapest: Magvető, 1985), p. 223, cited by Kadarkay, in *Georg Lukács, Life, Thought and Politics*, p. 127.

101. Zsuffa, *Béla Balázs*, p. 44. Kadarkay refers to the close association of the protagonists of the play to Lukács, Balázs and Seidler. He also refers to Lukács's indictment of Balázs's responsibility for Irma's death in Lukács's essay, "The Judgment"; see Kadarkay, *Georg Lukács*, p. 122.

102. Kadarkay, *Georg Lukács*, p. 132.

103. See ibid., p.131 (Béla Balázs to Lukács, 21 June 1915, LAK [Philosophical Institute of the Hungarian Academy of Sciences, Lukács Archive and Library], Budapest). Although the incident that is alluded to in this letter as well as Irma's suicide occurred after Balázs wrote the *Bluebeard* play, his pattern of casual and reckless involvement with women preceded the writing of the play.

104. Kadarkay refers to Lukács's use of the Hungarian folk-ballad, Kőműves Kelemen, in which the masons entomb a woman alive in a castle they are building because they believe human blood is stronger than cement (p. 129).

105. See Kahane, "The Woman with a Knife," p. 183.

106. Ernest Wolf, *Treating the Self* (New York: Guilford Press, 1988), p. 185.

107. See Jeremy Tambling, *Opera and the Culture of Fascism* (Oxford: Clarendon Press, 1996), p. 23. Tambling suggests that this dark side of modernism has been credited with the arousal of fascism. The liberal bourgeois was willing to give up the rational values of the Enlightenment for national unity. Accordingly, fascism is viewed as a refusal to accept the contradictions and uncertainties of modernity, which may be expressed in a sense of entitlement for spontaneous action without regard for established norms of human behavior.

108. Heinz Kohut, *How does Analysis cure?* ed. Arnold Goldberg (Chicago: University of Chicago Press, 1984), pp. 65–66.

109. Julia Kristeva, *Powers of Horror: An Essay on Abjection*, trans. Leon Roudiez (New York: Columbia University Press, 1982), pp. 1–9.

110. Benjamin, *Bonds of Love*, p. 82.

111. Ibid., p. 197, Benjamin suggests that Western society maintains the myth of autonomy and individuality by rejecting the person's needs for dependency and mutual recognition, which are first nurtured in the mother-child relationship. Benjamin suggests that the split between private life, where nurturance functions are provided by women, and public life, where men can then compete with other "autonomous beings" like themselves, contributes to the creation of the public world "as a place in which direct recognition and care for the needs of others is impossible—and this is tolerable as long as the private world [nurtured by women] cooperates."

4. *Pelléas et Mélisande: Polarity of Characterizations*

1. Early on in my research for this study, I formulated associations of the principles of symmetry and asymmetry to the psychological spheres of the unconscious (fate) and conscious, respectively, and extended these associations to the basic properties of symmetry and asymmetry in Debussy's and Bartók's musical language, as manifested in their operas. I am thankful to my wife for having brought to my attention the similarities between my formulations and Matte Blanco's identification of symmetry versus asymmetry as characteristics of conscious versus unconscious, respectively. See Ignacio Matte Blanco, *The Unconscious as Infinite Sets: An Essay in Bi-Logic* (London: Duckworth, 1975), p. 106.

2. See George Perle, *Serial Composition and Atonality* (6th ed., rev., Berkeley: University of California Press, 1991), p. 26.

3. On 17 May 1893, the day of the first performance of the original Maeterlinck play, *L'Echo de Paris* made a perceptive analogy of the play to painting, stating (with pejorative intention) that it "is not at all designed for the stage, [but] for the medium of painted canvas," as quoted in Marcel Dietschy, *A Portrait of Claude Debussy*, ed. and trans. William Ashbrook and Margaret G. Cobb (Oxford: Clarendon Press, 1990; original French publication, Neuchâtel, Suisse: Editions de la Baconnière, 1962), p. 80. This statement about the play may well be applied to the mood of Debussy's perceptive operatic setting.

4. Maurice Emmanuel, *Pelléas et Mélisande de Claude Debussy: Étude et Analyse* (Paris: Éditions Mellottée, 1926; 2nd ed., 1950), p. 36.

5. See Emmanuel, *"Pelléas et Mélisande,"* original French text of October, 1889: "Je rêve de poèmes qui ne me condamnent pas à perpétrer des actes longs, pesants; qui me fournissent des scènes mobiles, diverses par les lieux et le caractère; où les personnages ne discutent pas, mais subissent la vie et le sort."

6. Boulez, *"Pelléas* Reflected," in notes for the recording, *Boulez Conducts Debussy: "Pelléas et Mélisande,"* CBS M3 30119 (New York: CBS, 1970).

7. See also Debussy's note, "Why I Wrote *Pelléas*" (April 1902), in *Monsieur Croche et autres écrits* (Paris: Editions Gallimard, 1971); see the translation, *Debussy on Music: The Critical Writings of the Great Composer*, ed. François Lesure, trans. and ed. Richard Langham Smith (New York: Alfred A. Knopf; Ithaca, N.Y., 1977: Cornell University Press, 1977), p. 74.

8. "C'est pourquoi il n'y a pas de 'fil conducteur' dans Pelléas et que les personnages n'y subissent pas l'esclavage du 'leit-motive"; the entire original letter is reproduced in Roger Nichols and Richard Langham Smith, *Claude Debussy: "Pelléas et Mélisande"* (Cambridge: Cambridge University Press, 1989), pp. 184–185. See also Debussy's attack on what he considered to be Wagner's obsessive use of the leitmotif, in *Debussy on Music*, trans. Smith, p. 203.

9. See Adolphe Julien, *"Pelléas et Mélisande,"* *Le Théâtre* 84 (June 1902): 144, for handwritten evidence of Debussy's use of specific character motifs.

10. Subheadings in the following discussion are intended to draw attention to the local structural role of the main leitmotifs.

11. Jules Emile van Ackere, *"Pelléas et Mélisande" ou la rencontre miraculeuse d'une poésie et d'une musique* (Bruxelles: Les Editions de la Librairie Encyclopedique, 1952), p. 22. One may perhaps agree with Ackere (p. 44) that, because of these musical characteristics, it is difficult to assign precise meanings to the leitmotifs in *Pelléas*. Such ambiguity has led to different interpretations by scholars in their analyses of the opera. These divergences in interpretation will be cited and evaluated at the appropriate points in this study.

12. See Debussy, "Why I Wrote *Pelléas*," in *Debussy on Music*, p. 74.

13. See Richard Langham Smith, "Motives and Symbols," in *Claude Debussy: "Pelléas et Mélisande,"* p. 85.

14. Maurice Maeterlinck, "On Women," *The Treasure of the Humble*, trans. Alfred Sutro (New York: Dodd, Mead; London: George Allen, Ruskin House, 1902), p. 85.

15. For these and other convincing assignments of the basic motifs of the opera, see Lawrence Gilman, *Debussy's "Pelléas et Mélisande": A Guide to the Opera* (New York: Schirmer, 1907). Gilman's motivic designations are adhered to throughout the present study. Other detailed surveys of Debussy's motifs are given, for instance, by Emmanuel, in *Pelléas et Mélisande*, pp. 95–210, and Mary Jeanne van Appledorn, "A Stylistic Study of Claude Debussy's Opera *Pelléas et Mélisande*" (Ph.D. dissertation, University of Rochester, Eastman School of Music, 1966), pp. 407–434.

16. Cited page and measure numbers in the present study refer to the reprint edition (New York: Edwin F. Kalmus, n.d.) of the 1907 publication of the piano-vocal score, which is used for practical reasons of availability. One should also keep on hand the orchestral-vocal score of the opera (New York: Dover Publications, 1985) to facilitate the analytical references to instrumentation. David Grayson points out, in *The Genesis of Debussy's "Pelléas et Mélisande"* (Ann Arbor: UMI Research Press, 1986), p. 199 ff., that "the opera's complex publication history has considerably complicated the task of determining which score is the most authoritative source for the vocal parts. . . . The question is crucial here in order simply to determine for any given passage which of two divergent readings represents the original and which, the revision. The issue cannot just be settled by the chronology of publication dates." One might add that this question extends beyond the vocal parts of the various publications. Comparison of the various published editions of the vocal score (1902, 1905 rev., and 1907) and the full orchestral score (1904) reveals differences in the area of enharmonic pitch spellings, among others.

17. See Gilman, *Debussy's "Pelléas et Mélisande": A Guide to the Opera*, p. 58.

18. Emmanuel, *Pelléas et Mélisande*, pp. 135–136, in which this motif is associated with both Fate and Golaud, whereas Arthur B. Wenk, in *Claude Debussy and Twentieth-Century Music* (Boston: Twayne, 1983), pp. 38–39 (especially example 10), identifies the motif with Golaud, its altered form with the wedding ring that Golaud will give to Mélisande.

19. Grayson, *The Genesis of Debussy's "Pelléas et Mélisande,"* pp. 235–236; see also his exx. 2b and 3, the original and the new "Golaud" motifs, respectively.

20. Smith, "Motives and Symbols," p. 95.

21. The English translation of the opera's French libretto, which is based on the original Maeterlinck play, is that of Jean-Claude Poyet, translation Decca 1991 (Orchestre symphonique de Montréal, directed by Charles Dutoit). This literal translation is used in this study more for purposes of music-text analysis than for its poetic value. In contrast, the English translation given in the Kalmus piano-vocal score edition, cited above, is not used here because it does not provide a direct literal translation of the Maeterlinck text, but rather a more poetic approach designed to capture the atmosphere if not the precise meaning of Maeterlinck's lines. This "singing" translation is also designed to facilitate vocal performance.

22. See Perle's statement regarding symmetrical formations, in *Serial Composition and Atonality*, in n. 1.

23. René Terrasson, *"Pelléas et Mélisande," ou l'initiation* (Paris, 1982), p. 25.

24. See Nichols, "Synopsis," in *Claude Debussy*, p. 66.

25. See chap. 3, on "Trauma."

26. See Adorno, *Philosophy of Modern Music*, p. 156, as was cited in chap. 1.

27. According to Pasler, in "*Pelléas* and Power," p. 147, most of Debussy's supporters and friends were pro-Dreyfus and many of them in their published articles had protested Dreyfus's imprisonment, although Debussy himself held a neutral position on the matter.

28. Roger Shattuck, *The Banquet Years: The Origins of the Avant-Garde in France, 1885 to World War I* (New York: Vintage Books, 1955; rev. ed. 1968), pp. 3–4.

29. At the time of the first performance of *Pelléas*, Debussy's handwritten comment, which referred to this theme as it appeared at the opening of act 1, scene 3, was published with the corresponding musical excerpt in Julien, "Théâtre," p. 11. Furthermore, a Debussy letter printed in *The Daily Telegraph* of London, which was later published in his obituary, in "The Curtain Falls on Claude Debussy," *The New York Times* (May 5, 1918), part 4, p. 7, confirms the association of this theme with Mélisande: "the motive which accompanies 'Mélisande' is never altered . . . because, in reality, Mélisande is always unchanged in herself, and dies without any one . . . ever having understood her." See the reprint of the complete letter in Grayson, *The Genesis of Debussy's "Pelléas et Mélisande,"* p. 231.

30. Claude Debussy, *Segalen et Debussy*, ed. Annie Joly-Segalen and André Schaeffner (Monaco, 1961), p. 107.

31. See Stefan Jarocinski, "Quelques aspects de l'univers sonore de Debussy," in *Debussy et l'evolution de la musique au XXe siècle*, ed. Edith Weber (Paris, 1965), p. 168.

32. Wenk, *Claude Debussy*, p. 44, table 3.

33. The term "French sixth" chord and other such traditional designations in this discussion are to be understood only as convenient labels, as such traditional chord constructions are nonfunctional in this context.

34. Based on the following assignment of numbers to pitch-classes—C = 0, C♯ = 1, D = 2, E♭ = 3, and so on—we will refer to the whole-tone cycle containing pitch-class C as "WT-0," and the other whole-tone cycle containing pitch-class C♯ as "WT-1."

35. George Perle argues in *Serial Composition and Atonality* (6th ed., rev., Berkeley: University of California Press, 1991), p. 26, that "Because of its self-evident structure [a symmetrical] chord tends to have a somewhat stable character."

36. Maeterlinck, "On Women," pp. 83–84.

37. Wenk, in *Claude Debussy*, pp. 40–41, refers to this and several other dominant-tonic (perfect-cadence) resolutions associated with moments of "intimacy: approaching, touching, joining hands."

38. Wenk, in *Claude Debussy*, p. 37, points to Maeterlinck's use of "water, blindness, hair, and cold, as recurring symbols in a drama whose basic premise is the futility of human action in the face of implacable destiny."

39. Carl G. Jung, "Marriage as a Psychological Relationship," *The Portable Jung*, ed. Joseph Campbell (New York: The Viking Press), p. 165.

40. Henry Prunière, "A la Villa Médicis," *La Revue Musicale* 7 (1926): 23–42.

41. Wenk, *Claude Debussy*, p. 39.

42. See "Duke Bluebeard's Castle, Notes on the Text by Béla Balázs, Circa 1915," English translation by Carl Leafstedt from the Hungarian translation (for inclusion in Balázs, *Balázs Béla: Válogatott cikkek*, 34–37) of the original German, in Carl Leafstedt, *Inside Bluebeard's Castle: Music and Drama in Béla Bartók's Opera* (New York: Oxford University Press, 1999), p. 202.

43. See Nichols, "Synopsis," *Claude Debussy*, p. 64 ff.

44. W. D. Hall, *Maurice Maeterlinck: A Study of His Life and Thought* (Oxford: Clarendon Press, 1960), p. 38.

45. Ibid., p. 38.

46. The "Well scene" is discussed more thoroughly later.

47. See Maeterlinck, "The Star," *The Treasure of the Humble*, trans. Alfred Sutro (New York: Dodd, Mead; London: George Allen, Ruskin House, 1902), p. 141. Originally published in French as *Le Trésor des Humbles* (1897).

48. Introduction (p. 25), A (p. 26, m. 1), B (p. 26, m. 5), A' (p. 27, m. 5), B' (p. 27, m. 9 ff.).

49. Smith, "Tonalities of Darkness and Light," *Claude Debussy: "Pelléas et Mélisande,"* p. 108.

50. Maeterlinck, "The Pre-Destined," in *The Treasure of the Humble*, p. 48.

51. Maeterlinck, "Mystic Morality," in *The Treasure of the Humble*, p. 61.

52. See the discussion in chap. 5 regarding the symbolic association of the flute timbre with Pelléas throughout much of the opera and with the image of Pan in mythology, a god of the Greeks and Romans who became a symbol of pastoral love and music.

53. Maeterlinck, "Mystic Morality," in *The Treasure of the Humble*, p. 62.

54. Smith, "Tonalities of Darkness and Light," *Claude Debussy, Pelléas et Mélisande*, p. 109. Smith also points out that in a rejected fourth scene, which exists complete in manuscript form at the Pierpont Morgan Library in New York, this tendency was further manifested as Arkel, Pelléas, and Geneviève wait in the darkness of night for a ship to arrive.

55. Maeterlinck, "The Tragical in Daily Life," in *The Treasure of the Humble*, pp. 111–112.

56. Wenk, *Claude Debussy*, p. 40.

57. Ibid.

5. Pelléas et Mélisande: Fate and the Unconscious

1. Arnold Schoenberg, "The Whole-Tone Scale and Related Five- and Six-Part Chords," in *Theory of Harmony* (originally published as *Harmonielehre*, 1911), trans. Roy E. Carter (Berkeley: University of California Press, 1978), p. 390 ff. Speculative as well as practical theorists had also begun serious explorations of symmetrical pitch constructions as the basis for expanding compositional techniques. Among the most notable were the German theorists Bernard Ziehn, Georg Capellen, and Hermann Schroeder, all of whom were concerned specifically with procedures of symmetrical inversion, as discussed by David Bernstein, in "Symmetry and Symmetrical Inversion in Turn-of-the-Century Theory and Practice," paper given at a national meeting of the American Musicological Society (Baltimore, 3 November 1988).

2. Schoenberg assumes, in *Theory of Harmony*, p. 393, that it was in *Pelléas et Mélisande* that Debussy first used the whole-tone scale, but as the translator points out (p. 393, n. 1), Debussy had already employed it in works of the early 1890s. Although Schoenberg assumes Franz Liszt to have been the first to use the whole-tone scale (p. 390), there is evidence for whole-tone root progressions of triads in the music of Schubert, Glinka, and others of the early nineteenth century (see chap. 2, n. 9). One prominent example, as referred to by Felix Salzer and Carl Schachter in *Counterpoint in Composition: The Study of Voice Leading* (New York: McGraw-Hill, 1969), ex. 7-71 and ex. 7-71a, occurs in the "Sanctus" of Schubert's *Mass in E-Flat*, in which the initial E♭ tonic moves to the dominant at the end of the excerpt through a series of descending major thirds, E♭–C♭–(B)–G–E♭. By means of passing whole tones within the major thirds, a complete whole-tone scale is outlined in the bass. Certain more unusual adumbrations of the whole-tone scale are observed, by Philip Friedheim, in "Radical Harmonic Procedures in Berlioz," *Music Review* 21/4 (November 1960): 286, in such works as the *Francs-Juges* Overture (1827) of Berlioz, in which two chromatic scales (interval-1 cycles) ascend in parallel minor-thirds against both whole-tone scales (interval-2 cycles) that descend in parallel minor-thirds. The harmonic result is a series based on reiterations of the three diminished seventh chords (interval-3 cycles), this progression preventing any clear sense of tonal orientation.

3. Schoenberg, *Theory of Harmony*, p. 393.

4. Ibid., p. 397.

5. In the present piano-vocal score edition, this free translation of "l'hiver" as "ice" rather than "winter" conceals a fundamental symbolic connection between the well and Mélisande's ultimate fate. This symbolism is elaborated in the following paragraph.

6. Maeterlinck, "The Star," in *The Treasure of the Humble*, trans. Alfred Sutro (New York: Dodd, Mead; London: George Allen, Ruskin House, 1902), p. 141.

7. Arthur B. Wenk, *Claude Debussy and Twentieth-Century Music* (Boston, Mass.: Twayne, 1983), pp. 43–44.

8. Ibid., p. 44.

9. These symbolically related events are discussed in more detail in chap. 6.

10. Wenk, *Claude Debussy*, p. 44.

11. "Animal magnetism," is a treatment method developed by Franz Anton Mesmer (1734–1815), a student of philosophy and law who changed his interests to medicine. He completed his medical studies in Vienna in 1766. Mesmer's doctoral thesis studied the influence of planets on human diseases. He postulated that a fluid permeates the universe and connects everything, inanimate bodies as well as living beings. Disease was caused by an unequal distribution of this fluid and Mesmer used magnets and electrical devises to treat his patients in order to correct their imbalance. Mesmer discovered the importance of having rapport with the patient and realized that the personal power of the magnetizer was instrumental in promoting healing, hence the name "animal magnetism." Many practitioners of "animal magnetism" created altered states of consciousness in their patients and kept records of their findings that pioneered the scientific study of hypnosis, or mesmerism. See Henri F. Ellenberger, *The Discovery of the Unconscious: The History and Evolution of Dynamic Psychiatry* (New York: Basic Books, 1970), pp. 57–77.

12. Ellenberger, in *The Discovery of the Unconscious*, p. 77, refers to Pierre Janet's observations that some practitioners of animal magnetism were not trained physicians and used the techniques without appropriate care.

13. Peter Giovacchini, *A Clinician's Guide to Reading Freud* (New York: Jason Aronson, 1982), p. 3.

14. See the short introduction to Sigmund Freud, "A Note on the Concept of the Unconscious in Psychoanalysis [1912]," *Standard Edition*, vol. 12 (London: Hogarth Press, 1958), pp. 255–267.

15. Giovacchini, *A Clinician's Guide*, pp. 3–4.

16. Freud hypothesizes, in "Beyond the Pleasure Principle," *A General Selection from the Works of Sigmund Freud*, ed. John Rickman, M.D. (Garden City, N.Y.: Doubleday, 1957), p. 158, that "*an instinct would be a tendency innate in living organic matter impelling it towards the reinstatement of an earlier condition* [italics are Freud's], one which it had to abandon under the influence of external disturbing forces—a kind of organic elasticity, or, to put it another way, the manifestation of inertia in organic life." In the case of Pelléas, then, the notion of fate (equivalent to the unconscious) is an overriding factor, since there are no external forces strong enough to disturb, or divert the internal instinctual force from moving toward the inanimate condition, which was there before the animate. In other words, Pelléas cannot and does not struggle against destiny, that is, he cannot struggle against "the reinstatement of an earlier condition." This is due, as Freud points out, to the "expression of the conservative nature of living beings."

17. Maeterlinck, "The Star," p. 131.

18. For additional psychological interpretations, see chap. 3.

19. Freud, "Beyond the Pleasure Principle," p. 150.

20. Whole-tone transformations of complete dominant ninths in this crucial scene will be discussed later in more depth.

21. Mélisande's hair becomes the primary object of act 3, scene 1 (p. 127 ff.), which is the most seductive, sensual scene of the opera.

22. See Wenk, *Claude Debussy*, p. 44.

23. Maeterlinck, "On Women," *The Treasure of the Humble*, p. 84.

24. We also learn from the next scene (p. 77) that Golaud had fallen from his horse at noon, precisely the moment that Mélisande's ring had fallen into the well. The beast that Golaud was hunting was thus set free by Golaud's accident.

25. See Ignacio Matte-Blanco, *The Unconscious as Infinite Sets: An Essay in Bi-Logic* (London: Duckworth, 1975), pp. 160–61.

26. Maeterlinck, "On Women," p. 82.

27. Ibid., pp. 83–84.

28. We know this from Maeterlinck's *Ariane et Barbe-bleue*.

29. Maurice Denis, *Henri Lerolle et ses amis* (Paris, 1932), p. 32.

30. Maeterlinck, "The Star," p. 128.

31. *Debussy Letters*, eds. François Lesure and Roger Nichols, trans. Roger Nichols (Cambridge, Mass.: Harvard University Press, 1987), p. 62; originally published as *Claude Debussy: Lettres, 1884–1918* (Paris: Hermann, 1980).

32. Maeterlinck, "The Deeper Life," pp. 195–196.

33. Maeterlinck, "On Women," p. 78.

34. Maeterlinck, "The Pre-Destined," p. 51.

35. It is also significant that this reiterated note (D) is the opening tonic note of the opera.

36. According to Debussy's close friend, G. Jean-Aubry, the musical ideas of the Symbolist Jules Laforgue, poet of *Pan et la Syrinx*, were considered essential to Debussy's aesthetics. See *Debussy on Music: The Critical Writings of the Great Composer*, ed. François Lesure, trans. and ed. Richard Langham Smith (New York: Knopf, 1977; Ithaca, N.Y.: Cornell University Press, 1977) pp. 97–98, n. 1.

37. It is striking that in the legends of Pan and Mélusine, both creatures are half-human and half-animal. By means of symbolical association with these legends, one could assume that physical consummation of the love between Pelléas and Mélisande does not occur.

38. Giovacchini, in *A Narrative Textbook*, p. 17, refers to the laws of the unconscious (as opposed to the laws that govern coherent, rational thought), according to which everything has a purpose.

39. Lawrence Kramer, *Music as Cultural Practice, 1800–1900* (Berkeley: University of California Press, 1990), p. 22 ff. See also Smith, "Tonalities of Darkness and Light," chap. 5.

40. Kramer, *Music as Cultural Practice*, p. 30.

6. *Pelléas et Mélisande: Musico-Dramatic Turning Point*

1. David Grayson, "Waiting for Golaud: The Concept of Time in *Pelléas*," in *Debussy Studies*, ed. Richard Langham Smith (Cambridge: Cambridge University Press, 1997), p. 37.

2. There is evidence that such associations may sometimes be produced inadvertently on the part of the composer. Grayson discusses (in ibid.) the "modern concept of the 'free play of signifiers'" which, in one case in Debussy's setting (in act 3, scene 3: exit of the vaults) resulted from "an 'accident' of the compositional process." A motif accompanying one of the lines in the final passage of the play that was eventually cut from the opera was retained in the following interlude, so the motif was left without its original dramatic reference. Grayson points out that

"As a result, the motive appears in the opera without its dramatic *raison d'être:* the reverberation of a sentiment that has been left unexpressed. Once again, the key to unlocking the mystery has been shrouded in silence." Thus, the compositional "accident" itself evokes a symbolic meaning for the motif which, incidentally, "was not part of the original draft but was added, both within the scene and in the interlude, as a revision." In any case, the final form of the opera is, to use a truism, the composer's final decision, so that all elements become part of the symbolic message as they stand and must be considered as such.

3. Maurice Maeterlinck, "Cross Correspondence," in *Our Eternity,* trans. Alexander Teixeira de Mattos (New York: Dodd, Mead, 1913), p. 142.

4. Ibid., p. 135.

5. According to Sir William Crookes, in his article in the *Quarterly Journal of Science* (1874), as quoted by Maeterlinck, "Cross Correspondence," p. 142, "The difference between the advocates of Psychic Force and the Spiritualists consists in this—we contend that there is as yet insufficient proof of any other directing agent than the Intelligence of the Medium, and no proof whatever of the agency of Spirits of the Dead. . . . Thus the controversy resolves itself into a pure question of *fact,* only to be determined by a laborious and long-continued series of experiments and an extensive collection of psychological facts."

6. Maeterlinck, "Cross Correspondence," p. 144–145.

7. Arthur B. Wenk, in *Claude Debussy and Twentieth-Century Music* (Boston: Twayne, 1983), p. 42, asserts that "The harmonic blankness of the whole-tone scale renders it particularly appropriate to represent fear, confusion, dread, all of which convey a certain paralysis and immobility." Wenk demonstrates that Debussy's use of pedal points plays a similar role in creating a sense of staticism in connection with appropriate situations. Pedal points are used to reflect entrapment or a sense of imprisonment: Golaud pinned beneath his horse (act 2), Mélisande's hair caught in the branches (act 3), Yniold's complaint about the immovable rock (act 4), symbolization of the stagnant water in the castle vaults, and so on. Wenk also significantly identifies Debussy's use of pedal in connection with the "immobility of waiting," as when Arkel refers to fate (act 1), when Pelléas and Mélisande wait for Golaud's fatal attack on them (act 4), and when the characters face the immobility of death—tremolo pedal at Pelléas's violent death (act 4) and quiet pedal at Mélisande's peaceful death (act 5).

8. Béla Bartók, "Harvard Lectures," in *Béla Bartók Essays,* ed. Benjamin Suchoff (New York: St. Martin's Press, 1976), pp. 379–381.

9. Although D moves up to D♯ at these two cadential points in the arabesque, the D♯, which is prominent in the "Night" motif and its cadence, is replaced in the recitative by the pentatonic note D, so a descent is suggested on the more background level. In the dotted-quarter ostinato of the ritournelle that punctuates Pelléas's appearance (p. 117, mm. 6–7), we get a foreground-level manifestation of these relations (in enharmonic spelling, D♯–Cx–C♯).

10. Wenk, *Claude Debussy,* p. 41.

11. Wenk, *Claude Debussy,* pp. 41–42.

12. Smith, "Tonalities of Darkness and light," p. 112.

13. Maurice Maeterlinck, "The Deeper Life," in *The Treasure of the Humble,* trans. Alfred Sutro (New York: Dodd, Mead; London: George Allen, Ruskin House, 1902), p. 180.

14. Debussy, "Why I wrote Pelléas," (April 1902), originally in *Monsieur Croche et autres écrits* (Paris: Editions Gallimard, 1971; see the translation, Lesure, ed., *Debussy on Music,* p. 75.

15. Debussy, "Pelléas et Mélisande: A Reply to the Critics (Interview by Robert de Flers)," *Le Figaro* (May 16, 1902); in *Debussy on Music,* pp. 79–80.

16. See Kramer's conception of "expressive doublings," in *Music as Cultural Practice 1800–1900* (Berkeley: University of California Press, 1990), p. 22 ff., as discussed in chap. 5.

17. Wenk, *Claude Debussy,* p. 42.

18. In an interview, published in *Cahiers Debussy*, Bulletin du Centre de Documentation Claude Debussy, no. 1 (Geneva: Editions Minkoff, 1974), Debussy contrasts Edgar Allen Poe with Maeterlinck, which brings to our attention Debussy's plans for two unrealized operas on the tales of Poe. It is known that Maeterlinck was significantly influenced by Poe, and in the present scene in the underground vaults of the castle, the mood of horror also may reveal to us, as suggested in Lesure, ed., *Debussy on Music*, Smith, p. 222, "how the tales of Poe entered an area of Debussy's imagination close to that of Pelléas."

19. Wenk, *Claude Debussy*, p. 44.

20. Ibid.

21. Ibid., p. 45.

7. Pelléas et Mélisande: Mélisande as Christ Symbol

1. Unconscious forces that appear to lie at the heart of Pelléas's dilemma are discussed in connection with other events in the opera.

2. Marcellus is also one of those men who has the capacity to foresee events (for instance, the exact day of his own death) like Pelléas's father, who foresees his son's impending death.

3. Maeterlinck, "The Pre-Destined," in *The Treasure of the Humble*, trans. Alfred Sutro (New York: Dodd, Mead; London: George Allen, Ruskin House, 1902), pp. 51–52.

4. For a discussion of this instrumental timbre in accord with its contextual and symbolic association with Pelléas, like the syrinx (or panpipe) of Pan, see chap. 5.

5. Richard Langham Smith, "Tonalities of Darkness and Light," Roger Nichols and Richard Langham Smith, *Claude Debussy: "Pelléas et Mélisande"* (Cambridge: Cambridge University Press, 1989), p. 113.

6. Ibid., p. 128, ex. 14.

7. In the Bible, David sends Absalom, his favorite son, to his death for rebelling against his father. In the context of the present action, we may perhaps interpret this as a symbol of God sending Jesus, his favorite son, to his death at the crucifixion.

8. Wenk, *Claude Debussy*, p. 44.

9. Ibid.

10. Maeterlinck, "The Deeper Life," in *The Treasure of the Humble*, trans. Alfred Sutro (New York: Dodd, Mead; London: George Allen, Ruskin House, 1902), pp. 185–186.

11. Roy Howat, *Debussy in Proportion: A Musical Analysis* (Cambridge: Cambridge University Press, 1983), p. 164.

12. Ernő Lendvai, in *Béla Bartók: An Analysis of his Music* (London: Kahn and Averill, 1971), pp. 17–34, was the first to discover in works of Bartók formal proportions that belong either to the Golden Section system or the Fibonacci series (0, 1, 1, 2, 3, 5, 8, 13, 21, 34, 55, 89, . . .). The Golden Section formula is approximated in this series. In the Fibonacci series the largest of any three adjacent numbers is the sum of the two smaller ones. In the Golden Section system, the division of a given distance is such that the proportion of the whole length to the larger section geometrically corresponds to the proportion of the larger to the smaller section. The larger section (x) is .618 (ad inf.) of the entire length (1), and so the complementary smaller section (1 - x) is .382 (ad inf.). The larger section is the geometric mean of the whole and the smaller section. It follows that the specific Golden Section proportions of a given whole can be arrived at simply by multiplying the whole either by its larger section, x (= .618), or its smaller one, 1 - x (= .382). Thus, 1316 x .618 = 813.288, while 1316 x .382 = 502.712, which are almost the exact proportions of Debussy's Scene 4, as demonstrated by Howat, in ibid.

13. Howat, in *Debussy in Proportion*, p. 156, also points out that this was the first scene of the opera set by Debussy.

14. Maeterlinck, "The Deeper Life," pp. 180–181.

15. Wenk, *Claude Debussy*, p. 44.

16. Smith, "Tonalities of Darkness and Light," p. 114.

17. In ibid., p. 115 ff., Smith also provides many other pertinent manifestations of this tonal symbolism.

18. In ibid., p. 122, Smith identifies C major as well as the triplet figuration with darkness, as in the Grotto, in contrast to F♯ major. He also points to the octatonic scale as a means of exploiting the false-relation clash of combined major and minor and the light/dark duality of Lydian and Phrygian modes.

19. Ibid., pp. 131–132.

20. In ibid., pp. 130–132, Smith identifies the Lydian mode (i.e., with its sharp character) with "light" and "ecstasy," in contrast to the Phrygian mode and the more compressed octatonic scale, both identified with "darkness."

21. Wenk, *Claude Debussy*, p. 44.

22. Smith, "Tonalities of Darkness and Light," p. 131.

8. *Pelléas et Mélisande: Circuity of Fate*

1. Richard Langham Smith, "Tonalities of Darkness and Light," in Roger Nichols and Richard Langham Smith, *Claude Debussy: Pelléas et Mélisande* (Cambridge: Cambridge University Press, 1989), p. 122.

2. Maurice Maeterlinck, "The Foretelling of the Future," in *The Double Garden*, trans. Alexander Teixeira de Mattos (New York: Dodd, Mead, 1909), pp. 141–142.

3. Ibid., p. 143.

4. Ibid., pp. 142–143.

5. These principles of return accord with the more general concept of "circuity" in the play, as posited by David Grayson, in "Waiting for Golaud: The Concept of Time in Pelléas," *Debussy Studies*, ed. Richard Langham Smith (Cambridge: Cambridge University Press, 1997), p. 29 ff.

6. Arthur B. Wenk, in *Claude Debussy and Twentieth-Century Music* (Boston: Twayne Publishers, 1983), p. 44, associates the oboe with Mélisande's sadness.

7. The significance of this tonal relation will be addressed in more depth later. Suffice it to say at this point that the opera begins on D and ends on C♯, a long-range tonal relation which is essential to the opera's tonal symbolism.

8. These symbolic connections are developed in more detail by Grayson, in "Waiting for Golaud," pp. 29–30.

9. Wenk, *Claude Debussy*, pp. 47–50.

10. Smith, "Tonalities of Darkness and Light," p. 132 ff.

11. The musical importance of the C♯ major tonality is also discussed by Carolyn Abbate, in "Tristan in the composition of Pelléas," *Nineteenth-Century Music* 5 (1981): 117–141, in which she infers from the sketches for act 5 that the compositional process of this act "evolved backwards from the final cadence." Thus, as Smith also assumes, in "Tonalities of Darkness and Light," p. 136, "the 'goal' key of C♯ seems to have been clear in the composer's mind from the outset."

12. Grayson, "Waiting for Golaud," p. 29.

13. Henry J. Schmidt, *How Dramas End: Essays on the German "Sturm und Drang," Buchner, Hauptmann, and Fleisser* (Ann Arbor: University of Michigan Press, 1992), p. 19.

14. Edward Lockspeiser, *Debussy* (New York: McGraw-Hill, 1936; rev. J. M. Dent, 1963), pp. 209–210.

15. Such attempts are exemplified in the rhetorical symbolism of the German late Baroque aesthetic theory known as the *Affektenlehre*, or in the more ambiguous associations found in program music of the nineteenth century.

16. Wenk, *Claude Debussy and the Poets* (Berkeley: University of California Press, 1976), p. 274.

17. Ibid., p. 275.

9. Duke Bluebeard's Castle: Psychological Motivation

1. Theodor W. Adorno, *Philosophy of Modern Music*, trans. Anne G. Mitchell and Wesley V. Blomster (New York: Seabury Press, 1973), pp. 155–156, and the corresponding discussion in chap. 1.

2. The English translation of the original Hungarian text used in this study is that of Carl S. Leafstedt, "Music and Drama in Béla Bartók's Opera *Duke Bluebeard's Castle*" (Ph.D. dissertation, Harvard University, 1994), pp. 313–329. This translation is intended only for purposes of music-text analysis, and does not serve a poetic function. As pointed out by Leafstedt, p. 313, "Of the available published translations by Kallman, Davies, and others, none provides a direct, literal translation of the *Bluebeard* text. Theirs are more poetic translations, designed to capture the atmosphere if not the precise meaning of Balázs's portentous lines, and also to be sung to the eight-syllable rhythmic patterns of the Hungarian original."

The new Dover edition, first published in 2001, is an unabridged republication of *Herzog Blaubarts Burg (A kékszakállú herceg vára) / Oper in einem Akt von Béla Balázs / Musik von Béla Bartók, Op. 11 / Deutsche Übertragung von Wilhelm Ziegler*, originally published by Universal Edition A. G., Vienna, 1921. The piano-vocal score published by Universal Edition, 1921, renewed by Boosey and Hawkes, 1949, and the orchestral-vocal score published by Universal Edition, 1925, are both used as the basis of the musical discussions in the present study. In 1912, Kodály's wife, Emma Gruber, prepared the German translation of the Hungarian text in the piano-vocal score edition which, according to György Kroó, "Opera: Duke Bluebeard's Castle," *The Bartók Companion*, ed. Malcolm Gillies (London: Faber and Faber, 1993), p. 351, "was written into Bartók's autograph draft largely by Zoltán Kodály himself." The German translation of the orchestral-vocal score is by Wilhelm Ziegler. Rehearsal numbers are identical in these editions.

3. Judit Frigyesi, *Béla Bartók and Turn-of-the-Century Budapest* (Berkeley: University of California Press, 1998), pp. 227–228.

4. Joseph Zsuffa, *Béla Balázs: The Man and the Artist* (Berkeley: University of California Press, 1987), p. 13.

5. Ibid.

6. Zsuffa, in ibid., refers to Balázs's own diary notes as an important source for this personal information.

7. Béla Bartók Jr., "The Private Man," *The Bartók Companion*, ed. Malcolm Gillies (London: Faber and Faber, 1993): 18. A similar first-witness account is given by the composer/musicologist Paul A. Pisk, in Elliott Antokoletz, "A Survivor of the Vienna Schoenberg Circle: An Interview with Paul A. Pisk," *Tempo* 154 (September 1985): 20.

8. For a well-documented introduction to such a characterological study, see Bertalan Pethő, "Béla Bartók's Personality," *Studia Musicologica* 23 (1981): 443–458.

9. See *Béla Bartók: Briefe an Stefi Geyer, 1907–1908*, ed. Paul Sacher, German trans. Lajos Nyikos (Basle: Privatdruck Ltd., 1979), for the most extensive documentation of this relationship and of Bartók's innermost feelings and philosophical ideas (including his espousal of atheism and the principles of Nietzsche). In addition to the facsimiles of Bartók's letters and post-

cards, there is a poem, which appeared on the first page of the *First Violin Concerto*, op. posth. (begun in Jászberény, 1 July 1907, and completed in Budapest, 5 February 1908), entitled "My Confession for Stefi."

10. In ibid., introduction, p. 10, Lajos Nyikos refers to certain pessimistic notions of Bartók that were common to the era. These letters address, along with many other themes, Bartók's turn away from the Catholic Church and his criticism of the established morals of Hungarian bourgeois society in general.

11. Pethő, "Béla Bartók's Personality," p. 443.

12. Zoltán Kodály, *Visszatekintés: Összegyűjtött írások, beszédek, nyilatkozatok I–II* [Retrospection: collection of writings, speeches, statements], ed. Ferenc Bónis (Budapest: Zeneműkiadó, 1964), vol. 2, p. 443.

13. Pethő, "Béla Bartók's Personality," pp. 443–445.

14. Pál Gergely, *Bartók-emlékeim a Magyar Tudományos Akadémiáról*. [My Bartók Memories from the Hungarian Academy of the Sciences]. A Hungarológiai Intézet Tudományos Közleményei VI/19–20, Forum, Újvidék, 1974, pp. 257–264, See Kodály, *Visszatekintés*, vol. 2, p. 462.

15. *Bartók Béla levelei IV: Új dokumentumok* [Béla Bartók's Correspondence IV: new documents], ed. János Demény (Budapest: Zeneműkiadó Vállalat, 1971), p. 63.

16. *Bartók Béla levelei II: Magyar és külföldi dokumentumok (Az utolsó két év gyűjtése)* [Béla Bartók's Correspondence II: Hungarian and foreign documents (material collected during the last two years)], ed. János Demény (Budapest: Művelt Nép Könyvkiadó, 1951), p. 174.

17. B. Horváth, *Dürer "Melankólia" című metszetéről* [About Dürer's engraving "Melancholy"]. *Művészet* vol. 3 (1962), no. 11, pp. 4–8, vol. 4 (1963), no. 7, pp. 7–12, vol. 5 (1964), No. 3, pp. 6–10.

18. *Bartók Béla levelei II* (1951), p. 170.

19. *Béla Bartók Letters*, ed. János Demény (New York: St. Martin's Press, 1971), trans. Peter Balabán and István Farkas. Trans. rev. Elizabeth West and Colin Mason (London: Faber & Faber; Budapest: Corvina Press, 1971), p. 83.

20. Pethő points out, in "Béla Bartók's Personality," p. 445, that "Psychologically, the image of the melancholic type is completed by thriftiness and mania for collection. Both characteristics were very conspicuous in Bartók's mentality. Kodály wrote about Bartók as a folklorist that 'his mania for collection had reached such a high pitch that if it had aimed at money, he would have been a multi-millionaire long since" [Kodály, *Visszatekintés*, vol. 2, pp. 445–446]. He enthusiastically continued to enrich his collection of plants, beetles, butterflies and stones even at his adult age, he collected peasant embroidery, carvings, jugs, bowls, mis-directed envelopes and his interest in linguistics was also characterized by his being a collector."

21. Peter L. Giovacchini, M.D., *A Narrative Textbook of Psychoanalysis* (Northvale, N.J.: Jason Aronson, 1987), p. 323.

22. For systematic identification and description of the basic musical motifs of the opera, see Sándor Veress, "Bluebeard's Castle," in *Béla Bartók: A Memorial Review* (New York: Boosey and Hawkes, 1950): 45–49.

23. Veress, "Bluebeard's Castle," p. 53.

24. See n. 62 of this chapter.

25. Julian Grant, "A Foot in Bluebeard's Door," in *The Stage Works of Béla Bartók*, ed. Nicholas John (London: John Calder; New York: Riverrun Press, 1991), p. 26.

26. Grant, "A Foot in Bluebeard's Door," pp. 29–30.

27. Ibid., pp. 27–28.

28. Paul Banks, "Images of the Self: 'Duke Bluebeard's Castle,'" in *The Stage Works of Béla Bartók*, ed. Nicholas John (London: John Calder; New York: Riverrun Press, 1991), p. 10–11.

29. Veress, "Bluebeard's Castle," p. 38. For Frigyesi, in *Béla Bartók*, p. 228 (in accord with Veress's interpretation), the man's ambivalence toward his own secrets seeks its resolution in

Judith, whose "intrusion answers his need to be seen, and it is her blessed capacity to be able to see. As Bluebeard says to her, after having placed the first key into her hand: 'Blessed are thy hands, Judith'."

30. A thorough historical investigation of the name of Judith in both literary and artistic traditions is provided by Carl S. Leafstedt, *Inside Bluebeard's Castle: Music and Drama in Béla Bartók's Opera* (New York: Oxford University Press, 1999), esp. chap. 7, "Judith: The Significance of a Name"; see also Leafstedt, "Music and Drama" (Ph.D. diss.), chap. 3, "The figure of Judith in Early Twentieth-Century Art and Culture: The Significance of a Name." Several of the more salient points of his investigation are mentioned later.

31. Adorno, *Philosophy of Modern Music*, p. 156, describes "the overpoweringly intensified proportion in modern industrialism between the body of the individual and the things and forces in technical civilization."

32. Carl S. Leafstedt, "Music and Drama in Béla Bartók's Opera: *Duke Bluebeard's Castle*" (Ph.D. diss., Harvard University, 1994), p. 102.

33. Otto Weininger, *Geschlecht und Charakter* [Sex and Character] (London: William Heinemann, 1906), p. 236.

34. As the basis for understanding the characters' relation to the social structure, one may invoke certain principles relevant to Hegelian and Marxist dialectical concepts regarding the relative state of objects, for instance, as pertaining to the question of who we are and what we do as people. Do we change completely, partially, or not at all within a changing environment? See the discussion on Hegelian and Marxist dialectics by Michael Payne and M. A. R. Habbib in the introduction to Terry Eagleton, *The Significance of Theory* (Oxford: Blackwell, 1990), pp. 10–13. According to Debussy himself (see David Grayson, *The Genesis of Debussy's "Pelléas et Mélisande"* [Ann Arbor: UMI Research Press, 1986, 1983], p. 231), Mélisande retains certain immutable qualities (e.g., her own unique feelings as a woman) within the changing environment, and this seems to be true also for Judith, the relentless woman in the Bartók opera. These dialectical concepts are reconciled with the new awareness of the internal human level based on psychological motivation, that is, as interpreted in conjunction with the principles of Freudian psychoanalytical theory.

35. Frigyesi, *Béla Bartók*, p. 196.

36. Critical studies of the opera have been devoted almost entirely to the Bluebeard character, with little or no systematic attention given to that of Judith. A thorough historical investigation of the name of Judith in both literary and artistic traditions is provided by Leafstedt, in "Music and Drama in Béla Bartók's Opera," esp. chap. 3, "The figure of Judith in Early Twentieth-Century Art and Culture: The Significance of a Name." Several of the more salient points of his investigation are mentioned later. See also Leafstedt, *Inside Bluebeard's Castle: Music and Drama in Béla Bartók's Opera* (New York: Oxford University Press, 1999), pp. 185–199.

37. Leafstedt points out that, even today, the 1909 painting sometimes appears under the title of *Salome*, as in Carl Schorske's *Fin-de-Siècle Vienna: Politics and Culture* (New York: Vintage Books, 1981), p. 226, where it is referred to as "Salome (Judith II)." For a basic survey of the various Judith representations in art and literature before 1900, see Nadine Sine, "Cases of Mistaken Identity: Salome and Judith at the Turn of the Century," *German Studies Review* 11/1 (February 1988): 9–29. For a listing of other studies on Judith in nineteenth- and early twentieth-century paintings, see Leafstedt, *Inside Bluebeard's Castle*, p. 222, n. 2.

38. The mysterious role of the woman in Schoenberg's monodrama may be understood best by means of an autobiographical interpretation. Carl Schorske suggests, in *Fin-de-Siècle Vienna*, p. 226, a possible connection between Schoenberg's experience—his wife's affair with the young expressionist painter, Richard Gerstl, and Gerstl's suicide—and *Erwartung*.

39. See Bartók's letter of 15 August 1905 to Irmy Jurkovics, in *Béla Bartók Letters*, ed. Demény, p. 50.

40. See Bartók's letter of September 1907 to Stefi Geyer, *Béla Bartók Letters*, p. 83.

41. Frigyesi, *Béla Bartók*, p. 197.

42. Angelica Bäumer, *Gustav Klimt: Women* (London: Weidenfeld and Nicolson, 1986): 13.

43. These interactions are based almost exclusively on diatonic, whole-tone, and chromatic pitch-sets and their derivative subcollections or *intervallic cells*.

44. In the Hungarian folk music sources, the pentatonic scale always occurs in its (symmetrical) minor-mode form, as opposed to those permutations found, for instance, in Russian and Chinese sources; see Béla Bartók, *The Hungarian Folk Song*, ed. Benjamin Suchoff, trans. M. D. Calvocoressi (Albany: State University of New York Press, 1981), pp. 17–18.

45. Part of the following discussion of the relation between the semitonal "Blood" motif and the diatonic sphere is derived from Elliott Antokoletz, *The Music of Béla Bartók: A Study of Tonality and Progression in Twentieth-Century Music* (Berkeley: University of California Press, 1984), pp. 89–93, and also "Bartók's *Bluebeard*: The Sources of Its 'Modernism,'" *College Music Symposium* 30/1 (Spring 1990): 79 ff.

46. The first number refers to the two semitones that form the primary interval couple, G♯–A and A♯–B, the second number to the interval of their adjacency, in this case, semitone A/A♯).

47. Halsey Stevens, *The Life and Music of Béla Bartók* (London: Oxford University Press, 1953; 2nd ed. 1964; 3rd ed., ed. Malcolm Gillies, Oxford: Clarendon Press, 1993), p. 286.

48. *Béla Bartók Essays*, ed. Benjamin Suchoff (New York: St. Martin's Press, 1976), p. 386. As a primary manifestation of the French reaction to the Wagner *Tristan* idiom, *Pelléas* resulted in part from Debussy's interest in the French Baroque approach to recitative, in which the musical setting was geared to the precise and realistic declamation of the French text. In *Pelléas*, the recitative style is always sensitive to the rhythm and meaning of the text. Typical single-note repetitions and a constrained vocal range together form a vehicle primarily for the expression of the characters' intentions, the main melodic phrase remaining in the orchestra to express the musical emotion.

49. Bartók, *The Hungarian Folk Song*, p. 14.

50. Ibid.

51. The connection between this theme in several of Wagner's operas and the *Bluebeard* subject is posed by Ethan Mordden, in *Opera in the Twentieth Century: Sacred, Profane, Godot* (New York: Oxford University Press, 1978), p. 38.

52. I will refer to the initial whole-tone collection, WT-0, C–D–E–F♯–G♯–A♯ (or its enharmonic form, C–D–E–G♭–A♭–B♭), as "primary," the other whole-tone collection, WT-1, C♯–D♯–F–G–A–B (or its enharmonic form, D♭–E♭–F–G–A–B), as "secondary."

53. See Bartók's letter to Stefi Geyer, dated Wednesday, middle of September (1907), in *Béla Bartók Letters*, ed. Demény, pp. 86–87. Example 9-4 will be discussed later, in connection with a different set of motivic associations relevant to the opening F♯ pentatonic theme.

54. János Kárpáti, in *Bartók's String Quartets*, trans. Fred Macnicol (Budapest: Corvina Press, 1975), p. 173, informs us that a manuscript in the Budapest Bartók Archívum contains three themes from the *Violin Concerto* sketched on one side and four theme sketches from the *First Quartet* on the other.

55. The *Concerto* was published posthumously by Boosey and Hawkes (London) in 1958.

56. Letter to Stefi Geyer, dated Wednesday, middle of September (1907), in *Béla Bartók Letters*, ed. Demény, p. 87.

57. Letter to Stefi Geyer, dated 6 September 1907, in *Béla Bartók Letters*, ed. Demény, p. 76ff.

58. As pointed out by Kenneth Chalmers, in *Béla Bartók* (London: Phaedon Press, 1995), p. 68, Bartók's atheistic philosophy was quite common among the more educated classes around the turn of the century in Hungary. His explication of his philosophical perspective in his letter to Stefi Geyer seems to have been intended not only for the two of them but also to address it as a broader issue within the Hungarian cultural context at large.

59. Letter to Irmy Jurkovics, dated 15 August 1905, in *Béla Bartók Letters*, ed. Demény, p. 50.

60. Letter to his mother, dated 10 September 1905, in *Béla Bartók Letters*, ed. Demény, p. 53.

61. Denijs Dille, "Angaben zum Violinkonzert, 1907, den Deux Portraits, dem Quartett op. 7 und den Zwei Rumänischen Tänzen," in *Documenta Bartókiana*, vol. 2, ed. Denijs Dille (Mainz: Schott, 1965), p. 92. See also János Kárpáti, *Bartók vonósnégyesei* [Bartók's string quartets] (Budapest: Zeneműkiadó, 1967; English trans. Fred Macnicol, *Bartók's String Quartets*, Budapest: Corvina Press, 1975), p. 173.

62. Benjamin Suchoff, in "Program Notes for the Concerto for Orchestra," *Béla Bartók: A Celebration* (New York: Book-of-the-Month Records, 1981), p. 7, also points to thematic transformations of this "darkness music" in Bartók's *Concerto for Orchestra* (1943), in which the cyclical appearances of this music suggest that "the first and perhaps most important of the composer's extra-musical intentions [that is, in the *Bluebeard* opera] is thus made apparent." We may provide support for Suchoff's perceptive observation by pointing to Bartók's use of a funereal lament as the *Concerto's* third (central) movement: "Elegia."

63. Letter to his mother, dated 10 September 1905, in *Béla Bartók Letters*, ed. Demény, p. 53.

64. Letter to Stefi Geyer, dated 6 September 1907, in ibid, p. 77.

65. Letter to Stefi, in ibid., p. 83.

66. Letter to Stefi, in ibid., p. 81.

67. Malcolm Gillies, "Portraits, Pictures, and Pieces," *The Bartók Companion*, p. 479.

68. Banks, "Images of the Self," p. 12.

69. "Octatonic" refers to an eight-note symmetrical scale that alternates whole-steps and half-steps or half-steps and whole-steps.

70. See Béla Bartók, *Rumanian Folk Music*, vol. 4, ed. Benjamin Suchoff, trans. E. C. Teodorescu et al. (The Hague: Martinus Nijhoff, 1975), p. 19. See also Bartók, *The Hungarian Folk Song*, p. 18.

71. Frigyesi points out, in *Béla Bartók and Turn-of-the-Century Budapest*, p. 242, that "the ostinato halts when [Bluebeard] speaks, the tempo slows down, and there is a return to a dry and unemotional flow of even eighth notes."

72. For an outline of these occurrences, see Veress, "Bluebeard's Castle," pp. 45–49.

73. This structural outline of the scene occurs as follows: introduction (no. 30), a^1 (no. 33), b^1 (no. 34), a^2 (no. 36), b^2 (no. 37, m. 4), introduction (no. 40, m. 5).

10. Duke Bluebeard's Castle: Toward Character Reversal

1. Paul Banks, "Images of the Self: 'Duke Bluebeard's Castle,'" *The Stage Works of Béla Bartók* (London: John Calder, 1991; New York: Riverrun Press, 1991), pp. 10–11.

2. Judit Frigyesi, *Béla Bartók and Turn-of-the-Century Budapest* (Berkeley: University of California Press, 1998), p. 228.

3. Carl S. Leafstedt, *Inside Bluebeard's Castle: Music and Drama in Béla Bartók's Opera* (New York: Oxford University Press, 1999), pp. 111–112; see also Leafstedt, "Music and Drama in Béla Bartók's Opera" (Cambridge, Mass.: Ph.D. diss., 1994), p. 207.

4. This principle, based on the process of contraction from the pentatonic minor seventh chord of the "Castle" theme and Judith's initial hybrid diatonic/whole-tone statement of the

"Stefi'" seventh chord leitmotif to the chromatic cellular representation of "blood," has been discussed by Elliott Antokoletz, in *The Music of Béla Bartók: A Study of Tonality and Progression in Twentieth-Century Music* (Berkeley: University of California Press, 1984), pp. 89–93, and more extensively in "Bartók's *Bluebeard*: The Sources of Its 'Modernism'," *College Music Symposium* 30/1 (Spring 1990): 79–84.

5. *Béla Bartók Essays*, ed. Benjamin Suchoff (New York: St. Martin's Press, 1976), pp. 382–383.

6. *Béla Bartók Letters*, ed. János Demény (New York: St. Martin's Press, 1971), English trans. Peter Balabán and István Farkas. Trans. rev. Elizabeth West and Colin Mason (London: Faber & Faber; Budapest: Corvina Press, 1971), p. 87 (letter originally in Hungarian).

7. *Béla Bartók Letters*, ed. János Demény, p. 83.

8. According to János Kárpáti, *Bartók's String Quartets*, trans. Fred Macnicol (Budapest: Corvina Press, 1975; original Hungarian edition, Budapest: Zeneműkiadó, 1967), p. 173, this information, which appears in Bartók's last letter to Stefi Geyer, was obtained from the violinist herself. See also *Documenta bartókiana* 2 (Budapest, 1965), p. 92, where Bartók, in his letter to Stefi Geyer, identifies the transformed "funeral-dirge" theme of the *First Quartet* with the opening theme of movement 2 of the *Violin Concerto*.

9. Gunter Weiss-Aigner, "The 'Lost' Violin Concerto," in *The Bartók Companion*, ed. Malcolm Gillies (London: Faber and Faber, 1993; Portland, Ore.: Amadeus Press, 1994), p. 469.

10. See Alicja Usarek, "Béla Bartók's 1907 Violin Concerto: In the spirit of *Tristan*," *International Journal of Musicology*, 7 (1998), p. 311.

11. János Kárpáti, "Early String Quartets," *The Bartók Companion*, pp. 226–227.

12. Frigyesi, *Béla Bartók*, pp. 264–265.

13. *Béla Bartók Letters*, ed. Demény, p. 87.

14. See this "polar-axis" principle of Ernő Lendvai, in *Béla Bartók: An Analysis of His Music* (London: Kahn and Averill, 1971), pp. 1–15, for an explanation of the three traditional tonal functions—subdominant, tonic, dominant—in Bartók's music, each function supposedly established by a series of four minor third–related or tritone-related tonalities, respectively. This system assumes that any of the four nodes of the dominant axis can function as the dominant of any one of the four nodes of the tonic axis, a theoretical notion that is controversial at best.

15. *Documenta Bartókiana* 2, p. 92 ff.

16. Leafstedt, "Music and Drama" (diss.), p. 124

17. *Béla Bartók, Briefe an Stefi Geyer, 1907–1908*, ed. Paul Sacher, German trans. Lajos Nyikos, foreword and preface Paul Sacher, afterword Lajos Nyikos (Basle: Privatdruck, 1979), January and February, 1908.

18. György Kroó, "Duke Bluebeard's Castle," *Studia Musicologica* 1 (1961): 303–304, and 337.

19. In 1907, when Stefi Geyer was nineteen, Bartók was twenty-six. In 1910, when his new wife Márta Ziegler was sixteen, he was twenty-nine. In 1915, when Klára Gombossy (poet for three of the songs from his op. 15) was fourteen, he was thirty-five. These factors, together with several others, lead us to assume that the woman in the opera, who has just left her family and her betrothed to follow Bluebeard, is much younger than the man: Bluebeard, having acquired great wealth and power, has had three wives who came to him at the morning, noon, and evening phases of his life, while Judith, who has never been married, came to him at the midnight phase.

20. Bertalan Pethő, "Béla Bartók's Personality," *Studia Musicologica* 23 (1981): 456–457.

21. The source is *Bartók Béla levelei* II, ed. János Demény (Budapest: Művelt Nép Könyvkiadó, 1951), p. 80.

22. Ibid., p. 188.

23. Because we do not have Stefi's side of the correspondence, there is some question as to how much of an active role Bartók actually played in the demise of his relationship with Stefi.

24. The opera is pervaded by rhythms from Hungarian folk music, but Bartók informs us, in his "Harvard Lectures" (*Béla Bartók Essays*, ed. Suchoff, p. 384), that this long-short rhythm occurs very rarely in the genuine Hungarian folk music sources and is actually an "anti-Hungarian" pattern. According to Bartók, "This statement, again, does not mean that we never use such a pattern in our original works." Although it would appear that Bartók is more concerned with the symbolic imagery that the rhythm invokes rather than the strict adherence to the authentic folk music qualities per se, he goes on to say that "I must lay stress on the fact that these 'dotted' rhythm patterns originate in the metrical peculiarities and the accentuation of the Hungarian language."

25. See *Béla Bartók Essays*, ed. Suchoff, pp. 381–383.

26. This permutation of the pentatonic scale (that is, in its minor-modal or symmetrical position), which is the basis of the opening "Castle" motif of the opera (F♯–A–B–C♯–E), is characteristic of the Hungarian folk tunes, in contrast to the nonsymmetrical permutations found in Russian and Chinese folk music. See Bartók, *Essays*, p. 61, and *The Hungarian Folk Song*, ed. Benjamin Suchoff, trans. M. D. Calvocoressi (Albany: State University of New York Press, 1981), p. 17. Expansion of the symmetrical Hungarian pentatonic scale into larger poly-modal chromatic symmetries in these early Bartók songs is shown in Antokoletz, *The Music of Béla Bartók*, pp. 32–50.

27. This vocal statement of Judith is bounded registrally by the same major-seventh, F♯–F, of her opening theme (No. 3) based on the "Stefi" seventh chord, G♭–A–D♭–F (in enharmonic spelling, F♯–A–C♯–E♯), which seems to provide further support for the association of fate and blood to the composer's own unrequited love for Stefi Geyer.

28. János Kárpáti, "Alternative Structures in Bartók's 'Contrasts'," *Studia Musicologica* 23 (1981): 207.

29. In spite of the role played by the dual (major-minor) third in the transformation of the modal-diatonic sphere into the chromatic sphere, the individual modal identities that constitute a bimodal or polymodal combination are retained, as Bartók himself claimed: "bimodality led toward the use of diatonic scales or scale portions filled out with chromaticized degrees which have a totally new function. They are not altered degrees of a certain chord leading to a degree of a following chord. They can only be interpreted as the ingredients of the various modes used simultaneously and at a given time, a certain number of the seemingly chromaticized degrees belonging to one mode, other degrees to another mode. These degrees have absolutely no chordal function. This circumstance is clearly shown if the degrees are picked out and grouped into the modes to which they belong." See "Harvard Lectures," in *Béla Bartók Essays*, ed. Suchoff, p. 376; see also John Vinton, "Bartók on His Own Music," *Journal of the American Musicological Society* 19 (1966): 230. This view contrasts with that posed by Edwin von der Null, in *Béla Bartók: Ein Beitrag zur Morphologie der neuen Musik* (Halle: Mitteldeutsche Verlags A. G., 1930), p. 74, in which von der Null assumed that the simultaneous presence of both major and minor (modal) thirds produces sonic neutrality and the absence of mode. The significance of Bartók's contrasting assertion is seen in the maximal distinction between the polarized dramatic spheres of light and blood, the distinction of one (light) permitted by the clear modal identities within a polymodal construction (i.e., the distinct modal identities of the seventh chord diatonic variants in connection with Judith, who desires to bring light into the Castle), the distinction of the other (blood) produced by the abstraction of pure chromatic elements from the polymodal combinations as Bluebeard's wounds (castle doors) are opened.

30. See Kárpáti, *Bartók's String Quartets*, p. 233, for reference to this phenomenon in the *Fifth String Quartet*.

31. See János Kárpáti, "Tonal Divergences of Melody and Harmony: A Characteristic Device in Bartók's Musical Language," *Studia Musicologica* 24 (1982): 376.

32. Kárpáti, "Tonal Divergences," p. 376.

33. See n. 8 earlier.

34. Retention only of the sustained fifth degree (C♯) at this point leaves the structure unresolved. This modification of the Armory's opening F♯ tonality appears to be a microcosmic reflection of the large-scale tonal structure of the opera. At the return of the original F♯ pentatonic "Castle" theme at the end of the opera, the fifth degree (C♯) is left unresolved as Bluebeard faces "endless darkness." Judith's momentary hesitation is not due to fear, as she claims, but rather to the obscurity of the lock in the "shadow." The latter may be interpreted as a symbolic adumbration of their ultimate fate, as expressed by Bluebeard's final words in this scene.

35. The piling up of half-step dissonances in connection with Judith's reference to Bluebeard's "bloody" treasures recalls Richard Strauss's similar use of the half-step as the basis for the "Vengeance" motif when Orestes kills Klytemnestra.

36. Leafstedt, *Inside Bluebeard's Castle*, p. 106.

11. *Duke Bluebeard's Castle: The Nietzschean Condition*

1. *Béla Bartók Letters*, ed. János Demény (New York: St. Martin's Press, 1971), English trans. Peter Balabán and István Farkas. Trans. rev. Elizabeth West and Colin Mason (London: Faber & Faber; Budapest: Corvina Press, 1971), pp. 52–54.

2. Ibid., p. 54.

3. *Béla Bartók Letters*, ed. Demény, p. 81.

4. *Béla Bartók Letters*, ed. Demény, pp. 50–51.

5. The following is taken from Friedrich Nietzsche, *Human, All Too Human: A Book for Free Spirits*, trans. Marion Faber, with Stephen Lehmann (Lincoln: University of Nebraska Press, 1984), pp. 36–38, aphorisms 33 and 34. These passages have documentary significance in connection with Bartók's thinking since, as pointed out by Judit Frigyesi, in *Béla Bartók and Turn-of-the-Century Budapest* (Berkeley: University of California Press, 1998), p. 154, "Bartók marked these sections, underlined certain sentences, and added an exclamation mark in the margin."

6. See the letter to Stefi Geyer, 6 September 1907, in *Béla Bartók Letters*, p. 82.

7. See "*Duke Bluebeard's Castle*, Notes on the Text by Béla Balázs, Circa 1915," English translation by Carl Leafstedt from the Hungarian translation (for inclusion in Balázs, *Balázs Béla: Válogatott cikkek*, 34–37) of the original German, in Carl Leafstedt, *Inside Bluebeard's Castle: Music and Drama in Béla Bartók's Opera* (New York: Oxford University Press, 1999), p. 202.

8. The dilemma for Bartók and the Bluebeard character, as embodied in this philosophy, is explored later.

9. Friedrich Nietzsche, *Thus Spoke Zarathustra: A Book for None and All*, trans. Walter Kaufmann (New York: Viking Penguin, 1954), p. 42.

10. As the librettist himself tells us, the castle is not a real one made of stone, but the soul of Bluebeard. See "*Duke Bluebeard's Castle*, Notes on the Text by Béla Balázs, Circa 1915," p. 202.

11. See chap. 7, n. 12, regarding the "Golden Section" (GS) system or Fibonacci series in connection with Debussy's music. As pointed out by Lendvai, in "Nature Symbolism," *Bartók and Kodály*, vol. 1, rev. ed. (Budapest: Institute for Culture, 1979), p. 167, "[The Fibonacci series] covers the simplest golden section sequence which can be expressed in whole-numbers/ the golden section of 89 being 55, and that of 55 being 34, etc." Although representing the GS scheme on the most basic level, the placement of Bluebeard's Domain as the fifth door within the eight-section whole is striking in view of the frequency with which this formal relation occurs throughout Bartók's works.

12. For an alternative structural interpretation of this scene, see Carl Leafstedt, "Structure in the Fifth Door Scene of Bartrók's *Duke Bluebeard's Castle*: An Alternative Viewpoint," *College Music Symposium* 30/1 (Spring 1990): 96–102.

13. See Nietzsche, *Human, All Too Human*, pp. 231–232, aphorism 29.

14. These circumstances are discussed in detail by Frigyesi, in *Béla Bartók*, p. 157.

15. Ibid..

16. As discussed earlier, the gapped whole-tone cell serves the same symbology in Debussy's opera.

17. Béla Balázs Diary, MS 5023/12, 14–15, Manuscript Department, National Széchenyi Library. Frigyesi, in *Béla Bartók*, p. 325, informs us that "the text preceding this entry is found in Béla Balázs, *Napló* [Diary], vol. 1 (Budapest: Magvető, 1982), p. 344.

18. Béla Bartók, "La musique populaire hongroise" [Hungarian folk music], *La revue musicale* 2/1 (November 1921): 8–22. See also *Béla Bartók Essays*, ed. Benjamin Suchoff (New York: St. Martin's Press, 1976), pp. 61–62.

19. Nietzsche, *Human, All Too Human*, p. 277, aphorism 131.

20. Ibid., pp. 241–242, aphorism 41.

12. *Duke Bluebeard's Castle: Final Transformation*

1. György Kroó, "Opera: *Duke Bluebeard's Castle*," in *The Bartók Companion*, ed. Malcolm Gillies (London: Faber and Faber, 1993; Portland, Ore.: Amadeus Press, 1994), pp. 354–355.

2. Frank Whitford, *Klimt* (London: Thames and Hudson, 1990), p. 168.

3. Béla Balázs, *Hebbel Frigyes Pantragizmusa, mint a Romantikus Világnézlet Eredménye* [Friedrich Hebbel's pan-tragicness, as a result of the Romantic worldview] (Budapest: Franklin Társulat, 1909).

4. See Kroó, "Opera: *Duke Bluebeard's Castle*," and "Duke Bluebeard's Castle," *Studia Musicologica* 1 (1961): 251–340, for a more comprehensive survey of the literary sources of the *Bluebeard* tale.

5. Kroó, "Opera," p. 349.

6. Ibid., p. 350.

7. See "*Duke Bluebeard's Castle*, Notes on the Text by Béla Balázs, Circa 1915," English translation by Carl Leafstedt from the Hungarian translation (for inclusion in Balázs, *Balázs Béla: Válogatott cikkek*, 34–37) of the original German, in Carl Leafstedt, *Inside Bluebeard's Castle: Music and Drama in Béla Bartók's Opera* (New York: Oxford University Press, 1999), p. 202.

8. As pointed out by Dorothy Lamb Crawford, in "Love and Anguish: Bartók's Expressionism," in *Bartók Perspectives*, ed. Elliott Antokoletz, Victoria Fischer, and Benjamin Suchoff (New York: Oxford University Press, 2000), p. 130, Bartók, like the expressionists of the Vienna Schoenberg circle, belonged to the first generation of the twentieth century "to become aware of Freudian psychoanalysis and new knowledge of the subconscious; the first to live with escalating anxiety in relationships between men and women that resulted from the overturn of sexual mores."

9. Ibid., p. 130.

10. Ibid., p. 131, cites Bartók's statement to Stefi Geyer about the opening of the first movement of the *String Quartet no. 1* as his "funeral dirge."

11. *Béla Bartók Letters*, ed. János Demény (New York: St. Martin's Press, 1971, English trans. Peter Balabán and István Farkas; trans. rev. Elizabeth West and Colin Mason, London: Faber and Faber; Budapest: Corvina Press, 1971), p. 86.

12. Alexander Grinstein, *Freud's Rules of Dream Interpretation* (New York: International Universities Press, 1983), p. 143.

13. See letter to his mother dated 10 September 1905, in *Béla Bartók Letters*, ed. Demény, p. 53.

14. See Grinstein, *Freud's Rules*, p. 140.

15. One note, D (confined to no. 121, mm. 9–10), is the only element in the entire passage that falls outside the otherwise exclusive pitch content of these tritone-related seventh chords, on C and G♭. The D–C figure suggests an echo of Judith's "Danger" motif.

16. See Peter Giovacchini, "Beyond the Pleasure Principle," in *A Clinician's Guide to Reading Freud* (New York: Aronson, 1982), pp. 150–151.

17. See Grinstein, *Freud's Rules*, p. 143.

18. See Sigmund Freud, *Introductory Lectures on Psycho-Analysis* (London: Hogarth Press, 1963), p. 156, as quoted in Grinstein, *Freud's Rules*, p. 101.

19. Freud, *Introductory Lectures*, p. 158; see also Freud, *The Interpretation of Dreams* (1900; London: Hogarth Press, 1953), p. 354.

20. Freud, *The Interpretation of Dreams* (1900), p. 354.

21. See Grinstein, *Freud's Rules*, p. 102.

22. Friedrich Nietzsche, *The Gay Science*, trans. Walter Kaufmann (New York: Vintage Books, 1974), pp. 318–319, no. 363.

23. Ibid., p. 126, no. 68.

24. See n. 7 earlier.

25. Grinstein, *Freud's Rules*, p. 141.

26. Ibid.

27. In the first movement of the 1907 *Violin Concerto* and the first of the *Two Portraits for Orchestra*, this form of the seventh chord represents Stefi the "ideal," in contrast with the minor-modal funereal form of the *First String Quartet* or the "grotesque" form of the second *Portrait*.

28. According to Judit Frigyesi's interpretation, in *Béla Bartók and Turn-of-the-Century Budapest* (Berkeley: University of California Press, 1998, pp. 200–201, Bluebeard himself, however, was not aware of the mysteries within his soul. Frigyesi quotes Paula Hermann, who belonged to the small circle of Balázs, Kodály, and Aranka Bauer, who wrote on 20 July 1906, in *Napló*, p. 325, that "We tell everything, even what only we know about ourselves, we open the most inner doors. . . . All this is an effort to bring someone close to ourselves or grow close to someone. But we pour out the many inner images in vain—we are alone. We might as well have stolen each other's diary from the drawer. We remain strangers."

29. See *Béla Bartók Letters*, ed. Demény, p. 87.

30. See *Béla Bartók Letters*, ed. Demény, p. 83.

31. Letter to Irmy Jurkovics, dated 15 August 1905, in *Béla Bartók Letters*, pp. 50–51.

13. Symbolism and Expressionism in Other Early Twentieth-Century Operas

1. In contrast to Charcot, whose clinical work primarily reflected the Realism of Comte's Positivist philosophy, Freud's clinical studies, like those of Janet, primarily reflected the Symbolist conception, as seen, for instance, in his approach to free association and the interpretation of dreams.

2. Sigmund Freud, *Studien über Hysterie* [1895] (*Studies in Hysteria* [1955]) and *Die Traumdeutung* (1899; *The Interpretation of Dreams*, 1953).

3. William Mann, *Richard Strauss: A Critical Study of the Operas* (Cassell and London: Cassell & Company, 1964), p. 68.

4. This tonal organization is discussed later in connection with fig. 13–1, which appeared in Elliott Antokoletz, *The Music of Béla Bartók: A Study of Tonality and Progression in Twentieth-Century Music* (Berkeley: University of California Press, 1984), pp. 14-16, and in "Strauss' Elek-

tra: Toward Expressionism and the Transformation of Nineteenth-Century Chromatic Tonality," *Musik und Dichtung* (Frankfurt am Main: Verlag Peter Lang, 1990): 449. With regard to pitch indication by means of letter notation in the musical examples and diagrams of this work, major keys and triads are represented by uppercase letters, minor keys and triads by lowercase letters. In the text, however, all pitch names are represented by uppercase letters.

5. *Richard Strauss und Hugo von Hofmannsthal: Briefwechsel,* vol. 10 in *Gesamtausgabe,* ed. Franz and Alice Strauss, rev. Willi Schuh (Zurich: Atlantis Verlag AG, 1952, enlarged 2d ed., 1955; Eng. trans. Collins, 1961), letters from 1906 through 1909 passim.

6. Letter of 11 March 1906, in *Strauss und Hofmannsthal: Briefwechsel,* p. 15.

7. Letter of 22 December 1907, in *Strauss und Hofmannsthal: Briefwechsel,* p. 24. Original German text: "schaffen Sie mir ein recht handlungs- und gegensatzreiches Drama mit wenig Massenszenen, aber zwei bis drei sehr guten, ausgiebigen Rollen. Was unsere neuliche Unterredung über "Elektra" betrifft, so meine ich, dass wir Aigisth doch nicht ganz weglassen können. Er gehört unbedingt mit zur Handlung und muss mit erschlagen werden . . . Es ist nicht gut, dass nach dem Mord von Klytämnestra die ganzen Weiber gelaufen kommen, dann wieder verschwinden, dann, nach dem Morde des Aigisth, mit Chrysothemis wieder ankommen. Das sind zu stark gebrochene Linien. . . . Könnte man nicht Aigisth nach Hause kommen lassen, unmittelbar nachdem Orest ins Haus getreten ist? Und die Morde dann kurz hintereinander vollziehen?"

8. Letter of 22 June 1908, in *Strauss und Hofmannsthal: Briefwechsel,* p. 32. Original German text: "8, 16, 20 Verse, soviel Sie können, und alles in derselben ekstatischen Stimmung, immer sich steigernd."

9. The opera provides ample evidence of the Wagnerian orchestra brought to its highest point of development and expansion, not only in terms of its style and size but also instrumental technique. In addition to many subdivisions in the strings, the instrumental sections include eight horns (four being Wagnerian tubas), large traditional wind complements to which are added piccolo, English horn, bassett horns, heckelphon (a baritone type of oboe invented by Heckel in 1904), and highly diverse percussion. Strauss often employs mutes for all brass (including tubas), which creates a nervous, disembodied sound, flutter-tongue tones for brass, trills for all winds, and tremolos for strings playing harmonics.

10. All measure and rehearsal numbers are the same for the piano-vocal and orchestral scores. The musical excerpts are quoted from the piano-vocal score, arr. Carl Besl, Eng. trans. Alfred Kalisch (Adolph Fürstner, 1909–1910, 1937; New York: Boosey & Hawkes, 1943).

11. In the *Choephori* of Aeschylus, Orestes is taunted by the Furies of Klytemnestra and seeks purification at Delphi. We find the appearance of gods and goddesses in one of the sequels as well. In the Euripides version of *Elektra,* which differs in many respects from those of the other two ancient authors, the twin sons of Zeus, Castor and Pollux, are also present. The Euripides story begins in a remote part of the land, where Elektra has been forced to marry a peasant.

12. This has significant consequences regarding the special means by which Chrysothemis's tonality is absorbed ultimately into the "triumph" complex at the end of the opera (see fig. 13–1 earlier).

13. The opera is based on a complex network of leitmotifs, which are outlined by Ernest Hutcheson in *"Elektra" by Richard Strauss: A Guide to the Opera* (New York: G. Schirmer, 1910; Boston: Boston Music, 1910), pp. 17–61, and in the more detailed discussion by Norman Del Mar, *Richard Strauss,* vol. 1 (Ithaca, N.Y.: Cornell University Press, 1962, 1986), pp. 287–333.

14. Ethan Mordden, *Opera in the Twentieth Century: Sacred, Profane, Godot* (New York: Oxford University Press, 1978), p. 116.

15. Part of the following discussion of *Erwartung* is taken from Elliott Antokoletz and

George Perle, *Erwartung and Bluebeard*, program note for the performance by the New York Metropolitan Opera (16 January 1989).

16. Theodor Adorno, *Philosophy of Modern Music*, trans. Anne G. Mitchell and Wesley V. Blomster (New York: Seabury Press, 1973), pp. 155–156; see chap. 1, and Adorno's notion of "shock" in modern music.

17. Charles Rosen, *Arnold Schoenberg* (Princeton, N.J.: Princeton University Press, 1975), p. 41 ff.

18. Arnold Schoenberg, "New Music, My Music," *Style and Idea: Selected Writings of Arnold Schoenberg*, ed. Leonard Stein, trans. Leo Black (London: Faber and Faber, 1975; Los Angeles: Belmont Music Publishers, 1975; Berkeley: University of California Press, 1984), p. 105.

19. Letter from Berg to Webern, dated 19 August 1918. See Redlich, *Alban Berg: Versuch einer Würdigung* (Vienna: Universal Edition, 1957); Eng. trans. abridged as *Alban Berg: The Man and His Music* (London: John Calder; New York: Abelard-Schumann, 1957), p. 365, n. 205. See also Reich, *Alban Berg* (Zürich: Atlantis Verlag AG, 1963); trans. Cornelius Cardew (New York: Vienna House, 1974), pp. 43 and 45.

20. Karen Monson, *Alban Berg: A Modern Biography of the Composer of Wozzeck and Lulu* (Boston: Houghton Mifflin Company, 1979), p. 157.

21. See n. 19.

22. See "Postscript by Alban Berg, 1931," in Reich's *Wozzeck: A Guide to the Text and Music of the Opera* (New York: G. Schirmer, reprinted from the monograph originally published by the League of Composers, *Modern Music*, 1927, 1931, 1952), p. 22.

23. Reich, *Alban Berg*, pp. 120–121; see also Perle's discussion of "The Text and Formal Design," in *The Operas of Alban Berg*, vol. 1: *Wozzeck* (Berkeley: University of California Press, 1980), p. 38 ff.

24. George Perle, "Representation and Symbol in the Music of *Wozzeck*," *Music Review* 33/4 (November 1971): 281; see also Perle, *Wozzeck*, p. 93.

25. For a systematic outline and description of the main associative themes, motifs, and figures, see Reich, *Wozzeck*, pp. 8–21; see also Perle, *Wozzeck*, p. 94 ff.

26. See Jarman, *The Music of Alban Berg* (Berkeley: University of California Press, 1979), Perle, *Wozzeck*, and Schmalfeldt, *Berg's Wozzeck: Harmonic Language and Dramatic Design* (New Haven, Conn.: Yale University Press, 1983).

27. Perle, *Wozzeck*, p. 130.

28. Jarman, *The Music of Alban Berg*, p. 22.

29. Schmalfeldt, *Berg's Wozzeck*, preface.

30. Ibid., pp. ix–x. See Allen Forte's *The Structure of Atonal Music* (New Haven, Conn.: Yale University Press, 1973), as the basis of Schmalfeldt's method of harmonic analysis.

31. The significance of this cyclic interlocking is established more prominently in connection with the six-part canon that begins Variation 20 (mm. 620–623).

32. Perle, "Representation and Symbol," p. 304.

33. Reich, *Wozzeck*, p. 21.

Epilogue

1. Elliott Antokoletz, *The Music of Béla Bartók: A Study of Tonality and Progression in Twentieth-Century Music* (Berkeley: University of California Press, 1984), p. xi–xii.

2. Ignacio Matte Blanco, *The Unconscious as Infinite Sets: An Essay in Bi-Logic* (London: Duckworth, 1975).

3. Sigmund Freud, "The Interpretation of Dreams," *Standard Edition* 5 (London: Hogarth Press, 1953), p. 509.

4. See, for instance, my discussion in chapter 4, especially the discussion related to table 4-1, of how the interaction between contrasting diatonic and symmetrical pitch collections symbolizes the intrusion of the unconscious into the conscious realm in Debussy's musical setting of the timeless Kingdom of Allemonde and the tragic lives of the inhabitants.

5. See Georgette Leblanc, *Souvenirs*, p. 94.

6. See Adorno, *Essays on Music*, p.162.

7. Heinz Kohut, letter to Erich Heller, 1 December 1976, in *Selected Writings of Heinz Kohut: 1950–1978*, ed. Paul H. Ornstein (New York: International University Press, 1978), p. 908.

8. Balázs's *Bluebeard* play resonates with autobiographical references to the contrasting personalities of the intellectual, impenetrable Lukás and the passionate Balázs. Arpad Kadarkay alluded to the similarities between Balázs, Bluebeard, and Lukács's personality. See Kadarkay, *Georg Lukács: Life, Thought, and Politics* (Cambridge, Mass.: Blackwell, 1991), p. 132.

9. György Lukács, "My Socratic Mask," in *The Lukács Reader*, ed. Arpad Kadarkay (Oxford: Blackwell, 1995), pp. 58 and 61.

Works Cited

Abbate, Carolyn. "Tristan in the Composition of Pelléas." *Nineteenth-Century Music* 5 (1981): 117–141.

Adorno, Theodor W. *Essays on Music*, ed. Richard Leppert, trans. Susan H. Gillespie. Berkeley: University of California Press, 2002.

———. *Philosophy of Modern Music*, trans. Anne G. Mitchell and Wesley V. Blomster. New York: Seabury Press, 1973.

Antokoletz, Elliott. "A Survivor of the Vienna Schoenberg Circle: An Interview with Paul A. Pisk." *Tempo* 154 (September 1985): 8–16.

———. "Bartók's *Bluebeard*: The Sources of Its 'Modernism.'" *College Music Symposium* 30/1 (Spring 1990): 75–95.

———. "Organic Development and the Interval Cycles in Bartók's Three Studies, Op. 18." *Studia Musicologica* 36/3–4 (1995): 249–261.

———. "Organic Expansion and Classical Structure in Bartók's Sonata for Two Pianos and Percussion." In *Bartók Perspectives*, ed. Elliott Antokoletz, Victoria Fischer, and Benjamin Suchoff. New York: Oxford University Press, 2000, pp. 77–94.

———. "Strauss' *Elektra*: Toward Expressionism and the Transformation of Nineteenth-Century Chromatic Tonality." *Musik und Dichtung*. Frankfurt am Main: Peter Lang, 1990, pp. 443–467.

———. *The Music of Béla Bartók: A Study of Tonality and Progression in Twentieth-Century Music*. Berkeley: University of California Press, 1984.

Antokoletz, Elliott, and George Perle. "*Erwartung* and *Bluebeard*." Program Note in *Stagebill*, for the performance by the New York Metropolitan Opera (16 January 1989).

Ashman, Mike. "Around the Bluebeard Myth." In *The Stage Works of Béla Bartók*, ed. Nicholas John. Sponsor: Martini, *Operaguide* 44. New York: Riverrun; London: Calder, 1991, pp. 35–38.

Balakian, Anna. *Literary Origins of Surrealism: A New Mysticism in French Poetry*. New York: New York University Press, 1947; rev. ed. 1966.

Balázs, Béla. "Baratsag." In *Csend*. Budapest: Magvető, 1985, p. 223.

———. "Diary, MS 5023/12, 14–15," Manuscript Department, National Széchenyi Library. In *Béla Balázs, Napló* [Diary], vol. 1. Budapest: Magvető, 1982).

————. "Duke Bluebeard's Castle, Notes on the Text by Béla Balázs, Circa 1915." Eng. trans. by Carl Leafstedt from the Hungarian translation (for inclusion in Balázs, *Balázs Béla: Válogatott cikkek*, 34–37) of the original German. In Carl Leafstedt, *Inside Bluebeard's Castle: Music and Drama in Béla Bartók's Opera*. New York: Oxford University Press, 1999, pp. 201–203.

————. *Hebbel Frigyes Pantragizmusa, mint a Romantikus Világnézlet Eredménye* [Friedrich Hebbel's pan-tragicness, as a result of the Romantic worldview]. Budapest: Franklin Társulat, 1909.

————. *Theory of the Film: Character and Growth of a New Art*, trans. Edith Bone. London: Dennis Dobson., 1952.

Banks, Paul. "Images of the Self: Duke Bluebeard's Castle." In *The Stage Works of Béla Bartók*, ed. Nicholas John. New York: Riverrun; London: Calder, 1991, pp. 7–12.

Bäumer, Angelica. *Gustav Klimt: Women*. London: Weidenfeld and Nicolson, 1986.

Bartók, Béla. "Autobiography [1921]." In *Béla Bartók Essays*, ed. Benjamin Suchoff. New York: St. Martin's Press, 1976, p. 410. Originally appeared in several versions. in: *Musikblätter des Anbruch* (Vienna) 3/5 (March 1921): 87–90; *Magyar írás hármaskönyve* (Budapest) 1/2 (May, 1921): 33–36; *Az est hármaskönyve* (Budapest: Az Est Lapkiadó RT Kiadása, 1923): cols. 77–84; *Sovremennya muzyka* (Moscow) 2/7 (1925): 1–6; and *Színházi élet* (Budapest) 17/51 (December 1927): 49–51.

————. *Briefe an Stefi Geyer, 1907–1908*, ed. Paul Sacher, German trans. Lajos Nyikos. Basle: Privatdruck, 1979.

————. *Családi levelei* [Béla Bartók's family letters], ed. Béla Bartók, Jr. Budapest: Zeneműkiadó, 1981.

————. "Harvard Lectures." In *Béla Bartók Essays*, ed. Benjamin Suchoff. New York: St. Martin's Press, 1976. pp. 354–392. The original publication of the manuscripts of four lectures given during February 1943 was in *Journal of the American Musicological Society* 19/2 (Summer 1966): 232–243.

————. *Herzog Blaubarts Burg (A kékszakállú herceg vára) / Oper in einem Akt von Béla Balázs / Musik von Béla Bartók, Op. 11 / Deutsche Übertragung von Wilhelm Ziegler*, originally published by Universal Edition A. G., Vienna, 1921. The piano-vocal score published by Universal Edition, 1921, renewed by Boosey and Hawkes, 1949, and the orchestral-vocal score published by Universal Edition, 1925, are both used as the basis of the musical discussions in this study. The new Dover edition, first published in 2001, is an unabridged republication.

————. "La musique populaire hongroise" [Hungarian folk music]. *La revue musicale* 2/1 (November 1921): 8–22.

————. *Letters*, ed. János Demény. New York: St. Martin's Press, 1971. Eng. trans. Peter Balabán and István Farkas. Trans. rev. Elizabeth West and Colin Mason. London: Faber & Faber; Budapest: Corvina Press, 1971.

————. *Levelei II: Magyar és külföldi dokumentumok (Az utolsó két év gyűjtése)* [Béla Bartók's Correspondence II: Hungarian and foreign documents (material collected during the last two years)], ed. János Demény. Budapest: Művelt Nép Könyvkiadó, 1951.

————. *Levelei IV. Új dokumentumok* [Béla Bartók's Correspondence IV: new documents], ed. János Demény. Budapest: Zeneműkiadó Vállalat, 1971.

————. *Rumanian Folk Music*, vol. 4, ed. Benjamin Suchoff, trans. E. C. Teodorescu, Abram Loft, and Ernest H. Sanders. The Hague: Martinus Nijhoff, 1975.

————. "Temoignage (sur Ravel)." *Revue Musicale* 19/2 (December 1938): 436.

————. *The Hungarian Folk Song*, ed. Benjamin Suchoff, trans. M. D. Calvocoressi. Albany: State University of New York Press, 1981.

————. "The Relation of Folk Song to the Development of the Art Music of Our Time." In *Béla Bartók Essays*, ed. Benjamin Suchoff. New York: St. Martin's Press, 1976, pp. 320–330. Originally published in *The Sackbut* 2/1 (June, 1921): 5–11.

Bartók Jr., Béla. "The Private Man." In *The Bartók Companion*, ed. Malcolm Gillies. London: Faber and Faber, 1993, pp. 18–29.

Bauer, Herbert. *Hebbel Frigyes pántragizmusa, mint a romantikus világnézlet eredménye* (Friedrich Hebbel's Pan-tragicness, as the Result of the Romantic Worldview). Budapest: Franklin Társulat, 1909.

Beaunier, André. *Le poésie nouvelle*. Paris, 1920.

Benjamin, Jessica. *The Bonds of Love: Psychoanalysis, Feminism, and the Problem of Domination*. New York: Pantheon Books, 1988.

Berg, Alban. "Postscript by Alban Berg, 1931." In Willi Reich. *Wozzeck: A Guide to the Text and Music of the Opera*. New York: G. Schirmer, reprinted from the monograph originally published by the League of Composers, *Modern Music*, 1927, 1931.

Bernstein, David. "Symmetry and Symmetrical Inversion in Turn-of-the-Century Theory and Practice." Paper given at a national meeting of the American Musicological Society in Baltimore (3 November 1988).

Bosley, Keith, and Peter Sherwood, translators, "Annie Miller [The Ballad of Anna Molnár]." In *The Stage Works of Béla Bartók*, ed. Nicholas John. New York: Riverrun; London: Calder, 1991, pp. 23–24.

Boulez, Pierre. *"Pelléas Reflected."* In notes for the recording, *Boulez Conducts Debussy: "Pelléas et Mélisande."* CBS M3 30119. New York: CBS, 1970.

Breuer, Josef. "Theoretical." In Sigmund Freud and Josef Breuer, *Studies on Hysteria*, trans. and ed. James Strachey. New York: Discus Books/Avon Books, by arr. with Basic Books, 1966, p. 276.

Broughton, Simon. "Bartók and World Music." In *The Stage Works of Béla Bartók*, ed. Nicholas John. New York: Riverrun; London: Calder, 1991, pp. 13–22.

Chalmers, Kenneth. *Béla Bartók*. London: Phaedon Press, 1995.

Charles, Marilyn. "The Language of the Body: Allusions to Self-Experience in Women's Poetry." *Psychoanalytic Psychology* 18/2 (Spring 2001): 346.

Chodorow, Nancy J. *Feminism and Psychoanalytic Theory*. New Haven, Conn.: Yale University Press, 1989.

Comte, Auguste. *Cours de philosophie positive*. Paris: La Société Positiviste, 1892–1896; 1830–1842. Eng. trans., *The Course of Positive Philosophy*. New York: W. Gowans, 1868; 1853.

Crawford, Dorothy Lamb. "Love and Anguish: Bartók's Expressionism." In *Bartók Perspectives*, ed. Elliott Antokoletz, Victoria Fischer, and Benjamin Suchoff. New York: Oxford University Press, 2000, pp. 129–139.

Cross, Anthony. "Debussy and Bartók." *Musical Times* 108 (1967): 126.

Davies, John Langdon. *A Short History of Women*. New York: Viking, 1927.

Debussy, Claude. "Interview." In *Cahiers Debussy. Bulletin du Centre de Documentation Claude Debussy*, no. 1. Geneva: Editions Minkoff, 1974.

————. "Pelléas and Gil Blas: Claudine and Monsieur Croche." In François Lesure, ed. *Debussy on Music: The Critical Writings of the Great French Composer*, trans. and ed. Richard Langham Smith. Ithaca, N.Y.: Cornell University Press, 1977, pp. 59–218 .

————. "Pelléas et Mélisande: A Reply to the Critics (Interview by Robert de Flers)." *Le Figaro* (May 16, 1902). Originally in *Monsieur Croche et autres écrits*. Paris: Editions Gallimard, 1971, trans. in *Debussy on Music: The Critical Writings of the Great Composer*, ed. François Lesure, trans. and ed. Richard Langham Smith. New York: Knopf, 1977; Ithaca, N.Y.: Cornell University Press, 1977, pp. 79–82.

————. "Why I Wrote *Pelléas*" (April 1902). In *Monsieur Croche et autres écrits*. Paris: Editions Gallimard, 1971, pp. 74–78.

————. *Letters*, eds. François Lesure and Roger Nichols, trans. Roger Nichols. Cambridge, Mass.: Harvard University Press, 1987; originally published as *Claude Debussy: Lettres, 1884–1918*. Paris: Hermann, éditeurs des sciences et des arts, 1980.

————. *Pelléas et Mélisande*. New York: Edwin F. Kalmus, n.d. Reprint edition of the 1907 publication of the piano-vocal score.

————. *Pelléas et Mélisande*. New York: Dover Publications, 1985. Orchestral-vocal score of the opera.

Del Mar, Norman. *Richard Strauss*, vol. 1. Ithaca, N.Y.: Cornell University Press, 1962, 1986, pp. 287–333.

Dietschy, Marcel. *A Portrait of Claude Debussy*, ed. and trans. William Ashbrook and Margaret G. Cobb. Oxford: Clarendon Press, 1990; original French publication, Neuchâtel, Suisse: Editions de la Baconnière, 1962.

Dille, Denijs. "Angaben zum Violinkonzert, 1907, den Deux Portraits, dem Quartett op. 7 und den Zwei Rumänischen Tänzen." *Documenta Bartókiana*, vol. 2, ed. Denijs Dille. Mainz: Schott, 1965, p. 92.

Eagleton, Terry. *The Significance of Theory*. Oxford: Blackwell, 1990.

Ellenberger, Henri F. *The Discovery of the Unconscious: The History and Evolution of Dynamic Psychiatry*. New York: Basic Books, 1970.

Emmanuel, Maurice. *Pelléas et Mélisande de Claude Debussy: Étude et Analyse*. Paris: Éditions Mellottée, 1926, 2d ed., 1950.

Erichsen, Eric J. *On Concussion of the Spine, Nervous Shock, and Other Obscure Injuries to the Nervous System in Their Clinical and Medico-Legal Aspects*. New York: William Wood, 1886.

————. *On Railway and Other Injuries of the Nervous System*. London: Walton and Moberley, 1866.

Forte, Allen. *The Structure of Atonal Music*. New Haven, Conn.: Yale University Press, 1973.

Freud, Anna. *About Losing and Being Lost*. In *The Writings of Anna Freud, vol. 14, 1945–1956*. New York: International Universities Press, 1968, pp. 308–310.

Freud, Sigmund. "A Note on the Concept of the Unconscious in Psychoanalysis [1912]." *Standard Edition*, vol. 12. London: Hogarth Press, 1958, pp. 255–267.

————. "Beyond the Pleasure Principle [1920a]." *Standard Edition of the Complete Psychological Works of Sigmund Freud*, vol. 18. London: Hogarth Press, 1955, pp. 7–64.

————. *Introductory Lectures on Psycho-Analysis*. London: Hogarth Press, 1963.

————. "Some Psychical Consequences of the Anatomical Distinctions Between the Sexes" [1925], *Standard Edition*, vol. 19. London: Hogarth Press, 1961, p. 257.

————. *Die Traumdeutung* (1899; *The Interpretation of Dreams*, 1953). London: Hogarth Press, 1953. New trans. Joyce Crick. New York: Oxford Univesity Press, 1999.

Freud, Sigmund, and Josef Breuer. *Studien über Hysterie* [1895] (Studies on Hysteria [1955], trans. and ed. James Strachey. New York: Avon, 1966.

Friedheim, Philip. "Radical Harmonic Procedures in Berlioz." *Music Review* 21/4 (November 1960): 286.

Frigyesi, Judit. *Béla Bartók and Turn-of-the-Century Budapest*. Berkeley: University of California Press, 1998.

————. "In Search of Meaning in Context: Bartók's *Duke Bluebeard's Castle*," *Current Musicology* 70 (Fall 2000): 5–31.

Gilligan, Carol. *In a Different Voice: Psychological Theory and Women's Development*. Cambridge. Mass.: Harvard University Press, 1982.

Gilman, Lawrence. *Debussy's "Pelléas et Mélisande": A Guide to the Opera*. New York: G. Schirmer, 1907.

Giovacchini, Peter L. *A Clinician's Guide to Reading Freud*. New York: Jason Aronson, 1982.
_____. *A Narrative Textbook of Psychoanalysis*. Northvale, N.J.: Jason Aronson, 1987.
_____. "Beyond the Pleasure Principle." *A Clinician's Guide to Reading Freud*. New York: Aronson, 1982.
Gluck, Mary. *Georg Lukács and His Generation, 1900–1918*. Cambridge, Mass: Harvard University Press, 1985
Goetz, Christopher G., Michel Bonduelle, and Toby Gelfand. *Charcot: Constructing Neurology*. New York: Oxford University Press, 1995.
Grant, Julian. "A Foot in Bluebeard's Door." In *The Stage Works of Béla Bartók*, ed. Nicholas John. New York: Riverrun; London: Calder, 1991, pp. 25–34.
Grayson, David. *The Genesis of Debussy's "Pelléas et Mélisande."* Ann Arbor: UMI Research Press, 1986.
_____. "Waiting for Golaud: The Concept of Time in *Pelléas*." In *Debussy Studies*, ed. Richard Langham Smith. Cambridge: Cambridge University Press, 1997, pp. 26–45.
Grinstein, Alexander. *Freud's Rules of Dream Interpretation*. New York: International Universities Press, 1983.
Halls, W. D. *Maurice Maeterlinck*. Oxford: Clarendon Press, 1960.
Heller, Agnes. *Lukács Revalued*. Oxford: Basil Blackwell, 1983.
Horváth, B. Dürer. "*Melankólia*" *című metszetérol* [About Dürer's engraving "Melancholy"]. *Művészet* vol. 3 (1962), no. 11, pp. 4–8, vol. 4 (1963), no. 7, pp. 7–12, vol. 5 (1964), no. 3, pp. 6–10.
Howat, Roy. *Debussy in Proportion: A Musical Analysis* (Cambridge: Cambridge University Press, 1983), p. 164.
Huebner, Steven. *French Opera at the Fin de Siècle: Wagnerism, Nationalism, and Style*. New York: Oxford University Press, 1999.
Hutcheson, Ernest. "*Elektra*" *by Richard Strauss: A Guide to the Opera*. New York: G. Schirmer, 1910; Boston: Boston Music, 1910, pp. 17–61.
Irigaray, Luce. *The Speculum of the Other Woman*, trans. G. C. Gill. Ithaca, N.Y.: Cornell University Press, 1985.
Jarman, Douglas. *The Music of Alban Berg*. Berkeley: University of California Press, 1979.
Jarocinski, Stefan. *Debussy, Impressionism, and Symbolism*, trans. Rollo Myers. London: Eulenberg, 1976.
John, Nicholas, ed. *The Stage Works of Béla Bartók*. New York: Riverrun; London: Calder, 1991.
Jung, Carl G. "Marriage as a Psychological Relationship." In *The Portable Jung*, ed. Joseph Campbell. New York: Viking, 1971,p p. 163–177.
Kadarkay, Arpad. *Georg Lukács: Life , Thought, and Politics*. Cambridge, Mass.: Basil Blackwell, 1991.
Kahane, Claire. "The Woman with a Knife and the Chicken without a Head: Fantasies of Rage and Emptiness." In Peter L. Rudnytsky and Andrew M. Gordon, eds., *Psychoanalyses/Feminisms*. Albany: State University of New York Press, 2000, pp. 179–191.
Kárpáti, János. "Alternatív struktúrák Bartók Kontrasztok című művében" [Alternative structures in Bartók's *Contrasts*]. *Zeneelmélet, stíluselemzés*. Budapest: Zeneműkiadó, 1977), pp. 103–108. Also published in English in *Studia Musicologica* 23 (1981): 201–207.
_____. *Bartók vonósnégyesei* [Bartók's string quartets]. Budapest: Zeneműkiadó, 1967, trans. Fred Macnicol. *Bartók's String Quartets*. Budapest: Corvina Press, 1975. Revised and enlarged as *Bartók's Chamber Music*, trans. Fred Macnicol and Mária Steiner, trans. rev. Paul Merrick. Stuyvesant, N.Y.: Pendragon Press, 1994.
_____. "Tonal Divergences of Melody and Harmony: A Characteristic Device in Bartók's Musical Language." *Studia Musicologica* 24 (1982): 373–380.
Kernberg, Otto. *Borderline Conditions and Pathological Narcissism*. New York: Jason Aronson, 1975.

ED: New entry adds two lines. To prevent reflow, we reset John entry and Kernberg entry tighter to lose two lines. –Comp.

Kodály, Zoltán. "Béla Bartók." *La Revue Musicale* 2, no. 5 (March 1921): 213.

———. *Visszatekintés: Összegyűjtött írások, beszédek, nyilatkozatok 1–2.* [Retrospection: collection of writings, speeches, statements], ed. Ferenc Bónis. Budapest: Zeneműkiadó, 1964, vol. 2.

Kohut, Heinz. *How Does Analysis Cure?* ed. Arnold Goldberg and Paul Stepansky. Chicago: University of Chicago Press, 1984.

———. *Selected Writings of Heinz Kohut: 1950–1978,* ed. Paul H. Ornstein. New York: International University Press, 1978.

Kramer, Lawrence. *Music as Cultural Practice, 1800–1900.* Berkeley: University of California Press, 1990.

Kristeva, Julia. *Powers of Horror: An Essay on Abjection,* trans. Leon Roudiez. New York: Columbia University Press, 1982.

Kroó, György. "Duke Bluebeard's Castle." *Studia Musicologica* 1 (1961): 251–340.

———. "Monothematik und Dramaturgie in Bartóks Bühnenwerken." *Studia Musicologica* 5/1–4 (1963): 449–467.

———. "Adatok 'A kékszakállú herceg vára' keletkezéstörténetéhez" [Some data on the genesis of *Duke Bluebeard's Castle*]. *Magyar zenetörténeti tanulmányok: Szabolcsi Bence 70. születésnapjára* (1969): 333ff. English translation in *Studia Musicologica* 23 [1981]: 79–123.

———. "Opera: *Duke Bluebeard's Castle.*" In *The Bartók Companion,* ed. Malcolm Gillies. London: Faber and Faber, 1993; Portland, Ore.: Amadeus Press, 1994. pp. 349–359.

———. "Opera: *Duke Bluebeard's Castle.*" *Studia Musicologica* 1 (1961): 251–340.

Layton, Lynne. "Trauma, Gender Identity, and Sexuality: Discourses in Fragmentation." In *Psychoanalyses/Feminisms,* ed. Peter L.Rudnytsky and Andrew M. Gordon. Albany: State University of New York Press, 2000, pp. 211–227.

Leafstedt, Carl S. "*Bluebeard* as Theater: The Influence of Maeterlinck and Hebbel on Balázs's *Bluebeard* Drama." In *Bartók and His World,* ed. Peter Laki. Princeton, N.J.: Princeton University Press, 1995, pp. 119–48.

———. *Inside Bluebeard's Castle: Music and Drama in Bartók's Opera.* New York: Oxford University Press, 1999.

———. "Music and Drama in Béla Bartók's Opera *Duke Bluebeard's Castle.*" Ph.D. dissertation, Harvard University, Cambridge, Mass., 1994.

———. "Structure in the Fifth Door Scene of Bartrók's *Duke Bluebeard's Castle:* An Alternative Viewpoint." *College Music Symposium* 30/1 (Spring 1990): 96–102.

Leblanc, Georgette. *Souvenirs: My Life with Maeterlinck,* trans. Janet Flanner. New York: Dutton and Co., 1932.

Lendvai, Ernő. *Béla Bartók: An Analysis of his Music.* London: Kahn and Averill, 1971.

———. "Nature Symbolism." In *Bartók and Kodály,* vol. 1, rev. ed. Budapest: Institute for Culture, 1979, pp. 153–190.

Lesure, François, ed. *Debussy on Music: The Critical Writings of the Great Composer,* trans. and ed. Richard Langham Smith. New York: Knopf, 1977; Ithaca, N.Y.: Cornell University Press, 1977.

Limayrac, Paulin. "La Poèsie symboliste et socialiste." *Revue des Deux Mondes,* N.S. 5 (1844): 669–682.

Lisak, David. "Sexual Aggression, Masculinity, and Fathers." *Signs* 16/2 (Winter, 1991): 238–262.

Lockspeiser, Edward. *Debussy.* New York: McGraw-Hill, 1936; rev. J. M. Dent, 1963.

Lukács, György. "The Metaphysics of Tragedy." In *Soul and Form,* trans. Anna Bostock. London: Merlin, 1978, pp. 152–174

———. "My Socratic Mask." In *The Lukács Reader,* ed. Arpad Kadarkay. Oxford: Blackwell, 1995, pp. 57–62.

Maeterlinck, Maurice. *Bulles Bleues (souvenirs heureux).* Monaco: Éditions du Rocher, 1948.

————. "Cross Correspondence." In *Our Eternity*, trans. Alexander Teixeira de Mattos. New York: Dodd Mead, 1913, pp. 131–146.

————. "On Women." In *The Treasure of the Humble*, trans. Alfred Sutro. New York: Dodd, Mead; London: George Allen, Ruskin House, 1902, pp. 75–94. Originally published in French as *Le Trésor des Humbles* (1897).

————. "Silence." In *The Treasure of the Humble*, trans. Alfred Sutro. New York: Dodd, Mead; London: George Allen, Ruskin House, 1902, pp. 1–22.

————. "The Deeper Life." In *The Treasure of the Humble*, trans. Alfred Sutro. New York: Dodd, Mead; London: George Allen, Ruskin House, 1902, pp. 169–196.

————. *The Double Garden*, trans. Alexander Teixeira de Mattos. New York: Dodd Mead, 1904.

————. "The Pre-Destined." In *The Treasure of the Humble*, trans. Alfred Sutro. New York: Dodd, Mead; London: George Allen, Ruskin House, 1902, pp. 43–58.

————. "The Star." *The Treasure of the Humble*, trans. Alfred Sutro. New York: Dodd, Mead; London: George Allen, Ruskin House, 1902, pp. 121–146.

Magyar Zenetörténeti Tanulmányok 4. Kodály Zoltán Emlékére, ed. Ferenc Bónis. Budapest: Zeneműkiadó, 1977, p. 33.

Mann, William. *Richard Strauss: A Critical Study of the Operas*. Cassell and London: Cassell & Company., 1964.

Matte Blanco, Ignacio. *The Unconscious as Infinite Sets: An Essay in Bi-Logic*. London: Duckworth, 1975.

McClary, Susan. *Feminine Endings: Music, Gender, and Sexuality*. Minneapolis: University of Minnesota Press, 1991.

McWilliams, Nancy. *Psychoanalytic Diagnosis: Understanding the Personality Structure in the Clinical Process*. New York: Guilford Press, 1994.

Monson, Karen. *Alban Berg: A Modern Biography of the Composer of Wozzeck and Lulu*. Boston: Houghton Mifflin, 1979.

Mordden, Ethan. *Opera in the Twentieth Century: Sacred, Profane, Godot*. New York: Oxford University Press, 1978.

Mukařovsky, Jan. *Kapitoly z české poetiky*, vol. 2. Prague: Svoboda, 1948.

Nichols, Roger, and Richard Langham Smith. *Claude Debussy: Pelléas et Mélisande*. Cambridge: Cambridge University Press, 1989.

Nietzsche, Friedrich. *Human, All Too Human: A Book for Free Spirits*, trans. Marion Faber, with Stephen Lehmann. Lincoln: University of Nebraska Press, 1984.

————. *The Gay Science*, trans. Walter Kaufmann. New York: Vintage Books, 1974.

————. *Thus Spoke Zarathustra: A Book for None and All*, trans. Walter Kaufmann. New York: Viking Penguin, 1954.

Oppenheim, Herman. *Die traumatische Neurosen*. Berlin: Hirschwald, 1889.

Pasler, Jann. "Pelléas and Power: Forces Behind the Reception of Debussy's Opera." *Nineteenth Century Music* 10/3 (Spring 1987); repr. in *Music at the Turn of the Century*. Berkeley: University of California Press, 1990.

Perle, George. "Representation and Symbol in the Music of Wozzeck." *Music Review* 33/4 (November 1971): 281–308.

————. *Serial Composition and Atonality*, 6th ed. rev. Berkeley: University of California Press, 1991.

————. "Symmetrical Formations in the String Quartets of Béla Bartók." *Music Review* 16 (November 1955): 301–312.

————. *The Operas of Alban Berg*, vol. 1: *Wozzeck*. Berkeley: University of California Press, 1980.

Pethő, Bertalan. "Béla Bartók's Personality." *Studia musicologica* 23 (1981): 443–458.

Pór, Péter. "The Symbolist Turn in Endre Ady's Poetry." In *The Symbolist Movement in the Literature of European Languages: A Comparative History of Literatures in European Languages,* ed. Anna Balakian. Budapest: Akadémiai Kiadó, 1982; rev. ed. 1984, pp. 361–380.

Proctor, Gregory. "Technical Bases of Nineteenth-Century Chromatic Tonality: A Study in Chromaticism." Ph.D. diss., Princeton University, Princeton, N.J., 1977.

Prunière, Henry. "A la Villa Médicis," *La Revue Musicale* 7 (1926): 23–42

Redlich, Hans. *Alban Berg: Versuch einer Würdigung.* Vienna: Universal Edition, 1957; Eng. trans. abridged as *Alban Berg: The Man and His Music.* London: John Calder; New York: Abelard-Schumann, 1957. Letter from Berg to Webern, dated 19 August 1918.

Reich, Wilhelm. *The Mass Psychology of Fascism* (1933). New York: Simon and Schuster, 1970.

Reich, Willi. *Alban Berg.* Zürich: Atlantis Verlag AG, 1963, trans. Cornelius Cardew. New York: Vienna House, 1974.

Reiff, Philip. *The Feeling Intellect: Selected Writings,* ed. Jonathan B. Imber. Chicago: Chicago University Press, 1990.

Régnier, Henri de. "Poètes d'aujourd'hui et poèsie de demain." *Mercure de France,* 35 (1900): 342.

Rodenbach, Georges. *Le Rouet des brumes.* Paris: Sâeguier, 1900.

Rolland, Romain. "Pelléas et Mélisande." *Musiciens d'Aujourd'hui.* 17th ed. Paris: Librairie Hatchette, n.d., pp. 197–206.

Rosen, Charles. *Arnold Schoenberg.* Princeton, N.J.: Princeton University Press, 1975.

Rover, Constance. *Love, Morals and the Feminists.* London: Routledge, 1970.

Rudnytsky, Peter L., and Andrew M. Gordon. *Psychoanalyses/Feminisms.* Albany: State University of New York Press, 2000.

St. Augustine. *On Christian Doctrine,* trans. D. W. Robertson, Jr. Indianapolis: Bobbs-Merrill, 1958.

Saint-Denis, Marie-Jean-Leon Hervey de. *Les Rêves et les moyens de les diriger.* Paris: Amyot, 1867.

Salzer, Felix, and Carl Schachter. *Counterpoint in Composition: The Study of Voice Leading.* New York: McGraw-Hill, 1969, 215–221.

Schmidt, Henry J. *How Dramas End: Essays on the German "Sturm und Drang," Buchner, Hauptmann, and Fleisser.* Ann Arbor, MI.: University of Michigan Press, 1992.

Schneider, Marcel. "Symbolist Movement," trans. Edouard Roditi. In *The Symbolist Movement in the Literature of European Languages: A Comparative History of Literatures in European Languages,* ed. Anna Balakian. Budapest: Akadémiai Kiadó, 1982; rev. ed. 1984, pp. 471–482.

Schoenberg, Arnold. "New Music, My Music." In *Style and Idea: Selected Writings of Arnold Schoenberg,* ed. Leonard Stein, trans. Leo Black. London: Faber and Faber Ltd.; Los Angeles: Belmont Music Publishers, 1975; Berkeley: University of California Press, 1984, pp. 99–106.

———. "The Whole-Tone Scale and Related Five- and Six-Part Chords." In *Theory of Harmony* (originally published as *Harmonielehre,* 1911), trans. Roy E. Carter. Berkeley: University of California Press, 1978, pp. 390–398.

———. "Composition with Twelve Tones (I)" [1941]. In *Style and Idea, Selected Writings of Arnold Schoenberg,* ed. Leonard Stein, trans. Leo Black. London: Faber and Faber, 1975, pp. 214–244.

Schorske, Carl. *Fin-de-Siècle Vienna: Politics and Culture.* New York: Vintage Books, 1981.

Schmalfeldt, Janet. *Berg's Wozzeck: Harmonic Language and Dramatic Design.* New Haven, Conn.: Yale University Press, 1983.

Shattuck, Roger. *The Banquet Years: The Origins of the Avant-Garde in France, 1886 to World War I.* New York: Vintage Books, 1955; rev. ed. 1968.

Sine, Nadine. "Cases of Mistaken Identity: Salome and Judith at the Turn of the Century." *German Studies Review* 11/1 (February 1988): 9–29.

Smith, Richard Langham. "Tonalities of Darkness and Light." In Roger Nichols and Richard Langham Smith, *Claude Debussy: Pelléas et Mélisande*. Cambridge: Cambridge University Press, 1989, pp. 107–139.

Stern, Daniel N. *The Interpersonal World of the Infant: A View from Psychoanalysis and Developmental Psychology.* New York: Basic Books, 1985.

Stern, Daniel N., Beatrice Beebe, Joseph Jaffe, and Stephen Bennett, "The Infant's Stimulus World during Social Interaction: A Study of Caregiver Behaviors with Particular Reference to Repetition and Timing." In *Studies in Mother-Infant Interaction*, ed. H. R. Schaffer. London: Academic Press, 1977, pp. 177–193.

Stevens, Halsey. *The Life and Music of Béla Bartók.* London: Oxford University Press, 1953; 2nd ed. 1964; 3rd ed., ed. Malcolm Gillies, Oxford: Clarendon Press, 1993.

Strauss, Richard, and Hugo von Hofmannsthal. *Briefwechsel*, vol. X. In *Gesamtausgabe*, ed. Franz and Alice Strauss, rev. Willi Schuh. Zurich: Atlantis Verlag AG, 1952, enlarged 2d ed.,1955; Eng. trans. Collins, 1961. Letters from 1906 through 1909.

Stravinsky, Igor. *Autobiography* (New York: Simon and Schuster, 1936; New York: W. W. Norton, 1962).

Suchoff, Benjamin, ed. *Béla Bartók Essays.* New York: St. Martin's Press, 1976.

———. "Program Notes for the Concerto for Orchestra," *Béla Bartók: A Celebration.* New York: Book-of-the-Month Records, 1981.

Tambling, Jeremy. *Opera and the Culture of Fascism.* Oxford: Clarendon Press, 1966.

Taruskin, Richard. "Chernomoor to Kaschei: Harmonic Sorcery; or, Stravinsky's 'Angle.'" *Journal of the American Musicological Society* 38/1 (Spring 1985): 79–142.

Thematic Guide [to A *kékszakállú herceg vára (Duke Bluebeard's Castle)*]. "'A kékszakállú herceg vára' libretto by Béla Balázs, and 'Duke Bluebeard's Castle' translation by John Lloyd Davies." In *The Stage Works of Béla Bartók*, ed. Nicholas John. New York: Riverrun; London: Calder, 1991, pp. 39–44.

Theweleit, Klaus. *Male Fantasies.* Vol. 2. Minneapolis: University of Minnesota Press, 1989.

Turnbull, Michael. *Mary Garden.* Portland, Oregon: Amadeus Press, 1997.

Usarek, Alicja. "Béla Bartók's 1907 Violin Concerto: In the spirit of *Tristan.*'" *International Journal of Musicology*, 7 (1998), pp. 301–319.

———. "The Genesis and Fate of Béla Bartók's 1907 *Violin Concerto.*" D.M.A. diss., the University of Texas at Austin, 2000.

Vallas, Léon. *Claude Debussy: His Life and Works*, trans. Maire and Grace O'Brien. New York: Dover, 1973; New York: Oxford University Press, 1933.

Van Ackere, Jules Emile. *"Pelléas et Mélisande" ou la rencontre miraculeuse d'une poésie et d'une musique.* Bruxelles: Les Editions de la Librairie Encyclopedique, 1952.

Van Appledorn, Mary Jeanne. "A Stylistic Study of Claude Debussy's Opera *Pelléas et Mélisande.*" Ph.D. dissertation, University of Rochester, Eastman School of Music, Rochester, N.Y., 1966.

Van der Kolk, Bessel A. "The Body Keeps the Score: Approaches to the Psychobiology of Post-traumatic Stress Disorder." In *Traumatic Stress: The Effects of Overwhelming Experience on Mind, Body, and Society*, ed. Bessel A. Van der Kolk, Alexander C. MacFarlane, and Lars Weisaeth. New York: Guilford Press, 1996, pp. 214–241.

———. "Trauma and Memory," in *Traumatic Stress: The Effects of Overwhelming Experience on Mind, Body, and Society*, eds. Bessel A. van der Kolk, Alexander C. McFarlane, Lars Weisaeth. New York: Guilford Press, 1996, pp. 293–296.

Van der Kolk, Bessel A., Onno van der Hart, and Charles R. Marmar. "Dissociation and Information Processing in Post-Traumatic Stress Disorder." In *Traumatic Stress: The Effects of Overwhelming Experience on Mind, Body, and Society*, ed. Bessel A. van der Kolk, Alexander C. McFarlane, and Lars Weisaeth. New York: Guilford Press, 1996, pp. 303–327.

Van Eeden, Frederik. *De Nachtbruid* (1909). *The Bride of Dreams*, trans. Mellie von Auw. New York: Mitchell Kennerley, 1913.

Veress, Sándor. "Bluebeard's Castle." *Tempo* (London) 13 (1949): 32–38; reprinted in *Béla Bartók: A Memorial Review*. New York: Boosey & Hawkes, 1950, pp. 36–53.

Vinton, John. "Bartók on His Own Music." *Journal of the American Musicological Society* 19 (1966): 232–243.

Von der Nüll, Edwin. *Béla Bartók: Ein Beitrag zur Morphologie der neuen Musik*. Halle: Mitteldeutsche Verlags A. G., 1930.

Weininger, Otto. *Geschlecht und Charakter* [Sex and Character]. London: William Heinemann, 1906.

Weiss-Aigner, Gunter. "The 'Lost' Violin Concerto." In *The Bartók Companion*, ed. Malcolm Gillies. London: Faber and Faber, 1993; Portland, Ore.: Amadeus Press, 1994, pp. 468–476.

Wellek, René. "What is Symbolism?" In *The Symbolist Movement in the Literature of European Languages: A Comparative History of Literatures in European Languages*, ed. Anna Balakian. Budapest: Akadémiai Kiadó, 1982; rev. ed. 1984, pp. 26–27.

Wenk, Arthur B. *Claude Debussy and the Poets*. Berkeley: University of California Press, 1976.

———. *Claude Debussy and Twentieth-Century Music*. Boston: Twayne Publishers, 1983.

Whitebook, J. "Reflections on the Autonomous Individual and Decentered Subject." *American Imago* 49 (1992): 97–116.

Whitford, Frank. *Klimt*. London: Thames and Hudson, 1990.

Whittall, Arnold. "Tonality and the Whole-Tone Scale in the Music of Debussy." *Music Review* 36/4 (November 1975): 261.

Winnicott, Donald W. "Ego Distortion in Terms of True and False Self." In *The Maturational Processes and the Facilitating Environment*. New York: International University Press, 1965, pp. 140–152.

Wolf, Ernest. *Treating the Self*. New York and London: Guilford Press, 1988.

Youens, Susan. "An Unseen Player: Destiny in Pelléas et Mélisande." In *Reading Opera*, ed. Arthur Groos and Roger Parker. Princeton, N.J.: Princeton University Press, 1988, pp. 60–88.

Zsuffa, Joseph. *Béla Balázs: The Man and the Artist*. Berkeley: University of California Press, 1987.

Index

Academy of Music (Budapest), 14
Adorno, Theodor W., 12, 182, 292
Ady, Endre, 10, 238, 252
Aeschylus, 264
  Choephori of, 328n11
animal magnetism, 88, 313n11. *See also* consciousness, altered states of
Antokoletz, Elliott, 291, 300n5
Arcadia, 105
Aristotelian logic, 292
axis of symmetry, 19, 63, 66, 71, 98, 136, 149, 159, 216, 229, 232. *See also* symmetrical pitch constructions and relations

Balázs, Béla, 4, 7, 31, 43, 44, 45, 47, 52, 183, 187, 238, 251, 292, 293, 302n1, 302n3, 330n8
  "ballad of inner life," 44
  Bluebeard mystery play, 6, 7, 8, 27, 32, 43, 48, 50–53, 182, 183, 184, 196, 238, 259
  Don Juan and Bluebeard play, 43, 51
  on men and women, 44, 45
  political exile of, 306n66
  view of women, 44, 46, 189, 190, 243–244, 297n7
Banks, Paul, 187, 200
Bartók, Béla, 4, 15, 22, 24, 31, 43, 47, 52, 184, 185, 198–199, 234, 291
  ambivalence regarding gender relation of power, 234
  and atheism, 197, 199, 322n58
  and the Catholic Church, 197
  diatonic extension in range of chromatic themes and chromatic compression of diatonic themes, 121
  Concerto for Orchestra, 322n62
  Concerto for Violin and Orchestra, op. posth., 25, 184, 196, 199, 210, 211, 212
  Contrasts, 218
  Duke Bluebeard's Castle, 4, 8, 16, 22, 24, 30, 42, 46–50, 121, 182–261: autobiographical perspective, 50–52
  Eight Hungarian Folksongs, 214–215
  Fifth String Quartet, 25, 221
  First Sonata for violin and piano, 222, 223
  First String Quartet, 25, 210
  Four Dirges for Piano, op. 8b, 198
  Fourteen Bagatelles for Piano, op. 6, 196, 199, 211, 212
  on men and women, 198, 234, 252, 253
  Miraculous Mandarin, 252, 253
  mother of, 213, 234
  on Nietzsche, 238
  Quatre nénies, op. 9a, 14
  Sonata for piano, 214
  on suicide, 252
  Three Studies, op. 18, for piano, 25
  Two Portraits for Orchestra, op. 5, 184, 196, 199, 212
  Two Romanian Dances, op. 8a, 212
  on women, 244, 297n7
Bauer, Herbert, 44, 45. *See also* Balázs, Béla
Bauer, Simon, 44

Bäumer, Angelica, 190
Beaunier, André, 11
Beethoven, Ludwig van, use of "expressive doubling" in Scherzi of *Fifth Symphony* and *String Quartet*, op. 74 ("Harp"), 115
Bellini, Vincenzo, *Norma*, 15
Benjamin, Jessica, 32, 48, 54
Berg, Alban, 15, 280
   Lulu, 181
   Three Orchestral Pieces, op. 14, 279
   Wozzeck, 181, 263, 279–290
Berlioz, Hector, 16
   Francs-Juges Overture, 312n2
Bismarck, Otto Edouard Leopold von, 60
Blake, William, use of "expressive doubling" in *Songs of Innocence and Experience*, 115
Brahms, Johannes, 262
Breuer, Josef, 3, 6, 46
Bruckner, Anton, 262, 263
Büchner, Georg, *Woyzeck*, 279, 280
Budapest Bartók Archívum, Bartók's personal library in, 14

Capellen, Georg, 312n1
Carré, Albert. *See* Paris, Opéra-Comique
cell[s], pitch- or intervallic, 22–23, 29, 122, 138
   definition of, 301n17
   inversionally related, 22–23
chain of thirds, 24–27, 221–223
characterization, final musical transformation of, 248–250
Charcot, Jean-Martin, 5, 6, 46, 88, 327n1
Chausson, Ernest, 101
Chekhov, Anton, 7
Chodorow, Nancy, 32
Chopin, Frédérik, 16
chromatic compression
   of diatonic themes or constructions, 24, 121, 131, 200, 204–205, 209, 210, 214, 223–224, 250, 323n4
   of whole-tone to octatonic or chromatic, 222, 131–133, 165–168, 201, 227 (*see also* diatonic extension in range of chromatic themes)
chromatic saturation, 124, 220. *See also* Wenk, Arthur B.
composers, French, Russian, and Hungarian, 17, 18
Comte, Auguste, 5
   Positivist philosophy of, 5, 297n24, 327n1

conscious (mind), 57, 80, 94, 95, 126, 149, 330n4
consciousness, 89, 91, 173, 213
   altered states of, 313n11
Crawford, Dorothy Lamb, on Bartók's view of suicide, 252
Cross, Anthony, 15
crucifixion, symbol of, 147, 150, 152, 153, 154, 156, 316n7
cycles, interval. *See* interval cycle[s]

Dalmatia, 210
Darwin, Charles, 3
   theory of evolution of, 3
death wish. *See* instinct, death
Debussy, Claude, 4, 15, 20, 22, 31, 58, 61, 291
   cathédral engloutie, La, 125
   Images I and *II*, 14
   L'isle joyeux, 14
   Nocturnes, 17, 68
   Pelléas et Mélisande, 4, 8, 9, 16, 24, 68, 55–181, 182, 188, 190, 192
   Pour le piano, 14
   Prélude à l'après midi d'un faune, 68
   Préludes I, 14
   String Quartet, 14, 68
   Syrinx, 105
   on women, 37–38
developing variation, 279
diatonic extension in range, of chromatic themes or constructions, 24, 121, 167, 210, 223, 234. *See also* chromatic compression of diatonic themes or constructions
diatonic saturation, 124. *See also* Wenk, Arthur B.
dodecaphonic series, 24, 218. *See also* twelve-tone language
dominant-ninth chord, 18, 19, 84–116
drame lyrique, 9
Dreyfus, Alfred, 60
   movement, 302n3
Dukas, Paul, 9, 187
   Ariane et Barbe-Bleue, 187, 188, 190, 249

Emmanuel, Maurice, 56
equal-division system, 17
Eulenberg, H., *Ritter Blaubart*, 249
Euripedes, 264, 328n11
   Elektra, 328n11
Eve's nature, passion of, 248

Exposition Universelle (1889). *See* Paris,
　Exposition Universelle
Expressionism, 278–279, 290
expressive doubling, definition of, 115, 128

fate, 3, 7, 23, 30, 38, 56, 62, 64–65, 67, 74,
　76, 84, 94, 100, 104, 129, 135, 147–148,
　152, 159–160, 173, 180
　circle of light as symbol of, 101
　circuity of, 173–181
　Maeterlinck's view of, 64–65, 95
　notion of (equivalent to unconscious),
　　313n16
　submission to, 104, 169, 207
Fauré, Gabriel, 10, 55–83
feminist view, 48–52, 187
　movement, 188
femme fatale, 230. *See also* siren of destruction
Flaubert, Gustave
　Hérodias, 249
　Madame Bovary, 249
folk modalities, pentatonic-diatonic, 15, 16, 17
folk-music sources, from borderlands of
　Western culture, 15
Fourcaud, M., 9, 126
France, Anatole, *Les sept femmes de la
　Barbe-Bleue*, 249
Franco-Prussian War (1871), 60
free-atonality, 278
Freikorps, 31, 32
French Impressionists, 18
Freud, Sigmund, 3, 6, 7, 31, 36, 46, 88, 89,
　256, 278, 279, 292, 327n1
　Interpretation of Dreams, 8
　Studien über Hysterie, 262
　theory of psychoanalysis, 262, 303n7, 326n8
　Vienna of, 262
Frigyesi, Judit, 46, 47, 182, 208, 211, 212, 238

Gesamtkunstwerk, 9
Geyer, Stefi, 46, 47, 184, 185, 196–199, 208,
　210, 211, 212, 213, 234, 253, 258, 260,
　261, 322n58, 323n8, 323n19, 324n23
Gilman, Lawrence, 59
　"Fate" motif of, 58
Giovacchini, Peter L., 185, 256
　summary of Freud's hypothesis by, 256
Glinka, Mikhail, 16, 312n2
Golden Section proportions, 157–158, 236,
　316n12, 325n11
Grant, Julian, 187

Grayson, David, 179, 180, 181, 314n2
Grinstein, Alexander
　on patients contemplating suicide in
　　dreams, 252
　on "Death Symbols," 253, 257–258
Gruber, Emma, 43, 238
Guiraud, Ernest, 56

Halls, W. D., 40
Hebbel, Friedrich, 8, 48
　Judith, 8, 47, 52, 189, 249
Heller, Agnes, 51
Hlaváček, Karel, 11
Hoffmann, E. T. A., use of expressive
　doubling by in *The Golden Pot*, 115
Hofmannsthal, Hugo von, 7, 262, 263, 264
Howat, Roy, on Debussy's use of Golden
　Section proportions, 157–158
Hungarian linguistic syntax, archaic,
　191–193, 194–195, 244–245
　isometric stanzaic structure, 244
　octosyllabic phrase construction, 221,
　　244–246
　quaternary stanzaic structure of, 236
hysteria, 5, 6

Ibsen, Henryk, 7
Impressionism, 4
　aesthetics of, 68
　French Impressionist painting, 67
instinct
　death, 89, 251–256, 259
　definition of, 313n16
　sexual, 251, 256
instrumental timbre, as signifier, 56, 61,
　71–72, 86–88, 120, 121, 135, 137, 141,
　152–153, 161. *See also* Wenk, Arthur B.
interval cycle[s], 17, 18–21, 23–27, 57, 124,
　138, 282–287, 289, 301n20
　definition of, 299n47
　total complex of, 23, 301n21
interval-ratio, 24–27, 66, 191, 200–202, 203,
　214, 240, 250
　definition of, 301n23
Irigaray, Luce, 48
isometric stanzaic structure. *See* Hungarian
　linguistic syntax, archaic

Janet, Pierre, 3, 6, 31, 46, 327n1
　development of "psychological analysis," 6
Jarman, Douglas, on *Wozzeck*, 281

Joyce, James, 7, 181
Jungian dream symbolism, 47
Jurkovics, Irmy, 234, 235

Kafka, Franz, 181
Kahane, Claire, 48, 52
Kárpáti, János, 24, 25, 211, 218, 221, 222, 223
Kernberg, Otto, 48
Klimt, Gustav, 189
    Judith and Holofernes, 189
Kodály, Zoltán, 14, 43, 184, 185, 238
Kohut, Heinz, 185
Kramer, Lawrence, 115, 128
    definition of expressive doubling, 115, 128
Kretschmer, Ernst, theory of personality
    typology, 185
Kristeva, Julia, 54
Kroó, György, 212, 248

Laforgue, Jules
    musical ideas of, 314n36
    Pan et la Syrinx, 314n36
Layton, Lynne, 32
Leafstedt, Carl, 47, 212, 233
Leblanc, Georgette, 37
leitmotif, 10, 56, 57, 58–59, 186, , 264, 289,
    302n26, 309n8, 309n10, 310n15
    of Stefi Geyer, 197, 208, 209, 210, 220,
    226, 259, 260
leit-sound, 56, 121
Lendvai, Ernő, 25, 316n12
    Golden Section, 302n24, 316n12
    polar-axis system or principle, 212, 323n14
Lerolle, Henri, 99
Lisak, David, 32
Liszt, Franz, 16
Lockspeiser, Edward, 181
Lőcse, 45
Lukács, György, 8, 43, 45, 46, 47, 51, 52, 238,
    252, 293, 330n8
    view of women, 46, 297n7

Maeterlinck, Maurice, 4, 94, 292
    Ariane et Barbe-Bleue, 60, 188, 189, 249
    on catastrophe, 100
    Catholic upbringing of, 35
    on cross correspondence, 117, 118
    depression of, 35
    on fate, 95, 104
    insight of, 40, 77, 147–148, 156, 158
    Pelléas et Mélisande play, 4, 9, 27, 30, 32, 60,
    117, 182

symbolist message of, 73, 173
"The Tragical in Daily Life," 80
Treasure of the Humble, 101
on women, 4, 65, 93, 95, 302n2
Mahler, Gustav, 262, 263
Mallarmé, Stéphane, 8, 9, 11
Marks, Lawrence E., "the Doctrine of
    Equivalent Information," 8
Marschner, Heinrich, 10
Matte-Blanco, Ignacio, 55, 292
    symmetrical relationships, 55, 94, 292
Mélusine, 105, 189, 314n37
Mesmer, Franz Anton, 313n11
Mockel, Albert, 40
modernist conception
    definition of, 3
    gender and power in, 188–190
modernity, reflections on, 53–54, 308n107
modes and scales
    Chinese, 68
    Javanese, 68
    North African, 68
Mordden, Ethan, 278
Mozart, Wolfgang Amadeus, 61
Mukafovsky, Jan, 11
Mussorgsky, Modest, 18, 22
    Boris Godunov, 18, 68

Napoleon III, defeat of, 60
narcissistic defenses
    definition of, 31
    entitlement, 50
    pathology, 303n9
    psycho-dynamic qualities of, 53, 182, 185
Nichols, Roger, 72
Nietzsche, Friedrich, 10, 46, 184, 189, 197,
    211, 234–235, 238, 246, 257, 259–261
    conception of man's "Will to Power," 259
    on independence, 237–238, 246–247
    on love between men and women, 257
    on women, 245
    Zarathustra, 189, 210, 235, 261
Nietzschean condition, 234–236, 257

octosyllabic phrase construction. *See* Hungar-
    ian linguistic syntax, archaic
Oedipal principle, 264
Offenbach, Jacques, comic opera of, 249
Opéra-Comique. *See* Paris, Opéra-Comique

Pan, 105, 314n36, 314n37
panpipe, 105

Pappenheim, Marie, 189, 279
  Erwartung, 189
Paris
  Conservatory, 56
  Exposition Universelle, 68
  Opéra-Comique, 156
parlando rubato, 15, 16, 192, 244
Pásztory, Ditta, 184, 197
pentatonic/diatonic and whole-tone spheres,
    synthesis of, 248
Perle, George, on *Wozzeck*, 281
Perrault, Charles, 1697 tale by, 183, 249, 257
  *Histoires ou Contes du Temps passé, avec des
    Moralités*, 249
  Little Red Riding Hood, 45
Pethő, Bertalan
  on Bartók and personality types, 184–185,
    213
  on Bartók and women, 213
pleasure-principle, 89
Poe, Edgar Allen, Maeterlinck influenced by,
    316n18
polar-axis system or principle. *See* Lendvai,
    Ernő
political symbol, Golaud as, 60, 156, 177
polymodal chromaticism or combination, 191,
    194, 214–215, 219, 324n29
polytonality, pseudo- or quasi-, 271, 272
Pór, Péter, 10
Positivist philosophy, 5, 12, 327n1. *See also*
    Comte, Auguste
post-traumatic stress disorder, 5
proportional structure, geometrically
    expanding, 236. *See also* Golden
    Section proportions
psychoanalysis, 6, 11, 31, 262–263, 303n10
psychodynamic psychology, 31
Puccini, Giacomo, 10

quaternary stanzaic structure. *See* Hungarian
    linguistic syntax, archaic

recitative opera, 28, 192. *See also* parlando
    rubato
Régnier, Henri de, 11
Reiff, Philip, 46
Reinhardt, Max, 189, 262
repetition-compulsion, 89
Reznicek, E., after Eulenberg's *Ritter Blaubart*,
    249
Rimsky-Korsakov, Nicolay, 187
Russian nationalists, 15, 18, 20

Saint-Denis, Marquis Marie-Jean-Leon de
    Hervey de, 7
Salome, 189, 249
Salpetrière, 5, 6, 88
scale formations, new kinds of (pentatonic-
    diatonic, whole-tone, octatonic), 15
Schmalfeldt, Janet, on *Wozzeck*, 281
Schneider, Marcel, 7, 10
Schnitzler, Arthur, 7, 262
Schoenberg, Arnold, 10, 15, 20, 84, 85, 187,
    262
  Erwartung, 189, 263, 278–279, 320n38
  Four Orchestral Songs, op. 22, 279
  Glückliche Hand, Die, 187, 279
  Harmonielehre, 21, 84, 85
  Herzgewächse, 279
  Pelleas und Melisande, 85
  Pierrot Lunaire, op. 21, 279
  Sechs kleine Klavierstücke, op. 19, 279
  use of whole-tone scale, 85
Schopenhauer, Arthur, 211
Schroeder, Hermann, 312n1
Schubert, Franz, 16, 312n2
  Mass in E-Flat, 312n2
Scott, Cyril, 10
Scriabin, Alexander, 15, 187
  Prometheus, 187
Seidler, Irma, 46, 51, 308n98, 308n101,
    308n103
sets, interaction of pentatonic, diatonic,
    whole-tone, and octatonic, 22–23
sexual wishes, gratification of and death, 253.
  See also instinct, sexual
Sibelius, Jean, 10
signs, natural and conventional, 12, 300n58
siren of destruction, 38, 93, 95, 111, 189,
    190
Smith, Richard Langham, 11, 80, 151, 163,
    165, 180
Socialist ideology, 13
  interest in by some Symbolist writers, 13
Socrates, 293
Sophocles, *Elektra*, 263, 264
Stern, Daniel, 8, 32
Strauss, Richard, 14, 262
  Ariadne auf Naxos, 263
  Elektra, 14, 262–278: continuous inner
    action of Wagner in, 264; leitmotifs in,
    328n13
  Rosenkavalier, Der, 263
  Salome, 47
  Zarathustra, 210

Stravinsky, Igor, 15
Strindberg, August, 7
Symbolism, definition of, 11
symmetrical pitch constructions and relations,
    16, 17, 18–22, 55–57, 59, 132, 263,
    264, 265–271, 273–274, 292, 309n1,
    312n1, 324n26, 330n4
  definition of, 300n8
  derived by French, Russian, and Hungarian
    composers, 17, 18–21
  polymodal chromatic, 214–215, 292
  transformation into, 4, 20, 56, 159
synesthesia, definition of, 8, 295n4
Syrinx, 105, 314n36
Szeged, 45, 307n70

talking cure. *See* Freud, Sigmund, theory of
    psychoanalysis
telepathy, 117–118
tempo giusto, 15
Teyte, Maggie, in early dramatic role of
    Mélisande, 39
Theweleit, Klaus, 31–32
Third Republic, 60
Toller, Ernst, 7
traditional harmonic functions or construc-
    tions (major-minor scale system), 4, 18,
    22, 55, 75
  symmetrical transformation of, 4, 159
trauma, 4, 30–54, 60, 174, 182
  fate and, 34
  personal and social factors in the develop-
    ment of, 30–31
  psychological reconceptualizations of, 4–6
Turner, J. M. W., use of expressive doubling in
    *Shade and Darkness—The Evening of the
    Deluge* and *Light and Color (Goethe's
    Theory)—The Morning After the Deluge—
    Mosses [sic] Writing the Book
    of Genesis*, 115
twelve-tone language, 16, 23–27

ultrachromaticism, 14, 18, 263
unconscious, the, 3, 30–54, 55, 57, 67, 80,
    84, 89, 100, 117, 118, 126, 149, 173,
    174, 182, 184, 300n59, 313n16, 316n1,
    330n4
  darkness of, 101, 140, 181
  domination over conscious mind, 95, 262

laws of, 314n38
motivation, 71, 182, 251, 252, 253, 257
music as encoder of, 89–95
power of, 88–89, 117

Van der Kolk, Bessel A., 5
Van Eeden, Frederik, *The Bride of Dreams*, 7
Verdi, Giuseppe, 15
Veress, Sándor, 186, 187–188, 248
Verlaine, Paul, 8, 9
Vienna, as seat of Austro-Hungarian Empire,
    262
von der Nüll, Edwin, 25, 324n29

Wagner, Richard, 8, 9, 10, 263
  continuous inner action of, 264
  Fliegender Holländer, Der, 10, 193
  Gesamtkunstwerk of, 9
  Lohengrin, 10
  music dramas of, 58, 186
  Rienzi, 10
  Tannhäuser, 10
  Tristan und Isolde, 7, 14, 58, 169, 181, 210,
    279
Wagnerian formula, 57
Wagner-Strauss period, 14, 18, 184
Wassermann, Jacob, 7, 262
Weber, Carl Maria von, 10
Webern, Anton, 15
Wedekind, Frank, 189
  Lulu, 189
Weininger, Otto, 188, 252
  suicide of, 252
Wenk, Arthur B., 61, 82, 87, 124, 137, 141,
    154, 160 167, 169, 180, 181
  diatonic and chromatic saturation, 124, 125
Winnicott, Donald, 40
women, on, 188, 189, 252
  Paul's dictum, 3 (*see also* Maeterlink,
    Maurice)
Woolf, Virginia, 181
World War I, 14, 184, 278, 290

Yeats, William Butler, 7

Ziegler, Márta, 46, 47, 184, 197, 323n19
Ziehn, Bernard, 312n1
Zola, Emile, 5
Zsuffa, Joseph, 51

Printed in the United States
135353LV00004B/168/A

9 780195 365825

1936759R0021

Printed in Great Britain
by Amazon.co.uk, Ltd.,
Marston Gate.